SPSS

SPSS® Base System Syntax Reference Guide Release 5.0

SPSS Inc.

SPSS Inc.
444 N. Michigan Avenue
Chicago, Illinois 60611
Tel: (312) 329-2400
Fax: (312) 329-3668

SPSS Federal Systems (U.S.)
SPSS Latin America
SPSS Benelux BV
SPSS UK Ltd.
SPSS UK Ltd., New Delhi
SPSS GmbH Software
SPSS Scandinavia AB
SPSS Asia Pacific Pte. Ltd.
SPSS Japan Inc.
SPSS Australasia Pty. Ltd.

For more information about SPSS® software products, please write or call

Marketing Department
SPSS Inc.
444 North Michigan Avenue
Chicago, IL 60611
Tel: (312) 329-3500
Fax: (312) 329-3668

SPSS is a registered trademark and the other product names are the trademarks of SPSS Inc. for its proprietary computer software. No material describing such software may be produced or distributed without the written permission of the owners of the trademark and license rights in the software and the copyrights in the published materials.

The SOFTWARE and documentation are provided with RESTRICTED RIGHTS. Use, duplication, or disclosure by the Government is subject to restrictions as set forth in subdivision (c)(1)(ii) of The Rights in Technical Data and Computer Software clause at 52.227-7013. Contractor/manufacturer is SPSS Inc., 444 N. Michigan Avenue, Chicago, IL, 60611.

General notice: Other product names mentioned herein are used for identification purposes only and may be trademarks of their respective companies.

Windows is a trademark of Microsoft Corporation.

SPSS® Base System Syntax Reference Guide, Release 5.0
Copyright © 1992 by SPSS Inc.
All rights reserved.
Printed in the United States of America.

No part of this publication may be reproduced, stored in a retrieval system, or transmitted, in any form or by any means, electronic, mechanical, photocopying, recording, or otherwise, without the prior written permission of the publisher.

2 3 4 5 6 7 8 9 0   94 93 92

ISBN 0-923967-53-2

Library of Congress Catalog Card Number: 92-060766

Preface

SPSS® is a comprehensive, integrated system for statistical data analysis. It is available on a wide variety of computers and operating systems, including IBM PC, PS/2, and compatible computers running OS/2 or Microsoft Windows; Apple Macintosh computers; workstations, minicomputers, and larger systems under UNIX and VAX/VMS; and many other mainframes. All of these versions contain an SPSS Processor that reads and carries out commands in the well-known SPSS language. No matter which version you use, you can issue the same commands and expect the same results.

This manual is a reference to the command syntax for the SPSS Base system. It opens with an introduction which provides a brief overview that should help you determine which commands are best for the job at hand. Following the introduction is "Universals," which describes the rules of command syntax and documents those components of the command language that appear in many commands, such as the arithmetic, string, date, and other functions available in many data transformation commands. Following "Universals," SPSS commands are presented in alphabetical order, and the command syntax is illustrated with many examples. Appendixes provide additional information on command states, complex file defininition, the macro facility, and import/export character sets.

This reference guide does *not* provide an overview of SPSS, teach you how to create jobs and interpret results, or show you how to run SPSS on your computer and operating system. This information is supplied in a separate *Base System User's Guide* for your version of SPSS.

Manuals for the Base System. Documentation for SPSS Release 5 consists of:

- The *SPSS Base System User's Guide* provides detailed information on how to run SPSS on your computer's operating system, including complete documentation of the user interface provided for your system. It also explains many of the statistical concepts involved, how to use the statistical procedures correctly, and how to interpret the results.

- The *SPSS Base System Syntax Reference Guide* documents and provides examples of all the command syntax in the Base system. On some computer operating systems, the user interface makes it possible to obtain most of the features of SPSS without ever looking at command syntax. There are, however, some features that can be obtained only by entering and running SPSS commands.

SPSS Options. The following options are available as add-on enhancements to the SPSS Base system:

- **SPSS Professional Statistics**™ provides techniques to measure the similarities and differences in data, classify data, identify underlying dimensions, and more. It includes procedures for these analyses: cluster, k-means cluster, discriminant, factor, multidimensional scaling, proximity, and reliability.
- **SPSS Advanced Statistics**™ includes sophisticated techniques such as logistic regression, loglinear analysis, multivariate analysis of variance, constrained nonlinear regression, probit analysis, Cox regression, Kaplan-Meier and actuarial survival analysis.
- **SPSS Tables**™ creates a variety of presentation-quality tabular reports, including complex stub-and-banner tables and displays of multiple-response data.
- **SPSS Trends**™ performs comprehensive forecasting and time-series analyses with multiple curve-fitting models, smoothing models, and methods for estimating autoregressive functions.
- **SPSS Categories**™ performs conjoint analysis and optimal scaling procedures, including correspondence analysis.
- **SPSS CHAID**™ simplifies tabular analysis or categorical data, develops predictive models, screens out extraneous predictor variables, and produces easy-to-read tree diagrams that segment a population into subgroups that share similar characteristics.
- **SPSS**® **LISREL**® **7** analyses linear structural relations and simultaneous equation models.

If you would like to be on our mailing list and you did not buy your system directly from us, write to us at one of the addresses listed on the following page. We will send you a copy of our newsletter and let you know about SPSS Inc. activities in your area.

Contacting SPSS Inc.

If you would like to be on our mailing list, write to us at one of the addresses below. We will send you a copy of our newsletter and let you know about SPSS Inc. activities in your area.

SPSS Inc.
444 North Michigan Ave.
Chicago, IL 60611
Tel: (312) 329-3500
Fax: (312) 329-3668

SPSS Federal Systems
12030 Sunrise Valley Dr.
Suite 300
Reston, VA 22091
Tel: (703) 391-6020
Fax: (703) 391-6002

SPSS Latin America
444 North Michigan Ave.
Chicago, IL 60611
Tel: (312) 329-3556
Fax: (312) 329-3668

SPSS Benelux BV
P.O. Box 115
4200 AC Gorinchem
The Netherlands
Tel: +31.1830.36711
Fax: +31.1830.35839

SPSS UK Ltd.
SPSS House
5 London Street
Chertsey
Surrey KT16 8AP
United Kingdom
Tel: +44.932.566262
Fax: +44.932.567020

SPSS UK Ltd., New Delhi
c/o Ashok Business Centre
Ashok Hotel
50B Chanakayapuri
New Delhi 110 021
India
Tel: +91.11.600121 x1029
Fax: +91.11.6873216

SPSS GmbH Software
Steinsdorfstrasse 19
D-8000 Munich 22
Germany
Tel:+49.89.2283008
Fax: +49.89.2285413

SPSS Scandinavia AB
Sjöängsvägen 7
S-191 72 Sollentuna
Sweden
Tel: +46.8.7549450
Fax: +46.8.7548816

SPSS Asia Pacific Pte. Ltd.
10 Anson Road, #34-07
International Plaza
Singapore 0207
Singapore
Tel: +65.221.2577
Fax: +65.221.9920

SPSS Japan Inc.
Gyoen Sky Bldg.
2-1-11, Shinjuku
Shinjuku-ku
Tokyo 160
Japan
Tel: +81.3.33505261
Fax: +81.3.33505245

SPSS Australasia Pty. Ltd.
121 Walker Street
North Sydney, NSW 2060
Australia
Tel: +61.2.954.5660
Fax: +61.2.954.5616

Contents

Introduction: A Guide to SPSS Command Syntax 1

Universals 11
SPSS Commands 11
Files 21
Variables 32
Transformation Expressions 45
Date and Time in SPSS 59

Commands 74
ADD FILES 74
ADD VALUE LABELS 82
AGGREGATE 85
ANOVA 95
APPLY DICTIONARY 104
AUTORECODE 108
BEGIN DATA—END DATA 112
BREAK 114
CLEAR TRANSFORMATIONS 115
COMMENT 116
COMPUTE 117
CORRELATIONS 127
COUNT 133
CROSSTABS 135
DATA LIST 147

DEFINE—!ENDDEFINE 165
DESCRIPTIVES 183
DISPLAY 190
DOCUMENT 193
DO IF 195
DO REPEAT—END REPEAT 204
DROP DOCUMENTS 209
EDIT 210
END CASE 212
END FILE 220
ERASE 222
EXAMINE 223
EXECUTE 233
EXPORT 234
FILE HANDLE 240
FILE LABEL 241
FILE TYPE—END FILE TYPE 242
FILTER 257
FINISH 259
FLIP 261
FORMATS 265
FREQUENCIES 269
GET 279
GET BMDP 283
GET CAPTURE 289
GET OSIRIS 293

GET SAS   299
GET SCSS   305
GET TRANSLATE   309
GRAPH   317
HELP   337
HOST   339
IF   340
IMPORT   346
INCLUDE   350
INFO   352
INPUT PROGRAM—END INPUT PROGRAM   356
KEYED DATA LIST   360
LEAVE   366
LIST   368
LOOP—END LOOP   372
MATCH FILES   382
MATRIX DATA   390
MCONVERT   409
MEANS   412
MISSING VALUES   420
MULT RESPONSE   423
N OF CASES   433
NEW FILE   435
NONPAR CORR   436
NPAR TESTS   442
NUMERIC   459
ONEWAY   461
PARTIAL CORR   471
PLOT   479
POINT   487
PRESERVE   491

PRINT   492
PRINT EJECT   498
PRINT FORMATS   501
PRINT SPACE   504
PROCEDURE OUTPUT   506
RANK   508
RECODE   514
RECORD TYPE   520
REFORMAT   529
REGRESSION   531
REGRESSION: Residuals   549
RENAME VARIABLES   558
REPEATING DATA   560
REPORT   574
REREAD   601
RESTORE   607
SAMPLE   608
SAVE   611
SAVE SCSS   616
SAVE TRANSLATE   619
SELECT IF   625
SET   630
SHOW   644
SORT CASES   648
SPLIT FILE   650
STRING   653
SUBTITLE   655
SYSFILE INFO   657
TEMPORARY   658
TITLE   661
T-TEST   663

UPDATE 667

VALUE LABELS 674

VARIABLE LABELS 677

VECTOR 679

WEIGHT 685

WRITE 688

WRITE FORMATS 693

XSAVE 696

Appendix A
SPSS Commands and Program States 703

Program States 703

Determining Command Order 705

Appendix B
IMPORT/EXPORT Character Sets 711

Appendix C
Defining Complex Files 718

A Rectangular File 718

Nested Files 719

Grouped Data 721

Mixed Files 725

Repeating Data 728

Appendix D
Using the Macro Facility 732

Example 1: Automating a File-Matching Task 733

Example 2: Testing Correlation Coefficients 739

Example 3: Generating Random Data 743

Topical Index 747

Syntax Index 762

Introduction: A Guide to SPSS Command Syntax

SPSS runs on a wide variety of computers and operating systems. The user interface varies between operating systems—but the basic command syntax is essentially the same on all systems. Some (but probably not all) of the following methods for submitting commands will be available on your system:

- **Dialog box interface.** Pull-down menus and simple dialog boxes allow you to perform most tasks without ever looking at the underlying command syntax.
- **SPSS Manager.** Menus help you build commands, reducing or eliminating most syntax errors.
- **Interactive session.** Commands are executed as they are entered (or in selected groups) and the results appear on your computer screen.
- **Batch mode.** Commands are entered and saved in a file, and the command syntax file is then run as a batch job.

Both the dialog box interface and the SPSS Manager can be used in an interactive session or as a method for creating command syntax files for batch execution. The basic syntax rules for interactive and batch operation are provided in the Universals section of this syntax reference guide. Consult the *Base System User's Guide* for your version of SPSS for information on the methods available for running SPSS on your computer.

Overview

The syntax reference guide is arranged alphabetically by command name to provide quick access to detailed information on each command in the SPSS command language. This introduction is intended to help you determine which commands are best for the job at hand.

Most SPSS commands can be classified according to what they do to the **working data file**, which is simply the rectangular array of cases and variables with which SPSS is currently working. Operations with the working data file include:

- **Defining a working data file.** Data-definition commands define a new data file or read a previously-defined data file and make it available for analysis.
- **Describing the working data file.** These commands add labels or other optional information to the data in the file.
- **Modifying data values.** The SPSS transformation language allows you to specify calculations, simple or elaborate, to be carried out with your data.
- **Defining complex data files.** More powerful "programming" commands let you take control of the process by which SPSS builds the working data file.
- **Selecting cases for processing.** Capabilities for logical case selection and random sampling are essential in data analysis.
- **Modifying the structure of the working data file.** You can easily rearrange, combine, or split up your data files.
- **Saving the working data file.** Use SPSS format for efficiency or another format for portability.

- **Displaying data values**. Take a look at the data in your working data file.
- **Statistical analysis, tabulation, and graphics**. The analytical commands in SPSS calculate and display statistics, graphics, or tabulations. They are probably the reason you are using SPSS.
- **Other utilities**. This group includes utility commands that do not affect the working data file, but that enhance or simplify the operation of SPSS itself.

The remainder of this introduction provides overviews of the commands that perform these functions. For details on the operation of any command, consult the appropriate section of this syntax reference guide.

Defining a Working Data File

SPSS can read data files created in a wide variety of spreadsheet and database formats. Commands are also available for defining and reading data from simple, unformatted text files.

Data Files in SPSS, Spreadsheet, or Database Format

The easiest way to define a working data file is to open a data file that has already been defined, either in SPSS or in some other software. If you have data in such a file, use one of the following commands:

GET. Reads data files in SPSS format as created by the SAVE command in SPSS running under the same operating system or a compatible one. GET is the fastest way to define a working data file. Labels and missing-value definitions that were in effect when the file was saved are preserved.

IMPORT. Reads data files as created by the EXPORT command in SPSS on any machine under any operating system. IMPORT is noticeably slower than GET, but preserves labels and missing-value definitions.

GET TRANSLATE. Reads data files created by popular spreadsheet and database software. Field names may be preserved as SPSS variable names. (Other GET commands for other software formats are available under some operating systems. Consult the appropriate sections of this syntax reference guide for details.)

Unformatted Text Files

If your data are in an unformatted "text" file such as the ASCII files that can be saved by text editors or word processors, you must tell SPSS exactly where and how to read the variables in the file. Do this with:

DATA LIST. Specifies names, formats, and locations of variables to be read from a text file.

MATRIX DATA. Defines an SPSS matrix file to be read from a text or ASCII file. An SPSS matrix-format file can contain correlation, covariance, or other kinds of matrices. Statistical procedures are sometimes able to analyze a matrix-format file more efficiently than a case-oriented data file. The MCONVERT command converts between correlation and covariance matrix files.

Other Data Definition Commands

A utility command that can be useful in defining a data file is:

APPLY DICTIONARY. Applies labels, formats, and missing-value definitions to the working data file from a data file saved in SPSS format, when some or all of the variables in the two files have the same names.

If you are running SPSS under a suitable operating system, you can use:

KEYED DATA LIST and POINT. These commands read keyed (indexed sequential) or direct-access (VSAM) data files under certain operating systems.

Describing the Working Data File

Once you have defined a working data file, you can add other information to its dictionary. With the exception of the MISSING VALUES command, these commands are basically cosmetic and affect the appearance rather than the content of SPSS output.

MISSING VALUES. Specifies that certain values should be excluded from analysis. These are typically codes used to represent absent or irrelevant data.

FORMATS. Specifies the format (e.g., numeric, date, dollar) by which data values should be displayed. You can also use PRINT FORMATS to specify one format for displayed values, and WRITE FORMATS to specify another format (possibly nonprintable) for use with the WRITE command.

VARIABLE LABELS. Provides extended descriptive labels for variables. SPSS automatically uses variable labels to annotate its output.

VALUE LABELS. Provides extended descriptive labels for individual values of variables. These labels are particularly useful if you use numeric codes to represent categorical information, such as gender or race. SPSS automatically uses value labels to annotate its output.

ADD VALUE LABELS. Adds value labels without replacing those previously defined for a variable.

RENAME VARIABLES. Changes the names of variables in the working data file.

Related utilities include:

DISPLAY. Displays information on variables, documents, or macros defined in the working data file.

DOCUMENT. Adds documentary information to the working data file. Documents are preserved by the SAVE command.

Modifying Data Values

The SPSS transformation language makes it easy to change the values of your variables in almost any systematic way. (*Ad hoc* changes in individual values can be made in the Data Editor, available in some operating environments.)

Transformation commands are not executed immediately. Instead, they are stored in the computer's memory until a command is processed that needs the data. At that time SPSS executes all transformation commands that are pending since the last time it read the data file. (See EXECUTE to override this behavior.)

COMPUTE. Evaluates an expression and assigns the result to the values of a new or existing variable. The expression can involve constants, variables in the working data file, arithmetic or logical operators, and any of several dozen functions.

IF. Evaluates an expression conditionally (depending on whether a logical expression is true for a particular case) and assigns the result of the expression to a new or existing variable.

DO IF and related commands (ELSE IF, ELSE, END IF). Delimit a block of transformation commands which are to be executed conditionally, depending on whether a logical expression is true for each particular case.

RECODE. Reassigns the values of individual variables, or collapses ranges of values into single values, according to your specifications. This command can also create a new variable to contain the recoded or collapsed values.

AUTORECODE. Recodes values automatically into consecutive integers. This command works for both numeric and string (alphanumeric) variables.

COUNT. Counts how many of a set of variables have any of a set of specified values, and sets a variable equal to the count.

DO REPEAT. Replicates a block of transformation commands, substituting different variables or constants into each copy.

RANK. Assigns rank orders to cases, based on a variable in the working data file. Unlike other commands listed here, RANK requires SPSS to process the data file immediately.

TEMPORARY. Indicates that a group of transformation commands should modify the working data file only temporarily.

Two utility commands do nothing but add variable names to the dictionary:

NUMERIC. Adds a list of numeric variables to the dictionary. Since new variables are numeric by default, the main use of this command is to specify in advance the order of a group of new variables.

STRING. Adds a string (alphanumeric) variable or a list of string variables to the dictionary. Since new variables are numeric by default, this command is required before any transformation command that uses a new string variable.

Defining Complex Data Files

The above commands all read or modify rectangular data files in ways that handle typical situations. When your data are not arranged in one of these typical ways, you can use the more powerful programming facilities of SPSS to take control of the building of the working data file. With these facilities you can read a data file of almost any shape, or you can generate deterministic or random data in a file of your own creation.

INPUT PROGRAM. Marks the beginning of a program to define or create a working data file. The program usually includes control structures (such as LOOP or DO IF), one or more DATA LIST commands, and transformation commands (such as COMPUTE).

The following special-purpose commands are available within an input program:

END CASE. Sends a case to the working data file.

END FILE. Closes the working data file explicitly rather than waiting for the end of a data file being read by SPSS.

REREAD. Causes the next DATA LIST command executed to read the same record as the previously executed DATA LIST command. This lets you use part of a data record to determine the way in which the rest of the record is read.

REPEATING DATA. Allows more than one case to be defined by a single input record. This command can also be used in a FILE TYPE structure, described below.

LOOP. Marks the beginning of a group of transformation commands to be executed repeatedly. Loop termination can be controlled by a logical criterion, an index variable, or explicitly with the BREAK command. The LOOP command can also be used as a part of the transformation language, outside of an input program.

Certain commonly encountered data structures, where a data value on each record determines how that record should be treated, are handled automatically by the FILE TYPE and RECORD TYPE commands. Each variety of FILE TYPE provides "canned" logic for rereading data records, with automatic checks for such problems as invalid record types, missing or out-of-order records, and duplicate records. Subsequent RECORD TYPE commands provide the details for each record type.

FILE TYPE MIXED. Builds a case from each record that is read. Unwanted record types can be skipped, and each record type can be treated differently, but one case is built from each record processed.

FILE TYPE GROUPED. Builds a single case from a group of records.

FILE TYPE NESTED. Builds cases from hierarchical data files, spreading data values from higher-level (aggregated) records to lower-level records.

Utility commands that are particularly helpful in defining complex files include:

LEAVE. Retains the values of specified variables from one case to another, rather than reinitializing them between cases.

VECTOR. Defines a group of consecutive variables as a pseudo-vector. Transformation commands can then refer to individual variables by means of an index variable that is evaluated at run time. This facility is particularly helpful within a loop structure, since the loop index can also be used within the vector.

Selecting Cases for Processing

The following commands specify that subsequent processing should be based on selected cases only:

SELECT IF. Lets you specify a logical criterion for case selection.

FILTER. Lets you specify a logical criterion for temporary case selection.

SAMPLE. Lets you select a sample of the cases in the working data file, based on a pseudo-random number generated by SPSS.

N OF CASES. Specifies that only a certain number of cases from the beginning of the data file should be used.

Modifying the Structure of the Working Data File

The following commands, used singly or in combination, let you reorganize the working data file in almost any way you could want:

SORT CASES. Sorts the cases in the working data file into ascending or descending order of the values of one or more variables.

FLIP. Transposes the data matrix so that each variable becomes a case and each case becomes a variable.

WEIGHT. Simulates the replication of individual cases in statistical calculations and tables.

AGGREGATE. Combines groups of cases into single aggregated cases. Variables in the aggregated file contain statistical functions (such as sums or means) of the original variables, computed across a group of cases in the original, unaggregated file.

UPDATE. Replaces data values in a master file with values from one or more transaction files.

ADD FILES. Combines the cases in two or more data files, normally files containing many of the same variables.

MATCH FILES. Combines the variables in two or more data files, normally files containing many of the same cases. Can also perform table lookups, in which the value of a key variable is used to extract data from a table file.

SPLIT FILE. Specifies that analysis should be performed separately for each group of cases, as defined by one or more grouping variables.

Saving the Working Data File

A working data file exists only during the course of an SPSS session. The following commands save a copy of the working data file on any available storage device.

SAVE. Saves the working data file in native SPSS format, which can be read by the GET command under the same operating system or a compatible one. This is the best format in which to save data files that you will analyze repeatedly with SPSS. All dictionary information is preserved. SPSS reads and writes files much faster in its own format. Files in this format can be used only within SPSS.

XSAVE. Saves the working data file in native SPSS format while carrying out the next SPSS procedure, thus saving the processing time required to read the data file (provided that there is another SPSS procedure within the session).

EXPORT. Saves the working data file in SPSS portable format, which can be read by the SPSS Import command, on any machine under any operating system. EXPORT is noticeably slower than SAVE or XSAVE.

SAVE TRANSLATE. Saves the working data file in one of several formats that can be read by popular spreadsheet and database software.

WRITE. Saves the data values in the working data file in text (typically ASCII) format, with no dictionary information.

Displaying Data Values

The simplest thing that SPSS can do to the working data file is display it. The Data Editor (where available) provides the quickest and easiest way to view the contents of the working data file. The following commands display data in increasingly elaborate ways:

LIST. Displays the data in the working data file. This command offers minimal control over the data displayed or its format.

PRINT. Displays data values, or calculated values or constants, while carrying out the next SPSS procedure. This is an efficient and flexible way of displaying data, provided that there will be another procedure. It requires you to specify the format and to calculate any summary statistics using the transformation language.

REPORT. Produces reports containing summary statistics, listings of individual cases, or both. This is usually the easiest way to obtain reports more complex than simple case listings.

Statistical Analysis, Tabulation, and Graphics

The procedures performing these tasks are probably why you are using SPSS. Consult the *Base System User's Guide* for your version of SPSS for assistance in choosing the right procedure and interpreting the results.

Analytical procedures read the working data file. As they do so, SPSS carries out any transformation commands that have been specified since the data file was last read. If the working data file has been modified, a new copy is written for subsequent use.

Summary Measures, Frequency Tables, and Crosstabulation

CROSSTABS. Builds cross-classification tables and calculates tests of independence and measures of association for categorical variables.

DESCRIPTIVES. Efficiently calculates univariate statistics, such as means and variances, that do not require tabulation.

EXAMINE. Displays exploratory plots and statistics.

FREQUENCIES. Displays frequency tables, as well as univariate statistics and plots.

MULT RESPONSE. Displays frequency tables and crosstabulations for multiple-response and multiple-dichotomy variables.

Comparing Means and Analysis of Variance

ANOVA. Performs factorial analysis of variance for single dependent variables and multiple factors.

MEANS. Displays subgroup means based on one or more grouping variables.

ONEWAY. Performs analysis of variance with one factor, allowing user-specified contrasts and displaying any of several multiple-comparison tests. See also ANOVA.

T-TEST. Performs the t test for a difference between two means, for either independent or paired samples.

Correlation and Linear Regression

CORRELATIONS. Calculates Pearson correlation coefficients.

REGRESSION. Performs least-squares regression analysis, displaying coefficients, significance tests, and a variety of diagnostic plots, statistics, and listings.

PARTIAL CORR. Calculates matrices of partial correlation coefficients.

Nonparametric Measures

NONPAR CORR. Calculates Spearman and Kendall nonparametric correlation coefficients.

NPAR TESTS. Calculates a variety of significance tests and measures of association for ordinal and nominal variables.

Graphical Display

GRAPH. Produces high-resolution charts and plots. This facility varies greatly from one operating environment to another.

PLOT. Displays high- or low-resolution (character-based) scatterplots.

Other Utilities

The following commands perform miscellaneous useful tasks whose implementation often differs widely from one operating environment to another. Such differences are noted, where possible, in the reference section for each command.

SET. Controls any of numerous settings that can be used to tailor the behavior or output of SPSS.

SHOW. Displays the current settings of the specifications controlled by SET.

PRESERVE and RESTORE. Allow you to "remember" the current settings of the SET specifications and restore them later. They are chiefly used in macros.

DEFINE (macro). The DEFINE command lets you define a macro, which is a block of SPSS command syntax (a command, part of a command, or multiple commands) that can be invoked by name. You can pass parameters to a macro when invoking it. See Appendix D for examples of how to use the macro facility.

HELP. The basic HELP facility described in this syntax reference guide is replaced by a more powerful help system in some environments. Consult the *Base System User's Guide* for your version of SPSS.

EXECUTE. Causes SPSS to read the working data file and execute any commands that are pending, such as transformation commands. This is sometimes useful after commands that act like transformations (such as PRINT and XSAVE), carrying out their function during the next data pass.

INCLUDE. Reads and executes SPSS command syntax from a file.

HOST. Gives you access to native operating-system commands during an SPSS session, in operating systems where this facility is implemented.

ERASE. Deletes files during an SPSS session, in operating systems where this facility is implemented.

SYSFILE INFO. Displays information such as variable names from data files saved in SPSS format without disturbing the working data file.

TITLE and SUBTITLE. Include titles of your choice on each page of SPSS output.

COMMENT. Lets you annotate the listing of SPSS commands executed in a session. To save comments with a data file, use DOCUMENT.

Example

The following commands could be used in SPSS either as part of an SPSS session or as a complete batch job:

```
GET FILE=WEATHER.SAV.
COMPUTE AVTEMP=MEAN.2(TEMP1,TEMP2,TEMP3).
VARIABLE LABELS AVTEMP 'Average Daily Temperature'.
REGRESSION
 /DEPENDENT=NEWTEMP
 /ENTER=AVTEMP HUMID PRESSURE WINDDIR WINDSPD
 /SAVE=PRED(PREDICT).
SAVE OUTFILE=FORECAST.SAV.
```

- The GET command reads the SPSS data file *WEATHER.SAV* and uses it as the working data file.
- The COMPUTE command uses a statistical function to create a new variable, *AVTEMP*.
- The statistical function MEAN.2 indicates that the the value of *AVTEMP* should be the mean of the three variables (*TEMP1, TEMP2, TEMP3*) and that at least two of the variables must have nonmissing values.
- The VARIABLE LABELS command supplies a descriptive label for the new variable.
- The REGRESSION command initiates a statistical procedure.
- The SAVE subcommand saves the predicted values generated by the REGRESSION procedure and assigns the variable name *PREDICT* to these values.
- The SAVE command creates a new SPSS data file, *FORECAST.SAV*, which contains all the variables from *WEATHER.SAV* plus the two new variables, *AVTEMP* and *PREDICT*.

Universals

This part of the *SPSS Base System Syntax Reference Guide* discusses general topics pertinent to running SPSS using command syntax. The topics are divided into five sections:

- *SPSS Commands* explains command syntax, including command specification, command order, and running SPSS commands in different modes. In this section, you will learn how to read SPSS syntax charts, which summarize command syntax in diagrams and provide an easy reference. Discussions of individual commands are found in an alphabetical reference in the next part of this manual.
- *Files* discusses different types of files used by SPSS. Terms frequently mentioned in this manual are defined. This section provides an overview of how SPSS handles files so that you can make the best use of SPSS capabilities and increase your efficiency.
- *Variables* contains important information on general rules and conventions concerning variables and variable definition in SPSS. In this section, you will find detailed information on variable formats.
- *Transformation Expressions* describes expressions that can be used in data transformation. Functions and operators available in SPSS are defined and illustrated. In this section, you will find a complete list of available functions and how to use them with SPSS commands.
- *Date and Time in SPSS* deals with functions and formats used with date and time expressions. In this section, you will find ways to read and convert date and time, use them in analysis, and display them in output.

SPSS Commands

Commands are the instructions that you give SPSS to initiate an action. For SPSS to interpret your commands correctly, you must follow certain rules.

Syntax Diagrams

Each SPSS command described in this manual includes a syntax diagram that shows all the subcommands, keywords, and specifications allowed for that command. By recognizing symbols and different type fonts, you can use the syntax diagram as a quick reference for any command. Figure 1 is an example.

- Lines of text in italics indicate limitation or operation mode of the command.
- Elements shown in upper case are keywords defined by SPSS to identify commands, subcommands, functions, operators, and other specifications. In Figure 1, T-TEST is the command and GROUPS is a subcommand.

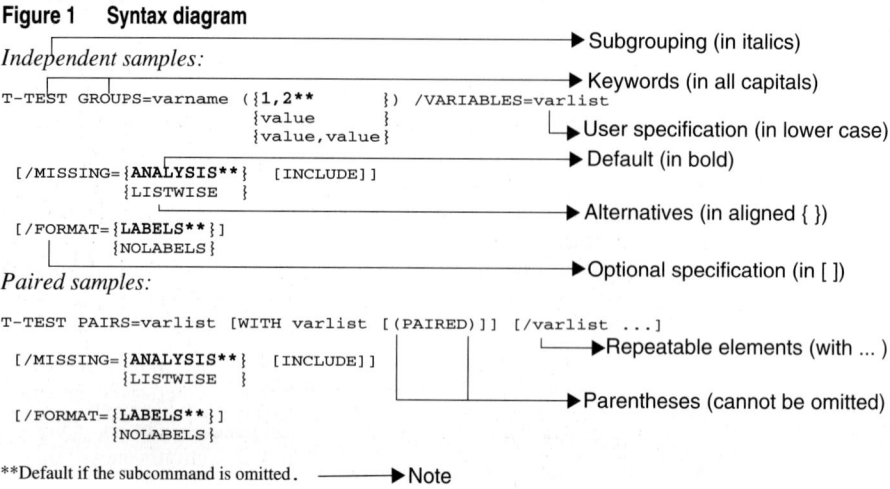

Figure 1 Syntax diagram

- Elements in lower case describe specifications you supply. For example, varlist indicates that you need to supply a list of variables.
- Elements in bold are defaults. SPSS supports two types of defaults. When the default is followed by **, as ANALYSIS** in Figure 1, the default (ANALYSIS) is in effect if the subcommand (MISSING) is not specified. If a default is not followed by **, it is in effect when the subcommand (or keyword) is specified by itself.
- Parentheses, apostrophes, and quotation marks are required where indicated.
- Elements enclosed in square brackets ([ ]) are optional. Wherever brackets would confuse the format, they are omitted. The command description explains which specifications are required and which are optional.
- Braces ({ }) indicate a choice between elements. You can specify any one of the elements enclosed within the aligned braces.
- Ellipses indicates that you can repeat an element in the specification. The specification

  T-TEST PAIRS=varlist [WITH varlist [(PAIRED)]] [/varlist ...]

  means that you can specify multiple variable lists with optional WITH variables and keyword PAIRED in parentheses.
- Most abbreviations are obvious; for example, varname stands for variable name and varlist stands for a variable list.
- The command terminator is not shown in the syntax diagram.

Command Specification

The following rules apply to all SPSS commands:

- Commands begin with a keyword that is the name of the command and often have additional specifications, such as subcommands and user specifications. Refer to the discus-

sion of each command to see which subcommands and additional specifications are required.
- Commands and any command specifications can be entered in upper and lower case. Commands, subcommands, keywords, and variable names are translated to upper case before processing. All user specifications, including labels and data values, preserve upper and lower case.
- Spaces can be added between specifications at any point where a single blank is allowed. In addition, lines can be broken at any point where a single blank is allowed. There are two exceptions: the END DATA command can have only one space between words, and string specifications on commands such as TITLE, SUBTITLE, VARIABLE LABELS, and VALUE LABELS can be broken across two lines only by specifying a + between string segments (see "String Values in Command Specifications" on p. 16).
- The first word of a command can be abbreviated to a minimum of three letters provided no duplicates result. For example, AGGREGATE can be abbreviated to AGG, but COMPUTE can only be abbreviated to COMP to avoid confusion with COMMENT. A very small number of commands can duplicate an internal command when abbreviated to three characters (for example, LIST) and at least four characters should be used. For internal command structure, DATA LIST cannot be abbreviated.
- If the first word of a multiple-word command has a duplicate (for example, FILE LABEL and FILE TYPE), the first word cannot be abbreviated.
- All keywords after the first command word can be abbreviated to three characters. For example, ADD VAL LAB is a valid abbreviation for ADD VALUE LABELS, and EXA VAR=varlist is valid for EXAMINE VARIABLES=varlist. END DATA is an exception: you must spell both command keywords in full; END DAT is *not* a valid abbreviation for END DATA.
- Three-character truncation does not apply to INFO command specifications. Spell out all keywords in full. For procedure names specified on INFO, spell out the first word in full and subsequent words through at least the first three characters.

Running SPSS Commands

You can run SPSS commands in either batch or interactive mode. In batch mode, SPSS commands are read and acted upon as a batch, so the system knows that a command is complete when it encounters a new command. In interactive mode, SPSS commands are executed immediately, and you must use a command terminator to tell SPSS when a command is complete.

Interactive Mode

The following rules apply to command specifications in interactive mode:
- Each command ends with a command terminator. The default command terminator is a period. It is best to omit the terminator on BEGIN DATA, however, so that SPSS will treat inline data as one continuous specification.
- The command terminator must be the last non-blank character in a command.

- Commands can begin in any column of a command line and continue for as many lines as needed. The exception is the END DATA command, which must begin in the first column of the first line after the end of data.
- The maximum length of any command line is 80 characters, including the prompt and the command terminator.

You should observe interactive rules when you

- Submit commands from a syntax window or with an SPSS Manager, either one command at a time or as a group.
- Enter commands at an SPSS prompt on those systems that run prompted sessions.

See the *Base System User's Guide* for your version of SPSS for more information.

Batch Mode

The following rules apply to command specifications in batch mode:

- All commands in the command file must begin in column 1. You can use plus (+) or minus (−) signs in the first column if you want to indent the command specification to make the command file more readable.
- If multiple lines are used for a command, column 1 of each continuation line must be blank.
- Command terminators are optional.
- An asterisk (*) in the first column indicates a comment line (see the COMMENT command).

You should observe batch rules when you

- Construct a command file that will be submitted to your operating system for execution.
- Construct a command file that will be included with the INCLUDE command. You can include a command file when you are working in interactive mode. The included command file, however, must follow batch rules.

The way you submit a command file for execution varies from operating system to operating system. Command files do not necessarily need to be submitted to a batch queue, although they can be on operating systems that have a batch queue. In batch mode, the commands in the file are executed one after the other, and SPSS output is displayed when all commands are executed. Consult the *SPSS User's Guide* for your system for specific information.

The following is a sample command file:

```
GET FILE=BANK.SAV /KEEP ID TIME SEX JOBCAT SALBEG SALNOW
     /RENAME SALNOW = SAL90.

DO IF TIME LT 82.
+   COMPUTE RATE=0.05.
ELSE.
+   COMPUTE RATE=0.04.
END IF.

COMPUTE SALNOW=(1+RATE)*SAL90.

EXAMINE VARIABLES=SALNOW BY SEX /PLOT=NONE.
```

Figure 2 shows an SPSS session in batch mode where the sample command file above (named *sample.sys*) was submitted to SPSS on UNIX:

Figure 2   An SPSS session on UNIX run in batch mode

```
$ spss -m sample.sps  ⏎Enter

For IBM AIX 3.1          SPSS for Unix -- Development          SPSS ID 333333
This software is functional through November 30, 1992.

Try the new SPSS Release 4.0 features:

* LOGISTIC REGRESSION procedure            * CATEGORIES Option:
* EXAMINE procedure to explore data        *     conjoint analysis
* FLIP to transpose data files             *     correspondence analysis
* MATRIX Transformations Language          * GRAPH interface to SPSS Graph

See the new SPSS documentation for more information on these new features.

   1   0     GET FILE=BANK.SAV /KEEP ID TIME SEX JOBCAT SALBEG SALNOW
   2   0              /RENAME SALNOW = SAL90.
   3   0

File bank.sav
   Label:  05.00.00
   Created:  13 Jan 92 15:36:45 - 11 variables and 474 cases

   4   0    DO IF TIME LT 82.
   5   1    +  COMPUTE RATE=0.05.
   6   1    ELSE.
   7   1    +  COMPUTE RATE=0.04.
   8   1    END IF.
   9   1
  10   0    COMPUTE SALNOW=(1+RATE)*SAL90.
  11   0
  12   0    EXAMINE VARIABLES=SALNOW BY SEX /PLOT=NONE.

       SALNOW

Valid cases:        474.0   Missing cases:         .0   Percent missing:         .0

Mean          14387.02   Std Err    327.4883   Min      6615.000   Skewness     2.1190
Median        12096.00   Variance   50835828   Max     56160.00    S E Skew      .1122
5% Trim       13567.90   Std Dev    7129.925   Range   49545.00    Kurtosis     5.3204
                                               IQR      5531.700   S E Kurt      .2238

       SALNOW
By     SEX          0         MALES

Valid cases:        258.0   Missing cases:         .0   Percent missing:         .0

Mean          17317.99   Std Err    506.8771   Min      8174.400   Skewness     1.6324
Median        13699.20   Variance   66286501   Max     56160.00    S E Skew      .1516
5% Trim       16486.12   Std Dev    8141.652   Range   47985.60    Kurtosis     2.7287
                                               IQR      9488.000   S E Kurt      .3021

       SALNOW
By     SEX          1         FEMALES

Valid cases:        216.0   Missing cases:         .0   Percent missing:         .0

Mean          10886.13   Std Err    214.9651   Min      6615.000   Skewness     1.8791
Median        10157.10   Variance    9981362   Max     24412.50    S E Skew      .1655
5% Trim       10557.46   Std Dev    3159.329   Range   17797.50    Kurtosis     4.7452
```

Subcommands

Many commands include additional specifications called *subcommands* for locating data, handling data, and formatting the output display.
- Subcommands begin with a keyword that is the name of the subcommand. Some subcommands include additional specifications.
- A subcommand keyword is separated from its specifications, if any, by an equals sign. The equals sign is usually optional but is required where ambiguity is possible in the specification. To avoid ambiguity, it is best to use the equals signs as shown in the syntax diagrams in this manual.
- Most subcommands can be named in any order. However, some commands require a specific subcommand order. The description of each command includes a section on subcommand order section.
- Subcommands are separated from each other by a slash. To avoid ambiguity, it is best to use the slashes as shown in the syntax diagrams in this manual.

Keywords

Keywords identify commands, subcommands, functions, operators, and other specifications in SPSS.
- Keywords, including commands and subcommands, can often be truncated to the first three characters of each word. An exception is the keyword WITH, which must be spelled in full. See "Command Specification" on p. 12 for additional rules for three-character truncation of commands.
- Keywords identifying logical operators (AND, OR, and NOT), relational operators (EQ, GE, GT, LE, LT, and NE), and ALL, BY, TO, and WITH are reserved words and cannot be used as variable names.

Values in Command Specifications

Values specified in commands follow the following rules:
- A single lowercase character in the syntax diagram, for example, *n*, *w*, and *d*, indicates a user-specified value.
- The value can be an integer or a real number within a restricted range, as required by the specific command or subcommand. For exact restrictions, read the individual command description.
- A number specified as an argument to a subcommand can be entered with or without leading zeros.

String Values in Command Specifications

- Each string specified in a command should be enclosed in a set of apostrophes or quotation marks.

- To specify an apostrophe within a string, either use quotation marks to enclose the string or specify double apostrophes. Both of the following specifications are valid:

  ```
  'Client''s Satisfaction'
  ```

  ```
  "Client's Satisfaction"
  ```

- To specify quotation marks within a string, use apostrophes to enclose the string:

  ```
  'Categories Labeled "UNSTANDARD" in the Report'
  ```

- String specifications can be broken across command lines by specifying each string segment within apostrophes or quotes and using a + sign to join segments. For example,

  ```
  'One, Two'
  ```

  can be specified as

  ```
  'One,'
  + ' Two'
  ```

  The plus sign can be specified on either the first or the second line of the broken string. Any blanks separating the two segments must be enclosed within one or the other string segment.

- Blanks within apostrophes or quotation marks are significant.

Delimiters

Delimiters are used to separate data values, keywords, arguments, and specifications.

- A blank is usually used to separate one specification from another, except when another delimiter serves the same purpose or when a comma is required.
- Commas are required to separate arguments to functions. Otherwise, blanks are generally valid substitutes for commas.
- Arithmetic operators (+, -, *, and /) serve as delimiters in expressions.
- Blanks can be used before and after operators or equals signs to improve readability, but commas cannot.
- Special delimiters include parentheses, apostrophes, quotation marks, the slash, and the equals sign. Blanks before and after special delimiters are optional.
- The slash is used primarily to separate subcommands and lists of variables. Although slashes are sometimes optional, it is a good practice to enter them as shown in the syntax diagrams.
- The equals sign is used between a subcommand and its specifications, as in STATISTICS= MEAN, and to show equivalence, as in COMPUTE target variable=expression. Equals signs following subcommands are frequently optional, but it is best to enter them for clarity.

Command Order

Command order in SPSS is more often than not a matter of common sense and follows the following logical sequence: variable definition, data transformation, and statistical analysis.

For example, you cannot label, transform, analyze, or use a variable in any way before it exists. The following general rules apply:

- Commands that define variables for a session (DATA LIST, GET, MATRIX DATA, etc.) must precede commands that assign labels or missing values to those variables; they must also precede transformation and procedure commands that use those variables.
- Transformation commands (IF, COUNT, COMPUTE, etc.) that are used to create and modify variables must precede commands that assign labels or missing values to those variables, and they must also precede the procedures that use those variables.
- Generally, the logical outcome of command processing determines command order. For example, a procedure that creates new variables in the working data file must precede a procedure that uses those new variables.
- Some commands, such as REREAD and END CASE, can appear only in an *input program* where the cases are created. Other commands, such as SELECT IF, can appear only in a *transformation program* after cases have been created. Still other commands, such as COMPUTE, can appear in an input or transformation program. For a discussion of these program states and command order, see Appendix A.

In addition to observing the rules above, it is important to distinguish between commands that cause the data to be read and those that do not. Table 1 shows the commands that cause the data to be read. Most of the remaining commands (those that do not cause the data to be read) do not take effect immediately; they are read by SPSS but are not executed until a command that causes the data to be read is encountered in the command sequence. This avoids unnecessary passes through the data.

Table 1 Commands that cause the data to be read*

AGGREGATE	FREQUENCIES	PARTIAL CORR
ALSCAL	GRAPH	PLOT
ANOVA	HILOGLINEAR	PROBIT
AUTORECODE	IMPORT	PROXIMITIES
BEGIN DATA	LIST	QUICK CLUSTER
CLUSTER	LOGISTIC REGRESSION	RANK
CNLR	LOGLINEAR	REGRESSION
CORRELATIONS	MANOVA	RELIABILITY
CROSSTABS	MATRIX	REPORT
DESCRIPTIVES	MCONVERT	SAVE
DISCRIMINANT	MEANS	SAVE SCSS
EXAMINE	MULTIPLE RESPONSE	SAVE TRANSLATE
EXECUTE	NLR	SORT
EXPORT	NONPAR CORR	SURVIVAL
FACTOR	NPAR TESTS	T-TEST
FLIP	ONEWAY	

* This table shows the procedures in the SPSS Base system and the Professional Statistics and Advanced Statistics options; it does not show commands in other SPSS options, such as SPSS Tables or SPSS Trends.

Transformation commands that alter the dictionary of the working data file, such as MISSING VALUES, and commands that do not affect the working data, such as SET, SHOW, and DISPLAY, take effect as soon as they are encountered in the command sequence, regardless of conditional statements that precede them. Table 2 lists all transformation commands that take effect immediately.

Table 2   Transformation commands that take effect immediately

ADD VALUE LABELS	PRINT FORMATS
DOCUMENT	SPLIT FILE
DROP DOCUMENTS	STRING
FORMATS	VALUE LABELS
LEAVE	VARIABLE LABELS
MISSING VALUES	VECTOR
N OF CASES	WEIGHT
NUMERIC	WRITE FORMATS

Since these transformations take effect regardless of the conditional statements that precede them, they cannot be applied selectively to individual cases, as shown in the following example:

```
DO IF AGE>69.
MISSING VALUES INCOME EXPENSES (0).
ELSE.
COMPUTE PROFIT=INCOME-EXPENSES.
END IF.
LIST.
```

The MISSING VALUES command is in effect when COMPUTE is executed, even if the condition defined on DO IF is false. To treat 0 income and expenses as missing only for those older than 69, use RECODE in the DO IF—END IF structure to selectively recode 0 to a negative number and declare the negative number as missing:

```
MISSING VALUES INCOME EXPENSES (-1).
DO IF (AGE>69).
RECODE INCOME EXPENSES (0=-1).
END IF.
COMPUTE PROFILE=INCOME-EXPENSES.
LIST.
```

In addition, the order of transformations that take effect immediately in the command sequence can be misleading. Consider the following:

```
COMPUTE PROFIT=INCOME-EXPENSES.
MISSING VALUES INCOME EXPENSES (0).
LIST.
```

- COMPUTE precedes MISSING VALUES and is processed first; however, SPSS delays its execution until the data are being read.
- MISSING VALUES takes effect as soon as it is encountered.

- LIST causes the data to be read; thus, SPSS executes both COMPUTE and LIST during the same data pass. Because MISSING VALUES is already in effect by this time, all cases with the value 0 for either *INCOME* or *EXPENSES* return a missing value for *PROFIT*.

To prevent the MISSING VALUES command from taking effect before COMPUTE is executed, you must position MISSING VALUES after the LIST command. Alternatively, place an EXECUTE command between COMPUTE and MISSING VALUES.

Files

SPSS reads, creates, and writes different types of files. This section provides an overview of the types of files used in SPSS and discusses concepts and rules that apply to all files. Conventions for naming, printing, deleting, or permanently saving files, and for submitting command files for processing, differ from one computer and operating system to another. For specific information, consult the *Base System User's Guide* for your version of SPSS.

Command File

Command files contain SPSS commands, sometimes with inline data. They can be created by a text editor. Wherever SPSS allows you to paste commands, either in a syntax window or with an SPSS manager, the resulting file is a command file. You can also edit a journal file to produce a command file (see "Journal File" below). Commands in a command file are run in batch mode and must follow the rules applicable to batch-mode commands (see "Batch Mode" on p. 14). All examples in this manual follow these rules. The following is an example of a simple command file that contains both commands and inline data:

```
DATA LIST /ID 1-3 SEX 4 (A) AGE 5-6 OPINION1 TO OPINION5 7-11.
BEGIN DATA
001F2621221
002M5611122
003F3422212
329M2121212
END DATA.
LIST.
```

- Case does not matter for commands but is significant for inline data. If you specified f for female and m for male in column 4 of the data line, the value of *SEX* would be f or m, instead of F or M as it is now.
- Commands can be in upper or lower case. SPSS converts all commands to upper case before processing. Uppercase characters are used for all commands throughout this manual only to distinguish them from other text.

Journal File

SPSS keeps a journal file to record all commands entered during an SPSS session, along with any error or warning messages generated by these commands. You can retrieve this file with any text editor and review it to learn how the SPSS session went. You can also edit the file to build a new command file and use it in another run. An edited and tested journal file can be saved and later used for repeated tasks.

The default name for the journal file is *SPSS.JNL* on most operating systems. You can turn off the journal or assign a different name to it (see SET). SPSS erases an existing journal file with the default name when it starts a new session. If you want to save a journal file for future use, rename it before you start another SPSS session. On some operating systems, SPSS allows you to append to journals from a previous session. Consult the *User's Guide* for your version of SPSS for specific information. Figure 3 is a journal file for a short SPSS session.

Figure 3 Records from an SPSS journal file

```
DATA LIST /ID 1-3 SEX 4 (A) AGE 5-6 OPINION1 TO OPINION5 7-11.
BEGIN DATA
001F2621221
002M5611122
003F3422212
004F45112L2
>Warning # 1102
>An invalid numeric field has been found.  The result has been set to the
>system-missing value.
END DATA.
LIST.
finish.
```

- The warning message, marked by the > symbol, tells you that an invalid numeric field has been found. Checking the last data line, you will notice that column 10 is *L*, which is probably a typographic error. You can correct the typo (for example, by changing the *L* to 1), delete the warning message, and submit the file again.
- The last command in the file, FINISH, is included in the journal when you exit an SPSS session. Delete this command if you want to continue your session after you submit the edited command file.

Data Files

SPSS is capable of reading and writing a wide variety of data files, including raw data files created by a data entry device or a text editor, formatted data files produced by a data management program, data files generated by other software packages, and SPSS data files. SPSS data files contain information in SPSS format and therefore are the fastest to retrieve, process, and save in SPSS.

Raw Data File

Raw data files contain only data, either generated by a programming language, such as COBOL, FORTRAN, and ASSEMBLER, or entered with a data entry device or a text editor. SPSS can read raw data arranged in almost any format, including raw matrix materials and nonprintable codes. User-entered data can be imbedded within an SPSS command file as inline data or saved on tape or disk as an external file. Nonprintable machine codes are usually stored in an external file.

Raw data must be defined before they can be used by SPSS procedures. Data definition commands such as DATA LIST, KEYED DATA LIST, and MATRIX DATA can be used to read in raw data. Appropriate input formats must be specified on these commands (see "Variable Formats" on p. 34). If for some reason you need to write a raw data file, use the WRITE command or specify WRITE on a procedure with that subcommand. On most operating systems, the default extension of a raw data file produced by SPSS is *.DAT*.

Files from Other Software Applications

SPSS can read files from a variety of other software applications, including dBASE, Lotus, SYLK, and Excel. It can also read simple tab-delimited spreadsheet files. Use GET TRANS-

LATE with different TYPE specifications to read files from common spreadsheet and database programs. To produce data files for these programs, use SAVE TRANSLATE.

On some operating systems, SPSS is also capable of converting data files produced by other statistical software packages, such as BMDP, OSIRIS, SAS, and SCSS. Use GET BMDP, GET OSIRIS, GET SAS, and GET SCSS to read these files, and use SAVE SCSS to save SCSS data files.

Consult the *User's Guide* for your version of SPSS for the types of files (if any) that your system can read and write.

SPSS Data File

An SPSS data file is a file specifically formatted for use by SPSS, containing both data and the dictionary that defines the data. The **dictionary** contains names for the variables, formats for reading and displaying values, and optional variable and value labels and missing-value specifications. SPSS data files are created by using a SAVE or XSAVE command during a session. The default extension of a saved SPSS data file is *.SAV*. An SPSS data file can also be a matrix file created with the MATRIX=OUT subcommand on procedures that write matrices.

To retrieve an SPSS data file, use GET. SPSS data files speed processing and are required as input for combining files during an SPSS session. For a discussion of the structure of SPSS data files, see "SPSS Data File Structure" on p. 25.

SPSS Portable File

A portable file contains all of the data and dictionary information stored in the working data file but is specially formatted for transporting files between installations with different versions of SPSS (such as the PRIME, VAX, or HONEYWELL GCOS computers) or for transporting files between SPSS, SPSS/PC+, and other software using the same portable file format. Use IMPORT to read a portable file and EXPORT to save the working data file as a portable file. On most operating systems, the default extension of a saved portable file is *.POR*. Since a portable file needs conversion, it is always simpler to transport a file as an SPSS data file whenever possible.

Working Data File

The working data file is the data file you build to use in the current session. You can retrieve an SPSS data file using GET, which in effect makes a working copy of the specified file. You can also build a new file with DATA LIST or other data definition commands.

The working data file is not created until SPSS encounters a command (usually a procedure) that causes it to read the data (see Table 1 on p. 18). At that point, SPSS executes all of the preceding data definition and transformation commands and the command that causes the data to be read. The working data file is then available for further transformations and procedures, and it remains available until replaced by a new working data file or until the end of the session.

Some procedures can add variables to the working data file. Others, such as AGGREGATE and procedures that write matrix materials, can replace the working data file.

Any transformations and statistical analyses you request during an SPSS session are performed on the working data file. Transformations performed during an SPSS session apply to the working data file only. Changes to the file are lost if the working data file is erased or replaced before you have saved it. See SAVE and XSAVE.

Listing File

An SPSS session generates a listing file unless you explicitly suppress it using the SET command. The listing file contains output generated by an SPSS session and is formatted for reading. It can be displayed on the terminal, printed on a printer, or saved on a disk to be retrieved as a text file. A listing file can contain any of the following output:

- *Resource utilization message.* This includes the SPSS header and session summaries. The following is a sample session summary:

```
Preceding task required .08 seconds CPU time;   1.00 seconds elapsed.
   10  0
        9 command lines read.
        0 errors detected.
        0 warnings issued.
        0 seconds CPU time.
        2 seconds elapsed time.
          End of job.
End of job:   9 command lines   0 errors   0 warnings   0 CPU seconds
STOP
```

- *Command printback.* When executing commands in batch mode, SPSS prints each command it reads regardless of whether the command is syntactically correct or whether it is executed. Unlike the commands in the SPSS journal file, command lines in the printback are numbered for easy reference.

- *Diagnostic messages.* Unless otherwise routed, these messages are printed directly under the command they diagnose and specify the problem element by its line or beginning column. SPSS issues three kinds of diagnostic messages during a session: notes, warnings, and error messages. **Notes** alert you to operations that may not have produced meaningful results:

```
>Note # 17570 on line 32.  Command name: EXAMINE
>The number of unique data values for this cell is equal to one.  The cell will
>be included in any boxplots produced but other output will be omitted.
```

Warnings result from minor syntax or data errors encountered during the execution of a command. SPSS informs you of the error, its location in the command, and the operation SPSS has performed. The following is an example of a warning message:

```
>Warning # 1110
>Embedded signs are invalid except under E format.  The result has been set to
>the system-missing value.
>Command line: 1   Current case: 2   Current splitfile group: 1
>Field contents: '1-2'
>Record number: 2   Starting column: 1   Record length: 80
```

An **error message** is issued when SPSS encounters a syntax or data error that invalidates any result from the procedure and thus makes the continuation of execution meaningless. The command will be bypassed but will be scanned for additional errors. Subsequent commands that do not use results from that command will be executed but the results may be unreliable. The following is an error message that stops the execution of a command:

```
>Error # 105.  Command name: LIST
>This command is not valid before an active file has been defined.  See the
>documentation on the INPUT PROGRAM command.
>This command not executed.
```

If SPSS detects conditions that make it impossible to continue, a **termination message** is displayed and the current session stops. This type of error message should rarely occur. An explanatory note usually accompanies such a message so that you can make an effort to correct the situation. Contact SPSS Technical Support when you encounter a termination message. The following is a termination message:

```
>This is an error from which SPSS cannot recover.
>The SPSS run will terminate now.
```

- *SPSS command results.* The results include those generated by SPSS procedures and those produced by DISPLAY or WRITE. Note that the results from a WRITE command can be saved as computer-readable data in an external file but they are listed in user-readable format in the listing file. Note also that on systems where high-resolution graphics are available, only character-based charts are included in the listing file. Consult the *User's Guide* for your version of SPSS for discussion of graphic output.

SPSS Data File Structure

An SPSS data file is a self-documented file containing data and descriptive information. The descriptive information is called the **dictionary**. It contains variable names and locations, variable and value labels, print and write formats, and missing-value indicators. To use an SPSS data file, you must retrieve it with GET, which creates a working data file from the SPSS data file. Only a few commands can use an SPSS data file directly without first specifying GET; they include MATCH FILES, ADD FILES, and procedures that can read SPSS matrix data files.

To view the contents of an SPSS data file, retrieve it with GET and then use LIST to display the variables in the working data file. Figure 4 shows a partial listing of a working file. The values are displayed using their print format, which is different from the way they are internally stored.

Figure 4   Part of a listed working data file

```
ID  SALBEG SEX TIME   AGE  SALNOW EDLEVEL  WORK JOBCAT MINORITY  SEXRACE
628   8400   0   81  28.50  16080    16     .25    4      0       1.00
630  24000   0   73  40.33  41400    16   12.50    5      0       1.00
632  10200   0   83  31.08  21960    15    4.08    5      0       1.00
633   8700   0   93  31.17  19200    16    1.83    4      0       1.00
635  17400   0   83  41.92  28350    19   13.00    5      0       1.00
637  12996   0   80  29.50  27250    18    2.42    4      0       1.00
641   6900   0   79  28.00  16080    15    3.17    1      0       1.00
649   5400   0   67  28.75  14100    15     .50    1      0       1.00
650   5040   0   96  27.42  12420    15    1.17    1      0       1.00
652   6300   0   77  52.92  12300    12   26.42    3      0       1.00
653   6300   0   84  33.50  15720    15    6.00    1      0       1.00
656   6000   0   88  54.33   8880    12   27.00    1      0       1.00
657  10500   0   93  32.33  22000    17    2.67    4      0       1.00
658  10800   0   98  41.17  22800    15   12.00    5      0       1.00
```

The dictionary is created when an SPSS data file is built. You can display or modify the dictionary of a working file. Use DISPLAY DICTIONARY to view the dictionary, and use commands such as VARIABLE LABELS, VALUE LABELS, and MISSING VALUES to modify specific information contained in the dictionary. Figure 5 shows part of the displayed dictionary information of the working data file displayed in Figure 4.

Figure 5 Displayed dictionary information

```
              List of variables on the active file
Name                                                              Position

ID          Employee Code                                            1
            Print Format: F4
            Write Format: F4

SALBEG      Beginning Salary                                         2
            Print Format: F5
            Write Format: F5
            Missing Values: 0

SEX         Sex of Employee                                          3
            Print Format: F1
            Write Format: F1
            Missing Values: 9

            Value     Label

                0     Males
                1     Females
TIME        Job Seniority                                            4
            Print Format: F2
            Write Format: F2
            Missing Values: 0
```

SPSS Matrix Data Files

An SPSS matrix data file is similar to any SPSS data file. It is a self-documented file containing data and descriptive information. The descriptive information, stored in the file dictionary, includes variable names, variable print and write formats, and optional variable and value labels. You can assign or change the names, labels, and formats of the variables in a matrix data file, just as you can in any SPSS data file. Many procedures in SPSS can read raw matrix data and write a representative matrix of the data values to an SPSS matrix data file, which can be used as input for subsequent analysis.

Table 3 shows the types of matrix materials written by SPSS procedures. The *ROWTYPE_* values (discussed below) of each matrix are also included so you can see which procedure matrices are readable by other procedures. If a procedure produces more than one type of matrix, the subcommands required for each type of matrix are listed.

Table 3 Types of matrices and their contents

Command	Subcommands/Notes	ROWTYPE_ values
ALSCAL		PROX
CLUSTER		PROX
CORRELATIONS		MEAN STDDEV N CORR

Table 3 Types of matrices and their contents (Continued)

Command	Subcommands/Notes	ROWTYPE_ values
DISCRIMINANT	/CLASSIFY=POOLED	N (1 per cell) COUNT (1 per cell) MEAN (1 per cell) STDDEV (pooled) CORR (pooled)
	/CLASSIFY=SEPARATE, /STATISTICS=BOXM, or /STATISTICS=GCOV	N (1 per cell) COUNT (1 per cell) MEAN (1 per cell) STDDEV (1 per cell) CORR (1 per cell)
FACTOR	/MATRIX=OUT(CORR=file) /MATRIX=IN(CORR=file)	CORR
	/MATRIX=OUT(FAC=file) /MATRIX=IN(FAC=file)	FACTOR
MANOVA		N (cell and pooled) MEAN (1 per cell) STDDEV (pooled) CORR (pooled)
NONPAR CORR	/PRINT=SPEARMAN	N RHO
	/PRINT=KENDALL	N TAUB
ONEWAY	Separate variance Can be input and output	MEAN (1 per cell) STDDEV (1 per cell) N (1 per cell)
	Pooled variance Can be input only	MEAN (1 per cell) N (1 per cell) MSE (pooled) DFE (pooled)
PARTIAL CORR		N CORR
PROXIMITIES		PROX
REGRESSION		MEAN STDDEV N CORR
RELIABILITY		N MEAN STDDEV CORR

- All SPSS procedures that handle matrix materials use the MATRIX subcommand. The MATRIX subcommand specifies the file from which the input matrix is read and/or the file to which the output matrix is written.
- Matrix materials can be read from an external file as long as a working data file has been created. The working file does not have to be the matrix data file.
- The procedures that read matrix materials cannot read every type of SPSS matrix data file. For example, REGRESSION cannot read a matrix data file written by NONPAR CORR.

Figure 6 lists the structure of a matrix file and Figure 7 shows the dictionary information for the same file.

Variable Order. The following variable order is standard for all SPSS matrix data files:

1. Split variables, if any. In Figure 6, the split variable is *SEX*.
2. *ROWTYPE_* variable. The values of the *ROWTYPE_* variable describe the contents of the matrix data file, such as MEAN, STDDEV, N, and CORR.
3. Factor or grouping variables, if any.
4. *VARNAME_* variable (or *FACTOR_* variable for factor-loading matrices). The values of the *VARNAME* variable are the names of the variable used to form the matrix.
5. Continuous variables used to form the matrix.

Split Files. When split-file processing is in effect, a full set of matrix materials is written for each split-file group defined by the split variables.

- A split variable cannot have the same variable name as any other variable written to the matrix data file. Not all procedures allow split-file variables in their matrices.
- If split-file processing is in effect when a matrix is written, the same split file must be in effect when that matrix is read by any procedure.

Additional Statistics. Some procedures include statistics with their matrix materials. For example, CORRELATION matrices always include the mean, standard deviation, and number of cases used to compute each coefficient, as shown in Figure 6. Other procedures, for example PROXIMITIES and FACTOR, include no statistics with their matrices. See Table 3 for a list of the statistics written by each procedure. Refer to the description of each command for its requirements for a matrix input file.

Missing Values. The treatment of missing values in a procedure affects the matrix materials written to the data file. With pairwise treatment of missing values, the matrix of N's used to compute each coefficient is included in the matrix. With any other missing-value treatment, the single N used to calculate all coefficients in the matrix is included in the form of a vector. Figure 6 includes the matrix of N's written by CORRELATIONS when missing values are excluded pairwise from the analysis. Figure 8 shows the single N written by CORRELATIONS when missing values are excluded listwise.

The missing-value treatment that was in effect when the matrix was written must be compatible with the missing-value treatment in effect when the matrix is read. For example, REGRESSION can read a matrix written by CORRELATIONS but only if the missing-value treatment of both procedures is consistent. Either both must refer to a matrix of N's or both must refer to a single N. For all procedures, pairwise treatment of missing values generates a matrix of N's; any other treatment of missing values generates a single vector of N's.

Figure 6 A matrix data file (LIST output)

```
FILE:        MATRIX FILE
SEX:    1    FEMALE

SEX ROWTYPE_ VARNAME_      FOOD         RENT      PUBTRANS      TEACHER         COOK     ENGINEER

  1 MEAN               73.3750000  134.500000   53.5000000   46.8000000   72.4375000  59.8125000
  1 STDDEV             15.4483009  115.534699   25.8173069   19.4209018   29.5746936  21.5196616
  1 N        FOOD      16.0000000   16.0000000   16.0000000   15.0000000   16.0000000  16.0000000
  1 N        RENT      16.0000000   16.0000000   16.0000000   15.0000000   16.0000000  16.0000000
  1 N        PUBTRANS  16.0000000   16.0000000   16.0000000   15.0000000   16.0000000  16.0000000
  1 N        TEACHER   15.0000000   15.0000000   15.0000000   15.0000000   15.0000000  15.0000000
  1 N        COOK      16.0000000   16.0000000   16.0000000   15.0000000   16.0000000  16.0000000
  1 N        ENGINEER  16.0000000   16.0000000   16.0000000   15.0000000   16.0000000  16.0000000
  1 CORR     FOOD       1.0000000    .3658643    .5372333    .1733358    .1378010    .3778351
  1 CORR     RENT        .3658643   1.0000000    .1045105   -.0735708    .2026299    .1237062
  1 CORR     PUBTRANS    .5372333    .1045105   1.0000000    .6097397    .3877995    .6413121
  1 CORR     TEACHER     .1733358   -.0735708    .6097397   1.0000000    .4314755    .7312415
  1 CORR     COOK        .1378010    .2026299    .3877995    .4314755   1.0000000    .7807327
  1 CORR     ENGINEER    .3778351    .1237062    .6413121    .7312415    .7807327   1.0000000

NUMBER OF CASES READ =     14     NUMBER OF CASES LISTED =     14


FILE:        MATRIX FILE
SEX:    2    MALE

SEX ROWTYPE_ VARNAME_      FOOD         RENT      PUBTRANS      TEACHER         COOK     ENGINEER

  2 MEAN               68.8620690  112.137931   45.1379310   33.9310345   60.2142857  60.1785714
  2 STDDEV             20.4148478   81.3430672   24.1819356   26.9588722   30.2952840  28.8752792
  2 N        FOOD      29.0000000   29.0000000   29.0000000   29.0000000   28.0000000  28.0000000
  2 N        RENT      29.0000000   29.0000000   29.0000000   29.0000000   28.0000000  28.0000000
  2 N        PUBTRANS  29.0000000   29.0000000   29.0000000   29.0000000   28.0000000  28.0000000
  2 N        TEACHER   29.0000000   29.0000000   29.0000000   29.0000000   28.0000000  28.0000000
  2 N        COOK      28.0000000   28.0000000   28.0000000   28.0000000   28.0000000  28.0000000
  2 N        ENGINEER  28.0000000   28.0000000   28.0000000   28.0000000   28.0000000  28.0000000
  2 CORR     FOOD       1.0000000    .2012077    .5977491    .6417034    .4898941    .5190702
  2 CORR     RENT        .2012077   1.0000000   -.1405952   -.0540657    .0727153    .3508598
  2 CORR     PUBTRANS    .5977491   -.1405952   1.0000000    .7172945    .7170419    .6580408
  2 CORR     TEACHER     .6417034   -.0540657    .7172945   1.0000000    .6711871    .6650047
  2 CORR     COOK        .4898941    .0727153    .7170419    .6711871   1.0000000    .7688210
  2 CORR     ENGINEER    .5190702    .3508598    .6580408    .6650047    .7688210   1.0000000

NUMBER OF CASES READ =     14     NUMBER OF CASES LISTED =     14
```

Matrix File Dictionaries. As shown in Figure 7, print and write formats of A8 are assigned to the matrix variables that SPSS creates (for example, *ROWTYPE_*, *VARNAME_*, and *FACTOR_*). No labels are assigned to these variables. Print and write formats of F10.7 are assigned to all the continuous variables in the matrix analysis; the names and variable labels defined for these variables in the original data file are retained, but their original values and value labels are dropped because they do not apply to the matrix data file. When split-file processing is in effect, the variable names, variable and value labels, and print and write formats of the split-file variables are read from the dictionary of the original data file.

Procedures read and write matrices in which each row corresponds to a single case in the matrix data file. For example, the matrix shown in Figure 8 has nine cases. The first three cases with the *ROWTYPE_* values of MEAN, STDDEV, and N have no values for *VARNAME_* but do have values for all the variables from *FOOD* to *ENGINEER*. The fourth case, CORR, in the matrix generated for the first split-file group has a value of FOOD for *VARNAME_*, a value of 0.3652366 when correlated with variable *RENT*, a value of 0.5371597 when correlated with variable *PUBTRANS*, and so forth.

For a more detailed discussion of SPSS matrix data files, see *SPSS Advanced Statistics*.

Figure 7 Dictionary of a matrix system file (DISPLAY output)

```
FILE:      MATRIX FILE
           LIST OF VARIABLES ON THE ACTIVE FILE

NAME                                                              POSITION

SEX                                                                  1
               PRINT FORMAT: F2
               WRITE FORMAT: F2

           VALUE     LABEL

             1       FEMALE
             2       MALE

ROWTYPE_                                                             2
               PRINT FORMAT: A8
               WRITE FORMAT: A8

VARNAME_                                                             3
               PRINT FORMAT: A8
               WRITE FORMAT: A8

FOOD       AVG FOOD PRICES                                           4
               PRINT FORMAT: F10.7
               WRITE FORMAT: F10.7

RENT       NORMAL RENT                                               5
               PRINT FORMAT: F10.7
               WRITE FORMAT: F10.7

PUBTRANS   PRICE FOR PUBLIC TRANSPORT                                6
               PRINT FORMAT: F10.7
               WRITE FORMAT: F10.7

TEACHER    NET TEACHER'S SALARY                                      7
               PRINT FORMAT: F10.7
               WRITE FORMAT: F10.7

COOK       NET COOK'S SALARY                                         8
               PRINT FORMAT: F10.7
               WRITE FORMAT: F10.7

ENGINEER   NET ENGINEER'S SALARY                                     9
               PRINT FORMAT: F10.7
               WRITE FORMAT: F10.7
```

Figure 8 Single N in the matrix system file

```
FILE:       MATRIX FILE
SEX:    1   FEMALE

SEX ROWTYPE_ VARNAME_       FOOD        RENT     PUBTRANS     TEACHER        COOK     ENGINEER

  1 MEAN               73.4666667 136.800000  54.0000000  46.8000000  73.8666667  60.0000000
  1 STDDEV             15.9860058 119.210019  26.6431444  19.4209018  30.0353760  22.2614337
  1 N                  15.0000000  15.0000000 15.0000000  15.0000000  15.0000000  15.0000000
  1 CORR     FOOD       1.0000000   .3652366    .5371597    .1733358    .1358120    .3773434
  1 CORR     RENT        .3652366  1.0000000    .0989524   -.0735708    .1914448    .1213899
  1 CORR     PUBTRANS    .5371597   .0989524   1.0000000    .6097397    .3811372    .6409265
  1 CORR     TEACHER     .1733358  -.0735708    .6097397   1.0000000    .4314755    .7312415
  1 CORR     COOK        .1358120   .1914448    .3811372    .4314755   1.0000000    .7893533
  1 CORR     ENGINEER    .3773434   .1213899    .6409265    .7312415    .7893533   1.0000000

NUMBER OF CASES READ =       9     NUMBER OF CASES LISTED =        9

                                                                                          2

FILE:       MATRIX FILE
SEX:    2   MALE

SEX ROWTYPE_ VARNAME_       FOOD        RENT     PUBTRANS     TEACHER        COOK     ENGINEER

  2 MEAN               69.6428571 114.464286  46.1428571  33.7500000  60.2142857  60.1785714
  2 STDDEV             20.3437392  81.8474109 24.0011023  27.4356149  30.2952840  28.8752792
  2 N                  28.0000000  28.0000000 28.0000000  28.0000000  28.0000000  28.0000000
  2 CORR     FOOD       1.0000000   .1752920    .5784136    .6638084    .4898941    .5190702
  2 CORR     RENT        .1752920  1.0000000   -.1817862   -.0491139    .0727153    .3508598
  2 CORR     PUBTRANS    .5784136  -.1817862   1.0000000    .7447511    .7170419    .6580408
  2 CORR     TEACHER     .6638084  -.0491139    .7447511   1.0000000    .6711871    .6650047
  2 CORR     COOK        .4898941   .0727153    .7170419    .6711871   1.0000000    .7688210
  2 CORR     ENGINEER    .5190702   .3508598    .6580408    .6650047    .7688210   1.0000000

NUMBER OF CASES READ =       9     NUMBER OF CASES LISTED =        9
```

Variables

To prepare data for processing in SPSS, you must define variables by assigning variable names and formats. You can also specify variable labels, value labels, and missing values, but they are optional. This section discusses the two essential components of variable definition in SPSS: variable names and formats.

Variable Names

Each variable must have a unique name. Variable names are stored in the dictionary of an SPSS data file or working data file. Observe the following rules when establishing variable names or referring to variables by their names on commands:

- Variable names can contain up to eight characters, the first of which must be a letter or one of the characters @, #, or $.
- A # character in the first position of a variable name defines a scratch variable (see "Scratch Variables" on p. 34).
- A $ sign in the first position indicates that the variable is a system variable (see "System Variables" on p. 33). The $ sign is not allowed as the initial character of a user-defined variable.
- The period, underscore, and the characters $, #, and @ can be used within variable names. For example, A._$@#1 is a valid variable name.
- Variable names ending with a period should be avoided, since the period may be interpreted as a command terminator.
- Variable names can be established on the DATA LIST, KEYED DATA LIST, MATRIX DATA, NUMERIC, STRING, COMPUTE, RECODE, and COUNT commands. They can be changed with the RENAME VARIABLES command.
- Reserved keywords cannot be used as variable names. SPSS reserved keywords are

    ALL   AND   BY   EQ   GE   GT   LE
    LT   NE   NOT   OR   TO   WITH

Keyword TO

SPSS allows you to establish names for a set of variables or to refer to any number of consecutive variables by specifying the beginning and the ending variables joined by keyword TO.

To establish names for a set of variables with keyword TO, use a character prefix with a numeric suffix:

- The prefix can be any valid name. Both the beginning and ending variable must use the same prefix.
- The numeric suffix can be any integer, but the first number must be smaller than the second. For example, ITEM1 TO ITEM5 establishes five variables named *ITEM1*, *ITEM2*, *ITEM3*, *ITEM4*, and *ITEM5*.

- Each variable name, including the number, must not exceed eight characters.
- Leading zeros used in numeric suffixes are included in the variable name. For example, V001 TO V100 establishes 100 variables, *V001, V002, V003,* . . . *V100*. V1 TO V100 establishes 100 variables, *V1, V2, V3,* . . . *V100*.

Keyword TO can also be used on procedures and other commands to refer to consecutive variables on the working data file. For example, AVAR TO VARB refers to the variables *AVAR* and all subsequent variables up to and including *VARB*.

- In most cases, the TO specification uses the variable order on the working data file. Use the DISPLAY command to see the order of variables on the working data file.
- On some subcommands, the order in which variables are named on a previous subcommand, usually the VARIABLES subcommand, is used to determine which variables are consecutive and therefore are implied by the TO specification. This is noted in the description of individual commands.

System Variables

System variables are special variables created by SPSS during a working session to keep system-required information, such as the number of cases read by the system, the system-missing value, and the current date. System variables can be used in data transformations.

- The names of system variables begin with a dollar sign ($).
- You cannot modify a system variable or alter its print or write format. Except for these restrictions, you can use system variables anywhere a normal variable is used in the transformation language.
- System variables are not available for procedures.

$CASENUM   *Permanent case sequence number.* For each case, *$CASENUM* is the number of permanent cases read up to and including that case. The format is F8.0. The value of *$CASENUM* is not necessarily the row number in a Data Editor window (available in windowed environments).

$SYSMIS   *System-missing value.* The system-missing value displays as a period (.) or whatever is used as the decimal point.

$JDATE   *Current date in number of days from October 14, 1582* (day 1 of the Gregorian calendar). The format is F6.0.

$DATE   *Current date in international date format.* The format is A9 in the form dd-mmm-yy.

$TIME   *Current date and time. $TIME* represents the number of seconds from midnight, October 14, 1582, to the date and time when the transformation command is executed. The format is F20.

$LENGTH   *The current page length.* The format is F11.0. For more information, see SET.

$WIDTH   *The current page width.* The format is F3.0. For more information, see SET.

Scratch Variables

Scratch variables are variables created for the sole purpose of facilitating SPSS operations during a session.
- To create a scratch variable, specify a variable name that begins with the # character, for example, *#ID*. Scratch variables can be either numeric or string.
- Scratch variables are initialized to 0 for numeric variables or blank for string variables.
- SPSS does not reinitialize scratch variables when reading a new case. Their values are always carried across cases. Therefore, a scratch variable is a good choice for a looping index.
- Do not use LEAVE with a scratch variable.
- Scratch variables cannot be used in procedures and cannot be saved in an SPSS data file.
- Scratch variables cannot be assigned missing values, variable labels, or value labels.
- Scratch variables can be created between procedures but are always discarded as the next procedure begins.
- Scratch variables are discarded once a TEMPORARY command is specified.
- Keyword TO cannot refer to scratch variables and permanent variables at the same time.
- Scratch variables cannot be named on a WEIGHT command.

Variable Formats

SPSS accepts two variable types: numeric and string (also referred to as alphanumeric). Numeric values are stored internally as double-precision floating-point numbers and string values as codes listed in the SPSS character set (see Appendix B). Variable formats determine how SPSS reads raw data into storage and how it displays and writes values out.

Input and Output Formats

Values are read according to their *input* format and displayed on your terminal or written to a file according to their *output* format. In SPSS, the input and output formats differ in several ways.
- The input format is either specified or implied on the DATA LIST, KEYED DATA LIST, or other data definition commands. It is in effect only when SPSS builds cases in a working data file. Figure 9 shows the command printback for DATA LIST, which includes input format specifications.

Figure 9   SPSS output showing input formats

```
   1   0   DATA LIST   /ID 1-4 SCORE 6-9 (F,2).

This command will read 1 records from the command file

Variable      Rec     Start      End        Format

ID             1        1         4         F4.0
SCORE          1        6         9         F4.2
```

- DATA LIST or any other data definition command automatically generates an output format from the input format and expands the output format to include punctuation characters such as decimal points, commas, dollar signs, and percent signs. To see the current output formats of variables in the working data file, use DISPLAY VARIABLES. The variables defined by the above DATA LIST command are displayed in Figure 10. Note that the output format for *SCORE* has been expanded one space to allow the display of the decimal point (the F4.2 input format indicates a four-character variable with two implied decimal places; the F5.2 output format includes one space for the decimal point).

Figure 10 SPSS output showing output formats

```
            List of variables on the active file
   Name      Pos   Print Fmt    Write Fmt     Missing Values
   ID         1    F4           F4
   SCORE      2    F5.2         F5.2
```

- The formats (specified or default) on NUMERIC, COMPUTE or other commands that create new variables are output formats. You must specify adequate widths to accommodate all punctuation characters.
- The output format is in effect during the entire working session (unless explicitly changed) and is saved in the dictionary of an SPSS data file.
- Output formats for numeric variables can be changed with the FORMATS, PRINT FORMATS, or WRITE FORMATS command.
- Output formats (widths) for string variables cannot be changed with command syntax. However, you can use STRING to declare a new variable with the desired format and then use COMPUTE to copy values from the existing string variable into the new variable.
- The format type cannot be changed from string to numeric, or vice versa, with command syntax. However, you can use RECODE to recode values from one variable into another variable of a different type.

See DATA LIST for information on specifying input data formats. See FORMATS, PRINT FORMATS, and WRITE FORMATS for information on specifying output data formats. See STRING for information on declaring new string variables.

Numeric Variable Formats

- The formats used in this manual use FORTRAN-like syntax, for example, Fw.d, where F denotes the format type (numeric), w represents the variable width, and d represents the number of decimal places.
- By default, the DATA LIST and KEYED DATA LIST commands assume that variables are numeric with an F format type. The default width depends on whether the data are in fixed or freefield format. For discussion of fixed data and freefield data, see DATA LIST.
- Numeric variables created by COMPUTE, COUNT, or other commands that create numeric variables are assigned a format type F8.2 (or the default format defined on SET FORMAT).
- If a data value exceeds its width specification, SPSS makes an attempt to display some value nevertheless. It first rounds the decimals, then takes out punctuation characters,

then tries scientific notation, and if there is still not enough space, produces asterisks (***) indicating that a value is present but cannot be displayed in the assigned width.
- The output format does not affect the value stored in the file. A numeric value is always stored in double precision.

F, N, and E Formats

Table 4 lists the formats most commonly used to read in and write out numeric data.

Table 4 Common numeric formats

Format type	Description	Sample format	Sample input	Output for fixed input		Output for freefield input	
				Format	Value	Format	Value
Fw.d	Standard numeric	F5.0	1234	F5.0	1234	F5.0	1234
			1.234		1		1[*]
		F5.2	1234	F6.2	12.34	F6.2	1234.0
			1.234		1.23		1.23
Nw.d	Restricted numeric	N5.0	00123	F5.0	123	F5.0	123
			1.234		.[†]		1
		N5.2	12345	F6.2	123.45	F6.2	12345
			12.34		.		12.34
Ew.d	Scientific notation	E8.0	1234E3	E10.3	1.234E+06	E10.3	1.234E+06[**]
			1234		1.234E+03		1.234E+03

---

* Only the display is truncated. The value is stored in full precision.
† System-missing value. In this case, the value entered contains an illegal decimal point.
** Scientific notation is accepted in input data with F, COMMA, DOLLAR, DOT, and PCT formats. The same rules apply as specified below.

For fixed data:
- If a value has no coded decimal point but the input format specifies decimal positions, the rightmost positions are interpreted as implied decimal digits. For example, if the input F format specifies two decimal digits, the value 1234 is interpreted as 12.34; however, the value 123.4 is still interpreted as 123.4.
- With N format, decimal places are always implied. Only unsigned integers are allowed. Values not padded with leading zeroes to the specified width or those containing decimal points are assigned the system-missing value. This format is useful for reading and checking values that should be integers containing leading zeroes.
- The E format reads all forms of scientific notation. If the sign is omitted, + is assumed. If the sign (+ or -) is specified before the exponent, the E or D can be omitted. A single space is permitted after the E or D and/or after the sign. If both the sign and the letter E or D are omitted, implied decimal places are assumed. For example, 1.234E3, 1.234+3, 1.234E+3, 1.234D3, 1.234D+3, 1.234E 3, and 1234 are all legitimate values. Only the last value can imply decimal places.

- E format input values can be up to 40 characters wide and include up to 15 decimal positions.
- The default output width (w) for the E format is either the specified input width or the number of specified decimal positions plus 7 ($d+7$), whichever is greater. The minimum width is 10 and the minimum decimal places are 3.

For freefield data:
- F format w and d specifications do not affect how data are read. They only determine the output formats (expanded, if necessary). 1234 is always read as 1234 in freefield data, but a specified F5.2 format will be expanded to F6.2 and the value will be displayed as 1234.0 (the last decimal place rounded for lack of space).
- The N format, when used for freefield data, is treated as F format.
- The E format for freefield data follows the same rules as for fixed data except that no blank space is permitted in the value. Thus, 1.234E3 and 1.234+3 are allowed, but the value 1.234 3 will cause mistakes when the data are read.
- The default output E format and the width and decimal place limitations are the same as with fixed data.

COMMA, DOT, DOLLAR, and PCT Formats

Table 5 lists the formats that read and write data with imbedded punctuation characters and symbols, such as commas, dots, dollar and percent signs. The input data may or may not contain such characters. The data values read in are stored as numbers but displayed using the appropriate formats. Other formats that use punctuation characters and symbols are date and time formats and currency formats. Date and time are discussed in "Date and Time in SPSS" on p. 59. Currency formats are output formats only. (See SET and FORMATS.)

Table 5 Numeric formats with punctuation and symbols

Format type	Description	Sample format	Sample input	Default output format	Displayed value
COMMAw.d	Commas in numbers	COMMA6.0	12345	COMMA7.0	12,345
			12,345		12,345
			123,45		12,345
		COMMA6.3	12345	COMMA7.3	12.345
			123,45		12.345
			1.2345		1.234
			1234.5		1234.50[*]
DOTw.d	Dots in numbers	DOT6.0	12345	DOT7.0	12.345
			123.45		12.345
			123.45		12.345
		DOT6.3	12345	DOT7.3	12,345
			123.45		12,345
			1,2345		1,234
			1234,5		1234,50*

Table 5   Numeric formats with punctuation and symbols (Continued)

Format type	Description	Sample format	Sample input	Default output format	Displayed value
DOLLARw.d	Dollar sign and comma in numbers	DOLLAR7.0	1234	DOLLAR10.0	$1,234
			1,234		$1,234
			$1234		$1,234
			$1,234		$1,234
		DOLLAR7.3	1234	DOLLAR10.3	$1.234
			1,234		$1.234
			$1,23.4		$123.400
			12345.6		$12345.600*
PCTw.d	Percent sign after numbers	PCT7.0	1234	PCT8.0	1234%
			12.34		12%
		PCT7.2	1234	PCT9.3	1.234%
			12.3		12.340%
			1234		12.34%

* When the decimal point is coded in input, SPSS displays all specified decimal places whether recorded in the data or note. When the width is inadequate, thousands separators are dropped before decimal places.

- Formats listed in Table 5 cannot be used to read freefield data.
- Data values can appear anywhere within the column specification. Both leading and trailing blanks are allowed.
- The sign (for example, "$" for DOLLAR format) or punctuation mark (for example, "." for DOT format) is ignored in the input data. Its position does not affect the value read into storage.
- The default output format expands the width of the input format by the number of the required signs or punctuation marks plus the decimal point if *d* is not 0. For example, COMMA9.2 is expanded to COMMA12.2 to accommodate two possible commas and one decimal point.
- DOT format is similar to COMMA format but reverses the symbols used for the thousands separator and the decimal point. For example, in DOT format, 1.234 has the value of one thousand two hundred and thirty-four.

Binary and Hexadecimal Formats

SPSS is capable of reading and writing data in formats used by a number of programming languages such as PL/1, COBOL, FORTRAN, and ASSEMBLER. The data can be binary, hexadecimal, or zoned decimal. Formats described in this section can be used both as input formats and output formats, but with fixed data only. The described formats are not available on all systems. Consult the *Base System User's Guide* for your version of SPSS for details.

The default output format for all formats described in this section is an equivalent F format, allowing the maximum number of columns for values with symbols and punctuation. To change the default, use FORMATS or WRITE FORMATS.

IBw.d (integer binary):

The IB format reads fields that contain fixed-point binary (integer) data. The data might be generated by COBOL using COMPUTATIONAL data items, by FORTRAN using INTEGER*2 or INTEGER*4, or by ASSEMBLER using fullword and halfword items. The general format is a signed binary number that is 16 or 32 bits in length.

The general syntax for IB format is IBw.d, where w is the field width in bytes (omitted for column-style specifications) and d is the number of digits to the right of the decimal point. Since the width is expressed in bytes and the number of decimal positions is expressed in digits, *d* can be greater than *w*. For example, both of the following commands are valid:

```
DATA LIST FIXED /VAR1 (IB4.8).
DATA LIST FIXED /VAR1 1-4 (IB,8).
```

Widths of 2 and 4 represent standard 16-bit and 32-bit integers, respectively. Fields read with IB format are treated as signed. For example, the one-byte binary value 11111111 would be read as −1.

PIBw.d (positive integer binary):

The PIB format is essentially the same as IB except that negative numbers are not allowed. This restriction allows one additional bit of magnitude. The same one-byte value 11111111 would be read as 255.

PIBHEXw (hexadecimal of PIB):

The PIBHEX format reads hexadecimal numbers as unsigned integers and writes positive integers as hexadecimal numbers. The general syntax for PIBHEX format is PIBHEXw, where w indicates the total number of hexadecimal characters. The w specification must be an even number, with a maximum of 16.

For input data, each hexadecimal number must consist of the exact number of characters. No signs, decimal points, or leading and trailing blanks are allowed. For some operating systems (such as IBM CMS), hexadecimal characters must be uppercase. The following example illustrates the kind of data PIBHEX format can read:

```
DATA LIST FIXED
 /VAR1 1-4 (PIBHEX) VAR2 6-9 (PIBHEX) VAR3 11-14 (PIBHEX).
BEGIN DATA
0001 0002 0003
0004 0005 0006
0007 0008 0009
000A 000B 000C
000D 000E 000F
00F0 0B2C FFFF
END DATA.
LIST.
```

The values for *VAR1*, *VAR2*, and *VAR3* are listed in Figure 11. PIBHEX format can also be used to write decimal values as hexadecimal numbers, which may be useful for programmers.

Figure 11 Output displaying values read in PIBHEX format

```
VAR1    VAR2    VAR3

   1       2       3
   4       5       6
   7       8       9
  10      11      12
  13      14      15
 240    2860   65535
```

Zw.d (zoned decimal):

The Z format reads data values that contain zoned decimal data. Such numbers may be generated by COBOL systems using DISPLAY data items, by PL/1 systems using PICTURE data items, or by ASSEMBLER using zoned decimal data items.

In zoned decimal format, one digit is represented by one byte, generally hexadecimal F1 representing 1, F2 representing 2, and so on. The last byte, however, combines the sign for the number with the last digit. In the last byte, hexadecimal A, F, or C assigns +, and B, D, or E assigns –. For example, hexadecimal D1 represents 1 for the last digit and assigns the minus sign (-) to the number.

The general syntax of Z format is Zw.d, where w is the total number of bytes (which is the same as columns) and d is the number of decimals. For input data, values can appear anywhere within the column specifications. Both leading and trailing blanks are allowed. Decimals can be implied by the input format specification or explicitly coded in the data. Explicitly coded decimals override the input format specifications.

The following example illustrates how Z format reads zoned decimals in their printed forms on IBM mainframe and PC systems. The printed form for the sign zone (A to I for +1 to +9, and so on) may vary from system to system.

```
DATA LIST FIXED /VAR1 1-5 (Z) VAR2 7-11 (Z,2) VAR3 13-17 (Z)
  VAR4 19-23 (Z,2) VAR5 25-29 (Z) VAR6 31-35 (Z,2).
BEGIN DATA
1234A 1234A 1234B 1234B 1234C 1234C
1234D 1234D 1234E 1234E 1234F 1234F
1234G 1234G 1234H 1234H 1234I 1234I
1234J 1234J 1234K 1234K 1234L 1234L
1234M 1234M 1234N 1234N 1234O 1234O
1234P 1234P 1234Q 1234Q 1234R 1234R
1234{ 1234{ 1234} 1234} 1.23M 1.23M
END DATA.
LIST.
```

The values for *VAR1* to *VAR6* are listed in Figure 12.

Figure 12 Output displaying values read in Z format

```
VAR1    VAR2    VAR3    VAR4    VAR5    VAR6

 12341  123.41   12342  123.42   12343  123.43
 12344  123.44   12345  123.45   12346  123.46
 12347  123.47   12348  123.48   12349  123.49
-12341 -123.41  -12342 -123.42  -12343 -123.43
-12344 -123.44  -12345 -123.45  -12346 -123.46
-12347 -123.47  -12348 -123.48  -12349 -123.49
 12340  123.40  -12340 -123.40      -1   -1.23
```

The default output format for Z format is the equivalent F format, as shown on Figure 12. The default output width is based on the input width specification plus one column for the sign and one column for the implied decimal point (if specified). For example, an input format of Z4.0 generates an output format of F5.0 and an input format of Z4.2 generates an output format of F6.2.

Pw.d (packed decimal):

The P format is used to read fields with packed decimal numbers. Such numbers are generated by COBOL using COMPUTATIONAL–3 data items, and by ASSEMBLER using packed decimal data items. The general format of a packed decimal field is two four-bit digits in each byte of the field except the last. The last byte contains a single digit in its four leftmost bits and a four-bit sign in its rightmost bits. If the last four bits are 1111 (hexadecimal F), the value is positive; if they are 1101 (hexadecimal D), the value is negative. One byte under P format can represent numbers from –9 to 9.

The general syntax of P format is Pw.d, where w is the number of bytes (not digits) and d is the number of digits to the right of the implied decimal point. The number of digits in a field is (2*w–1).

PKw.d (unsigned packed decimal):

The PK format is essentially the same as P except that there is no sign. That is, even the rightmost byte contains two digits, and negative data cannot be represented. One byte under PK format can represent numbers from 0 to 99. The number of digits in a field is 2*w.

RBw (real binary):

The RB format is used to read data values which contain internal format floating-point numbers. Such numbers are generated by COBOL using COMPUTATIONAL–1 or COMPUTATIONAL–2 data items, by PL/1 using FLOATING DECIMAL data items, by FORTRAN using REAL or REAL*8 data items, or by ASSEMBLER using floating-point data items.

The general syntax of RB format is RBw, where w is the total number of bytes. The width specification must be an even number between 2 and 8. Normally, a width specification of 8 is used to read double-precision values, and a width of 4 is used to read single-precision values.

RBHEXw (hexadecimal of RB):

The RBHEX format interprets a series of hexadecimal characters as a number that represents a floating-point number. This representation is system-specific. If the field width is less than twice the width of a floating-point number, the value is right-padded with binary zeros. For some operating systems (for example, IBM CMS), letters in hexadecimal values must be upper case.

The general syntax of RBHEX format is RBHEXw, where w indicates the total number of columns. The width must be an even number. The values are real ("floating point") numbers. Leading and trailing blanks are not allowed. Any data values shorter than the specified input width must be padded with leading zeros.

String Variable Formats

- The values of string variables can contain numbers, letters, and special characters and can be up to 255 characters long.
- SPSS differentiates between long strings and short strings. Long strings can be displayed by some procedures and by the PRINT command, and they can be used as break variables to define subgroups in REPORT. They cannot, however, be tabulated in procedures such as CROSSTABS, and they cannot have user-missing values. Short strings, on the other hand, can be tabulated and can have user-missing values. The maximum length of a short string depends on the computer and operating system; it is typically 8 characters.
- System-missing values cannot be generated for string variables, since any character is a legal string value.
- When a transformation command that creates or modifies a string variable yields a missing or undefined result, a null string is assigned. The variable displays as blanks and is not treated as missing.
- String formats are used to read and write string variables. The input values can be alphanumeric characters (A format) or the hexadecimal representation of alphanumeric characters (AHEX format).
- For fixed data, the width can be explicitly specified on DATA LIST or KEYED DATA LIST or implied if column-style specifications are used. For freefield data, the default width is 1; if the input string may be longer, w must be explicitly specified. Input strings shorter than the specified width are right-padded with blanks.
- The output format for a string variable is always A. The width is determined by the input format or the format assigned on the STRING command. String formats can be displayed with DISPLAY VARIABLES but cannot be changed.

Aw (Standard Characters)

The A format is used to read standard characters. Characters can include letters, numbers, punctuation marks, blanks, and most other characters on your keyboard. Numbers entered as values for string variables cannot be used in calculations unless you convert them to numeric format with the NUMBER function (see "String Functions" on p. 49).

Fixed data:

With fixed-format input data, any punctuation—including leading, trailing, and imbedded blanks—within the column specifications is included in the string value. For example, a string value of "Mr. Ed" (with one imbedded blank) is distinguished from a value of "Mr. Ed" (with two imbedded blanks). It is also distinguished from a string value of "MR. ED" (all upper case), and all three are treated as separate values. These can be important considerations for any procedures, transformations, or data selection commands involving string variables. Consider the following example:

```
DATA LIST FIXED /ALPHAVAR 1-10 (A).
BEGIN DATA
Mr. Ed
Mr. Ed
MR. ED
Mr.  Ed
 Mr. Ed
END DATA.
AUTORECODE ALPHAVAR /INTO NUMVAR.
LIST.
```

AUTORECODE recodes the values into consecutive integers. Figure 13 shows the recoded values.

Figure 13 Different string values illustrated

```
ALPHAVAR    NUMVAR

Mr. Ed         4
Mr. Ed         4
MR. ED         2
Mr.  Ed        3
 Mr. Ed        1
```

Freefield data:

With freefield data, blanks and commas are treated as delimiters for A format variables unless the value is enclosed in apostrophes or quotation marks. For example,

```
Ed, Mr.
```

is read as two separate values (Ed and Mr.). To include blanks and/or commas in a string value, enclose the value in apostrophes or quotation marks. For example, the following command file will generate a list of values as shown in Figure 14:

```
DATA LIST FREE /ALPHAVAR (A10).
BEGIN DATA
Mr.  Ed
Ed,Mr.
'Mr.  Ed'
'Ed, Mr.'
END DATA.
LIST.
```

Figure 14 Blanks and commas in freefield string input

```
ALPHAVAR

Mr.
Ed
Ed
Mr.
Mr.  Ed
Ed, Mr.
```

AHEXw (Hexadecimal Characters)

The AHEX format is used to read the hexadecimal representation of standard characters. Each set of two hexadecimal characters represents one standard character. For codes used on different operating systems, see Appendix B.

- The w specification refers to columns of the hexadecimal representation and must be an even number. Leading, trailing, and imbedded blanks are not allowed, and only valid hexadecimal characters can be used in input values.
- For some operating systems (for example, IBM CMS), letters in hexadecimal values must be upper case.
- The default output format for variables read with AHEX input format is A format. The default width is half the specified input width. For example, an input format of AHEX14 generates an output format of A7.
- Used as an output format, the AHEX format displays the printable characters in the hexadecimal characters specific to your system. The following commands run on a UNIX system (where A=41 (decimal 65), a=61 (decimal 97), and so forth) produce the output shown in Figure 15:

```
DATA LIST FIXED
  /A,B,C,D,E,F,G,H,I,J,K,L,M,N,O,P,Q,R,S,T,U,V,W,X,Y,Z 1-26 (A).
FORMATS ALL (AHEX2).
BEGIN DATA
ABCDEFGHIJKLMNOPQRSTUVWXYZ
abcdefghijklmnopqrstuvwxyz
END DATA.
LIST.
```

Figure 15 Display of hexadecimal representation of the character set with AHEX format

```
A  B  C  D  E  F  G  H  I  J  K  L  M  N  O  P  Q  R  S  T  U  V  W  X  Y  Z
41 42 43 44 45 46 47 48 49 4A 4B 4C 4D 4E 4F 50 51 52 53 54 55 56 57 58 59 5A
61 62 63 64 65 66 67 68 69 6A 6B 6C 6D 6E 6F 70 71 72 73 74 75 76 77 78 79 7A
```

FORTRAN-Like Format Specifications

You can use FORTRAN-like format specifications to define formats for a set of variables, as in the following example:

```
DATA LIST FILE=HUBDATA RECORDS=3
      /MOHIRED, YRHIRED, DEPT1 TO DEPT4 (T12, 2F.0, 4(1X,F1.0)).
```

- The specification T12 in parentheses tabs to the 12th column. The first variable (*MOHIRED*) will be read beginning from column 12.
- The specification 2F2.0 assigns the format F2.0 to two adjacent variables (*MOHIRED* and *YRHIRED*).
- The next four variables (*DEPT1* to *DEPT4*) are each assigned the format F1.0. The 4 in 4(1X,F1.0) distributes the same format to four consecutive variables. 1X skips one column before each variable. (The column-skipping specification placed within the parentheses is distributed to each variable.)

Transformation Expressions

Transformation expressions are used in commands like COMPUTE, IF, DO IF, LOOP IF, and SELECT IF. This section describes the three types of expressions: numeric, string, and logical, as well as available operators. For date and time functions, see "Date and Time in SPSS" on p. 59.

Numeric Expressions

Numeric expressions can be used with the COMPUTE and IF command and as part of a logical expression for commands such as IF, DO IF, LOOP IF, and SELECT IF. Arithmetic expressions can also appear in the index portion of a LOOP command, on the REPEATING DATA command, and on the PRINT SPACES command.

Arithmetic Operations

The following arithmetic operators are available in SPSS:

+   *Addition.*
-   *Subtraction.*
*   *Multiplication.*
/   *Division.*
** *Exponentiation.*

- No two operators can appear consecutively.
- Arithmetic operators cannot be implied. For example, (VAR1)(VAR2) is not a legal specification; you must specify VAR1*VAR2.
- Arithmetic operators and parentheses serve as delimiters. To improve readability, blanks (not commas) can be inserted before and after an operator.
- To form complex expressions, you can use variables, constants, and functions with arithmetic operators.
- The order of execution is functions first, then exponentiation, then multiplication, division, and unary –, and then addition and subtraction.
- Operators at the same level are executed from left to right.
- To override the order of operation, use parentheses. Execution begins with the innermost set of parentheses and progresses out.

Numeric Constants

- Constants used in numeric expressions or as arguments to functions can be integer or noninteger, depending on the application or function.

- You can specify as many digits in a constant as needed, as long as you understand the precision restrictions of your computer.
- Numeric constants can be signed (+ or –) but cannot contain any other special characters such as the comma or dollar sign.
- Numeric constants can be expressed with scientific notation. Thus, the exponent for a constant in scientific notation is limited to two digits. The range of values allowed for exponents in scientific notation is from –99 to +99.

Complex Numeric Arguments

- Except where explicitly restricted, complex expressions can be formed by nesting functions and arithmetic operators as arguments to functions.
- The order of execution for complex numeric arguments is functions first, then exponentiation, then multiplication, division, and unary –, and then addition and subtraction.
- To control the order of execution in complex numeric arguments, use parentheses.

Numeric Functions

Numeric functions can be used in any numeric expression on IF, SELECT IF, DO IF, ELSE IF, LOOP IF, END LOOP IF, and COMPUTE. Numeric functions always return numbers (or the system-missing value whenever the result is indeterminate). The expression to be transformed by a function is called the *argument*. Most functions have a variable or a list of variables as arguments.

- In numeric functions with two or more arguments, each argument must be separated by a comma. Blanks alone cannot be used to separate variable names, expressions, or constants in transformation expressions.
- Arguments should be enclosed in parentheses, as in TRUNC(INCOME), where the TRUNC function returns the integer portion of variable *INCOME*.
- Multiple arguments should be separated by commas, as in MEAN(Q1,Q2,Q3), where the MEAN function returns the mean of variables *Q1, Q2,* and *Q3*.

Arithmetic Functions

- All arithmetic functions except MOD have single arguments; MOD has two. The arguments to MOD must be separated by a comma.
- Arguments can be numeric expressions, as in RND(A**2/B).

ABS(arg)   *Absolute value.* ABS(SCALE) is 4.7 when *SCALE* equals 4.7 or –4.7.

RND(arg)   *Round the absolute value to an integer and reaffix the sign.* RND(SCALE) is –5 when *SCALE* equals –4.7.

TRUNC(arg)   *Truncate to an integer.* TRUNC(SCALE) is –4 when *SCALE* equals -4.7.

MOD(arg,arg)   *Remainder (modulo) of the first argument divided by the second.* When *YEAR* equals 1983, MOD(YEAR,100) is 83.

SQRT(arg)	*Square root.* SQRT(SIBS) is 1.41 when *SIBS* equals 2.
EXP(arg)	*Exponential. e is raised to the power of the argument.* EXP(VARA) is 7.39 when *VARA* equals 2.
LG10(arg)	*Base 10 logarithm.* LG10(VARB) is 0.48 when *VARB* equals 3.
LN(arg)	*Natural or Naperian logarithm (base e).* LN(VARC) is 2.30 when *VARC* equals 10.
ARSIN(arg)	*Arcsine.* (Alias ASIN.) *The result is given in radians.* ARSIN(ANG) is 1.57 when *ANG* equals 1.
ARTAN(arg)	*Arctangent.* (Alias ATAN.) *The result is given in radians.* ARTAN(ANG2) is 0.79 when *ANG2* equals 1.
SIN(arg)	*Sine. The argument must be specified in radians.* SIN(VARD) is 0.84 when *VARD* equals 1.
COS(arg)	*Cosine. The argument must be specified in radians.* COS(VARE) is 0.54 when *VARE* equals 1.

Statistical Functions

- Each argument to a statistical function (expression, variable name, or constant) must be separated by a comma.
- The *.n* suffix can be used with all statistical functions to specify the number of valid arguments. For example, MEAN.2(A,B,C,D) returns the mean of the valid values for variables *A, B, C,* and *D* only if at least two of the variables have valid values. The default for *n* is 2 for SD, VARIANCE, and CFVAR, and 1 for other statistical functions.
- Keyword TO can be used to refer to a set of variables in the argument list.

SUM(arg list)	*Sum of the nonmissing values across the argument list.*
MEAN(arg list)	*Mean of the nonmissing values across the argument list.*
SD(arg list)	*Standard deviation of the nonmissing values across the argument list.*
VARIANCE(arg list)	*Variance of the nonmissing values across the argument list.*
CFVAR(arg list)	*Coefficient of variation of the nonmissing values across the argument list. The coefficient of variation is the standard deviation divided by the mean.*
MIN(arg list)	*Minimum nonmissing value across the argument list.*
MAX(arg list)	*Maximum nonmissing value across the argument list.*

Random Number and Distribution Functions

UNIFORM(arg)	*Return a uniform pseudo-random number with values varying between 0 and the value of the argument.* For example, SAMP1 = UNIFORM(150) assigns a

value to *SAMP1* for each case in the file. All values are sampled from a uniform distribution between 0 and 150.

NORMAL(arg) *Return a normal pseudo-random number with a mean of 0 and a standard deviation equal to the argument.* For example, SAMP2 = NORMAL(2.5) assigns a value to *SAMP2* for each case in the file. All values are sampled from a normal distribution with a mean of 0 and a standard deviation of 2.5.

CDFNORM(arg) *Standard normal cumulative distribution.* This function returns the probability that a random variable with the standard normal distribution (mean of 0 and standard deviation equal to 1) falls below the value of the argument. For example, PROBVAL = CDFNORM(1.96) yields a probability of 0.975.

PROBIT(arg) *Inverse of the standard normal cumulative distribution.* The value of the argument must be a probability greater than 0 and less than 1. The function returns the standard normal value having a cumulative probability equal to the argument. For example, IPROBVAL = PROBIT(0.975) yields a value of 1.96.

Missing Values in Numeric Expressions

- Most numeric expressions receive the system-missing value when any one of the values in the expression is missing.
- Some arithmetic operations involving 0 can be evaluated even when the variables have missing values. These operations are:

Expression	Result
0 * missing	0
0 / missing	0
MOD(0,missing)	0

- The *.n* suffix can be used with the statistical functions SUM, MEAN, MIN, MAX, SD, VARIANCE, and CFVAR to specify the number of valid arguments you consider acceptable. The default of *n* is 2 for SD, VARIANCE, and CFVAR, and 1 for other statistical functions. For example,

  COMPUTE FACTOR = SUM.2(SCORE1 TO SCORE3).

  computes variable *FACTOR* only if a case has valid information for at least two scores. *FACTOR* is assigned the system-missing value if a case has valid values for fewer than two scores.

Domain Errors

Domain errors occur when numeric expressions are mathematically undefined or cannot be represented numerically on the computer for reasons other than missing data. Two common examples are division by zero and the square root of a negative number. When SPSS detects a domain error, it issues a warning and assigns the system-missing value to the expression. For example, the command COMPUTE TESTVAR = TRUNC(SQRT(X/Y) * .5) returns system-missing if *X/Y* is negative or if *Y* is 0.

The following are domain errors in numeric expressions:

**	*A negative number to a noninteger power.*
/	*A divisor of 0.*
MOD	*A divisor of 0.*
SQRT	*A negative argument.*
EXP	*An argument that produces a result too large to be represented on the computer.*
LG10	*A negative or 0 argument.*
LN	*A negative or 0 argument.*
ARSIN	*An argument whose absolute value exceeds 1.*
NORMAL	*A negative or 0 argument.*
PROBIT	*A negative or 0 argument, or an argument 1 or greater.*

String Expressions

Expressions involving string variables can be used on COMPUTE and IF commands and in logical expressions on commands such as IF, DO IF, LOOP IF, and SELECT IF.

- A string expression can be a constant enclosed in apostrophes (for example, 'IL'), a string function (see "String Functions" below), or a string variable.
- An expression must return a string if the target variable is a string.
- The string returned by a string expression does not have to be the same length as the target variable; no warning messages are issued if the lengths are not the same. If the target variable produced by a COMPUTE command is shorter, the result is right-trimmed. If the target variable is longer, the result is right-padded.

String Functions

- The target variable for each string function must be a string and *must have already been declared* (see STRING).
- Multiple arguments in a list must be separated by commas.
- When two strings are compared, the case in which they are entered is significant. The LOWER and UPCASE functions are useful for making comparisons of strings regardless of case.
- For certain functions (for example, MIN, MAX, ANY, and RANGE), the outcome will be affected by case and by whether the string includes numbers or special characters. The character set in use varies by system. With the ASCII character set, lower case follows upper case in the sort order. Therefore, if *NAME1* is in upper case and *NAME2* is in lower case, MIN(NAME1,NAME2) will return *NAME1* as the minimum. The reverse is true with the EBCDIC character set, which sorts lower before upper case.

CONCAT(arg list) — *Concatenate the arguments into a string.* String variables and strings can be intermixed as arguments. For example, CONCAT(A,'**') creates the string ABCD** for a case with value ABCD for the string variable *A*.

LOWER(arg) — *Convert upper case to lower case.* All other characters remain unchanged. The argument can be a string variable or value. For example, LOWER(NAME1) returns charles if the value of *NAME1* is CHARLES.

LPAD(a1, a2, a3) — *Left-pad.* Variable a1 is left-padded up to the length specified by a2 using the optional single character a3 as the pad character. a2 must be a positive integer from 1 to 255. The default pad character is a blank. For example, LPAD(ALPHA1,10) adds four leading blanks to the target variable if *ALPHA1* has an A6 format. a3 can be any character enclosed in apostrophes or any expression that yields a single character.

LTRIM(a1, a2) — *Left-trim.* The character a2 is trimmed from the beginning of a1. For example, LTRIM(ALPHA2,'0') trims leading zeros from variable *ALPHA2*. a2 can be any character enclosed in apostrophes or any expression that yields a single character. The default for a2 is a blank.

RPAD(a1, a2, a3) — *Right-pad.* Variable a1 is right-padded up to the length of a2 using the optional single character a_3 as the pad character. a2 must be a positive integer from 1 to 255. The default pad character is a blank. For example, RPAD(ALPHA3,8,'*') adds two trailing asterisks to the target variable if *ALPHA3* has an A6 format. a3 can be any character enclosed in apostrophes or any expression that yields a single character.

RTRIM(a1, a2) — *Right-trim.* The character a2 is trimmed from the end of a1. For example, RTRIM(ALPHA4,'*') trims trailing asterisks from variable *ALPHA4*. a2 can be any character enclosed in apostrophes or any expression that yields a single character. The default for a2 is a blank.

SUBSTR(a1, a2, a3) — *Substring.* This function returns the substring within a1 beginning with the position specified by a2 and optionally for a length of a3. a2 can be a positive integer from 1 to the length of a1. a3, when added to a2, should not exceed the length of a1. If a3 is not specified, the substring is returned up to the end of a1. For example, if variable *ALPHA5* has an A6 format, SUBSTR(ALPHA5,3) returns the last four characters of *ALPHA5*. SUBSTR (ALPHA5,3,1) returns the third character of *ALPHA5*.

When used on the left side of an equals sign, the substring is replaced by the string specified on the right side of the equals sign. The rest of the original string remains intact. For example, SUBSTR(ALPHA6,3,1)='*' changes the third character of all values for *ALPHA6* to *. If the replacement string is longer or shorter than the substring, the replacement is truncated or padded with blanks on the right to an equal length.

UPCASE(arg) — *Convert lower case to upper case.* The argument can be a string variable or a string. For example, UPCASE(NAME1) returns CHARLES if the value of *NAME1* is Charles.

Search Functions

- The values returned by INDEX and/or RINDEX can be used as arguments to SUBSTR to pull out substrings with the same beginning or ending character but with varying position and length.

INDEX(a1, a2, a3) — *Return a number that indicates the position of the first occurrence of a2 in a1.* a1 is the string that is searched. a2 is the string variable or string that is used in the search. If a3 is not specified, all of a2 is used. For example, INDEX(ALPHA8,'*X*') returns 2 for a case with value X**X**X* for variable *ALPHA8*. The optional a3 is the number of characters used to divide a2 into separate strings. Each substring is used for searching and the function returns the first occurrence of any of the substrings. With the same value X**X**X* for *ALPHA8*, both INDEX(ALPHA8, '*X*', 2) and INDEX(ALPHA8, '*X*', 1) return 1. a3 must be a positive integer and must divide evenly into the length of a_2. The target variable must be numeric. If a2 is not found within a1, the value 0 is returned.

LENGTH(arg) — *Return the length of the specified string.* The argument can be a string variable or a string. For example, LENGTH(LNAME) always returns 6 if *LNAME* has an A6 format. The target variable must be numeric.

MAX(arg list) — *Return the maximum value across the argument list.* For example, MAX(LNAME,FNAME) selects the name that comes last in the sort order, the first or the last name. MAX is also available as a numeric function.

MIN(arg list) — *Return the minimum value across the argument list.* For example, MIN(LNAME,FNAME) selects the name that comes first in the sort order, the first or the last name. MIN is also available as a numeric function.

RINDEX(a1,a2,a3) — *Return a number indicating the position of the last occurrence of a2 in a1.* a1 is the string that is searched. a2 is the string variable or string that is used in the search. If a3 is not specified, all of a2 is used. For example, RINDEX(ALPHA8,'*X*') returns 5 for a case with value X**X**X* for variable *ALPHA8*. The optional a3 is the number of characters used to divide a2 into separate strings. Each substring is used for searching and the function returns the last occurrence of any of the substrings. With same value X**X**X* for *ALPHA8*, RINDEX (ALPHA8, '*X*', 2) returns 7, and RINDEX (ALPHA8, '*X*', 1) returns 8. a3 must be a positive integer and must divide evenly into the length of a2. The target variable must be numeric. If a2 is not found within a1, the value 0 is returned.

Conversion Functions

NUMBER(arg,format) *Convert the argument into a number using the specified format.* The argument is string, the format is a numeric format, and the result is numeric. The string is essentially reread using the format and returned as a number. For example, NUMBER (XALPHA,F3.1) converts all values for *XALPHA* to numbers using the F3.1 format. The function returns the system-missing value if the conversion is invalid.

STRING(arg,format) *Converts the argument into a string using the specified format.* The argument is numeric, the format is a numeric format, and the result is a string. The number is converted from internal representation according to the format and then stored as a string. For example, STRING (INCOME, DOLLAR8) converts the numeric values for *INCOME* to the dollar format and returns it as a string value. If the result is shorter than the string variable that receives the values, it is right-justified. If the result is longer, it is right-trimmed.

Missing Values in String Expressions

- If the numeric argument (which can be an expression) for functions LPAD and RPAD is illegal or missing, the result is a null string. If the padding or trimming is the only operation, the string is then padded to its entire length with blanks. If the operation is nested, the null string is passed to the next nested level.

- If a numeric argument to SUBSTR is illegal or missing, the result is a null string. If SUBSTR is the only operation, the string is blank. If the operation is nested, the null string is passed to the next nested level.

- If a numeric argument to INDEX or RINDEX is illegal or missing, the result is system-missing.

Logical Expressions

Logical expressions can appear on the IF, SELECT IF, DO IF, ELSE IF, LOOP IF, and END LOOP IF commands. SPSS evaluates a logical expression as true or false, or as missing if it is indeterminate. A logical expression returns 1 if the expression is true, 0 if it is false, or system-missing if it is missing. Thus, logical expressions can be any expressions that yield this three-value logic.

- The simplest logical expression is a logical variable. A logical variable is any numeric variable that has values 1, 0, or system-missing. Logical variables cannot be strings.

- Logical expressions can be simple logical variables or relations, or they can be complex logical tests involving variables, constants, functions, relational operators, logical operators, and parentheses to control the order of evaluation.

- On an IF command, a logical expression that is true causes the assignment expression to be executed. A logical expression that returns missing has the same effect as one that is false: the assignment expression is not executed and the value of the target variable is not altered.

- On a DO IF command, a logical expression that is true causes SPSS to execute the commands immediately following the DO IF, up to the next ELSE IF, ELSE, or END IF. If it is false, SPSS looks for the next ELSE IF or ELSE command. If the logical expression returns missing for each of these, SPSS skips the entire structure.
- On a SELECT IF command, a logical expression that is true causes the case to be selected. A logical expression that returns missing has the same effect as one that is false: the case is not selected.
- On a LOOP IF command, a logical expression that is true causes looping to begin (or continue). A logical expression that returns missing has the same effect as one that is false: the structure is skipped.
- On an END LOOP IF command, a logical expression that is false returns control to the LOOP command for that structure and looping continues. If it is true, looping stops and the structure is terminated. A logical expression that returns a missing value has the same effect as one that is true: the structure is terminated.

String Variables in Logical Expressions

String variables, like numeric variables, can be tested in logical expressions.
- String variables must be declared before they can be used in a string expression.
- String variables cannot be compared to numeric variables.
- If strings of different lengths are compared, the shorter string is right-padded with blanks to equal the length of the longer.
- The magnitude of strings can be compared using LT, GT, and so forth, but the outcome depends on the sorting sequence of the computer. Use with caution.

Logical Functions

- Each argument to a logical function (expression, variable name, or constant) must be separated by a comma.
- The target variable for a logical function must be numeric.
- Functions RANGE and ANY can be useful shortcuts to more complicated specifications on the IF, DO IF, and other conditional commands. For example, the command

    SELECT IF ANY(REGION,'NW','NE','SE').

    is equivalent to

    SELECT IF (REGION EQ 'NW' OR REGION EQ 'NE' OR REGION EQ 'SE').

RANGE(arg,arg list)   *Return 1 or true if the value of the first argument is in the inclusive ranges; return 0 or false if not.* The first argument is usually a variable, and the second argument is a list of one or more pairs of values. The variable can be either numeric or string. For example, RANGE (AGE,1,17,62,99) returns 1 for ages 1 through 17 and 62 through 99, inclusive, and 0 for any other ages. RANGE (LNAME,'A','MZZZZZZ') returns 1 for last names that begin with a letter between A and M, inclusive, and 0 for last names beginning with other letters.

ANY(arg,arg list)   *Return 1 or true if the value of the first argument matches one of the arguments in the list; return 0 or false if not.* The first argument is usually a variable, either numeric or string. For example, ANY(PROJECT,3,4,7,9) returns 1 if the value for variable *PROJECT* is 3, 4, 7, or 9, and 0 for other values of *PROJECT*. Similarly, ANY (LNAME,'MARTIN','JONES','EVANS') returns 1 for people whose last names are MARTIN, JONES, or EVANS, and 0 for all other last names.

Relational Operators

A relation is a logical expression that compares two values using a *relational operator*. In the command

```
IF (X EQ 0) Y=1
```

variable *X* and 0 are expressions that yield the values to be compared by the EQ relational operator. Relational operators are

EQ or =	*Equal to.*
NE or ~= ¬= or <>	*Not equal to.*
LT or <	*Less than.*
LE or <=	*Less than or equal to.*
GT or >	*Greater than.*
GE or >=	*Greater than or equal to.*

- The symbols representing NE (~= or ¬=) are system dependent (see "NOT Logical Operator" below).
- The expressions in a relation can be variables, constants, or more complicated arithmetic expressions.
- Blanks (not commas) must be used to separate the relational operator from the expressions. To make the command more readable, use extra blanks or parentheses.

NOT Logical Operator

The NOT logical operator reverses the true/false outcome of the expression that immediately follows.
- The NOT operator affects only the expression that immediately follows, unless a more complex logical expression is enclosed in parentheses.
- The valid substitute for NOT varies from operating system to operating system. In general, the tilde (~) is valid for ASCII systems while ¬ (or the symbol over number 6 on the keyboard) is valid for IBM EBCDIC systems. See the *Base System User's Guide* for your version of SPSS.

- NOT can be used to check whether a numeric variable has the value 0, 1, or any other value. For example, all scratch variables are initialized to 0. Therefore, NOT (#ID) returns false or missing when *#ID* has been assigned a value other than 0.

AND and OR Logical Operators

Two or more relations can be logically joined using the logical operators AND and OR. Logical operators combine relations according to the following rules:

- The ampersand (&) symbol is a valid substitute for the logical operator AND. The vertical bar (|) is a valid substitute for the logical operator OR.
- Only one logical operator can be used to combine two relations. However, multiple relations can be combined into a complex logical expression.
- Regardless of the number of relations and logical operators used to build a logical expression, the result is either true, false, or indeterminate because of missing values.
- Operators or expressions cannot be implied. For example, X EQ 1 OR 2 is illegal; you must specify X EQ 1 OR X EQ 2.
- The ANY and RANGE functions can be used to simplify complex expressions.

AND *Both relations must be true for the complex expression to be true.*

OR *If either relation is true, the complex expression is true.*

Table 6 lists the outcome for AND and OR combinations.

Table 6 Outcome for AND and OR combinations

Expression	Outcome	Expression	Outcome
true AND true	= true	true OR true	= true
true AND false	= false	true OR false	= true
false AND false	= false	false OR false	= false
true AND missing	= missing	true OR missing	= true[*]
missing AND missing	= missing	missing OR missing	= missing
false AND missing	= false[*]	false OR missing	= missing

[*] Expressions where SPSS can evaluate the outcome with incomplete information. See "Missing Values in Logical Expressions" on p. 56.

Order of Evaluation

- When arithmetic operators and functions are used in a logical expression, the order of operations is functions and arithmetic operations first, then relational operators, and then logical operators.
- When more than one logical operator is used, NOT is evaluated first, then AND, and then OR.
- To change the order of evaluation, use parentheses.

Missing Values in Logical Expressions

In a simple relation, the logic is indeterminate if the expression on either side of the relational operator is missing. When two or more relations are joined by logical operators AND and OR, SPSS always returns a missing value if all of the relations in the expression are missing. However, if any one of the relations can be determined, SPSS tries to return true or false according to the logical outcomes shown in Table 6.

- When two relations are joined with the AND operator, the logical expression can never be true if one of the relations is indeterminate. The expression can, however, be false.
- When two relations are joined with the OR operator, the logical expression can never be false if one relation returns missing. The expression, however, can be true.

Other Functions

SPSS also includes a lag function and several missing-value functions.

Across-Case LAG Function

LAG(arg,n) *The value of the variable* n *cases before.* The first argument is a variable. The second argument, if specified, is a constant and must be a positive integer; the default is 1. For example, PREV4=LAG(GNP,4) returns the value of *GNP* for the fourth case before the current one. The first four cases have system-missing values for *PREV4*.

- The result is of the same type (numeric or string) as the variable specified as the first argument.
- The first *n* cases for string variables are set to blanks. For example, if PREV2=LAG (LNAME,2) is specified, blanks will be assigned to the first two cases for *PREV2*.
- When LAG is used with commands that select cases (for example, SELECT IF and SAMPLE), LAG counts cases *after* case selection, even if specified before these commands (see "Command Order" on p. 17).

Missing-Value Functions

- Each argument to a missing-value function (expression, variable name, or constant) must be separated by a comma.
- Only numeric values can be used as arguments in missing-value functions.
- Keyword TO can be used to refer to a set of variables in the argument list for functions NMISS and NVALID.
- Functions MISSING and SYSMIS are logical functions and can be useful shortcuts to more complicated specifications on the IF, DO IF, and other conditional commands.

VALUE(arg) *Ignore user-defined missing values.* The value is treated as is. The argument must be a variable name.

MISSING(arg)	*True or 1 if the value is user-missing or system-missing; false or 0 otherwise.*
SYSMIS(arg)	*True or 1 if the value is system-missing; false or 0 otherwise.*
NMISS(arg list)	*Number of system-missing values in the argument list.* The function does not count user-missing values.
NVALID(arg list)	*Number of valid values in the argument list.*

Treatment of Missing Values in Arguments

If the logic of an expression is indeterminate because of missing values, the expression returns a missing value, and the command is not executed. Table 7 summarizes how SPSS handles missing values in arguments to various functions.

Table 7   Missing values in arguments

Function	Returns system-missing if
MOD (x1,x2)	x1 is missing, or x2 is missing and x1 is not 0
MAX.n (x1,x2,...xk) MEAN.n (x1,x2,...xk) MIN.n (x1,x2,...x1) SUM.n (x1,x2,...xk)	fewer than *n* arguments are valid; the default *n* is 1
CFVAR.n (x1,x2,...xk) SD.n (x1,x2,...xk) VARIANCE.n (x1,x2,...xk)	fewer than *n* arguments are valid; the default *n* is 2
LPAD(x1,x2,x3) LTRIM(x1,x2) RTRIM(x1,x2) RPAD(x1,x2,x3)	x1 or x2 is illegal or missing
SUBSTR(x1,x2,x3)	x2 or x3 is illegal or missing
NUMBER(x,format) STRING(x,format)	the conversion is invalid
INDEX(x1,x2,x3) RINDEX(x1,x2,x3)	x3 is invalid or missing

Table 7   Missing values in arguments (Continued)

Function	Returns system-missing if
LAG (x,n)	x is missing *n* cases previously (and always for the first *n* cases); the default *n* is 1
ANY (x,x1,x2,...xk) RANGE (x,x1,x2,...xk)	x or all of x1, x2, ... xk are missing
VALUE (x)	x is system-missing
MISSING (x) NMISS (x1,x2,...xk) NVALID (x1,x2,...xk) SYSMIS (x)	never

- Any function that is not listed in Table 7 returns the system-missing value when the argument is missing.
- The system-missing value is a displayed as a period (.) for numeric variables.
- String variables do not have system-missing values. An invalid string expression nested within a complex transformation yields a null string, which is passed to the next level of operation and treated as missing. However, an invalid string expression that is not nested is displayed as a blank string and is *not* treated as missing.

Date and Time in SPSS

SPSS reads and writes date and time in many different formats but stores them as floating-point numbers. You can perform arithmetic operations on them, use them in statistical procedures, and display or print them in a format of your choice. This section discusses the input and output formats for date and time, arithmetic operations using date and time variables, and date and time functions.

Date and Time Formats

Date and time formats are both input and output formats. They can be used on DATA LIST and other variable definition commands to read in values representing dates or times or date-time combinations. Like numeric formats, each input format generates a default output format, automatically expanded (if necessary) to accommodate display width. In addition, you can assign or modify output formats using FORMATS, WRITE FORMATS, and PRINT FORMATS commands. The output formats are effective only with LIST, REPORT, and TABLES procedures and the PRINT and WRITE transformation commands. Other procedures use the F format and display the values as numbers.

- All date and time formats have a minimum input width and some have a different minimum output. Wherever the input minimum width is less than the output minimum, SPSS expands the width automatically when displaying or printing values. However, when you specify output formats, you must allow enough space for displaying the date and time in the format you choose.
- Input data shorter than the specified width are correctly evaluated as long as all the necessary elements are present. For example, with the TIME format, 1:2, 01 2, and 01:02 are all correctly evaluated even though the minimum width is 5. However, if only one element (hours or minutes) is present, you must use a time function to aggregate or convert the data (see "Date and Time Functions" on p. 66).
- If a date or time value cannot be completely displayed in the specified width, values are truncated in the output. For example, an input time value of 1:20:59 (1 hour, 20 minutes, 59 seconds) displayed with a width of 5 will generate an output value of 01:20, not 01:21. The truncation of output does not affect the numeric value stored in the working file.

Table 8 shows all date and time formats available in SPSS, where w indicates the total number of columns and d (if present) the number of decimal places for fractional seconds. The example shows the output format with the minimum width and default decimal positions (if applicable). The format allowed in the input data is much less restrictive (see "Input Data Specification" on p. 60).

Table 8 Date and time formats in SPSS

Format type	Description	Min w In	Min w Out	Max w	Max d	General form	Example
DATEw	International date	8	9	40		dd-mmm-yy	28-OCT-90
		10	11			dd-mmm-yyyy	28-OCT-1990
ADATEw	American date	8	8	40		mm/dd/yy	10/28/90
		10	10			mm/dd/yyyy	10/28/1990
EDATEw	European date	8	8	40		dd/mm/yy	28/10/90
		10	10			dd/mm/yyyy	28/10/1990
JDATEw	Julian date	5	5	40		yyddd	90301
		7	7			yyyyddd	1990301
SDATEw	Sortable date*	8	8	40		yy/mm/dd	90/10/28
		10	10			yyyy/mm/dd	1990/10/28
QYRw	Quarter and year	4	6	40		q Q yy	4 Q 90
		6	8			q Q yyyy	4 Q 1990
MOYRw	Month and year	6	6	40		mmm yy	OCT 90
		8	8			mmm yyyy	OCT 1990
WKYRw	Week and year	6	8	40		ww WK yy	43 WK 90
		8	10			ww WK yyyy	43 WK 1990
WKDAYw	Day of the week	2	2	40		(name of the day)	SU
MONTHw	Month	3	3	40		(name of the month)	JAN
TIMEw	Time	5	5	40		hh:mm	01:02
TIMEw.d		10	10	40	16	hh:mm:ss.s	01:02:34.75
DTIMEw	Days and time	8	8	40		dd hh:mm	20 08:03
DTIMEw.d		13	13	40	16	dd hh:mm:ss.s	20 08:03:00
DATETIMEw	Date and time	17	17	40		dd-mmm-yyyy hh:mm	20-JUN-1990 08:03
DATETIMEw.d		22	22	40	16	dd-mmm-yyyy hh:mm:ss.s	20-JUN-1990 08:03:00

* All date and time formats in SPSS produce sortable data. SDATE, a date format used in a number of Asian countries, can be sorted in its character form and is used as a sortable format by many programmers.

Input Data Specification

The following general rules apply to date and time input formats:

- Input data must be fixed. Data can appear anywhere within the specified columns. Leading and trailing blanks are allowed. If column-style specifications are used, the width specification can be omitted (see DATA LIST). For example,

```
DATA LIST /BIRTHDAY 1-8 (DATE).
```

is equivalent to

```
DATA LIST /BIRTHDAY (DATE8).
```

- You cannot use date and time formats to read freefield data.
- Two-digit years are assumed to have the prefix 19. Whether all four digits or only two digits are displayed in output depends on the width specification on the format.
- Dashes, periods, commas, slashes, or blanks can be used as delimiters in the date-month-year input. For example, with DATE format, the following input forms are all acceptable:

```
28-10-90        28/10/1990        28.OCT.90        October 28, 1990
```

The displayed values, however, will be the same: 28-OCT-90 or 28-OCT-1990, depending on whether the specified width allows 11 characters in output.

- The JDATE format does not allow internal delimiters and requires leading zeros for day values less than 100 and two-digit year values less than 10. For example, for January 1, 1990, the following two specifications are acceptable:

```
90001                  1990001
```

However, neither of the following is acceptable:

```
90 1                   90/1
```

- Months can be represented in digits, Roman numerals, or three-character abbreviations, and they can be fully spelled out. For example, all of the following specifications are acceptable for October:

```
10        X        OCT        October
```

- The quarter in QYR format is expressed as 1, 2, 3, or 4. It must be separated from the year by the letter Q. Blanks can be used as additional delimiters. For example, for the fourth quarter of 1990, all the following specifications are acceptable:

```
4Q90        4Q1990        4 Q 90        4 Q 1990
```

On some operating systems, such as IBM CMS, Q must be upper case. The displayed output is 4 Q 90 or 4 Q 1990, depending on whether the width specified allows all four digits of the year.

- The week in the WKYR format is expressed as a number from 1 to 53. Week 1 begins on January 1, week 2 on January 8, and so forth. The value may be different from the number of the calendar week. The week and year must be separated by the string WK. Blanks can be used as additional delimiters. For example, for the 43rd week of 1990, all the following specifications are acceptable:

```
43WK90        43WK1990        43 WK 90        43 WK 1990
```

On some operating systems, such as IBM CMS, WK must be upper case. The displayed output is 43 WK 90 or 43 WK 1990, depending on whether the specified width allows enough space for all four digits of the year.

- In time specifications, colons can be used as delimiters between hours, minutes, and seconds. Hours and minutes are required but seconds are optional. A period is required to separate seconds from fractional seconds. Hours can be of unlimited magnitude, but the maximum value for minutes is 59 and for seconds 59.999. . . .

- Data values can contain a sign (+ or −) in TIME and DTIME formats to represent time intervals before or after a point in time.

Example

```
DATA LIST FIXED
 /VAR1 1-17 (DATE) VAR2 21-37 (ADATE) VAR3 41-47 (JDATE).
BEGIN DATA
28-10-90             10/28/90              90301
28.OCT.1990          X 28 1990             1990301
28 October, 2001     Oct.  28, 2001        2001301
END DATA.
LIST.
```

- Internally, all date format variables are stored as the number of seconds from 0 hours 0 minutes and 0 seconds of Oct. 14, 1582.

The LIST output from these commands is shown in Figure 16.

Figure 16 Output illustrating DATE, ADATE, and JDATE formats

```
        VAR1              VAR2          VAR3

    28-OCT-1990        10/28/1990     1990301
    28-OCT-1990        10/28/1990     1990301
    28-OCT-2001        10/28/2001     2001301
```

Example

```
DATA LIST FIXED /VAR1 1-10 (QYR) VAR2 12-25 (MOYR) VAR3 28-37 (WKYR).
BEGIN DATA
4Q90         10/90          43WK90
4 Q 90       Oct-1990       43 WK 1990
4 Q 2001     October, 2001  43 WK 2001
END DATA.
LIST.
```

- Internally, the value of a QYR variable is stored as midnight of the first day of the first month of the specified quarter, the value of a MOYR variable is stored as midnight of the first day of the specified month, and the value of a WKYR format variable is stored as midnight of the first day of the specified week. Thus, 4Q90 and 10/90 are both equivalent to October 1, 1990, and 43WK90 is equivalent to October 22, 1990.

The LIST output from these commands is shown in Figure 17.

Figure 17 Output illustrating QYR, MOYR, and WKYR formats

```
     VAR1         VAR2           VAR3

   4 Q 1990     OCT 1990      43 WK 1990
   4 Q 1990     OCT 1990      43 WK 1990
   4 Q 2001     OCT 2001      43 WK 2001
```

Example

```
DATA LIST FIXED
  /VAR1 1-11 (TIME,2) VAR2 13-21 (TIME) VAR3 23-28 (TIME).
BEGIN DATA
1:2:34.75    1:2:34.75 1:2:34
END DATA.
LIST.
```

- TIME reads and writes time of the day or a time interval.
- Internally, the TIME values are stored as the number of seconds from midnight of the day or of the time interval.

The LIST output from these commands is shown in Figure 18.

Figure 18 Output illustrating TIME format

```
    VAR1       VAR2     VAR3
1:02:34.75  1:02:34    1:02
```

Example

```
DATA LIST FIXED
  /VAR1 1-9 (WKDAY) VAR2 10-18 (WKDAY)
   VAR3 20-29 (MONTH) VAR4 30-32 (MONTH) VAR5 35-37 (MONTH).
BEGIN DATA
Sunday    Sunday    January     1    Jan
Monday    Monday    February    2    Feb
Tues      Tues      March       3    Mar
Wed       Wed       April       4    Apr
Th        Th        Oct        10    Oct
Fr        Fr        Nov        11    Nov
Sa        Sa        Dec        12    Dec
END DATA.
FORMATS VAR2 VAR5 (F2).
LIST.
```

- WKDAY reads and writes the day of the week; MONTH reads and writes the month of the year.
- Values for WKDAY are entered as strings but stored as numbers. They can be used in arithmetic operations but not in string functions.
- Values for MONTH can be entered either as strings or as numbers, but are stored as numbers. They can be used in arithmetic operations but not in string functions.
- To display the values as numbers, assign an F format to the variable, as was done for *VAR2* and *VAR5* in the above example.

The LIST output from these commands is shown in Figure 19.

Figure 19 Output illustrating WKDAY and MONTH formats

```
    VAR1  VAR2      VAR3      VAR4  VAR5

SUNDAY      1    JANUARY     JAN    1
MONDAY      2    FEBRUARY    FEB    2
TUESDAY     3    MARCH       MAR    3
WEDNESDAY   4    APRIL       APR    4
THURSDAY    5    OCTOBER     OCT   10
FRIDAY      6    NOVEMBER    NOV   11
SATURDAY    7    DECEMBER    DEC   12
```

Example

```
DATA LIST FIXED /VAR1 1-14 (DTIME) VAR2 18-42 (DATETIME).
BEGIN DATA
20 8:3             20-6-90 8:3
20:8:03:46         20/JUN/1990 8:03:46
20 08 03 46.75     20 June, 2001 08 03 46.75
END DATA.
LIST.
```

- DTIME and DATETIME read and write time intervals.
- The decimal point explicitly coded in the input data for fractional seconds.
- The DTIME format allows a – or + sign in the data value to indicate a time interval before or after a point in time.
- Internally, values for a DTIME variable are stored as the number of seconds of the time interval while those for a DATETIME variable are stored as the number of seconds from 0 hours 0 minutes and 0 seconds of Oct. 14, 1852.

The LIST output from these commands is shown in Figure 20.

Figure 20 Output illustrating DTIME and DATETIME formats

```
         VAR1                   VAR2

    20 08:03:00         20-JUN-1990 08:03:00
    20 08:03:46         20-JUN-1990 08:03:46
    20 08:03:46         20-JUN-2001 08:03:46
```

Arithmetic Operations with Date and Time Variables

Most date and time variables are stored internally as the number of seconds from a particular date or as a time interval and therefore can be used in arithmetic operations:

- In SPSS, a *date* is a floating-point number representing the number of seconds from midnight, October 14, 1582. Dates, which represent a particular point in time, are stored as the number of seconds to that date. For example, November 8, 1957, is stored as 1.2E+10.
- A date includes the time of day, which is the time interval past midnight. When time of day is not given, it is taken as 00:00 and the date is an even multiple of 86,400 (the number of seconds in a day).

- A *time interval* is a floating-point number representing the number of seconds in a time period, for example, an hour, minute, or day. For example, the value representing 5.5 days is 475,200; the value representing the time interval 14:08:17 is 50,897.
- QYR, MOYR, and WKYR variables are stored as midnight of the first day of the respective quarter, month, and week of the year. Therefore, 1 Q 90, 1/90, and 1 WK 90 are all equivalents of January 1, 1990 0:0:00. See "Date and Time Functions" on p. 66 for information on how to determine the quarter, month, or week of a year for a certain date.
- WKDAY variables are stored as 1 to 7, and MONTH variables as 1 to 12. For information on how to determine the day of the week or the month of the year for a certain date, see "Date and Time Functions" on p. 66.
- Both dates and time intervals can be used in arithmetic expressions. The results are stored as the number of seconds or days (see Table 9).
- Do not mix time variables (TIME and DTIME) with date variables (DATE, ADATE, EDATE, and so forth) in computations. Since date variables have an implicit time value of 00:00:00, calculations involving time values that are not multiples of a whole day (e.g, 24 hours, 0 minutes, 0 seconds) will yield unreliable results.
- Mixing a DATETIME variable with a date variable may yield an unreliable results. Operations involving date variables are accurate only to the days. To avoid possible misinterpretation, use the DTIME format and ignore the hours and minutes portion of the resulting value.

You can perform virtually any arithmetic operation with them. Of course, not all of these operations are particularly useful. You can calculate the number of days between two dates by subtracting one date from the other—but adding two dates does not produce a very meaningful result.

By default, any new numeric variables you compute are displayed in F format. In the case of calculations involving time and date variables, this means the default output is expressed as a number of seconds or days. Use the FORMATS (or PRINT FORMATS) command to specify an appropriate format for the computed variable. Table 9 shows the recommended output formats for some of the calculations possible with date and time variables.

Table 9 Recommended output formats for date and time calculations

Arithmetic operation	Result	Recommended output format
time ± time[*]	time	TIME, DTIME
date - date [†]	time	DTIME
DATETIME - DATETIME	time	TIME, DTIME
DATETIME ± time	date	DATETIME

* Including TIME and DTIME formats.
† Including DATE, ADATE, EDATE, JDATE, and SDATE formats.

Example

```
DATA LIST RECORDS=2
 /TIME 1-8 (TIME) DTIME 10-19 (DTIME) DATE 21-29 (DATE)
  ADATE 31-38 (ADATE)
 /DATTIME1 1-18 (DATETIME) DATTIME2 20-37 (DATETIME).
BEGIN DATA
1:10:15   1 0:25:10   13-8-90   10/21/90
28-OCT-90 9:15:17  29/OCT/90 10:30:22
END DATA.
COMPUTE ADDTIME=TIME+DTIME.
COMPUTE DATEDIF1=ADATE-DATE.
COMPUTE DATEDIF2=DATTIME2-DATTIME1.
COMPUTE DATETIME=DATTIME2+DTIME.
LIST VARIABLES=ADDTIME DATEDIF1 DATEDIF2 DATETIME.
FORMATS ADDTIME DATEDIF2 (TIME15) DATEDIF1 (DTIME15)
 DATETIME (DATETIME25).
LIST VARIABLES=ADDTIME DATEDIF1 DATEDIF2 DATETIME.
```

The results of these commands are shown in Figure 21.

Figure 21 Results of arithmetic operations with date and time variables

```
   ADDTIME       DATEDIF1       DATEDIF2              DATETIME

   25:35:25     69 00:00:00     25:15:05        30-OCT-1990 10:55:32
```

Date and Time Functions

Date and time functions provide aggregation, conversion, and extraction routines for dates and time intervals. Each function transforms an expression consisting of one or more arguments. Arguments can be complex expressions, variable names, or constants. Date and time expressions and variables are legitimate arguments.

Aggregation Functions

Aggregation functions generate dates and time intervals from values that were not read by SPSS date and time input formats.

- All aggregation functions begin with DATE or TIME, depending on whether a date or a time interval is requested. This is followed by a subfunction that corresponds to the type of values found in the data.
- The subfunctions are separated from the function by a period (.) and are followed by an argument list specified in parentheses.
- The arguments to the DATE and TIME functions must be separated by commas and must contain integer values.

DATE.DMY(d,m,y)   *Combine day, month, and year.* The value of the argument for day must be expressed as an integer between 1 and 31. The value of the argument for month must be expressed as an integer between 1 and 13 (13 returns January of the following year). Years are expressed in two or four digits. A two-digit specification implies a prefix of 19. For example, the command

```
COMPUTE BIRTHDAY=DATE.DMY(DAY,MONTH,YEAR).
```

stores the value of approximately 1.184E+10 in *BIRTHDAY* when *DAY* is 8, *MONTH* is 11, and *YEAR* is 57. This value can be displayed with a DATE9 format as 08-NOV-57.

DATE.MDY(m,d,y) *Combine month, day, and year.* This function follows the same rules as DATE.DMY, except for the order of the arguments. For example, the command

```
COMPUTE BIRTHDAY=DATE.MDY(MONTH,DAY,YEAR).
```

stores the same value as the previous example in *BIRTHDAY* for the same values of *MONTH*, *DAY*, and *YEAR*. The value can be displayed as 11/08/57 with an ADATE8 format.

DATE.YRDAY(y,d) *Combine year and day of the year.* The year can be expressed as either two or four digits. Two-digit years are assumed to have a prefix of 19. The day can be expressed as any integer between and including 1 and 366. For example, the command

```
COMPUTE BIRTHDAY=DATE.YRDAY(1688,301).
```

when combined with a DATE11 print format produces the date 27-OCT-1688 for *BIRTHDAY*.

DATE.QYR(q,y) *Combine quarter and year.* The quarter must be expressed as a single digit between and including 1 and 4. The year can contain two or four digits. Two-digit values are assumed to have a prefix of 19. For example, the command

```
COMPUTE QUART=DATE.QYR(QTR,YEAR).
```

with a QDATE6 print format produces a value of 4 Q 57 for *QUART* when *QTR* is 4 and *YEAR* is 57. Since each quarter is assumed to begin on the first day of the first month of the quarter, a DATE9 print format for the same value is displayed as 01-OCT-57.

DATE.MOYR(m,y) *Combine month and year.* The value of the month must be expressed as an integer between and including 1 and 12. The year can be expressed as two or four digits. For example, the command

```
COMPUTE START=DATE.MOYR(MONTH,YEAR).
```

displays NOV 57 for *START* when *MONTH* is 11 and *YEAR* is 57 and the print format is MOYR.

DATE.WKYR(w,y) *Combine week and year.* The week must be an integer between and including 1 and 53. The year can be represented by two or four digits. For example, the command

```
COMPUTE WEEK=DATE.WKYR(WK,YEAR).
```

displays 26-NOV-57 for *WEEK* when *WK* is 48 and *YEAR* is 57 and the print format is DATE9. The number of the week in the WKYR format is calculated beginning with the first day of the year. It may be different from the number of calendar week.

TIME.HMS(h,m,s) *Combine hour, minute, and second into a time interval.* For example, the command

```
COMPUTE PERIOD1= TIME.HMS (HR,MIN,SEC).
```

produces an interval of 45,030 seconds for *PERIOD1* when *HR* equals 12, *MIN* equals 30, and *SEC* equals 30. The value can be displayed as 12:30:30 with a TIME8 print format.

You can supply one, two, or three arguments. Trailing arguments can be omitted and default to 0. The value of the first nonzero argument can spill over into the next higher argument. For example, the command

```
COMPUTE PERIOD2=TIME.HMS(HR,MIN).
```

produces an interval of 5400 seconds for *PERIOD2* when *HR* is 0 and *MIN* is 90. The value can be displayed as 01:30 with a TIME5 print format.

You can have a noninteger value for the last argument. For example, the command

```
COMPUTE PERIOD3=TIME.HMS(HR).
```

produces an interval of 5400 seconds for *PERIOD3* when *HR* equals 1.5 and is displayed as 01:30 with a TIME5 format. When you supply a nonzero argument to a function, each of the lower-level units must be within the range of –60 to +60.

TIME.DAYS(d) *Aggregate days into a time interval.* The argument can be expressed as any numeric value. For example, the command

```
COMPUTE NDAYS=TIME.DAYS(SPELL).
```

with a value of 2.5 for *SPELL* generates a value for *NDAYS* that is displayed as 2 12:00 with a DTIME7 format.

Conversion Functions

The conversion functions convert time intervals from one unit of time to another. Time intervals are stored as the number of seconds in the interval; the conversion functions provide a means for calculating more appropriate units, for example, converting seconds to days.

Each conversion function consists of the CTIME function followed by a period (.), the target time unit, and an argument. The argument can consist of expressions, variable names, or constants. The argument must already be a time interval (see "Aggregation Functions" on p. 66). Time conversions produce noninteger results with a default format of F8.2.

Since time and dates are stored internally as seconds, a function that converts to seconds is not necessary.

CTIME.DAYS(arg)   *Convert a time interval to the number of days.* For example, the command

```
COMPUTE NDAYS=CTIME.DAYS(TIME.HMS(HR,MIN,SEC)).
```

with 12 for *HR*, 30 for *MIN*, and 30 for *SEC* yields a value of 0.52 for *NDAYS*. `CTIME.DAYS(45030)` yields the same result.

CTIME.HOURS(arg)   *Convert a time interval to the number of hours.* For example, the command

```
COMPUTE NHOURS=CTIME.HOURS(TIME.HMS(HR,MIN,SEC)).
```

using the same values as the previous example produces a value of 12.51 for *NHOURS*.

CTIME.MINUTES(arg)   *Convert a time interval to the number of minutes.* Using the same values as the previous example for *HR*, *MIN*, and, *SEC*, the command

```
COMPUTE NMINS=CTIME.MINUTES(TIME.HMS(HR,MIN,SEC)).
```

converts the interval to minutes and produces a value of 750.50 for *NMINS*.

YRMODA Function

YRMODA(arg list)   *Convert year, month, and day to a day number.* The number returned is the number of days since October 14, 1582 (day 1 of the Gregorian calendar).

- Arguments for YRMODA can be variables, constants, or any other type of numeric expression but must yield integers.
- Year, month, and day must be specified in that order.
- The first argument can be any year between 0 and 99, or between 1582 to 47516.
- If the first argument yields a number between 00 and 99, 1900 through 1999 is assumed.
- The month can range from 1 through 13. Month 13 with day 0 yields the last day of the year. For example, YRMODA(1990,13,0) produces the day number for December 31, 1990. Month 13 with any other day yields the day of the first month of the coming year, for example, YRMODA(1990,13,1) produces the day number for January 1, 1991.
- The day can range from 0 through 31. Day 0 is the last day of the previous month regardless of whether it is 28, 29, 30, or 31. For example, YRMODA(1990,3,0) yields 148791.00, the day number for February 28, 1990.
- The function returns the system-missing value if any of the three arguments is missing or if the arguments do not form a valid date *after* October 14, 1582.
- Since YRMODA yields the number of days instead of seconds, you can not display it in date format unless you convert it to the number of seconds.

Extraction Functions

The extraction functions extract subfields from dates or time intervals, targeting the day or a time from a date value. This permits you to classify events by day of the week, season, shift, and so forth.

- Each extraction function begins with XDATE, followed by a period, the subfunction name (what you want to extract), and an argument.
- The argument can be an expression, a variable name, or a constant, provided the argument is already in date form.
- In the following examples, the value for variable *BIRTHDAY* is 05-DEC-1954 5:30:15, read with a DATE20 input format.

XDATE.MDAY(arg) *Return day number in a month from a date.* The result is an integer between 1 and 31. The date must have occurred after October 14, 1582. For example, you can extract the day number from *BIRTHDAY*, as in:

```
COMPUTE DAYNUM=XDATE.MDAY(BIRTHDAY).
```

When the value for *BIRTHDAY* is 05-DEC-1954 5:30:15, *DAYNUM* is 5.

XDATE.MONTH(arg) *Return month number from a date.* The result is an integer between 1 and 12. The date must have occurred after October 14, 1582. For example, you can extract the month number from *BIRTHDAY*, as in:

```
COMPUTE MONTHNUM=XDATE.MONTH(BIRTHDAY).
```

When the value for *BIRTHDAY* is 05-DEC-1954 5:30:15, this command yields 12 for *MONTHNUM*. If you provide a print format of MONTH12, as in

```
PRINT FORMAT MONTHNUM(MONTH12).
```

the value would be displayed as DECEMBER.

XDATE.YEAR(arg) *Return a four-digit year from a date.* The date must have occurred after October 14, 1582. For example, you can extract the year from *BIRTHDAY*, as in:

```
COMPUTE YEAR=XDATE.YEAR(BIRTHDAY).
```

When the value for *BIRTHDAY* is 05-DEC-1954 5:30:15, this command returns 1954 for *YEAR*.

XDATE.HOUR(arg) *Return the hour from a date or time of day.* The result is an integer between 0 and 23. For example, you can extract the hour from *BIRTHDAY*, as in:

```
COMPUTE HOUR=XDATE.HOUR(BIRTHDAY).
```

When the value for *BIRTHDAY* is 05-DEC-1954 5:30:15, this command returns 5 for *HOUR*.

XDATE.MINUTE(arg) *Return the minute of the hour from a date or time of day.* The result is an integer from 0 through 59. For example, you can extract the minute of the hour from *BIRTHDAY*, as in:

    COMPUTE MIN=XDATE.MINUTE(BIRTHDAY).

When the value for *BIRTHDAY* is 05-DEC-1954 5:30:15, this command returns 30 for *MIN*.

XDATE.SECOND(arg) *Return the second of the minute from a date or time of day.* The result is an integer or, if there are fractional seconds, a value with decimals. For example, you can extract the second of the minute from *BIRTHDAY*, as in:

    COMPUTE SEC=XDATE.SECOND(BIRTHDAY).

When the value for *BIRTHDAY* is 05-DEC-1954 5:30:15, this command returns a value of 15.00 for *SEC*.

XDATE.WKDAY(arg) *Return the day within a week from a date.* The result is an integer between and including 1 and 7, with Sunday being 1 and Saturday being 7. The date must have occurred after October 14, 1582. For example, you can extract the day of the week from *BIRTHDAY*, as in:

    COMPUTE DAYNAME=XDATE.WKDAY(BIRTHDAY).

When the value for *BIRTHDAY* is 05-DEC-1954 5:30:15, this command returns the value 1 for *DAYNAME*. If you provide an output format of WKDAY, as in

    PRINT FORMAT DAYNAME (WKDAY9).

the value for *DAYNAME* would display as SUNDAY.

XDATE.JDAY(arg) *Return the day of the year from the date.* The result is an integer between 1 and 366 inclusive. The date must have occurred after October 14, 1582. For example, you can extract the day of the year from *BIRTHDAY*, as in:

    COMPUTE DAYNUM=XDATE.JDAY(BIRTHDAY).

When the value for *BIRTHDAY* is 05-DEC-1954 5:30:15, this command returns the value 339 for *DAYNUM*.

XDATE.QUARTER(arg) *Return quarter number within a year for a date.* The result is 1, 2, 3, or 4. The date must have occurred after October 14, 1582. To extract the quarter in which *BIRTHDAY* occurred, use the command:

    COMPUTE Q=XDATE.QUARTER(BIRTHDAY).

When *BIRTHDAY* equals 5-DEC-1954 05:30:15, the value of *Q* is 4.

XDATE.WEEK(arg) *Return the week number of a date.* The result is an integer between 1 and 53. The date must have occurred after October 14, 1582. For example, you can extract the week number from *BIRTHDAY,* as in:

    COMPUTE WEEKNUM=XDATE.WEEK(BIRTHDAY).

When the value for *BIRTHDAY* is 5-DEC-1954 05:30:15, this command returns the value 49 for *WEEKNUM*.

XDATE.TDAY(arg)   *Return number of days in a time interval or from October 14, 1582.* The value returned is an integer (the fractional portion of a day is ignored). For example, the command

```
COMPUTE NDAYS=XDATE.TDAY(BIRTHDAY).
```

returns the value 135922 when the value for *BIRTHDAY* is 05-DEC-1954 5:30:15, indicating the number of days between October 14, 1582 and December 5, 1954. The hours, minutes, and seconds are ignored.

XDATE.TIME(arg)   *Return time of day from a date.* The result is expressed as the number of elapsed seconds since midnight of that date. For example, when the value for *BIRTHDAY* is 05-DEC-1954 5:30:15, the command

```
COMPUTE ELSEC=XDATE.TIME(BIRTHDAY).
```

returns the value 19815 for *ELSEC*. If you provide a TIME print format, as in

```
PRINT FORMAT ELSEC(TIME8).
```

the value is displayed as 5:30:15.

XDATE.DATE(arg)   *Return the date portion of a date.* The result is the integral date portion of a date, which is the number of elapsed seconds between midnight October 14, 1582 and midnight of the date in question. The date must have occurred after October 14, 1582. To extract the date from variable *BIRTHDAY*, use:

```
COMPUTE BRTHDATE=XDATE.DATE(BIRTHDAY).
```

The value for *BIRTHDATE* can then be displayed as 12/05/54 using ADATE8 format.

Precautions with Date and Time Variables

Dates and times are represented internally as seconds. The numbers for dates are very large, and arithmetic overflows can result. For instance, dates in the 20th century are on the order of 10 to the 10th power (11 digits). For that reason, a few precautions are in order:

- Some machine environments cannot accommodate the computation of higher powers of date and time variables. For example, computations higher than the sixth power may cause overflows on some machines.
- The magnitude of the values may cause inaccuracies in some statistical procedures. It is advisable to subtract a fixed date if you want to keep seconds as the unit, or to convert days using the XDATE.TDAYS function. REGRESSION, CORRELATIONS, ANOVA, and ONEWAY use an adaptive centering method, so their accuracy will not be affected.
- LIST, REPORT, and TABLES are the only procedures that display values in date and time formats. The PRINT and WRITE transformation commands can also display and write date and time formats. However, some summary variables in REPORT and calculated vari-

ables in TABLES display in F format, regardless of the print formats of variables used as arguments.
- All other procedures use F format in all cases. The default width and number of decimal places is taken from the print format, but the format type is ignored. For example, in a frequency table, the date 1/09/57 with a print format of DATE9 will be displayed as 11830147200, not 01-SEP-57.
- Changing the print format in no way alters the values that are stored in SPSS. For example, if you assign a print format of DATE9 for a variable read with DATETIME format, the time of day will not display but continues to be part of the value. This means that seemingly identical values can be displayed as separate entries within SPSS procedures.

Commands

ADD FILES

```
ADD FILES FILE={file}
               {*   }

[/RENAME=(old varnames=new varnames)...]

[/IN=varname]

/FILE=... [/RENAME=...] [/IN=...]

[/BY varlist]

[/MAP]

[/KEEP={ALL**  }] [/DROP=varlist]
       {varlist}

[/FIRST=varname]  [/LAST=varname]
```

**Default if the subcommand is omitted.

Example:

```
ADD FILES FILE=SCHOOL1 /FILE=SCHOOL2.
```

Overview

ADD FILES combines cases from two up to fifty SPSS data files by concatenating or interleaving cases. When cases are **concatenated,** all cases from one file are added to the end of all cases from another file. When cases are **interleaved,** cases in the resulting file are ordered according to the values of one or more key variables.

The files specified on ADD FILES can be SPSS data files created by the SAVE or XSAVE commands or the working data file. The combined file becomes the new working file. Statistical procedures following ADD FILES use this combined file unless you replace it by building another working file. You must use the SAVE or XSAVE commands if you want to save the combined file as an SPSS data file.

In general, ADD FILES is used to combine files containing the same variables but different cases. To combine files containing the same cases but different variables, use MATCH FILES. To update existing SPSS data files, use UPDATE. ADD FILES cannot concatenate raw data files. To concatenate raw data files, use DATA LIST within an INPUT PROGRAM structure (see p. 155 for an example). Alternatively, convert the raw data files to SPSS data files with the SAVE or XSAVE commands and then use ADD FILES to combine them.

Options

Variable Selection. You can specify which variables from each input file are included in the new working file using the DROP and KEEP subcommands.

Variable Names. You can rename variables in each input file before combining the files using the RENAME subcommand. This permits you to combine variables that are the same but whose names differ in different input files, or to separate variables that are different but have the same name.

Variable Flag. You can create a variable that indicates whether a case came from a particular input file using IN. When interleaving cases, you can use the FIRST or LAST subcommands to create a variable that flags the first or last case of a group of cases with the same value for the key variable.

Variable Map. You can request a map showing all variables in the new working file, their order, and the input files from which they came using the MAP subcommand.

Basic Specification

- The basic specification is two or more FILE subcommands, each of which specifies a file to be combined. If cases are to be interleaved, the BY subcommand specifying the key variables is also required.
- All variables from all input files are included in the new working file unless DROP or KEEP is specified.

Subcommand Order

- RENAME and IN must immediately follow the FILE subcommand to which they apply.
- BY, FIRST, and LAST must follow all FILE subcommands and their associated RENAME and IN subcommands.

Syntax Rules

- RENAME can be repeated after each FILE subcommand. RENAME applies only to variables in the file named on the FILE subcommand immediately preceding it.
- BY can be specified only once. However, multiple key variables can be specified on BY. When BY is used, all files must be sorted in ascending order by the key variables (see SORT CASES).
- FIRST and LAST can be used only when files are interleaved (when BY is used).
- MAP can be repeated as often as desired.

Operations

- ADD FILES reads all input files named on FILE and builds a new working data file that replaces any working file created earlier in the session. ADD FILES is executed when the data are read by one of the procedure commands or the EXECUTE, SAVE, or SORT CASES commands.
- The resulting file contains complete dictionary information from the input files, including variable names, labels, print and write formats, and missing-value indicators. It also contains the documents from each input file. See DROP DOCUMENTS for information on deleting documents.
- Variables are copied in order from the first file specified, then from the second file specified, and so on. Variables that are not contained in all files receive the system-missing value for cases that do not have values for those variables.
- If the same variable name exists on more than one file but the format type (numeric or string) does not match, the command is not executed.
- If a numeric variable has the same name but different formats (for example, F8.0 and F8.2) on different input files, the format of the variable in the first-named file is used.
- If a string variable has the same name but different formats (for example, A24 and A16) on different input files, the command is not executed.
- If the working file is named as an input file, any N and SAMPLE commands that have been specified are applied to the working file before files are combined.

Limitations

- Maximum 50 files can be combined on one ADD FILES command.
- The TEMPORARY command cannot be in effect if the working data file is used as an input file.

Example

```
ADD FILES FILE=SCHOOL1 /FILE=SCHOOL2.
```

- ADD FILES concatenates cases from the SPSS data files *SCHOOL1* and *SCHOOL2*. All cases from *SCHOOL1* precede all cases from *SCHOOL2* in the resulting file.

Example

```
SORT CASES BY LOCATN DEPT.
ADD FILES   FILE=SOURCE /FILE=* /BY LOCATN DEPT
 /KEEP AVGHOUR AVGRAISE LOCATN DEPT SEX HOURLY RAISE /MAP.
SAVE OUTFILE=PRSNNL.
```

- SORT CASES sorts cases in the working file in ascending order of their values for *LOCATION* and *DEPT*.

- ADD FILES combines two files: the SPSS data file *SOURCE* and the sorted working file. File *SOURCE* must also be sorted by *LOCATN* and *DEPT*.
- BY indicates that the keys for interleaving cases are *LOCATN* and *DEPT*, the same variables used on SORT CASES.
- KEEP specifies the variables to be retained in the resulting file.
- MAP produces a list of variables in the resulting file and the two input files.
- SAVE saves the resulting file as a new SPSS data file named *PRSNNL*.

FILE Subcommand

FILE identifies the files to be combined. A separate FILE subcommand must be used for each input file.
- An asterisk may be specified on FILE to indicate the working data file.
- The order in which files are named determines the order of cases in the resulting file.

Raw Data Files

To add cases from a raw data file, you must first define the file as the working data file using the DATA LIST command. ADD FILES can then combine the working file with an SPSS data file.

Example

```
DATA LIST FILE=GASDATA/1 OZONE 10-12 CO 20-22 SULFUR 30-32.
ADD FILES  FILE=PARTICLE /FILE=*.
SAVE  OUTFILE=POLLUTE.
```

- The *GASDATA* file is a raw data file and is defined on the DATA LIST command.
- The *PARTICLE* file is a previously saved SPSS data file.
- FILE=* on ADD FILES specifies the working data file, which contains the gas data. FILE=PARTICLE specifies the SPSS data file *PARTICLE*.
- SAVE saves the resulting file as an SPSS data file with the filename *POLLUTE*. Cases from the *GASDATA* file follow cases from the *PARTICLE* file.

RENAME Subcommand

RENAME renames variables in input files *before* they are processed by ADD FILES. RENAME follows the FILE subcommand that specifies the file containing the variables to be renamed.
- RENAME applies only to the FILE subcommand immediately preceding it. To rename variables from more than one input file, enter a RENAME subcommand after each FILE subcommand that specifies a file with variables to be renamed.
- Specifications for RENAME consist of a left parenthesis, a list of old variable names, an equals sign, a list of new variable names, and a right parenthesis. The two variable lists

must name or imply the same number of variables. If only one variable is renamed, the parentheses are optional.
- More than one such specification can be entered on a single RENAME subcommand, each enclosed in parentheses.
- The TO keyword can be used to refer to consecutive variables in the file and to generate new variable names (see "Keyword TO" on p. 32).
- RENAME takes effect immediately. KEEP and DROP subcommands entered prior to RENAME must use the old names, while those entered after RENAME must use the new names.
- All specifications within a single set of parentheses take effect simultaneously. For example, the specification RENAME (A,B = B,A) swaps the names of the two variables.
- Variables cannot be renamed to scratch variables.
- Input data files are not changed on disk; only the copy of the file being combined is affected.

Example

```
ADD FILES FILE=CLIENTS /RENAME=(TEL_NO, ID_NO = PHONE, ID)
 /FILE=MASTER /BY ID.
```

- ADD FILES adds new client cases from file *CLIENTS* to existing client cases in file *MASTER*.
- Two variables on *CLIENTS* are renamed prior to the match. *TEL_NO* is renamed *PHONE* to match the name used for phone numbers in the master file. *ID_NO* is renamed *ID* so that it will have the same name as the identification variable in the master file and can be used on the BY subcommand.
- The BY subcommand orders the resulting file according to client ID number.

BY Subcommand

BY specifies one or more key variables that determine the order of cases in the resulting file. When BY is specified, cases from the input files are interleaved according to their values for the key variables.

- BY must follow the FILE subcommands and any associated RENAME and IN subcommands.
- The key variables specified on BY must be present and have the same names in all input files.
- Key variables can be long or short string variables or numerics.
- All input files must be sorted in ascending order of the key variables. If necessary, use SORT CASES before ADD FILES.
- Cases in the resulting file are ordered by the values of the key variables. All cases from the first file with the first value for the key variable are first, followed by all cases from the second file with the same value, followed by all cases from the third file with the same value, and so forth. These cases are followed by all cases from the first file with the next value for the key variable, and so on.

- Cases with system-missing values are first in the resulting file. User-missing values are interleaved with other values.

DROP and KEEP Subcommands

DROP and KEEP are used to include only a subset of variables in the resulting file. DROP specifies a set of variables to exclude and KEEP specifies a set of variables to retain.
- DROP and KEEP do not affect the input files on disk.
- DROP and KEEP must follow all FILE and RENAME subcommands.
- DROP and KEEP must specify one or more variables. If RENAME is used to rename variables, specify the new names on DROP and KEEP.
- DROP and KEEP take effect immediately. If a variable specified on DROP or KEEP does not exist in the input files, was dropped by a previous DROP subcommand, or was not retained by a previous KEEP subcommand, SPSS displays an error message and does not execute the ADD FILES command.
- DROP cannot be used with variables created by the IN, FIRST, or LAST subcommands.
- KEEP can be used to change the order of variables in the resulting file. With KEEP, variables are kept in the order they are listed on the subcommand. If a variable is named more than once on KEEP, only the first mention of the variable is in effect; all subsequent references to that variable name are ignored.
- Keyword ALL can be specified on KEEP. ALL must be the last specification on KEEP, and it refers to all variables not previously named on that subcommand. It is useful when you want to arrange the first few variables in a specific order.

Example

```
ADD FILES FILE=PARTICLE /RENAME=(PARTIC=POLLUTE1)
 /FILE=GAS /RENAME=(OZONE TO SULFUR=POLLUTE2 TO POLLUTE4)
 /KEEP=POLLUTE1 POLLUTE2 POLLUTE3 POLLUTE4.
```

- The renamed variables are retained in the resulting file. KEEP is specified after all the FILE and RENAME subcommands, and it refers to the variables by their new names.

IN Subcommand

IN creates a new variable in the resulting file that indicates whether a case came from the input file named on the preceding FILE subcommand. IN applies only to the file specified on the immediately preceding FILE subcommand.
- IN has only one specification, the name of the flag variable.
- The variable created by IN has value 1 for every case that came from the associated input file and value 0 for every case that came from a different input file.
- Variables created by IN are automatically attached to the end of the resulting file and cannot be dropped. If FIRST or LAST are used, the variable created by IN precedes the variables created by FIRST or LAST.

Example

```
ADD FILES  FILE=WEEK10 /FILE=WEEK11 /IN=INWEEK11 /BY=EMPID.
```

- IN creates the variable *INWEEK11*, which has value 1 for all cases in the resulting file that came from the input file *WEEK11* and value 0 for those cases that were not in file *WEEK11*.

Example

```
ADD FILES  FILE=WEEK10 /FILE=WEEK11 /IN=INWEEK11 /BY=EMPID.
IF  (NOT INWEEK11) SALARY1=0.
```

- The variable created by IN is used to screen partially missing cases for subsequent analyses.
- Since IN variables have either value 1 or 0, they can be used as logical expressions, where 1=true and 0=false. The IF command sets variable *SALARY1* equal to 0 for all cases that came from file *INWEEK11*.

FIRST and LAST Subcommands

FIRST and LAST create logical variables that flag the first or last case of a group of cases with the same value on the BY variables. FIRST and LAST must follow all FILE subcommands and their associated RENAME and IN subcommands.

- FIRST and LAST have only one specification, the name of the flag variable.
- FIRST creates a variable with value 1 for the first case of each group and value 0 for all other cases.
- LAST creates a variable with value 1 for the last case of each group and value 0 for all other cases.
- Variables created by FIRST and LAST are automatically attached to the end of the resulting file and cannot be dropped.

Example

```
ADD FILES  FILE=SCHOOL1 /FILE=SCHOOL2
 /BY=GRADE /FIRST=HISCORE.
```

- The variable *HISCORE* contains value 1 for the first case in each grade in the resulting file and value 0 for all other cases.

MAP Subcommand

MAP produces a list of the variables included in the new working file and the file or files from which they came. Variables are listed in the order they exist in the resulting file. MAP has no specifications and must follow after all FILE and RENAME subcommands.

- Multiple MAP subcommands can be used. Each MAP shows the current status of the working file and reflects only the subcommands that precede the MAP subcommand.
- To obtain a map of the working data file in its final state, specify MAP last.

- If a variable is renamed, its original and new names are listed. Variables created by IN, FIRST, and LAST are not included in the map since they are automatically attached to the end of the file and cannot be dropped.
- MAP can be used with the EDIT command to obtain a listing of the variables in the resulting file without actually reading the data and combining the files.

ADD VALUE LABELS

```
ADD VALUE LABELS varlist value 'label' value 'label'...[/varlist...]
```

Example:
```
ADD VALUE LABELS JOBGRADE 'P' 'Parttime Employee'
                          'C' 'Customer Support'.
```

Overview

ADD VALUE LABELS adds or alters value labels without affecting other value labels already defined for that variable. In contrast, VALUE LABELS adds or alters value labels but deletes all existing value labels for that variable when it does so.

Basic Specification

The basic specification is a variable name and individual values with associated labels.

Syntax Rules

- Labels can be assigned to values of any previously defined variable. It is not necessary to enter value labels for all of a variable's values.
- Each value label must be enclosed in apostrophes or quotation marks.
- When an apostrophe occurs as part of a label, enclose the label in quotation marks or enter the internal apostrophe twice with no intervening space.
- Value labels can contain any characters, including blanks.
- The same labels can be assigned to the same values of different variables by specifying a list of variable names. For string variables, the variables in the list must have the same defined width (for example, A8).
- Multiple sets of variable names and value labels can be specified on one ADD VALUE LABELS command as long as each set is separated from the previous one by a slash.
- To continue a label from one command line to the next, specify a plus (+) sign before the continuation of the label and enclose each segment of the label, including the blank between them, in apostrophes or quotes.

Operations

- Unlike most transformations, ADD VALUE LABELS takes effect as soon as it is encountered in the command sequence. Thus, special attention should be paid to its position among commands. See "Command Order" on p. 17 for more information.
- The added value labels are stored in the working file dictionary.

- ADD VALUE LABELS can be used for variables that have no previously assigned value labels.
- Adding labels to some values does not affect labels previously assigned to other values.

Limitations

- Value labels cannot exceed 60 characters. Most procedures display only 20 characters.
- Value labels cannot be assigned to long string variables.

Example

```
ADD VALUE LABELS V1 TO V3 1 'Officials & Managers'
                          6 'Service Workers'
             /V4 'N' 'New Employee'.
```

- Labels are assigned to the values 1 and 6 of the variables between and including *V1* and *V3* on the working data file.
- Following the required slash, a label for value N for variable *V4* is specified. N is a string value and must be enclosed in apostrophes or quotation marks.
- If labels already exist for these values, they are changed in the dictionary. If labels do not exist for these values, new labels are added to the dictionary.
- Existing labels for other values for these variables are not affected.

Example

```
ADD VALUE LABELS OFFICE88 1 "EMPLOYEE'S OFFICE ASSIGNMENT PRIOR"
    + " TO 1988".
```

- The label for value 1 for *OFFICE88* is specified on two command lines. The plus sign concatenates the two string segments and a blank is included at the beginning of the second string in order to maintain correct spacing in the label.

Value Labels for String Variables

- For short string variables, the values and the labels must be enclosed in apostrophes or quotation marks.
- If a specified value is longer than the defined width of the variable, SPSS displays a warning and truncates the value. The added label will be associated with the truncated value.
- If a specified value is shorter than the defined width of the variable, SPSS adds blanks to right-pad the value without warning. The added label will be associated with the padded value.
- If a single set of labels is to be assigned to a list of string variables, the variables must have the same defined width (for example, A8).

Example

```
ADD VALUE LABELS  STATE 'TEX' 'TEXAS' 'TEN' 'TENNESSEE'
                        'MIN' 'MINNESOTA'.
```

- ADD VALUE LABELS assigns labels to three values of variable *STATE*. Each value and each label is specified in apostrophes.
- Assuming variable *STATE* is defined as three characters wide, the labels *TEXAS*, *TENNESSEE*, and *MINNESOTA* will be appropriately associated with values TEX, TEN, and MIN. However, if *STATE* were defined as two characters wide, SPSS would truncate the specified values to two characters and would not be able to associate the labels correctly. Both TEX and TEN would be truncated to TE and would first be assigned label *TEXAS*, which would then be changed to *TENNESSEE* by the second specification.

Example

```
ADD VALUE LABELS=STATE REGION "U" "UNKNOWN".
```

- Label *UNKNOWN* is assigned to value U for both *STATE* and *REGION*.
- *STATE* and *REGION* must have the same defined width. If they do not, a separate specification must be made for each, as in:

```
ADD VALUE LABELS STATE "U" "UNKNOWN" / REGION "U" "UNKNOWN".
```

AGGREGATE

```
AGGREGATE OUTFILE={file} [/MISSING=COLUMNWISE] [/DOCUMENT]
               {*   }

 [/PRESORTED] /BREAK=varlist[({A})][varlist...]
                              {D}

 /aggvar['label']aggvar['label']...=function(arguments)

 [/aggvar ...]
```

Available functions:

SUM	Sum	MEAN	Mean
SD	Standard deviation	MAX	Maximum
MIN	Minimum	PGT	% of cases greater than value
PLT	% of cases less than value	PIN	% of cases between values
POUT	% of cases not in range	FGT	Fraction greater than value
FLT	Fraction less than value	FIN	Fraction between values
FOUT	Fraction not in range	N	Weighted number of cases
NU	Unweighted number of cases	NMISS	Weighted n of missing
NUMISS	Unweighted number of missing cases	FIRST	First nonmissing
LAST	Last nonmissing		

Example:
```
AGGREGATE OUTFILE=AGGEMP /BREAK=LOCATN DEPT /COUNT=N
  /AVGSAL AVGRAISE = MEAN(SALARY RAISE)
  /SUMSAL SUMRAISE = SUM(SALARY RAISE)
  /BLACKPCT 'Percentage Black' = PIN(RACE,1,1)
  /WHITEPCT 'Percentage White' = PIN(RACE,5,5).
```

Overview

AGGREGATE aggregates groups of cases in the working data file into single cases and creates a new, aggregated file. The values of one or more variables in the working file define the case groups. These variables are called **break variables.** A set of cases with identical values for each break variable is called a **break group.** A series of aggregate functions are applied to **source variables** in the working file to create new, aggregated variables that have one value for each break group.

AGGREGATE is often used with MATCH FILES to add variables with summary measures (sum, mean, etc.) to a file. Transformations performed on the combined file can create composite summary measures. With the REPORT procedure, the composite variables can be used to write reports with nested composite information.

Options

Aggregated File. You can produce either an SPSS data file or a new working file.

Documentary Text. You can copy documentary text from the original file into the aggregated file using the DOCUMENT subcommand. By default, documentary text is dropped.

Sorting. By default, cases in the aggregated file are sorted in ascending order of the values of each break variable. Alternatively, you can specify descending order. If the working file is already sorted by the break variables, you can skip this final sorting pass through the file using the PRESORTED subcommand.

Aggregated Variables. You can create aggregated variables using any of 19 aggregate functions. Functions SUM, MEAN, and SD can aggregate only numeric variables. All other functions can use both numeric and string variables.

Labels and Formats. You can specify variable labels for the aggregated variables. Variables created with functions MAX, MIN, FIRST, and LAST assume the formats and value labels of their source variables. All other variables assume the default formats described under "Aggregate Functions" on p. 89.

Basic Specification

The basic specification is OUTFILE, BREAK, and at least one aggregate function and source variable. OUTFILE specifies a name for the aggregated file. BREAK names the case grouping (break) variables. The aggregate function creates a new aggregated variable.

Subcommand Order

- OUTFILE must be specified first.
- If specified, DOCUMENT and PRESORTED must precede BREAK. No other subcommand can be specified between these two subcommands.
- MISSING, if specified, must immediately follow OUTFILE.
- The aggregate functions must be specified last.

Operations

- When AGGREGATE produces an SPSS data file, the working file remains unchanged and is still available for analysis. When AGGREGATE creates a new working file, it replaces the old working file. Only the new working file is available for analysis.
- The aggregated file contains the break variables plus the variables created by the aggregate functions.
- AGGREGATE excludes cases with missing values from all aggregate calculations except those involving functions N, NU, NMISS, and NUMISS.
- Unless otherwise specified, AGGREGATE sorts cases in the aggregated file in ascending order of the values of the grouping variables.
- If PRESORTED is specified, a new aggregate case is created each time a different value or combination of values is encountered on variables named on the BREAK subcommand.

- AGGREGATE ignores split-file processing. To achieve the same effect, name the variable or variables used to split the file as break variables before any other break variables. AGGREGATE produces one file, but the aggregated cases are in the same order as the split files.

Example

```
AGGREGATE OUTFILE=AGGEMP /BREAK=LOCATN DEPT
 /COUNT=N
 /AVGSAL AVGRAISE = MEAN(SALARY RAISE)
 /SUMSAL SUMRAISE = SUM(SALARY RAISE)
 /BLACKPCT 'Percentage Black' = PIN(RACE,1,1)
 /WHITEPCT 'Percentage White' = PIN(RACE,5,5).
```

- AGGREGATE creates a new SPSS data file *AGGEMP*. *AGGEMP* contains two break variables (*LOCATN* and *DEPT*) and all the new aggregate variables (*COUNT*, *AVGSAL*, *AVGRAISE*, *SUMSAL*, *SUMRAISE*, *BLACKPCT*, and *WHITEPCT*).
- BREAK specifies *LOCATN* and *DEPT* as the break variables. In the aggregated file, cases are sorted in ascending order of *LOCATN* and in ascending order of *DEPT* within *LOCATN*. The working data file remains unsorted.
- Variable *COUNT* is created as the weighted number of cases in each break group. *AVGSAL* is the mean of *SALARY* and *AVGRAISE* is the mean of *RAISE*. *SUMSAL* is the sum of *SALARY* and *SUMRAISE* is the sum of *RAISE*. *BLACKPCT* is the percentage of cases with value 1 for *RACE*. *WHITEPCT* is the percentage of cases with value 5 for *RACE*.

Example

```
GET FILE=HUBEMPL /KEEP=LOCATN DEPT HOURLY RAISE SEX.
AGGREGATE OUTFILE=AGGFILE /BREAK=LOCATN DEPT
 /AVGHOUR AVGRAISE=MEAN(HOURLY RAISE).
SORT CASES BY LOCATN DEPT.
MATCH FILES   TABLE=AGGFILE /FILE=* /BY LOCATN DEPT
 /KEEP AVGHOUR AVGRAISE LOCATN DEPT SEX HOURLY RAISE /MAP.

COMPUTE HOURDIF=HOURLY/AVGHOUR.
COMPUTE RAISEDIF=RAISE/AVGRAISE.
LIST.
```

- GET reads SPSS data file *HUBEMPL* and keeps a subset of variables.
- AGGREGATE creates a file aggregated by *LOCATN* and *DEPT* with the two new variables *AVGHOUR* and *AVGRAISE*, containing the means by location and department for *HOURLY* and *RAISE*. The aggregated file is saved as an SPSS data file named *AGGFILE*. Only the aggregated data file *AGGFILE* is sorted by *LOCATN* and *DEPT*; the working data file remains unchanged.
- SORT CASES sorts the working data file in ascending order of *LOCATN* and *DEPT*, the same variables used as AGGREGATE break variables.
- MATCH FILES specifies a table lookup match with *AGGFILE* as the table file and the sorted working data file as the case file.
- BY indicates that the keys for the match are *LOCATN* and *DEPT*.

- KEEP specifies the subset and order of variables to be retained in the resulting file.
- MAP provides a listing of the variables in the resulting file and the two input files.
- The COMPUTE commands calculate the ratios of each employee's hourly wage and raise to the department averages for wage and raise. The results are stored in variables *HOURDIF* and *RAISEDIF*.
- LIST displays the resulting file.

OUTFILE Subcommand

OUTFILE specifies a name for the file created by AGGREGATE. If an asterisk is specified on OUTFILE, the aggregated file replaces the working file. OUTFILE must be the first subcommand specified on AGGREGATE.

- If the aggregated file replaces the working file, the file is not automatically saved on disk. To save the file, use the SAVE command.

Example

```
AGGREGATE OUTFILE=AGGEMP
 /BREAK=LOCATN
 /AVGSAL = MEAN(SALARY).
```

- OUTFILE creates an SPSS data file named *AGGEMP*. The working file remains unchanged and is available for further analysis.
- File *AGGEMP* contains two variables, LOCATN and AVGSAL.

BREAK Subcommand

BREAK lists the grouping variables, also called the break variables. Each unique combination of values of the break variables defines one break group.
- The variables named on BREAK can be any combination of variables in the working data file.
- Unless PRESORTED is specified, AGGREGATE sorts cases after aggregating. By default, cases are sorted in ascending order of the values of the break variables. AGGREGATE sorts first on the first break variable, then on the second break variable within the groups created by the first, and so on.
- Sort order can be controlled by specifying an A (for ascending) or D (for descending) in parentheses after any break variables.
- The designations A and D apply to all preceding undesignated variables.
- Subcommand PRESORTED overrides all sorting specifications.

Example

```
AGGREGATE OUTFILE=AGGEMP
 /BREAK=LOCATN DEPT (A) TENURE (D)
 /AVGSAL = MEAN(SALARY).
```

- BREAK names variables *LOCATN*, *DEPT*, and *TENURE* as the break variables.

- Cases in the aggregated file are sorted in ascending order of *LOCATN*, in ascending order of *DEPT* within *LOCATN*, and in descending order of *TENURE* within *LOCATN* and *DEPT*. For each group defined by these variables, *AVGSAL* is computed as the mean of salary.

DOCUMENT Subcommand

DOCUMENT copies documentation from the original file into the aggregated file. By default, documents are dropped from the aggregated file, whether the file is the working file or an SPSS data file. DOCUMENT must appear after OUTFILE but before BREAK.

PRESORTED Subcommand

PRESORTED indicates that cases in the working data file are sorted according to the values of the break variables. This prevents AGGREGATE from sorting cases that have already been sorted and can save a considerable amount of processing time.

- If specified, PRESORTED must precede BREAK. The only specification is keyword PRESORTED. PRESORTED has no additional specifications.
- When PRESORTED is specified, SPSS forms an aggregate case out of each group of *adjacent* cases with the same values for the break variables.
- If the working file is not sorted by the break variables in ascending order and PRESORTED is specified, a warning message is generated but the procedure is executed. Each group of adjacent cases with the same values for break variables forms a case in the aggregated file, which may produce multiple cases with the same values for the break variables.

Example

```
AGGREGATE OUTFILE=AGGEMP
 /PRESORTED
 /BREAK=LOCATN DEPT
 /AVGSAL = MEAN(SALARY).
```

- PRESORTED indicates that cases are already sorted by variables *LOCATN* and *DEPT*.
- AGGREGATE does not make an extra data pass to sort the cases.

Aggregate Functions

An aggregated variable is created by applying an aggregate function to a variable in the working file. The variable in the working file is called the **source** variable, and the new aggregated variable is the **target** variable.

- The aggregate functions must be specified last on AGGREGATE.
- The simplest specification is a target variable list, followed by an equals sign, a function name, and a list of source variables.
- The number of target variables named must match the number of source variables.

- When several aggregate variables are defined at once, the first-named target variable is based on the first-named source variable, the second-named target is based on the second-named source, and so on.
- Only functions MAX, MIN, FIRST, and LAST copy complete dictionary information from the source variable. For all other functions, new variables do not have labels and are assigned default dictionary print and write formats. The default format for a variable depends on the function used to create it (see list of functions below).
- You can provide a variable label for a new variable by specifying the label in apostrophes immediately following the new variable name. Value labels cannot be assigned in AGGREGATE.
- To change formats or add value labels to a working data file created by AGGREGATE, use the PRINT FORMATS, WRITE FORMATS, FORMATS, or VALUE LABELS commands. If the aggregate file is written to disk, first retrieve the file using GET, specify the new labels and formats, and resave the file.

The following is a list of available functions:

SUM(varlist) — *Sum across cases.* Default formats are F8.2.

MEAN(varlist) — *Mean across cases.* Default formats are F8.2.

SD(varlist) — *Standard deviation across cases.* Default formats are F8.2.

MAX(varlist) — *Maximum value across cases.* Complete dictionary information is copied from the source variables to the target variables.

MIN(varlist) — *Minimum value across cases.* Complete dictionary information is copied from the source variables to the target variables.

PGT(varlist,value) — *Percentage of cases greater than the specified value.* Default formats are F5.1.

PLT(varlist,value) — *Percentage of cases less than the specified value.* Default formats are F5.1.

PIN(varlist,value1,value2) — *Percentage of cases between value1 and value2, inclusive.* Default formats are F5.1.

POUT(varlist,value1,value2) — *Percentage of cases not between value1 and value2.* Cases where the source variable equals value1 or value2 are not counted. Default formats are F5.1.

FGT(varlist,value) — *Fraction of cases greater than the specified value.* Default formats are F5.3.

FLT(varlist,value) — *Fraction of cases less than the specified value.* Default formats are F5.3.

FIN(varlist,value1,value2) — *Fraction of cases between value1 and value2, inclusive.* Default formats are F5.3.

FOUT(varlist,value1,value2)	*Fraction of cases not between value1 and value2.* Cases where the source variable equals value1 or value2 are not counted. Default formats are F5.3.
N(varlist)	*Weighted number of cases in break group.* Default formats are F7.0 for unweighted files and F8.2 for weighted files.
NU(varlist)	*Unweighted number of cases in break group.* Default formats are F7.0.
NMISS(varlist)	*Weighted number of missing cases.* Default formats are F7.0 for unweighted files and F8.2 for weighted files.
NUMISS(varlist)	*Unweighted number of missing cases.* Default formats are F7.0.
FIRST(varlist)	*First nonmissing observed value in break group.* Complete dictionary information is copied from the source variables to the target variables.
LAST(varlist)	*Last nonmissing observed value in break group.* Complete dictionary information is copied from the source variables to the target variables.

- Functions SUM, MEAN, and SD can be applied only to numeric source variables. All other functions can use short and long string variables as well as numeric ones.
- The N and NU functions do not require arguments. Without arguments, they return the number of weighted and unweighted valid cases in a break group. If you supply a variable list, they return the number of weighted and unweighted valid cases for the variables specified.
- For several functions, the argument includes values as well as a source variable designation. Either blanks or commas can be used to separate the components of an argument list.
- For PIN, POUT, FIN, and FOUT, the first value should be less than or equal to the second. If the first is greater, AGGREGATE automatically reverses them and prints a warning message. If the two values are equal, PIN and FIN calculate the percentages and fractions of values equal to the argument. POUT and FOUT calculate the percentages and fractions of values not equal to the argument.
- String values specified in an argument should be enclosed in apostrophes. They are evaluated in alphabetical order.

Example

```
AGGREGATE OUTFILE=AGGEMP /BREAK=LOCATN
 /AVGSAL 'Average Salary' AVGRAISE = MEAN(SALARY RAISE).
```

- AGGREGATE defines two aggregate variables, *AVGSAL* and *AVGRAISE*.
- *AVGSAL* is the mean of *SALARY* for each break group and *AVGRAISE* is the mean of *RAISE*.
- The label *Average Salary* is assigned to *AVGSAL*.

Example
```
AGGREGATE OUTFILE=* /BREAK=DEPT
 /LOWVAC,LOWSICK = PLT (VACDAY SICKDAY,10).
```
- AGGREGATE creates two aggregated variables: *LOWVAC* and *LOWSICK*. *LOWVAC* is the percentage of cases with values less than 10 for *VACDAY* and *LOWSICK* is the percentage of cases with values less than 10 for *SICKDAY*.

Example
```
AGGREGATE OUTFILE=GROUPS /BREAK=OCCGROUP
 /COLLEGE = FIN(EDUC,13,16).
```
- AGGREGATE creates variable *COLLEGE*, which is the fraction of cases with 13 to 16 years of education (variable *EDUC*).

Example
```
AGGREGATE OUTFILE=* /BREAK=CLASS
 /LOCAL = PIN(STATE,'IL','IO').
```
- AGGREGATE creates variable *LOCAL*, which is the percentage of cases in each break group whose two-letter state code represents Illinois, Indiana, or Iowa. (The abbreviation for Indiana, IN, is between IL and IO in an alphabetical sort sequence.)

MISSING Subcommand

By default, AGGREGATE uses all nonmissing values of the source variable to calculate aggregated variables. An aggregated variable will have a missing value only if the source variable is missing for every case in the break group. You can alter the default missing-value treatment by using the MISSING subcommand. You can also specify the inclusion of user-missing values on any function.

- MISSING must immediately follow OUTFILE.
- COLUMNWISE is the only specification available for MISSING.
- If COLUMNWISE is specified, the value of an aggregated variable is missing for a break group if the source variable is missing for any case in the group.
- COLUMNWISE does not affect the calculation of the N, NU, NMISS, or NUMISS functions.
- COLUMNWISE does not apply to break variables. If a break variable has a missing value, cases in that group are processed and the break variable is saved in the file with the missing value. Use SELECT IF if you want to eliminate cases with missing values for the break variables.

Including Missing Values

You can force a function to include user-missing values in its calculations by specifying a period after the function name.

- AGGREGATE ignores periods used with functions N, NU, NMISS, and NUMISS if these functions have no argument.

- User-missing values are treated as valid when these four functions are followed by a period and have a variable as an argument. NMISS.(AGE) treats user-missing values as valid and this gives the number of cases for which *AGE* has the system-missing value only.

The effect of specifying a period with N, NU, NMISS, and NUMISS is illustrated by the following:

N = N. = N(AGE) + NMISS(AGE) = N.(AGE) + NMISS.(AGE)
NU = NU. = NU(AGE) + NUMISS(AGE) = NU.(AGE) + NUMISS.(AGE)

- The function N (the same as N. with no argument) yields a value for each break group that equals the number of cases with valid values (N(AGE)) plus the number of cases with user- or system-missing values (NMISS(AGE)).
- This in turn equals the number of cases with either valid or user-missing values (N.(AGE)) plus the number with system-missing values (NUMISS.(AGE)).
- The same identities hold for the NU, NMISS, and NUMISS functions.

Example

```
AGGREGATE OUTFILE=AGGEMP /MISSING=COLUMNWISE /BREAK=LOCATN
 /AVGSAL = MEAN(SALARY).
```

- *AVGSAL* is missing for an aggregated case if *SALARY* is missing for any case in the break group.

Example

```
AGGREGATE OUTFILE=* /BREAK=DEPT
 /LOVAC = PLT.(VACDAY,10).
```

- *LOVAC* is the percentage of cases within each break group with values less than 10 for *VACDAY*, even if some of those values are defined as user-missing.

Example

```
AGGREGATE OUTFILE=CLASS /BREAK=GRADE
 /FIRSTAGE = FIRST.(AGE).
```

- The first value of *AGE* in each break group is assigned to variable *FIRSTAGE*.
- If the first value of *AGE* in a break group is user-missing, that value will be assigned to *FIRSTAGE*. However, the value will retain its missing-value status, since variables created with FIRST take dictionary information from their source variables.

Comparing Missing-Value Treatments

Table 1 demonstrates the effects of specifying the MISSING subcommand and a period after the function name. Each entry in the table is the number of cases used to compute the specified function for variable *EDUC*, which has 10 nonmissing cases, 5 user-missing cases, and 2 system-missing cases for the group. Note that columnwise treatment produces the same results as the default for every function except the MEAN function.

Table 1   Default vs. columnwise missing-value treatments

Function	Default	Columnwise
N	17	17
N.	17	17
N(EDUC)	10	10
N.(EDUC)	15	15
MEAN(EDUC)	10	0
MEAN.(EDUC)	15	0
NMISS(EDUC)	7	7
NMISS.(EDUC)	2	2

ANOVA

```
ANOVA [VARIABLES=] varlist BY varlist(min,max)...varlist(min,max)
      [WITH varlist] [/VARIABLES=...]

 [/COVARIATES={FIRST**}]
              {WITH   }
              {AFTER  }

 [/MAXORDERS={ALL**}]
             {n    }
             {NONE }

 [/METHOD={UNIQUE**    }]
          {EXPERIMENTAL}
          {HIERARCHICAL}

 [/STATISTICS=[MCA] [REG†] [MEAN] [ALL] [NONE]]

 [/MISSING={EXCLUDE**}]
           {INCLUDE  }

 [/FORMAT={LABELS**}]
          {NOLABELS}
```

**Default if the subcommand is omitted.
†REG (table of regression coefficients) is displayed only if the design is relevant.

Example:

```
ANOVA VARIABLES=PRESTIGE BY REGION(1,9) SEX,RACE(1,2)
  /MAXORDERS=2
  /STATISTICS=MEAN.
```

Overview

ANOVA performs analysis of variance for factorial designs. The default is the full factorial model if there are five or fewer factors. Analysis of variance tests the hypothesis that the group means of the dependent variable are equal. The dependent variable is interval level, and one or more categorical variables define the groups. These categorical variables are termed **factors**. ANOVA also allows you to include continuous explanatory variables, termed **covariates**. Other SPSS procedures that perform analysis of variance are ONEWAY, MEANS, and MANOVA. To perform a comparison of two means, use TTEST.

Options

Specifying Covariates. You can introduce covariates into the model using the WITH keyword on the VARIABLES subcommand.

Order of Entry of Covariates. By default, covariates are processed before main effects for factors. You can process covariates with or after main effects for factors using the COVARIATES subcommand.

Suppressing Interaction Effects. You can suppress the effects of various orders of interaction using the MAXORDERS subcommand.

Methods for Decomposing Sums of Squares. By default, the regression approach (keyword UNIQUE) is used. You can request the regression or hierarchical approach using the METHOD subcommand.

Statistical Display. Using the STATISTICS subcommand, you can request means and counts for each dependent variable for groups defined by each factor and each combination of factors up to the fifth level. You also can request unstandardized regression coefficients for covariates and multiple classification analysis (MCA) results. In the MCA table, effects are expressed as deviations from the grand mean. The table includes a listing of unadjusted category effects for each factor, category effects adjusted for other factors, category effects adjusted for all factors and covariates, and eta and beta values.

Formatting Options. You can suppress both variable and value labels in the displayed results using the FORMAT subcommand.

Basic Specification

- The basic specification is a single VARIABLES subcommand with an analysis list. The minimum analysis list specifies a list of dependent variables, the keyword BY, a list of factor variables, and the minimum and maximum integer values of the factors in parentheses.
- By default, the model includes all interaction terms up to five-way interactions. The sums of squares are decomposed using the regression approach, in which all effects are assessed simultaneously, with each effect adjusted for all other effects in the model. A case that has a missing value for any variable in an analysis list is omitted from the analysis.

Subcommand Order

- The variable list must be first if keyword VARIABLES is omitted from the specification.
- The remaining subcommands can be named in any order.

Operations

- A separate analysis of variance is performed for each dependent variable in an analysis list, using the same factors and covariates.
- All ANOVA output, except that produced by STATISTICS=MEANS, fits in 80 columns. If you want to limit the width of the means and counts table, use the SET WIDTH command (see SET).

Limitations

- Maximum 5 analysis lists.
- Maximum 5 dependent variables per analysis list.
- Maximum 10 factor variables per analysis list.
- Maximum 10 covariates per analysis list.

- Maximum 5 interaction levels.
- Maximum 25 value labels per variable displayed in the MCA table.
- The combined number of categories for all factors in an analysis list plus the number of covariates must be less than the sample size.

Example

```
ANOVA VARIABLES=PRESTIGE BY REGION(1,9) SEX, RACE(1,2)
 /MAXORDERS=2
 /STATISTICS=MEAN.
```

- VARIABLES specifies a three-way analysis of variance: *PRESTIGE* by *REGION*, *SEX*, and *RACE*.
- Variables *SEX* and *RACE* each have two categories with values 1 and 2 included in the analysis. *REGION* has nine categories valued 1 through 9.
- MAXORDERS examines interaction effects up to and including the second order. All three-way interaction terms are pooled into the error sum of squares.
- STATISTICS requests a table of means of *PRESTIGE* within the combined categories of *REGION*, *SEX*, and *RACE*.

Example

```
ANOVA VARIABLES=PRESTIGE BY REGION(1,9) SEX,RACE(1,2)
  /RINCOME BY SEX,RACE(1,2).
```

- ANOVA specifies a three-way analysis of variance of *PRESTIGE* by *REGION*, *SEX*, and *RACE*, and a two-way analysis of variance of *RINCOME* by *SEX* and *RACE*.

VARIABLES Subcommand

VARIABLES specifies the analysis list. The actual keyword VARIABLES can be omitted.

- More than one design can be specified on the same ANOVA command by separating the analysis lists with a slash.
- Variables named before keyword BY are dependent variables. Value ranges are not specified for dependent variables.
- Variables named after BY are factor (independent) variables.
- Every factor variable must have a value range indicating its minimum and maximum values. The values must be separated by a space or comma and enclosed in parentheses.
- Factor variables must have integer values. Noninteger values for factors are truncated.
- Cases with values outside the range specified for a factor are excluded from the analysis.
- If two or more factors have the same value range, you can specify the value range once following the last factor to which it applies. You can specify a single range that encompasses the ranges of all factors in the list. For example, if you have two factors, one with values 1 and 2 and the other with values 1 through 4, you can specify the range for both

as 1,4. However, this may reduce performance and cause memory problems if the specified range is larger than some of the actual ranges.
- Variables named after keyword WITH are covariates.
- Each analysis list can include only one BY and one WITH keyword.

COVARIATES Subcommand

COVARIATES specifies the order for assessing blocks of covariates and factor main effects.
- The order of entry is irrelevant when METHOD=UNIQUE.

FIRST *Process covariates before factor main effects.* This is the default.

WITH *Process covariates concurrently with factor main effects.*

AFTER *Process covariates after factor main effects.*

MAXORDERS Subcommand

MAXORDERS suppresses the effects of various orders of interaction.

ALL *Examine all interaction effects up to and including the fifth order.* This is the default.

n *Examine all interaction effects up to and including the nth order.* For example, MAXORDERS=3 examines all interaction effects up to and including the third order. All higher-order interaction sums of squares are pooled into the error term.

NONE *Delete all interaction terms from the model.* All interaction sums of squares are pooled into the error sum of squares. Only main and covariate effects appear in the ANOVA table.

METHOD Subcommand

METHOD controls the method for decomposing sums of squares.

UNIQUE *Regression approach.* UNIQUE overrides any keywords on the COVARIATES subcommand. All effects are assessed simultaneously for their partial contribution. The MCA and MEAN specifications on the STATISTICS subcommand are not available with the regression approach. This is the default if METHOD is omitted.

EXPERIMENTAL *Classic experimental approach.* Covariates, main effects, and ascending orders of interaction are assessed separately in that order.

HIERARCHICAL *Hierarchical approach.*

Regression Approach

All effects are assessed simultaneously, with each effect adjusted for all other effects in the model. This is the default when the METHOD subcommand is omitted. Since multiple classification analysis (MCA) tables cannot be produced when the regression approach is used, specifying MCA or ALL on STATISTICS with the default method triggers a warning.

Some restrictions apply to the use of the regression approach:

- The lowest specified categories of all the independent variables must have a marginal frequency of at least 1, since the lowest specified category is used as the reference category. If this rule is violated, no ANOVA table is produced and a message is displayed identifying the first offending variable.
- Given an n-way crosstabulation of the independent variables, there must be no empty cells defined by the lowest specified category of any of the independent variables. If this restriction is violated, one or more levels of interaction effects are suppressed and a warning message is issued. However, this constraint does not apply to categories defined for an independent variable but not occurring in the data. For example, given two independent variables, each with categories of 1, 2, and 4, the (1,1), (1,2), (1,4), (2,1), and (4,1) cells must not be empty. The (1,3) and (3,1) cells will be empty but the restriction on empty cells will not be violated. The (2,2), (2,4), (4,2), and (4,4) cells may be empty, although the degrees of freedom will be reduced accordingly.

To comply with these restrictions, specify precisely the lowest nonempty category of each independent variable. Specifying a value range of (0,9) for a variable that actually has values of 1 through 9 results in an error, and no ANOVA table is produced.

Classic Experimental Approach

Each type of effect is assessed separately in the following order (unless WITH or AFTER is specified on the COVARIATES subcommand):

- Effects of covariates.
- Main effects of factors.
- Two-way interaction effects.
- Three-way interaction effects.
- Four-way interaction effects.
- Five-way interaction effects.

The effects within each type are adjusted for all other effects of that type and also for the effects of all prior types (see Table 2).

Hierarchical Approach

The hierarchical approach differs from the classic experimental approach only in the way it handles covariate and factor main effects. In the hierarchical approach, factor main effects and covariate effects are assessed hierarchically: factor main effects are adjusted only for the factor main effects already assessed, and covariate effects are adjusted only for the covariates already assessed (see Table 2). The order in which factors are listed on the ANOVA command determines the order in which they are assessed.

Example

The following analysis list specifies three factor variables named *A*, *B*, and *C*:

```
ANOVA VARIABLES=Y BY A,B,C(0,3).
```

Table 2 summarizes the three methods for decomposing sums of squares for this example.

- With the default *regression approach,* each factor or interaction is assessed with all other factors and interactions held constant.
- With the *classic experimental* approach, each main effect is assessed with the two other main effects held constant, and two-way interactions are assessed with all main effects and other two-way interactions held constant. The three-way interaction is assessed with all main effects and two-way interactions held constant.
- With the *hierarchical approach,* the factor main effects A, B, and C are assessed with all prior main effects held constant. The order in which the factors and covariates are listed on the ANOVA command determines the order in which they are assessed in the hierarchical analysis. The interaction effects are assessed the same way as in the experimental approach.

Table 2   Terms adjusted for under each option

Effect	Regression (UNIQUE)	Experimental	Hierarchical
A	All others	B,C	None
B	All others	A,C	A
C	All others	A,B	A,B
AB	All others	A,B,C,AC,BC	A,B,C,AC,BC
AC	All others	A,B,C,AB,BC	A,B,C,AB,BC
BC	All others	A,B,C,AB,AC	A,B,C,AB,AC
ABC	All others	A,B,C,AB,AC,BC	A,B,C,AB,AC,BC

Summary of Analysis Methods

Table 3 describes the results obtained with various combinations of methods for controlling entry of covariates and decomposing the sums of squares.

STATISTICS Subcommand

STATISTICS requests additional statistics. STATISTICS can be specified by itself or with one or more keywords.

- If you specify STATISTICS without keywords, ANOVA calculates MEAN and REG (each defined below).

Table 3 Combinations of COVARIATES and METHOD subcommands

	Assessments between types of effects	Assessments within the same type of effect
METHOD=UNIQUE	**Covariates, Factors,** and **Interactions** simultaneously	**Covariates**: adjust for factors, interactions, and all other covariates **Factors**: adjust for covariates, interactions, and all other factors **Interactions**: adjust for covariates, factors, and all other interactions
METHOD=EXPERIMENTAL	**Covariates** then **Factors** then **Interactions**	**Covariates**: adjust for all other covariates **Factors**: adjust for covariates and all other factors **Interactions**: adjust for covariates, factors, and all other interactions of the same and lower orders
METHOD=HIERARCHICAL	**Covariates** then **Factors** then **Interactions**	**Covariates**: adjust for covariates that are preceding in the list **Factors**: adjust for covariates and factors preceding in the list **Interactions**: adjust for covariates, factors, and all other interactions of the same and lower orders
COVARIATES=WITH and METHOD=EXPERIMENTAL	**Factors** and **Covariates** concurrently then **Interactions**	**Covariates**: adjust for factors and all other covariates **Factors**: adjust for covariates and all other factors **Interactions**: adjust for covariates, factors, and all other interactions of the same and lower orders
COVARIATES=WITH and METHOD=HIERARCHICAL	**Factors** and **Covariates** concurrently then **Interactions**	**Factors**: adjust only for preceding factors **Covariates**: adjust for factors and preceding covariates **Interactions**: adjust for covariates, factors, and all other interactions of the same and lower orders
COVARIATES=AFTER and METHOD=EXPERIMENTAL	**Factors** then **Covariates** then **Interactions**	**Factors**: adjust for all other factors **Covariates**: adjust for factors and all other covariates **Interactions**: adjust for covariates, factors, and all other interactions of the same and lower orders

Table 3 Combinations of COVARIATES and METHOD subcommands (Continued)

	Assessments between types of effects	Assessments within the same type of effect
COVARIATES=AFTER and METHOD=HIERARCHICAL	Factors then Covariates then Interactions	**Factors**: adjust only for preceding factors **Covariates**: adjust factors and preceding covariates **Interactions**: adjust for covariates, factors, and all other interactions of the same and lower orders

- If you specify a keyword or keywords on the STATISTICS subcommand, ANOVA calculates only the additional statistics you request.

MEAN *Means and counts table.* This statistic is not available when METHOD is omitted or when METHOD=UNIQUE. See "Cell Means" below.

REG *Unstandardized regression coefficients.* Displays unstandardized regression coefficients for the covariates. See "Regression Coefficients for the Covariates" below.

MCA *Multiple classification analysis.* The MCA table is not produced when METHOD is omitted or when METHOD=UNIQUE. See "Multiple Classification Analysis" below.

ALL *Means and counts table, unstandardized regression coefficients, and multiple classification analysis.*

NONE *No additional statistics.* ANOVA calculates only the statistics needed for analysis of variance. This is the default if the STATISTICS subcommand is omitted.

Cell Means

STATISTICS=MEAN displays means and counts of each dependent variable for each cell defined by the factors and combinations of factors.

- This statistic is not available with METHOD=UNIQUE.
- For each dependent variable, a separate table is displayed for each effect, showing the means and cell counts for each combination of values of the factors that define the effect, ignoring all other factors.
- If MAXORDERS is used to suppress higher-order interactions, cell means corresponding to suppressed interaction terms are not displayed.
- The means displayed are the observed means in each cell, and they are produced only for dependent variables, not for covariates.

Regression Coefficients for the Covariates

STATISTICS=REG requests the unstandardized regression coefficients for the covariates.

- The regression coefficients are computed at the point where the covariates are entered into the equation. Thus, their values depend on the type of design specified by the COVARIATES or METHOD subcommands.

- The coefficients are displayed immediately below the summary table in the output.

Multiple Classification Analysis

STATISTICS=MCA displays the grand mean of the dependent variable and a table of category means for each factor expressed as deviations from the grand mean. The latter are sometimes termed **treatment effects.**

- For each category of each factor, the MCA table presents the unadjusted mean of the dependent variable expressed as a deviation from the grand mean, the deviation from the grand mean of the category mean adjusted for other factors, and the deviation from the grand mean of the category mean adjusted for both factors and covariates.
- For each factor, the output displays the correlation ratio (eta) with the unadjusted deviations (the square of eta indicates the proportion of variance explained by all categories of the factor), a partial beta equivalent to the standardized partial regression coefficient that would be obtained by assigning the unadjusted deviations to each factor category and regressing the dependent variable on the resulting variables, the parallel partial betas from a regression that includes covariates in addition to the factors, and the multiple R and R^2 from this regression.
- The MCA table cannot be produced if METHOD is omitted or if METHOD=UNIQUE. When produced, the MCA table does not display values adjusted for factors if COVARIATES is omitted, if COVARIATES=FIRST, or if COVARIATES=WITH and METHOD=EXPERIMENTAL. A full MCA table is produced only if METHOD=HIERARCHICAL or if METHOD=EXPERIMENTAL and COVARIATES=AFTER.

MISSING Subcommand

By default, a case that is missing for any variable named in the analysis list is deleted for all analyses specified by that list. Use MISSING to include cases with user-missing data.

EXCLUDE   *Exclude cases with missing data.* This is the default.

INCLUDE   *Include cases with user-defined missing data.*

FORMAT Subcommand

By default, ANOVA displays variable or value labels if they have been defined. Use the FORMAT subcommand to suppress variable and value labels.

LABELS   *Display variable and value labels.* This is the default.

NOLABELS *Suppress variable and value labels.*

References

Andrews, F., J. Morgan, J. Sonquist, and L. Klein. *Multiple classification analysis.* 2nd ed. 1973. Ann Arbor: Univ. of Michigan.

APPLY DICTIONARY

```
APPLY DICTIONAY FROM=file
```

Example:
```
APPLY DICTIONARY FROM = 'MASTER.SAV'.
```

Overview

APPLY DICTIONARY applies dictionary information from an external SPSS data file to the working data file. The applied dictionary information includes variable and value labels, missing-value flags, print and write formats, and weight. APPLY DICTIONARY does not add or remove variables, and it cannot apply dictionary information selectively to individual variables.

Basic Specification

The basic specification is the FROM subcommand and the name of an SPSS data file. The file specification may vary from operating system to operating system, but enclosing the filename in apostrophes generally works.

Syntax Rules

- The equals sign after FROM is optional.
- The file containing the dictionary information to be applied (the **source file**) must be an SPSS data file.
- The file to which the dictionary information is applied (the **target file**) must be the working data file. You cannot specify another file.

Operation

- APPLY DICTIONARY adds or replaces dictionary information variable by variable by matching variables that have the same name and the same type (string or numeric) in both files. Variables in the working data file that do not have a match in the source file are not changed.
- APPLY DICTIONARY does not add or remove variables from the working data file.
- If no matched variables are found, SPSS displays a warning message.
- Variables that have the same name but different types are not considered matching. SPSS displays a warning message and lists the variables with nonmatching types.

Variable Labels

APPLY DICTIONARY adds labels or replaces old labels with new ones. It cannot be used to remove a defined variable label in the working data file.
- If the variable label in the source file is blank, it will not replace an existing variable label, even if the blanks are in quotes.

Table 4 shows how variable labels are replaced between matched variables.

Table 4 Variable label replacement

Variable	Label in working file (target file)	Label in SPSS file (source file)	Label in resulting file
VAR1	"AGE 86"	"AGE 91"	"AGE 91"
VAR2		"JOBCAT91"	"JOBCAT91"
VAR3	"WORK ID"		"WORK ID"
VAR4	"RACE"	" "	"RACE"

Value Labels

APPLY DICTIONARY treats the value labels of a variable as a set. It adds or replaces the entire set of value labels for a matched variable in the working data file. You cannot remove the defined value label set from a variable or selectively add or replace individual value labels.

- APPLY DICTIONARY does not merge the set of value labels for a variable in the SPSS data file with the labels for a matched variable in the working data file. The variable in the resulting file uses the labels from the SPSS data file only.
- If the variable in the SPSS data file does not have any defined value labels, the matching variable in the working data file keeps its original value labels.
- If the matched variable in the working data file is a long string, value labels are not applied even if the source variable is a short string and has value labels defined. SPSS displays a message when this occurs.
- If the matched variables are both short strings but the target variable is longer than the source variable, the values for the source variable are right-padded before their labels are applied to the target variable.
- If the matched variables are both short strings but the source variable is longer, the values for the source variable are right-trimmed if there are enough blank spaces on the right. If any one of the values that has labels defined does not have enough blank spaces to be trimmed, the entire set of value labels is not applied and the variable in the working data file maintains its original value label specifications.

Missing Values

APPLY DICTIONARY treats the missing-value specifications of a variable as a set. It adds or replaces the entire set of missing values for a matched variable in the working data file. You can remove the entire set of missing-value specifications from a variable but cannot selectively add or replace individual missing-value specifications.

- APPLY DICTIONARY does not merge the set of missing values for a variable in the SPSS data file with the missing-value specifications for a matched variable in the working data file. The variable in the resulting file uses the missing values defined in the SPSS data file only.
- If the variable in the SPSS data file does not define any missing values, the variable in the working data file keeps its missing-value specifications.
- If the matched variable in the working data file is a long string, missing-value specifications are not applied even if the source variable is a short string and has missing values defined. SPSS displays a message specifying the missing value and information about the length of the matched variables.
- If the matched variables are both short strings but the target variable is longer than the source variable, the missing values from the source variable are right-padded.
- If the matched variables are both short strings but the source variable is longer, the missing values from the source variable are right-trimmed if there are enough blank spaces on the right. If any one of the defined missing values does not have enough blank spaces to be trimmed, the entire set will not be applied. The variable in the working data file maintains its original missing-value specifications.

Print and Write Formats

APPLY DICTIONARY always replaces the print and write formats of matched numeric variables in the working data file.
- The print and write formats of string variables are not changed. They keep the original length defined on the DATA LIST or STRING command. To change the length of a string variable, define a new variable using STRING and then use the COMPUTE command.

Weight

APPLY DICTIONARY adds or replaces the weighting information in the working data file. Table 5 summarizes how weighting information is applied. In the table, *WTWORK* refers to the weight variable in the working file and *WTSPSS* to the weight variable in the SPSS data file:
- SPSS displays a message when either the weight status or the weight variable is changed.

Table 5   Weight information

Working file		SPSS file		Resulting file	
Status	Weight	Status	Weight	Status	Weight
Weighted	*WTWORK*	Unweighted	N/A	Weighted	*WTWORK*
		Weighted	*WTSPSS*	Weighted	*WTSPSS** *WTWORK*†
Unweighted	N/A	Weighted	*WTSPSS*	Weighted Unweighted†	*WTSPSS** N/A

*If *WTSPSS* exists in the working file.
†If *WTSPSS* does not exist in the working file.

FROM Subcommand

FROM specifies an SPSS data file as the source file whose dictionary information is to be applied to the working file.
- FROM is required.
- Only one SPSS data file can be specified on FROM.
- The SPSS data file from which the current working file was built can be specified on FROM. This will restore dictionary information from the most recently saved version of the file.

AUTORECODE

```
AUTORECODE VARIABLES=varlist

 /INTO new varlist

[/DESCENDING]

[/PRINT]
```

Example:
```
AUTORECODE VARIABLES=COMPANY /INTO RCOMPANY.
```

Overview

AUTORECODE recodes the values of string and numeric variables to consecutive integers and puts the recoded values into a new variable called a **target variable**. The value labels or values of the original variable are used as value labels for the target variable. AUTORECODE is useful for creating numeric independent (grouping) variables from string variables for procedures like ONEWAY, ANOVA, MANOVA, and DISCRIMINANT. AUTORECODE can also recode the values of factor variables to consecutive integers, which is required by MANOVA and which reduces the amount of workspace needed by other statistical procedures like ANOVA. AUTORECODE is also useful with the TABLES procedure, where string values are truncated to eight characters but value labels can be displayed in full. (See the *SPSS Tables* manual for more information.)

AUTORECODE is similar to the RECODE command. The main difference is that AUTORECODE automatically generates the values. In RECODE, you must specify the new values.

Options

Displaying Recoded Variables. You can display the values of the original and recoded variables using the PRINT subcommand.

Ordering of Values. By default, values are recoded in ascending order (lowest to highest). You can recode values in descending order (highest to lowest) using the DESCENDING subcommand.

Basic Specification

The basic specification is VARIABLES and INTO. VARIABLES specifies the variables to be recoded. INTO provides names for the target variables that store the new values. VARIABLES and INTO must name or imply the same number of variables.

Subcommand Order

- VARIABLES must be specified first.

- INTO must immediately follow VARIABLES.

Syntax Rules

A variable cannot be recoded into itself. More generally, target variable names cannot duplicate any variable names already in the working file.

Operations

- The values of each variable to be recoded are sorted and then assigned numeric values. By default, the values are assigned in ascending order: 1 is assigned to the lowest nonmissing value of the original variable, 2 to the second-lowest nonmissing value, and so on for each value of the original variable.
- Values of the original variables are unchanged.
- Missing values are recoded into values higher than any nonmissing values, with their order preserved. For example, if the original variable has 10 nonmissing values, the first missing value is recoded as 11 and retains its user-missing status. System-missing values remain system-missing.
- AUTORECODE does not sort the cases in the working file. As a result, the consecutive numbers assigned to the target variables may not be in order in the file.
- Target variables are assigned the same variable labels as the original source variables. To change the variable labels, use the VARIABLE LABELS command after AUTORECODE.
- Value labels are automatically generated for each value of the target variables. If the original value had a label, that label is used for the corresponding new value. If the original value did not have a label, the old value itself is used as the value label for the new value. The defined print format of the old value is used to create the new value label.
- AUTORECODE ignores SPLIT FILE specifications. However, any SELECT IF specifications are in effect for AUTORECODE.

Example

```
DATA LIST / COMPANY 1-21 (A) SALES 24-28.
BEGIN DATA
CATFOOD JOY            10000
OLD FASHIONED CATFOOD  11200
  . . .
PRIME CATFOOD          10900
CHOICE CATFOOD         14600
END DATA.

AUTORECODE VARIABLES=COMPANY /INTO=RCOMPANY /PRINT.

TABLES TABLE = SALES BY RCOMPANY
  /TTITLE='CATFOOD SALES BY COMPANY'.
```

- Because TABLES truncates string variables to eight characters, AUTORECODE is used to recode the string variable *COMPANY*, which contains the names of various hypothetical cat food companies.
- AUTORECODE recodes *COMPANY* into a numeric variable *RCOMPANY*. Values of *RCOMPANY* are consecutive integers beginning with 1 and ending with the number of different values entered for *COMPANY*. The values of *COMPANY* are used as value labels for *RCOMPANY*'s numeric values. The *PRINT* subcommand displays a table of the original and recoded values.
- Variable *RCOMPANY* is used as the banner variable in the TABLES procedure to produce a table of sales figures for each cat food company. The value labels for *RCOMPANY* are used as column headings. Since TABLES does not truncate value labels, the full company names appear.

Example

```
AUTORECODE VARIABLES=REGION /INTO=RREGION /PRINT.
ANOVA Y BY RREGION (1,5).
```

- In statistical procedures, empty cells can reduce performance and increase memory requirements. In this example, assume factor *REGION* has only five nonempty categories, represented by the numeric codes 1, 4, 6, 14, and 20. AUTORECODE recodes those values into 1, 2, 3, 4, and 5 for target variable *RREGION*.
- Variable *RREGION* is used in ANOVA. If the original variable *REGION* were used, the amount of memory required by ANOVA would be 4429 bytes. Using variable *RREGION*, ANOVA requires only 449 bytes of memory.

Example

```
DATA LIST / RELIGION 1-8 (A) Y 10-13.
MISSING VALUES RELIGION (' ').
BEGIN DATA
CATHOLIC 2013
PROTEST  3234
JEWISH   5169
NONE      714
OTHER    2321
 . . .
END DATA.
AUTORECODE VARIABLES=RELIGION /INTO=NRELIG /PRINT /DESCENDING.
MANOVA Y BY NRELIG(1,5).
```

- Because MANOVA requires consecutive integer values for factor levels, string variable *RELIGION* is recoded into a numeric variable. The five values for *RELIGION* are first sorted in descending order (Z to A) and are then assigned values 1, 2, 3, 4, and 5 in target variable *NRELIG*.
- Since a blank space is specified as a user-missing value, it is assigned the value 6. In the table produced by PRINT, value 6 is displayed as 6M for variable *NRELIG* to flag it as a user-missing value.

- The values of *RELIGION* are used as value labels for the corresponding new values in *NRELIG*.
- Target variable *NRELIG* is used as a factor variable in MANOVA.

VARIABLES Subcommand

VARIABLES specifies the variables to be recoded. VARIABLES is required and must be specified first. The actual keyword VARIABLES is optional.

- Values from the specified variables are recoded and stored in the target variables listed on INTO. Values of the original variables are unchanged.

INTO Subcommand

INTO provides names for the target variables that store the new values. INTO is required and must immediately follow VARIABLES.

- The number of target variables named or implied on INTO must equal the number of source variables listed on VARIABLES.

Example

```
AUTORECODE VARIABLES=V1 V2 V3 /INTO=NEWV1 TO NEWV3 /PRINT.
```

- AUTORECODE stores the recoded values of *V1*, *V2*, and *V3* into target variables named *NEWV1*, *NEWV2*, and *NEWV3*.

PRINT Subcommand

PRINT displays a correspondence table of the original values of the source variables and the new values of the target variables. The new value labels are also displayed.

- The only specification is keyword PRINT. There are no additional specifications.
- If the width is set to less than 132, the table is displayed in 80 columns. If the width has been previously set to 132 (by the SET WIDTH command), the table is displayed in 132 columns.
- Only the first 18 characters of the values of the source variables and the first 48 characters of the value labels of the target variables are displayed.

DESCENDING Subcommand

By default, values for the source variable are recoded in ascending order (from lowest to highest). DESCENDING assigns the values to new variables in descending order (from highest to lowest). The largest value is assigned 1, the second-largest 2, and so on.

- The only specification is keyword DESCENDING. There are no additional specifications.

BEGIN DATA—END DATA

```
BEGIN DATA
data records
END DATA
```

Example:

```
BEGIN DATA
1   3424   274 ABU DHABI  2
2  39932    86 AMSTERDAM  4
3   8889   232 ATHENS
4   3424   294 BOGOTA     3
END DATA.
```

Overview

BEGIN DATA and END DATA are used when data are entered within the command sequence (inline data). BEGIN DATA and END DATA are also used for inline matrix data. BEGIN DATA signals the beginning of data lines and END DATA signals the end of data lines.

Basic Specification

The basic specification is BEGIN DATA, the data lines, and END DATA. BEGIN DATA must be specified by itself on the line that immediately precedes the first data line. END DATA is specified by itself on the line that immediately follows the last data line.

Syntax Rules

- BEGIN DATA, the data, and END DATA must precede the first SPSS procedure.
- The command terminator after BEGIN DATA is optional. It is best to leave it out so that SPSS will treat inline data as one continuous specification.
- END DATA must always begin in column 1. It must be spelled out in full and can have only one space between the words END and DATA. Procedures and additional transformations can follow the END DATA command.
- Data lines must *not* have a command terminator. For inline data formats, see DATA LIST.
- Inline data records are limited to a maximum of 80 columns. (On certain IBM systems, UNNUMBERED must be in effect to read 80 columns. On other systems, the maximum may be fewer than 80 columns.) If data records exceed 80 columns, they must be stored in an external file that is specified on the FILE subcommand of the DATA LIST (or similar) command.

Operations

- When SPSS encounters BEGIN DATA, it begins to read and process data on the next input line. All preceding transformation commands are processed as the working file is built.
- SPSS continues to evaluate input lines as data until it encounters END DATA, at which point it begins evaluating input lines as SPSS commands.
- No other SPSS commands are recognized between BEGIN DATA and END DATA.
- The INCLUDE command can specify a file that contains BEGIN DATA, data lines, and END DATA. The data in such a file are treated as inline data. Thus, the FILE subcommand should be omitted from the DATA LIST (or similar) command.
- When running SPSS from prompts, the prompt DATA> appears immediately after BEGIN DATA is specified. After END DATA is specified, the prompt SPSS> returns.

Example

```
DATA LIST /XVAR 1 YVAR ZVAR 3-12 CVAR 14-22(A) JVAR 24.
BEGIN DATA
1  3424   274 ABU DHABI  2
2 39932    86 AMSTERDAM  4
3  8889   232 ATHENS
4  3424   294 BOGOTA     3
5 11323   332 HONG KONG  3
6   323   232 MANILA     1
7  3234   899 CHICAGO    4
8 78998  2344 VIENNA     3
9  8870   983 ZURICH     5
END DATA.
MEANS XVAR BY JVAR.
```

- DATA LIST defines the names and column locations of the variables. The FILE subcommand is omitted because the data are inline.
- There are nine cases in the inline data. Each line of data completes a case.
- END DATA signals the end of data lines. It begins in column 1 and has only a single space between END and DATA.

BREAK

```
BREAK
```

Overview

BREAK controls looping that cannot be fully controlled with IF clauses. Generally, BREAK is used within a DO IF—END IF structure. The expression on the DO IF command specifies the condition in which BREAK is executed.

Basic Specification

- The only specification is keyword BREAK. There are no additional specifications.
- BREAK must be specified within a loop structure. Otherwise, an error results.

Operations

- A BREAK command inside a loop structure but not inside a DO IF—END IF structure terminates the first iteration of the loop for all cases, since no conditions for BREAK are specified.
- A BREAK command within an inner loop terminates only iterations in that structure, not in any outer loop structures.

Example

```
VECTOR          #X(10).
LOOP            #I = 1 TO #NREC.
+   DATA LIST       NOTABLE/ #X1 TO #X10 1-20.
+   LOOP            #J = 1 TO 10.
+       DO IF           SYSMIS(#X(#J)).
+           BREAK.
+       END IF.
+       COMPUTE         X = #X(#J).
+       END CASE.
+   END LOOP.
END LOOP.
```

- The inner loop terminates when there is a system-missing value for any of the variables #X1 to #X10.
- The outer loop continues until all records are read.

CLEAR TRANSFORMATIONS

```
CLEAR TRANSFORMATIONS
```

Overview

CLEAR TRANSFORMATIONS discards previous data transformation commands.

Basic Specification

The only specification is the command itself. CLEAR TRANSFORMATIONS has no additional specifications.

Operations

- CLEAR TRANSFORMATIONS discards all data transformation commands that have accumulated since the last procedure.
- CLEAR TRANSFORMATIONS has no effect if a command file is submitted to your operating system for execution. It generates a warning when present.
- Be sure to delete CLEAR TRANSFORMATIONS and any unwanted transformation commands from an SPSS journal file if you plan to submit the file to the operating system for batch-mode execution. Otherwise, the unwanted transformations will cause problems.

Example

```
GET FILE=QUERY.
FREQUENCIES=ITEM1 ITEM2 ITEM3.
RECODE ITEM1, ITEM2, ITEM3 (0=1) (1=0) (2=-1).
COMPUTE INDEXQ=(ITEM1 + ITEM2 + ITEM3)/3.
VARIABLE LABELS INDEXQ 'SUMMARY INDEX OF QUESTIONS'.
CLEAR TRANSFORMATIONS.
DISPLAY DICTIONARY.
```

- The GET and FREQUENCIES commands are executed.
- The RECODE, COMPUTE, and VARIABLE LABELS commands are transformations. They do not affect the data until the next procedure is executed.
- The CLEAR TRANSFORMATIONS command discards the RECODE, COMPUTE, and VARIABLE LABELS commands.
- The DISPLAY command displays the working file dictionary. Data values and labels are exactly as they were when the FREQUENCIES command was executed. Variable INDEXQ does not exist because CLEAR TRANSFORMATIONS discarded the COMPUTE command.

COMMENT

```
{COMMENT} text
{   *    }
```

Overview

COMMENT inserts explanatory text within the command sequence. Comments are included among the commands printed back in the output; they do not become part of the information saved in an SPSS data file. To include commentary in the dictionary of a data file, use the DOCUMENT command.

Syntax Rules

- The first line of a comment can begin with the keyword COMMENT or with an asterisk (*). Comment text can extend for multiple lines and can contain any characters.
- Use /* and */ to set off a comment within a command. The comment can be placed wherever a blank is valid (except within strings) and should be preceded by a blank. Comments within a command cannot be continued on the next line.
- The closing */ is optional when the comment is at the end of the line. The command can continue on the next line just as if the inserted comment was a blank.
- Comments cannot be inserted within data lines.

Example

```
* Create a new variable as a combination of two old variables;
  the new variable is a scratch variable used later in the
  session;  it will not be saved with the data file.
COMPUTE #XYVAR=0.
IF (XVAR EQ 1 AND YVAR EQ 1) #XYVAR=1.
```

- The three-line comment will be included in the display file but will not be part of the data file if the working data file is saved.

Example

```
IF (RACE EQ 1 AND SEX EQ 1) SEXRACE = 1  /*White males.
```

- The comment is entered on a command line. The closing */ is not needed because the comment is at the end of the line.

COMPUTE

```
COMPUTE target variable=expression
```

Arithmetic operators:

+ Addition   - Subtraction
* Multiplication   / Division
** Exponentiation

Arithmetic functions:

ABS(arg)	Absolute value
RND(arg)	Round
TRUNC(arg)	Truncate
MOD(arg)	Modulus
SQRT(arg)	Square root
EXP(arg)	Exponential
LG10(arg)	Base 10 logarithm
LN(arg)	Natural logarithm
ARSIN(arg)	Arcsine
ARTAN(arg)	Arctangent
SIN(arg)	Sine
COS(arg)	Cosine

Statistical functions:

SUM[.n](arg list)	Sum of values across argument list
MEAN[.n](arg list)	Mean value across argument list
SD[.n](arg list)	Standard deviation of values across list
VAR[.n](arg list)	Variance of values across list
CFVAR[.n](arg list)	Coefficient of variation of values across list
MIN[.n](arg list)	Minimum value across list
MAX[.n](arg list)	Maximum value across list

Missing-value functions:

VALUE(varname)	Ignore user-missing
MISSING(varname)	True if missing
SYSMIS(varname)	True if system-missing
NMISS(arg list)	Number of missing values across list
NVALID(arg list)	Number of valid values across list

Cross-case function:

LAG(varname,n)   Value of variable *n* cases before

Logical functions:

RANGE(varname,range)   True if value of variable is in range
ANY(arg,arg list)   True if value of first argument is included in argument list

Other functions:

UNIFORM(arg)   Uniform pseudo-random number between 0 and *n*
NORMAL(arg)   Normal pseudo-random number with mean of 0 and standard deviation of *n*
CDFNORM(arg)   Probability that random variable falls below *n*
PROBIT(arg)   Inverse of CDFNORM

Date and time aggregation functions:

DATE.DMY(d,m,y)   Read day, month, year, and return date
DATE.MDY(m,d,y)   Read month, day, year, and return date
DATE.YRDAY(y,d)   Read year, day, and return date
DATE.QYR(q,y)   Read quarter, year, and return quarter start date
DATE.MOYR(m,y)   Read month, year, and return month start date
DATE.WKYR(w,y)   Read week, year, and return week start date
TIME.HMS(h,m,s)   Read hour, minutes, seconds, and return time interval
TIME.DAYS(d)   Read days and return time interval

Date and time conversion functions:

YRMODA(yr,mo,da)   Convert year, month, day to day number
CTIME.DAYS(arg)   Convert time interval to days
CTIME.HOURS(arg)   Convert time interval to hours
CTIME.MINUTES(arg)   Convert time interval to minutes

Date and time extraction functions:

XDATE.MDAY(arg)   Return day of the month
XDATE.MONTH(arg)   Return month of the year
XDATE.YEAR(arg)   Return four-digit year
XDATE.HOUR(arg)   Return hour of a day
XDATE.MINUTE(arg)   Return minute of an hour
XDATE.SECOND(arg)   Return second of a minute
XDATE.WKDAY(arg)   Return weekday number
XDATE.JDAY(arg)   Return day number of day in given year
XDATE.QUARTER(arg)   Return quarter of date in given year

XDATE.WEEK(arg)	Return week number of date in given year
XDATE.TDAY(arg)	Return number of days in time interval
XDATE.TIME(arg)	Return time portion of given date and time
XDATE.DATE(arg)	Return integral portion of date

String functions:

ANY(arg,arg list)	Return 1 if value of argument is included in argument list
CONCAT(arg list)	Join the arguments into a string
INDEX(a1,a2,a3)	Return number indicating position of first occurrence of *a2* in *a1*; optionally, *a2* in *a3* evenly divided substrings of *a1*
LAG(arg,n)	Return value of argument *n* cases before
LENGTH(arg)	Return length of argument
LOWER(arg list)	Convert upper case to lower case
LPAD(a1,a2,a3)	Left-pad beginning of *a1* to length *a2* with character *a3*
LTRIM(a1,a2)	Trim character *a2* from beginning of *a1*
MAX(arg list)	Return maximum value of argument list
MIN(arg list)	Return minimum value of argument list
NUMBER(arg,format)	Convert argument into number using format
RANGE(arg,arg list)	Return 1 if value of argument is in inclusive range of argument list
RINDEX(a1,a2,a3)	Return number indicating rightmost occurrence of *a2* in *a1*; optionally, *a2* in *a3* evenly divided substrings of *a1*
RPAD(a1,a2,a3)	Right-pad end of *a1* to length *a2* with character *a3*
RTRIM(a1,a2)	Trim character *a2* from end of *a1*
STRING(arg,format)	Convert argument into string using format
SUBSTR(a1,a2,a3)	Return substring of *a1* beginning with position *a2* for length *a3*
UPCASE(arg list)	Convert lower case to upper case

Example:
```
COMPUTE NEWVAR=RND((V1/V2)*100).
STRING DEPT(A20).
COMPUTE DEPT='PERSONNEL DEPARTMENT'.
```

Overview

COMPUTE creates new numeric variables or modifies the values of existing string or numeric variables. The variable named on the left of the equals sign is the **target variable**. The variables, constants, and functions on the right side of the equals sign form an **assignment expression**. For a complete discussion of functions, see "Transformation Expressions" on p. 45.

Numeric Transformations

Numeric variables can be created or modified with COMPUTE. The assignment expression for numeric transformations can include combinations of constants, variables, numeric operators, and functions.

String Transformations

String variables can be modified but cannot be created with COMPUTE. However, a new string variable can be declared and assigned a width with the STRING command and then assigned values by COMPUTE. The assignments expression can include string constants, string variables, and any of the string functions. All other functions are available for numeric transformations only.

Basic Specification

The basic specification is a target variable, an equals sign (required), and an assignment expression.

Syntax Rules

- The target variable must be named first, and the equals sign is required. Only one target variable is allowed per COMPUTE command.
- Numeric and string variables cannot be mixed in an expression. In addition, if the target variable is numeric, the expression must yield a numeric value; if the target variable is a string, the expression must yield a string value.
- Each function must specify at least one argument enclosed in parentheses. If a function has two or more arguments, the arguments must be separated by commas. For a complete discussion of the functions and their arguments, see "Transformation Expressions" on p. 45.
- You can use the TO keyword to refer to a set of variables where the argument is a list of variables.

Numeric Variables

- Parentheses are used to indicate the order of execution and to set off the arguments to a function.
- Numeric functions use simple or complex expressions as arguments. Expressions must be enclosed in parentheses.

String Variables

- String values and constants must be enclosed in apostrophes or quotation marks.

- When strings of different lengths are compared using the ANY or RANGE functions, the shorter string is right-padded with blanks so that its length equals that of the longer.

Operations

- If the target variable already exists, its values are replaced.
- If the target variable does not exist and the assignment expression is numeric, SPSS creates a new variable.
- If the target variable does not exist and the assignment expression is a string, SPSS displays an error message and does not execute the command.
- COMPUTE is not executed if it contains invalid syntax. New variables are not created and existing target variables remain unchanged.

Numeric Variables

- New numeric variables created with COMPUTE are assigned a dictionary format of F8.2 and are initialized to the system-missing value for each case (unless the LEAVE command is used). Existing numeric variables transformed with COMPUTE retain their original dictionary formats. The format of a numeric variable can be changed with the FORMATS command.
- All expressions are evaluated in the following order: first, functions, then exponentiation, and then arithmetic operations. The order of operations can be changed with parentheses.
- COMPUTE returns the system-missing value when it doesn't have enough information to properly evaluate a function. Arithmetic functions that take only one argument cannot be evaluated if that argument is missing. The date and time functions cannot be evaluated if any argument is missing. Statistical functions are evaluated if a sufficient number of arguments are valid. For example, in the command

    COMPUTE FACTOR = SCORE1 + SCORE2 + SCORE3

    FACTOR is assigned the system-missing value for a case if any of the three score values is missing. It is assigned a valid value only when all score values are valid. In the command

    COMPUTE FACTOR = SUM(SCORE1 TO SCORE3).

    FACTOR is assigned a valid value if at least one score value is valid. It is system-missing only when all three score values are missing.

String Variables

- String variables can be modified but not created on COMPUTE. However, a new string variable can be created and assigned a width with the STRING command and then assigned new values with COMPUTE.
- Existing string variables transformed with COMPUTE retain their original dictionary formats. String variables declared on STRING and transformed with COMPUTE retain the formats assigned to them on STRING.

- The format of string variables cannot be changed with FORMATS. Instead, use STRING to create a new variable with the desired width and then use COMPUTE to set the values of the new string equal to the values of the original.
- The string returned by a string expression does not have to be the same width as the target variable. If the target variable is shorter, the result is right-trimmed. If the target variable is longer, the result is right-padded. SPSS displays no warning messages when trimming or padding.
- To control the width of strings, use the functions are available for padding (LPAD, RPAD), trimming (LTRIM, RTRIM), and selecting a portion of strings (SUBSTR).

Examples

The following examples illustrate the use of COMPUTE. For a complete discussion of each function, see "Transformation Expressions" on p. 45.

Arithmetic Operations

```
COMPUTE V1=25-V2.
COMPUTE V3=(V2/V4)*100.

DO IF TENURE GT 5.
COMPUTE RAISE=SALARY*.12.
ELSE IF TENURE GT 1.
COMPUTE RAISE=SALARY*.1.
ELSE.
COMPUTE RAISE=0.
END IF.
```

- *V1* is 25 minus *V2* for all cases. *V3* is the percentage *V2* is of *V4*.
- *RAISE* is 12% of *SALARY* if *TENURE* is greater than 5. For remaining cases, *RAISE* is 10% of *SALARY* if *TENURE* is greater than 1. For all other cases, *RAISE* is 0.

Arithmetic Functions

```
COMPUTE WTCHANGE=ABS(WEIGHT1-WEIGHT2).
COMPUTE NEWVAR=RND((V1/V2)*100).
COMPUTE INCOME=TRUNC(INCOME).
COMPUTE MINSQRT=SQRT(MIN(V1,V2,V3,V4)).

COMPUTE TEST = TRUNC(SQRT(X/Y)) * .5.
COMPUTE PARENS = TRUNC(SQRT(X/Y) * .5).
```

- *WTCHANGE* is the absolute value of *WEIGHT1* minus *WEIGHT2*.
- *NEWVAR* is the percentage of *V1* is of *V2*, rounded to an integer.
- *INCOME* is truncated to an integer.
- *MINSQRT* is the square root value of the minimum value of the four variables *V1* to *V4*. MIN determines the minimum value of the four variables, and SQRT computes the square root.

- The last two examples illustrate the use of parentheses to control the order of execution. For a case with value 2 for *X* and *Y*, *TEST* equals 0.5, since 2 divided by 2 (X/Y) is 1, the square root of 1 is 1, truncating 1 returns 1, and 1 times 0.5 is 0.5. However, *PARENS* equals 0 for the same case, since SQRT(*X/Y*) is 1, 1 times 0.5 is 0.5, and truncating 0.5 returns 0.

Statistical Functions

```
COMPUTE NEWSAL = SUM(SALARY,RAISE).
COMPUTE MINVAL = MIN(V1,V2,V3,V4).
COMPUTE MEANVAL = MEAN(V1,V2,V3,V4).
COMPUTE NEWMEAN = MEAN.3(V1,V2,V3,V4).
```

- *NEWSAL* is the sum of *SALARY* plus *RAISE*.
- *MINVAL* is the minimum of the values for *V1* to *V4*.
- *MEANVAL* is the mean of the values for *V1* to *V4*. Since the mean can be computed for one, two, three, or four values, *MEANVAL* is assigned a valid value as long as any one of the four variables has a valid value for that case.
- In the last example, the .3 suffix specifies the minimum number of valid arguments required. *NEWMEAN* is the mean of variables *V1* to *V4* *only* if at least 3 of these variables have valid values. Otherwise, *NEWMEAN* is system-missing for that case.

Missing-Value Functions

```
MISSING VALUE V1 V2 V3 (0).
COMPUTE ALLVALID=V1 + V2 + V3.
COMPUTE UM=VALUE(V1) + VALUE(V2) + VALUE(V3).
COMPUTE SM=SYSMIS(V1) + SYSMIS(V2) + SYSMIS(V3).
COMPUTE M=MISSING(V1) + MISSING(V2) + MISSING(V3).
```

- The MISSING VALUE command declares value 0 as missing for *V1*, *V2*, and *V3*.
- *ALLVALID* is the sum of three variables only for cases with valid values for all three variables. *ALLVALID* is assigned the system-missing value for a case if any variable in the assignment expression has a system- or user-missing value.
- The VALUE function overrides user-missing value status. Thus, *UM* is the sum of *V1*, *V2*, and *V3* for each case, including cases with value 0 (the user-missing value) for any of the three variables. Cases with the system-missing value for *V1*, *V2*, and *V3* are system-missing.
- The SYSMIS function on the third COMPUTE returns value 1 if the variable is system-missing. Thus, *SM* ranges from 0 to 3 for each case, depending on whether variables *V1*, *V2*, and *V3* are system-missing for that case.
- The MISSING function on the fourth COMPUTE returns the value 1 if the variable named is system- or user-missing. Thus, *M* ranges from 0 to 3 for each case, depending on whether variables *V1*, *V2*, and *V3* are user- or system-missing for that case.

- Alternatively, you could use the COUNT command to create variables *SM* and *M*.

```
* Test for listwise deletion of missing values.
DATA LIST /V1 TO V6 1-6.
BEGIN DATA
213 56
123457
123457
9234 6
END DATA.
MISSING VALUES V1 TO V6(6,9).

COMPUTE NOTVALID=NMISS(V1 TO V6).
FREQUENCIES VAR=NOTVALID.
```

- COMPUTE determines the number of missing values for each case. For each case without missing values, the value of *NOTVALID* is 0. For each case with one missing value, the value of *NOTVALID* is 1, and so forth. Both system- and user-missing values are counted.
- FREQUENCIES generates a frequency table for *NOTVALID*. The table gives a count of how many cases have all valid values, how many cases have one missing value, how many cases have two missing values, and so forth, for variables *V1* to *V6*. This table can be used to determine how many cases would be dropped in an analysis that uses listwise deletion of missing values. See pp. 200 and 344 for other ways to check listwise deletion.

Cross-Case Operations

```
COMPUTE LV1=LAG(V1).
COMPUTE LV2=LAG(V2,3).
```

- *LV1* is the value of *V1* for the previous case.
- *LV2* is the value of *V2* for three cases previous. The first 3 cases of *LV2* receive the system-missing value.

Logical Functions

```
COMPUTE WORKERS=RANGE(AGE,18,65).
COMPUTE QSAME=ANY(Q1,Q2).
```

- *WORKERS* is 1 for cases where *AGE* is from 18 through 65, 0 for all other valid values of *AGE*, and system-missing for cases with a missing value for *AGE*.
- *QSAME* is 1 whenever *Q1* equals *Q2* and 0 whenever they are different.

Other Functions

```
COMPUTE V1=UNIFORM(10).
COMPUTE V2=NORMAL(1.5).
```

- *V1* is a pseudo-random number from a distribution with values ranging between 0 and the specified value of 10.

- *V2* is a pseudo-random number from a distribution with a mean of 0 and a standard deviation of the specified value of 1.5.
- You can change the seed value of the pseudo-random-number generator with the SEED specification on SET.

Date and Time Aggregation Functions

```
COMPUTE OCTDAY=DATE.YRDAY(1688,301).
COMPUTE QUART=DATE.QYR(QTR,YEAR).
COMPUTE WEEK=DATE.WKYR(WK,YEAR).
```

- *OCTDAY* is the 301st day of year 1688. With a DATE format, *OCTDAY* displays as 27-OCT-1688.
- *QUART* reads values for quarter from variable *QTR* and values for year from variable *YEAR*. If *QTR* is 3 and *YEAR* is 88, *QUART* with a QDATE format displays as 3 Q 88.
- *WEEK* takes the value for week from variable *WK*, and the value for year from variable *YEAR*. If *WK* is 48 and *YEAR* is 57, *WEEK* with a DATE format displays as 26-NOV-57.

Date and Time Conversion Functions

```
COMPUTE NMINS=CTIME.MINUTES(TIME.HMS(HR,MIN,SEC)).
COMPUTE AGER=(YRMODA(1992,10,01)-
              YRMODA(YRBIRTH,MOBIRTH,DABIRTH))/365.25.
```

- The CTIME.MINUTES function converts a time interval to number of minutes. If *HR* equals 12, *MIN* equals 30, and *SEC* equals 30, the TIME.HMS function returns and interval of 45,030, which CTIME.MINUTES converts to minutes. *NMINS* equals 750.50.
- The YRMODA function converts the current date (in this example, October 1, 1992) and birthdate to a number of days. Birthdate is subtracted from current date and the remainder is divided by the number of days in a year to yield age in years.

Date and Time Extraction Functions

```
COMPUTE MONTHNUM=XDATE.MONTH(BIRTHDAY).
COMPUTE DAYNUM=XDATE.JDAY(BIRTHDAY).
```

- The XDATE.MONTH function reads a date and returns the month number expressed as an integer from 1 to 12. If *BIRTHDAY* is formatted as DATETIME20 and contains the value 05-DEC-1954 5:30:15, *MONTHNUM* equals 12.
- The XDATE.JDAY function returns the day of the year, expressed as an integer between 1 and 366. For the value *BIRTHDAY* used by the first COMPUTE, *DAYNUM* equals 339.

Equivalence

```
STRING DEPT(A20).
COMPUTE DEPT='Personnel Department'.
COMPUTE OLDVAR=NEWVAL.
```

- *DEPT* is a new string variable and must be specified on STRING before it can be specified on COMPUTE. STRING assigns *DEPT* a width of 20 characters, and COMPUTE assigns the value Personnel Department to *DEPT* for each case.
- *OLDVAR* must already exist; otherwise it would have to be declared on STRING. The values of *OLDVAR* are modified to equal the values of *NEWVAL*. *NEWVAL* must be an existing string variable. If the dictionary width of *NEWVAL* is longer than the dictionary width of *OLDVAR*, the modified values of *OLDVAR* are truncated.

String Functions

```
STRING NEWSTR(A7) / DATE(A8) / #MO #DA #YR (A2).
COMPUTE NEWSTR=LAG(OLDSTR,2).

COMPUTE #MO=STRING(MONTH,F2.0).
COMPUTE #DA=STRING(DAY,F2.0).
COMPUTE #YR=STRING(YEAR,F2.0).
COMPUTE DATE=CONCAT(#MO,'/',#DA,'/',#YR).

COMPUTE LNAME=UPCASE(LNAME).
```

- STRING declares *NEWSTR* as a new string variable with a width of 7 characters, *DATE* with a width of 8 characters, and scratch variables *#MO*, *#DA*, and *#YR* with a width of 2 characters each.
- The first COMPUTE sets *NEWSTR* equal to the value of *OLDSTR* for two cases previous. The first two cases receive the system-missing value for *NEWSTR*.
- The next three COMPUTE commands convert existing numeric variables *MONTH*, *DAY*, and *YEAR* to the temporary string variables *#MO*, *#DA*, and *#YR* so they can be used with the CONCAT function. The next COMPUTE assigns the concatenated value of *#MO*, *#DA*, and *#YR*, separated by slashes, to *DATE*. If *#MO* is 10, *#DA* is 16, and *#YR* is 49, *DATE* is 10/16/49.
- The final COMPUTE converts lowercase letters for the existing string variable *LNAME* to uppercase letters.

CORRELATIONS

```
CORRELATIONS [VARIABLES=] varlist [WITH varlist] [/varlist...]

[/MISSING={PAIRWISE**}    [{INCLUDE}]]
          {LISTWISE  }     {EXCLUDE}

[/PRINT={TWOTAIL**}  {SIG**}]
        {ONETAIL  }  {NOSIG }

[/FORMAT={MATRIX**}]
         {SERIAL  }

[/MATRIX=OUT({*   })]
             {file}

[/STATISTICS=[DESCRIPTIVES] [XPROD] [ALL]]
```

**Default if the subcommand is omitted.

Example:
```
CORRELATIONS VARIABLES=FOOD RENT PUBTRANS TEACHER COOK ENGINEER
   /MISSING=INCLUDE.
```

Overview

CORRELATIONS (alias PEARSON CORR) produces Pearson product-moment correlations with significance levels and, optionally, univariate statistics, covariances, and cross-product deviations. Other procedures that produce correlation matrices are PARTIAL CORR, REGRESSION, DISCRIMINANT, and FACTOR.

Options

Types of Matrices. A simple variable list on the VARIABLES subcommand produces a square matrix. You can also request a rectangular matrix of correlations between specific pairs of variables or between variable lists using the keyword WITH on VARIABLES.

Significance Levels. By default, CORRELATIONS displays the number of cases and significance levels for each coefficient. Significance levels based on a two-tailed test. You can request a one-tailed test and you can suppress the number of cases and significance level for each coefficient using the PRINT subcommand.

Additional Statistics. You can obtain the mean, standard deviation, and number of nonmissing cases for each variable, and the cross-product deviations and covariance for each pair of variables using the STATISTICS subcommand.

Formatting Options. By default, CORRELATIONS uses matrix format and displays redundant coefficients. You can use serial string format and display only nonredundant coefficients using the FORMAT subcommand.

Matrix Output. You can write matrix materials to a data file using the MATRIX subcommand. The matrix materials include the mean, standard deviation, number of cases used to compute each coefficient, and Pearson correlation coefficient for each variable. The matrix data file can be read by several other SPSS procedures.

Basic Specification

- The basic specification is the VARIABLES subcommand, which specifies the variables to be analyzed. The actual keyword VARIABLES can be omitted.
- By default, CORRELATION produces a matrix of correlation coefficients. The number of cases and significance level are displayed for each coefficient. The significance level is based on a two-tailed test.

Subcommand Order

- The VARIABLES subcommand must be first.
- The remaining subcommands can be specified in any order.

Operations

- The correlation of a variable with itself is displayed as 1.0000.
- A correlation that cannot be computed is displayed as a period (.).
- CORRELATIONS does not execute if long or short string variables are specified on the variable list.
- The display uses the width set on the SET command.

Limitations

- Maximum 40 variable lists.
- Maximum 500 variables total per command.
- Maximum 250 syntax elements. Each individual occurrence of a variable name, keyword, or special delimiter counts as 1 toward this total. Variables implied by the TO convention do not count toward this total.

Example

```
CORRELATIONS VARIABLES=FOOD RENT PUBTRANS TEACHER COOK ENGINEER
 /VARIABLES=FOOD RENT WITH COOK TEACHER MANAGER ENGINEER
 /MISSING=INCLUDE.
```

- The first VARIABLES subcommand requests a square matrix of correlation coefficients among variables *FOOD*, *RENT*, *PUBTRANS*, *TEACHER*, *COOK*, and *ENGINEER*.
- The second VARIABLES subcommand requests a rectangular correlation matrix in which variables *FOOD* and *RENT* are the rows and *COOK*, *TEACHER*, *MANAGER*, and *ENGINEER* are the columns.

- MISSING requests that user-missing values be included in the computation of each coefficient.

VARIABLES Subcommand

VARIABLES specifies the variable list. The actual keyword VARIABLES is optional.
- A simple variable list produces a square matrix of correlations of each variable with every other variable.
- Variable lists joined by keyword WITH produce a rectangular correlation matrix. Variables before WITH define the rows of the matrix and variables after WITH define the columns.
- Keyword ALL can be used in the variable list to refer to all user-defined variables.
- You can specify multiple VARIABLES subcommands on a single CORRELATIONS command. The slash between the subcommands is required; the keyword VARIABLES is not.

PRINT Subcommand

PRINT controls whether the significance level is based on a one- or two-tailed test and whether the number of cases and the significance level for each correlation coefficient are displayed.

TWOTAIL *Two-tailed test of significance.* This test is appropriate when the direction of the relationship cannot be determined in advance, as is often the case in exploratory data analysis. This is the default.

ONETAIL *One-tailed test of significance.* This test is appropriate when the direction of the relationship between a pair of variables can be specified in advance of the analysis.

SIG *Display the number of cases and significance level.* SIG is the default.

NOSIG *Suppress the display of the number of cases and significance level.* A single asterisk (*) following a coefficient indicates a significance level of ≤ 0.05. Two asterisks (**) following a coefficient indicate a significance level of ≤ 0.01. NOSIG cannot be used if FORMAT=SERIAL. If both NOSIG and FORMAT=SERIAL are specified, only FORMAT=SERIAL is in effect.

STATISTICS Subcommand

The correlation coefficient is automatically displayed for every pair of variables. STATISTICS requests additional statistics. The statistics for each variable list precede the corresponding correlation matrices.

DESCRIPTIVES *Mean, standard deviation, and number of nonmissing cases for each variable.* Missing values are handled on a variable-by-variable basis regardless of the missing-value option in effect for the correlations.

XPROD *Cross-product deviations and covariance for each pair of variables.*

ALL *All additional statistics.* This produces the same statistics as DESCRIPTIVES and XPROD together.

MISSING Subcommand

MISSING controls the treatment of missing values.

- The PAIRWISE and LISTWISE keywords are alternatives; however, each can be specified with INCLUDE or EXCLUDE.
- The default is LISTWISE and EXCLUDE.

PAIRWISE *Exclude missing values pairwise.* Cases missing values for one or both of a pair of variables for a specific correlation coefficient are excluded from the computation of that coefficient. Since each coefficient is based on all cases that have valid values for that particular pair of variables, this can result in a set of coefficients based on a varying number of cases. This is the default.

LISTWISE *Exclude missing values listwise.* Cases that have missing values for any variable named in a list are excluded from the computation of all coefficients defined by that list. Each variable list is evaluated separately.

INCLUDE *Include user-missing values.* User-missing values are included in the analysis.

EXCLUDE *Exclude all missing values.* Both user- and system-missing values are excluded from the analysis.

FORMAT Subcommand

By default, CORRELATIONS includes redundant coefficients in the correlation and displays in matrix format. FORMAT controls matrix format.

- PRINT=NOSIG is ignored when FORMAT=SERIAL is specified.

MATRIX *Matrix format with redundant coefficients.* This is the default.

SERIAL *Serial string format with nonredundant coefficients.* Coefficients from the first row of the matrix are displayed first, followed by all unique (not already displayed) coefficients from the second row, and so on for all rows in the matrix. Each coefficient is identified by the pair of variables for which it was calculated. The number of cases and significance level are displayed below the correlations.

MATRIX Subcommand

MATRIX writes matrix materials to a data file. The matrix materials include the mean and standard deviation for each variable, the number of cases used to compute each coefficient, and the Pearson correlation coefficients. Several SPSS procedures can read matrix materials produced by CORRELATIONS, including PARTIAL CORR, REGRESSION, FACTOR, and CLUSTER (see "SPSS Matrix Data Files" on p. 26).

- CORRELATIONS cannot write rectangular matrices (those specified with keyword WITH) to a file.
- If you specify more than one variable list on CORRELATIONS, only the last list that does not use keyword WITH is written to the matrix data file.
- Keyword OUT specifies the file to which the matrix is written. The filename must be specified in parentheses.
- Documents from the original file will not be included in the matrix file and will not be present if the matrix file becomes the working data file.

OUT (filename) *Write a matrix data file.* Specify either a file or an asterisk (*), enclosed in parentheses. If you specify a file, the file is stored on disk and can be retrieved at any time. If you specify an asterisk, the matrix data file replaces the working file but is not stored on disk unless you use SAVE or XSAVE.

Format of the Matrix Data File

- The matrix data file has two special variables created by SPSS: *ROWTYPE_* and *VARNAME_*. Variable *ROWTYPE_* is a short string variable with values MEAN, STDDEV, N, and CORR (for Pearson correlation coefficient). The next variable, *VARNAME_*, is a short string variable whose values are the names of the variables used to form the correlation matrix. When *ROWTYPE_* is CORR, *VARNAME_* gives the variable associated with that row of the correlation matrix.
- The remaining variables in the file are the variables used to form the correlation matrix.

Split Files

- When split-file processing is in effect, the first variables in the matrix file will be split variables, followed by *ROWTYPE_*, *VARNAME_*, and the variables used to form the correlation matrix.
- A full set of matrix materials is written for each subgroup defined by the split variables.
- A split variable cannot have the same name as any other variable written to the matrix data file.
- If split-file processing is in effect when a matrix is written, the same split-file specifications must be in effect when that matrix is read by another procedure.

Missing Values

- With pairwise treatment of missing values (the default), a matrix of the number of cases used to compute each coefficient is included with the matrix materials.
- With listwise treatment, a single number indicating the number of cases used to calculate all coefficients is included.

Example

```
GET FILE=CITY /KEEP FOOD RENT PUBTRANS TEACHER COOK ENGINEER.
CORRELATIONS VARIABLES=FOOD TO ENGINEER
 /MATRIX OUT(CORRMAT).
```

- **CORRELATIONS** reads data from the file *CITY* and writes one set of matrix materials to the file *CORRMAT*. The working file is still *CITY*. Subsequent commands are executed on *CITY*.

Example

```
GET FILE=CITY /KEEP FOOD RENT PUBTRANS TEACHER COOK ENGINEER.
CORRELATIONS VARIABLES=FOOD TO ENGINEER
 /MATRIX OUT(*).
LIST.
DISPLAY DICTIONARY.
```

- **CORRELATIONS** writes the same matrix as in the example above. However, the matrix data file replaces the working file. The **LIST** and **DISPLAY** commands are executed on the matrix file, not on the *CITY* file.

Example

```
CORRELATIONS VARIABLES=FOOD RENT COOK TEACHER MANAGER ENGINEER
 /FOOD TO TEACHER /PUBTRANS WITH MECHANIC
 /MATRIX OUT(*).
```

- Only the matrix for *FOOD* TO *TEACHER* is written to the matrix data file because it is the last variable list that does not use keyword **WITH**.

COUNT

```
COUNT varname=varlist(value list) [/varname=...]
```

Keywords for numeric value lists:
LOWEST, LO, HIGHEST, HI, THRU, MISSING, SYSMIS

Example:
```
COUNT TARGET=V1 V2 V3 (2).
```

Overview

COUNT creates a numeric variable that, for each case, counts the occurrences of the same value (or list of values) across a list of variables. The new variable is called the *target* variable. The variables and values that are counted are the *criterion* variables and values. Criterion variables can be either numeric or string.

Basic Specification

The basic specification is the target variable, an equals sign, the criterion variable(s), and the criterion value(s) enclosed in parentheses.

Syntax Rules

- Use a slash to separate the specifications for each target variable.
- The criterion variables specified for a single target variable must be either all numeric or all string.
- Each value in a list of criterion values must be separated by a comma or space. String values must be enclosed in apostrophes.
- Keywords THRU, LOWEST (LO), HIGHEST (HI), SYSMIS, and MISSING can only be used with numeric criterion variables.
- A variable can be specified in more than one criterion variable list.
- You can use keyword TO to specify consecutive criterion variables that have the same criterion value or values.
- You can specify multiple variable lists for a single target variable to count different values for different variables.

Operations

- Target variables are always numeric and are initialized to 0 for each case. They are assigned a dictionary format of F8.2.
- If the target variable already exists, its previous values are replaced.

- COUNT ignores the missing-value status of user-missing values. It counts a value even if that value has been previously declared as missing.
- The target variable is never system-missing. To define user-missing values for target variables, use the RECODE or MISSING VALUES command.
- SYSMIS counts system-missing values for numeric variables.
- MISSING counts both user- and system-missing values for numeric variables.

Example

```
COUNT TARGET=V1 V2 V3 (2).
```

- The value of *TARGET* for each case will be either 0, 1, 2, or 3, depending on the number of times the value 2 occurs across the three variables for each case.
- *TARGET* is a numeric variable with an F8.2 format.

Example

```
COUNT QLOW=Q1 TO Q10 (LO THRU 0)
     /QSYSMIS=Q1 TO Q10 (SYSMIS).
```

- Assuming there are 10 variables between and including *Q1* and *Q10* on the working data file, *QLOW* ranges from 0 to 10, depending on the number of times a case has a negative or 0 value across variables *Q1* to *Q10*.
- *QSYSMIS* ranges from 0 to 10, depending on how many system-missing values are encountered for *Q1* to *Q10* for each case. User-missing values are not counted.
- Both *QLOW* and *QSYSMIS* are numeric variables and have F8.2 formats.

Example

```
COUNT SVAR=V1 V2 ('male  ') V3 V4 V5 ('female').
```

- *SVAR* ranges from 0 to 5, depending on the number of times a case has a value of male for *V1* and *V2* and a value of female for *V3*, *V4*, and *V5*.
- *SVAR* is a numeric variable with an F8.2 format.

CROSSTABS

General mode:

```
CROSSTABS [TABLES=]varlist BY varlist [BY...] [/varlist...]

 [/MISSING={TABLE**}]
          {INCLUDE}

 [/WRITE[={NONE**}]]
         {CELLS }
```

Integer mode:

```
CROSSTABS VARIABLES=varlist(min,max) [varlist...]

 /TABLES=varlist BY varlist [BY...] [/varlist...]

 [/MISSING={TABLE**}]
          {INCLUDE}
          {REPORT }

 [/WRITE[={NONE**}]]
         {CELLS }
         {ALL   }
```

Both modes:

```
[/FORMAT={LABELS** }  {AVALUE**}  {NOINDEX**}  {TABLES**} {BOX**}]
         {NOLABELS }  {DVALUE  }  {INDEX    }  {NOTABLES} {NOBOX}
         {NOVALLABS}

[/CELLS=[{COUNT**}] [ROW    ] [EXPECTED] [SRESID ]]
         {NONE   }  [COLUMN ] [RESID   ] [ASRESID]
                    [TOTAL  ]            [ALL    ]

[/STATISTICS=[CHISQ]  [LAMBDA]  [BTAU]  [GAMMA]  [ETA ]]
             [PHI  ]  [UC    ]  [CTAU]  [D    ]  [CORR]
             [CC   ]  [NONE  ]  [RISK]  [KAPPA]  [ALL ]
```

**Default if the subcommand is omitted.

Example:

```
CROSSTABS TABLES=FEAR BY SEX
 /CELLS=ROW COLUMN EXPECTED RESIDUALS
 /STATISTICS=CHISQ.
```

Overview

CROSSTABS produces contingency tables showing the joint distribution of two or more variables that have a limited number of distinct values. The frequency distribution of one variable is subdivided according to the values of one or more variables. The unique combination of values for two or more variables defines a cell. To analyze contingency tables using hierarchical log-linear models, use HILOGLINEAR; to analyze contingency tables using a general linear model approach, use LOGLINEAR (both in the SPSS Advanced Statistics option).

CROSSTABS can operate in two different modes: *general* and *integer*. Integer mode builds some tables more efficiently but requires more specifications than general mode. Some subcommand specifications and statistics are available only in integer mode.

Options

Methods for Building Tables. To build tables in general mode, use the TABLES subcommand. Integer mode requires the TABLES and VARIABLES subcommands and minimum and maximum values for the variables.

Cell Contents. By default, CROSSTABS displays only the number of cases in each cell. You can request row, column, and total percentages, and also expected values and residuals using the CELLS subcommand.

Statistics. In addition to the tables, you can obtain measures of association and tests of hypotheses for each subtable using the STATISTICS subcommand.

Formatting Options. With the FORMAT subcommand you can control the order in which rows are displayed and suppress the display of variable labels, value labels, and the table itself. In addition, you can display a list of the tables produced by CROSSTABS with the page number where each table begins.

Writing and Reproducing Tables. You can write cell frequencies to a file and reproduce the original tables with the WRITE subcommand.

Basic Specification

In general mode, the basic specification is TABLES with a table list. The actual keyword TABLES can be omitted. In integer mode, the minimum specification is the VARIABLES subcommand specifying the variables to be used and their value ranges, and the TABLES subcommand with a table list.

- The minimum table list specifies a list of row variables, the keyword BY, and a list of column variables.
- In integer mode, all variables must be numeric with integer values. In general mode, variables can be numeric (integer or noninteger) or string.
- The default table shows cell counts.

Subcommand Order

- In general mode, the table list must be first if keyword TABLES is omitted. If keyword TABLES is explicitly used, subcommands can be specified in any order.
- In integer mode, VARIABLES must precede TABLES. Keyword TABLES must be explicitly specified.

Operations

- Integer mode builds tables more quickly but requires more workspace if the table has many empty cells.
- If a long string variable is used in general mode, only the short-string portion (first eight characters) is tabulated.
- Statistics are calculated separately for each two-way table or two-way subtable. Missing values are reported for the table as a whole.
- If only percentages and/or cell counts are requested, percentages are displayed without a percent sign and zero values are displayed as blanks. If percentages and expected values or residuals are requested, the percent sign is used in percentages and zero values are displayed as zeros.
- Scientific notation is used for cell counts when necessary.
- The output uses the width defined on the SET command.
- The BOX subcommand on SET controls the characters used in the table display.
- In general mode, keyword TO on the TABLES subcommand refers to the order of variables in the working file. ALL refers to all variables in the working file. In integer mode, TO and ALL refer to the position and subset of variables specified on the VARIABLES subcommand.

Limitations

The following limitations apply to CROSSTABS in *general mode*:
- Maximum 200 variables named or implied on the TABLES subcommand.
- Maximum 1000 nonempty rows or columns for each table.
- Maximum 20 table lists per CROSSTABS command.
- Maximum 10 dimensions (9 BY keywords) per table.
- Maximum 400 value labels displayed on any single table.

The following limitations apply to CROSSTABS in *integer mode*:
- Maximum 100 variables named or implied on the VARIABLES subcommand.
- Maximum 100 variables named or implied on the TABLES subcommand.
- Maximum 1000 nonempty rows or columns for each table.
- Maximum 20 table lists per CROSSTABS command.
- Maximum 8 dimensions (7 BY keywords) per table.
- Maximum 20 rows or columns of missing values when REPORT is specified on MISSING.
- Minimum value that can be specified is -99,999.
- Maximum value that can be specified is 999,999.

Example

```
CROSSTABS TABLES=FEAR BY SEX
 /CELLS=ROW COLUMN EXPECTED RESIDUALS
 /STATISTICS=CHISQ.
```

- CROSSTABS generates a bivariate table. Variable *FEAR* defines the rows of the table and variable *SEX* defines the columns.
- CELLS requests row and column percentages, expected cell frequencies, and residuals.
- STATISTICS requests the chi-square statistic.

Example

```
CROSSTABS TABLES=JOBCAT BY EDCAT BY SEX BY INCOME3.
```

- This table list produces a subtable of *JOBCAT* by *EDCAT* for each combination of values of *SEX* and *INCOME3*.

VARIABLES Subcommand

The VARIABLES subcommand is required for integer mode. VARIABLES specifies a list of variables to be used in the crosstabulations and the lowest and highest values for each variable. Values are specified in parentheses and must be integers. Noninteger values are truncated.

- Variables can be specified in any order. However, the order in which they are named on VARIABLES determines their implied order on TABLES (see the TABLES subcommand on p. 139).
- A range must be specified for each variable. If several variables can have the same range, it can be specified once after the last variable to which it applies.
- CROSSTABS uses the specified ranges to allocate tables. One cell is allocated for each possible combination of values of the row and column variables before the data are read. Thus, if the specified ranges are larger than the actual ranges, workspace will be wasted.
- Cases with values outside the specified range are considered missing and are not used in the computation of the table. This allows you to select a subset of values within CROSSTABS.
- If the table is sparse because the variables do not have values throughout the specified range, consider using general mode or recoding the variables.

Example

```
CROSSTABS VARIABLES=FEAR SEX RACE (1,2) MOBILE16 (1,3)
    /TABLES=FEAR BY SEX MOBILE16 BY RACE.
```

- VARIABLES defines values 1 and 2 for *FEAR*, *SEX*, and *RACE*, and values 1, 2, and 3 for *MOBILE16*.

TABLES Subcommand

TABLES specifies the table lists and is required in both integer and general mode. The following rules apply to both modes.

- You can specify multiple TABLES subcommands on a single CROSSTABS command. The slash between the subcommands is required; the keyword TABLES is required only in integer mode.
- Variables named before the first BY in a table list are row variables, and variables named after the first BY in a table list are column variables.
- When the table list specifies two dimensions (one BY keyword), the first variable before BY is crosstabulated with each variable after BY, then the second variable before BY with each variable after BY, and so forth.
- Each subsequent use of the keyword BY in a table list adds a new dimension (or layer) to the tables requested. Variables named after the second (or subsequent) BY are control variables.
- When the table list specifies more than two dimensions, a two-way subtable is produced for each combination of values of control variables. The value of the last specified control variable changes the most slowly in determining the order in which tables are displayed.
- You can name more than one variable in each dimension.

General Mode

- The actual keyword TABLES can be omitted in general mode.
- In general mode, both numeric and string variables can be specified. Long strings are truncated to short strings for defining categories.
- Keywords ALL and TO can be specified in any dimension. In general mode, TO refers to the order of variables in the working file and ALL refers to all variables defined in the working file.

Example

```
CROSSTABS   TABLES=FEAR BY SEX BY RACE.
```

- This example crosstabulates *FEAR* by *SEX* controlling for *RACE*. In each subtable, *FEAR* is the row variable and *SEX* is the column variable.
- A subtable is produced for each value of the control variable *RACE*.

Example

```
CROSSTABS   TABLES=CONFINAN TO CONARMY BY SEX TO REGION.
```

- This command produces crosstabulations of all variables in the working file between and including *CONFINAN* and *CONARMY* by all variables between and including *SEX* and *REGION*.

Integer Mode

- In integer mode, variables specified on TABLES must be first named on VARIABLES.
- Keywords TO and ALL can be specified in any dimension. In integer mode, TO and ALL refer to the position and subset of variables specified on the VARIABLES subcommand, not to the variables in the working file.

Example

```
CROSSTABS  VARIABLES=FEAR (1,2) MOBILE16 (1,3)
  /TABLES=FEAR BY MOBILE16.
```

- VARIABLES names two variables, *FEAR* and *MOBILE16*. Values 1 and 2 for *FEAR* are used in the tables, and values 1, 2, and 3 are used for variable *MOBILE16*.
- TABLES specifies a bivariate table with two rows (values 1 and 2 for *FEAR*) and three columns (values 1, 2, and 3 for *MOBILE16*). *FEAR* and *MOBILE16* can be named on TABLES because they were named on the previous VARIABLES subcommand.

Example

```
CROSSTABS  VARIABLES=FEAR SEX RACE DEGREE (1,2)
  /TABLES=FEAR BY SEX BY RACE BY DEGREE.
```

- This command produces four subtables. The first subtable crosstabulates *FEAR* by *SEX*, controlling for the first value of *RACE* and the first value of *DEGREE*; the second subtable controls for the second value of *RACE* and the first value of *DEGREE*; the third subtable controls for the first value of *RACE* and the second value of *DEGREE*; and the fourth subtable controls for the second value of *RACE* and the second value of *DEGREE*.

CELLS Subcommand

By default, CROSSTABS displays only the number of cases in each cell. Use CELLS to display row, column or total percentages, expected counts, or residuals. These are calculated separately for each bivariate table or subtable.

- CELLS specified without keywords displays cell counts plus row, column, and total percentages for each cell.
- If CELLS is specified with keywords, CROSSTABS displays only the requested cell information.
- The key located at the top left corner of each table describes the information contained in each cell.
- Scientific notation is used for cell contents when necessary.

COUNT *Observed cell counts.* This is the default if CELLS is omitted.

ROW *Row percentages.* The number of cases in each cell in a row is expressed as a percentage of all cases in that row.

COLUMN *Column percentages.* The number of cases in each cell in a column is expressed as a percentage of all cases in that column.

TOTAL	*Two-way table total percentages.* The number of cases in each cell of a subtable is expressed as a percentage of all cases in that subtable.
EXPECTED	*Expected counts.* Expected counts are the number of cases expected in each cell if the two variables in the subtable are statistically independent.
RESID	*Residuals.* Residuals are the difference between the observed and expected cell counts.
SRESID	*Standardized residuals* (Haberman, 1978).
ASRESID	*Adjusted standardized residuals* (Haberman, 1978).
ALL	*All cell information.* This includes cell counts; row, column and total percentages; expected counts; residuals; standardized residuals; and adjusted standardized residuals.
NONE	*No cell information.* Use NONE when you want to write tables to a procedure output file without displaying them (see the WRITE subcommand on p. 143). This is the same as specifying NOTABLES on FORMAT.

STATISTICS Subcommand

STATISTICS requests measures of association and related statistics. By default, CROSSTABS does not display any additional statistics.

- STATISTICS without keywords displays the chi-square test.
- If STATISTICS is specified with keywords, CROSSTABS calculates only the requested statistics.
- In integer mode, values that are not included in the specified range are *not* used in the calculation of the statistics, even if these values exist in the data.
- If user-missing values are included with MISSING, cases with user-missing values are included in the calculation of statistics as well as in the tables.

CHISQ	*Chi-square.* Includes Pearson chi-square, likelihood-ratio chi-square, and Mantel-Haenszel chi-square. Mantel-Haenszel is valid only if both variables are numeric. For 2×2 tables, Fisher's exact test is computed when a table that does not result from missing rows or columns in a larger table has a cell with an expected frequency less than 5. Yates' corrected chi-square is computed for all other 2×2 tables. This is the default if STATISTICS is specified with no keywords.
PHI	*Phi and Cramér's V.*
CC	*Contingency coefficient.*
LAMBDA	*Lambda (symmetric and asymmetric) and Goodman and Kruskal's tau.*
UC	*Uncertainty coefficient (symmetric and asymmetric).*
BTAU	*Kendall's tau-b.*
CTAU	*Kendall's tau-c.*

GAMMA	*Gamma.* Zero-order gammas are displayed for 2-way tables and conditional gammas are displayed for 3-way to 10-way tables in general mode and 3-way to 8-way tables in integer mode. Partial and zero-order gammas for 3-way to 8-way tables are available in integer mode only.
D	Somers' d *(symmetric and asymmetric).*
ETA	*Eta.* Available for numeric data only.
CORR	*Pearson's* r *and Spearman's correlation coefficient.* This is available for numeric data only.
KAPPA	*Kappa coefficient* (Kraemer, 1982). Kappa can be computed only for square tables in which the row and column values are identical. If there is a missing row or column, use integer mode to specify the square table, since a missing column or row in general mode would keep the table from being square.
RISK	*Relative risk* (Bishop et al., 1975). Relative risk can be calculated only for 2×2 tables.
ALL	*All statistics available.*
NONE	*No summary statistics.* This is the default if STATISTICS is omitted.

MISSING Subcommand

By default, CROSSTABS deletes cases with missing values on a table-by-table basis. Cases with missing values for any variable specified for a table are not used in the table or in the calculation of statistics. Use MISSING to specify alternative missing-value treatments.

- The only specification is a single keyword.
- The number of missing cases is always displayed at the end of the table, following the last subtable and any requested statistics.
- If the missing values are not included in the range specified on VARIABLES, they are excluded from the table regardless of the keyword you specify on MISSING.

TABLE	*Delete cases with missing values on a table-by-table basis.* When multiple table lists are specified, missing values are handled separately for each list. This is the default.
INCLUDE	*Include user-missing values.*
REPORT	*Report missing values in the tables.* This option includes missing values in tables but not in the calculation of percentages or statistics. The letter *M* is used to indicate that cases within a cell are missing. REPORT is available only in integer mode.

FORMAT Subcommand

By default, CROSSTABS displays tables and subtables with variable and value labels when they are available (only the first 16 characters of value labels are displayed). The values for the row variables are displayed in order from lowest to highest. Use FORMAT to modify the default table display.

LABELS — *Display both variable and value labels for each table.* This is the default.

NOLABELS — *Suppress variable and value labels.*

NOVALLABS — *Suppress value labels but display variable labels.*

AVALUE — *Display row variables from lowest to highest value.* This is the default.

DVALUE — *Display row variables from highest to lowest.*

NOINDEX — *Suppress the table index.* This is the default.

INDEX — *Display an index of tables.* The index follows the last page of tables. It lists all tables produced and the beginning page number of each table.

TABLES — *Display tables.* This is the default.

NOTABLES — *Suppress tables.* If STATISTICS is specified, only the statistics are displayed. If STATISTICS is omitted, no output is displayed. NOTABLES is useful when you want to write tables to a file without displaying them. This is the same as specifying NONE on CELLS.

BOX — *Use box characters around every cell.* This is the default.

NOBOX — *Suppress box characters around each cell.* The row and column headings are still separated from the table by box characters.

WRITE Subcommand

Use the WRITE subcommand to write cell frequencies to a file for subsequent use by SPSS or another program. CROSSTABS can also use these cell frequencies as input to reproduce tables and compute statistics.

- The only specification is a single keyword.
- The name of the file must be specified on the PROCEDURE OUTPUT command prior to CROSSTABS.
- If both CELLS and ALL are specified, CELLS is in effect and only the contents of nonempty cells are written to the file.
- If you include missing values with INCLUDE or REPORT on MISSING, no values are considered missing and all nonempty cells, including those with missing values, are written, even if CELLS is specified.
- If you exclude missing values on a table-by-table basis (the default), no records are written for combinations of values that include a missing value.
- If multiple tables are specified, the tables are written in the same order as they are displayed.

NONE — *Do not write cell counts to a file.* This is the default.

CELLS *Write cell counts for nonempty and nonmissing cells to a file.* Combinations of values that include a missing value are not written to the file.

ALL *Write cell counts for all cells to a file.* A record for each combination of values defined by VARIABLES and TABLES is written to the file. ALL is available only in integer mode.

The file contains one record for each cell. Each record contains the following:

Columns Contents

1–4 *Split-file group number, numbered consecutively from 1.* Note that this is not the value of the variable or variables used to define the splits.

5–8 *Table number.* Tables are defined by the TABLES subcommand.

9–16 *Cell frequency.* The number of times this combination of variable values occurred in the data, or, if case weights are used, the sum of case weights for cases having this combination of values.

17–24 *The value of the row variable* (the one named before the first BY).

25–32 *The value of the column variable* (the one named after the first BY).

33–40 *The value of the first control variable* (the one named after the second BY).

41–48 *The value of the second control variable* (the one named after the third BY).

49–56 *The value of the third control variable* (the one named after the fourth BY).

57–64 *The value of the fourth control variable* (the one named after the fifth BY).

65–72 *The value of the fifth control variable* (the one named after the sixth BY).

73–80 *The value of the sixth control variable* (the one named after the seventh BY).

- The split-file group number, table number, and frequency are written as integers.
- In integer mode, the values of variables are also written as integers. In general mode, the values are written according to the print format specified for each variable. Alphanumeric values are written at the left end of any field in which they occur.
- Within each table, records are written from one column of the table at a time, and the value of the last control variable changes most slowly.

Example

```
PROCEDURE OUTPUT   OUTFILE=CELLDATA.
CROSSTABS VARIABLES=FEAR SEX (1,2)
 /TABLES=FEAR BY SEX
 /WRITE=ALL.
```

- CROSSTABS writes a record for each cell in the table *FEAR* by *SEX* to the file *CELLDATA*. Figure 1 shows the contents of the *CELLDATA* file.

Figure 1   Cell records

```
1       1          551     1
1       1         1722     1
1       1         1801     2
1       1          892     2
```

Example

```
PROCEDURE OUTPUT   OUTFILE=XTABDATA.
CROSSTABS    TABLES=V1 TO V3 BY V4 BY V10 TO V15
  /WRITE=CELLS.
```

- CROSSTABS writes a set of records for each table to file *XTABDATA*.
- Records for the table *V1* by *V4* by *V10* are written first, followed by records for *V1* by *V4* by *V11*, and so forth. The records for *V3* by *V4* by *V15* are written last.

Reading a CROSSTABS Procedure Output File

You can use the file created by WRITE in a subsequent SPSS session to reproduce a table and compute statistics for it. Each record in the file contains all the information used to build the original table. The cell frequency information can be used as a weight variable on the WEIGHT command to replicate the original cases.

Example

```
DATA LIST FILE=CELLDATA
  /WGHT 9-16 FEAR 17-24 SEX 25-32.
VARIABLE LABELS FEAR 'AFRAID TO WALK AT NIGHT IN NEIGHBORHOODS'.
VALUE LABELS   FEAR 1 'YES' 2 'NO'/ SEX 1 'MALE' 2 'FEMALE'.
WEIGHT BY WGHT.
CROSSTABS TABLES=FEAR BY SEX
  /STATISTICS=ALL.
```

- DATA LIST reads the cell frequencies and row and column values from the *CELLDATA* file shown in Figure 1. The cell frequency is read as a weighting factor (variable *WGHT*). The values for the rows are read as *FEAR*, and the values for the columns as *SEX*, the two original variables.
- The WEIGHT command recreates the sample size by weighting each of the four cases (cells) by the cell frequency.

If you do not have the original data or the CROSSTABS procedure output file, you can reproduce a crosstabulation and compute statistics by simply entering the values from the table:

```
DATA LIST  /FEAR 1 SEX 3 WGHT 5-7.
VARIABLE LABELS  FEAR 'AFRAID TO WALK AT NIGHT IN NEIGHBORHOOD'.
VALUE LABELS   FEAR 1 'YES' 2 'NO'/ SEX 1 'MALE' 2 'FEMALE'.
 WEIGHT  BY WGHT.
BEGIN DATA
1 1   55
2 1  172
1 2  180
2 2   89
END DATA.
 CROSSTABS   TABLES=FEAR BY SEX
  /STATISTICS=ALL.
```

References

Bishop, Y. M. M., S. E. Feinberg, and P. W. Holland. 1975. *Discrete multivariate analysis: Theory and practice*. Cambridge: MIT Press.

Haberman, S. J. 1978. *Analysis of qualitative data*. Vol. 1. London: Academic Press.

Kraemer, H. C. 1982. Kappa coefficient. In *Encyclopedia of statistical sciences,* ed. S. Katz and N.L. Johnson. New York: John Wiley & Sons.

DATA LIST

```
DATA LIST [FILE=file] [{FIXED}] [RECORDS={1}] [{TABLE   }]
                      {FREE  }            {n}  {NOTABLE}
                      {LIST  }

/{1    } varname {col location [(format)]} [varname ...]
 {rec #}         {(FORTRAN-like format)   }

[/{2    } ...] [/ ...]
  {rec #}
```

Numeric and string input formats:

Type	Column-style format	FORTRAN-like format
Numeric (default)	d or F,d	Fw.d
Restricted numeric	N,d	Nw.d
Scientific notation	E,d	Ew.d
Numeric with commas	COMMA,d	COMMAw.d
Numeric with dots	DOT,d	DOTw.d
Numeric with commas and dollar sign	DOLLAR,d	DOLLARw.d
Numeric with percent sign	PCT,d	PCTw.d
Zoned decimal	Z,d	Zw.d
String	A	Aw

Some formats are not available on all implementations of SPSS.

Format elements to skip columns:

Type	Column-style format	FORTRAN-like format
Tab to column n		Tn
Skip n columns		nX

Date and time input formats:

Type	Data input	Format	FORTRAN-like format
International date	dd-mmm-yyyy	DATE	DATEw
American date	mm/dd/yyyy	ADATE	ADATEw
European date	dd/mm/yy	EDATE	EDATEw
Julian date	yyddd	JDATE	JDATEw
Sorted date	yy/mm/dd	SDATE	SDATEw
Quarter and year	qQyyyy	QYR	QYRw
Month and year	mm/yyyy	MOYR	MOYRw
Week and year	wkWKyyyy	WKYR	WKYRw
Date and time	dd-mmm-yyyy hh:mm:ss.ss	DATETIME	DATETIMEw.d

Time	hh:mm:ss.ss	TIME	TIMEw.d
Days and time	ddd hh:mm:ss.ss	DTIME	DTIMEw.d
Day of the week	string	WKDAY	WKDAYw
Month	string	MONTH	MONTHw

Example:

```
DATA LIST /ID 1-3 SEX 5 (A) AGE 7-8 OPINION1 TO OPINION5 10-14.
```

Overview

DATA LIST defines a raw data file (a raw data file contains numbers and other alphanumeric characters) by assigning names and formats to each variable in the file. Raw data can be inline (entered with your commands between BEGIN DATA and END DATA) or stored in an external file. They can be in fixed format (values for the same variable are always entered in the same location on the same record for each case) or in freefield format (values for consecutive variables are not in particular columns but are entered one after the other, separated by blanks or commas).

For information on defining matrix materials, see MATRIX DATA. For information on defining complex data files that cannot be defined with DATA LIST, see FILE TYPE and REPEATING DATA. For information on reading SPSS data files and SPSS portable files, see GET and IMPORT.

SPSS can also read data files created by other software applications. Commands that read these files include GET SCSS, GET SAS, GET BMDP, GET OSIRIS, and GET TRANSLATE.

Options

Data Source. You can use inline data or data from an external file.

Data Formats. You can define numeric (with or without decimal places) and string variables using an array of input formats (percent, dollar, date and time, and so forth). You can also specify column binary and unaligned positive integer binary formats (available only if used with the MODE=MULTIPUNCH setting on the FILE HANDLE command). For a complete list of available formats, see "Variable Formats" on p. 34.

Data Organization. You can define data that are in fixed format (values in the same location on the same record for each case), in freefield format with multiple cases per record, or in freefield format with one case on each record using the FIXED, FREE, and LIST keywords.

Multiple Records. For fixed-format data, you can indicate the number of records per case on the RECORDS subcommand. You can specify which records to read in the variable definition portion of DATA LIST.

Summary Table. For fixed-format data, you can display a table that summarizes the variable definitions using the TABLE subcommand. You can suppress this table using NOTABLE.

End-of-File Processing. You can specify a logical variable that indicates the end of the data using the END subcommand. This logical variable can be used to invoke special processing after all the cases from the data file have been read.

Basic Specification

- The basic specification is the FIXED, LIST, or FREE keyword, followed by a slash that signals the beginning of variable definition.
- FIXED is the default.
- If the data are in an external file, the FILE subcommand must be used.
- If the data are inline, the FILE subcommand is omitted and the data are specified between the BEGIN DATA and END DATA commands.
- Variable definition for fixed-format data includes a variable name, a column location, and a format (unless the default numeric format is used). The column location is not specified if FORTRAN-like formats are used, since these formats include the variable width.
- Variable definition for freefield data includes a variable name and, optionally, a FORTRAN-like format specification.

Subcommand Order

Subcommands can be named in any order. However, all subcommands must precede the first slash, which signals the beginning of variable definition.

Syntax Rules

Subcommands on DATA LIST are separated by spaces or commas, not by slashes.

Operations

- DATA LIST clears the working data file and defines a new working file.
- Variable names are stored in the working file dictionary.
- Formats are stored in the working file dictionary and are used to display and write the values. To change output formats of numeric variables defined on DATA LIST, use the FORMATS command.

Fixed-Format Data

- The order of the variables in the working file dictionary is the order in which they are defined on DATA LIST, not their sequence in the input data file. This order is important if you later use the TO keyword to refer to variables on subsequent commands.
- In numeric format, blanks to the left or right of a number are ignored; imbedded blanks are invalid. When SPSS encounters a field that contains one or more blanks interspersed among the numbers, it issues a warning message and assigns the system-missing value to that case.
- Alphabetical and special characters, except the decimal point and leading plus and minus signs, are not valid in numeric variables and are set to system-missing if encountered in the data.

- The system-missing value is assigned to a completely blank field for numeric variables. The value assigned to blanks can be changed using the BLANKS specification on the SET command.
- SPSS ignores data contained in columns and records that are not specified in the variable definition.

Freefield Data

- FREE can read freefield data with multiple cases recorded on one record or with one case recorded on more than one record. LIST can read freefield data with one case on each record.
- Leading and trailing blanks are ignored, and multiple blanks or commas are treated as a single delimiter.

Example

```
* Column-style format specifications.

DATA LIST /ID 1-3 SEX 5 (A) AGE 7-8 OPINION1 TO OPINION5 10-14.
BEGIN DATA
001 m 28 12212
002 f 29 21212
003 f 45 32145
  ...
128 m 17 11194
END DATA.
```

- The data are inline between the BEGIN DATA and END DATA commands, so the FILE subcommand is not specified. The data are in fixed format. Keyword FIXED is not specified because it is the default.
- Variable definition begins after the slash. Variable *ID* is in columns 1 through 3. Because no format is specified, numeric format is assumed. Variable *ID* is therefore a numeric variable that is three characters wide.
- Variable *SEX* is a short string variable in column 5. Variable *SEX* is one character wide.
- *AGE* is a two-column numeric variable in columns 7 and 8.
- Variables *OPINION1*, *OPINION2*, *OPINION3*, *OPINION4*, and *OPINION5* are named using the TO keyword (see "Keyword TO" on p. 32). Each is a one-column numeric variable, with *OPINION1* located in column 10 and *OPINION5* located in column 14.
- The BEGIN DATA and END DATA commands enclose the inline data. Note that the values of *SEX* are lowercase letters and must be specified as such on subsequent commands.

FILE Subcommand

FILE specifies the raw data file. FILE is required when data are stored in an external data file. FILE must not be used when the data are stored in a file that is included with the INCLUDE command or when the data are inline (see INCLUDE and BEGIN DATA—END DATA).

Syntax Reference Guide   DATA LIST   151

- FILE must be separated from other DATA LIST subcommands by at least one blank or comma.
- FILE must precede the first slash, which signals the beginning of variable definition.

FIXED, FREE, and LIST Keywords

FIXED, FREE, or LIST indicate the format of the data. Only one of these keywords can be used on each DATA LIST. The default is FIXED.

FIXED *Fixed-format data.* Each variable is recorded in the same column location on the same record for each case in the data. FIXED is the default.

FREE *Freefield data.* The variables are recorded in the same order for each case but not necessarily in the same column locations. More than one case can be entered on the same record. Values are separated by blanks or commas.

LIST *Freefield data with one case on each record.* The variables are recorded in freefield format as described for keyword FREE except that the variables for each case must be recorded on one record.

- FIXED, FREE, or LIST must be separated from other DATA LIST subcommands by at least one blank or comma.
- FIXED, FREE, or LIST must precede the first slash, which signals the beginning of data definition.
- For fixed-format data, you can use column-style or FORTRAN-like formats, or a combination of both. For freefield data, you can use only FORTRAN-like formats.
- For fixed-format data, SPSS reads values according to the column locations specified or implied by the FORTRAN-like format. Values in the data do *not* have to be in the same order as the variables named on DATA LIST and do *not* have to be separated by a space or column.
- For freefield data, SPSS reads values sequentially in the order in which the variables are named on DATA LIST. Values in the data *must* be in the order in which the variables are named on DATA LIST and *must* be separated by at least one blank or comma.
- For freefield data, a blank value cannot be used to indicate missing information. A value must be assigned to the missing information with the MISSING VALUES command.
- In freefield format, the end of a data record is the same as a blank or comma. This means that a value cannot be split across records. Multiple blank columns at the end of a record are interpreted as one delimiter between values.

Example

```
* Data in fixed format.

DATA LIST FILE=HUBDATA FIXED RECORDS=3
  /1 YRHIRED 14-15 DEPT 19 SEX 20.
```

- FIXED indicates explicitly that the *HUBDATA* file is in fixed format. Because FIXED is the default, keyword FIXED could have been omitted.

- Variable definition begins after the slash. Column locations are specified after each variable. Since formats are not specified, the default numeric format is used. Variable widths are determined by the column specifications: *YRHIRED* is two characters wide, *DEPT* and *SEX* are each one character wide.

Example

```
* Data in freefield format.

DATA LIST FREE / POSTPOS NWINS.
BEGIN DATA
2 19 7 5 10 25 5 17 8 11 3 18 6 8 1 29
END DATA.
```

- Data are inline, so FILE is omitted. Keyword FREE is used because data are in freefield format with multiple cases on a single record. Two variables, *POSTPOS* and *NWINS*, are defined. Since formats are not specified, both variables receive the default F8.2 format.
- All of the data are recorded on one record. The first two values build the first case in the working data file. For the first case, *POSTPOS* has value 2 and *NWINS* has value 19. For the second case, *POSTPOS* has value 7 and *NWINS* has value 5, and so forth. The working data file will contain eight cases.

Example

```
* Data in list format.

DATA LIST LIST / POSTPOS NWINS.
BEGIN DATA
2 19
7 5
10 25
5 17
8 11
3 18
6 8
1 29
END DATA.
```

- This example defines the same data as the previous example, but LIST is used because each case is recorded on a separate record. FREE could also be used. However, LIST is less prone to errors in data entry. If you leave out a value in the data with FREE format, all values after the missing value are assigned to the wrong variable. Since LIST format reads a case from each record, a missing value will affect only one case.

TABLE and NOTABLE Subcommands

TABLE displays a table summarizing the variable definitions supplied on DATA LIST. NOTABLE suppresses the summary table. TABLE is the default.
- TABLE and NOTABLE can only be used for fixed-format data.
- TABLE and NOTABLE must be separated from other DATA LIST subcommands by at least one blank or comma.

- TABLE and NOTABLE must precede the first slash, which signals the beginning of variable definition.

RECORDS Subcommand

RECORDS indicates the number of records per case for fixed-format data. In the variable definition portion of DATA LIST, each record is preceded by a slash. By default, DATA LIST reads one record per case.

- The only specification on RECORDS is a single integer, which indicates the number of records. The integer must indicate the *total* number of records for each case even if the variable definition portion of DATA LIST does not define all the records.
- RECORDS can be used only for fixed-format data and must be separated from other DATA LIST subcommands by at least one blank or comma. RECORDS must precede the first slash, which signals the beginning of variable definition.
- Each slash in the variable definition portion of DATA LIST indicates the beginning of a new record. The first slash indicates the first (or only) record. The second and any subsequent slashes tell SPSS to go to a new record.
- To skip a record, specify a slash without any variables for that record.
- The number of slashes in the variable definition cannot exceed the value of the integer specified on RECORDS.
- The sequence number of the record being defined can be specified after each slash. DATA LIST reads the number to determine which record to read. If the sequence number is used, you *do not* have to use a slash for any skipped records.
- The slashes for the second and subsequent records can be specified within the variable list, or they can be specified in a format list following the variable list (see example below).
- All variables to be read from one record should be defined before you proceed to the next record.
- Since RECORDS can be used only with fixed format, it is not necessary to define all the variables on a given record or to follow their order in the input data file.

Example

```
DATA LIST FILE=HUBDATA RECORDS=3
 /2 YRHIRED 14-15 DEPT 19 SEX 20.
```

- DATA LIST defines fixed-format data. RECORDS can only be used for fixed-format data.
- RECORDS indicates there are three records per case in the data. Only one record per case is defined in the data definition.
- The sequence number (2) before the first variable definition indicates that the variables being defined are on the second record. Because the sequence number is provided, a slash is not required for the first record, which is skipped.
- Variables *YRHIRED*, *DEPT*, and *SEX* are defined and will be included in the working data file. Any other variables on the second record or on the other records are not defined and are not included in the working file.

Example

```
DATA LIST FILE=HUBDATA RECORDS=3
 / /YRHIRED 14-15 DEPT 19 SEX 20.
```

- This command is equivalent to the one in the previous example. Because the record sequence number is omitted, a slash is required to skip the first record.

Example

```
DATA LIST FILE=HUBDATA RECORDS=3
 /YRHIRED (T14,F2.0) /  /NAME (T25,A24).
```

- RECORDS indicates there are three records for each case in the data.
- *YRHIRED* is the only variable defined on the first record. The FORTRAN-like format specification T14 means tab over 14 columns. Thus, *YRHIRED* begins in column 14 and has format F2.0.
- The second record is skipped. Because the record sequence numbers are not specified, a slash must be used to skip the second record.
- *NAME* is the only variable defined for the third record. *NAME* begins in column 25 and is a string variable with a width of 24 characters (format A24).

Example

```
DATA LIST FILE=HUBDATA RECORDS=3
 /YRHIRED NAME (T14,F2.0 /  / T25,A24).
```

- This command is equivalent to the one in the previous example. *YRHIRED* is located on the first record, and *NAME* is located on the third record.
- The slashes that indicate the second and third records are specified within the format specifications. The format specifications follow the complete variable list.

END Subcommand

END provides control of end-of-file processing by specifying a variable that is set to a value of 0 until the end of the data file is encountered, at which point the variable is set to 1. The values of all variables named on DATA LIST are left unchanged. The logical variable created with END can then be used on DO IF and LOOP to invoke special processing after all the cases from a particular input file have been built.

- DATA LIST and the entire set of commands used to define the cases must be enclosed within an INPUT PROGRAM—END INPUT PROGRAM structure. The END FILE command must also be used to signal the end of case generation.
- END can only be used with fixed-format data. An error is generated if the END subcommand is used with FREE or LIST.

Example

```
INPUT PROGRAM.
NUMERIC         TINCOME (DOLLAR8.0).               /* Total income
LEAVE           TINCOME.
DO IF           $CASENUM EQ 1.
+   PRINT       EJECT.
+   PRINT       / 'Name         Income'.
END IF
DATA LIST       FILE=INCOME END=#EOF NOTABLE / NAME 1-10(A)
                                              INCOME 16-20(F).
DO IF           #EOF.
+   PRINT       / 'TOTAL      ', TINCOME.
+   END FILE.
ELSE.
+   PRINT       / NAME, INCOME (A10,COMMA8).
+   COMPUTE     TINCOME = TINCOME+INCOME.   /* Accumulate total income
END IF.
END INPUT PROGRAM.

EXECUTE.
```

- The data definition commands are enclosed within an INPUT PROGRAM—END INPUT PROGRAM structure.
- NUMERIC indicates that a new numeric variable, *TINCOME*, will be created.
- LEAVE tells SPSS to leave variable *TINCOME* at its value for the previous case as each new case is read, so that it can be used to accumulate totals across cases.
- The first DO IF structure, enclosing the PRINT EJECT and PRINT commands, tells SPSS to display the headings *Name* and *Income* at the top of the display (when *$CASENUM* equals 1).
- DATA LIST defines variables *NAME* and *INCOME*, and it specifies the scratch variable *#EOF* on the END subcommand.
- The second DO IF prints the values for *NAME* and *INCOME* and accumulates the variable *INCOME* into *TINCOME* by passing control to ELSE as long as *#EOF* is not equal to 1. At the end of the file, *#EOF* equals 1, and the expression on DO IF is true. The label *TOTAL* and the value for *TINCOME* are displayed, and control is passed to END FILE.

Example

```
* Concatenate three raw data files.

INPUT PROGRAM.
NUMERIC #EOF1 TO #EOF3.   /*These will be used as the END variables.

DO IF #EOF1 & #EOF2 & #EOF3.
+    END FILE.
ELSE IF #EOF1 & #EOF2.
+    DATA LIST   FILE=THREE END=#EOF3 NOTABLE / NAME 1-20(A)
             AGE 25-26 SEX 29(A).
+    DO IF NOT #EOF3.
+       END CASE.
+    END IF.
ELSE IF #EOF1.
+    DATA LIST  FILE=TWO END=#EOF2 NOTABLE / NAME 1-20(A)
             AGE 21-22 SEX 24(A).
```

```
+       DO IF NOT #EOF2.
+          END CASE.
+       END IF.
ELSE.
+       DATA LIST  FILE=ONE END=#EOF1 NOTABLE /1 NAME 1-20(A)
                 AGE 21-22 SEX 24 (A).
+       DO IF NOT #EOF1.
+          END CASE.
+       END IF.
END IF.
END INPUT PROGRAM.

REPORT FORMAT AUTOMATIC LIST /VARS=NAME AGE SEX.
```

- The input program contains a DO IF—ELSE IF—END IF structure.
- Scratch variables are used on each END subcommand so the value will not be reinitialized to the system-missing value after each case is built.
- Three data files are read, two of which contain data in the same format. The third requires a slightly different format for the data items. All three DATA LIST commands are placed within the DO IF structure.
- END CASE builds cases from each record of the three files. END FILE is used to trigger end-of-file processing once all data records have been read.
- This application can also be handled by creating three separate SPSS data files and using ADD FILES to put them together. The advantage of using the input program is that additional files are not required to store the separate data files prior to performing ADD FILES. In addition, the files remain raw data files: they need not be converted to SPSS data files.

Variable Definition

The variable definition portion of DATA LIST assigns names and formats to the variables in the data. Depending on the format of the file, you may also need to specify record and column location. The following sections describe variable names, location, and formats.

Variable Names

- Variable names can contain up to eight characters. All variable names must begin with a letter or the @ or # character. A # symbol as the first character of the variable name defines the variable as a scratch variable. System variables (beginning with a $) cannot be defined on DATA LIST. An underscore can be used within a variable name, provided the underscore is not the first character.
- Keyword TO can be used to generate names for consecutive variables in the data. Leading zeros in the number are preserved in the name. *X1* TO *X100* and *X001* TO *X100* both generate 100 variable names, but the first 99 names are not the same in the two lists. *X01* TO *X9* is not a valid specification. For more information on the TO keyword and other variable-naming rules, see "Variable Names" on p. 32.
- The order in which variables are named on DATA LIST determines their order in the working data file. If the working file is saved as an SPSS data file, the variables are saved in this order unless they are explicitly reordered on the SAVE or XSAVE command.

Syntax Reference Guide   DATA LIST   157

Example

```
DATA LIST FREE / ID SALARY #V1 TO #V4.
```

- The FREE keyword indicates the data are in freefield format. Six variables are defined: *ID*, *SALARY*, *#V1*, *#V2*, *#V3*, and *#V4*. *#V1* to *#V4* are scratch variables that are not stored in the working data file. Their values can be used in transformations but not in procedure commands.

Variable Location

For fixed-format data, variable locations are specified either explicitly using column locations or implicitly using FORTRAN-like formats. For freefield data, variable locations are not specified. Values are read sequentially in the order variables are named on the variable list.

Fixed-Format Data

- If column-style formats are used, you must specify the column location of each variable after the variable name. If the variable is one column wide, specify the column number. Otherwise, specify the first column number followed by a dash (–) and the last column number.
- If several adjacent variables on the same record have the same width and format type, you use one column specification after the last variable name. Specify the beginning column location of the first variable, a dash, and the ending column location of the last variable. SPSS divides the total number of columns specified equally among the variables. If the number of columns does not divide equally, an error message is issued.
- The same column locations can be used to define multiple variables.
- For FORTRAN-like formats, column locations are implied by the width specified on the formats (see "Variable Formats" on p. 159). To skip columns, use the T*n* or *n*X format specifications.
- With fixed format, column-style and FORTRAN-like specifications can be mixed on the same DATA LIST command.
- Record location is indicated by a slash or a slash and record number before the names of the variables on that record. See the RECORDS subcommand on p. 153 for information on specifying record location.
- SPSS ignores data in columns and on records that are not specified on DATA LIST.
- In the data, values do not have to be separated by a space or comma.

Example

```
DATA LIST   FILE=HUBDATA RECORDS=3
  /1 YRHIRED 14-15 DEPT 19 SEX 20
  /2 SALARY 21-25.
```

- The data are in fixed format (the default) and are read from file *HUBDATA*.

- Three variables, *YRHIRED*, *DEPT*, and *SEX*, are defined on the first record of the *HUBDATA* file. One variable, *SALARY*, is read from columns 21 through 25 on the second record. The total number of records per case is specified as 3 even though no variables are defined on the third record. The third record is simply skipped in data definition.

Example

```
DATA LIST  FILE=HUBDATA RECORDS=3
   /1 DEPT 19 SEX 20 YRHIRED 14-15 MOHIRED 12-13 HIRED 12-15
   /2 SALARY 21-25.
```

- The first two defined variables are *DEPT* and *SEX*, located in columns 19 and 20 on record 1. The next three variables, *YRHIRED*, *MOHIRED*, and *HIRED*, are also located on the first record.
- *YRHIRED* is read from columns 14 and 15, *MOHIRED* from columns 12 and 13, and *HIRED* from columns 12 through 15. Variable *HIRED* is a four-column variable with the first two columns representing the month when an employee was hired (the same as *MOHIRED*) and the last two columns representing the year of employment (the same as *YRHIRED*).
- The order of the variables in the dictionary is the order in which they are defined on DATA LIST, not their sequence in the *HUBDATA* file.

Example

```
DATA LIST  FILE=HUBDATA RECORDS=3
   /1 DEPT 19 SEX 20 MOHIRED YRHIRED 12-15
   /2 SALARY 21-25.
```

- A single column specification follows *MOHIRED* and *YRHIRED*. DATA LIST divides the total number of columns specified equally between the two variables. Thus, each variable has a width of two columns.

Example

```
* Mixing column-style and FORTRAN-like format specifications.

DATA LIST FILE=PRSNL / LNAME M_INIT STREET (A20,A1,1X,A10)
    AGE 35-36.
```

- FORTRAN-like format specifications are used for string variables *LNAME*, *M_INIT*, and *STREET*. These variables must be adjacent in the data file. *LNAME* is twenty characters wide and is located in columns 1–20. *M_INIT* is one character wide in column 21. The 1X specification defines a blank column between *M_INIT* and *STREET*. *STREET* is ten characters wide and is located in columns 23–32.
- A column-style format is used for variable *AGE*. *AGE* begins in column 35, ends in column 36, and by default has numeric format.

Freefield Data

- In freefield data, column location is irrelevant, since values are not in fixed column positions. Instead, values are simply separated from each other by blanks or by commas. Any number of consecutive blanks or commas (except blanks or commas within a string value) are interpreted as one delimiter. A value cannot be split across records.

- If there are not enough values to complete the last case, a warning is issued and the incomplete case is dropped.
- Neither commas nor blanks can be used within numeric values.
- Using a blank field for a missing numeric value causes values from that point on to be assigned to the wrong variable. With LIST format, only one case is affected. With FREE format, all remaining cases are affected.
- String values that contain blanks or commas must be enclosed in apostrophes or quotation marks. The apostrophes or quotation marks are not read as part of the string value. To include an apostrophe in a string value, enclose the value in quotation marks. To include quotation marks in a value, enclose the value in apostrophes (see "String Values in Command Specifications" on p. 16).

Example

```
DATA LIST FREE / ID (F3.0) NAME (A8).
BEGIN DATA
122    SMITH
234,,,"O'BRIAN"
354,,,'VAN DYKE'
END DATA.
```

- Data are in freefield format, so column locations are not specified. Formats are specified for the variables because the default format F8.2 is not appropriate for the data. There are two defined variables, *ID* and *NAME*. *ID* is a numeric variable three characters wide with no decimal places. *NAME* is a string variable eight characters wide.
- For the first case in the data, spaces are used between values. For the second and third cases, commas are used between values. Multiple commas or spaces are interpreted as a single delimiter.
- For the second case, the quotation marks enclosing the string value make it possible to include an apostrophe in the name. Apostrophes enclosing the string value in the third case make it possible to include a space in the name. The space is interpreted as part of the string value, not as a delimiter.

Variable Formats

Two types of format specifications are available: column-style and FORTRAN-like. With each type you can specify both numeric and string formats. The difference between the two types is that FORTRAN-like formats include the width of the variable and column-style formats do not.

- Column-style formats are available only for fixed-format data.
- Column-style and FORTRAN-like formats can be mixed on the same DATA LIST to define fixed-format data.
- A value that cannot be read according to the format type specified is assigned the system-missing value and a warning message is issued.

The following sections discuss the rules for specifying column-style and FORTRAN-like formats, followed by additional considerations for numeric and string formats. See p. 147 for a partial list of available formats. For a complete discussion of formats, see "Variable Formats" on p. 34).

Column-Style Format Specifications

The following rules apply to column-style formats:
- Data must be in a fixed format.
- Column locations must be specified after variable names. The width of a variable is determined by the number of specified columns. See "Fixed-Format Data" on p. 157 for information on specifying column location.
- Following the column location, specify the format type in parentheses. The format type applies only to the variable or the list of variables associated with the column location specification immediately before it. If no format type is specified, numeric (F) format is used.
- To include decimal positions in the format, specify the format type followed by a comma and the number of decimal positions. For example, (DOLLAR) specifies only whole dollar amounts; (DOLLAR,2) specifies DOLLAR format with two decimal positions.
- Since column positions are explicitly specified, the variables can be named in any order.

FORTRAN-like Format Specifications

The following rules apply to FORTRAN-like formats:
- Data can be in either fixed or freefield format.
- Column locations cannot be specified. The width of a variable is determined by the width portion (w) of the format specification. The width must specify the number of characters in the widest value.
- One format specification applies to only one variable. The format is specified in parentheses after the variable to which it applies. Alternatively, a variable list can be followed by an equal number of format specifications contained in one set of parentheses. When a number of consecutive variables have the same format, the number can be used as a multiplying factor preceding the format. For example, (3F5.2) assigns the format F5.2 to three consecutive variables.
- For fixed data, the number of formats specified (either explicitly or implied by the multiplication factor) must be the same as the number of variables. Otherwise, SPSS issues an error message. If no formats are specified, all variables have the default format F8.2.
- For freefield data, variables with no specified formats take the default F8.2 format. However, an asterisk (*) must be used to indicate where the default format stops. Otherwise, SPSS tries to apply the next specified format to every variable before it and issues an error message if the number of formats specified is less than the number of variables.
- For freefield data, only A and F formats can be used; any other formats may cause SPSS to misread the data.
- For fixed data, Tn can be used before a format to indicate that the variable begins at the nth column, and nX can be used to skip n columns before reading the variable. When Tn is specified, variables named do not have to follow the order of the variables in the data.

Syntax Reference Guide DATA LIST 161

- For freefield data, variables are located according to the sequence in which they are named on DATA LIST. The order of variables on DATA LIST must correspond to the order of variables in the data.
- To include decimal positions in the format, specify the total width followed by a decimal point and the number of decimal positions. For example, (DOLLAR5) specifies a five-column DOLLAR format without decimal positions; (DOLLAR5.2) specifies a five-column DOLLAR format, two columns of which are decimal positions.

Numeric Formats

- Format specifications on DATA LIST are input formats. Based on the width specification and format type, SPSS generates output (print and write) formats for each variable. SPSS automatically expands the output format to accommodate punctuation characters such as decimal points, commas, dollar signs, or date and time delimiters. (SPSS does not automatically expand the output formats you assign on the FORMATS, PRINT FORMATS, and WRITE FORMATS commands. For information on assigning output formats, refer to these commands.)
- Scientific notation is accepted in input data with F, COMMA, DOLLAR, DOT, and PCT formats. The same rules apply to these formats as to E format. The values 1.234E3, 1.234+3, and 1.234E 3 are all legitimate. The last value (with a blank space) will cause freefield data to be misread and therefore should be avoided when LIST or FREE is specified.

Implied Decimal Positions

- For fixed-format data, decimal positions can be coded in the data or implied by the format. If decimal positions are implied but are not entered in the data, SPSS interprets the rightmost digits in each value as the decimal digits. A coded decimal point in a value overrides the number of implied decimal places. For example, (DOLLAR,2) specifies two decimal positions. The value 123 is interpreted as 1.23; however, the value 12.3 is interpreted as 12.3 because the coded decimal position overrides the number of implied decimal positions.
- For freefield data, decimal positions cannot be implied but must be coded in the data. If decimal positions are specified in the format but a data value does not include a decimal point, SPSS fills the decimal places with zeros. For example, with F3.1 format (three columns with one decimal place), the value 22 is displayed as 22.0. If a value in the data has more decimal digits than are specified in the format, the additional decimals are truncated in displayed output (but not in calculations). For example, with F3.1 format, the value 2.22 is displayed as 2.2 even though in calculations it remains 2.22.

Table 6 compares how values are interpreted for fixed and freefield formats. Values in the table are for a four-column numeric variable.

Table 6 Interpretation of values in fixed and freefield format

	Fixed		Freefield	
Values	Default	Two defined decimal places	Default	Two defined decimal places
2001	2001	20.01	2001.00	2001.00
201	201	2.01	201.00	201.00
-201	-201	-2.01	-201.00	-201.00
2	2	.02	2.00	2.00
20	20	.20	20.00	20.00
2.2	2.2	2.2	2.20	2.20
.201	.201	.201	.201	.201
2 01	Undefined	Undefined	Two values	Two values

Example

```
DATA LIST
   /MODEL 1 RATE 2-6(PCT,2) COST 7-11(DOLLAR) READY 12-21(ADATE).
BEGIN DATA
1935   7878811-07-1988
2 16754654606-08-1989
3 17684783612-09-1989
END DATA.
```

- Data are inline and in fixed format (the default).
- Each variable is followed by its column location. After the column location, a column-style format is specified in parentheses.
- *MODEL* begins in column 1, is one column wide, and receives the default numeric F format.
- *RATE* begins in column 2 and ends in column 6. The PCT format is specified with two decimal places. A comma is used to separate the format type from the number of decimal places. Decimal points are not coded in the data. Thus, SPSS reads the rightmost digits of each value as decimal digits. The value 935 for the first case in the data is interpreted as 9.35. Note that it does not matter where numbers are entered within the column width.
- *COST* begins in column 7 and ends in column 11. DOLLAR format is specified.
- *READY* begins in column 12 and ends in column 21. ADATE format is specified.

Example

```
DATA LIST FILE=DATA1
   /MODEL (F1) RATE (PCT5.2) COST (DOLLAR5) READY (ADATE10).
```

- In this example, the FILE subcommand is used because the data are in an external file.
- The variable definition is the same as in the preceding example except that FORTRAN-like format specifications are used rather than column-style. Column locations are not specified. Instead, the format specifications include a width for each format type.
- The width (w) portion of each format must specify the total number of characters in the widest value. DOLLAR5 format for *COST* accepts the five-digit value 78788, which dis-

plays as $78,788. Thus, the specified input format DOLLAR5 generates an output format DOLLAR7. SPSS automatically expands the width of the output format to accommodate the dollar sign and comma in displayed output.

String Formats

String (alphanumeric) variables can contain any numbers, letters, or characters, including special characters and imbedded blanks. Numbers entered as values for string variables cannot be used in calculations unless you convert them to numeric format (see RECODE). On DATA LIST, a string variable is defined with an A format if data are in standard character form or an AHEX format if data are in hexadecimal form. For further discussion of string formats, see "String Variable Formats" on p. 42.

- For fixed-format data, the width of a string variable is either implied by the column location specification or specified by the *w* on the FORTRAN-like format. For freefield data, the width must be specified on the FORTRAN-like format.
- The string formats defined on DATA LIST are both input and output formats. You cannot change the format of a defined string variable in SPSS. However, you can use the STRING command to define a new string variable and COMPUTE to copy the values from the old variable (see COMPUTE).
- AHEX format is available only for fixed-format data. Since each set of two hexadecimal characters represents one standard character, the width specification must be an even number. The output format for a variable in AHEX format is A format with half the specified width.
- If a string in the data is longer than its specified width, the string is truncated and a warning message is displayed. If the string in the data is shorter, it is right-padded with blanks and no warning message is displayed.
- For fixed-format data, all characters within the specified or implied columns, including leading, trailing, and imbedded blanks and punctuation marks, are read as the value of the string.
- For freefield data, string values in the data must be enclosed in apostrophes or quotation marks if the string contains a blank or a comma. Otherwise, the blank or comma is treated as a delimiter between values. Apostrophes can be included in a string by enclosing the string in quotation marks. Quotation marks can be included in a string by enclosing the string in apostrophes.

Example

```
DATA LIST FILE=WINS FREE /POSTPOS NWINS * POSNAME (A24).
```

- *POSNAME* is specified as a 24-character string. The asterisk preceding *POSNAME* indicates that *POSTPOS* and *NWINS* are read with the default format. If the asterisk was not specified, SPSS would apply the A24 format to *POSNAME* and then issue an error message indicating that there are more variables than specified formats.

Example

```
DATA LIST FILE=WINS FREE /POSTPOS * NWINS (A5) POSWINS.
```

- Both *POSTPOS* and *POSWINS* receive the default numeric format F8.2.
- *NWINS* receives the specified format of A5.

DEFINE—!ENDDEFINE

```
DEFINE macro name
 ([{argument name=} [!DEFAULT (string)] [!NOEXPAND] {!TOKENS   (n)                }]
  {!POSITIONAL=   }                                 {!CHAREND  ('char')          }
                                                    {!ENCLOSE  ('char', 'char')  }
                                                    {!CMDEND                     }

 [/{argument name=} ...])
  {!POSITIONAL=   }

macro body

!ENDDEFINE
```

SET command controls:

```
PRESERVE
RESTORE
```

Assignment:

```
!LET var=expression
```

Conditional processing:

```
!IF (expression) !THEN statements
   [!ELSE statements]
!IFEND
```

Looping constructs:

```
!DO !varname=start !TO finish [BY step]
   statements  [!BREAK]
!DOEND

!DO !varname !IN (list)
   statements  [!BREAK]
!DOEND
```

Macro directives:

```
!OFFEXPAND
!ONEXPAND
```

String manipulation functions:

```
!LENGTH (string)
!CONCAT (string1,string2
!SUBSTRING (string,from,[length])
!INDEX (string1,string2)
!HEAD (string)
!TAIL (string)
!QUOTE (string)
!UNQUOTE (string)
!UPCASE (string)
!BLANKS (n)
!NULL
!EVAL (string)
```

Example:
```
DEFINE sesvars ().
  age sex educ religion.
!ENDDEFINE.
```

Overview

DEFINE—!ENDDEFINE defines an SPSS macro, which can then be used within a command sequence. A macro can be useful in several different contexts. For example, it can be used to

- Issue a series of the same or similar commands repeatedly, using looping constructs rather than redundant specifications.
- Specify a set of variables.
- Produce output from several SPSS procedures with a single command.
- Create complex input programs, procedure specifications, or whole sessions that can then be executed.

An SPSS macro is defined by specifying any part of a valid SPSS command and giving it a macro name. This name is then specified in a macro call within an SPSS command sequence. When SPSS encounters the macro name, it expands the macro.

In the examples of macro definition throughout this reference, the macro name, body, and arguments are shown in lower case for readability. Macro keywords, which are always preceded by an exclamation point (!), are shown in upper case. For additional examples of the macro facility in SPSS, see Appendix D.

Options

Macro Arguments. You can declare and use arguments in the macro definition and then assign specific values to these arguments in the macro call. You can define defaults for the arguments and indicate whether an argument should be expanded when the macro is called. (See pp. 169 to 176.)

Macro Directives. You can turn macro expansion on and off (see p. 176).

String Manipulation Functions. You can process one or more character strings and produce either a new character string or a character representation of a numeric result (see pp. 176 to 178).

Conditional Processing. You can build conditional and looping constructs (see p. 180).

Macro Variables. You can directly assign values to macro variables (see p. 182).

Basic Specification

All macros must start with the DEFINE command and end with the macro command !ENDDEFINE. These commands identify the beginning and end of a macro definition and are used to separate the macro definition from the rest of the command sequence.

Example

```
* Macro without arguments: Specify a group of variables.

DEFINE sesvars ().
   age sex educ religion.
!ENDDEFINE.

FREQUENCIES VARIABLES=sesvars.
```

- The macro name is **sesvars**. Because the parentheses are empty, sesvars has no arguments. The macro body defines four variables: *AGE, SEX, EDUC,* and *RELIGION*.
- The macro call is specified on FREQUENCIES. When the call is executed, sesvars is expanded into variables *AGE, SEX, EDUC,* and *RELIGION*.
- After the macro expansion, FREQUENCIES is executed.

Example

```
* Macro without arguments: Repeat a sequence of commands.

DATA LIST FILE = MAC4D /GROUP 1    REACTIME 3-5 ACCURACY 7-9.
VALUE LABELS GROUP      1'normal'
                        2'learning disabled'.
* Macro definition.
DEFINE check ().
split file by group.
frequencies variables = reactime accuracy
  /histogram.
descriptives reactime accuracy.
list.
split file off.
regression variables = group reactime accuracy
  /dependent = accuracy
  /enter
  /scatterplot (reactime, accuracy).
!ENDDEFINE.

check.                     /* First call of defined macro check

COMPUTE REACTIME = SQRT (REACTIME).
COMPUTE ACCURACY = SQRT (ACCURACY).

check.                     /* Second call of defined macro check

COMPUTE REACTIME = lg10 (REACTIME * REACTIME).
COMPUTE ACCURACY = lg10 (ACCURACY * ACCURACY).

check.                     /* Third call of defined macro check
```

- The name of the macro is *CHECK*. The empty parentheses indicate that there are no arguments to the macro.
- The macro definition (between DEFINE and !ENDDEFINE) contains the command sequence to be repeated, SPLIT FILE, FREQUENCIES, DESCRIPTIVES, LIST, SPLIT FILE, and REGRESSION.

- Immediately after DEFINE, specify the **macro name**. All macros must have a name. The name is used in the macro call to refer to the macro. Macro names can begin with an exclamation point (!), but other than this follow the usual SPSS naming conventions. Starting a name with an ! ensures that it will not conflict with the other text or variables in the session.
- Immediately after the macro name, specify an optional **argument** definition in parentheses. This specification indicates the arguments that will be read when the macro is called. If you do not want to include arguments, specify just the parentheses; *the parentheses are required, whether or not they enclose an argument.*
- Next specify the body of the macro. The **macro body** can include SPSS commands, parts of SPSS commands, or macro statements (macro directives, string manipulation statements, and looping and conditional processing statements).
- At the end of the macro body, specify the !ENDDEFINE command.

To invoke the macro, issue a **macro call** in the command sequence. To call a macro, specify the macro name and any necessary arguments. If there are no arguments, only the macro name is required.

Operations

- When macros are used in a prompted session, the SPSS> prompt changes to DEFINE> between the DEFINE and !ENDDEFINE commands.
- When SPSS reads the macro definition, it translates into upper case all text (except arguments) not enclosed in quotation marks. Arguments are read in upper and lower case.
- The macro facility does not build and execute commands; rather, it expands strings in a process called **macro expansion**. A macro call initiates macro expansion. After the strings are expanded, the commands (or parts of commands) that contain the expanded strings are executed as part of the SPSS command sequence.
- Any elements on the macro call that are not used in the macro expansion are read and combined with the expanded strings.
- The expanded strings and the remaining elements from the macro call, if any, must conform to SPSS syntax rules. If not, SPSS generates either a warning or an error message, depending on the nature of the syntax problem.

Limitations

- The BEGIN DATA—END DATA commands are not allowed within a macro.
- The DEFINE command is not allowed within a macro.

- The macro is called three times. Every time check is encountered, it is replaced with the command sequence SPLIT FILE, FREQUENCIES, DESCRIPTIVES, LIST, SPLIT FILE OFF, and REGRESSION. The command sequence using the macro facility is identical to the command sequence in which the specified commands are explicitly stated three separate times.

Example

```
* Macro with an argument.

DEFINE myfreq (vars = !CHAREND('/')).
frequencies variables = !vars
  /format = notable
  /hbar = normal
  /statistics = default skewness kurtosis.
!ENDDEFINE.

myfreq vars = AGE SEX EDUC RELIGION /.
```

- The macro definition defines vars as the macro argument. In the macro call, four variables are specified as the argument to the macro myfreq. When SPSS expands the myfreq macro, it substitutes the argument, AGE, SEX, EDUC, and RELIGION, for !vars and executes the resulting commands.

Macro Arguments

The macro definition can include macro arguments, which can be assigned specific values in the macro call. There are two types of arguments: keyword and positional. *Keyword arguments* are assigned names in the macro definition; in the macro call, they are identified by name. *Positional arguments* are defined after keyword !POSITIONAL in the macro definition; in the macro call, they are identified by their relative position within the macro definition.

- There is no limit to the number of arguments that can be specified in a macro.
- All arguments are specified in parentheses and must be separated by slashes.
- If both keyword and positional arguments are defined in the same definition, the positional arguments must be defined, used in the macro body, and invoked in the macro call before the keyword arguments.

Example

```
* A keyword argument.

DEFINE macname (arg1 = !TOKENS(1)).
frequencies variables = !arg1.
!ENDDEFINE.

macname arg1 = V1.
```

- The macro definition defines macname as the macro name and arg1 as the argument. arg1 has one token and can be assigned any value in the macro call.

- The macro call expands the macname macro. The argument is identified by its name, arg1, and is assigned the value V1. V1 is substituted wherever !arg1 appears in the macro body. The macro body in this example is the FREQUENCIES command.

Example

```
* A positional argument.

DEFINE macname (!POSITIONAL !TOKENS(1)
              /!POSITIONAL !TOKENS(2)).
frequencies variables = !1 !2.
!ENDDEFINE.

macname V1 V2 V3.
```

- The macro definition defines macname as the macro name with two positional arguments. The first argument has one token and the second argument has two tokens. The tokens can be assigned any values in the macro call.
- The macro call expands the macname macro. The arguments are identified by their positions. V1 is substituted for !1 wherever !1 appears in the macro body. V2 and V3 are substituted for !2 wherever !2 appears in the macro body. The macro body in this example is the FREQUENCIES command.

Keyword Arguments

Keyword arguments are called with user-defined keywords that can be specified in any order. In the macro body, the argument name is preceded by an exclamation point. On the macro call, the argument is specified without the exclamation point.

- Keyword argument definitions contain the argument name, an equals sign, and the !TOKENS, !ENCLOSE, !CHAREND, or !CMDEND keyword (see "Assigning Tokens to Arguments" on p. 172).
- Argument names are limited to seven characters and cannot match the character portion of a macro keyword, such as DEFINE, TOKENS, CHAREND, and so forth. See the syntax chart on p. 165 for a list of SPSS macro keywords.
- The keyword !POSITIONAL cannot be used in keyword argument definitions.
- Keyword arguments do not have to be called in the order they were defined.

Example

```
DATA LIST FILE=MAC / V1 1-2 V2 4-5 V3 7-8.

* Macro definition.
DEFINE macdef2 (arg1 = !TOKENS(1)
              /arg2 = !TOKENS(1)
              /arg3 = !TOKENS(1)).
frequencies  variables = !arg1 !arg2 !arg3.
!ENDDEFINE.

* Macro call.
macdef2 arg1=V1   arg2=V2   arg3=V3.
macdef2 arg3=V3   arg1=V1   arg2=V2.
```

- Three arguments are defined: arg1, arg2, and arg3, each with one token. In the first macro call, arg1 is assigned the value V1, arg2 is assigned the value V2, and arg3 is assigned the value V3. V1, V2, and V3 are then used as the variables in the FREQUENCIES command.
- The second macro call yields the same results as the first one. With keyword arguments, you do not need to call the arguments in the order they were defined.

Positional Arguments

Positional arguments must be defined in the order they will be specified on the macro call. In the macro body, the first positional argument is referred to by !1, the second positional argument defined is referred to by !2, and so on. Similarly, the value of the first argument in the macro call is assigned to !1, the value of the second argument is assigned to !2, and so on.

- Positional arguments can be collectively referred to in the macro body by specifying !*. The !* specification concatenates arguments, separating individual arguments with a blank.

Example

```
DATA LIST FILE=MAC / V1 1-2 V2 4-5 V3 7-8.

* Macro definition.
DEFINE macdef (!POS !TOKENS(1).
              /!POS !TOKENS(1).
              /!POS !TOKENS(1)).
frequencies variables = !1 !2 !3.
!ENDDEFINE.

* Macro call.
macdef   V1    V2    V3.
macdef   V3    V1    V2.
```

- Three positional arguments with one token each are defined. The first positional argument is referred to by !1 on the FREQUENCIES command, the second by !2, and the third by !3.
- When the first call expands the macro, the first positional argument (!1) is assigned the value V1, the second positional argument (!2) is assigned the value V2, and the third positional argument (!3) is assigned the value V3.
- In the second call, the first positional argument is assigned the value V3, the second positional argument is assigned the value V1, and the third positional argument is assigned the value V2.

Example

```
DEFINE macdef (!POS !TOKENS(3)).
frequencies variables = !1.
!ENDDEFINE.

macdef   V1    V2    V3.
```

- This example is the same as the previous one, except that it assigns three tokens to one argument instead of assigning one token to each of three arguments. The result is the same.

Example

```
DEFINE macdef (!POS !TOKENS(1)
              /!POS !TOKENS(1)
              /!POS !TOKENS(1)).
frequencies variables = !*.
!ENDDEFINE.

macdef   V1    V2    V3.
```

- This is a third alternative for achieving the macro expansion shown in the previous two examples. It specifies three arguments but then joins them all together on one FREQUENCIES command using the symbol !*.

Assigning Tokens to Arguments

A **token** is a character or group of characters that has a predefined function in a specified context. The argument definition must include a keyword that indicates which tokens following the macro name are associated with each argument.

- Any SPSS keyword, variable name, or delimiter (a slash, comma, etc.) is a valid token.
- The arguments for a given macro can use a combination of the token keywords.

!TOKENS (n)   *Assign the next* n *tokens to the argument.* The value *n* can be any positive integer and must be enclosed in parentheses. !TOKENS allows you to specify exactly how many tokens are desired.

!CHAREND ('char')   *Assign all tokens up to the specified character to the argument.* The character must be a one-character string specified in apostrophes and enclosed in parentheses. !CHAREND specifies the character that ends the argument assignment. This is useful when the number of assigned tokens is arbitrary or not known in advance.

!ENCLOSE ('char','char')   *Assign all tokens between the indicated characters to the argument.* The starting and ending characters can be any one-character strings, and they do not need to be the same. The characters are each enclosed in apostrophes and separated by a comma. The entire specification is enclosed in parentheses. !ENCLOSE allows you to group multiple tokens within a specified pair of symbols. This is useful when the number of tokens to be assigned to an argument is indeterminate, or when the use of an ending character is not sufficient.

!CMDEND   *Assign to the argument all the remaining text on the macro call, up to the start of the next command.* !CMDEND is useful for changing the defaults on an existing SPSS command. Since !CMDEND reads up to the next command, only the last argument in the argument list can be specified with !CMDEND. If !CMDEND is not the final argument, the arguments following !CMDEND are read as text.

Example

```
* Keyword !TOKENS.

DEFINE macname (!POSITIONAL !TOKENS (3)).
frequencies variables = !1.
!ENDDEFINE.

macname ABC DEFG HI.
```

- The three tokens following macname (ABC, DEFG, and HI) are assigned to the positional argument !1, and FREQUENCIES is then executed.

Example

```
* Keyword !TOKENS.

* Macro definition.
DEFINE earnrep (varrep = !TOKENS (1)).
sort cases by !varrep.
report variables = earnings
  /break = !varrep
  /summary = mean.
!ENDDEFINE.

* Call the macro three times.
earnrep varrep= SALESMAN.   /*First macro call
earnrep varrep = REGION.    /*Second macro call
earnrep varrep = MONTH.     /*Third macro call
```

- This macro runs a REPORT command three times, each time with a different break variable.
- The macro name is earnrep, and there is one keyword argument, varrep, which has one token.
- In the first macro call, the token SALESMAN is substituted for !varrep when the macro is expanded. REGION and MONTH are substituted for !varrep when the macro is expanded in the second and third calls.

Example

```
* Keyword !CHAREND'.

DEFINE macname (!POSITIONAL !CHAREND ('/')
               /!POSITIONAL !TOKENS(2)).
frequencies variables = !1.
correlations variables= !2.
!ENDDEFINE.

macname A B C D / E F.
```

- When the macro is called, all tokens up to the slash (A, B, C, and D) are assigned to the positional argument !1. E and F are assigned to the positional argument !2.

Example

```
* Keyword !CHAREND.

DEFINE macname (!POSITIONAL !CHAREND ('/')).
frequencies variables = !1.
!ENDDEFINE.

macname A B C D / E F.
```

- Although E and F are not part of the positional argument and not used in the macro expansion, SPSS still reads them as text and interprets them in relation to where the macro definition ends. In this example, macro definition ends after the expanded variable list (D). E and F are names of variables. Thus, E and F are added to the variable list and FREQUENCIES is executed with six variables: *A, B, C, D, E*, and *F*.

Example

```
* Keyword !ENCLOSE.

DEFINE macname (!POSITIONAL !ENCLOSE('(',')')).
frequencies variables = !1
  /statistics = default skewness.
!ENDDEFINE.

macname (A B C) D E.
```

- When the macro is called, the three tokens enclosed in parentheses, A, B, and C, are assigned to the positional argument !1 in the macro body.
- After macro expansion is complete, SPSS reads the remaining characters on the macro call as text. In this instance, the macro definition ends with keyword SKEWNESS on the STATISTICS subcommand. Adding variable names to the STATISTICS subcommand is not valid SPSS syntax. SPSS generates a warning message but is still able to execute the frequencies command. Frequency tables and the specified statistics are generated for variables *A, B*, and *C*.

Example

```
* Keyword !CMDEND'.

DEFINE macname (!POSITIONAL !TOKENS(2)
                /!POSITIONAL !CMDEND).
frequencies variables = !1.
correlations variables= !2.
!ENDDEFINE.

macname A B C D E.
```

- When the macro is called, the first two tokens following macname (A and B) are assigned to the positional argument !1. C, D, and E are assigned to the positional argument !2. Thus, the variables used for FREQUENCIES are *A* and *B*, and the variables used for CORRELATION are *C, D*, and *E*.

Example

```
* Incorrect order for !CMDEND.

DEFINE macname  (!POSITIONAL !CMDEND
                /!POSITIONAL !tokens(2)).
frequencies variables = !1.
correlations variables= !2.
!ENDDEFINE.

macname  A B C D E.
```

- When the macro is called, all five tokens, A, B, C, D, and E, are assigned to the first positional argument. No variables are included on the variable list for CORRELATIONS, causing SPSS to generate an error message. The previous example declares the arguments in the correct order.

Example

```
* Using !CMDEND.
SUBTITLE 'CHANGING DEFAULTS ON A COMMAND'.

DEFINE myfreq (!POSITIONAL !CMDEND ).
frequencies !1
   /statistics=default skewness   /* Modify default statistics.
!ENDDEFINE.

myfreq VARIABLES = A B /HIST.
```

- The macro myfreq contains options for the FREQUENCIES command. When the macro is called, myfreq is expanded to perform a FREQUENCIES analysis on variables *A* and *B*. The analysis produces default statistics and the skewness statistic, plus a histogram, as requested on the macro call.

Example

```
* Keyword arguments: Using a combination of token keywords.

DATA LIST FREE / A B C D E.
DEFINE macdef3 (arg1 = !TOKENS(1)
               /arg2 = !ENCLOSE ('(',')')
               /arg3 = !CHAREND('%')).
frequencies variables = !arg1  !arg2 !arg3.
!ENDDEFINE.
macdef arg1 = A   arg2=(B C)   arg3=DE %.
```

- Because arg1 is defined with the !TOKENS keyword, the value for arg1 is simply specified as A. arg2 is specified in parentheses, as indicated by !ENCLOSE. The value for arg3 is followed by a percent sign, as indicated by !CHAREND.

Defining Defaults

The optional !DEFAULT keyword in the macro definition establishes default settings for arguments.

!DEFAULT *Default argument.* After !DEFAULT, specify the value you want to use as a default for that argument. A default can be specified for each argument.

Example

```
DEFINE macdef (arg1 = !DEFAULT (V1) !TOKENS(1)
              /arg2 = !TOKENS(1)
              /arg3 = !TOKENS(1)).
frequencies variables = !arg1 !arg2 !arg3.
!ENDDEFINE.

macdef arg2=V2  arg3=V3.
```

- V1 is defined as the default value for argument arg1. Since arg1 is not specified on the macro call, it is set to V1.
- If !DEFAULT (V1) were not specified, the value of arg1 would be set to a null string.

Controlling Expansion

!NOEXPAND indicates that an argument should not be expanded when the macro is called.

!NOEXPAND *Do not expand the specified argument.* !NOEXPAND applies to a single argument and is useful only when a macro calls another macro (imbedded macros).

Macro Directives

!ONEXPAND and !OFFEXPAND determine whether macro expansion is on or off. !ONEXPAND activates macro expansion and !OFFEXPAND stops macro expansion. All symbols between !OFFEXPAND and !ONEXPAND in the macro definition will not be expanded when the macro is called.

!ONEXPAND *Turn macro expansion on.*

!OFFEXPAND *Turn macro expansion off.* !OFFEXPAND is effective only when SET MEXPAND is ON (the default).

Macro Expansion in Comments

When macro expansion is on, a macro is expanded when its name is specified in a comment line beginning with *. To use a macro name in a comment, specify the comment within slashes and asterisks (/* ...*/) to avoid unwanted macro expansion. (See COMMENT.)

String Manipulation Functions

String manipulation functions process one or more character strings and produce either a new character string or a character representation of a numeric result.

- The result of any string manipulation function is treated as a character string.

- The arguments to string manipulation functions can be strings, variables, or even other macros. A macro argument or another function can be used in place of a string.
- The strings within string manipulation functions must be either single tokens, such as ABC, or delimited by apostrophes or quotation marks, as in 'A B C'. See Table 7 for a set of expressions and their results.

Table 7 Expressions and results

Expression	Result
!UPCASE(abc)	ABC
!UPCASE('abc')	ABC
!UPCASE(a b c)	error
!UPCASE('a b c')	A B C
!UPCASE(a/b/c)	error
!UPCASE('a/b/c')	A/B/C
!UPCASE(!CONCAT(a,b,c))	ABC
!UPCASE(!CONCAT('a','b','c'))	ABC
!UPCASE(!CONCAT(a, b, c))	ABC
!UPCASE(!CONCAT('a ','b ','c '))	A B C
!UPCASE(!CONCAT('a,b,c'))	A,B,C
!QUOTE(abc)	'ABC'
!QUOTE('abc')	abc
!QUOTE('Bill"s')	'Bill"s'
!QUOTE("Bill's")	"Bill's"
!QUOTE(Bill's)	error
!QUOTE(!UNQUOTE('Bill"s'))	'Bill"s'

!LENGTH (str)   *Return the length of the specified string.* The result is a character representation of the string length. !LENGTH(abcdef) returns 6. If the string is specified with apostrophes around it, each apostrophe adds 1 to the length. !LENGTH ('abcdef') returns 8. If an argument is used in place of a string and it is set to null, this function will return 0.

!CONCAT(str1,str2 . . .)   *Return a string that is the concatenation of the strings.* For example, !CONCAT (abc,def) returns abcdef.

!SUBSTRING (str,from,[length])   *Return a substring of the specified string.* The substring starts at the *from* position and continues for the specified *length*. If the length is not specified, the substring ends at the end of the input string. For example, !SUBSTRING (abcdef, 3, 2) returns cd.

!INDEX (haystack,needle)   *Return the position of the first occurrence of the needle in the haystack.* If the needle is not found in the haystack, the function returns 0. !INDEX (abcdef,def) returns 4.

!HEAD (str)   *Return the first token within a string.* The input string is not changed. !HEAD ('a b c') returns a.

!TAIL (str)   *Return all tokens except the head token.* The input string is not changed. !TAIL('a b c') returns b c.

!QUOTE (str)   *Put apostrophes around the argument.* !QUOTE replicates any imbedded apostrophe. !QUOTE(abc) returns 'abc'. If !1 equals Bill's, !QUOTE(!1) returns 'Bill''s'.

!UNQUOTE (str)   *Remove quotes and apostrophes from the enclosed string.* If !1 equals 'abc', !UNQUOTE(!1) is abc. Internal paired quotes are unpaired; if !1 equals 'Bill''s', !UNQUOTE(!1) is Bill's. The specification !UNQUOTE(!QUOTE(Bill)) returns Bill.

!UPCASE (str)   *Convert all lowercase characters in the argument to uppercase.* !UPCASE('abc def') returns ABC DEF.

!BLANKS (n)   *Generate a string containing the specified number of blanks.* The *n* specification must be a positive integer. !BLANKS(5) returns a string of five blank spaces. Unless the blanks are quoted, they cannot be processed, since the macro facility compresses blanks.

!NULL   *Generate a string of length 0.* This can help determine whether an argument was ever assigned a value, as in !IF (!1 !EQ !NULL) !THEN . . . .

!EVAL (str)   *Scan the argument for macro calls.* During macro definition, an argument to a function or an operand in an expression is not scanned for possible macro calls unless the !EVAL function is used. It returns a string that is the expansion of its argument. For example, if mac1 is a macro, then !EVAL(mac1) returns the expansion of mac1. If mac1 is not a macro, !EVAL(mac1) returns mac1.

SET Subcommands for Use with Macro

Four subcommands on the SET command were designed for use with the macro facility.

MPRINT   *Display a list of commands after macro expansion.* The specification on MPRINT is YES or NO (alias ON or OFF). By default, the output does not include a list of commands after macro expansion (MPRINT NO). The MPRINT subcommand on SET is independent of the PRINTBACK command.

MEXPAND   *Macro expansion.* The specification on MEXPAND is YES or NO (alias ON or OFF). By default, MEXPAND is on. SET MEXPAND OFF prevents macro expansion. Specifying SET MEXPAND ON reestablishes macro expansion.

MNEST   *Maximum nesting level for macros.* The default number of levels that can be nested is 50. The maximum number of levels depends on storage capacity.

MITERATE   *Maximum loop iterations permitted in macro expansions.* The default number of iterations is 1000.

Restoring SET Specifications

The PRESERVE and RESTORE commands bring more flexibility and control over SET. PRESERVE and RESTORE are available generally within SPSS but are especially useful with macros.

- The settings of all SET subcommands—those set explicitly and those set by default (except MEXPAND)—are saved with PRESERVE. PRESERVE has no further specifications.
- With RESTORE, all SET subcommands are changed to what they were when the PRESERVE command was executed. RESTORE has no further specifications.
- PRESERVE...RESTORE sequences can be nested up to five levels.

PRESERVE   *Store the SET specifications that are in effect at this point in the SPSS session.*

RESTORE   *Restore the SET specifications to what they were when PRESERVE was specified.*

Example

```
* Two nested levels of preserve and restore'.

DEFINE macdef ().
preserve.
set format F5.3.
descriptives v1 v2.
+ preserve.
set format F3.0 blanks=999.
descriptives v3 v4.
+ restore.
descriptives v5 v6.
restore.
!ENDDEFINE.
```

- The first PRESERVE command saves all the current SET conditions. If none have been specified, the default settings are saved.
- Next, the format is set to F5.3 and descriptive statistics for *V1* and *V2* are obtained.
- The second PRESERVE command saves the F5.3 format setting and all other settings in effect.
- The second SET command changes the format to F3.0 and sets BLANKS to 999 (the default is SYSMIS). Descriptive statistics are then obtained for *V3* and *V4*.
- The first RESTORE command restores the format to F5.3 and BLANKS to the default, the setting in effect at the second PRESERVE. Descriptive statistics are then obtained for *V5* and *V6*.
- The last RESTORE restores the settings in effect when the first PRESERVE was specified.

Conditional Processing

The !IF construct specifies conditions for processing. The syntax is as follows:

```
!IF (expression) !THEN statements
                [!ELSE statements]
!IFEND
```

- !IF, !THEN, and !IFEND are all required. !ELSE is optional.
- If the result of the expression is true, the statements following !THEN are executed. If the result of the expression is false and !ELSE is specified, the statements following !ELSE are executed. Otherwise, the program continues.
- Valid operators for the expressions include !EQ, !NE, !GT, !LT, !GE, !LE, !OR, !NOT, and !AND, or =, ~= (¬=), >, <, >=, <=, |, ~ (¬), and & (see "Relational Operators" on p. 54).
- When a macro is expanded, conditional processing constructs are interpreted after arguments are substituted and functions are executed.
- !IF statements can be nested whenever necessary. Parentheses can be used to specify the order of evaluation. The default order is the same as for transformations: !NOT has precedence over !AND, which has precedence over !OR.

Looping Constructs

Looping constructs accomplish repetitive tasks. Loops can be nested to whatever depth is required, but loops cannot be crossed. The macro facility has two looping constructs: the index loop (DO loop) and the list-processing loop (DO IN loop).

- When a macro is expanded, looping constructs are interpreted after arguments are substituted and functions are executed.

Index Loop

The syntax of an index loop is as follows:

```
!DO !var = start !TO finish [ !BY step ]
    statements
!BREAK
!DOEND
```

- !var is the indexing variable and must begin with an exclamation point.
- The start, finish, and step values must be numbers or expressions that evaluate to numbers.
- The loop begins at the start value and continues until it reaches the finish value (unless a !BREAK statement is encountered). The step value is optional and can be used to specify a subset of iterations. If start is set to 1, finish to 10, and step to 3, the loop will be executed four times with the index variable assigned values 1, 4, 7, and 10.
- The statements can be any valid SPSS commands or macro keywords. !DOEND specifies the end of the loop.
- !BREAK is an optional specification. It can be used in conjunction with conditional processing to exit the loop.

Example

```
DEFINE macdef (arg1 = !TOKENS(1)
              /arg2 = !TOKENS(1)).
!DO !i = !arg1 !TO !arg2.
frequencies variables = !CONCAT(var,!i).
!DOEND.
!ENDDEFINE.
macdef arg1 = 1 arg2 = 3.
```

- The variable *!i* is initially assigned the value 1 (arg1) and is incremented until it equals 3 (arg2), at which point the loop ends.
- The first loop concatenates var and the value for *!i*, which is 1 in the first loop. The second loop concatenates var and 2, and the third concatenates var and 3. The result is that FREQUENCIES is executed three times, with variables *VAR1, VAR2,* and *VAR3,* respectively.

List-Processing Loop

The syntax of a list processing loop is as follows:

```
!DO !var !IN (list)
    statements
!BREAK
!DOEND
```

- The !DO and !DOEND statements begin and end the loop. !BREAK is used to exit the loop.
- The !IN function requires one argument, which must be a list of items. The number of items in the list determines the number of iterations. At each iteration, the index variable *!var* is set to each item in the list.
- The list can be any expression, although it is usually a string. Only one list can be specified in each list-processing loop.

Example

```
DEFINE macdef (!POS !CHAREND('/') ).
!DO !i !IN ( !1).
frequencies variables = !i.
!DOEND.
!ENDDEFINE.
macdef VAR1 VAR2 VAR3  /.
```

- The macro call assigns three variables, *VAR1, VAR2,* and *VAR3,* to the positional argument !1. Thus, the loop completes three iterations.
- In the first iteration, *!i* is set to value *VAR1*. In the second and third iterations, *!i* is set to *VAR2* and *VAR3*, respectively. Thus, FREQUENCIES is executed three times, respectively with *VAR1, VAR2,* and *VAR3*.

Example

```
DEFINE macdef (!POS !CHAREND('/') ).
!DO !i !IN ( !1).
sort cases by !i.
report var = earnings
   /break = !i
   /summary = mean.
!DOEND.
!ENDDEFINE.

macdef SALESMAN REGION MONTH /.
```

- The positional argument !1 is assigned the three variables *SALESMAN*, *REGION*, and *MONTH*. The loop is executed three times and the index variable *!i* is set to each of the variables in succession. The macro creates three reports.

Direct Assignment of Macro Variables

The macro command !LET assigns values to macro variables. The syntax is as follows:

```
!LET !var = expression
```

- The expression must be either a single token or enclosed in parentheses.
- The macro variable *!var* cannot be a macro keyword (see the syntax chart on p. 165 for a list of macro keywords), and it cannot be the name of one of the arguments within the macro definition. Thus, !LET cannot be used to change the value of an argument.
- *!var* can be a new variable or one previously assigned by a !DO command or another !LET command.

Example

```
!LET !a = 1.
!LET !b = !CONCAT(ABC,!SUBSTR(!1,3,1),DEF).
!LET !c = (!2 ~= !NULL).
```

- The first !LET sets *!a* equal to 1.
- The second !LET sets *!b* equal to ABC followed by 1 character taken from the third position of !1 followed by DEF.
- The last !LET sets *!c* equal to 0 (false) if !2 is a null string or to 1 (true) if !2 is not a null string.

DESCRIPTIVES

```
DESCRIPTIVES [VARIABLES=] varname[(zname)] [varname...]

 [/MISSING={VARIABLE**}   [INCLUDE]]
           {LISTWISE  }

 [/SAVE]

 [/FORMAT={LABELS**}   {NOINDEX**}  {LINE**}]
          {NOLABELS}   {INDEX   }   {SERIAL}

 [/STATISTICS=[DEFAULT**]   [MEAN**]    [MIN**]   [SKEWNESS]]
              [STDDEV** ]   [SEMEAN]    [MAX**]   [KURTOSIS]
              [VARIANCE ]   [SUM   ]    [RANGE]   [ALL]

 [/SORT=[{MEAN    }]  [{(A)}]]
         {SMEAN   }    {(D)}
         {STDDEV  }
         {VARIANCE}
         {KURTOSIS}
         {SKEWNESS}
         {RANGE   }
         {MIN     }
         {MAX     }
         {SUM     }
         {NAME    }
```

**Default if the subcommand is omitted.

Example:
```
DESCRIPTIVES VARIABLES=FOOD RENT, APPL TO COOK, TELLER, TEACHER
  /STATISTICS=VARIANCE DEFAULT
  /MISSING=LISTWISE.
```

Overview

DESCRIPTIVES computes univariate statistics, including the mean, standard deviation, minimum, and maximum, for numeric variables. Because it does not sort values into a frequency table, DESCRIPTIVES is an efficient means of computing descriptive statistics for continuous variables. Other procedures that display descriptive statistics include FREQUENCIES, MEANS, and EXAMINE.

Options

Z Scores. You can create new variables that contain Z scores (standardized deviation scores from the mean) and add them to the working data file by specifying Z-score names on the VARIABLES subcommand or by using the SAVE subcommand.

Display Format. With the FORMAT subcommand you can display statistics in serial format and restrict the width to narrow format regardless of the width defined on SET. You can also control the display of variable labels and names.

Statistical Display. Optional statistics available with the STATISTICS subcommand include the standard error of the mean, variance, kurtosis, skewness, range, and sum. DESCRIPTIVES does not compute the median or mode (see FREQUENCIES or EXAMINE).

Display Order. You can list variables in ascending or descending alphabetical order or by the numerical value of any of the available statistics using the SORT subcommand.

Basic Specification

The basic specification is the VARIABLES subcommand with a list of variables. The actual keyword VARIABLES can be omitted. All cases with valid values for a variable are included in the calculation of statistics for that variable. Statistics include the mean, standard deviation, minimum, maximum, and number of cases with valid values.

Subcommand Order

- Subcommands can be used in any order.

Operations

- If a string variable is specified on the variable list, no statistics are displayed for that variable.
- The available width and the statistics and formats requested determine whether the statistics are displayed in tabular or serial form. If the width is insufficient to display the statistics requested, DESCRIPTIVES first truncates the variable label and then adopts serial format.

Limitations

- If there is insufficient memory available to calculate statistics for all variables requested, DESCRIPTIVES truncates the variable list.

Example

```
DESCRIPTIVES VARIABLES=FOOD RENT, APPL TO COOK, TELLER, TEACHER
  /STATISTICS=VARIANCE DEFAULT
  /MISSING=LISTWISE.
```

- DESCRIPTIVES requests statistics for variables *FOOD*, *RENT*, *TELLER*, *TEACHER*, and all the variables between and including *APPL* and *COOK* in the working data file.
- STATISTICS requests the variance and the default statistics: mean, standard deviation, minimum, and maximum.
- MISSING specifies that cases with missing values for any variable in the variable list will be omitted from the calculation of statistics for all variables.

Example

```
DESCRIPTIVES VARS=ALL.
```

- DESCRIPTIVES requests statistics for all variables in the working file.
- Because no STATISTICS subcommand is included, only the mean, standard deviation, minimum, and maximum are displayed.

VARIABLES Subcommand

VARIABLES names the variables for which you want to compute statistics. The actual keyword VARIABLES can be omitted.
- Keyword ALL can be used to refer to all user-defined variables in the working data file.
- Variables named more than once appear in the display more than once.
- Only one variable list can be specified.

Z Scores

The Z-score transformation standardizes variables to the same scale, producing new variables with a mean of 0 and a standard deviation of 1. These variables are added to the working data file.
- To obtain Z scores for all specified variables, use the SAVE subcommand.
- To obtain Z scores for a subset of variables, name the new variable in parentheses following the source variable on the VARIABLES subcommand and do not use the SAVE subcommand.
- Specify new names individually; a list in parentheses is not recognized.
- The new variable name can be any acceptable eight-character name that is not already part of the working data file.

Example

```
DESCRIPTIVES VARIABLES=NTCSAL NTCPUR (PURCHZ) NTCPRI (PRICEZ).
```

- DESCRIPTIVES creates Z-score variables named *PURCHZ* and *PRICEZ* for *NTCPUR* and *NTCPRI*, respectively. No Z-score variable is created for *NTCSAL*.

SAVE Subcommand

SAVE creates a Z-score variable for each variable specified on the VARIABLES subcommand. The new variables are added to the working data file.
- When DESCRIPTIVES creates new Z-score variables, it displays a table containing the source variable names, the new variable names, their labels, and the number of cases for which each Z-score variable is computed.

- DESCRIPTIVES automatically supplies variable names for the new variables. The new variable name is created by prefixing the letter *Z* to the first seven characters of the source variable name. For example, *ZNTCPRI* is the *Z*-score variable for *NTCPRI*.
- If the default naming convention duplicates variable names in the working data file, DESCRIPTIVES uses an alternative naming convention: first *ZSC001* through *ZSC099*, then *STDZ01* through *STDZ09*, then *ZZZZ01* through *ZZZZ09*, then *ZQZQ01* through *ZQZQ09*.
- Variable labels are created by prefixing *ZSCORE* to the first 31 characters of the source variable label. If the alternative naming convention is used, DESCRIPTIVES prefixes *ZSCORE(varname)* to the first 31 characters of the label. If the source variable does not have a label, DESCRIPTIVES uses *ZSCORE(varname)* for the label.
- If you specify new names on the VARIABLES subcommand *and* use the SAVE subcommand, DESCRIPTIVES creates one new variable for each variable on the VARIABLES subcommand, using default names for variables not assigned names on VARIABLES.
- If at any time you want to change any of the variable names, whether those DESCRIPTIVES created or those you previously assigned, you can do so with the RENAME VARIABLES command.

Example

```
DESCRIPTIVES VARIABLES=ALL
   /SAVE.
```

- SAVE creates a *Z*-score variable for all variables in the working file. All *Z*-score variables receive the default name.

Example

```
DESCRIPTIVES VARIABLES=NTCSAL NTCPUR (PURCHZ) NTCPRI (PRICEZ)
   /SAVE.
```

- DESCRIPTIVES creates three *Z*-score variables named *ZNTCSAL* (the default name), *PURCHZ*, and *PRICEZ*.

Example

```
DESCRIPTIVES VARIABLES=SALARY86 SALARY87 SALARY88
   /SAVE.
```

- In this example the default naming convention would produce duplicate names. Thus, the names of the three *Z*-score variables are *ZSALARY8*, *ZSC001*, and *ZSC002*.

FORMAT Subcommand

FORMAT controls formatting options.
- By default, DESCRIPTIVES displays a 40-character variable label and the statistics for each variable on one line. If requested statistics do not fit in the available width, DESCRIPTIVES first truncates variable labels to 21 characters and then, if necessary, uses serial format.
- To view DESCRIPTIVES output on a computer monitor, you may need to reduce the output width to 80 columns on the SET WIDTH command. However, this will reduce the num-

ber of columns available for displaying statistics. You can make more space available for statistics by specifying the NOLABELS keyword to suppress variable labels and by specifying listwise deletion of missing values on the MISSING subcommand, which suppresses the column for valid number of cases.

LABELS *Display variable labels.* This is the default.

NOLABELS *Suppress variable labels.*

INDEX *Display reference indexes.* INDEX displays a positional and an alphabetic reference index following the statistical display. The index shows the page location in the output of the statistics for each variable. The variables are listed by their position in the working data file and alphabetically.

NOINDEX *Suppress reference indexes.* This is the default.

LINE *Displays statistics in line format.* In line format, statistics are displayed on the same line as the variable name. This is the default.

SERIAL *Displays statistics in serial format.* In serial format, statistics are displayed below the variable name, permitting larger field widths and more decimal digits for very large or very small numbers. DESCRIPTIVES automatically uses this format if the number of statistics requested does not fit in the column format.

Example

```
SET WIDTH=80.
DESCRIPTIVES VARIABLES=TEACHER FTEX FSALES SECRET
  /STATISTICS=ALL
  /FORMAT=INDEX SERIAL.
```

- SET WIDTH limits the output to 80 columns.
- FORMAT requests reference indexes and displays the statistics in serial-style format.

STATISTICS Subcommand

By default, DESCRIPTIVES displays the mean, standard deviation, minimum, and maximum. Use the STATISTICS subcommand to request other statistics.

- When you use STATISTICS, DESCRIPTIVES displays *only* those statistics you request.
- Keyword ALL obtains all statistics.
- You can specify keyword DEFAULT to obtain the default statistics without having to name MEAN, STDDEV, MIN, and MAX.
- The median and mode, which are available in FREQUENCIES and EXAMINE, are not available in DESCRIPTIVES. These statistics require that values be sorted, and DESCRIPTIVES does not sort values (the SORT subcommand does not sort values, it simply lists variables in the order you request).
- If you request a statistic that is not available, DESCRIPTIVES issues an error message and the command is not executed.

- The maximum column width for skewness, kurtosis, and their standard error is 10; the maximum width for mean, standard error of the mean, minimum, maximum, and range is 11; the maximum width for standard deviation is 12; the maximum width for variance is 13; the maximum width for sum is 14. These widths include a blank between statistics.
- Except for the minimum and maximum values, DESCRIPTIVES displays all statistics with three decimal positions if it can fit them into the maximum width. Large numbers are rounded to fit the column width. If the integer portion still exceeds the column width, DESCRIPTIVES uses scientific notation. Extremely small numbers are also displayed with scientific notation.

MEAN *Mean.*

SEMEAN *Standard error of the mean.*

STDDEV *Standard deviation.*

VARIANCE *Variance.*

KURTOSIS *Kurtosis and standard error of kurtosis.*

SKEWNESS *Skewness and standard error of skewness.*

RANGE *Range.*

MIN *Minimum observed value.*

MAX *Maximum observed value.*

SUM *Sum.*

DEFAULT *Mean, standard deviation, minimum, and maximum. These are the default statistics.*

ALL *All statistics available in DESCRIPTIVES.*

SORT Subcommand

By default, DESCRIPTIVES lists variables in the order they are specified on VARIABLES. Use SORT to list variables in ascending or descending alphabetical order of variable name or in ascending or descending order of numeric value of any of the statistics.

- If you specify SORT without any keywords, variables are sorted in ascending order of the mean.
- SORT can sort variables by the value of any of the statistics available with DESCRIPTIVES, but only those statistics specified on STATISTICS (or the default statistics) are displayed.

Only one of the following keywords can be specified on SORT:

MEAN *Sort by mean. This is the default when SORT is specified without keywords.*

SEMEAN *Sort by standard error of the mean.*

STDDEV *Sort by standard deviation.*

VARIANCE	*Sort by variance.*
KURTOSIS	*Sort by kurtosis.*
SKEWNESS	*Sort by skewness.*
RANGE	*Sort by range.*
MIN	*Sort by minimum observed value.*
MAX	*Sort by maximum observed value.*
SUM	*Sort by sum.*
NAME	*Sort by variable name.*

Sort order can be specified in parentheses following the specified keyword:

A *Sort in ascending order.* This is the default when SORT is specified without keywords.

D *Sort in descending order.*

Example

```
DESCRIPTIVES VARIABLES=A B C
 /STATISTICS=DEFAULT RANGE
 /SORT=RANGE (D).
```

- DESCRIPTIVES sorts variables *A*, *B*, and *C* in descending order of range and displays the mean, standard deviation, minimum and maximum values, range number of cases, and value labels.

MISSING Subcommand

MISSING controls missing values.

- By default, DESCRIPTIVES deletes cases with missing values on a variable-by-variable basis. A case with a missing value for a variable will not be included in the summary statistics for that variable, but the case *will* be included for variables where it is not missing.
- The VARIABLE and LISTWISE keywords are alternatives; however, each can be specified with INCLUDE.
- When either the keyword VARIABLE or the default missing-value treatment is used, DESCRIPTIVES reports the number of valid cases for each variable. It always displays the number of cases that would be available if listwise deletion of missing values had been selected.

VARIABLE *Exclude cases with missing values on a variable-by-variable basis.* This is the default.

LISTWISE *Exclude cases with missing values listwise.* Cases with missing values for any variable named are excluded from the computation of statistics for all variables.

INCLUDE *Include user-missing values.*

DISPLAY

```
DISPLAY [SORTED] [{NAMES**  }] [/VARIABLES=varlist]
                 {INDEX     }
                 {VARIABLES }
                 {LABELS    }
                 {DICTIONARY}

                 {[SCRATCH]  }
                 {[VECTOR]   }
                 {[MACROS]   }
                 {[DOCUMENTS]}
```

**Default if the subcommand is omitted.

Example:

```
DISPLAY SORTED DICTIONARY /VARIABLES=DEPT SALARY SEX TO JOBCAT.
```

Overview

DISPLAY exhibits information from the dictionary of the working data file. The information can be sorted, and it can be limited to selected variables.

Basic Specification

The basic specification is simply the command keyword, which displays an unsorted list of the variables in the working data file.

Syntax Rules

DISPLAY can be specified by itself or with one of the keywords defined below. NAMES is the default. To specify two or more keywords, use multiple DISPLAY commands.

NAMES *Variable names.* A list of the variables in the working data file is displayed. The names are not sorted and display in a compressed format, about eight names across the page. This is the default.

DOCUMENTS *Documentary text.* Documentary text is provided on the DOCUMENT command. No error message is issued if there is no documentary information in the working data file.

DICTIONARY *Complete dictionary information for variables.* Information includes variable names, labels, sequential position of each variable in the file, print and write formats, missing values, and value labels. Up to 60 characters can be displayed for variable and value labels.

INDEX *Variable names and positions.*

VARIABLES *Variable names, positions, print and write formats, and missing values.*

LABELS *Variable names, positions, and variable labels.*

SCRATCH	*Scratch variable names.*
VECTOR	*Vector names.*
MACROS	*Currently defined macros.* The macro names are always sorted.

Operations

- DISPLAY directs information to the output.
- If SORTED is not specified, information is displayed according to the order of variables in the working data file.
- DISPLAY is executed as soon as it is encountered in the command sequence, as long as a dictionary has been defined.

Example

```
GET FILE=HUB.
DISPLAY DOCUMENTS.
DISPLAY DICTIONARY.
```

- Each DISPLAY command specifies only one keyword. The first requests documentary text and the second requests complete dictionary information for the *HUB* file.

SORTED Keyword

SORTED alphabetizes the display by variable name. SORTED can precede keywords NAMES, DICTIONARY, INDEX, VARIABLES, LABELS, SCRATCH, or VECTOR.

Example

```
DISPLAY SORTED DICTIONARY.
```

- This command displays complete dictionary information for variables in the working data file, sorted alphabetically by variable name.

VARIABLES Subcommand

VARIABLES (alias NAMES) limits the displayed information to a set of specified variables. VARIABLES must be the last specification on DISPLAY and can follow any specification that requests information about variables (all except VECTOR, SCRATCH, DOCUMENT, and MACROS).

- The only specification is a slash followed by a list of variables. The slash is optional.
- If keyword SORTED is not specified, information is displayed in the order variables are stored in the working data file, regardless of the order variables are named on VARIABLES.

Example

```
DISPLAY SORTED DICTIONARY
 /VARIABLES=DEPT, SALARY, SEX TO JOBCAT.
```

- DISPLAY exhibits dictionary information only for the variables named and implied by keyword TO on the VARIABLES subcommand and sorts them alphabetically by variable name.

DOCUMENT

```
DOCUMENT text
```

Example:
```
DOCUMENT   This file contains a subset of variables from the
           General Social Survey data.  For each case it records
           only the age, sex, education level, marital status,
           number of children, and type of medical insurance
           coverage.
```

Overview

DOCUMENT saves a block of text of any length in an SPSS data file. The documentation can be displayed with the DISPLAY command.

When GET retrieves a data file, or when ADD FILES, MATCH FILES, or UPDATE is used to combine data files, all documents from each specified file are copied into the working file. DROP DOCUMENTS can be used to drop those documents from the working file. Whether or not DROP DOCUMENTS is used, new documents can be added to the working file with the DOCUMENT command.

Basic Specification

The basic specification is DOCUMENT followed by any length of text. The text is stored in the file dictionary when the data are saved in an SPSS data file.

Syntax Rules

- The text can be entered on as many lines as needed.
- Blank lines can be used to separate paragraphs.
- Multiple DOCUMENT commands can be used within the command sequence. However, the DISPLAY command cannot be used to exhibit the text from a particular DOCUMENT command. DISPLAY shows all existing documentation.

Operations

- The documentation and the date it was entered are saved in the data file's dictionary. New documentation is saved along with any documentation already in the working data file.
- If a DROP DOCUMENTS command *follows* a DOCUMENT command anywhere in the command sequence, the documentation added by that DOCUMENT command is dropped from the working file along with all other documentation.

Example

```
GET FILE=GENSOC /KEEP=AGE SEX EDUC MARITAL CHILDRN MED_INS.
FILE LABEL   General Social Survey subset.

DOCUMENT     This file contains a subset of variables from the
             General Social Survey data.  For each case it records
             only the age, sex, education level, marital status,
             number of children, and type of medical insurance
             coverage.

SAVE OUTFILE=SUBSOC.
```

- GET keeps only a subset of variables from file *GENSOC*. All documentation from file *GENSOC* is copied into the working file.
- FILE LABEL creates a label for the new working file.
- DOCUMENT specifies the new document text. Both existing documents from file *GENSOC* and the new document text are saved in file *SUBSOC*.

Example

```
GET FILE=GENSOC /KEEP=AGE SEX EDUC MARITAL CHILDRN MED_INS.

DROP DOCUMENTS.

FILE LABEL   General Social Survey subset.

DOCUMENT     This file contains a subset of variables from the
             General Social Survey data.  For each case it records
             only the age, sex, education level, marital status,
             number of children, and type of medical insurance
             coverage.

SAVE OUTFILE=SUBSOC.
```

- DROP DOCUMENTS drops the documentation from file *GENSOC* as data are copied into the working file. Only the new documentation specified on DOCUMENT is saved in file *SUBSOC*.

DO IF

```
DO IF [(]logical expression[)]
transformation commands
[ELSE IF [(]logical expression[)]]
transformation commands
[ELSE IF [(]logical expression[)]]
   .
   .
   .
[ELSE]
transformation commands
END IF
```

The following relational operators can be used in logical expressions:

Symbol	Definition	Symbol	Definition
EQ or =	Equal to	NE or <>[*]	Not equal to
LT or <	Less than	LE or <=	Less than or equal to
GT or >	Greater than	GE or >=	Greater than or equal to

---

* On ASCII systems (for example, UNIX, VAX, and all PC's) you can also use ~=; on IBM EBCDIC systems (for example, IBM 360 and IBM 370) you can also use ¬=.

The following logical operators can be used in logical expressions:

Symbol	Definition
AND or &	Both relations must be true
Or or |	Either relation can be true
Not[*]	Reverses the outcome of an expression

---

* On ASCII systems you can also use ~; on IBM EBCDIC systems you can also use ¬ (or the symbol above number 6).

Example:
```
DO IF (YRHIRED GT 87).
COMPUTE              BONUS = 0.
ELSE IF (DEPT87 EQ 3).
COMPUTE              BONUS = .1*SALARY87.
ELSE IF (DEPT87 EQ 1).
COMPUTE              BONUS = .12*SALARY87.
ELSE IF (DEPT87 EQ 4).
COMPUTE              BONUS = .08*SALARY87.
ELSE IF (DEPT87 EQ 2).
COMPUTE              BONUS = .14*SALARY87.
END IF.
```

Overview

The DO IF—END IF structure conditionally executes one or more transformations on subsets of cases based on one or more logical expressions. The ELSE command can be used within the structure to execute one or more transformations when the logical expression on DO IF is not true. The ELSE IF command within the structure provides further control.

The DO IF—END IF structure is best used for conditionally executing multiple transformation commands, such as COMPUTE, RECODE, and COUNT. IF is more efficient for executing a single conditional COMPUTE-like transformation. DO IF—END IF transforms data for *subsets* of cases defined by logical expressions. To perform repeated transformations on the *same* case, use LOOP—END LOOP.

A DO IF—END IF structure can be used within an input program to define complex files that cannot be handled by standard file definition facilities. See "Complex File Structures" on p. 202 for an example.

See END FILE for information on using DO IF—END IF to instruct SPSS to stop reading data before it encounters the end of the file or to signal the end of the file when creating data. See p. 155 for an example of using DO IF—END IF with END FILE to concatenate raw data files.

Basic Specification

The basic specification is DO IF followed by a logical expression, a transformation command, and the END IF command, which has no specifications.

Syntax Rules

- The ELSE IF command is optional and can be repeated as many times as needed.
- The ELSE command is optional. It can be used only once and must follow any ELSE IF commands.
- The END IF command must follow any ELSE IF and ELSE commands.
- A logical expression must be specified on the DO IF and ELSE IF commands. Logical expressions are not used on the ELSE and END IF commands.
- String values used in expressions must be specified in quotes and must include any leading or trailing blanks. Lowercase letters are considered distinguished from uppercase letters.
- To create a new string variable within a DO IF—END IF structure, you must first declare the variable on the STRING command.
- DO IF—END IF structures can be nested to any level permitted by available memory. They can be nested within LOOP—END LOOP structures, and loop structures can be nested within DO IF structures.

Logical Expressions

- Logical expression can be simple logical variables or relations, or they can be complex logical tests involving variables, constants, functions, relational operators, and logical operators. Logical expressions can use any of the numeric or string functions allowed in COMPUTE transformations (see COMPUTE).
- Parentheses can be used to enclose the logical expression itself and to specify the order of operations within a logical expression. Extra blanks or parentheses can be used to make the expression easier to read.
- Blanks (*not* commas) are used to separate relational operators from expressions.
- A relation can include variables, constants, or more complicated arithmetic expressions. Relations cannot be abbreviated. For example, the first relation below is valid; the second is not:

    Valid: (A EQ 2 OR A EQ 5)
    Not valid: (A EQ 2 OR 5)
- A relation cannot compare a string variable to a numeric value or variable, or vice versa. A relation cannot compare the result of a logical function (SYSMIS, MISSING, ANY, or RANGE) to a number.

Operations

- DO IF marks the beginning of the control structure and END IF marks the end. Control for a case is passed out of the structure as soon as a logical condition is met on a DO IF, ELSE IF, or ELSE command.
- A logical expression is evaluated as true, false, or missing. A transformation specified for a logical expression is executed only if the expression is true.
- Logical expressions are evaluated in the following order: functions, exponentiation, arithmetic operations, relations, and finally logical operators. (For strings, the order is functions, relations, and then logical operators.) When more than one logical operator is used, NOT is evaluated first, followed by AND and then OR. You can change the order of operations using parentheses.
- Numeric variables created within a DO IF structure are initially set to the system-missing value. By default, they are assigned an F8.2 format.
- New string variables created within a DO IF structure are initially set to a blank value and are assigned the format specified on the STRING command that creates them.
- If the transformed value of a string variable exceeds the variable's defined format, the value is truncated. If the value is shorter than the format, the value is right-padded with blanks.
- If WEIGHT is specified within a DO IF structure, it takes effect unconditionally.
- Commands like SET, DISPLAY, SHOW, and so forth specified within a DO IF structure are executed when they are encountered in the command file.
- The DO IF—END IF structure (like LOOP—END LOOP) can include commands such as DATA LIST, END CASE, END FILE, and REREAD, which define complex file structures.

Flow of Control

- If the logical expression on DO IF is true, the commands immediately following DO IF are executed up to the next ELSE IF or ELSE or END IF command. Control then passes to the first statement following END IF.
- If the expression on DO IF is false, control passes to the following ELSE IF command. Multiple ELSE IF commands are evaluated in the order they are specified until the logical expression on one of them is true. Commands following that ELSE IF command are executed up to the ELSE or END IF command, and control passes to the first statement following END IF.
- If none of the expressions are true on the DO IF or any of the ELSE IF commands, the commands following ELSE are executed and control passes out of the structure. If there is no ELSE command, a case goes through the entire structure with no change.
- Missing values returned by the logical expression on DO IF or on any ELSE IF cause control to pass to the END IF command at that point.

Missing Values and Logical Operators

When two or more relations are joined by logical operators AND and OR, SPSS always returns missing if all of the relations in the expression are missing. However, if any one of the relations can be determined, SPSS tries to return true or false according to the logical outcomes shown in Table 8. The asterisk indicates situations where SPSS can evaluate the outcome with incomplete information.

Table 8 Logical outcome

Expression	Outcome	Expression	Outcome
true AND true	= true	true OR true	= true
true AND false	= false	true OR false	= true
false AND false	= false	false OR false	= false
true AND missing	= missing	true OR missing	= true*
missing AND missing	= missing	missing OR missing	= missing
false AND missing	= false*	false OR missing	= missing

Example

```
DO IF  (YRHIRED LT 87).
RECODE RACE(1=5)(2=4)(4=2)(5=1).
END IF.
```

- The RECODE command recodes *RACE* for those individuals hired before 1987 (*YRHIRED* is less than 87). The *RACE* variable is not recoded for individuals hired in 1987 or later.
- The RECODE command is skipped for any case with a missing value for *YRHIRED*.

Example

```
DATA LIST     FREE / X(F1).
NUMERIC       #QINIT.
DO IF         NOT #QINIT.
+  PRINT EJECT.
+  COMPUTE      #QINIT = 1.
END IF.
PRINT         / X.

BEGIN DATA
1 2 3 4 5
END DATA.
EXECUTE.
```

- This example shows how to execute a command only once.
- The NUMERIC command creates scratch variable *#QINIT*, which is initialized to 0.
- The NOT logical operator on DO IF reverses the outcome of a logical expression. In this example, the logical expression is a numeric variable that takes only 0 (false) or 1 (true) as its values. The PRINT EJECT command is executed only once, when the value of scratch variable *#QINIT* equals 0. After the COMPUTE command sets *#QINIT* to 1, the DO IF structure is skipped for all subsequent cases. A scratch variable is used because it is initialized to 0 and is not reinitialized after each case.

ELSE Command

ELSE executes one or more transformations when none of the logical expression on DO IF or any ELSE IF commands is true.

- Only one ELSE command is allowed within a DO IF—END IF structure.
- ELSE must follow all ELSE IF commands (if any) in the structure.
- If the logical expression on DO IF or any ELSE IF command is true, SPSS ignores the commands following ELSE.

Example

```
DO IF (X EQ 0).
COMPUTE Y=1.
ELSE.
COMPUTE Y=2.
END IF.
```

- *Y* is set to 1 for all cases with value 0 for *X*, and *Y* is 2 for all cases with any other valid value for *X*.
- The value of *Y* is not changed by this structure if *X* is missing.

Example

```
DO IF  (YRHIRED GT 87).
COMPUTE             BONUS = 0.
ELSE.
IF  (DEPT87 EQ 1) BONUS = .12*SALARY87.
IF  (DEPT87 EQ 2) BONUS = .14*SALARY87.
IF  (DEPT87 EQ 3) BONUS = .1*SALARY87.
IF  (DEPT87 EQ 4) BONUS = .08*SALARY87.
END IF.
```

- If an individual was hired after 1987 (*YRHIRED* is greater than 87), *BONUS* is set to 0 and control passes out of the structure. Otherwise, control passes to the IF commands following ELSE.
- Each IF command evaluates every case. The value of *BONUS* is transformed only when the case meets the criteria specified on IF. Compare this structure with ELSE IF in the example on p. 201, which performs the same task more efficiently.

Example

```
* Test for listwise deletion of missing values.

DATA LIST / V1 TO V6 1-6.
BEGIN DATA
123456
    56
1 3456
123456
123456
END DATA.

DO IF NMISS(V1 TO V6)=0.
+   COMPUTE SELECT='V'.
ELSE
+   COMPUTE SELECT='M'.
END IF.

FREQUENCIES VAR=SELECT.
```

- If there are no missing values for any of the variables *V1* to *V6*, COMPUTE sets the value of *SELECT* equal to V (for valid). Otherwise, COMPUTE sets the value of *SELECT* equal to M (for missing).
- FREQUENCIES generates a frequency table for *SELECT*. The table gives a count of how many cases have missing values for one or more variables, and how many cases have valid values for all variables. Commands in this example can be used to determine how many cases are dropped from an analysis that uses listwise deletion of missing values. See pp. 124 and 344 for alternative ways to check listwise deletion of missing values.

ELSE IF Command

ELSE IF executes one or more transformations when the logical expression on DO IF is not true.

- Multiple ELSE IF commands are allowed within the DO IF—END IF structure.

- If the logical expression on DO IF is true, SPSS executes the commands immediately following DO IF up to the first ELSE IF. Then control passes to the command following the END IF command.
- If the result of the logical expression on DO IF is false, control passes to ELSE IF.

Example

```
STRING STOCK(A9).
DO IF (ITEM EQ 0).
COMPUTE STOCK='New'.
ELSE IF (ITEM LE 9).
COMPUTE STOCK='Old'.
ELSE.
COMPUTE STOCK='Cancelled'.
END IF.
```

- STRING declares string variable *STOCK* and assigns it a width of 9 characters.
- The first COMPUTE is executed for cases with value 0 for *ITEM*, and then control passes out of the structure. Such cases are not reevaluated by ELSE IF, even though 0 is less than 9.
- When the logical expression on DO IF is false, control passes to the ELSE IF command, where the second COMPUTE is executed only for cases with *ITEM* less than or equal to 9. Then control passes out of the structure.
- If the logical expressions on both the DO IF and ELSE IF commands are false, control passes to ELSE, where the third COMPUTE is executed.
- The DO IF—END IF structure sets *STOCK* equal to New when *ITEM* equals 0, to Old when *ITEM* is less than or equal to 9 but not equal to 0 (including negative numbers if they are valid), and to Cancelled for all valid values of *ITEM* greater than 9. The value of *STOCK* remains blank if *ITEM* is missing.

Example

```
DO IF (YRHIRED GT 87).
COMPUTE            BONUS = 0.
ELSE IF (DEPT87 EQ 3).
COMPUTE            BONUS = .1*SALARY87.
ELSE IF (DEPT87 EQ 1).
COMPUTE            BONUS = .12*SALARY87.
ELSE IF (DEPT87 EQ 4).
COMPUTE            BONUS = .08*SALARY87.
ELSE IF (DEPT87 EQ 2).
COMPUTE            BONUS = .14*SALARY87.
END IF.
```

- For cases hired after 1987, *BONUS* is set to 0 and control passes out of the structure. For a case that was hired before 1987 with value 3 for *DEPT87*, *BONUS* equals 10% of salary. Control then passes out of the structure. The other three ELSE IF commands are not evaluated for that case. This differs from the example on p. 200, where the IF command is evaluated for every case. The DO IF—ELSE IF structure shown here is more efficient.
- If Department 3 is the largest, Department 1 the next largest, and so forth, control passes out of the structure quickly for many cases. For a large number of cases or an SPSS com-

mand file that will be executed frequently, these efficiency considerations can be important.

Nested DO IF Structures

To perform transformations involving logical tests on two variables, you can use nested DO IF—END IF structures.

- There must be an END IF command for every DO IF command in the structure.

Example

```
DO IF  (RACE EQ 5).        /*Do whites
+   DO IF  (SEX EQ 2).     /*White female
+   COMPUTE SEXRACE=3.
+   ELSE.                  /*White male
+   COMPUTE SEXRACE=1.
+   END IF.                /*Whites done
ELSE IF (SEX EQ 2).        /*Nonwhite female
COMPUTE SEXRACE=4.
ELSE.                      /*Nonwhite male
COMPUTE SEXRACE=2.
END IF.                    /*Nonwhites done
```

- This structure creates variable *SEXRACE*, which indicates both the sex and minority status of an individual.
- An optional plus sign, minus sign, or period in the first column allows you to indent commands so you can easily see the nested structures.

Complex File Structures

Some complex file structures may require you to imbed more than one DATA LIST command inside a DO IF—END IF structure. For example, consider a data file that has been collected from various sources. The information from each source is basically the same, but it is in different places on the records:

```
111295100FORD      CHAPMAN AUTO SALES
121199005VW        MIDWEST VOLKSWAGEN SALES
11 395025FORD      BETTER USED CARS
11        CHEVY 195005     HUFFMAN SALES & SERVICE
11        VW    595020     MIDWEST VOLKSWAGEN SALES
11        CHEVY 295015     SAM'S AUTO REPAIR
12        CHEVY 210 20     LONGFELLOW CHEVROLET
  9555032 VW                HYDE PARK IMPORTS
```

In the above file, an automobile part number always appears in columns 1 and 2, and the automobile manufacturer always appears in columns 10 through 14. The location of other information, such as price and quantity, depends on both the part number and the type of automobile. The DO IF—END IF structure in the following example reads records for part type 11.

Example

```
INPUT PROGRAM.
DATA LIST FILE=CARPARTS /PARTNO 1-2 KIND 10-14 (A).

DO IF (PARTNO EQ 11 AND KIND EQ 'FORD').
+ REREAD.
+ DATA LIST /PRICE 3-6 (2) QUANTITY 7-9 BUYER 20-43 (A).
+ END CASE.

ELSE IF (PARTNO EQ 11 AND (KIND EQ 'CHEVY' OR KIND EQ 'VW')).
+ REREAD.
+ DATA LIST /PRICE 15-18 (2) QUANTITY 19-21 BUYER 30-53 (A).
+ END CASE.
END IF.
END INPUT PROGRAM.

PRINT FORMATS PRICE (DOLLAR6.2).
PRINT /PARTNO TO BUYER.
WEIGHT BY QUANTITY.
DESCRIPTIVES PRICE.
```

- The first DATA LIST extracts the part number and the type of automobile.
- Depending on the information from the first DATA LIST, the records are reread, pulling the price, quantity, and buyer from different places.
- The two END CASE commands limit the working file to only those cases with Part 11 and automobile type Ford, Chevrolet, or Volkswagen. Without the END CASE commands, cases would be created in the working file for other part numbers and automobile types with missing values for price, quantity, and buyer.
- The results of the PRINT command are shown in Figure 2.

Figure 2   Printed information for part 11

```
11 FORD   $12.95 100 CHAPMAN AUTO SALES
11 FORD    $3.95  25 BETTER USED CARS
11 CHEVY   $1.95   5 HUFFMAN SALES & SERVICE
11 VW      $5.95  20 MIDWEST VOLKSWAGEN SALES
11 CHEVY   $2.95  15 SAM'S AUTO REPAIR
```

DO REPEAT—END REPEAT

```
DO REPEAT stand-in var={varlist    } [/stand-in var=...]
                     {value list}

transformation commands

END REPEAT [PRINT]
```

Example:

```
DO REPEAT R=REGION1 TO REGION5.
COMPUTE R=0.
END REPEAT.
```

Overview

The DO REPEAT—END REPEAT structure repeats the same transformations on a specified set of variables, reducing the number of commands you must enter to accomplish a task. This utility does not reduce the number of commands SPSS executes, just the number of commands you enter. To display the expanded set of commands SPSS generates, specify PRINT on END REPEAT.

DO REPEAT uses a *stand-in variable* to represent a *replacement list* of variables or values. The stand-in variable is specified as a place holder on one or more transformation commands within the structure. When SPSS repeats the transformation commands, the stand-in variable is replaced, in turn, by each variable or value specified in the replacement list.

The following commands can be used within a DO REPEAT—END REPEAT structure:

- Data transformations: COMPUTE, RECODE, IF, COUNT, and SELECT IF.
- Data declarations: VECTOR, STRING, NUMERIC, and LEAVE.
- Data definition: DATA LIST, MISSING VALUES (but not VARIABLE LABELS or VALUE LABELS).
- Loop structure commands: LOOP, END LOOP, and BREAK.
- Do-if structure commands: DO IF, ELSE IF, ELSE, and END IF.
- Print and write commands: PRINT, PRINT EJECT, PRINT SPACE, and WRITE.
- Format commands: PRINT FORMATS, WRITE FORMATS, and FORMATS.

Basic Specification

The basic specification is DO REPEAT, a stand-in variable followed by a required equals sign and a replacement list of variables or values, and at least one transformation command. The structure must end with the END REPEAT command. On the transformation commands, a single stand-in variable represents every variable or value specified in the replacement list.

Syntax Rules

- Multiple stand-in variables can be specified on a DO REPEAT command. Each stand-in variable must have its own equals sign and associated variable or value list and must be separated from other stand-in variables by a slash. All lists must name or generate the same number of items.
- Stand-in variables can be assigned any valid variable names: permanent, temporary, scratch, system, and so forth. A stand-in variable does not exist outside the DO REPEAT— END REPEAT structure and has no effect on variables with the same name that exist outside the structure. However, two stand-in variables cannot have the same name within the same DO REPEAT structure.
- A replacement *variable* list can include new or existing variables, and they can be string or numeric. Keyword TO can be used to name consecutive existing variables and to create a set of new variables. New string variables must be declared on the STRING command either before DO REPEAT or within the DO REPEAT structure. All replacement variable and value lists must have the same number of items.
- A replacement *value* list can be a list of strings or numeric values, or it can be of the form n_1 TO n_2, where n_1 is less than n_2 and both are integers. (Note that the keyword is TO, not THRU.)

Operations

- DO REPEAT marks the beginning of the control structure and END REPEAT marks the end. Once control passes out of the structure, all stand-in variables defined within the structure cease to exist.
- SPSS repeats the commands between DO REPEAT and END REPEAT once for each variable or value in the replacement list.
- Numeric variables created within the structure are initially set to the system-missing value. By default, they are assigned an F8.2 format.
- New string variables declared within the structure are initially set to a blank value and are assigned the format specified on the STRING command that creates them.
- If DO REPEAT is used to create new variables, the order in which they are created depends on how the transformation commands are specified. Variables created by specifying the TO keyword (for example, *V1* TO *V5*) are not necessarily consecutive on the working data file. See the PRINT subcommand on p. 207 for examples.

Example

```
DO REPEAT R=REGION1 TO REGION5.
COMPUTE R=0.
END REPEAT.
```

- DO REPEAT defines the stand-in variable *R*, which represents five new numeric variables: *REGION1*, *REGION2*, *REGION35*, *REGION4*, and *REGION5*.

- The five variables are initialized to 0 by a single COMPUTE specification that is repeated for each variable in the replacement list. Thus, SPSS generates five COMPUTE commands from the one specified.
- Stand-in variable *R* ceases to exist once control passes out of the DO REPEAT structure.

Example

```
* This example shows a typical application of INPUT PROGRAM, LOOP,
  and DO REPEAT. A data file containing random numbers is generated.
 INPUT PROGRAM.
+   LOOP #I = 1 TO 1000.
+     DO REPEAT RESPONSE = R1 TO R400.
+        COMPUTE RESPONSE = UNIFORM(1) > 0.5.
+     END REPEAT.
+     COMPUTE AVG = MEAN(R1 TO R400).
+     END CASE.
+   END LOOP.
+   END FILE.
END INPUT PROGRAM.

FREQUENCIES VARIABLE=AVG
 /FORMAT=CONDENSE
 /HISTOGRAM
 /STATISTICS=MEAN MEDIAN MODE STDDEV MIN MAX.
```

- The INPUT PROGRAM—END INPUT PROGRAM structure encloses an input program that builds cases from transformation commands.
- The indexing variable (*#I*) on LOOP—END LOOP indicates that the loop should be executed 1000 times.
- The DO REPEAT—END REPEAT structure generates 400 variables, each with a 50% chance of being 0 and a 50% chance of being 1. This is accomplished by specifying a logical expression on COMPUTE that compares the values returned by UNIFORM(1) to the value 0.5. (UNIFORM(1) generates random numbers between 0 and 1.) Logical expressions are evaluated as false (0), true (1), or missing. Thus, each random number returned by UNIFORM that is 0.5 or less is evaluated as false and assigned the value 0, and each random number returned by UNIFORM that is greater than 0.5 is evaluated as true and assigned the value 1.
- The second COMPUTE creates variable *AVG*, which is the mean of *R1* to *R400* for each case.
- END CASE builds a case with the variables created within each loop. Thus, the loop structure creates 1000 cases, each with 401 variables (*R1* to *R400*, and *AVG*).
- END FILE signals the end of the data file generated by the input program. If END FILE were not specified in this example, the input program would go into an infinite loop. No working file would be built, and SPSS would display an error message for every procedure that follows the input program.
- FREQUENCIES produces a condensed frequency table, histogram, and statistics for *AVG*. The histogram for *AVG* shows a normal distribution.

PRINT Subcommand

The PRINT subcommand on END REPEAT displays the commands generated by the DO REPEAT—END REPEAT structure. PRINT can be used to verify the order in which commands are executed.

Example

```
DO REPEAT Q=Q1 TO Q5/ R=R1 TO R5.
COMPUTE Q=0.
COMPUTE R=1.
END REPEAT PRINT.
```

- The DO REPEAT—END REPEAT structure initializes one set of variables to 0 and another set to 1.
- The output from the PRINT subcommand is shown in Figure 3. The generated commands are preceded by plus signs.
- The COMPUTE commands are generated in such a way that variables are created in alternating order: *Q1*, *R1*, *Q2*, *R2*, and so forth. If you plan to use the TO keyword to refer to *Q1* to *Q5* later, you should use two separate DO REPEAT utilities; otherwise, *Q1* to *Q5* will include four of the five *R* variables. Alternatively, use the NUMERIC command to predetermine the order in which variables are added to the working file, or specify the replacement value lists as shown in the next example.

Figure 3   Output from the PRINT subcommand

```
 2   0      DO REPEAT Q=Q1 TO Q5/ R=R1 TO R5
 3   0      COMPUTE Q=0
 4   0      COMPUTE R=1
 5   0      END REPEAT PRINT

 6   0      +COMPUTE Q1=0
 7   0      +COMPUTE R1=1
 8   0      +COMPUTE Q2=0
 9   0      +COMPUTE R2=1
10   0      +COMPUTE Q3=0
11   0      +COMPUTE R3=1
12   0      +COMPUTE Q4=0
13   0      +COMPUTE R4=1
14   0      +COMPUTE Q5=0
15   0      +COMPUTE R5=1
```

Example

```
DO REPEAT Q=Q1 TO Q5,R1 TO R5/ N=0,0,0,0,0,1,1,1,1,1.
COMPUTE Q=N.
END REPEAT PRINT.
```

- In this example, a series of constants are specified as a stand-in value list for *N*. All the *Q* variables are initialized first, and then all the *R* variables, as shown in Figure 4.

Figure 4 Output from the PRINT subcommand

```
 2   0           DO REPEAT Q=Q1 TO Q5,R1 TO R5/ N=0,0,0,0,0,1,1,1,1,1
 3   0           COMPUTE Q=N
 4   0           END REPEAT PRINT

 5   0           +COMPUTE Q1=0
 6   0           +COMPUTE Q2=0
 7   0           +COMPUTE Q3=0
 8   0           +COMPUTE Q4=0
 9   0           +COMPUTE Q5=0
10   0           +COMPUTE R1=1
11   0           +COMPUTE R2=1
12   0           +COMPUTE R3=1
13   0           +COMPUTE R4=1
14   0           +COMPUTE R5=1
```

Example

```
DO REPEAT R=REGION1 TO REGION5/ X=1 TO 5.
COMPUTE R=REGION EQ X.
END REPEAT PRINT.
```

- In this example, stand-in variable *R* represents the variable list *REGION1* to *REGION5*. Stand-in variable *X* represents the value list 1 to 5.
- The DO REPEAT—END REPEAT structure creates dummy variables *REGION1* to *REGION5* that equal 0 or 1 for each of 5 regions, depending on whether variable *REGION* equals the current value of stand-in variable *X*.
- PRINT on END REPEAT causes SPSS to display the commands generated by the structure, as shown in Figure 5.

Figure 5 Commands generated by DO REPEAT

```
2  0  DO REPEAT R=REGION1 TO REGION5/ X=1 TO 5
3  0  COMPUTE R=REGION EQ X
4  0  END REPEAT PRINT

5  0  +COMPUTE REGION1=REGION EQ 1
6  0  +COMPUTE REGION2=REGION EQ 2
7  0  +COMPUTE REGION3=REGION EQ 3
8  0  +COMPUTE REGION4=REGION EQ 4
9  0  +COMPUTE REGION5=REGION EQ 5
```

DROP DOCUMENTS

    DROP DOCUMENTS

Overview

When GET retrieves an SPSS data file, or when ADD FILES, MATCH FILES, or UPDATE are used to combine SPSS data files, all documents from each specified file are copied into the working file. DROP DOCUMENTS is used to drop these or any documents added with the DOCUMENT command from the working file. Whether or not DROP DOCUMENTS is used, new documents can be added to the working file with the DOCUMENT command.

Basic Specification

The only specification is DROP DOCUMENTS. There are no additional specifications.

Operations

- Documents are dropped from the working data file only. The original data file is unchanged, unless it is resaved.
- DROP DOCUMENTS drops all documentation, including documentation added by any DOCUMENT commands specified prior to the DROP DOCUMENTS command.

Example

```
GET FILE=GENSOC /KEEP=AGE SEX EDUC MARITAL CHILDRN MED_INS.

DROP DOCUMENTS.

FILE LABEL   General Social Survey Subset.
DOCUMENT     This file contains a subset of variables from the
             General Social Survey data.  For each case it records
             only the age, sex, education level, marital status,
             number of children, and type of medical insurance
             coverage.

SAVE OUTFILE=SUBSOC.
```

- DROP DOCUMENTS drops the documentation text from file *GENSOC*. Only the new documentation added with the DOCUMENT command is saved on file *SUBSOC*.
- The original file *GENSOC* is unchanged.

EDIT

This command is not available on all operating systems.

```
EDIT
```

Example:
```
EDIT.
GET FILE=QUERY.
RECODE ITEM1, ITEM2, ITEM3 (0=1) (1=0) (2=-1).
COMPUTE INDEXQ=(ITEM1 + ITEM2 + ITEM3)/3.
VARIABLE LABELS INDEXQ 'Summary Index of Questions'.
FREQUENCIES=ITEM1 ITEM2 ITEM3.
```

Overview

EDIT causes SPSS to evaluate a sequence of commands without actually running the commands. EDIT is available only for batch mode.

Syntax Rules

The minimum specification is simply the command keyword. EDIT has no additional specifications.

- EDIT can be positioned anywhere within the sequence of commands and checks all the commands that follow it.

Operations

- EDIT checks for syntax errors, and it checks to see if all variables used in the commands have been defined. EDIT will look for variable definitions in a specified SPSS data file, on a DATA LIST command, and on any commands that create variables.
- EDIT cannot determine whether a DATA LIST command correctly defines the data. It can only determine whether the syntax is correct.
- If the variable definitions are contained in an SPSS data file that is not available to SPSS for checking, you can replicate data definitions in the EDIT session by using the DATA LIST, NUMERIC, or STRING commands. The DATA LIST does not need to correspond exactly with the data, but it must name all the variables to be used in the remainder of the session in the same order and with the same format as the variables in the data file.
- If data are inline, the BEGIN DATA and END DATA commands must be in their appropriate positions within the sequence of commands. However, EDIT does not check the data records.
- EDIT reports when a string variable is used where a numeric variable is required and vice versa.

- Some SPSS procedures create variables such as standard scores and residuals and add them to the working data file. EDIT does not know about these variables and issues error messages when it encounters them in subsequent commands.
- EDIT *does not* detect every possible error. For example, it will not recognize that a computation is impossible.

Example

```
EDIT.
DATA LIST  FILE=HUBDATA RECORDS=3
 /1 EMPLOYID 1-5 MOHIRED YRHIRED 12-15 DEPT79 TO DEPT82 SEX 16-20
 /2 SALARY79 TO SALARY82 6-25 HOURLY81 HOURLY82 40-53(2)
     PROMO81 72 AGE 54-55 RAISE82 66-70
 /3 JOBCAT 6 NAME 25-48 (A).
LIST VARIABLES=MOHIRED YRHIRED DEPT82
     SALARY79 TO SALARY82 NAME /FORMAT=NUMBERED.
```

- EDIT ensures that syntax on DATA LIST and LIST is correct and that all variables specified on LIST have been defined.
- The DATA LIST and LIST commands are not executed and the data are not read.

Example

```
EDIT.
GET FILE=HUBDATA.
COMPUTE   CASESEQ2=CASESEQ+1.
LEAVE CASESEQ2.
PRINT FORMATS CASESEQ2 (F3).

SELECT IF DEPT82 EQ 4.
LIST VARIABLES=CASESEQ2 MOHIRED YRHIRED DEPT82
     SALARY79 TO SALARY82 NAME /FORMAT=NUMBERED.
```

- All commands following EDIT are checked for syntax and variable names.
- SPSS reads the dictionary of the *HUBDATA* data file (specified on the GET command) so that it can check variables used throughout the session.
- EDIT is able to recognize *CASESEQ2* when it is specified on the LIST command because *CASESEQ2* is defined on the COMPUTE command. However, *CASESEQ2* is not created.
- The commands in this session are not executed and the data are not read.

END CASE

```
END CASE
```

Example:
```
* Restructure a data file to make each data item into a single case.

INPUT PROGRAM.
DATA LIST /#X1 TO #X3 (3(F1,1X)).

VECTOR V=#X1 TO #X3.

LOOP #I=1 TO 3.
- COMPUTE X=V(#I).
- END CASE.
END LOOP.
END INPUT PROGRAM.
```

Overview

END CASE is used in an INPUT PROGRAM—END INPUT PROGRAM structure to signal that a case is complete. Control then passes to the commands immediately following the input program. After these commands are executed for the newly created case, SPSS returns to the input program and continues building cases by processing the commands immediately after the last END CASE command that was executed. For more information about the flow control in an input program, see INPUT PROGRAM—END INPUT PROGRAM.

END CASE is especially useful for restructuring files, either building a single case from several cases or building several cases from a single case. It can also be used to generate data without any data input (see p. 206 for an example).

Basic Specification

The basic specification is simply END CASE. There are no additional specifications.

Syntax Rules

- END CASE is available only within an input program and is generally specified within a loop.
- Multiple END CASE commands can be used within an input program. Each builds a case from the transformation and data definition commands executed since the last END CASE command.
- If no END CASE is explicitly specified, an END CASE command is implied immediately before END INPUT PROGRAM and the input program loops until an end-of-file is encountered or specified (see END FILE).

Operations

- When an END CASE command is encountered, SPSS suspends execution of the rest of the commands before the END INPUT PROGRAM command and passes control to the commands after the input program. After these commands are executed for the new case, control returns to the input program. SPSS continues building cases by processing the commands immediately after the most recent END CASE command. Use a loop to build cases from the same set of transformation and data definition commands.
- When multiple END CASE commands are specified, SPSS follows the flow of the input program and builds a case whenever it encounters an END CASE command, using the set of commands executed since the last END CASE.
- Unless LEAVE is specified, all variables are reinitialized each time the input program is resumed.
- When transformations such as COMPUTE, definitions such as VARIABLE LABELS, and utilities such as PRINT are specified between the last END CASE command and END INPUT PROGRAM, they are executed while a case is being initialized, not when it is complete. This may produce undesirable results (see the example beginning on p. 218).

Example

```
* Restructuring a data file to make each data item a single case.

INPUT PROGRAM.
DATA LIST /#X1 TO #X3 (3(F1,1X)).

VECTOR V=#X1 TO #X3.

LOOP #I=1 TO 3.
- COMPUTE X=V(#I).
- END CASE.
END LOOP.
END INPUT PROGRAM.

BEGIN DATA
2 1 1
3 5 1
END DATA.
FORMAT X(F1.0).
PRINT / X.
EXECUTE.
```

- The input program encloses the commands that build cases from the input file. An input program is required because END CASE is used to create multiple cases from single input records.
- DATA LIST defines three variables. In the format specification, the number 3 is a repetition factor that repeats the format in parentheses three times, once for each variable. The specified format is F1 and the 1X specification skips 1 column.
- VECTOR creates vector *V* with the original scratch variables as its three elements. The indexing expression on the LOOP command increments variable #I three times to control the number of iterations per input case and to provide the index for vector *V*.

- COMPUTE sets *X* equal to each of the scratch variables. END CASE tells SPSS to build a case. Thus, the first loop (for the first case) sets *X* equal to the first element of vector *V*. Since *V(1)* references *#X1*, and *#X1* is 2, the value of *X* is 2. Variable *X* is then formatted and printed before control returns to the command END LOOP. The loop continues, since indexing is not complete. Thus SPSS then sets *X* to *#X2*, which is 1, builds the second case, and passes it to the FORMAT and PRINT commands. After the third iteration, which sets *X* equal to 1, SPSS formats and prints the case and terminates the loop. Since the end of the file has not been encountered, END INPUT PROGRAM passes control to the first command in the input program, DATA LIST, to read the next input case. After the second loop, however, SPSS encounters END DATA and completes building the working data file.
- The six new cases are shown in Figure 6.

Figure 6 Outcome for multiple cases read from a single case

```
2
1
1
3
5
1
```

Example

```
*Restructuring a data file to create a separate case for
 each book order.

INPUT PROGRAM.
DATA LIST  /ORDER 1-4 #X1 TO #X22 (1X,11(F3.0,F2.0,1X)).

LEAVE ORDER.
VECTOR BOOKS=#X1 TO #X22.

LOOP #I=1 TO 21 BY 2 IF NOT SYSMIS(BOOKS(#I)).
- COMPUTE ISBN=BOOKS(#I).
- COMPUTE QUANTITY=BOOKS(#I+1).
- END CASE.
END LOOP.
END INPUT PROGRAM.
BEGIN DATA
1045 182 2 155 1 134 1 153 5
1046 155 3 153 5 163 1
1047 161 5 182 2 163 4 186 6
1048 186 2
1049 155 2 163 2 153 2 074 1 161 1
END DATA.

SORT CASES ISBN.
DO IF $CASENUM EQ 1.
- PRINT EJECT /'Order ISBN Quantity'.
- PRINT SPACE.
END IF.

FORMATS ISBN (F3)/ QUANTITY (F2).
PRINT /' ' ORDER ' ' ISBN '  ' QUANTITY.

EXECUTE.
```

- Data are extracted from a file whose records store values for an invoice number and a series of book codes and quantities ordered. For example, invoice 1045 is for four different titles and a total of nine books: two copies of book 182, one copy each of 155 and 134, and five copies of book 153. The task is to break each individual book order into a record, preserving the order number on each new case.
- The input program encloses the commands that build cases from the input file. They are required because the END CASE command is used to create multiple cases from single input records.
- DATA LIST specifies *ORDER* as a permanent variable and defines 22 scratch variables to hold the book numbers and quantities (this is the maximum number of numbers and quantities that will fit in 72 columns). In the format specification, the first element skips 1 space after the value for variable *ORDER*. The number 11 repeats the formats that follow it 11 times: once for each book number and quantity pair. The specified format is F3.0 for book numbers and F2.0 for quantities. The 1X specification skips 1 column after each quantity value.
- LEAVE preserves the value of variable *ORDER* across the new cases to be generated.
- VECTOR sets up vector *BOOKS* with the 22 scratch variables as its elements. The first element is *#X1*, the second is *#X2*, and so forth.
- If the element for vector *BOOKS* is not system-missing, LOOP initiates the loop structure that moves through vector *BOOKS*, picking off the book numbers and quantities. The indexing clause initiates the indexing variable *#I* at 1, to be increased by 2 to a maximum of 21.
- The first COMPUTE command sets variable *ISBN* equal to the element in vector *BOOKS* indexed by *#I*, which is the current book number. The second COMPUTE sets variable *QUANTITY* equal to the next element in vector *BOOKS*, *#I* +1, which is the quantity associated with the book number in *BOOKS(#I)*.
- END CASE tells SPSS to write out a case with the current values of the three variables: *ORDER*, *ISBN*, and *QUANTITY*.
- END LOOP terminates the loop structure and control is returned to the LOOP command, where *#I* is increased by 2 and looping continues until the entire input case is read or until *#I* exceeds the maximum value of 21.
- SORT CASES sorts the new cases by book number.
- The DO IF structure encloses a PRINT EJECT command and a PRINT SPACE command to set up titles for the output.
- FORMATS establishes dictionary formats for new variables *ISBN* and *QUANTITY*. PRINT displays the new cases.
- EXECUTE runs the commands. The output is shown in Figure 7.

Figure 7   PRINT output showing new cases

```
Order ISBN Quantity

1049    74   1
1045   134   1
1045   153   5
1046   153   5
1049   153   2
1045   155   1
1046   155   3
1049   155   2
1047   161   5
1049   161   1
1046   163   1
1047   163   4
1049   163   2
1045   182   2
1047   182   2
1047   186   6
1048   186   2
```

Example

```
* Create variable that approximates a log-normal distribution.

SET FORMAT=F8.0.

INPUT PROGRAM.
LOOP I=1 TO 1000.
+ COMPUTE SCORE=EXP(NORMAL(1)).
+ END CASE.
END LOOP.
END FILE.
END INPUT PROGRAM.

FREQUENCIES VARIABLES=SCORE /FORMAT=NOTABLE /HISTOGRAM
  /PERCENTILES=1 10 20 30 40 50 60 70 80 90 99
  /STATISTICS=ALL.
```

- The input program creates 1000 cases with a single variable *SCORE*. Values for *SCORE* approximate a log-normal distribution.

Example

```
* Restructure a data file to create a separate case for each
  individual.
INPUT PROGRAM.
DATA LIST  /#RECS 1 HEAD1 HEAD2 3-4(A).    /*Read header info
LEAVE  HEAD1 HEAD2.

LOOP  #I=1 TO #RECS.
DATA LIST  /INDIV 1-2(1).                  /*Read individual info
PRINT  /#RECS HEAD1 HEAD2 INDIV.
END CASE.                                  /*Create combined case
END LOOP.
END INPUT PROGRAM.
```

```
BEGIN DATA
1 AC
91
2 CC
35
43
0 XX
1 BA
34
3 BB
42
96
37
END DATA.
LIST.
```

- Data are in a file with header records that indicate the type of record and the number of individual records that follow. The number of records following each header record varies. For example, the 1 in the first column of the first header record (AC) says that only one individual record (91) follows. The 2 in the first column of the second header record (CC) says that two individual records (35 and 43) follow. The next header record has no individual records, indicated by the 0 in column 1, and so on.
- The first DATA LIST reads the expected number of individual records for each header record into temporary variable *#RECS*. *#RECS* is then used as the terminal value in the indexing variable to read the correct number of individual records using the second DATA LIST.
- Variables *HEAD1* and *HEAD2* contain the information in columns 3 and 4, respectively, in the header records. The LEAVE command retains *HEAD1* and *HEAD2* so that this information can be spread to the individual records.
- Variable *INDIV* is the information from the individual record. *INDIV* is combined with *#RECS*, *HEAD1*, and *HEAD2* to create the new case. Notice in the output from the PRINT command in Figure 8 that no case is created for the header record with 0 for *#RECS*.
- END CASE passes each case out of the input program to the LIST command. Without END CASE, the PRINT command would still display the cases as shown in Figure 8 because it is inside the loop. However, only one (the last) case per header record would pass out of the input program. The outcome for LIST will be quite different (compare Figure 9 with Figure 10).

Figure 8   PRINT output

```
1 A C 9.1
2 C C 3.5
2 C C 4.3
1 B A 3.4
3 B B 4.2
3 B B 9.6
3 B B 3.7
```

Figure 9　LIST output when END CASE is specified

```
HEAD1 HEAD2 INDIV

A     C     9.1
C     C     3.5
C     C     4.3
B     A     3.4
B     B     4.2
B     B     9.6
B     B     3.7
```

Figure 10　LIST output when END CASE is not specified

```
HEAD1 HEAD2 INDIV

A     C     9.1
C     C     4.3
X     X     .
B     A     3.4
B     B     3.7
```

Example

```
* Note: the following is an erroneous program! The COMPUTE and
  PRINT commands that follow END CASE are misplaced. They should
  be specified after the END INPUT PROGRAM command.

INPUT PROGRAM.
DATA LIST   /#X1 TO #X3 (3(F1,1X)).

VECTOR V=#X1 TO #X3.

LOOP #I=1 TO 3.
COMPUTE X=V(#I).
END CASE.
END LOOP.

COMPUTE Y=X**2.    /* This should be specified after the input program
VARIABLE LABELS X 'TEST VARIABLE' Y 'SQUARE OF X'.
PRINT FORMATS X Y (F2).
END INPUT PROGRAM.

BEGIN DATA
2 1 1
3 5 1
END DATA.

FREQUENCIES VARIABLES=X Y.
```

- No error or warning is issued for these commands, but the result is not what was intended. The computed value for *X* is passed out of the input program when the END CASE command is encountered. Thus, *Y* is computed from the initialized value of *X*, which is the system-missing value. As Figure 11 shows, all six cases computed for *Y* within the input program have the system-missing value, represented by a period (.).

- The frequencies table for *X* is as expected, because *X* is computed from inline data and no computation is done between END CASE and END INPUT PROGRM.
- The VARIABLE LABELS and PRINT FORMATS commands have their desired effects even though they are executed with the COMPUTE command, because they do not act on any data read in.
- Moving COMPUTE before END CASE will solve the problem, but the preferred solution is to specify END INPUT PROGRAM before all commands in the transformation program, since they operate on the cases created by the input program.

Figure 11 FREQUENCIES output

```
X         TEST VARIABLE

                                                VALID    CUM
    VALUE LABEL            VALUE  FREQUENCY  PERCENT  PERCENT  PERCENT

                             1         3       50.0     50.0    50.0
                             2         1       16.7     16.7    66.7
                             3         1       16.7     16.7    83.3
                             5         1       16.7     16.7   100.0
                                    -------  -------  -------
                           TOTAL      6       100.0    100.0

VALID CASES     6    MISSING CASES    0
- - - - - - - - - - - - - - - - - - - - - - - - - - - - - - - - - -

Y         SQUARE OF X

                                                VALID    CUM
    VALUE LABEL            VALUE  FREQUENCY  PERCENT  PERCENT  PERCENT

                             .         6      100.0   MISSING
                                    -------  -------  -------
                           TOTAL      6       100.0    100.0
```

END FILE

```
END FILE
```

Example:
```
INPUT PROGRAM.
DATA LIST FILE=PRICES /YEAR 1-4 QUARTER 6 PRICE 8-12(2).
DO IF (YEAR GE 1881).   /*Stop reading before 1881
END FILE.
END IF.
END INPUT PROGRAM.
```

Overview

END FILE is used in an INPUT PROGRAM—END INPUT PROGRAM structure to tell SPSS to stop reading data before it actually encounters the end of the file. END FILE can be used with END CASE to concatenate raw data files by causing SPSS to delay end-of-file processing until it has read multiple data files (see p. 155 for an example). END FILE can also be used with LOOP and END CASE to generate data without any data input (see p. 206 for an example).

Basic Specification

The basic specification is simply END FILE. There are no additional specifications. The end of file is defined according to the conditions specified for END FILE in the input program.

Syntax Rules

- END FILE is available only within an INPUT PROGRAM structure.
- Only one END FILE command can be executed per input program. However, multiple END FILE commands can be specified within a conditional structure in the input program.

Operations

- When END FILE is encountered, SPSS stops reading data and puts an end of file in the working data file it was building. The case that causes the execution of END FILE is not read. To include this case, use the END CASE command before END FILE (see examples below).
- END FILE has the same effect as the end of the input data file. It terminates the input program (see INPUT PROGRAM—END INPUT PROGRAM).

Example

```
*Select cases.

INPUT PROGRAM.
DATA LIST FILE=PRICES /YEAR 1-4 QUARTER 6 PRICE 8-12(2).

DO IF (YEAR GE 1881).   /*Stop reading before 1881
END FILE.
END IF.

END INPUT PROGRAM.

LIST.
```

- This example assumes that data records are entered chronologically by year. The DO IF—END IF structure specifies an end of file when the first case with a value of 1881 or later for *YEAR* is reached.
- LIST executes the input program and lists cases in the working data file. The case that causes the end of the file is not included in the working data file.
- As an alternative to an input program with END FILE, you can use N OF CASES to select cases if you know the exact number of cases. Another alternative is to use SELECT IF to select cases before 1881, but then SPSS would unnecessarily read the entire input file.

Example

```
Select cases but retain the case that causes end-of-file processing.

INPUT PROGRAM.
DATA LIST FILE=PRICES /YEAR 1-4 QUARTER 6 PRICE 8-12(2).

DO IF (YEAR GE 1881).   /*Stop reading before 1881 (or at end of file)
END CASE.               /*Create case 1881
END FILE.

ELSE.
END CASE.               /*Create all other cases
END IF.
END INPUT PROGRAM.

LIST.
```

- The first END CASE command forces SPSS to retain the case that causes end-of-file processing.
- The second END CASE indicates the end of case for all other cases and passes them out of the input program one at a time. It is required because the first END CASE command causes SPSS to abandon default end-of-case processing (see END CASE).

ERASE

```
ERASE FILE='file'
```

Example:
```
ERASE FILE='PRSNL.DAT'.
```

Overview

ERASE removes a file from a disk.

Basic Specification

The basic specification is the keyword FILE followed by a file specification. The specified file is erased from the disk. The file specification may vary from operating system to operating system, but enclosing the filename in apostrophes generally works.

Syntax Rules

- The keyword FILE is required but the equals sign is optional.
- ERASE allows one file specification only and does not accept wildcard characters. To erase more than one file, specify multiple ERASE commands.
- The file to be erased must be specified in full. ERASE does not recognize any default file extension.

Operations

ERASE deletes the specified file regardless of its type. No message is displayed unless the command cannot be executed. Use ERASE with caution.

Example

```
ERASE FILE 'PRSNL.DAT'.
```

- File *PRSNL.SAV* is deleted from the current directory. Whether it is an SPSS data file or a file of any other type makes no difference.

EXAMINE

```
EXAMINE VARIABLES=varlist [[BY varlist] [varname BY varname]]

 [/COMPARE={GROUPS**  }]
          {VARIABLES }

 [/SCALE={PLOTWISE**}]
         {UNIFORM   }

 [/{TOTAL**}]
   {NOTOTAL}

 [/ID={case number**}]
      {varname      }

 [/FREQUENCIES [FROM(initial value)] [BY(increment)]]

 [/PERCENTILES [[({5,10,25,50,75,90,95})=[{HAVERAGE }] [NONE]]
                 {value list          }   {WAVERAGE }
                                          {ROUND    }
                                          {AEMPIRICAL}
                                          {EMPIRICAL}

 [/PLOT=[STEMLEAF**] [BOXPLOT**] [NPPLOT] [SPREADLEVEL(n)] [HISTOGRAM]]
        [{ALL }]
         {NONE}

 [/STATISTICS=[DESCRIPTIVES**] [EXTREME({5})]]
                                       {n}
              [{ALL }]
               {NONE}

 [/MESTIMATOR=[{NONE**}]]
              {ALL   }

              [HUBER({1.339})] [ANDREW({1.34})]
                    {c    }           {c   }

              [HAMPEL({1.7,3.4,8.5})]
                     {a  ,b  ,c   }

              [TUKEY({4.685})]
                    {c    }

 [/MISSING=[{LISTWISE**}] [{EXCLUDE**}] [{NOREPORT**}]]
            {PAIRWISE  }   {INCLUDE  }   {REPORT    }
```

**Default if the subcommand is omitted.

Examples:

```
EXAMINE VARIABLES=ENGSIZE,COST.
EXAMINE VARIABLES=MIPERGAL BY MODEL,MODEL BY CYLINDERS.
```

Overview

EXAMINE provides stem-and-leaf plots, boxplots, robust estimates of location, tests of normality and other descriptive statistics and plots. Separate analyses can be obtained for subgroups of cases.

Options

Cells. You can subdivide cases into cells based on their values for grouping (factor) variables using the BY keyword on the VARIABLES subcommand.

Output. You can control the display of output using the COMPARE subcommand and the scale of plots using the SCALE subcommand. You can produce frequency tables and control their format with the FREQUENCIES subcommand. You can specify the computational method and break points for percentiles with the PERCENTILES subcommand, and you can assign a variable to be used for labeling outliers on the ID subcommand.

Plots. You can request stem-and-leaf plots, histograms, vertical boxplots, spread-and-level plots with the Levene test for homogeneity of variance, and normal and detrended probability plots with tests for normality. These plots are available through the PLOT subcommand.

Statistics. You can request univariate statistical output with the STATISTICS subcommand and maximum-likelihood estimators with the MESTIMATORS subcommand.

Basic Specification

- The basic specification is VARIABLES and at least one dependent variable.
- For each dependent variable named on VARIABLES, the default output includes univariate statistics (mean, median, standard deviation, standard error, variance, kurtosis, kurtosis standard error, skewness, skewness standard error, sum, interquartile range (IQR), range, minimum, maximum, and 5% trimmed mean), a vertical boxplot, and a stem-and-leaf plot. Outliers are labeled on the boxplot with the system variable *$CASENUM*.

Subcommand Order

Subcommands can be named in any order.

Limitations

When string variables are used as factors, only the first eight characters are used to form cells. String variables cannot be specified as dependent variables.

Example

```
EXAMINE VARIABLES=ENGSIZE,COST.
```

- *ENGSIZE* and *COST* are the dependent variables.
- EXAMINE produces univariate statistics, a vertical boxplot, and a stem-and-leaf plot for each dependent variable.

Example

```
EXAMINE VARIABLES=MIPERGAL BY MODEL,MODEL BY CYLINDERS.
```

- *MIPERGAL* is the dependent variable. The cell specification follows the first BY keyword. Cases are subdivided based on values of *MODEL* and also based on the combination of values of *MODEL* and *CYLINDERS*.
- Assuming there are three values for *MODEL* and two values for *CYLINDERS*, this example produces univariate statistics, boxplots, and stem-and-leaf plots for all cases considered together, for the three cells defined by *MODEL*, and for the six cells defined by *MODEL* and *CYLINDERS* together.

VARIABLES Subcommand

VARIABLES specifies the dependent variables and the cells. The dependent variables are specified first, followed by keyword BY and the variables that define the cells. Repeated models on the same EXAMINE are discarded.

- To create cells defined by the combination of values of two or more factors, specify the factor names separated by keyword BY.
- Each value of a factor produces at least one separate page of output. If factors are combined with keyword BY, each combination of values will also produce at least one page of output.

Caution. Large amounts of output can be produced if many cells are specified. If there are many factors or if the factors have many values, EXAMINE will produce a large number of separate analyses.

Example

```
EXAMINE VARIABLES=SALARY,YRSEDUC BY RACE,SEX,DEPT,RACE BY SEX.
```

- *SALARY* and *YRSEDUC* are dependent variables.
- Cells are formed first for the values of *RACE*, *SEX*, and *DEPT* individually and then by the combination of values for *RACE* and *SEX*.
- EXAMINE produces univariate statistics, a boxplot, and a stem-and-leaf plot for cases as a whole and for each cell specified. If *RACE* and *SEX* each have two possible values and *DEPT* has three possible values, this produces 1 page of output for cases as a whole, 2 pages for subgroups defined by *RACE*, 2 for *SEX*, 3 for *DEPT*, and 4 for *RACE* by *SEX*, for a total of 12 pages for each dependent variable, or 24 pages in all.

COMPARE Subcommand

COMPARE controls how boxplots are displayed. This subcommand is most useful if there is more than one dependent variable and at least one factor in the design.

GROUPS   *For each dependent variable, boxplots for all cells are displayed together.* With this display, comparisons across cells for a single dependent variable are easily made. This is the default.

VARIABLES *For each cell, boxplots for all dependent variables are displayed together.* With this display, comparisons of several dependent variables are easily made. This is useful in situations where the dependent variables are repeated measures of the same variable (see the following example) or have similar scales, or when the dependent variable has very different values for different cells, and plotting all cells on the same scale would cause information to be lost.

Example

```
EXAMINE VARIABLES=GPA1 GPA2 GPA3 GPA4 BY MAJOR   /COMPARE=VARIABLES.
```

- The four GPA variables are summarized for each value of *MAJOR*.
- COMPARE=VARIABLES groups the boxplots for the four GPA variables together for each value of *MAJOR*.

Example

```
EXAMINE VARIABLES=GPA1 GPA2 GPA3 GPA4 BY MAJOR /COMPARE=GROUPS.
```

- COMPARE=GROUPS groups the boxplots for *GPA1* for all majors together, followed by boxplots for *GPA2* for all majors, and so on.

SCALE Subcommand

SCALE controls whether boxplots, stem-and-leaf plots, and histograms are constructed on the same scale for each cell in the analysis.
- EXAMINE does not use a uniform scale for boxplots of separate dependent variables unless they are plotted in the same plot with COMPARE=VARIABLES.
- SCALE is ignored when SET HIGHRES=ON.

PLOTWISE *Construct scales according to the values in each plot.* Boxplots for each cell are constructed on the basis of the values of the dependent variable for cases in that plot only. This is the default.

UNIFORM *Display plots using a common scale.* Scales for boxplots and histograms are the same for each cell in the model. The common scale is constructed on the basis of the values of the dependent variable values of all cases.

Examples

```
EXAMINE VARIABLES=SALARY BY SEX
   /SCALE=UNIFORM.
```

- The stem-and-leaf plots for *SALARY* are plotted on the same scale for both values of *SEX*.

```
EXAMINE VARIABLES=SALARY BONUS BY SEX
   /COMPARE=VARIABLES
   /SCALE=UNIFORM.
```

- *SALARY* and *BONUS* are plotted in the same boxplot for each value of *SEX*. The scale is the same in each boxplot.

TOTAL and NOTOTAL Subcommands

TOTAL and NOTOTAL control the amount of output produced by EXAMINE when factor variables are specified.

- TOTAL is the default. By default, or when TOTAL is specified, EXAMINE produces statistics and plots for each dependent variable overall and for each cell specified by the factor variables.
- NOTOTAL suppresses overall statistics and plots.
- TOTAL and NOTOTAL are alternatives.
- NOTOTAL is ignored when the VARIABLES subcommand does not specify factor variables.

ID Subcommand

ID assigns a variable from the working data file to identify the cases in the output. By default the case number is used for labeling outliers and extreme cases in boxplots.

- The identification variable can be either string or numeric. If it is numeric, value labels are used to label cases. If no value labels exist, the values are used.
- Up to 25 characters of the identification variable are displayed.
- Only one identification variable can be specified.

Example

```
EXAMINE VARIABLES=SALARY BY RACE BY SEX /ID=LASTNAME.
```

- ID displays up to 25 characters of the value of *LASTNAME* for outliers and extreme cases in the boxplots.

FREQUENCIES Subcommand

The FREQUENCIES subcommand generates frequency tables. Two keywords are available:

FROM(value)   *The lowest value for the frequency table.* Frequency tables are generated for values between the cutoff value and the maximum value for the dependent variable. All cases with values smaller than the cutoff value are reported as one group in the first row of the table. The default is the minimum value.

BY(increment)   *The increment for frequency display.* The default increment is the same as that selected for stems in the stem-and-leaf plot. If the increment is 0, frequencies for each distinct value are produced.

- Each row in the frequency table is identified by its center value. All values below the cutoff value, if specified, are represented in the first row, which is identified with a less-than sign (<).

Example

```
EXAMINE VARIABLE=DEGREES
  /FREQUENCIES FROM (90) BY (10).
```

- FREQUENCIES produces a frequency table for the dependent variable *DEGREES*.
- The cutoff value for the frequency table is 90. If there are cases with values smaller than 90, they are reported as a group on the first row of the frequency table.
- BY specifies increments of 10. The first frequency bin contains all cases with values greater than or equal to 90 but less than 100. The midpoint of the bin is 95. The next bin contains all cases with values greater than or equal to 100 but less than 110, with a midpoint of 105.
- Frequencies continue in increments of 10 until the maximum value for *DEGREES* is included in a bin.

PERCENTILES Subcommand

PERCENTILES controls the method and break points for percentile computations. If PERCENTILES is omitted, no percentiles are produced. If PERCENTILES is specified without keywords, HAVERAGE is used with default break points of 5, 10, 25, 50, 75, 90, and 95.

- Values for break points are specified in parentheses following the subcommand.
- The method keywords for follow the specifications for break points.

In the following formulas, cases are assumed to be ranked in ascending order. The following notation is used: w is the sum of the weights for all nonmissing cases, p is the specified percentile divided by 100, i is the rank of each case, and X_i is the value of the ith case.

HAVERAGE   *Weighted average at* $X_{(w+1)p}$. The percentile value is the weighted average of X_i and X_{i+1} using the formula $(1-f)X_i + fX_{i+1}$, where $(w+1)p$ is decomposed into an integer part i and a fractional part f. This is the default if PERCENTILES is specified without a keyword.

WAVERAGE   *Weighted average at* X_{wp}. The percentile value is the weighted average of X_i and $X_{(i+1)}$ using the formula $(1-f)X_i + fX_{i+1}$, where i is the integer part of wp and f is the fractional part of wp.

ROUND   *Observation closest to* wp. The percentile value is X_i, where i is the integer part of $(wp + 0.5)$.

EMPIRICAL   *Empirical distribution function.* The percentile value is X_i when the fractional part of wp is equal to 0. The percentile value is X_{i+1} when the fractional part of wp is greater than 0.

AEMPIRICAL   *Empirical distribution with averaging.* The percentile value is $(X_i + X_{i+1})/2$ when the fractional part of wp equals 0. The percentile value is X_{i+1} when the fractional part of wp is greater than 0.

NONE   *Suppress percentile output.* This is the default if PERCENTILES is omitted.

Example

```
EXAMINE VARIABLE=SALARY /PERCENTILES(10,50,90)=EMPIRICAL.
```

- PERCENTILES produces the 10th, 50th, and 90th percentiles for the dependent variable *SALARY* using the EMPIRICAL distribution function.

PLOT Subcommand

PLOT controls plot output. The default is a vertical boxplot and a stem-and-leaf plot for each dependent variable for each cell in the model.
- Spread-and-level plots can be produced only if there is at least one factor variable on the VARIABLES subcommand. If you request a spread-and-level plot and there are no factor variables, SPSS issues a warning and no spread-and-level plot is produced.
- If you specify the PLOT subcommand, only those plots explicitly requested are produced.

BOXPLOT *Vertical boxplot.* The boundaries of the box are Tukey's hinges. The median is identified by an asterisk. The length of the box is the interquartile range (IQR) computed from Tukey's hinges. Values more than three IQR's from the end of a box are labeled as extreme (E). Values more than 1.5 IQR's but less than 3 IQR's from the end of the box are labeled as outliers (O).

STEMLEAF *Stem-and-leaf plot.* In a stem-and-leaf plot, each observed value is divided into two components—leading digits (stem) and trailing digits (leaf).

HISTOGRAM *Histogram.*

SPREADLEVEL(n) *Spread-and-level plot.* If the keyword appears alone, the natural logs of the interquartile ranges are plotted against the natural logs of the medians for all cells. If a power for transforming the data (*n*) is given, the IQR and median of the transformed data are plotted. If 0 is specified for *n*, a natural log transformation of the data is done. The slope of the regression line and the Levene test for homogeneity of variance are also displayed. The Levene test is based on the original data if no transformation is specified and on the transformed data if a transformation is requested.

NPPLOT *Normal probability and detrended probability plots.* NPPLOT calculates Shapiro-Wilk's statistic and a Kolmogorov-Smirnov statistic with a Lilliefors significance level for testing normality. Shapiro-Wilk's statistic is not calculated when the sample size exceeds 50.

ALL *All available plots.*

NONE *No plots.*

Example

```
EXAMINE VARIABLES=CYCLE BY TREATMNT /PLOT=NPPLOT.
```

- PLOT produces normal probability plots and detrended probability plots for each value of *TREATMNT*.

Example

```
EXAMINE VARIABLES=CYCLE BY TREATMNT /PLOT=SPREADLEVEL(.5).
```

- PLOT produces a spread-and-level plot of the medians and interquartile ranges of the square root of *CYCLE*. Each point on the plot represents one of the *TREATMNT* groups.

Example

```
EXAMINE VARIABLES=CYCLE BY TREATMNT /PLOT=SPREADLEVEL(0).
```

- PLOT generates a spread-and-level plot of the medians and interquartile ranges of the natural logs of *CYCLE* for each *TREATMENT* group.

Example

```
EXAMINE VARIABLES=CYCLE BY TREATMNT /PLOT=SPREADLEVEL.
```

- PLOT generates a spread-and-level plot of the natural logs of the medians and interquartile ranges of *CYCLE* for each *TREATMNT* group.

STATISTICS Subcommand

STATISTICS requests univariate statistics and determines how many extreme values are displayed. DESCRIPTIVES is the default. If you specify keywords on STATISTICS, only the requested statistics are displayed.

DESCRIPTIVES *Univariate statistics only.* This includes the mean, median, 5% trimmed mean, standard error, variance, standard deviation, minimum, maximum, range, interquartile range, skewness, skewness standard error, kurtosis, and kurtosis standard error. This is the default.

EXTREME(n) *The cases with the n largest and n smallest values.* If n is omitted, the five largest and five smallest values are displayed. Extreme cases are labeled with their values for the identification variable if the ID subcommand is used or with their values for the system variable *$CASENUM* if ID is not specified.

ALL *Univariate statistics and cases with the five largest and five smallest values.*

NONE *No univariate statistics or extreme values.*

Example

```
EXAMINE VARIABLE=FAILTIME /ID=BRAND
  /STATISTICS=EXTREME(10) /PLOT=NONE.
```

- STATISTICS identifies the cases with the 10 lowest and 10 highest values for *FAILTIME*. These cases are labeled with the first 15 characters of their values for variable *BRAND*. Univariate statistics are not displayed.

MESTIMATORS Subcommand

M-estimators are robust maximum-likelihood estimators of location. Four M-estimators are available. They differ in the weights they apply to the cases. MESTIMATORS with no keywords produces Huber's M-estimator with $c=1.339$; Andrews' wave with $c=1.34\pi$; Hampel's M-estimator with $a=1.7$, $b=3.4$, and $c=8.5$; and Tukey's biweight with $c=4.685$.

HUBER(c)	*Huber's M-estimator.* The value of weighting constant c can be specified in parentheses following the keyword. The default is $c=1.339$.
ANDREW(c)	*Andrews' wave estimator.* The value of weighting constant c can be specified in parentheses following the keyword. Constants are multiplied by π. The default is 1.34π.
HAMPEL(a,b,c)	*Hampel's M-estimator.* The values of weighting constants a, b, and c can be specified in order in parentheses following the keyword. The default values are $a=1.7$, $b=3.4$, and $c=8.5$.
TUKEY(c)	*Tukey's biweight estimator.* The value of weighting constant c can be specified in parentheses following the keyword. The default is $c=4.685$.
ALL	*All four above M-estimators.* This is the default when MESTIMATORS is specified with no keyword. The default values for weighting constants are used.
NONE	*No M-estimators.* This is the default if MESTIMATORS is omitted.

Example

```
EXAMINE VARIABLE=CASTTEST /MESTIMATORS.
```

- MESTIMATORS generates all four M-estimators computed with the default constants.

Example

```
EXAMINE VARIABLE=CASTTEST /MESTIMATORS=HAMPELS(2,4,8).
```

- MESTIMATOR produces Hampel's M-estimator with weighting constants $a=2$, $b=4$, and $c=8$.

MISSING Subcommand

MISSING controls the processing of missing values in the analysis. The default is LISTWISE, EXCLUDE, and NOREPORT.

- LISTWISE and PAIRWISE are alternatives and apply to all variables. They are modified for dependent variables by INCLUDE/EXCLUDE and for factor variables by REPORT/NOREPORT.
- INCLUDE and EXCLUDE are alternatives; they apply only to dependent variables.
- REPORT and NOREPORTare alternatives; they determine if missing values for factor variables are treated as valid categories.

LISTWISE	*Delete cases with missing values listwise.* A case with missing values for any dependent variable or any factor in the model specification is excluded from statistics and plots unless modified by INCLUDE or REPORT. This is the default.
PAIRWISE	*Delete cases with missing values pairwise.* A case is deleted from the analysis only if it has a missing value for the dependent variable or factor being analyzed.

EXCLUDE *Exclude user-missing values.* User-missing values and system-missing values for dependent variables are excluded. This is the default.

INCLUDE *Include user-missing values.* Only system-missing values for dependent variables are excluded from the analysis.

NOREPORT *Exclude user- and system-missing values for factor variables.* This is the default.

REPORT *Include user- and system-missing values for factor variables.* User- and system-missing values for factors are treated as valid categories and are labeled as missing.

Example

EXAMINE VARIABLES=RAINFALL MEANTEMP BY REGION.

- MISSING is not specified and the default is used. Any case with a user- or system-missing value for *RAINFALL*, *MEANTEMP*, or *REGION* is excluded from the analysis and display.

Example

EXAMINE VARIABLES=RAINFALL MEANTEMP BY REGION
  /MISSING=PAIRWISE.

- Only cases with missing values for *RAINFALL* are excluded from the analysis of *RAINFALL*, and only cases with missing values for *MEANTEMP* are excluded from the analysis of *MEANTEMP*. Missing values for *REGION* are not used.

Example

EXAMINE VARIABLES=RAINFALL MEANTEMP BY REGION
  /MISSING=REPORT.

- Missing values for *REGION* are considered valid categories and are labeled as missing.

References

Frigge, M., D. C. Hoaglin, and B. Iglewicz. 1987. Some implementations of the boxplot. In Heiberger, R. M., and M. Martin, ed., *Computer science and statistics proceedings of the 19th symposium on the interface.* Alexandria, Virginia: American Statistical Association.

Hoaglin, D. C., F. Mosteller, J. W. Tukey. 1985. *Exploring data tables, trends, and shapes.* New York: John Wiley & Sons.

Hoaglin, D. C., F. Mosteller, J. W. Tukey. 1983. *Understanding robust and exploratory data analysis.* New York: John Wiley & Sons.

Tukey, John W. 1977. *Exploratory data analysis.* Reading, Mass.: Addison-Wesley.

Velleman, P. F., and D.C. Hoaglin. 1981. *Applications, basics, and computing of exploratory data analysis.* Boston: Duxbury Press.

EXECUTE

```
EXECUTE
```

Overview

EXECUTE forces the data to be read and executes the transformations that precede it in the command sequence.

Basic Specification

The basic specification is simply the command keyword. EXECUTE has no additional specifications.

Operations

- EXECUTE causes the data to be read but has no other influence on the session.
- EXECUTE is designed for use with transformation commands and facilities such as ADD FILES, MATCH FILES, UPDATE, PRINT, and WRITE, which do not read data and are not executed unless followed by a data-reading procedure.

Example

```
DATA LIST    FILE=RAWDATA / 1 LNAME 1-13 (A) FNAME 15-24 (A)
   MMAIDENL 40-55.
VAR LABELS   MMAIDENL 'MOTHER''S MAIDEN NAME'.
DO IF (MMAIDENL EQ 'Smith').
WRITE OUTFILE=SMITHS/LNAME FNAME.
END IF.
EXECUTE.
```

- This example writes the last and first names of all people whose mother's maiden name was Smith to the data file *SMITHS*.
- DO IF—END IF and WRITE do not read data and are only executed when data are read for a procedure. Because there is no procedure in this session, EXECUTE is used to read the data and execute all of the preceding transformation commands. Otherwise, the commands would not be executed.

EXPORT

```
EXPORT OUTFILE=file

[/TYPE={COMM**}]
       {TAPE  }

[/KEEP={ALL**  }] [/DROP=varlist]
       {varlist}

[/RENAME=(old varnames=new varnames)...]

[/MAP]

[/DIGITS=n]
```

**Default if the subcommand is omitted.

Example:

```
EXPORT OUTFILE=NEWDATA /RENAME=(V1 TO V3=ID, SEX, AGE) /MAP.
```

Overview

EXPORT produces a portable data file. A portable data file is a data file created by SPSS and used to transport data between different types of computers and operating systems (such as between IBM CMS and Digital VAX/VMS) or between SPSS, SPSS/PC+, or other software using the same portable file format. Like an SPSS data file, a portable file contains all of the data and dictionary information stored in the working data file from which it was created. (To send data to a computer and operating system the same as your own, send an SPSS data file, which is easier and faster to process than a portable file.)

EXPORT is similar to the SAVE command. It can occur in the same position in the command sequence as the SAVE command and saves the working data file. The file includes the results of all permanent transformations and any temporary transformations made just prior to the EXPORT command. The working data file is unchanged after the EXPORT command.

Options

Format. You can control the format of the portable file using the TYPE subcommand.

Variables. You can save a subset of variables from the working file and rename the variables using the DROP, KEEP, and RENAME subcommands. You can also produce a record of all variables and their names on the exported file with the MAP subcommand.

Precision. You can specify the number of decimal digits of precision for the values of all numeric variables on the DIGITS subcommand.

Basic Specification

The basic specification is the OUTFILE subcommand with a file specification. All variables from the working data file are written to the portable file, with variable names, variable and value labels, missing-value flags, and print and write formats.

Subcommand Order

Subcommands can be named in any order.

Operations

- Portable files are written with 80-character record lengths.
- Portable files may contain some unprintable characters.
- The working data file is still available for SPSS transformations and procedures after the portable file is created.
- The system variables *$CASENUM* and *$DATE* are assigned when the file is read by IMPORT.
- If the WEIGHT command is used before EXPORT, the weighting variable is included in the portable file.

Example

```
EXPORT OUTFILE=NEWDATA /RENAME=(V1 TO V3=ID,SEX,AGE) /MAP.
```

- The portable file is written to *NEWDATA*.
- Variables *V1*, *V2*, and *V3* are renamed *ID*, *SEX*, and *AGE* in the portable file. Their names remain *V1*, *V2*, and *V3* in the working file. None of the other variables written to the portable file are renamed.
- MAP requests a display of the variables in the portable file.

Methods of Transporting Portable Files

Portable files can be transported on magnetic tape or by a communications program.

Magnetic Tape

Before transporting files on a magnetic tape, make sure the receiving computer can read the tape being sent. The following tape specifications must be known before you write the portable file on the tape:

- Number of tracks—either 7 or 9.
- Tape density—200, 556, 800, 1600, or 6250 bits per inch (BPI).

- Parity—even or odd. This must be known only when writing a 7-track tape.
- Tape labeling—labeled or unlabeled. Check whether the site can use tape labels. Also make sure that the site has the ability to read multivolume tape files if the file being written uses more than one tape.
- Blocksize—the maximum blocksize the receiving computer can accept.

A tape written with the following characteristics can be read by most computers: 9-track, 1600 BPI, unlabeled, and a blocksize of 3200 characters. However, there is no guarantee that a tape written with these characteristics can be read successfully. The best policy is to know the requirements of the receiving computer ahead of time.

The following advice may help ensure successful file transfers by magnetic tape:

- Unless you are certain that the receiving computer can read labels, prepare an unlabeled tape.
- Make sure the record length of 80 is not changed.
- Do not use a separate character translation program, especially ASCII/EBCDIC translations. EXPORT/IMPORT takes care of this for you.
- Make sure the same blocking factor is used when writing and reading the tape. A blocksize of 3200 is frequently a good choice.
- If possible, write the portable file directly to tape to avoid possible interference from copy programs. Read the file directly from the tape for the same reason.
- Use the INFO LOCAL command to find out about using SPSS on your particular computer and operating system. INFO LOCAL generally includes additional information about reading and writing portable files.

Communications Programs

Transmission of a portable file by a communications program may not be possible if the program misinterprets any characters in the file as control characters (for example, as a line feed, carriage return, or end of transmission). This can be prevented by specifying TYPE=COMM on EXPORT. This specification replaces each control character with the character 0. The affected control characters are in positions 0–60 of the IMPORT/EXPORT character set (see Appendix B).

The line length that the communications program uses must be set to 80 to match the 80-character record length of portable files. A transmitted file must be checked for blank lines or special characters inserted by the communications program. These must be edited out prior to reading the file with the IMPORT command.

Character Translation

Portable files are character files, not binary files, and they have 80-character records so they can be transmitted over data links. A receiving computer may not use the same character set as the computer where the portable file was written. When it imports a portable file, SPSS translates characters in the file to the character set used by the receiving computer. Depending on the character set in use, some characters in labels and in string data may be lost in the translation. For example, if a file is transported from a computer using a seven-bit ASCII character set to a computer using a six-bit ASCII character set, some characters in the file may have no matching characters in six-bit ASCII. For a character that has no match, SPSS generates an appropriate nonprintable character (the null character in most cases).

For a table of the character-set translations available with IMPORT and EXPORT, refer to Appendix B. A blank in a column of the table means that there is no matching character for that character set and an appropriate nonprintable character will be generated by SPSS when you import a file.

OUTFILE Subcommand

OUTFILE specifies the portable file. OUTFILE is the only required subcommand on EXPORT.

TYPE Subcommand

TYPE indicates whether the portable file should be formatted for magnetic tape or for a communications program. You can specify either COMM or TAPE. See "Methods of Transporting Portable Files" on p. 235 for more information on magnetic tapes and communications programs.

- All portable files created by releases earlier than SPSS-X 2.1 are in tape format and may not be suitable for transmission by communications programs.

COMM *Transport portable files by a communications program.* When COMM is specified on TYPE, SPSS removes all control characters and replaces them with the character 0. This is the default.

TAPE *Transport portable files on magnetic tape.*

Example

```
EXPORT TYPE=TAPE /OUTFILE=HUBOUT.
```

- File *HUBOUT* is saved as a tape-formatted portable file.

DROP and KEEP Subcommands

DROP and KEEP save a subset of variables in the portable file.

- DROP excludes a variable or list of variables from the portable file. All variables not named are included in the portable file.
- KEEP includes a variable or list of variables in the portable file. All variables not named are excluded.
- Variables can be specified on DROP and KEEP in any order. With the DROP subcommand, the order of variables in the portable file is the same as their order in the working file. With the KEEP subcommand, the order of variables in the portable file is the order they are named on KEEP. Thus, KEEP can be used to reorder variables in the portable file.
- Both DROP and KEEP can be used on the same EXPORT command; the effect is cumulative. If you specify a variable already named on a previous DROP or one not named on a

previous KEEP, the variable is considered nonexistent and SPSS displays an error message. The command is aborted and no portable file is saved.

Example

```
EXPORT OUTFILE=NEWSUM /DROP=DEPT TO DIVISION.
```

- The portable file is written to file *NEWSUM*. Variables between and including *DEPT* and *DIVISION* in the working file are excluded from the portable file.
- All other variables are saved in the portable file.

RENAME Subcommand

RENAME renames variables being written to the portable file. The renamed variables retain their original variable and value labels, missing-value flags, and print formats. The names of the variables are not changed in the working data file.

- To rename a variable, specify the name of the variable in the working data file, an equals sign, and the new name.
- A variable list can be specified on both sides of the equals sign. The number of variables on both sides must be the same, and the entire specification must be enclosed in parentheses.
- Keyword TO can be used for both variable lists (see "Keyword TO" on p. 32).
- If you specify a renamed variable on a subsequent DROP or KEEP subcommand, the new variable name must be used.

Example

```
EXPORT OUTFILE=NEWSUM /DROP=DEPT TO DIVISION
   /RENAME=(NAME,WAGE=LNAME,SALARY).
```

- RENAME renames *NAME* and *WAGE* to *LNAME* and *SALARY*.
- *LNAME* and *SALARY* retain the variable and value labels, missing-value flags, and print formats assigned to *NAME* and *WAGE*.

MAP Subcommand

MAP displays any changes that have been specified by the RENAME, DROP, or KEEP subcommands.

- MAP can be specified as often as desired.
- Each MAP subcommand maps the results of subcommands that precede it; results of subcommands that follow it are not mapped. When MAP is specified last, it also produces a description of the portable file.

Example

```
EXPORT OUTFILE=NEWSUM /DROP=DEPT TO DIVISION /MAP
   /RENAME NAME=LNAME WAGE=SALARY /MAP.
```

- The first MAP subcommand produces a listing of the variables in the file after DROP has dropped the specified variables.
- RENAME renames *NAME* and *WAGE*.
- The second MAP subcommand shows the variables in the file after renaming. Since this is the last subcommand, the listing will show the variables as they are written in the portable file.

DIGITS Subcommand

DIGITS specifies the degree of precision for all noninteger numeric values written to the portable file.
- DIGITS has the general form DIGITS=n, where n is the number of digits of precision.
- DIGITS applies to all numbers for which rounding is required.
- Different degrees of precision *cannot* be specified for different variables. Thus, DIGITS should be set according to the requirements of the variable that needs the most precision.
- Default precision methods used by EXPORT work perfectly for integers that are not too large and for fractions whose denominators are products of 2, 3, and 5 (all decimals, quarters, eighths, sixteenths, thirds, thirtieths, sixtieths, and so forth.) For other fractions and for integers too large to be represented exactly in the working data file (usually more than 9 digits, often 15 or more), the representation used in the working file contains some error already, so no exact way of sending these numbers is possible. SPSS sends enough digits to get very close. The number of digits sent in these cases depends on the originating computer: on mainframe IBM versions of SPSS, it is the equivalent of 13 decimal digits (integer and fractional parts combined). If many numbers on a file require this level of precision, the file can grow quite large. If you do not need the full default precision, you can save some space in the portable file by using the DIGITS subcommand.

Example

```
EXPORT OUTFILE=NEWSUM /DROP=DEPT TO DIVISION /MAP /DIGITS=4.
```

- DIGITS guarantees the accuracy of values to four significant digits. For example, 12.34567890876 will be rounded to 12.35.

FILE HANDLE

```
FILE HANDLE handle /NAME=file specifications [/MODE={CHARACTER }]  [/LRECL=n]
                                                    {BINARY    }
                                                    {MULTIPUNCH}
                                                    {IMAGE     }
```

Overview

FILE HANDLE assigns a unique *file handle* to a file and supplies operating system specifications for the file. A defined file handle can be specified on any subsequent FILE, OUTFILE, MATRIX, or WRITE subcommands of various procedures.

Syntax Rules

- A file handle cannot exceed eight characters and must begin with an alphabetical character (A–Z) or a $, #, or @. It can contain numeric digits (0–9) but not imbedded blanks.
- FILE HANDLE is required for reading IBM VSAM data sets, any binary data files, and character data files that are not delimited by ASCII line feeds.

NAME Subcommand

NAME specifies the file you want to refer to by the file handle. The file specifications depend on the type of computer and operating system on which SPSS is run. Details on writing the file specifications for your operating system are documented in the *Base System User's Guide* for your version of SPSS.

MODE Subcommand

MODE specifies the type of file you want to refer to by the file handle.

CHARACTER *Character file whose logical records are delimited by ASCII line feeds.*

BINARY *Unformatted binary file generated by Microsoft Fortran.*

MULTIPUNCH *Column binary file.*

IMAGE *Binary file consisting of fixed length records.*

LRECL Subcommand

LRECL specifies the length of each record in the file. When you specify IMAGE under UNIX, OS/2, or Microsoft Windows, you must specify LRECL. You can specify a record length greater than the default (1024) for an image file, a character file, or a binary file. Do not use LRECL with MULTIPUNCH.

FILE LABEL

```
FILE LABEL label
```

Overview

FILE LABEL provides a descriptive label for a data file.

Syntax Rules

The only specification is a label up to 60 characters long.

Operations

- The file label is printed on the first line of each page of output displayed by SPSS.
- If the specified label is longer than 60 characters, SPSS truncates the label to 60 characters without warning.
- If the file is saved, the label is included in the dictionary of the SPSS data file.

Example

```
FILE LABEL  Hubbard Industrial Consultants Inc. employee data.
SAVE OUTFILE=HUBEMPL
   /RENAME=(AGE JOBCAT=AGE80 JOBCAT82) /MAP.
```

- FILE LABEL assigns a file label to the Hubbard Consultants Inc. employee data.
- The SAVE command saves the file as an SPSS data file, renaming two variables and mapping the results to check the renamed variables.

FILE TYPE—END FILE TYPE

For mixed file types:

```
FILE TYPE MIXED [FILE=file] RECORD=[varname] col loc [WILD={NOWARN}]
                                                           {WARN  }
```

For grouped file types:

```
FILE TYPE GROUPED [FILE=file] RECORD=[varname] col loc

  CASE=[varname] col loc [WILD={WARN  }] [DUPLICATE={WARN  }]
                               {NOWARN}              {NOWARN}

  [MISSING={WARN  }] [ORDERED={YES}]
           {NOWARN}            {NO }
```

For nested file types:

```
FILE TYPE NESTED [FILE=file] RECORD=[varname] col loc

  [CASE=[varname] col loc] [WILD={NOWARN}] [DUPLICATE={NOWARN}]
                                 {WARN  }              {WARN  }
                                                       {CASE  }

  [MISSING={NOWARN}]
           {WARN  }

END FILE TYPE
```

Example:

```
FILE TYPE  MIXED RECORD=RECID 1-2.
RECORD TYPE 23.
DATA LIST   /SEX 5 AGE 6-7 DOSAGE 8-10 RESULT 12.
END FILE TYPE.

BEGIN DATA
21   145010 1
22   257200 2
25   235  250    2
35   167             300     3
24   125150 1
23   272075 1
21   149050 2
25   134  035    3
30   138             300     3
32   229             500     3
END DATA.
```

Overview

The FILE TYPE—END FILE TYPE structure defines data for any one of the three types of complex raw data files: *mixed files,* which contain several types of records that define different types of cases; *hierarchical* or *nested files,* which contain several types of records with a defined relationship among the record types; or *grouped files,* which contain several records for each case with some records missing or duplicated. A fourth type of complex file, files with *repeating groups* of information, can be defined with the REPEATING DATA command.

FILE TYPE must be followed by at least one RECORD TYPE and one DATA LIST command. Each pair of RECORD TYPE and DATA LIST commands defines one type of record in the data. END FILE TYPE signals the end of file definition.

Within the FILE TYPE structure, the lowest-level record in a nested file can be read with a REPEATING DATA command rather than a DATA LIST command. In addition, any record in a mixed file can be read with REPEATING DATA.

Basic Specification

The basic specification on FILE TYPE is one of the three file type keywords (MIXED, GROUPED, or NESTED) and the RECORD subcommand. RECORD names the record identification variable and specifies its column location. If keyword GROUPED is specified, the CASE subcommand is also required. CASE names the case identification variable and specifies its column location.

The FILE TYPE—END FILE TYPE structure must enclose at least one RECORD TYPE and one DATA LIST command. END FILE TYPE is required to signal the end of file definition.

- RECORD TYPE specifies the values of the record type identifier (see RECORD TYPE).
- DATA LIST defines variables for the record type specified on the preceding RECORD TYPE command (see DATA LIST).
- Separate pairs of RECORD TYPE and DATA LIST commands must be used to define each different record type.

The resulting working data file is always a rectangular file, regardless of the structure of the original data file.

Specification Order

- FILE TYPE must be the first command in the FILE TYPE—END FILE TYPE structure. FILE TYPE subcommands can be named in any order.
- Each RECORD TYPE command must precede its corresponding DATA LIST command.
- END FILE TYPE must be the last command in the structure.

Syntax Rules

- For mixed files, if the record types have different variables or if they have the same variables recorded in different locations, separate RECORD TYPE and DATA LIST commands are required for each record type.
- For mixed files, the same variable name can be used on different DATA LIST commands, since each record type defines a separate case.
- For mixed files, if the same variable is defined for more than one record type, the format type and length of the variable should be the same on all DATA LIST commands. SPSS re-

fers to the *first* DATA LIST command that defines a variable for the print and write formats to include in the dictionary of the working data file.

- For grouped and nested files, the variable names on each DATA LIST must be unique, since a case is built by combining all record types together into a single record.
- For nested files, the order of the RECORD TYPE commands defines the hierarchical structure of the file. The first RECORD TYPE defines the highest-level record type, the next RECORD TYPE defines the next highest-level record, and so forth. The last RECORD TYPE command defines a case in the working data file. By default, variables from higher-level records are spread to the lowest-level record.
- For nested files, the SPREAD subcommand on RECORD TYPE can be used to spread the values in a record type only to the *first* case built from each record of that type. All other cases associated with that record are assigned the system-missing value for the variables defined on that type. See RECORD TYPE for more information.
- String values specified on the RECORD TYPE command must be enclosed in apostrophes or quotation marks.

Operations

- For mixed file types, SPSS skips all records that are not specified on one of the RECORD TYPE commands.
- If different variables are defined for different record types in mixed files, the variables are assigned the system-missing value for those record types on which they are not defined.
- For nested files, the first record in the file should be the type specified on the first RECORD TYPE command—the highest level of the hierarchy. If the first record in the file is not the highest-level type, SPSS skips all records until it encounters a record of the highest-level type. If MISSING or DUPLICATE have been specified, these records may produce warning messages but will not be used to build a case in the working file.
- When defining complex files, you are effectively building an input program and can use only commands that are allowed in the input state. See Appendix A for information on program states.

Example

```
* Reading multiple record types from a mixed file.
FILE TYPE  MIXED FILE=TREATMNT RECORD=RECID 1-2.
+ RECORD TYPE 21,22,23,24.
+ DATA LIST    /SEX 5 AGE 6-7 DOSAGE 8-10 RESULT 12.
+ RECORD TYPE 25.
+ DATA LIST    /SEX 5 AGE 6-7 DOSAGE 10-12 RESULT 15.
END FILE TYPE.
```

- Variable *DOSAGE* is read from columns 8–10 for record types 21, 22, 23, and 24 and from columns 10–12 for record type 25. *RESULT* is read from column 12 for record types 21, 22, 23, and 24, and from column 15 for record type 25.

- The working data file contains values for all variables defined on the DATA LIST commands for record types 21 through 25. All other record types are skipped.

Example

```
* Reading only one record type from a mixed file.

FILE TYPE  MIXED RECORD=RECID 1-2.
RECORD TYPE 23.
DATA LIST   /SEX 5 AGE 6-7 DOSAGE 8-10 RESULT 12.
END FILE TYPE.

BEGIN DATA
21  145010 1
22  257200 2
25  235   250   2
35  167         300    3
24  125150 1
23  272075 1
21  149050 2
25  134   035   3
30  138         300    3
32  229         500    3
END DATA.
```

- FILE TYPE begins the file definition and END FILE TYPE indicates the end of file definition. FILE TYPE specifies a mixed file type. Since the data are included between BEGIN DATA—END DATA, the FILE subcommand is omitted. The record identification variable *RECID* is located in columns 1 and 2.
- RECORD TYPE indicates that records with value 23 for variable *RECID* will be copied into the working data file. All other records are skipped. SPSS does not issue a warning when it skips records in mixed files.
- DATA LIST defines variables on records with the value 23 for variable *RECID*.

Example

```
* A grouped file of student test scores.

FILE TYPE GROUPED RECORD=#TEST 6 CASE=STUDENT 1-4.
RECORD TYPE 1.
DATA LIST   /ENGLISH 8-9 (A).
RECORD TYPE 2.
DATA LIST /READING 8-10.
RECORD TYPE 3.
DATA LIST /MATH 8-10.
END FILE TYPE.

BEGIN DATA
0001 1 B+
0001 2   74
```

```
0001 3   83
0002 1 A
0002 2 100
0002 3   71
0003 1 B-
0003 2   88
0003 3   81
0004 1 C
0004 2   94
0004 3   91
END DATA.
```

- FILE TYPE identifies the file as a grouped file. As required for grouped files, all records for a single case are together in the data. The record identification variable *#TEST* is located in column 6. A scratch variable is specified so it won't be saved in the working data file. The case identification variable *STUDENT* is located in columns 1–4.
- Because there are three record types, there are three RECORD TYPE commands. For each RECORD TYPE there is a DATA LIST to define variables on that record type.
- END FILE TYPE signals the end of file definition.
- SPSS builds four cases—one for each student. Each case includes the case identification variable plus the variables defined for each record type (the test scores). The values for *#TEST* are not saved in the working data file. Thus, each case in the working file has four variables: *STUDENT*, *ENGLISH*, *READING*, and *MATH*.

Example

```
* A nested file of accident records.

FILE TYPE NESTED RECORD=6 CASE=ACCID 1-4.
RECORD TYPE 1.
DATA LIST /ACC_ID 9-11 WEATHER 12-13 STATE 15-16 (A) DATE 18-24 (A).
RECORD TYPE 2.
DATA LIST /STYLE 11 MAKE 13 OLD 14 LICENSE 15-16(A) INSURNCE 18-21 (A).
RECORD TYPE 3.
DATA LIST /PSNGR_NO 11 AGE 13-14 SEX 16 (A) INJURY 18 SEAT 20-21 (A)
          COST 23-24.
END FILE TYPE.

BEGIN DATA
0001 1   322 1 IL 3/13/88    /* Type 1:   accident record
0001 2     1 44MI 134M        /* Type 2:   vehicle record
0001 3     1 34 M 1 FR  3     /* Type 3:    person record
0001 2     2 16IL 322F        /*            vehicle record
0001 3     1 22 F 1 FR 11     /*             person record
0001 3     2 35 M 1 FR  5     /*             person record
0001 3     3 59 M 1 BK  7     /*             person record
0001 2     3 21IN 146M        /*            vehicle record
0001 3     1 46 M 0 FR  0     /*             person record
END DATA.
```

- FILE TYPE specifies a nested file type. The record identifier, located in column 6, is not assigned a variable name, so the default scratch variable name *####RECD* is used. The case identification variable *ACCID* is located in columns 1–4.

- Because there are three record types, there are three RECORD TYPE commands. For each RECORD TYPE there is a DATA LIST command to define variables on that record type. The order of the RECORD TYPE commands defines the hierarchical structure of the file.
- END FILE TYPE signals the end of file definition.
- SPSS builds a case for each lowest-level (type 3) record, representing each person in the file. There can be only one type 1 record for each type 2 record, and one type 2 record for each type 3 record. Each vehicle can be in only one accident, and each person can be in only one vehicle. The variables from the type 1 and type 2 records are spread to their corresponding type 3 records.

Types of Files

The first specification on FILE TYPE is a file type keyword, which defines the structure of the data file. There are three file type keywords: MIXED, GROUPED, and NESTED. Only one of the three types can be specified on FILE TYPE.

MIXED *Mixed file type.* MIXED specifies a file in which each record type named on a RECORD TYPE command defines a case. You do not need to define all types of records in the file. In fact, FILE TYPE MIXED is useful for reading only one type of record because SPSS can decide whether to execute the DATA LIST for a record by simply reading the variable that identifies the record type.

GROUPED *Grouped file type.* GROUPED defines a file in which cases are defined by grouping together record types with the same identification number. Each case usually has one record of each type. All records for a single case must be together in the file. By default, SPSS assumes that the records are in the same sequence within each case.

NESTED *Nested file type.* NESTED defines a file in which the record types are related to each other hierarchically. The record types are grouped together by a case identification number that identifies the highest level—the first record type—of the hierarchy. Usually, the last record type specified—the lowest level of the hierarchy—defines a case. For example, in a file containing household records and records for each person living in the household, each person record defines a case. Information from higher record types may be *spread* to each case. For example, the value for a variable on the household record, such as *CITY*, can be spread to the records for each person in the household.

Subcommands and their Defaults for Each File Type

The specifications on the FILE TYPE differ for each type of file. Table 9 shows whether each subcommand is required or optional and, where applicable, what the default specification is for each file type. N/A indicates that the subcommand is not applicable to that type of file.

- FILE is required unless data are inline (included between BEGIN DATA—END DATA).
- RECORD is always required.
- CASE is required for grouped files.

Table 9 Summary of FILE TYPE subcommands for different file types

Subcommand	Mixed	Grouped	Nested
FILE	Conditional	Conditional	Conditional
RECORD	Required	Required	Required
CASE	Not Applicable	Required	Optional
WILD	NOWARN	WARN	NOWARN
DUPLICATE	N/A	WARN	NOWARN
MISSING	N/A	WARN	NOWARN
ORDERED	N/A	YES	N/A

- The subcommands CASE, DUPLICATE, and MISSING can also be specified on the associated RECORD TYPE commands for grouped files. However, DUPLICATE=CASE is invalid.
- For nested files, CASE and MISSING can be specified on the associated RECORD TYPE commands.
- If the subcommands CASE, DUPLICATE, or MISSING are specified on a RECORD TYPE command, the specification on the FILE TYPE command (or the default) is overridden only for the record types listed on that RECORD TYPE command. The FILE TYPE specification or default applies to all other record types.

FILE Subcommand

FILE specifies a text file containing the data. FILE is not used when the data are inline.

Example

```
FILE TYPE  MIXED FILE=TREATMNT RECORD=RECID 1-2.
```

- Data are in file *TREATMNT*. The file type is mixed. The record identification variable *RECID* is located in columns 1 and 2 of each record.

RECORD Subcommand

RECORD specifies the name and column location of the record identification variable.
- The column location of the record identifier is required. The variable name is optional.
- If you do not want to save the record type variable, you can assign a scratch variable name by using the # character as the first character of the name. If a variable name is not specified on RECORD, the record identifier is defined as the scratch variable *####RECD*.
- The value of the identifier for each record type must be unique and must be in the same location on all records. However, records do not have to be sorted according to type.

- A column-style format can be specified for the record identifier. For example, the following two specifications are valid:
```
RECORD=V1 1-2(N)
RECORD=V1 1-2(F,1)
```
FORTRAN-like formats cannot be used because the column location must be specified explicitly.
- Specify A in parentheses after the column location to define the record type variable as a string variable.

Example
```
FILE TYPE  MIXED FILE=TREATMNT RECORD=RECID 1-2.
```
- The record identifier is variable *RECID*, located in columns 1 and 2 of the hospital treatment data file.

CASE Subcommand

CASE specifies a name and column location for the case identification variable. CASE is required for grouped files and optional for nested files. It cannot be used with mixed files.
- For grouped files, each unique value for the case identification variable defines a case in the working data file.
- For nested files, the case identification variable identifies the highest-level record of the hierarchy. SPSS issues a warning message for each record with a case identification number not equal to the case identification number on the last highest-level record. However, the record with the invalid case number is used to build the case.
- The column location of the case identifier is required. The variable name is optional.
- If you do not want to save the case identification variable, you can assign a scratch variable name by using the # character as the first character of the name. If a variable name is not specified on CASE, the case identifier is defined as the scratch variable *####CASE*.
- A column-style format can be specified for the case identifier. For example, the following two specifications are valid:
```
CASE=V1 1-2(N)
CASE=V1 1-2(F,1)
```
FORTRAN-like formats cannot be used because the column location must be specified explicitly.
- Specify A in parentheses after the column location to define the case identification variable as a string variable.
- If the case identification number is not in the same columns on all record types, use the CASE subcommand on the RECORD TYPE commands as well as on the FILE TYPE command (see RECORD TYPE).

Example

```
* A grouped file of student test scores.

FILE TYPE GROUPED RECORD=#TEST 6 CASE=STUDENT 1-4.
RECORD TYPE 1.
DATA LIST   /ENGLISH 8-9 (A).
RECORD TYPE 2.
DATA LIST /READING 8-10.
RECORD TYPE 3.
DATA LIST /MATH 8-10.
END FILE TYPE.

BEGIN DATA
0001 1  B+
0001 2   74
0001 3   83
0002 1  A
0002 2  100
0002 3   71
0003 1  B-
0003 2   88
0003 3   81
0004 1  C
0004 2   94
0004 3   91
END DATA.
```

- CASE is required for grouped files. CASE specifies variable *STUDENT*, located in columns 1–4, as the case identification variable.
- The data contain four different values for *STUDENT*. The working data file therefore has four cases, one for each value of *STUDENT*. In a grouped file, each unique value for the case identification variable defines a case in the working file.
- Each case includes the case identification variable plus the variables defined for each record type. The values for *#TEST* are not saved in the working data file. Thus, each case in the working file has four variables: *STUDENT, ENGLISH, READING*, and *MATH*.

Example

```
* A nested file of accident records.

FILE TYPE NESTED RECORD=6 CASE=ACCID 1-4.
RECORD TYPE 1.
DATA LIST    /ACC_ID 9-11 WEATHER 12-13 STATE 15-16 (A) DATE 18-24 (A).
RECORD TYPE 2.
DATA LIST /STYLE 11 MAKE 13 OLD 14 LICENSE 15-16 (A) INSURNCE 18-21 (A).
RECORD TYPE 3.
DATA LIST /PSNGR_NO 11 AGE 13-14 SEX 16 (A) INJURY 18 SEAT 20-21 (A)
           COST 23-24.
END FILE TYPE.
```

```
BEGIN DATA
0001 1    322 1 IL 3/13/88   /* Type 1:   accident record
0001 2      1 44MI 134M      /* Type 2:   vehicle record
0001 3      1 34 M 1 FR  3   /* Type 3:   person record
0001 2      2 16IL 322F      /*           vehicle record
0001 3      1 22 F 1 FR 11   /*           person record
0001 3      2 35 M 1 FR  5   /*           person record
0001 3      3 59 M 1 BK  7   /*           person record
0001 2      3 21IN 146M      /*           vehicle record
0001 3      1 46 M 0 FR  0   /*           person record
END DATA.
```

- CASE specifies variable *ACCID*, located in columns 1–4, as the case identification variable. *ACCID* identifies the highest level of the hierarchy: the level for the accident records.
- As each case is built, the value of the variable *ACCID* is checked against the value of *ACCID* on the last highest-level record (record type 1). If the values do not match, a warning message is issued. However, the record is used to build the case.
- The data in this example contain only one value for *ACCID*, which is spread across all cases. In a nested file, the lowest-level record type determines the number of cases in the working data file. In this example, the working file has five cases because there are five person records.

Example

```
* Specifying case on the RECORD TYPE command.

FILE TYPE GROUPED FILE=HUBDATA RECORD=#RECID 80 CASE=ID 1-5.
RECORD TYPE 1.
DATA LIST   /MOHIRED YRHIRED 12-15 DEPT79 TO DEPT82 SEX 16-20.
RECORD TYPE 2.
DATA LIST   /SALARY79 TO SALARY82 6-25 HOURLY81 HOURLY82 40-53 (2)
             PROMO81 72   AGE 54-55 RAISE82 66-70.
RECORD TYPE 3   CASE=75-79.
DATA LIST   /JOBCAT 6 NAME 25-48 (A).
END FILE TYPE.
```

- The CASE subcommand on FILE TYPE indicates the case identification number is located in columns 1–5. However, for type 3 records the case identification number is located in columns 75–79. The CASE subcommand is therefore specified on the third RECORD TYPE command to override the case setting for type 3 records.
- The format of the case identification variable must be the same on all records. If the case identification variable is defined as a string on the FILE TYPE command, it cannot be defined as a numeric variable on the RECORD TYPE command, and vice versa.

WILD Subcommand

WILD determines whether SPSS issues a warning when it encounters undefined record types in the data file. Regardless of whether SPSS issues the warning, undefined records are not included in the working data file.

- The only specification on WILD is keyword WARN or NOWARN.

- WARN cannot be specified if keyword OTHER is specified on the last RECORD TYPE command to indicate all other record types (see RECORD TYPE).

WARN *Issue warning messages.* SPSS displays a warning message and the first 80 characters of the record for each record type that is not mentioned on a RECORD TYPE command. This is the default for grouped file types.

NOWARN *Suppress warning messages.* SPSS simply skips all record types not mentioned on a RECORD TYPE command and does not display warning messages. This is the default for mixed and nested file types.

Example

```
FILE TYPE  MIXED FILE=TREATMNT RECORD=RECID 1-2 WILD=WARN.
```

- WARN is specified on the WILD subcommand. SPSS displays a warning message and the first 80 characters of the record for each record type that is not mentioned on a RECORD TYPE command.

DUPLICATE Subcommand

DUPLICATE determines how SPSS responds when it encounters more than one record of each type for a single case. DUPLICATE is optional for grouped and nested files. DUPLICATE cannot be used with mixed files.

- The only specification on DUPLICATE is keyword WARN, NOWARN, or CASE.

WARN *Issue warning messages.* SPSS displays a warning message and the first 80 characters of the last record of the duplicate set of record types. Only the *last* record from a set of duplicates is included in the working data file. This is the default for grouped files.

NOWARN *Suppress warning messages.* SPSS does not display warning messages when it encounters duplicate record types. Only the *last* record from a set of duplicates is included in the working data file. This is the default for nested files.

CASE *Build a case in the working data file for each duplicate record.* SPSS builds *one* case in the working file for each duplicate record, spreading information from any higher-level records and assigning system-missing values to the variables defined on lower-level records. This option is available only for nested files.

Example

```
* A nested file of accident records.
* Issue a warning for duplicate record types.
FILE TYPE NESTED RECORD=6 CASE=ACCID 1-4 DUPLICATE=WARN.
RECORD TYPE 1.
DATA LIST    /ACC_ID 9-11 WEATHER 12-13 STATE 15-16 (A) DATE 18-24 (A).
RECORD TYPE 2.
DATA LIST /STYLE 11 MAKE 13 OLD 14 LICENSE 15-16 (A) INSURNCE 18-21 (A).
RECORD TYPE 3.
DATA LIST /PSNGR_NO 11 AGE 13-14 SEX 16 (A) INJURY 18 SEAT 20-21 (A)
          COST 23-24.
END FILE TYPE.

BEGIN DATA
0001 1  322 1 IL 3/13/88    /*          accident record
0001 2    1 44MI 134M       /*           vehicle record
0001 3    1 34 M 1 FR  3    /*            person record
0001 2    1 31IL 134M       /* duplicate vehicle record
0001 2    2 16IL 322F       /*           vehicle record
0001 3    1 22 F 1 FR 11    /*            person record
0001 3    2 35 M 1 FR  5    /*            person record
0001 3    3 59 M 1 BK  7    /*            person record
0001 2    3 21IN 146M       /*           vehicle record
0001 3    1 46 M 0 FR  0    /*            person record
END DATA.
```

- In the data there are two vehicle (type 2) records above the second set of person (type 3) records. This implies that an empty (for example, parked) vehicle was involved, or that each of the three persons was in two vehicles, which is impossible.
- DUPLICATE specifies keyword WARN. SPSS displays a warning message and the first 80 characters of the second of the duplicate set of type 2 records. The first duplicate record is skipped, and only the second is included in the working data file. This assumes that no empty vehicles were involved in the accident.
- If the duplicate record represents an empty vehicle, it can be included in the working data file by specifying keyword CASE on DUPLICATE. SPSS builds one case in the working data file for the first duplicate record, spreading information to that case from the previous type 1 record and assigning system-missing values to the variables defined for type 3 records. The second record from the duplicate set is used to build the three cases for the associated type 3 records.

MISSING Subcommand

MISSING determines whether SPSS issues a warning when it encounters a missing record type for a case. Regardless of whether SPSS issues the warning, it builds the case in the working file with system-missing values for the variables defined on the missing record. MISSING is optional for grouped and nested files.

- MISSING cannot be used with mixed files and is optional for grouped and nested files.
- For grouped and nested files, SPSS verifies that each defined case includes one record of each type.
- The only specification is keyword WARN or NOWARN.

WARN *Issue a warning message when a record type is missing for a case.* This is the default for grouped files.

NOWARN *Suppress the warning message when a record type is missing for a case.* This is the default for nested files.

Example

```
* A grouped file with missing records.

FILE TYPE GROUPED RECORD=#TEST 6 CASE=STUDENT 1-4 MISSING=NOWARN.
RECORD TYPE 1.
DATA LIST   /ENGLISH 8-9 (A).
RECORD TYPE 2.
DATA LIST /READING 8-10.
RECORD TYPE 3.
DATA LIST /MATH 8-10.
END FILE TYPE.

BEGIN DATA
0001 1 B+
0001 2  74
0002 1 A
0002 2 100
0002 3  71
0003 3  81
0004 1 C
0004 2  94
0004 3  91
END DATA.
```

- The data contain records for three tests administered to four students. However, not all students took all tests. The first student took only the English and reading tests. The third student took only the math test.
- One case in the working data file is built for each of the four students. If a student did not take a test, the system-missing value is assigned in the working file to the variable for the missing test. Thus, the first student has the system-missing value for the math test, and the third student has missing values for the English and reading tests.
- Keyword NOWARN is specified on MISSING. Therefore, no warning messages are issued for the missing records.

Example

```
* A nested file with missing records.

FILE TYPE NESTED RECORD=6 CASE=ACCID 1-4 MISSING=WARN.
RECORD TYPE 1.
DATA LIST   /ACC_ID 9-11 WEATHER 12-13 STATE 15-16 (A) DATE 18-24 (A).
RECORD TYPE 2.
DATA LIST /STYLE 11 MAKE 13 OLD 14 LICENSE 15-16 (A) INSURNCE 18-21 (A).
RECORD TYPE 3.
DATA LIST /PSNGR_NO 11 AGE 13-14 SEX 16 (A) INJURY 18 SEAT 20-21 (A)
           COST 23-24.
END FILE TYPE.
```

```
BEGIN DATA
0001 1   322 1 IL 3/13/88   /*         accident record
0001 3     1 34 M 1 FR  3   /*          person record
0001 2     2 16IL 322F      /*         vehicle record
0001 3     1 22 F 1 FR 11   /*          person record
0001 3     2 35 M 1 FR  5   /*          person record
0001 3     3 59 M 1 BK  7   /*          person record
0001 2     3 21IN 146M      /*         vehicle record
0001 3     1 46 M 0 FR  0   /*          person record
END DATA.
```

- The data contain records for one accident. The first record is a type 1 (accident) record, and the second record is a type 3 (person) record. However, there is no type 2 record, and therefore no vehicle, associated with the first person. The person may have been a pedestrian, but it is also possible that the vehicle record is missing.
- One case is built for each person record. The first case has missing values for the variables specified on the vehicle record.
- Keyword WARN is specified on MISSING. A warning message is issued for the missing record.

ORDERED Subcommand

ORDERED indicates whether the records are in the same order as they are defined on the RECORD TYPE commands. Regardless of the order of the records in the data file and the specification on ORDERED, SPSS builds cases in the working data file with records in the order defined on the RECORD TYPE commands.

- ORDERED can be used only for grouped files.
- The only specification is keyword YES or NO.
- If YES is in effect but the records are not in the order defined on the RECORD TYPE commands, SPSS issues a warning for each record that is out of order. SPSS still uses these records to build cases.

YES   *Records for each case are in the same order as they are defined on the RECORD TYPE commands.* This is the default.

NO   *Records are not in the same order within each case.*

Example

```
* A grouped file with records out of order.

FILE TYPE GROUPED RECORD=#TEST 6 CASE=STUDENT 1-4  MISSING=NOWARN
   ORDERED=NO.
RECORD TYPE 1.
DATA LIST   /ENGLISH 8-9 (A).
RECORD TYPE 2.
DATA LIST /READING 8-10.
RECORD TYPE 3.
DATA LIST /MATH 8-10.
END FILE TYPE.
```

```
BEGIN DATA
0001 2   74
0001 1   B+
0002 3   71
0002 2  100
0002 1   A
0003 2   81
0004 2   94
0004 1   C
0004 3   91
END DATA.
```

- The first RECORD TYPE command specifies record type 1, the second specifies record type 2, and the third specifies record type 3. However, records for each case are not always ordered type 1, type 2, and type 3.
- NO is specified on ORDERED. SPSS builds cases without issuing a warning that they are out of order in the data.
- Regardless of whether YES or NO is in effect for ORDERED, SPSS builds cases in the working data file in the same order specified on the RECORD TYPE commands.

FILTER

```
FILTER  {BY var}
        {OFF    }
```

Example:
```
FILTER BY SEX.
FREQUENCIES BONUS.
```

Overview

FILTER is used to exclude cases from SPSS procedures without deleting them from the working data file. When FILTER is in effect, cases with a 0 or missing value for the specified variable are not used in SPSS procedures. Those cases are not actually deleted and are available again if the filter is turned off. To see the current filter status, use the SHOW command.

Basic Specification

The basic specification is keyword BY followed by a variable name. Cases that have a 0 or missing value for the filter variable are excluded from subsequent procedures.

Syntax Rules

- Only one numeric variable can be specified. The variable can be one of the original variables in the data file or a variable computed with transformation commands.
- Keyword OFF turns off the filter. All cases in the working data file become available to subsequent procedures.
- If FILTER is specified without a keyword, FILTER OFF is assumed but SPSS displays a warning message.
- FILTER can be specified anywhere in the command sequence. Unlike SELECT IF, FILTER has the same effect within an input program as it does outside an input program. Attention must be paid to the placement of any transformation command used to compute values for the filter variable (see INPUT PROGRAM).

Operations

- FILTER performs case selection without changing the working data file. Cases that have a 0 or missing value are excluded from subsequent procedures but are not deleted from the file.
- Both system-missing and user-missing values are treated as missing. The FILTER command does not offer options for changing selection criteria. To set up different criteria for exclusion, create a numeric variable and conditionally compute its values before specifying it on FILTER.

- If FILTER is specified after TEMPORARY, FILTER affects the next procedure only. After that procedure, the filter status reverts to whatever it was before the TEMPORARY command.
- The filter status does not change until another FILTER command is specified or the working data file is replaced.
- If the specified filter variable is renamed, it is still in effect. The SHOW command will display the new name of the filter variable. However, the filter is turned off if the filter variable is recoded into a string variable or is deleted from the file.
- If the working data file is replaced after a MATCH FILES, ADD FILES, or UPDATE command and the working file is one of the input files, the filter remains in effect if the new working file has a numeric variable with the name of the filter variable. If the working data file does not have a numeric variable with that name (for example, if the filter variable was dropped or renamed), the filter is turned off.
- If the working data file is replaced by an entirely new data file (for example, by a DATA LIST, GET, and IMPORT command), the filter is turned off.
- The FILTER command changes the filter status and takes effect when a procedure is executed or an EXECUTE command is encountered.

Example

```
FILTER BY SEX.
FREQUENCIES BONUS.
```

- This example assumes that *SEX* is a numeric variable, with male and female coded as 0 and 1, respectively. The FILTER command excludes males and cases with missing values for *SEX* from the subsequent procedures. The FREQUENCIES command generates a frequency table of *BONUS* for females only.

Example

```
RECODE SEX (1=0)(0=1).
FILTER BY SEX.
FREQUENCIES BONUS.
```

- This example assumes the same coding scheme for *SEX* as the previous example. Before FILTER is specified, variable *SEX* is recoded. The FILTER command then excludes females and cases with missing values for *SEX*. The FREQUENCIES command generates a frequency table of *BONUS* for males only.

FINISH

```
FINISH
```

Overview

FINISH causes SPSS to stop reading commands.

Basic Specification

The basic specification is keyword FINISH. There are no additional specifications.

Command Files

- FINISH is optional in a command file and is used to mark the end of a session.
- FINISH causes SPSS to stop reading commands. Anything following FINISH in the command file is ignored. Any commands following FINISH in an INCLUDE file are ignored.
- FINISH cannot be used within a DO IF structure to end a session conditionally. FINISH within a DO IF structure will end the session unconditionally.

Prompted Sessions

- FINISH is required in a prompted session to terminate the session.
- Because FINISH is an SPSS command, it can be used only after the SPSS> prompt, which expects a procedure name. FINISH cannot be used to end a prompted session from a DATA>, CONTINUE>, HELP>, or DEFINE> prompt.

Operations

- FINISH immediately causes SPSS to stop reading commands.
- The appearance of FINISH on the printback of commands on the display file indicates that the session has been completed.
- When issued within the SPSS Manager (not available on all systems), FINISH terminates command processing and causes SPSS to query whether you want to continue working. If you answer *yes*, you can continue creating and editing files in both the input window and the output window; however, you can no longer run commands.

Example

```
* A command file.

DATA LIST FILE=RAWDATA /NAME 1-15(A) V1 TO V15 16-30.
LIST.
FINISH.
REPORT FORMAT=AUTO LIST /VARS=NAME V1 TO V10.
```

- FINISH causes SPSS to stop reading commands after LIST is executed. The REPORT command is not executed.

Example

```
SPSS> * A prompted session.

SPSS> DATA LIST FILE=RAWDATA /NAME 1-15(A) V1 TO V15 16-30.
SPSS> LIST.
SPSS> FINISH.
```

- FINISH terminates the prompted session.

FLIP

```
FLIP [[VARIABLES=] {ALL     }]
                   {varlist}

[/NEWNAMES=variable]
```

Example:
```
FLIP VARIABLES=WEEK1 TO WEEK52 /NEWNAMES=DEPT.
```

Overview

SPSS requires a file structure in which the variables are the columns and observations (cases) are the rows. If a file is organized such that variables are in rows and observations are in columns, you need to use FLIP to reorganize it. FLIP transposes the rows and columns of the data in the working data file so that, for example, row 1, column 2 becomes row 2, column 1, and so forth.

Options

Variable Subsets. You can transpose specific variables (columns) from the original file using the VARIABLES subcommand.

Variable Names. You can use the values of one of the variables from the original file as the variable names in the new file using the NEWNAMES subcommand.

Basic Specification

The basic specification is the command keyword FLIP, which transposes all rows and columns.

- By default, FLIP assigns variable names *VAR001* to *VARn* to the variables in the new file. It also creates the new variable *CASE_LBL*, whose values are the variable names that existed before transposition.

Subcommand Order

VARIABLES must precede NEWNAMES.

Operations

- FLIP replaces the working data file with the transposed file and displays a list of variable names in the transposed file.

- FLIP discards any previous VARIABLE LABELS, VALUE LABELS, and WEIGHT settings. Values defined as user-missing in the original file are translated to system-missing in the transposed file.
- FLIP obeys any SELECT IF, N, and SAMPLE commands in effect.
- FLIP does not obey the TEMPORARY command. Any transformations become permanent when followed by FLIP.
- String variables in the original file are assigned system-missing values after transposition.
- Numeric variables are assigned a default format of F8.2 after transposition (with the exceptions of *CASE_LBL* and the variable specified on NEWNAMES).
- The variable *CASE_LBL* is created and added to the working data file each time FLIP is executed.
- If *CASE_LBL* already exists as the result of a previous FLIP, its current values are used as the names of variables in the new file (if NEWNAMES is not specified).

Example

The following is the LIST output for a data file arranged in a typical spreadsheet format, with variables in rows and observations in columns:

```
A              B          C          D

Income      22.00      31.00      43.00
Price       34.00      29.00      50.00
Year      1970.00    1971.00    1972.00
```

The command

```
FLIP.
```

transposes all variables in the file. The LIST output for the transposed file is as follows:

```
CASE_LBL    VAR001    VAR002    VAR003

A              .         .         .
B           22.00     34.00   1970.00
C           31.00     29.00   1971.00
D           43.00     50.00   1972.00
```

- The values for the new variable *CASE_LBL* are the variable names from the original file.
- Case A has system-missing values, since variable *A* had the string values Income, Price, and Year.
- The names of the variables in the new file are *CASE_LBL, VAR001, VAR002,* and *VAR003*.

VARIABLES Subcommand

VARIABLES names one or more variables (columns) to be transposed. The specified variables become observations (rows) in the new working file.

- The VARIABLES subcommand is optional. If it is not used, all variables are transposed.
- The actual keyword VARIABLES can be omitted.
- If the VARIABLES subcommand is specified, variables that are not named are discarded.

Example

Using the untransposed file from the previous example, the command

```
FLIP VARIABLES=A TO C.
```

transposes only variables *A* through *C*. Variable *D* is not transposed and is discarded from the working data file. The LIST output for the transposed file is as follows:

```
CASE_LBL      VAR001      VAR002      VAR003
A                .           .           .
B              22.00       34.00     1970.00
C              31.00       29.00     1971.00
```

NEWNAMES Subcommand

NEWNAMES specifies a variable whose values are used as the new variable names.

- The NEWNAMES subcommand is optional. If it is not used, the new variable names are either *VAR001* to *VARn*, or the values of *CASE_LBL* if it exists.
- Only one variable can be specified on NEWNAMES.
- The variable specified on NEWNAMES does not become an observation (case) in the new working data file, regardless of whether it is specified on the VARIABLES subcommand.
- If the variable specified is numeric, its values become a character string beginning with the letter *V*.
- If the variable specified is a long string, only the first eight characters are used.
- Lowercase character values of a string variable are converted to uppercase, and any bad character values, such as blank spaces, are replaced with underscore (_) characters.
- If the variable's values are not unique, a numeric extension *n* is added to the end of a value after its first occurrence, with *n* increasing by 1 at each subsequent occurrence.

Example

Using the untransposed file from the first example, the command

```
FLIP NEWNAMES=A.
```

uses the values for variable *A* as variable names in the new file. The LIST output for the transposed file is as follows:

```
CASE_LBL      INCOME      PRICE       YEAR
B              22.00       34.00     1970.00
C              31.00       29.00     1971.00
D              43.00       50.00     1972.00
```

- Variable *A* does not become an observation in the new file. The string values for *A* are converted to upper case.

The following command transposes this file back to a form resembling its original structure:

```
FLIP.
```

The LIST output for the transposed file is as follows:

```
CASE_LBL       B          C          D

INCOME      22.00      31.00      43.00
PRICE       34.00      29.00      50.00
YEAR      1970.00    1971.00    1972.00
```

- Since the NEWNAMES subcommand is not used, the values of *CASE_LBL* from the previous FLIP (*B, C,* and *D*) are used as variable names in the new file.
- The values of *CASE_LBL* are now INCOME, PRICE, and YEAR.

FORMATS

```
FORMATS varlist(format) [varlist...]
```

Example:
```
FORMATS SALARY (DOLLAR8) / HOURLY (DOLLAR7.2) / RAISE BONUS (PCT2).
```

Overview

FORMATS changes variable print and write formats. In SPSS, print and write formats are *output* formats. Print formats, also called display formats, control the form in which values are displayed by a procedure or by the PRINT command; write formats control the form in which values are written by the WRITE command.

FORMATS changes both print and write formats. To change only print formats, use PRINT FORMATS. To change only write formats, use WRITE FORMATS. For information on assigning input formats during data definition, see DATA LIST.

Table 10 shows the output formats that can be assigned with the FORMATS, PRINT FORMATS, and WRITE FORMATS commands. For additional information on formats, see "Variable Formats" on p. 34.

Basic Specification

The basic specification is a variable list followed by a format specification in parentheses. All variables in the list receive the new format.

Syntax Rules

- You can specify more than one variable or variable list, followed by a format in parentheses. Only one format can be specified after each variable list. For clarity, each set of specifications can be separated by a slash.
- You can use keyword TO to refer to consecutive variables in the working data file.
- The specified width of a format must include enough positions to accommodate any punctuation characters such as decimal points, commas, dollar signs, or date and time delimiters. (This differs from assigning an *input* format on DATA LIST, where SPSS automatically expands the input format to accommodate punctuation characters in output.)
- Custom currency formats (CCw, CCw.d) must first be defined on the SET command before they can be used on FORMATS.
- FORMATS cannot be used with string variables. To change the length of a string variable, declare a new variable of the desired length with the STRING command and then use COMPUTE to copy values from the existing string into the new variable.
- To save the new print and write formats, you must save the working data file as an SPSS data file with the SAVE or XSAVE commands.

Table 10 shows the formats that can be assigned by FORMATS, PRINT FORMATS, or WRITE FORMATS. The first column of the table lists the FORTRAN-like specification. The column labeled *PRINT* indicates whether the format can be used to display values. The columns labeled *Min w* and *Max w* refer to the minimum and maximum widths allowed for the format type. The column labeled *Max d* refers to the maximum decimal places.

Table 10 Output data formats

Type	PRINT	Min w	Max w	Max d	Resulting form
Numeric					
Fw, Fw.d	yes	1*	40	16	
COMMAw, COMMAw.d	yes	1*	40	16	
DOTw, DOTw.d	yes	1*	40	16	
DOLLARw, DOLLARw.d	yes	2*	40	16	
CCw, CCw.d	yes	2*	40	16	
PCTw, PCTw.d	yes	1*	40	16	
PIBHEXw	yes	2†	16†		
RBHEXw	yes	4†	16†		
Zw, Zw.d	yes	1	40	16	
IBw, IBw.d	no	1	8	16	
PIBw, PIBw.d	no	1	8	16	
Nw.d	yes	1	40	16	
Pw, Pw.d	no	1	16	16	
Ew, Ew.d	yes	6	40		
PKw, PKw.d	no	1	16	16	
RBw	no	2	8		
String					
Aw	yes	1	254		
AHEXw	yes	2†	510		
Date and time					
DATEw	yes	9	40		dd-mmm-yy
		11			dd-mmm-yyyy
ADATEw	yes	8	40		mm/dd/yy
		10			mm/dd/yyyy
EDATEw	yes	8	40		dd/mm/yy
		10			dd/mm/yyyy
JDATEw	yes	5	40		yyddd
		7			yyyyddd
SDATEw	yes	8	40		yy/mm/dd
		10			yyyy/mm/dd
QYRw	yes	6	40		q Q yy

Table 10 Output data formats (Continued)

Type	PRINT	Min w	Max w	Max d	
		8			q Q yyyy
MOYRw	yes	6	40		mmm yy
		8			mmm yyyy
WKYRw	yes	8	40		ww WK yy
		10			ww WK yyyy
WKDAYw	yes	2**	40		
MONTHw	yes	3**	40		
TIMEw	yes	5††	40		hh:mm
TIMEw.d	yes	10	40	16	hh:mm:ss.s
DTIMEw	yes	8††	40		dd hh:mm
DTIMEw.d	yes	13	40	16	dd hh:mm:ss.s
DATETIMEw	yes	17††	40		dd-mmm-yyyy hh:mm
DATETIMEw.d	yes	22	40	16	dd-mmm-yyyy hh:mm:ss.s

*Add number of decimals plus 1 if number of decimals is more than 0. Total width cannot exceed 40 characters.
†Must be multiple of 2.
**As the field width is expanded, the output string is expanded until the entire name of the day or month is produced.
††Add 3 to display seconds.

Operations

- Unlike most transformations, FORMATS takes effect as soon as it is encountered in the command sequence. Special attention should be paid to its position among commands. For more information, see "Command Order" on p. 17.
- Variables not specified on FORMATS retain their current print and write formats in the working file. To see the current formats, use the DISPLAY command.
- The new formats are changed only in the working file and are in effect for the duration of the SPSS session or until changed again with a FORMATS, PRINT FORMATS, or WRITE FORMATS command. Formats in the original data file (if one exists) are not changed unless the file is resaved with the SAVE or XSAVE command.
- New numeric variables created with transformation commands are assigned default print and write formats of F8.2 (or the format specified on the FORMAT subcommand of SET). The FORMATS command can be used to change the new variable's print and write formats.
- New string variables created with transformation commands are assigned the format specified on the STRING command that declares the variable. FORMATS cannot be used to change the format of a new string variable.
- Date and time formats are effective only with the LIST, REPORT, and TABLES procedures and the PRINT and WRITE transformation commands. All other procedures use F format regardless of the date and time formats specified. See "Date and Time in SPSS" on p. 59.

- If a numeric data value exceeds its width specification, SPSS attempts to display some value nevertheless. First SPSS rounds decimal values, then removes punctuation characters, then tries scientific notation, and finally, if there is still not enough space, produces asterisks indicating that a value is present but cannot be displayed in the assigned width.

Example

```
FORMATS SALARY (DOLLAR8) /HOURLY (DOLLAR7.2)
        /RAISE BONUS (PCT2).
```

- The print and write formats for *SALARY* are changed to DOLLAR format with eight positions, including the dollar sign and comma when appropriate. The value 11550 is displayed as $11,550. An eight-digit number would require a DOLLAR11 format: 8 characters for the digits, 2 characters for commas, and 1 character for the dollar sign.
- The print and write formats for *HOURLY* are changed to DOLLAR format with seven positions, including the dollar sign, decimal point, and two decimal places. The value 115 is displayed as $115.00. If DOLLAR6.2 had been specified, the value 115 would be displayed as $115.0. SPSS would truncate the last 0 because a width of 6 is not enough to display the full value.
- The print and write formats for both *RAISE* and *BONUS* are changed to PCT with two positions: one position for the percentage and one position for the percent sign. The value 9 is displayed as 9%. Since the width allows for only two positions, the value 10 is displayed as 10, since the percent sign is truncated.

Example

```
COMPUTE V3=V1 + V2.
FORMATS V3 (F3.1).
```

- COMPUTE creates the new numeric variable *V3*. By default, *V3* is assigned an F8.2 format (or the default format specified on SET).
- FORMATS changes both the print and write formats for *V3* to F3.1.

Example

```
SET CCA='-/-.Dfl ..-'.
FORMATS COST (CCA14.2).
```

- SET defines a European currency format for the custom currency format type CCA.
- FORMATS assigns format CCA to variable *COST*. With the format defined for CCA on SET, the value 37419 is displayed as Dfl 37.419,00. See the SET command for more information on custom currency formats.

FREQUENCIES

```
FREQUENCIES [VARIABLES=]varlist[(min,max)] [varlist...]

 [/FORMAT=[{CONDENSE}]] [{NOTABLE }] [NOLABELS] [WRITE]
          {ONEPAGE  }   {LIMIT(n) }

          [{AVALUE}] [DOUBLE] [NEWPAGE] [INDEX]]
           {DVALUE}
           {AFREQ }
           {DFREQ }

 [/MISSING=INCLUDE]

 [/BARCHART=[MINIMUM(n)] [MAXIMUM(n)] [{FREQ(n)   }]]
                                      {PERCENT(n)}

 [/HISTOGRAM=[MINIMUM(n)] [MAXIMUM(n)] [{FREQ(n)   }]
                                       {PERCENT(n)}

             [{NONORMAL}] [INCREMENT(n)]]
              {NORMAL  }

 [/HBAR=same as HISTOGRAM]

 [/GROUPED=varlist [{(width)       }]]
                   {(boundary list)}

 [/NTILES=n]

 [/PERCENTILES=value list]

 [/STATISTICS=[DEFAULT] [MEAN] [STDDEV] [MINIMUM] [MAXIMUM]
              [SEMEAN] [VARIANCE] [SKEWNESS] [SESKEW] [RANGE]
              [MODE] [KURTOSIS] [SEKURT] [MEDIAN] [SUM] [ALL]
              [NONE]]
```

Example:
```
FREQUENCIES VAR=RACE /STATISTICS=ALL.
```

Overview

FREQUENCIES produces tables of frequency counts and percentages of the values of individual variables. FREQUENCIES is used to obtain frequencies and statistics for categorical variables and to obtain statistics and graphical displays for continuous variables.

Options

Display Format. You can condense, expand, or suppress tables and alter the order of values within tables using the FORMAT subcommand.

Statistical Display. Percentiles and ntiles are available for numeric variables with the PERCENTILES and NTILES subcommands. The following statistics are available with the STATISTICS subcommand: mean, median, mode, standard deviation, variance, skewness, kurtosis, and sum.

Plots. Histograms can be specified for numeric variables on the HISTOGRAM subcommand. Bar charts can be specified for numeric or string variables on the BARCHART subcommand.

Input Data. On the GROUPED subcommand you can indicate whether the input data are grouped (or collapsed) so that a better estimate can be made of percentiles.

Basic Specification

The basic specification is the VARIABLES subcommand and the name of at least one variable. By default, FREQUENCIES produces a frequency table.

Subcommand Order

Subcommands can be named in any order.

Syntax Rules

- You can specify multiple NTILES subcommands.
- BARCHART, HISTOGRAM, and HBAR are mutually exclusive. HBAR is used whenever any two of these subcommands are specified on the same FREQUENCIES command.
- FREQUENCIES operates in integer or general mode, depending on the VARIABLES specification.

General Mode

- FREQUENCIES runs in general mode if VARIABLES specifies a variable list without value ranges.
- You can specify numeric variables (with or without decimal values) or string variables. Only the short-string portion of long string variables are tabulated.
- Keyword ALL can be used on VARIABLES to refer to all user-defined variables in the working data file.

Integer Mode

- FREQUENCIES runs in integer mode if VARIABLES specifies a variable list and a value range in parentheses after each variable name.
- Specified variables must be numeric. Numeric variables with decimal positions are truncated to their whole number value.

Operations

- Variables are tabulated in the order that they are mentioned on the VARIABLES subcommand. If a variable is mentioned more than once, it is tabulated more than once.

- If a requested ntile or percentile cannot be calculated, a period (.) is displayed.
- The display always uses narrow format regardless of the width defined on SET.

General vs. Integer Mode

- In general mode, FREQUENCIES dynamically builds the table, setting up one cell for each unique value encountered in the data.
- In integer mode, the table for each variable includes only values within the specified range. Values outside the range are grouped into an out-of-range category and are considered missing for the calculation of percentages and statistics.
- Integer mode usually takes less computation time. (Computation time depends upon the range of values and the order in which values are read.)
- Integer mode requires less memory than does general mode, except when variables are sparsely distributed.
- In integer mode, the value range specification can eliminate extremely low or high values.
- Since integer mode truncates decimal positions, you can obtain grouped frequency tables for continuous variables without having to recode them to integers. General mode does not truncate nonintegers and can tabulate short strings.

Limitations

- Maximum 500 variables total per FREQUENCIES command.
- Maximum value range of 32,767 for a variable in integer mode.
- Maximum of 32,767 observed values over all variables.

Example

```
FREQUENCIES VAR=RACE /STATISTICS=ALL.
```

- FREQUENCIES requests a frequency table and all statistics for the categorical variable *RACE*.
- General mode is used because there is no range specified for *RACE*.

Example

```
FREQUENCIES STATISTICS=ALL /HISTOGRAM
  /VARIABLES=SEX (1,2) TVHOURS (0,24) SCALE1 TO SCALE5 (1,7)
  /FORMAT=NOTABLE.
```

- FREQUENCIES requests statistics and histograms for *SEX*, *TVHOURS*, and all variables between and including *SCALE1* and *SCALE5* in the working data file.
- Integer mode is used because a value range is specified for each variable.
- FORMAT suppresses the frequency tables, which are not useful for continuous variables.

VARIABLES Subcommand

VARIABLES names the variables to be tabulated and is the only required subcommand. VARIABLES also determines whether FREQUENCIES runs in general or integer mode. The actual keyword VARIABLES can be omitted.

- If value ranges are specified in parentheses after each variable name, FREQUENCIES runs in *integer* mode.
- If no value ranges are specified, FREQUENCIES runs in *general* mode.
- You cannot mix general and integer modes.

FORMAT Subcommand

FORMAT controls various features of the output, including frequency table format, order of categories, suppression of tables, table indexes, and output destination.

- The minimum specification is a single keyword.

Table Formats

By default, FREQUENCIES displays as many single-spaced frequency tables with complete labeling information as fit within the page length.

CONDENSE *Condensed format.* Counts are displayed in three columns without value labels and with valid and cumulative percentages rounded to integers. CONDENSE overrides ONEPAGE.

ONEPAGE *Conditional condensed format.* Condensed format is used for tables that would otherwise require more than one page.

NEWPAGE *Start each table on a new page.*

NOLABELS *Suppress value labels.*

DOUBLE *Double space frequency tables.*

Table Order

AVALUE *Sort categories in ascending order of values (numeric variables) or in alphabetical order (string variables).* This is the default.

DVALUE *Sort categories in descending order of values (numeric variables) or in reverse alphabetical order (string variables).* This is ignored when HISTOGRAM, HBAR, NTILES, or PERCENTILES is requested.

AFREQ *Sort categories in ascending order of frequency.* This is ignored when HISTOGRAM, HBAR, NTILES, or PERCENTILES is requested.

DFREQ *Sort categories in descending order of frequency.* This is ignored when HISTOGRAM, HBAR, NTILES, or PERCENTILES is requested.

Table Suppression

LIMIT(n) *Suppress frequency tables with more than n categories.* The number of missing and valid cases and requested statistics are displayed for suppressed tables.

NOTABLE *Suppress all frequency tables.* The number of missing and valid cases are displayed for suppressed tables. NOTABLE overrides LIMIT.

Table Index

INDEX *Display indexes of tables.* Two indexes are displayed: a positional index of frequency tables and an index arranged alphabetically by variable name.

Writing Tables to a File

WRITE *Direct procedure output (frequency tables and plots) to a separate file.* The file must be specified on a PROCEDURE OUTPUT command before the FREQUENCIES command. If WRITE is specified, frequency tables and plots are not shown in the displayed output.

Example

```
PROCEDURE OUTPUT  OUTFILE=CODEBOOK.
FREQUENCIES  VARIABLES=ALL /FORMAT=ONEPAGE WRITE.
```

- PROCEDURE OUTPUT specifies *CODEBOOK* as the file to receive the frequency tables.
- FREQUENCIES uses conditional condensed format and writes the frequency tables to file *CODEBOOK*, specified on PROCEDURE OUTPUT.
- Frequency tables are not shown in the output.

BARCHART Subcommand

BARCHART produces a bar chart for each variable named on the VARIABLES subcommand. By default, the horizontal axis for each bar chart is scaled in frequencies, and the interval width is determined by the largest frequency count for the variable being plotted. Bar charts are labeled with value labels or with the value if no label is defined.

- The minimum specification is the keyword BARCHART, which generates default bar charts.
- BARCHART cannot be used with HISTOGRAM or HBAR. HBAR is used whenever any two of these subcommands appear on the same FREQUENCIES command.

MIN(n) *Lower bound below which values are not plotted.*

MAX(n) *Upper bound above which values are not plotted.*

PERCENT(n)   *Horizontal axis scaled in percentages, where optional* n *is the maximum.* If n is not specified or if it is too small, FREQUENCIES chooses 5, 10, 25, 50, or 100, depending on the frequency count for the largest category.

FREQ(n)   *Horizontal axis scaled in frequencies, where optional* n *is the maximum.* If n is not specified or if it is too small, FREQUENCIES chooses 5, 10, 20, 50, 100, 200, 500, 1000, 2000, and so forth, depending on the largest category. This is the default.

Example

```
FREQUENCIES VAR=RACE /BARCHART.
```

- FREQUENCIES produces a frequency table and the default bar chart for variable *RACE*.

Example

```
FREQUENCIES VAR=V1 V2 /BAR=MAX(10).
```

- FREQUENCIES produces a frequency table and bar chart with values through 10 for each of variables *V1* and *V2*.

HISTOGRAM Subcommand

HISTOGRAM displays a plot for each numeric variable named on the VARIABLES subcommand. By default, the horizontal axis of each histogram is scaled in frequencies and the interval width is determined by the largest frequency count of the variable being plotted.

- The minimum specification is the keyword HISTOGRAM, which generates default histograms.
- The HISTOGRAM subcommand on the SET command controls the character used to draw histograms.
- HISTOGRAM cannot be used with BARCHART or HBAR. HBAR is used whenever any two of these subcommands appear on the same FREQUENCIES command.

MIN(n)   *Lower bound below which values are not plotted.*

MAX(n)   *Upper bound above which values are not plotted.*

PERCENT(n)   *Horizontal axis scaled in percentages, where optional* n *is the maximum.* If n is not specified or if it is too small, FREQUENCIES chooses 5, 10, 25, 50, or 100, depending on the largest category.

FREQ(n)   *Horizontal axis scaled in frequencies, where optional* n *is the scale.* If n is not specified or if it is too small, FREQUENCIES chooses 5, 10, 20, 50, 100, 200, 500, 1000, 2000, and so forth, depending on the largest category. This is the default.

INCREMENT(n)   *Interval width, where* n *is the size of the interval.* This specification overrides the default number of intervals on the vertical axis, which depends on the system page length. For a variable that ranges from 1 to 100, INCREMENT(2) produces 50 intervals with 2 values each.

NORMAL *Superimpose a normal curve.* The curve is based on all valid values for the variable, including values excluded by MIN and MAX.

NONORMAL *Suppress the normal curve.* This is the default.

Example

```
FREQUENCIES VAR=V1 /HIST=NORMAL INCREMENT(4).
```

- FREQUENCIES requests a histogram with a superimposed normal curve and an interval width of 4.

HBAR Subcommand

HBAR produces a plot for each numeric and string variable named on the VARIABLES subcommand. For numeric variables, HBAR produces a bar chart if the number of categories fits within the page length (see SET). Otherwise, HBAR produces a histogram. For short string variables and for the short-string portion of long string variables, HBAR produces bar charts regardless of the number of values.

By default, the horizontal axis of each plot is scaled in frequencies and the interval is determined by the largest frequency count. All keyword specifications for HISTOGRAM and BARCHART work with HBAR.

GROUPED Subcommand

When the values of a variable represent grouped or collapsed data, it is possible to estimate percentiles for the original, ungrouped data from the grouped data. The GROUPED subcommand specifies which variables have been grouped. It affects only the output from the PERCENTILES and NTILES subcommands and the MEDIAN statistic from the STATISTICS subcommand.

- Multiple GROUPED subcommands can be used on a single FREQUENCIES command. Multiple variable lists, separated by slashes, can appear on a single GROUPED subcommand.
- The variables named on GROUPED must have been named on the VARIABLES subcommand.
- The value or value list in the parentheses is optional. When it is omitted, SPSS treats the values of the variables listed on GROUPED as midpoints. If the values are not midpoints, they must first be recoded with the RECODE command.
- A single value in parentheses specifies the width of each grouped interval. The data values must be group midpoints, but there can be empty categories. For example, if you have data values of 10, 20, and 30 and specify an interval width of 5, the categories are 10 ± 2.5, 20 ± 2.5, and 30 ± 2.5. The categories 15 ± 2.5 and 25 ± 2.5 are empty.
- A value list in the parentheses specifies interval boundaries. The data values do not have to represent midpoints, but the lowest boundary must be lower than any value in the data. If any data values exceed the highest boundary specified (the last value within the parentheses), they will be assigned to an open-ended interval. In this case, some percentiles cannot be calculated.

Example

```
RECODE AGE  (1=15)  (2=25)  (3=35)  (4=45)  (5=55)
            (6=65)  (7=75)  (8=85)  (9=95)
   /INCOME  (1=5)   (2=15)  (3=25)  (4=35)  (5=45)
            (6=55)  (7=65)  (8=75)  (9=100).

FREQUENCIES VARIABLES=AGE, SEX, RACE, INCOME
   /GROUPED=AGE, INCOME
   /PERCENTILES=5,25,50,75,95.
```

- The *AGE* and *INCOME* categories of 1, 2, 3, and so forth are recoded to category midpoints. Note that data can be recoded to category midpoints on any scale; here *AGE* is recoded in years, but *INCOME* is recoded in thousands of dollars.
- The GROUPED subcommand on FREQUENCIES allows more accurate estimates of the requested percentiles.

Example

```
FREQUENCIES VARIABLES=TEMP
   /GROUPED=TEMP (0.5)
   /NTILES=10.
```

- The values of *TEMP* (temperature) in this example were recorded using an inexpensive thermometer whose readings are precise only to the nearest half degree.
- The observed values of 97.5, 98, 98.5, 99, and so on, are treated as group midpoints, smoothing out the discrete distribution. This yields more accurate estimates of the deciles.

Example

```
FREQUENCIES VARIABLES=AGE
   /GROUPED=AGE (17.5, 22.5, 27.5, 32.5, 37.5, 42.5, 47.5
                52.5, 57.5, 62.5, 67.5, 72.5, 77.5, 82.5)
   /PERCENTILES=5, 10, 25, 50, 75, 90, 95.
```

- The values of *AGE* in this example have been estimated to the nearest five years. The first category is 17.5 to 22.5, the second is 22.5 to 27.5, and so forth. The artificial clustering of age estimates at multiples of five years is smoothed out by treating *AGE* as grouped data.
- It is not necessary to recode the ages to category midpoints, since the interval boundaries are explicitly given.

PERCENTILES Subcommand

PERCENTILES displays the value below which the specified percentage of cases falls. The desired percentiles must be explicitly requested. There are no defaults.

Example

```
FREQUENCIES VAR=V1 /PERCENTILES=10 25 33.3 66.7 75.
```

- FREQUENCIES requests the values for percentiles 10, 25, 33.3, 66.7, and 75 for *V1*.

NTILES Subcommand

NTILES calculates the percentages that divide the distribution into the specified number of categories and displays the values below which the requested percentages of cases fall. There are no default ntiles.

- Multiple NTILES subcommands are allowed. Each NTILES subcommand generates separate percentiles. Any duplicate percentiles generated by different NTILES subcommands are consolidated in the output.

Example

```
FREQUENCIES VARIABLE=V1 /NTILES=4.
```

- FREQUENCIES requests quartiles (percentiles 25, 50, and 75) for *V1*.

Example

```
FREQUENCIES VARIABLE=V1 /NTILES=4 /NTILES=10.
```

- The first NTILES subcommand requests percentiles 25, 50, and 75.
- The second NTILES subcommand requests percentiles 10 through 90 in increments of 10.
- The 50th percentile is produced by both specifications but is displayed only once in the output.

STATISTICS Subcommand

STATISTICS controls the display of statistics. By default, cases with missing values are excluded from the calculation of statistics.

- The minimum specification is the keyword STATISTICS, which generates the mean, standard deviation, minimum, and maximum (these statistics are also produced by keyword DEFAULT).
- In integer mode, only cases with values in the specified range are used in the computation of statistics.

MEAN	*Mean.*
SEMEAN	*Standard error of the mean.*
MEDIAN	*Median.* Ignored when AFREQ or DFREQ are specified on the FORMAT subcommand.
MODE	*Mode.* If there is more than one mode, only the first mode is displayed.
STDDEV	*Standard deviation.*
VARIANCE	*Variance.*
SKEWNESS	*Skewness.*
SESKEW	*Standard error of the skewness statistic.*
KURTOSIS	*Kurtosis.*

SEKURT	*Standard error of the kurtosis statistic.*
RANGE	*Range.*
MINIMUM	*Minimum.*
MAXIMUM	*Maximum.*
SUM	*Sum.*
DEFAULT	*Mean, standard deviation, minimum, and maximum.*
ALL	*All available statistics.*
NONE	*No statistics.*

Example

```
FREQUENCIES VAR=AGE /STATS=MODE.
```

- STATISTICS requests the mode of *AGE*.

Example

```
FREQUENCIES VAR=AGE /STATS=DEF MODE.
```

- STATISTICS requests the default statistics (mean, standard deviation, minimum, and maximum) plus the mode of *AGE*.

MISSING Subcommand

By default, both user- and system-missing values are labeled as missing in the table but are not included in the valid and cumulative percentages, in the calculation of descriptive statistics, or in bar charts and histograms.

INCLUDE	*Include cases with user-missing values.* Cases with user-missing values are included in statistics and plots.

GET

```
GET FILE=file

 [/KEEP={ALL** }] [/DROP=varlist]
        {varlist}

 [/RENAME=(old varnames=new varnames)...]

 [/MAP]
```

**Default if the subcommand is omitted.

Example:
```
GET FILE=EMPL.
```

Overview

GET reads an SPSS data file that was created by the SAVE or XSAVE command. An SPSS data file is in a format only SPSS can read and contains data plus a dictionary. The dictionary contains a name for each variable in the data file, plus any assigned variable and value labels, missing-value flags, and variable print and write formats. The dictionary also contains document text created with the DOCUMENTS command.

GET is used only for reading SPSS data files. See DATA LIST for information on reading and defining data in a text data file. See MATRIX DATA for information on defining matrix materials in a text data file. For information on defining complex data files that cannot be defined with DATA LIST alone, see FILE TYPE and REPEATING DATA.

SPSS can also read data files created for other software applications. See IMPORT for information on reading *portable files* created with EXPORT in SPSS or SPSS/PC+. See commands such as GET TRANSLATE, GET SCSS, GET SAS, GET BMDP, and GET OSIRIS for information on reading files created by other software programs.

Options

Variable Subsets and Order. You can read a subset of variables and reorder the variables that are copied into the working data file using the DROP and KEEP subcommands.

Variable Names. You can rename variables as they are copied into the working data file with the RENAME subcommand.

Variable Map. To confirm the names and order of variables in the working data file, use the MAP subcommand. MAP displays the variables in the working file next to their corresponding names in the SPSS data file.

Basic Specification

- The basic specification is the FILE subcommand, which specifies the SPSS data file to be read.

- By default, GET copies all variables from the SPSS file into the working data file. Variables in the working file are in the same order and have the same names as variables in the SPSS data file. Documentary text from the SPSS file is copied into the dictionary of the working file.

Subcommand Order

- FILE must be specified first.
- The remaining subcommands can be specified in any order.

Syntax Rules

- FILE is required and can be specified only once.
- KEEP, DROP, RENAME, and MAP can be used as many times as needed.
- Documentary text copied from the SPSS data file can be dropped from the working data file with the DROP DOCUMENTS command.
- GET cannot be used inside a DO IF—END IF or LOOP—END LOOP structure.

Operations

- GET reads the dictionary of the SPSS data file.
- If KEEP is not specified, variables in the working data file are in the same order as variables in the SPSS data file.
- A file saved with weighting in effect maintains the values of variable *$WEIGHT*. For a discussion of turning off weights, see WEIGHT.
- The order of cases in the working data file is the same as their order in the SPSS data file. The values of *$CASENUM* are those from the original text data file before any selecting (see SELECT IF) or sorting (see SORT). The value of *$CASENUM* may differ from the actual number of a case after selecting or sorting.

FILE Subcommand

FILE specifies the SPSS data file to be read. FILE is required and can be specified only once. It must be the first specification on GET.

DROP and KEEP Subcommands

DROP and KEEP are used to copy a subset of variables into the working data file. DROP specifies variables that should not be copied into the working file. KEEP specifies variables that should be copied. Variables not specified on KEEP are dropped.

- Variables can be specified in any order. The order of variables on KEEP determines the order of variables in the working file. The order on DROP does not affect the order of variables in the working file.
- Keyword ALL on KEEP refers to all remaining variables not previously specified on KEEP. ALL must be the last specification on KEEP.
- If a variable is specified twice on the same subcommand, only the first mention is recognized.
- Multiple DROP and KEEP subcommands are allowed. However, specifying a variable named on a previous DROP or not named on a previous KEEP results in an error and the GET command is not executed.
- Keyword TO can be used to specify a group of consecutive variables in the SPSS data file.

Example

```
GET FILE=HUBTEMP /DROP=DEPT79 TO DEPT84 SALARY79.
```

- The working data file is copied from SPSS file *HUBTEMP*. All variables between and including *DEPT79* and *DEPT84*, as well as *SALARY79*, are excluded from the working file. All other variables are copied into the working file.
- Variables in the working data file are in the same order as the variables in the *HUBTEMP* file.

Example

```
GET FILE=PRSNL /DROP=GRADE STORE
               /KEEP=LNAME NAME TENURE JTENURE ALL.
```

- Variables *GRADE* and *STORE* are dropped when file *PRSNL* is copied into the working data file.
- KEEP specifies that LNAME, NAME, TENURE, and JTENURE are the first four variables in the working file, followed by all remaining variables (except those dropped by the previous DROP). These remaining variables are copied into the working file in the same sequence in which they appear in the *PRSNL* file.

RENAME Subcommand

RENAME changes the names of variables as they are copied into the working data file.
- The specification on RENAME is a list of old variable names followed by an equals sign and a list of new variable names. The same number of variables must be specified on both lists. Keyword TO can be used in the first list to refer to consecutive variables in the SPSS data file and in the second list to generate new variable names (see "Keyword TO" on p. 32). The entire specification must be enclosed in parentheses.
- Alternatively, you can specify each old variable name individually, followed by an equals sign and the new variable name. Multiple sets of variable specifications are allowed. The parentheses around each set of specifications are optional.
- Old variable names do not need to be specified according to their order in the SPSS data file.

- Name changes take place in one operation. Therefore, variable names can be exchanged between two variables.
- Variables cannot be renamed to scratch variables.
- Multiple RENAME subcommands are allowed.
- On a subsequent DROP or KEEP subcommand, variables are referred to by their new names.

Example

```
GET FILE=EMPL88 /RENAME  AGE=AGE88 JOBCAT=JOBCAT88.
```

- RENAME specifies two name changes for the working data file. *AGE* is renamed to *AGE88* and *JOBCAT* is renamed to *JOBCAT88*.

Example

```
GET FILE=EMPL88 /RENAME (AGE JOBCAT=AGE88 JOBCAT88).
```

- The name changes are identical to those in the previous example. *AGE* is renamed to *AGE88* and *JOBCAT* is renamed to *JOBCAT88*. The parentheses are required with this method.

MAP Subcommand

MAP displays a list of the variables in the working data file and their corresponding names in the SPSS data file.

- The only specification is keyword MAP. There are no additional specifications.
- Multiple MAP subcommands are allowed. Each MAP subcommand maps the results of subcommands that precede it; results of subcommands that follow it are not mapped.

Example

```
GET FILE=EMPL88 /RENAME=(AGE=AGE88) (JOBCAT=JOBCAT88)
 /KEEP=LNAME NAME JOBCAT88 ALL /MAP.
```

- MAP is specified to confirm the new names for variables *AGE* and *JOBCAT* and the order of variables in the working data file (*LNAME*, *NAME*, and *JOBCAT88*, followed by all remaining variables in the SPSS data file).

GET BMDP

This command is not available on all operating systems.

```
GET BMDP FILE=file

 [/SCAN={YES }] [/CODE=name]
       {ONLY}

 [/CONTENT=name] [/LABEL=quoted string]

 [/KEEP={ALL** }] [/DROP=varlist]
       {varlist}

 [/RENAME=(old varnames=new varnames)...]

 [/MAP]
```

**Default if the subcommand is omitted.

Example:
```
GET BMDP FILE=BMDPFIL3.
```

Overview

GET BMDP reads a save file from a BMDP data set. The specified save file from the data set becomes the SPSS working data file. If necessary, BMDP variable names and missing values are automatically converted to comply with SPSS conventions.

Options

Save Files. You can read a particular save file within the data set to read using the CONTENT, CODE, and LABEL subcommands.

Variable Subsets and Order. You can read a subset of variables and reorder the variables that are copied into the working data file using the DROP and KEEP subcommands.

Variable Names. You can rename variables as they are copied into the working data file with the RENAME subcommand.

Variable Map. To confirm the names and order of variables copied into the working data file, use the MAP subcommand. MAP displays the variables in the working file next to their corresponding names in the BMDP save file.

Basic Specification

- The basic specification is the FILE subcommand, which specifies the BMDP data set.
- By default, SPSS reads the first save file within the data set with the content field *DATA*. All variables from the BMDP save file are copied into the SPSS working data file. However, SPSS may have to rename BMDP variables so they conform to SPSS naming conventions (see "BMDP to SPSS Data Conversion" on p. 284).

Subcommand Order

- FILE is required and must be specified first.
- If specified, SCAN must immediately follow FILE.
- CONTENT, CODE, and LABEL can appear in any order but must follow FILE and SCAN.
- KEEP, DROP, RENAME, and MAP can be specified more than once and in any order but must follow all other subcommands.

Operations

- If KEEP is not specified, variables in the working data file are in the same order as variables in the BMDP save file.
- SPSS makes assumptions about the record format and other characteristics of the BMDP data set based on your computer and operating system. See the *Base System User's Guide* for your version of SPSS for information.
- Although it is possible for SPSS to read files with content other than *DATA*, such files are likely to be interpreted incorrectly. A certain amount of trial and error may be necessary to read and redefine such files.
- Information generated by the BMDP GROUPS paragraph is ignored.

Case Selection

In a BMDP save file, each case includes an automatic variable *USE*, whose value determines whether the case is included in an analysis. Only cases in which *USE* has a positive, nonmissing value are included in BMDP analyses. GET BMDP retains all cases, and it retains the variable *USE* unless the KEEP or DROP subcommands indicate otherwise. SPSS can use the same case selection as if the SELECT IF command is used before an analysis, as in SELECT IF USE > 0.

BMDP to SPSS Data Conversion

SPSS makes the following conversions to force BMDP data to comply with SPSS conventions.

Variable Names

- Initial blanks and special characters are changed to @. For example, *$VAR*, *.VAR*, */VAR*, and *VAR* preceded by a blank all become *@VAR* (see below about duplicate names).
- Internal blanks and special characters are changed to underscores. *VAR ONE* and *VAR/ONE* both become *VAR_ONE*.
- Parentheses are removed. *X(1)* becomes *X1*.
- If an SPSS reserved keyword is used as a BMDP variable name, SPSS appends the # symbol to the name and issues a warning message. The SPSS reserved keywords are ALL,

AND, BY, GE, GT, LE, LT, NE, NOT, OR, TO, and WITH. A BMDP variable named *AND*, for example, would be converted to *AND#*.
- If conversion produces duplicate variable names, SPSS creates names of the form *Vn*, in which *n* is an integer.

Missing Values

All three BMDP missing values (missing, lower than the minimum, and higher than the maximum) are converted to the SPSS system-missing value.

Print and Write Formats

- GET BMDP supplies print and write formats of F8.2 for all numeric variables and A4 for all string variables. FORMATS, PRINT FORMATS, and WRITE FORMATS in SPSS can be used to change these numeric formats if they are inappropriate.
- SPSS recognizes as string variables only those identified by the LABEL clause of BMDP's VARIABLE paragraph. Other string variables might not be detected and may be read as numeric. You can change these variables back to string using the REFORMAT command (see REFORMAT).

FILE Subcommand

FILE specifies the BMDP data set, which can include more than one BMDP save file. Unless the CODE, CONTENT, or LABEL subcommands are specified, SPSS reads the first save file within the specified data set with the content field *DATA*.

- FILE is required and must be the first specification on GET BMDP.

SCAN Subcommand

SCAN displays information about the save files within the BMDP data set. The information includes the content, code, and label fields for the save files. Code and label are specified by the user within BMDP; content is supplied by BMDP to identify the type of file (data, correlation matrix, and so on).

- When used, SCAN must immediately follow FILE.

YES *Read the save file and display the code, content, and label fields and other information from the file.*

ONLY *Do not read the save file but display the code, content, and label fields and other information from the file.*

Example

```
GET BMDP FILE=BMDPFIL3  /SCAN ONLY.
```

- FILE specifies the *BMDPFIL3* data set.

- SCAN displays information about the save files within the data set. However, no files are read. Information about the save file can be used on the CONTENT, CODE, or LABEL subcommands of another GET BMDP command.

CONTENT, CODE, and LABEL Subcommands

CONTENT, CODE, and LABEL are used to specify a particular save file within a single data set. The specification is a name or a string enclosed in apostrophes, according to BMDP conventions.

- If CONTENT is not specified, SPSS assumes DATA.
- If CODE or LABEL are not specified, SPSS reads the first save file with the specified content (DATA by default).
- If CODE or LABEL are specified, SPSS reads the first file that matches all of the information provided.

Example

```
GET BMDP FILE=BMDPFIL /LABEL= 'OLD DATA'.
```

- SPSS reads the first save file in data set *BMDPFIL* with content DATA and label OLD DATA.

DROP and KEEP Subcommands

DROP and KEEP are used to copy a subset of variables into the SPSS working data file. DROP specifies variables that should not be copied into the working file. KEEP specifies variables that should be copied. Variables not specified on KEEP are dropped.

- DROP and KEEP cannot precede the FILE, CONTENT, CODE, or LABEL subcommands.
- DROP and KEEP must use SPSS variable names, not BMDP variable names (see "BMDP to SPSS Data Conversion" on p. 284).
- Variables can be specified in any order. The order of variables on KEEP determines the order of variables in the working file. The order on DROP does not affect the order of variables in the working file.
- Keyword ALL on KEEP refers to all remaining variables not previously specified. ALL must be the last specification on KEEP.
- If a variable is specified twice on the same subcommand, only the first mention is recognized.
- Multiple DROP and KEEP subcommands are allowed. However, specifying a variable named on a previous DROP or not named on a previous KEEP results in an error and the command is not executed.
- Keyword TO can be used to specify a group of consecutive variables in the BMDP save file.

Example

```
GET BMDP FILE=BMDPFIL /DROP=X1 TO X4, X9 /KEEP=X7 X6 ALL.
```

- GET BMDP reads the BMDP data set *BMDPFIL*; the first save file with content *DATA* is copied into the SPSS working data file. The save file contains variables *X(1)* to *X(20)*. Note that DROP and KEEP use the SPSS variable names, not the BMDP variable names: the parentheses are dropped from the variable names.
- DROP excludes from the working data file all variables between and including *X1* and *X4*, as well as *X9*. All other variables are copied into the working file.
- KEEP specifies that *X7* and *X6* are the first two variables in the working data file, followed by all remaining variables (except those specified on DROP). The remaining variables are copied into the working file in the same sequence they appear in the original BMDP save file.

RENAME Subcommand

RENAME changes the names of variables as they are copied into the working data file.
- RENAME cannot precede the FILE, CONTENT, CODE, or LABEL subcommands.
- The specification on RENAME is a list of old variable names followed by an equals sign and a list of new variable names. The same number of variables must be specified on both lists, and you can use keyword TO. The entire specification must be enclosed in parentheses.
- Alternatively, you can specify each old variable name individually, followed by an equals sign and the new variable name. Multiple sets of variable specifications are allowed. The parentheses around each set of specifications are optional.
- The list of old variable names must use SPSS variable names, not BMDP variable names (see "BMDP to SPSS Data Conversion" on p. 284).
- Old variable names do not need to be specified according to their order in the BMDP save file.
- Name changes take place in one operation. Therefore, variable names can be exchanged between two variables.
- Variables cannot be renamed to scratch variables.
- Multiple RENAME subcommands are allowed.
- On a subsequent DROP or KEEP subcommand, variables are referred to by their new names.

Example

```
GET BMDP FILE= BMDPFIL4   /SCAN YES
  /KEEP = X1 X2 V1 V2
  /RENAME = (X1 X2 V1 V2 = X1_A X2_A X1_B X2_B).
```

- Assume the save file within data set *BMDPFIL4* contains variables named *X(1)*, *X(2)*, *X1*, and *X2* (and some others), in that order. SPSS converts the variable names *X(1)* and *X(2)* to *X1* and *X2*. Then, because of duplication, it converts *X1* and *X2* to *V1* and *V2* (see "BMDP to SPSS Data Conversion" on p. 284). Note that the KEEP and RENAME specifications use the SPSS names.
- RENAME changes variable names *X1* to *X1_A*, *X2* to *X2_A*, *V1* to *X1_B*, and *V2* to *X2_B*.

MAP Subcommand

MAP displays a list of the variables in the working data file and their corresponding names in the BMDP save file.

- MAP cannot precede the FILE, CONTENT, CODE, or LABEL subcommands.
- The only specification is keyword MAP. There are no additional specifications.
- Multiple MAP subcommands are allowed. Each MAP subcommand maps the results of subcommands that precede it; results of subcommands that follow it are not mapped.

Example

```
GET BMDP FILE=BMDPFIL4  /SCAN YES
  /KEEP=X1 X2 V1 V2 ALL
  /RENAME=(X1 X2 V1 V2 = X1_A X2_A X1_B X2_B)
  /MAP.
```

- MAP is specified to confirm the new names and the order of variables in the working data file (*X1_A*, *X2_A*, *X1_B*, and *X2_B*, followed by all remaining variables in the BMDP save file).

GET CAPTURE

```
GET CAPTURE  {INFORMIX}*
             {INGRES  }
             {ORACLE  }
             {SYBASE  }
             {SQL     }

 [/LOGIN=login]  [/PASSWORD=password]
 [/SERVER=host]  [/DATABASE=database name]†

 /SELECT=any select statement
```

* Not all subcommands specifying database types are available on all systems.
† Optional subcommands are database-specific. See "Syntax Rules" below for the subcommand(s) required by a database type.

Example:

```
GET CAPTURE INFORMIX
 /SELECT=customer.fname,
         customer.lname,
         customer.phone,
         orders.order_date
         from customer, orders
         where customer.customer_num=orders.customer_num
         and orders.backlog = "y"
         order by orders.order_date.
```

Overview

GET CAPTURE retrieves data from an INFORMIX, ORACLE, INGRES, SYBASE, or SQL SERVER database and converts them to a format that can be used by SPSS procedures. GET CAPTURE retrieves data and data information and builds a working data file for the current SPSS session.

Basic Specification

The basic specification is one of the subcommands specifying the database type followed by the SELECT subcommand and any SQL select statement.

Subcommand Order

The subcommand specifying the type of database must be the first specification. The SELECT subcommand must be the last.

Syntax Rules

- Only one subcommand specifying the database type can be used.

- The LOGIN and PASSWORD subcommands must be specified for ORACLE unless the environment variables *DBLOGIN* and *DBPASSWORD* are defined.
- The DATABASE subcommand must be specified for INGRES and SYBASE.
- The SERVER subcommand is used with SYBASE to specify a server other than the default.

Operations

- GET CAPTURE retrieves the data specified on SELECT.
- The variables are in the same order as they are specified on the SELECT subcommand.
- The data definition information captured from the database is stored in the working data file dictionary.

Limitations

Maximum 3800 characters (approximately) can be specified on the SELECT subcommand. This translates to 76 lines of 50 characters. Characters beyond the limit are ignored.

LOGIN and PASSWORD Subcommands

LOGIN and PASSWORD are required to access an ORACLE database unless the environmental variables *DBLOGIN* and *DBPASSWORD* are defined.

- The specification on LOGIN and PASSWORD is your login id and password, respectively.
- For database types other than ORACLE, these subcommands are ignored.

SERVER Subcommand

SERVER specifies the host server for the SYBASE database you want to access.

- If the subcommand is omitted, the default server is used. If no default server is defined, SPSS issues an error message and GET CAPTURE is not executed.
- For database types other than SYBASE, the specification on SERVER is ignored.

DATABASE Subcommand

DATABASE specifies the database you want to access and is required for accessing INGRES or SYBASE databases.

SELECT Subcommand

SELECT specifies any SQL select statement accepted by the database you access.

Example

```
GET CAPTURE INFORMIX
 /SELECT=customer.fname,
        customer.lname,
        customer.phone,
        orders.order_date
        from customer, orders
        where customer.customer_num=orders.custmer_num
        and orders.backlog = "y"
        order by orders.order_date.
```

- This example retrieves data from an INFORMIX database.
- The SQL select statement retrieves the customer's first and last names, phone numbers, and the date when an order was placed from two related data sets (*CUSTOMER* and *ORDERS*), selecting cases that have the same customer number in both data sets and that have backlog orders. The cases are sorted by the date an order was placed.
- GET CAPTURE converts the data to a format used by SPSS procedures and builds a working data file.

Data Conversion

GET CAPTURE converts variable names, labels, missing values, and data types, wherever necessary, to a format that conforms to SPSS conventions.

Variable Names and Labels

Database columns are read as SPSS variables.

- A column name is converted to an SPSS variable name if it conforms to SPSS naming conventions and is different from all other names created for the working data file. If not, GET CAPTURE gives the column a name formed from the first few letters of the column and its column number. If this is not possible, the letters COL followed by the column number are used. For example, the seventh column specified in the select statement could be *COL7*.
- GET CAPTURE labels each variable with its full column name specified in the original database.
- You can display a table of variable names with their original database column names using the DISPLAY LABELS command.

Missing Values

Null values in the database are transformed into the system-missing value in numeric variables or into blanks in string variables.

Data Types

Subcommand Order

- DATA and DICTIONARY must precede all other subcommands.
- KEEP, DROP, RENAME, and MAP can be specified in any order but must follow DATA and DICTIONARY.

Syntax Rules

- DATA and DICTIONARY are required and are not separated by a slash.
- KEEP, DROP, RENAME, and MAP can be specified as many times as needed and must be separated by a slash.

Operations

- If KEEP is not specified, variables in the working data file are in the same order as variables in the OSIRIS data set.
- There are three types of OSIRIS data sets: types 1, 3, and 5. SPSS can currently read only types 1 and 3. Type 1 data sets are the usual form for distribution; they are produced only by the OSIRIS system after many edit checks have been made. Type 3 data sets may be produced using ordinary text-editing software (or a card punch). Each data set consists of a fixed-format text data file and a dictionary file containing data definitions associated with OSIRIS variables.
- Variable label information is read from the OSIRIS dictionary. Type 1 data sets may include a dictionary codebook containing value label information, which GET OSIRIS automatically converts into SPSS value labels. Missing-value specifications are read from the OSIRIS data set.

OSIRIS to SPSS Data Conversion

SPSS makes the following conversions to force OSIRIS data sets to comply with SPSS conventions.

Variable Types

Both SPSS and OSIRIS recognize two variable types: numeric and string. OSIRIS numeric variables become SPSS numeric variables, and OSIRIS string variables become SPSS string variables of the same length.

Variable Names

OSIRIS variable numbers refer to responses to single- or multiple-response survey questions. SPSS converts a single response variable with the number n to the SPSS variable name Vn, and a multiple-response variable n with k possible responses to k variables named Mn.1 through Mn.k. An SPSS variable name is limited to eight characters. Thus, with the form Mn.k, if n has four digits, k can have no more than two, and if n has five digits, k can have only one. The form M*nk* is used, without the decimal point, when *n* has five digits and *k* has two.

Variable Labels

In OSIRIS, the term *variable name* has the same meaning as the term *variable label* in SPSS. OSIRIS variable names are converted to SPSS variable labels of the same length.

Missing Values

- For missing values, OSIRIS allows single values or size limits to be specified. Single values, if specified, are used as missing values for the corresponding variables in SPSS.
- An OSIRIS negative size limit *x* becomes the SPSS missing range (LO THRU *x*), and a positive size limit *y* becomes the SPSS missing range (*y* THRU HI).
- Range-missing values are not used for string variables. No missing values are used for long string variables. Warnings are issued if missing values occur in violation of these rules.

Value Labels

The dictionary codebook in an OSIRIS type 1 data set may include value label information. This information will be associated with the corresponding SPSS variables using the same values. When converted, labels longer than 60 characters are truncated.

Print and Write Formats

- OSIRIS string variables with length *l* are given an A format with width *w* for print and write formats.
- OSIRIS numeric variables are assigned one of three formats corresponding to the three forms of OSIRIS data values: numeric character, fixed-point binary, and floating-point binary.

Table 12 shows the assignment of numeric print and write formats. The width *w* and the number of decimal places *d* are taken from the OSIRIS data set.

Table 12   Print and write formats for numeric variables

OSIRIS data format	SPSS print format	SPSS write format
Numeric character	F*w.d*	F*w.d*
Fixed-point binary	F*w.d*	IB*w.d*
Floating-point binary	E*w.d*	RB*w*

Limitations

- Type 3 OSIRIS data sets can contain multiple logical records per case and values that span logical records. GET OSIRIS can handle type 3 data sets when there is only one logical record per case.

- GET OSIRIS can handle a logical record length of 80.
- Because SPSS treats OSIRIS multiple-response variables as separate variables, GET OSIRIS can handle a multiple-response variable that spans different logical records provided no corresponding individual SPSS variable spans different logical records.

DATA and DICTIONARY Subcommands

DATA and DICTIONARY together specify the OSIRIS data set. DATA identifies the OSIRIS data file. DICTIONARY identifies the OSIRIS dictionary file.

- DATA and DICTIONARY are required and must be the first specifications on GET OSIRIS.
- A slash cannot be used between the DATA and DICTIONARY specifications. However, slashes are used to separate any other subcommands used on GET OSIRIS.

Example

```
GET OSIRIS DATA=DATA48 DICTIONARY=DICT48.
```

- DATA identifies *DATA48* as the OSIRIS data file and DICTIONARY identifies *DICT48* as the OSIRIS dictionary file.

DROP and KEEP Subcommands

DROP and KEEP are used to copy a subset of variables into the working data file. DROP specifies variables that should not be copied into the working file. KEEP specifies variables that should be copied. Variables not specified on KEEP are dropped.

- DROP and KEEP cannot precede the DATA or DICTIONARY subcommands.
- DROP and KEEP specifications must use SPSS variable names, not OSIRIS variable numbers (see "OSIRIS to SPSS Data Conversion" on p. 294).
- Variables can be specified in any order. The order of variables on KEEP determines the order of variables in the working file. The order on DROP does not affect the order of variables in the working file.
- Keyword ALL on KEEP refers to all remaining variables not previously specified. ALL must be the last specification on KEEP.
- If a variable is specified twice on the same subcommand, only the first mention is recognized.
- Multiple DROP and KEEP subcommands are allowed. However, specifying a variable named on a previous DROP or not named on a previous KEEP results in an error and the command is not executed.
- Keyword TO can be used to specify a group of consecutive variables in the OSIRIS file.

Example

```
GET OSIRIS DATA=DATA48 DICTIONARY=DICT48
  /DROP=M5.1 TO M5.3 M5.9 /KEEP=M5.7 M5.6 ALL.
```

- DROP excludes from the working data file all variables between and including *M5.1* to *M5.3*, as well as *M5.9*. All other variables are copied into the working data file.
- KEEP specifies that *M5.7* and *M5.6* are the first two variables in the working file, followed by all remaining variables (except those specified on DROP). The remaining variables are copied into the working file in the same sequence in which they appear in the original OSIRIS data set.
- Note that DROP and KEEP use the SPSS variable names, not the OSIRIS variable numbers.

RENAME Subcommand

RENAME changes the names of variables as they are copied into the working data file. RENAME can be used to change the default names assigned by GET OSIRIS (see "OSIRIS to SPSS Data Conversion" on p. 294).

- The specification on RENAME is a list of old variable names followed by an equals sign and a list of new variable names. The same number of variables must be specified on both lists, and you can use keyword TO. The entire specification must be enclosed in parentheses.
- Alternatively, you can specify each old variable name individually, followed by an equals sign and the new variable name. Multiple sets of variable specifications are allowed. The parentheses around each set of specifications are optional.
- The list of old names must use the SPSS variable names, not OSIRIS variable names.
- Old variable names do not need to be specified according to their order in the OSIRIS data set.
- Name changes take place in one operation. Therefore, variable names can be exchanged between two variables.
- Variables cannot be renamed to scratch variables.
- Multiple RENAME subcommands are allowed.
- On a subsequent DROP or KEEP, variables are referred to by their new names.

Example

```
GET OSIRIS DATA=DATA48 DICTIONARY=DICT48
  /DROP=M5.1 TO M5.3 M5.9 /KEEP=M5.7 M5.6 ALL
  /RENAME (M5.7 M5.6=CHOICE1 CHOICE2).
```

- RENAME changes variable name *M5.7* to *CHOICE1* and *M5.6* to *CHOICE2*.

MAP Subcommand

MAP prints a list of the variables in the SPSS working data file and their corresponding names in the OSIRIS data set.

- The only specification is keyword MAP. There are no additional specifications.
- Multiple MAP subcommands are allowed. Each MAP subcommand maps the results of subcommands that precede it; results of subcommands that follow it are not mapped.

Example
```
GET OSIRIS DATA=DATA48 DICTIONARY=DICT48
  /DROP=M5.1 TO M5.3 M5.9  /KEEP=M5.7 M5.6 ALL
  /RENAME (M5.7 M5.6=CHOICE1 CHOICE2)
  /MAP.
```
- MAP is specified to confirm the new names and the order of variables in the working data file (*CHOICE1* and *CHOICE2*, followed by the remaining variables that are copied from the OSIRIS data set).

GET SAS

```
GET SAS DATA=file [DSET(data set)]
 [/FORMATS=file [FSET(data set)]]
```

Example:
```
GET SAS DATA='ELECT' DSET(Y1948).
```

Overview

GET SAS builds an SPSS working data file from a data set contained in a SAS XPORT file. A SAS XPORT file uses a portable file format and can be created by most versions of SAS. In most instances, GET SAS retrieves data and data definition items stored in the SAS XPORT file, including the file label, variable labels, print and write formats, and missing values, and it automatically modifies these data definition items where necessary to conform with SPSS conventions. It can also retrieve user-defined formats from a separate SAS data set and use them as value labels in the working data file.

Basic Specification

The basic specification is the DATA subcommand followed by the name of the SAS XPORT file to read. The SAS data set is copied into the working data file and any necessary data conversions are made (see "SAS to SPSS Data Conversion" on p. 300).

- By default, GET SAS assumes that the first data set in the XPORT file contains the data to be read and that no user-defined formats are to be applied.

Syntax Rules

- DATA is required and must be specified first.
- The files specified on DATA and FORMATS can be the same or different. The data sets containing data and formats in SAS can be in the same file or in different files.
- GET SAS does not allow KEEP, DROP, RENAME, and MAP subcommands. To use a subset of the variables, rename them, or display the file content, specify the appropriate commands after the working data file is created.

Operations

- GET SAS reads the data from the data set specified on the DATA subcommand.
- When GET SAS encounters an unknown format name, it inspects the data set specified on the FORMATS subcommand. If the format exists, it is applied after any necessary modifications are made (see "SAS to SPSS Data Conversion" on p. 300); otherwise, GET SAS applies the default format for the SPSS session (see SET).

- All variables from the SAS data set are included in the working data file, and they are in the same order as in the SAS data set.

DATA Subcommand

DATA specifies the file that contains the SAS data set to be read.

- DATA is required and must be the first specification on GET SAS.
- The file specification varies from operating system to operating system. Enclosing the filename within apostrophes always works.
- The optional DSET keyword on DATA specifies the data set to read. The default is the first data set within the specified SAS file.

DSET (data set) *Data set to read.* Specify the name of the data set in parentheses. If the specified data set does not exist in the SAS file, GET SAS displays a message informing you that the data set was not found. Names of the data sets in the file are then listed.

Example

```
GET SAS DATA='ELECT' DSET(Y1948).
```

- The SAS XPORT file *ELECT* is opened and the data set named *Y1948* is used to build the working file for the SPSS session.

FORMATS Subcommand

FORMATS specifies the SAS file with the data set containing formats to be applied to the data.

- FORMATS is optional. If it is omitted, user-defined formats are not applied.
- The file specification on FORMATS follows the same rules as for DATA.
- The file named on FORMATS and DATA can be the same or different. The filename cannot be omitted on FORMATS even if the data and formats reside in the same file.
- The data set named on FORMATS must be different from the data set named on DATA.

The optional keyword FSET specifies the data set containing the formats. The default is the first data set in the specified file.

FSET (data set) *Data set containing formats.* Specify the data set from which formats are to be obtained. The data set name must be enclosed in parentheses. If the specified data set does not exist in the SAS file, GET SAS displays a message informing you that the data set was not found. Names of the data sets in the file are then listed.

SAS to SPSS Data Conversion

Although SAS and SPSS data files have similar attributes, they are not identical. SPSS makes the following conversions to force SAS data sets to comply with SPSS conventions.

File Label

The file label for the SPSS file is obtained from the name specified on the LABEL option of the SAS DATA statement.

Variable Names

- Like SPSS, SAS allows variable names up to eight characters long, but the SAS naming conventions are somewhat different from those in SPSS. A SAS variable name must begin with a letter or an underscore. The underscore can be used within SPSS variable names but not at the beginning of a name. All leading underscores in SAS files are changed to the @ symbol.
- If an SPSS reserved keyword is used as a SAS variable name, SPSS appends the # symbol to the name and issues a warning message. The SPSS reserved keywords are ALL, AND, BY, GE, GT, LE, LT, NE, NOT, OR, TO, and WITH. A SAS variable named *AND*, for example, would be converted to *AND#*.

Variable Labels

SAS variable labels specified on the LABEL statement in the DATA step are used as variable labels in SPSS.

Value Labels

SAS value formats that assign value labels are read from the data set specified on the FORMATS subcommand. The SAS value labels are then converted to SPSS value labels in the following manner:
- Labels assigned to single values are retained.
- Labels assigned to a range of values are assigned to the beginning and end points of the range. For example, if SAS assigns the label *LOW* to values 1–3, in the resulting SPSS working data file the label *LOW* is assigned only to values 1 and 3.
- Labels assigned to SAS keywords LOW, HIGH, and OTHER are ignored.
- Labels assigned to long string variables are ignored.
- Labels over 60 characters long are truncated.

Missing Values

Since SAS has no user-defined missing values, all SAS missing codes are converted to SPSS system-missing values.

Variable Types

- Both SAS and SPSS allow two types of variables: numeric and character string. During conversion, SAS numeric variables become SPSS numeric variables, and SAS string variables become SPSS string variables of the same length.
- Values for SAS variables that can be identified in date format are converted to the number of seconds from October 15, 1582, to the given date. Similarly, values for any SAS variables that are clearly in date-time format are converted to the number of seconds from October 15, 1582, to the given date and time.

Print and Write Formats

SAS formats are converted to their closest representation within SPSS. Esoteric formats are converted to the default print format and the closest write format. If a numeric variable does not have a SAS format, the default SPSS format is used for both print and write formats. (The default numeric format for an SPSS session can be specified on SET FORMAT. If SET FORMAT is not specified for the session, the default numeric format is F8.2.)

Table 13 shows the correspondence between SPSS and SAS formats.

Table 13   Output format correspondence

SAS	SPSS print format	SPSS write format	Notes
BEST	default	default	
BINARYw.d	PIBHEXk	IBw.d	k=ceil(w/4)
Fw.d	Fw.d	Fw.d	
NEGPARENw.d	Fw.d	Fw.d	Prints negative numbers in parentheses in SAS
COMMAw.d	COMMAw.d	COMMAw.d	
COMMAXw.d	DOTw.d	DOTw.d	
DOLLARw.d	DOLLARw.d	DOLLARw.d	
DOLLARXw.d	DOTw.d	DOTw.d	Prints dollar format with comma as decimal delimiter in SAS
Ew.d	Ew.d	Ew.d	
FRACT	default	default	Prints n/m format in SAS
HEXw	IBHEXw	IBHEXw	
IBw	Fk.0	IBw	k=2w+1
OCTALw	IBHEXk.d	IBHEXk.d	k=3/4w
PDw	Fk.d	PW	k=2w+1
PERCENTw.d	PCTw.d	PCTw.d	
PIBw.d	default	PIBw.d	
PKw.d	Fk.d	PKw.d	k=2w+1
RBw	default	RBw	
ROMAN	F8.0	F8.0	

Table 13 Output format correspondence (Continued)

SAS	SPSS print format	SPSS write format	Notes
SSNw	Fw.0	Fw.0	
WORDFw.d	Fw.d	Fw.d	Prints numeric values as words in SAS
WORDSw.d	Fw.d	Fw.d	Prints numeric values as words and decimals as fractions in SAS
Zw	Nw	Nw	
ZDw	Zw	Zw	
$w	Aw	Aw	
$CHARw	Aw	Aw	
$ASCIIw	Aw	Aw	
$EBCDIC	Aw	Aw	
$HEXw	AHEXw	AHEXw	
$OCTALw	AHEXk	AHEXk	k=2/3w
$BINARYw	AHEXk	AHEXk	k=w/4
$VARYINGw	Aw	Aw	
DATEw	DATEw	DATEw	Minimum width for SPSS is 9
DATETIMEw	DATETIMEw	DATETIMEw	Minimum width for SPSS is 17
DAYw	DATE9	DATE9	Prints day of month in SAS
DDMMYYw	EDATEw	EDATEw	Minimum width for SPSS is 9
DOWNAMEw	WKDAYw	WKDAYw	
HHMMw.d	TIMEw+d	TIMEw+d	Minimum width for SPSS is 5
HOURw.d	TIME5.0	TIME5.0	No equivalent format for fractions of an hour in SPSS
JULIANw	JDATEw	JDATEw	
JULDAYw	JDATEw	JDATEW	
MMDDYYw	ADATEw	ADATEw	Minimum width for SPSS is 8
MMSSw.d	TIMEw.d	TIMEw.d	
MMYYw	MOYRw+1	MOYRw+1	
MONNAMEw	MONTHw	MONTHw	Prints name of the month in SAS
MONTH	MONTHw	MONTHw	
MONYYw	MOYRw+1	MOYRw+1	
NENGOw	JDATEw	JDATEw	Prints Japanese date format in SAS
QTRw	QYR8	QYR8	SPSS assumes the current year
QTRRw	QYR8	QYR8	Prints quarter in Roman numerals in SAS
TIMEw.d	TIMEw.d	TIMEw.d	Minimum width for SPSS is 5
TODw	DATETIMEw	DATETIMEw	Minimum width for SPSS is 21
WEEKDATEw	DATE12	DATE12	Prints day of week and date in SAS (day-of-week, month-name dd yy)
WEEKDATEXw	EDATE12	EDATE12	Prints day of week and date in SAS (day-of-week, dd month-name yy)

Table 13 Output format correspondence (Continued)

SAS	SPSS print format	SPSS write format	Notes
WEEKDAYw	WKDAYw	WKDAYw	
WORDDATEw	DATE12	DATE12	
WORDDATXw	DATE12	DATE12	
YEARw	SDATE10	SDATE10	
YYMMw	MOYR8	MOYR8	
YYMONw	MOYR8	MOYR8	
YYMMDDw	MOYR6	MOYR6	SDATE10 if width is 6 or more
YYQw	QYRw+2	QYRw+2	
YYQRw	QYRw+2	QYRw+2	Prints quarter in Roman numerals in SAS

GET SCSS

This command is not available on all operating systems.

```
GET SCSS MASTERFILE=file [/WORKFILE=file]

               {ALL**                       }
               {$ALL**                      }
 [/VARIABLES= {varlist                      }
               {$varlist                    }]
               {(old varnames=new varnames) }
```

**Default if the subcommand is omitted.

Example:

```
GET SCSS MASTERFILE=MHUBIN  WORKFILE=WHUBIN.
```

Overview

GET SCSS reads an SCSS masterfile or a workfile/masterfile combination.

Options

Workfiles. You can specify a workfile to read with the masterfile on the WORKFILE subcommand.

Variable Subsets, Order, and Names. You can read a subset of variables and reorder and/or rename variables that are copied into the SPSS working data file using the VARIABLES subcommand.

Basic Specification

The basic specification is the MASTERFILE subcommand, which specifies the SCSS masterfile to be read. The masterfile is copied into the SPSS working file.

Subcommand Order

- If both MASTERFILE and WORKFILE are specified, they can be used in either order.
- If VARIABLES is used, it must be the last specification.

Operations

In most instances, GET SCSS is able to retrieve the information in the SCSS masterfile. SPSS may need to recode data as explained below.

Missing Values

- SPSS and SCSS have different rules for defining user-missing values. First, SCSS allows more than three missing values per variable. Second, SCSS variables can have missing-value ranges that include valid values. Finally, SCSS allows you to specify a range of missing values for string variables as well as for numeric variables. When it encounters missing-value specifications that are not allowed in SPSS, GET SCSS recodes numeric values to the system-missing value and string values to blanks.
- In SCSS a value can be missing for some cases (via value revision) and not for others. SPSS considers such a value missing for all cases when reading the file with GET SCSS.
- Any time SPSS recodes a missing value, a warning message is issued to indicate the action taken.

Formats

Numeric variables copied from the SCSS masterfile are assigned print and write formats based on the length of the values. Variables with original alphanumeric values are assigned print and write formats of A1, A2, or A4 (for variables with three or four characters). Alphanumeric values cannot occur in a variable in a masterfile created using the SAVE SCSS command in SPSS but can occur in a masterfile defined directly in SCSS where the original values are alphanumeric but were revised as the masterfile was created.

MASTERFILE Subcommand

MASTERFILE specifies the masterfile to be read. If the masterfile alone is specified, only masterfile information is copied.

- MASTERFILE is required and must precede VARIABLES (if used).
- If WORKFILE is not specified, revisions or additions recorded in any of the workfiles associated with the specified masterfile are not available to SPSS.

Example

```
GET SCSS MASTERFILE=HUBIN.
```

- GET SCSS retrieves the SCSS masterfile *HUBIN*.

WORKFILE Subcommand

WORKFILE specifies a workfile associated with the masterfile being read. If WORKFILE is specified, the SPSS working data file reflects changes recorded in the workfile, including labels, revisions to existing variables, and computed variables.

- MASTERFILE and WORKFILE can be used in either order. The slash between these variables is optional.
- Both MASTERFILE and WORKFILE must precede VARIABLES.

- If the workfile alone is specified, SPSS tries to locate the masterfile but cannot always succeed (depending on the completeness of the specification in the workfile and on the operating system).

Example

```
GET SCSS WORKFILE=WHUBIN  MASTERFILE=MHUBIN.
```

- WORKFILE specifies workfile *WHUBIN*, which stores changes made to the masterfile *MHUBIN*.

VARIABLES Subcommand

VARIABLES limits the number of variables SPSS copies from the SCSS files. VARIABLES can also be used to determine the order of variables in the SPSS working file and to rename variables.

- VARIABLES must be the last specification on GET SCSS. VARIABLES can specify a variable list or keywords ALL or $ALL. ALL is the default if a workfile is specified. $ALL is the default if no workfile is specified and refers to the unrevised masterfile version of all of the variables.
- Variables are copied in the order specified on VARIABLES.
- You can copy the unrevised masterfile version of any variable, even if WORKFILE is specified, by specifying a dollar sign before the variable name. Since variable names beginning with dollar signs are not allowed in SPSS, such variables should be renamed.
- Variable name *THRU* is allowed in SCSS but not in SPSS, so it must be renamed.
- To rename variables, specify a list of old variable names followed by an equals sign and a list of new variable names. The same number of variables must be specified on both lists, and you can use keyword TO. The entire specification must be enclosed in parentheses.
- Alternatively, you can specify each old variable name individually, followed by an equals sign and the new variable name. Multiple sets of variable specifications are allowed. The parentheses around each set of specifications are optional.
- Name changes take place in one operation. Therefore, variable names can be exchanged between two variables.
- Variables cannot be renamed to scratch variables.

Example

```
GET SCSS WORKFILE=WHUBIN MASTERFILE=MHUBIN
  /VARIABLES=MOHIRED TO SEX, JOBCAT.
```

- Variables copied into the SPSS working data file are those between and including *MOHIRED* and *SEX*, and *JOBCAT*.

Example

```
GET SCSS WORKFILE=WHUBIN MASTERFILE=MHUBIN
  /VARIABLES=MOHIRED TO SEX ($SEX=SEX$) JOBCAT.
```

- This example uses the dollar sign to copy the unrevised masterfile version of variable *SEX* into the working data file. Since variable names beginning with dollar signs are not allowed in SPSS, the variable has to be renamed.
- The working data file contains both the revised and unrevised version of variable *SEX*.

Example
```
GET SCSS WORKFILE=WHUBIN MASTERFILE=MHUBIN
  /VARIABLES=(DEPT,SALARY,HOURLY=DEPT1,SALARY1,HOURLY1).
```

- Variables *DEPT*, *SALARY*, and *HOURLY* are copied into the SPSS data file and are renamed *DEPT1*, *SALARY1*, and *HOURLY1*, respectively. The parentheses are required.

GET TRANSLATE

This command is not available on all operating systems.

```
GET TRANSLATE FILE=file

 [/TYPE={WK  }]
        {WK1 }
        {WKS }
        {WR1 }
        {WRK }
        {SLK }
        {XLS }
        {DBF }
        {TAB }

 [/FIELDNAMES]*

 [/RANGE={range name }]*
         {start..stop}
         {start:stop }

 [/KEEP={ALL**  }] [/DROP=varlist]
        {varlist}

 [/RENAME=(old varnames=new varnames)...]

 [/MAP]
```

*Available only for spreadsheet and tab-delimited ASCII files.
**Default if the subcommand is omitted.

Keyword	Type of file
WK	Any Lotus 1-2-3 or Symphony file
WK1	1-2-3 Release 2.0
WKS	1-2-3 Release 1A
WR1	Symphony Release 2.0
WRK	Symphony Release 1.0
SLK	Microsoft Excel and Multiplan in SYLK (symbolic link) format
XLS	Microsoft Excel
DBF	All dBASE files
TAB	Tab-delimited ASCII file

Example:

```
GET TRANSLATE FILE='PROJECT.WKS'
 /FIELDNAMES
 /RANGE=D3..J279.
```

Overview

GET TRANSLATE creates an SPSS working data file from files produced by other software applications. Supported formats are 1-2-3, Symphony, Multiplan, Excel, dBASE II, dBASE III, dBASE IV, and tab-delimited ASCII files.

Options

Variable Subsets. You can use the DROP and KEEP subcommands to specify variables to omit or retain in the resulting working data file.

Variable Names. You can rename variables as they are translated using the RENAME subcommand.

Variable Map. To confirm the names and order of the variables in the working data file, use the MAP subcommand. MAP displays the variables in the working data file and their corresponding names in the other application.

Spreadsheet Files. You can use the RANGE subcommand to translate a subset of cells from a spreadsheet file. You can use the FIELDNAMES subcommand to translate field names in the spreadsheet file to SPSS variable names.

Basic Specification

- The basic specification is FILE with a file specification enclosed in apostrophes.
- If the file's extension is not the default for the type of file you are reading, TYPE must also be specified.

Subcommand Order

Subcommands can be named in any order.

Operations

GET TRANSLATE replaces an existing working data file.

Spreadsheets

A spreadsheet file suitable for SPSS should be arranged so that each row represents a case and each column a variable.
- By default, the new working data file contains all rows and up to 256 columns from Lotus 1-2-3, Symphony, or Excel, or up to 255 columns from Multiplan.
- By default, GET TRANSLATE uses the column letters as variable names in the working data file.
- The first row of a spreadsheet or specified range may contain field labels immediately followed by rows of data. These names can be transferred as SPSS variable names (see the FIELDNAMES subcommand on p. 314).
- The current value of a formula is translated to the SPSS working data file.
- Blank, ERR, and NA values in 1-2-3 and Symphony and error values such as #N/A in Excel are translated as system-missing in the SPSS working data file.

- Hidden columns and cells in 1-2-3 Release 2 and Symphony files are translated and copied into the SPSS working data file.
- Column width and format type are transferred to the dictionary of the SPSS working data file.
- The format type is assigned from values in the first data row. By default, the first data row is row 1. If RANGE is specified, the first data row is the first row in the range. If FIELD-NAMES is specified, the first data row follows immediately after the single row containing field names.
- If a cell in the first data row is empty, the variable is assigned the global default format from the spreadsheet.

The formats from 1-2-3, Symphony, Excel, and Multiplan are translated as follows:

1-2-3/Symphony	Excel	SYLK	SPSS
Fixed	0.00; #,##0.00	Fixed	F
	0; #,##00	Integer	F
Scientific	0.00E+00	Exponent	E
Currency	$#,##0_);...	$ (dollar)	DOLLAR
,(comma)			COMMA
General	General	General	F
+/ -		* (bargraph)	F
Percent	0%; 0.00%	Percent	PCT
Date	m/d/yy;d-mmm-yy...		DATE
Time	h:mm; h:mm;ss...		TIME
Text/Literal			F
Label		Alpha	String

If a string is encountered in a column with numeric format, it is converted to the system-missing value in the SPSS working data file.
- If a numeric value is encountered in a column with string format, it is converted to a blank in the SPSS working data file.
- Blank lines are translated as cases containing the system-missing value for numeric variables and blanks for string variables.
- 1-2-3 and Symphony date and time indicators (shown at the bottom of the screen) are not transferred from *WKS*, *WK1*, *WRK*, or *WR1* files.

Databases

Database files are logically very similar to SPSS data files.
- By default, all fields and records from dBASE II, dBASE III, or dBASE IV files are included in the SPSS working data file.
- Field names are automatically translated into SPSS variable names. If the FIELDNAMES subcommand is used with database files, it is ignored.

- Field names to be translated should comply with SPSS variable-naming conventions. Names longer than eight characters are truncated. If a field name is not unique in the first eight characters, the field will be dropped.
- Colons used in dBASE II field names are translated to underscores.
- Records in dBASE II, dBASE III, or dBASE IV that have been marked for deletion but that have not actually been purged are included in the working data file. To differentiate these cases, GET TRANSLATE creates a new string variable *D_R*, which contains an asterisk for cases marked for deletion. Other cases contain a blank for *D_R*.
- Character, floating, and numeric fields are transferred directly to SPSS variables. Date and logical fields are converted into string variables. Memo fields are ignored.

dBASE formats are translated to SPSS as follows:

dBASE	SPSS
Character	String
Logical	String
Date	Number
Numeric	Number
Floating	Number
Memo	Ignored

Tab-Delimited ASCII Files

Tab-delimited ASCII files are simple spreadsheets produced by a text editor, with the columns delimited by tabs and rows by carriage returns. The first row is usually occupied by column headings.

- By default all columns of all rows are treated as data. Default variable names *VAR1*, *VAR2*, and so forth are assigned to each column. The data type (numeric or string) for each variable is determined by the first data value in the column.
- If FIELDNAMES is specified, SPSS reads in the first row as variable names and determines data type by the values in from the second row.
- Any value that contains non-numeric characters is considered a string value. Dollar and date formats are not recognized and are treated as strings. When string values are encountered for a numeric variable, they are converted to the system-missing value.
- For numeric variables, the assigned format is F8.2 or the format of the first data value in the column, whichever is wider. Values that exceed the defined width are rounded for display, but the entire value is stored internally.
- For string variables, the assigned format is A8 or the format of the first data value in the column, whichever is wider. Values that exceed the defined width are truncated.
- ASCII data files delimited by space (instead of tabs) or in fixed format should be read by DATA LIST.

Limitations

The maximum number of variables that can be translated into the SPSS working data file depends on the maximum number of variables the other software application can handle:

Application	Maximum variables
1-2-3	256
Symphony	256
Multiplan	255
Excel	256
dBASE IV	255
dBASE III	128
dBASE II	32

FILE Subcommand

FILE names the file to read. The only specification is the name of the file.

- On some systems, file specifications should be enclosed in quotes or apostrophes.

Example

```
GET TRANSLATE FILE='PROJECT.WKS'.
```

- GET TRANSLATE creates a working data file from the 1-2-3 Release 1.0 spreadsheet with the name *PROJECT.WKS*.
- The working file contains all rows and columns and uses the column letters as variable names.
- The format for each variable is determined by the format of the value in the first row of each column.

TYPE Subcommand

TYPE indicates the format of the file.

- TYPE can be omitted if the file extension named on FILE is the default for the type of file you are reading.
- The TYPE subcommand takes precedence over the file extension.
- You can create a Lotus format file in Multiplan and translate it to an SPSS working data file by specifying WKS on TYPE.

WK	*Any Lotus 1-2-3 or Symphony file.*
WK1	*1-2-3 Release 2.0.*
WKS	*1-2-3 Release 1A.*
WR1	*Symphony Release 2.0.*

WRK   *Symphony Release 1.0.*

SLK   *Microsoft Excel and Multiplan saved in SYLK (symbolic link) format.*

XLS   *Excel.*

DBF   *All dBASE files.*

TAB   *Tab-delimited ASCII data file.*

Example

```
GET TRANSLATE FILE='PROJECT.OCT' /TYPE=SLK.
```

- GET TRANSLATE creates a working data file from the Multiplan file *PROJECT.OCT*.

FIELDNAMES Subcommand

FIELDNAMES translates spreadsheet field names into SPSS variable names.

- FIELDNAMES can be used with spreadsheet and tab-delimited ASCII files only. FIELDNAMES is ignored when used with database files.
- Each cell in the first row of the spreadsheet file (or the specified range) must contain a field name. If a column does not contain a name, the column is dropped.
- Field names to be translated into SPSS should conform to SPSS naming conventions. They must be unique in the first eight characters and cannot have leading blanks.
- Field names that exceed eight characters are truncated.
- If two or more columns in the spreadsheet have the same field name, only the first is translated to the working data file.
- Illegal characters in field names are changed to underscores in SPSS.
- If the spreadsheet file uses SPSS reserved words (ALL, AND, BY, EQ, GE, GT, LE, LT, NE, NOT, OR, TO, or WITH) as field names, GET TRANSLATE appends a dollar sign ($) to the variable name. For example, columns named *GE, GT, EQ,* and *BY* will be renamed *GE$, GT$, EQ$,* and *BY$* in the SPSS working data file.

Example

```
GET TRANSLATE FILE='MONTHLY.WRK' /FIELDNAMES.
```

- GET TRANSLATE creates a working data file from a Symphony 1.0 spreadsheet. The first row in the spreadsheet contains field names that are used as variable names in the SPSS working file.

RANGE Subcommand

RANGE translates a specified set of cells from a spreadsheet file.

- RANGE cannot be used for translating database files.
- For 1-2-3 or Symphony, specify the beginning of the range with a column letter and row number followed by two periods and the end of the range with a column letter and row

number, as in A1..K14.
- For Multiplan spreadsheets, specify the beginning and ending cells of the range separated by a colon, as in R1C1:R14C11.
- You can also specify the range using range names supplied in Symphony, 1-2-3, or Multiplan.
- If you specify FIELDNAMES with RANGE, the first row of the range must contain field names.

Example

```
GET TRANSLATE FILE='PROJECT.WKS' /FIELDNAMES /RANGE=D3..J279.
```

- GET TRANSLATE creates an SPSS working data file from the 1-2-3 Release 1A file *PROJECT.WKS*.
- The field names in the first row of the range (row 3) are used as variable names.
- Data from cells D4 through J279 are transferred to the working data file.

DROP and KEEP Subcommands

DROP and KEEP are used to copy a subset of variables into the SPSS working data file. DROP specifies the variables not to copy into the working file. KEEP specifies variables to copy. Variables not specified on KEEP are dropped.

- DROP and KEEP cannot precede the FILE or TYPE subcommands.
- DROP and KEEP specifications use SPSS variable names. By default, SPSS uses the column letters from spreadsheets and the field names from databases as variable names.
- If FIELDNAMES is specified when translating from a spreadsheet, the DROP and KEEP subcommands must refer to the field names, not the default column letters.
- Variables can be specified in any order. Neither DROP nor KEEP affects the order of variables in the resulting file. Variables are kept in their original order.
- If a variable is referred to twice on the same subcommand, only the first mention of the variable is recognized.
- Multiple DROP and KEEP subcommands are allowed; the effect is cumulative. Specifying a variable named on a previous DROP or not named on a previous KEEP results in an error and the command is not executed.
- If you specify both RANGE and KEEP, the resulting file contains only variables that are both within the range and specified on KEEP.
- If you specify both RANGE and DROP, the resulting file contains only variables within the range and excludes those mentioned on DROP, even if they are within the range.

Example

```
GET TRANSLATE FILE='ADDRESS.DBF' /DROP=PHONENO, ENTRY.
```

- GET TRANSLATE creates an SPSS working data file from the dBASE file *ADDRESS.DBF*, omitting the fields named *PHONENO* and *ENTRY*.

Example

```
GET TRANSLATE FILE='PROJECT.OCT' /TYPE=WK1 /FIELDNAMES
 /KEEP=NETINC, REP, QUANTITY, REGION, MONTH, DAY, YEAR.
```

- GET TRANSLATE creates an SPSS working data file from the 1-2-3 Release 2.0 file called *PROJECT.OCT*.
- Subcommand FIELDNAMES indicates that the first row of the spreadsheet contains field names, which will be translated into variable names in the SPSS working file.
- Subcommand KEEP translates columns with the field names *NETINC, REP, QUANTITY, REGION, MONTH, DAY,* and *YEAR* to the SPSS working file.

RENAME Subcommand

RENAME changes the names of variables as they are copied into the SPSS working data file.

- The specification on RENAME is a list of old variable names, an equals sign, and a list of new variable names. The same number of variables must be specified on both lists, and you can use keyword TO. The entire specification must be enclosed in parentheses.
- Alternatively, you can specify each old variable name individually, followed by an equals sign and the new variable name. Multiple sets of variable specifications are allowed. The parentheses around each set of specifications are optional.
- Name changes take place in one operation. Therefore, variable names can be exchanged between two variables.
- Variables cannot be renamed to scratch variables.
- Multiple RENAME subcommands are allowed.

Example

```
GET TRANSLATE FILE='PROJECT.WK'
     /RENAME  (A TO D = LNAME FNAME AGE SEX).
```

- RENAME changes the first four column letters to *LNAME, FNAME, AGE,* and *SEX* in the SPSS working data file.

MAP Subcommand

MAP displays a list of the variables in the SPSS working data file and their corresponding names in the other application.

- The only specification is keyword MAP. There are no additional specifications.
- Multiple MAP subcommands are allowed. Each MAP subcommand maps the results of subcommands that precede it; results of subcommands that follow it are not mapped.

Example

```
GET TRANSLATE FILE='ADDRESS.DBF' /DROP=PHONENO, ENTRY /MAP.
```

- MAP is specified to confirm that variables *PHONENO* and *ENTRY* have been dropped.

GRAPH

This command is available only on systems with high-resolution graphics capabilities.

```
GRAPH

  [/TITLE='line 1' ['line 2']]
  [/SUBTITLE='line 1']
  [/FOOTNOTE='line 1' ['line 2']]

  {/BAR [{(SIMPLE) }]=function/variable specification† }
        {(GROUPED)}
        {(STACKED)}

  {/LINE [{(SIMPLE)  }]                                 }
         {(MULTIPLE)}
         {(AREA)    }

  {/PIE†††                                              }

  {/HISTOGRAM [(NORMAL)]=var                            }

  {/SCATTERPLOT[{(BIVARIATE)}]=variable specification††}
               {(OVERLAY)  }
               {(MATRIX)   }
               {(XYZ)      }

  [/TEMPLATE=file]

  [/MISSING=[{LISTWISE**}{REPORT**}{EXCLUDE**}]]
            {VARIABLE  }{NOREPORT}{INCLUDE  }
```

** Default if the subcommand is omitted.
† Function/variable specification is required on all types of charts except scatterplots. The following table shows all possible specifications, where value_fun refers to the value function, count_fun refers to the count functions, and sum_fun refers to the summary functions.

	Simple Bars, Simple Lines, Simple Area Lines or Pies	Grouped/Stacked Bars or Multiple Area Lines
Categorical Charts	[count_fun BY] var	[count_fun BY] var BY var
	sum_fun(var) BY var	sum_fun(var) BY var BY var
	sum_fun(varlist)	sum_fun(varlist) BY var
	sum_fun(var) sum_fun(var)...	sum_fun(var) sum_fun(var)... BY var
Non-categorical Charts	value_fun(var) [BY var]	value_fun(varlist) [BY var]

†† Variable specification is required on all types of scatterplots. The following table shows all possible specifications:

BIVARIATE	var WITH var [BY var] [BY var (NAME)]
OVERLAY	varlist WITH varlist [(PAIR)] [BY var (NAME)]
MATRIX	varlist [BY var] [BY var(NAME)]
XYZ	var WITH var WITH var [BY var] [BY var (NAME)]

††† Cumulative functions (CUPCT, CUFREQ, and CUSUM) are inappropriate for pie charts but are not prohibited. When specified, all cases except those in the last category are counted more than once in the resulting pie.

Value function:

The VALUE function yields the value of the specified variable for each case. It always produces one bar, point, or slice for each case. The VALUE(X) specification implies the value of *X* by *n*, where *n* is the number of each case. You can specify multiple variables, as in:

```
GRAPH /BAR = VALUE(SALARY BONUS BENEFIT).
```

This command draws a bar chart with the values of *SALARY*, *BONUS*, and *BENEFIT* for each employee (case). The VALUE function always produces one bar/point/slice for each case. A BY variable can be used to supply case labels, but the BY variable does not affect the layout of the chart, even if values of the BY variable are the same for multiple cases.

Aggregation functions:

Two groups of aggregation functions are available: **count functions** and **summary functions**.

Count functions:

COUNT   *Frequency of cases in each category.*

PCT   *Frequency of cases in each category expressed as a percentage of the whole.*

CUPCT   *Cumulative percentage sorted by category value.*

CUFREQ   *Cumulative frequency sorted by category value.*

- Count functions yield the count or percentage of valid cases within categories determined by one or more BY variables, as in:

    ```
    GRAPH /BAR (SIMPLE) = PCT BY REGION.
    ```

- Count functions do not have any arguments.
- You can omit the keyword COUNT and subsequent keyword BY and specify just a variable, as in:

    ```
    GRAPH /BAR = DEPT.
    ```

    This command is interpreted as

    ```
    GRAPH /BAR = COUNT BY DEPT.
    ```

Summary functions:

MINIMUM   *Minimum value of the variable.*

MAXIMUM   *Maximum value of the variable.*

N   *Number of cases for which the variable has a nonmissing value.*

SUM   *Sum of the values of the variable.*

CUSUM   *Sum of the summary variable accumulated across values of the category variable.*

MEAN   *Mean.*

STDDEV   *Standard deviation.*

VARIANCE	*Variance.*
MEDIAN	*Median.*
MODE	*Mode.*
PTILE(x)	*xth percentile value of the variable. x must be greater than 0 and less than 100.*
PLT(x)	*Percentage of cases for which the value of the variable is less than x.*
PGT(x)	*Percentage of cases for which the value of the variable is greater than x.*
NLT(x)	*Number of cases for which the value of the variable is less than x.*
NGT(x)	*Number of cases for which the value of the variable is greater than x.*
PIN(x1,x2)	*Percentage of cases for which the value of the variable is greater than or equal to x1 and less than or equal to x2. x1 cannot exceed x2.*
NIN(x1,x2)	*Number of cases for which the value of the variable is greater than or equal to x1 and less than or equal to x2. x1 cannot exceed x2.*

- Summary functions are usually used with summary variables (variables that record continuous values, like age or expenses). To use a summary function, specify the name of one or more variables in parentheses after the name of the function, as in:

```
GRAPH /BAR = SUM(SALARY) BY DEPT.
```

- You can specify multiple summary functions for more chart types. For example, the same function can be applied to a list of variables, as in:

```
GRAPH /BAR = SUM(SALARY BONUS BENEFIT) BY DEPT.
```

This syntax is equivalent to

```
GRAPH /BAR = SUM(SALARY) SUM(BONUS) SUM(BENEFIT) BY DEPT.
```

Different functions can be applied to the same variable, as in:

```
 GRAPH /BAR = MEAN(SALARY) MEDIAN(SALARY) BY DEPT.
```

Different functions and variables can be combined, as in:

```
GRAPH /BAR = MIN(SALARY81) MAX(SALARY81)
             MIN(SALARY82) MAX(SALARY82) BY JOBCAT.
```

The effect of multiple summary functions on the structure of the charts is illustrated under the discussion of specific chart types.

Overview

GRAPH generates a high-resolution chart by computing statistics from variables in the working data file and constructing the chart according to your specification. The chart can be a bar chart, pie chart, line chart, histogram, or scatterplot. The chart is displayed where high-resolution display is available and can be edited with a chart editor and saved as a chart file.

Options

Titles and Footnotes. You can specify a title, subtitle, and footnote for the chart using the TITLE, SUBTITLE, and FOOTNOTE subcommands.

Chart Type. You can request a specific type of chart using the BAR, PIE, LINE, HISTOGRAM, or SCATTERPLOT subcommand. You can also specify the subtype of the requested chart with a keyword on the subcommand.

Chart Content. You can specify an aggregated categorical chart using various aggregation functions or a non-aggregated categorical chart using the VALUE function (see pp. 318–319 for a list of available aggregation functions).

Templates. You can specify a template to override the default chart attribute settings on your system using the TEMPLATE subcommand.

Basic Specification

The basic specification is a chart type subcommand. By default, the generated chart will have no title, subtitle, or footnote.

Subcommand Order

Subcommands can be specified in any order.

Syntax Rules

- Only one chart type subcommand can be specified.
- The function/variable specification is required for all subtypes of bar, line, and pie charts; the variable specification is required for histograms and all subtypes of scatterplots.
- The function/variable or variable specifications should match the subtype keywords. If there is a discrepancy, GRAPH produces the default chart for the function/variable or variable specification regardless of the specified keyword.
- When a nonaggregated categorical chart is requested, the VALUE function must be used.
- When an aggregated categorical chart is requested, one of the aggregated functions must be used.

Operations

- GRAPH computes aggregated functions to obtain the values needed for the requested chart and calculates an optimal scale for charting.
- The chart title, subtitle, and footnote are assigned as they are specified on TITLE, SUBTITLE, and FOOTNOTE subcommands. If you do not use these subcommands, none is assigned.

- GRAPH creates labels that provide information on the source of the values being plotted. Labeling conventions vary for different subtypes. Where variable or value labels are defined in the working data file, GRAPH uses the labels; otherwise, variable names or values are used.

Example

```
GRAPH /BAR = SUM(MURDER) BY CITY.
```

- This command requests a simple (default) bar chart showing the number of murders in each city.
- The category (*x* axis) labels are defined by the value labels (or values if no value labels exist) of the variable *CITY*.

TITLE, SUBTITLE, and FOOTNOTE Subcommands

TITLE, SUBTITLE, and FOOTNOTE specify lines of text placed at the top or bottom of the graph.
- One or two lines of text can be specified for TITLE or FOOTNOTE, and one line of text for SUBTITLE.
- Each line of text must be enclosed in apostrophes or quotation marks. The maximum length of any line is 72 characters.
- The default font sizes and types are used for the title, subtitle, and footnote.
- By default, the title, subtitle, and footnote are left-aligned with the *y* axis.
- If you do not specify TITLE, SUBTITLE, or FOOTNOTE, the default title, subtitle, and footnote are null, which leaves more space for the chart or plot.

Example

```
GRAPH TITLE = 'Murder in Major U.S Cities'
  /SUBTITLE = 'per 100,000 people'
  /FOOTNOTE = 'The above data was reported on August 26, 1987'
  /BAR = SUM(MURDER) BY CITY.
```

BAR Subcommand

BAR creates one of three types of bar charts.
- Keywords SIMPLE, GROUPED, and STACKED determine the kind of bar chart generated.
- Only one keyword can be specified, and it must be specified in the parentheses.
- When no keyword is specified, the default is either SIMPLE or GROUPED, depending on the type of function or variable specification.

SIMPLE   *Simple bar chart.* This is the default if no keyword is specified on the BAR subcommand and the variables defined a simple bar chart. A simple bar chart can be defined by a single summary or count function and a single BY variable, or by multiple summary functions and no BY variable (see Figure 12 to Figure 15).

GROUPED *Clustered bar chart.* A clustered bar chart is defined by a single function and two BY variables, or by multiple functions and a single BY variable. This is the default if no keyword is specified on the BAR subcommand and the variables define a clustered bar chart (see Figure 16 to Figure 19).

STACKED *Stacked bar chart.* A stacked bar chart displays a series of bars, each divided into segments stacked one on top of the other. The height of each segment represents the value of the category. Like a clustered bar chart, it is defined by a single function and two BY variables or by multiple functions and a single BY variable (see Figure 20 to Figure 22).

Figure 12 /BAR=COUNT BY JOBCAT

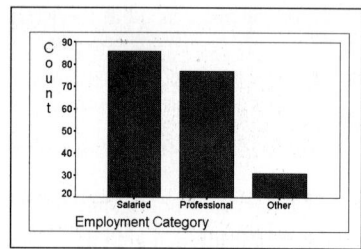

Specification: count_function BY var
          or summary_function(var) BY var

y axis title:	fn name [+fn var label]
y axis labels:	fn value scale
x axis title:	BY var label
x axis labels:	BY var value labels

Each bar shows the number of cases in the indicated job categories.

Figure 13 /BAR=MEAN(SALBEG, SALNOW)

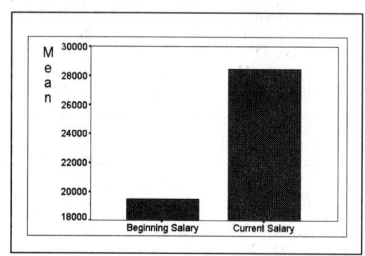

Specification: summary_function (varlist)

y axis title:	fn name
y axis labels:	fn value scale
x axis labels:	none
x axis labels:	fn var labels

One bar is produced for each variable, representing the summary function of that variable across all cases.

Syntax Reference Guide

Figure 14 /BAR=MEAN(SALARY) MEDIAN(INCOME)

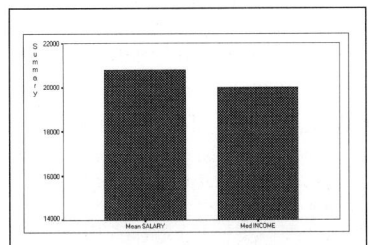

Specification: summary function list

y axis title:	Summary
y axis labels:	fn value scale
x axis title:	none
x axis labels:	fn names +var names

One bar is produced for each summary function. The argument can be the same or different.

Figure 15 /BAR=VALUE(VAR00001)

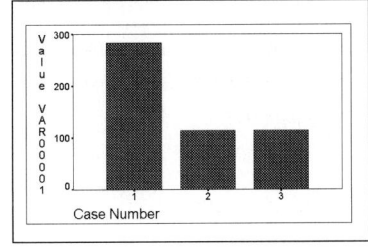

Specification: value_function(var) [BY var]

y axis title:	value + var label
y axis labels:	fn value scale
x axis title:	vase number
x axis labels:	case numbers

Each bar shows the value of a single case. If a BY variable is specified, the BY variable label will be *x* axis title and its value labels *x* axis labels.

Figure 16 /BAR=COUNT BY JOBCAT BY SEX

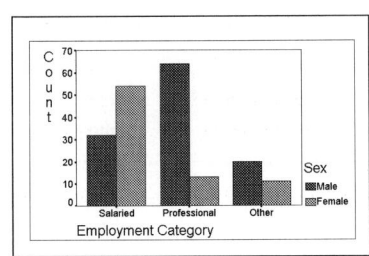

Specification: count_function BY var1 BY var2
or summary_function(var) BY var1 BY var2

Legend title:	2nd BY var label
Legend labels:	2nd BY value labels
y axis title:	fn name [+var label]
y axis labels:	fn value scale
x axis title:	1st BY var label
x axis labels:	1st BY value labels

Cases are broken down into categories by *VAR1* and then by *VAR2*. Each bar shows the valid number of cases within each subcategory.

Figure 17   /BAR=MEAN(SALBEG SALNOW) BY JOBCAT

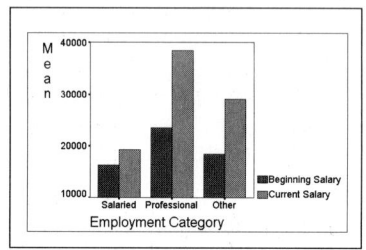

Specification: summary_function (varlist) BY var

Legend title:	none
Legend labels:	fn var labels
y axis title:	fn name
y axis labels:	fn value scale
x axis title:	var label
x axis labels:	BY value labels

The variables are broken down into categories. Within a category, each bar shows the value of the function for each variable.

Figure 18   /BAR=MEAN(SALNOW) MEDIAN(SALNOW) BY SEX

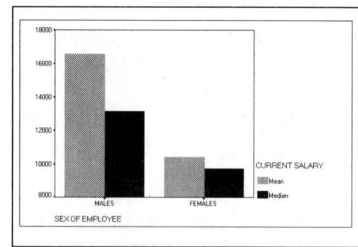

Specification: summary_function list BY var

Legend title:	fn var label (if only one fn var)
Legend labels:	fn name
y axis title:	none
y axis labels:	fn value scale
x axis title:	BY var label
x axis labels:	BY var value label

The variable is broken down into categories. Within a category, each bar shows a different function of the same variable.

Figure 19   /BAR=VALUE(SALBEG SALNOW) BY ID

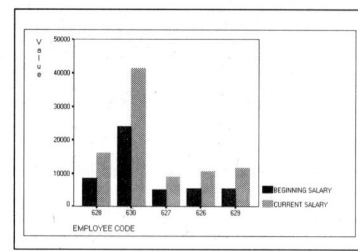

Specification: VALUE (varlist) [BY var]

Legend title:	none
Legend labels:	fn var name
y axis title:	value
y axis labels:	values
x axis title:	BY var label
x axis labels:	BY var value label

Each group shows one case identified by the category variable following BY. Each bar within the case shows the value of one variable for that case.

Figure 20 /BAR(STACKED)=COUNT BY JOBCAT BY SEX

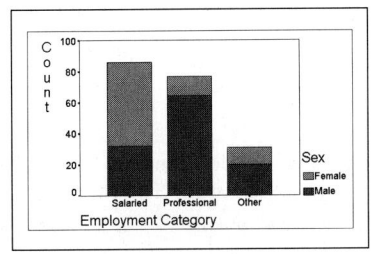

Specification: count_function BY var1 BY var2
or summary_function(var) BY var1 BY var2

Legend title:	2nd BY var label
Legend labels:	2nd BY var value labels
y axis title:	fn name [+fn var label]
y axis labels:	fn value
x axis title:	1st BY var label
x axis labels:	1st BY value labels

Each bar represents one subcategory defined by the two category variables. The bars are stacked within each category defined by the first category variable.

Figure 21 /BAR(STACKED)=SUM(THEFT AUTO BURGLARY) BY YEAR

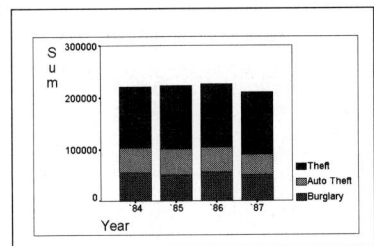

Specification: summary_function (varlist) BY var

Legend title:	none
Legend labels:	fn var labels
y axis title:	fn name
y axis labels:	fn value scale
x axis title:	BY var label
x axis labels:	BY var value labels

Each bar represents the function value of one variable broken down into categories. Bars within each category are stacked.

Figure 22 /BAR(STACKED)=VALUE(VAR00001 VAR00002)

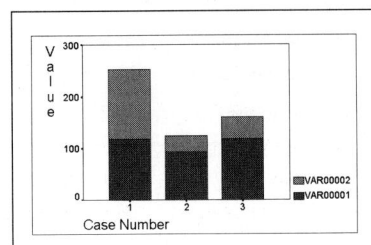

Specification: VALUE (varlist)

Legend title:	none
Legend labels:	var labels
y axis title:	fn name
y axis labels:	fn value scale
x axis title:	case number
x axis labels:	case numbers

Each bar shows the value of each variable for the indicated case.

LINE Subcommand

LINE creates one of three types of line charts using keywords SIMPLE, MULTIPLE, or AREA.

SIMPLE *Simple line chart.* A simple line chart is defined by a single function and a single BY variable or by multiple functions and no BY keyword. This is the default if no keyword is specified on LINE and the data define a simple line (Figure 23 to Figure 25).

MULTIPLE *Multiple line chart.* A multiple line chart is defined by a single function and two BY variables or by multiple functions and a single BY variable. This is the default if no keyword is specified on LINE and the data define a multiple line (Figure 26 to Figure 28).

AREA *Area line chart.* An area line chart fills the area beneath each line with a color or pattern. When multiple lines are specified, the second line is the sum of the first and second variables, the third line is the sum of the first, second, and third variables, and so on. The specification is the same as that for a simple or multiple line chart. Figure 29 to Figure 31 show area line charts with multiple lines.

Figure 23 /LINE=COUNT BY TIME

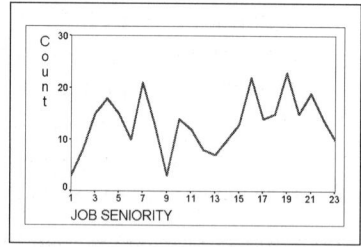

Specification: count_function BY var
or summary_function(var) BY var

y axis title:	fn name [+fn var label]
y axis labels:	fn value scale
x axis title:	BY var label
x axis labels:	BY var value labels

Each point on the line represents the number of valid cases for one category.

Figure 24 /LINE=MEAN(WINTER SPRING SUMMER FALL)

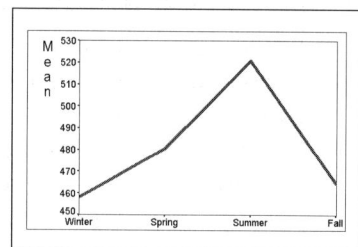

Specification: summary_function (varlist)

y axis title:	fn name
y axis labels:	fn value scale
x axis title:	none
x axis labels:	fn var labels

Each point on the line shows the function value for one variable across all valid cases.

Figure 25 /LINE=VALUE(VAR00001)

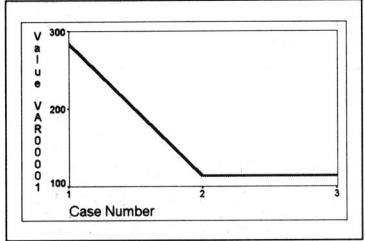

Specification: VALUE (var) [BY var]

y axis title:	value + var name
y axis labels:	value labels
x axis title:	case number
x axis label:	case numbers

Each point on the line shows the value of a single case. If a BY variable is specified, the *x* axis title will be the BY variable label and the *x* axis labels will be the BY variable value labels.

Figure 26 /LINE=COUNT BY TIME BY SEX

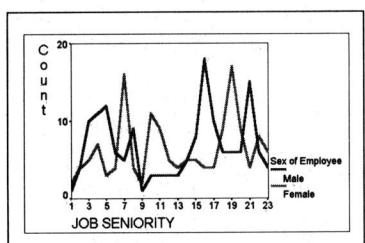

Specification: count_function BY var1 BY var2
or summary_function(var) BY var1 BY var2

Legend title:	2nd BY var label
Legend labels:	2nd BY var value labels
y axis title:	fn name [+fn var label]
y axis labels:	fn value scale
x axis title:	1st BY var label
x axis labels:	1st BY var value labels

Each line represents one category defined by the second BY variable. Each point on the line shows the number of valid cases for one category defined by the first BY variable.

Figure 27 /LINE=MEAN(VIOLENT PROPERTY) BY YEAR

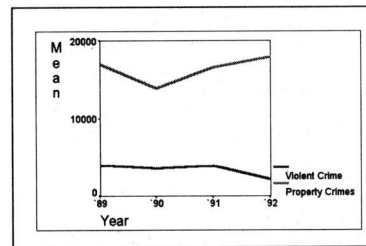

Specification: summary_function (varlist) BY var

Legend title:	none
Legend labels:	fn var labels
y axis title:	fn name
y axis labels:	fn value scale
x axis title:	BY var label
x axis labels:	BY var value labels

Each line represents one variable. Each point on the line shows the value for one category.

Figure 28 /LINE=VALUE(VAR0001 VAR0002)

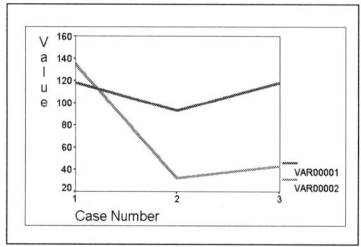

Specification: VALUE (varlist) [BY var]

Legend title:	none
Legend labels:	var labels
y axis title:	value
y axis labels:	values
x axis title:	case number
x axis labels:	case numbers

Each line represents one variable. Each point shows the value of each case for the variable. If a BY variable is specified, the x axis title will be the BY variable label and the x axis labels the BY variable value labels.

Figure 29 /LINE(AREA)=COUNT BY TIME

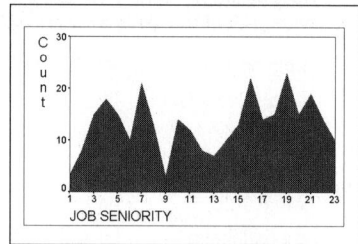

Specification: count_function BY var
or summary_function(var) BY var

y axis title:	fn name [+fn var label]
y axis labels:	fn value scale
x axis title:	BY var label
x axis labels:	BY var value labels

The area shows the number of valid cases for categories defined by the BY variable.

Figure 30 /LINE(AREA)=COUNT BY TIME BY SEX

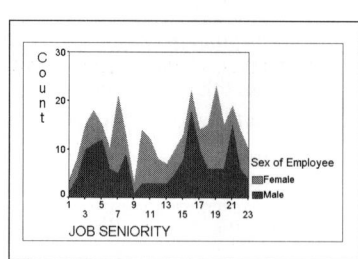

Specification: count_function BY var1 BY var2
or summary_function(var) BY var1 BY var2

Legend title:	2nd BY var label
Legend labels:	2nd BY var value labels
y axis title:	fn name [+fn var label]
y axis labels:	fn value scale
x axis title:	1st BY var label
x axis labels:	1st BY var value labels

The two areas represent the categories defined by the second category variable.

Figure 31 /LINE(AREA)=SUM(VIOLENT PROPERTY) BY YEAR

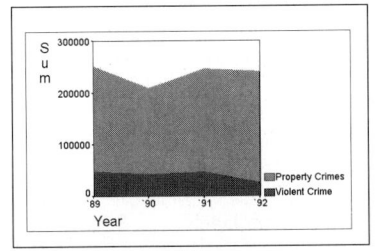

Specification:	summary_function (varlist) BY var
Legend title:	none
Legend labels:	fn var labels
y axis title:	fn name
y axis labels:	fn value
x axis Title:	category var label
x axis Labels:	category value [label]

Each area represents one function variable.

PIE Subcommand

PIE creates pie charts. A pie chart can be defined by a single function and a single BY variable or by multiple summary functions and no BY variable. A pie chart divides a circle into slices. The size of each slice indicates the value of the category relative to the whole (Figure 32 to Figure 34).

Figure 32 /PIE=COUNT BY JOBCAT

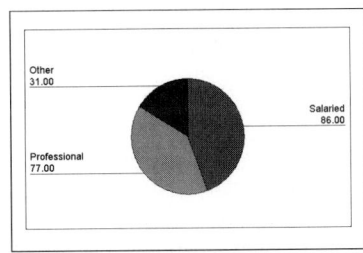

Specification:	count_function BY var
Top labels:	BY var value labels
Bottom labels:	fn values

Each pie slice shows the number of cases in one category defined by the BY variable.

Figure 33 /PIE=SUM(BURGLARY AUTO THEFT)

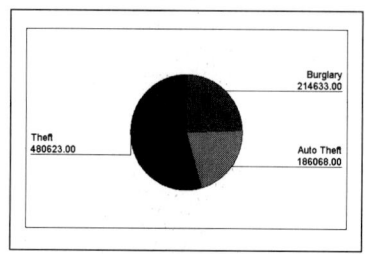

Specification: summary_function(varlist)

Top labels: fn var labels
Bottom labels: fn values

Each pie slice shows the function value for one variable.

Figure 34 /PIE=VALUE(VAR00001)

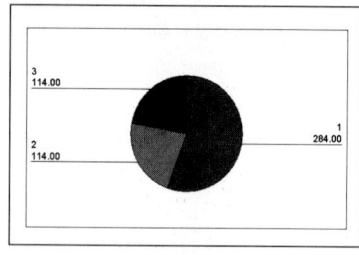

Specification: VALUE(var)

Top labels: case numbers
Bottom labels: case values

Each pie slice shows the value of one case.

SCATTERPLOT Subcommand

SCATTERPLOT produces two- or three-dimensional scatterplots. Multiple two-dimensional plots can be plotted within the same frame or as a scatterplot matrix. Only variables can be specified; aggregated functions cannot be plotted. When SCATTERPLOT is specified without keywords, the default is BIVARIATE.

BIVARIATE *One two-dimensional scatterplot.* A basic scatterplot is defined by two variables separated by the keyword WITH (see Figure 35 to Figure 37). This is the default when SCATTERPLOT is specified without keywords.

OVERLAY *Multiple plots drawn within the same frame.* Specify a variable list on both sides of WITH. By default, one scatterplot is drawn for each combination of variables on the left of WITH with variables on the right (see Figure 38). You can specify PAIR in parentheses to indicate that the first variable on the left is paired with the first variable on the right, the second variable on the left

Syntax Reference Guide

GRAPH 331

MATRIX	*Scatterplot matrix.* Specify at least two variables. One scatterplot is drawn for each combination of the specified variables above the diagonal and a second below the diagonal in a square matrix (see Figure 39).
XYZ	*One three-dimensional plot.* Specify three variables, each separated from the next with the keyword WITH (see Figure 40).

with the second variable on the right, and so on. All plots are drawn within the same frame and are differentiated by color or pattern. The axes are scaled to accommodate the minimum and maximum values across all variables.

- If you specify a control variable using BY, GRAPH produces a control scatterplot where values of the BY variable are indicated by different colors or patterns. A control variable cannot be specified for overlay plots.
- You can display the value label of an identification variable at the plotting position for each case. Add BY *var* (NAME) to the end of any valid scatterplot specification. Figure 37 shows a simple scatterplot with a label variable.

Figure 35 /SCATTERPLOT=COMPS WITH PROFITS

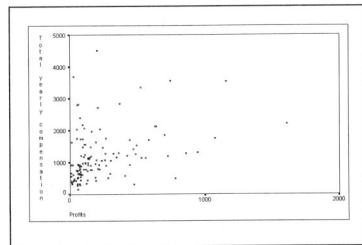

Specification: var1 WITH var2
              [BY var] [BY var (NAME)]

y axis title:	var1 var label
y axis labels:	scaled values
x axis title:	var2 var label
x axis labels:	scaled values

Figure 36 /SCATTERPLOT=SALNOW WITH SALBEG BY SEX

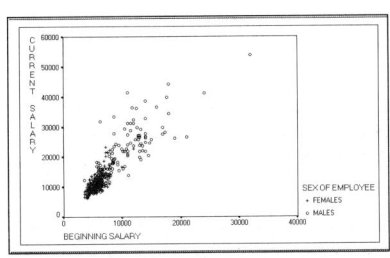

Specification: var1 WITH var2 BY var3*

Legend title	marker var (var3) label
Legend labels:	marker var value [label]
y axis title:	var1 var label
y axis labels:	scaled values
x axis title:	var2 var label
x axis labels:	scaled values

*VAR3 is a marker variable. For specification of a label variable, see Figure 37.

Figure 37   /SCATTERPLOT=SALNOW WITH JOBCAT BY ID (NAME)

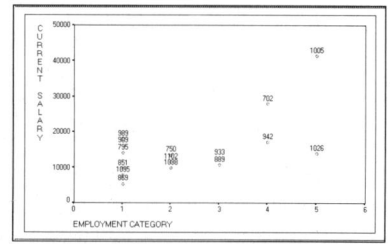

Specification: var1 WITH var2 BY var3(NAME)*

Point labels	Label var (*VAR3*) value labels
y axis title:	var1 var label
y axis labels:	scaled values
x axis title:	var2 var label
x axis labels:	scaled values

*When keyword NAME is specified, *VAR3* serves as a label variable. For the specification of a marker variable, see Figure 36. You can specify both a marker variable and a label variable for a simple scatterplot.

Figure 38   /SCATTERPLOT(OVERLAY)=VERBAL MATH WITH AARATIO)

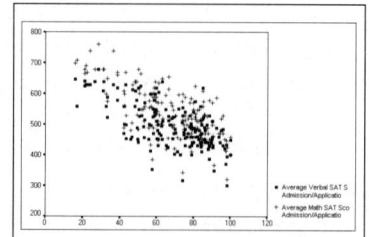

Specification: varlist WITH varlist [BY var(NAME)]*

Legend title	none
Legend labels:	pairs of var names
y axis title:	none
y axis labels:	scaled values**
x axis title:	none
x axis labels:	scaled values**

*You can specify only a label variable after BY for an overlay scatterplot. The keyword NAME is required if a BY variable is specified.
**Values are scaled to accommodate the maximum and minimum values of each pair.

Figure 39 /SCATTERPLOT(MATRIX)=SCORE COST SFRATIO

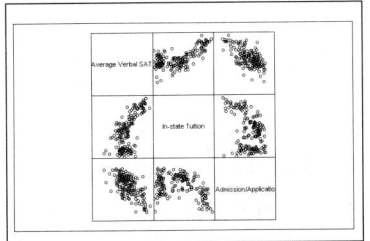

Specification: varlist [BY var] [BY var(NAME)]*

Legend title	marker var name
Legend labels	marker var value labels
Point labels:	label value labels
Diagonal titles:	var labels

*Matrix scatterplots can have both marker variable and label variable specifications.

Figure 40 /SCATTERPLOT(XYZ)=JOBCAT WITH SALARY WITH EDLEVEL BY SEX BY ID (NAME)

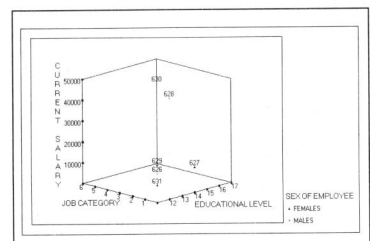

Specification:
xvar WITH yvar WITH zvar [BY var][BY var(NAME)]

Legend title	1st BY var label
Legend labels:	1st BY var value labels
Point labels:	2nd BY var value labels
x axis title:	xvar label
y axis title:	yvar label
z axis title:	zvar label

* 3-D scatterplots allow both marker variable and label variable specifications.

HISTOGRAM Subcommand

HISTOGRAM creates a histogram (see Figure 41 and Figure 42).
- Only one variable can be specified on this subcommand.
- GRAPH divides the values of the variable into several evenly spaced intervals and produces a bar chart showing the number of times the values for the variable fall within each interval.

- You can request a normal distribution line by specifying the keyword NORMAL in parentheses (Figure 42).

Figure 41 /HISTOGRAM=RATIO

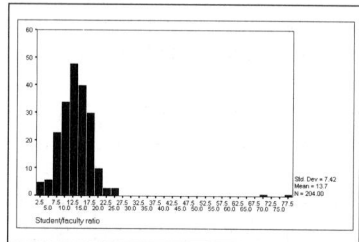

Specification: var

y axis title:	none
y axis label:	number of valid cases
x axis title:	var label
x axis label:	scaled values

The standard deviation, mean, and number of valid cases are displayed.

Figure 42 /HISTOGRAM(NORMAL)=VERBAL

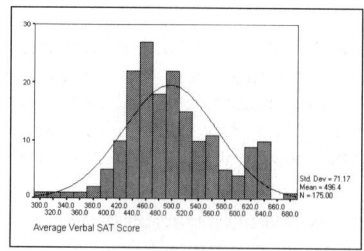

Specification: var

y axis title:	none
y axis labels:	number of valid cases
x axis title:	var label
x axis labels:	scaled values

The normal distribution line as well as the standard deviation, mean, and number of valid cases are displayed.

TEMPLATE Subcommand

TEMPLATE uses an existing chart as a template and applies it to the chart requested by the current GRAPH command.

- The specification on TEMPLATE is a chart file saved during a previous SPSS session.
- The general rule of application is that the template overrides the default setting, but the specifications on the current GRAPH command override the template. Nonapplicable elements and attributes are ignored.
- Three types of elements and attributes can be applied from a chart template: those dependent on data, those dependent on the chart type, and those dependent on neither.

Elements and Attributes Independent of Chart Types or Data

Elements and attributes common to all chart types are always applied unless overridden by the specifications on the current GRAPH command.

- The title, subtitle, and footnote, including text, color, font type and size, and line alignment are always applied. To give your chart a new title, subtitle, or footnote, specify the text on the TITLE, SUBTITLE, or FOOTNOTE subcommand. You cannot change other attributes.
- The outer frame of the chart, including line style, color, and fill pattern, is always applied. The inner frame is applied except for those charts that do not have an inner frame. The template overrides the system default.
- Label formats are applied wherever applicable. The template overrides the system default. Label text, however, is not applied. GRAPH automatically provides axis labels according to the function/variable specification.
- Legends and the legend title attributes, including color, font type and size, and alignment, are applied provided the current chart requires legends. The legend title text, however, is not applied. GRAPH provides the legend title according to the function/variable specification.

Elements and Attributes Dependent on Chart Type

Elements and attributes dependent on the chart type are those that exist only in a specific chart type. They include bars (in bar charts), lines and areas (in line charts), markers (in scatterplots), boxes (in boxplots), and pie sectors (in pie charts). These elements and their attributes are usually applied only when the template chart and the requested chart are of the same type. Some elements or their attributes may override the default settings across chart type.

- Color and pattern are always applied except for pie charts. The template overrides the system default.
- Scale axis lines are applied across chart types. Scale axis range is never applied.
- Interval axis lines are applied from interval axis to interval axis. Interval axis bins are never applied.
- If the template is a 3-D bar chart and you request a chart with one category axis, attributes of the first axis are applied from the template. If you request a 3-D bar chart and the template is not a 3-D chart, no category axis attributes are applied.

Elements and Attributes Dependent on Data

Data-dependent elements and attributes are applied only when the template and the requested chart are of the same type and the template has at least as many series assigned to the same types of chart elements as the requested chart.

- Category attributes and elements, including fill, border, color, pattern, line style, weight of pie sectors, pie sector explosion, reference lines, projection lines, and annotations, are applied only when category values in the requested chart match those in the template.

- The attributes of data-related elements with on/off states are always applied. For example, the line style, weight, and color of a quadratic fit in a simple bivariate scatterplot are applied if the requested chart is also a simple bivariate scatterplot. The specification on the GRAPH command, for example, HISTOGRAM(NORMAL), overrides the applied on/off status; in this case, a normal curve is displayed regardless of whether the template displays a normal curve.
- In bar, line, and area charts, the assignment of series to bars, lines, and areas is not applied.
- Case weighting status for histograms and scatterplots is not applied. You must turn weighting on or off before specifying the GRAPH command.

MISSING Subcommand

MISSING controls the treatment of missing values in the chart drawn by GRAPH.
- The default is LISTWISE, REPORT, and EXCLUDE.
- The MISSING subcommand has no effect on variables used with the VALUE function to create nonaggregated charts. User- and system-missing values create empty cells.
- LISTWISE and VARIABLE are alternatives and apply to variables used in summary functions for a chart or to variables being plotted in a scatterplot.
- REPORT and NOREPORT are alternatives and apply only to category variables. They control whether categories and series with missing values are created.
- INCLUDE and EXCLUDE are alternatives and apply to both summary and category variables.
- When a case has a missing value for the name variable but contains valid values for the dependent variable in a scatterplot, the case is always included. User-missing values are displayed as point labels; system-missing values are not displayed.
- For an aggregated categorical chart, if every aggregated series is empty in a category, the empty category is excluded.
- A nonaggregated categorical chart created with the VALUE function can contain completely empty categories. There are always as many categories as rows of data. However, at least one nonempty cell must be present; otherwise the chart is not created.

LISTWISE *Listwise deletion of cases with missing values.* A case with a missing value for any dependent variable is excluded from computations and graphs.

VARIABLE *Variable-wise deletion.* A case is deleted from the analysis only if it has a missing value for the dependent variable being analyzed.

REPORT *Report and graph missing-value categories.*

NOREPORT *Suppress missing-value categories.*

EXCLUDE *Exclude user-missing values.* Both user- and system-missing values for dependent variables are excluded from computations and graphs.

INCLUDE *Include user-missing values.* Only system-missing values for dependent variables are excluded from computations and graphs.

HELP

This command is not available on all operating systems.

```
{HELP} [{topic    [subtopic   }]] [SYNTAX]
{ ?  }  {command [subcommand]}
```

Example:

```
SPSS> HELP REGRESSION SYNTAX.
```

Overview

HELP (alias ?) provides online help during an SPSS prompted session. The HELP command is not allowed in command files. Consult the *Base System User's Guide* for your version of SPSS for the types of online help available.

HELP messages describe the function, syntax, and operation of commands. HELP also gives information about files, command order, and subcommands for complex procedures.

Syntax Rules

- The minimum specification is simply the command keyword or a question mark, either of which obtains a listing of available help topics.
- From any help screen that offers subtopics, type the number corresponding to the subtopic and press (←Enter). Use the number keys to type the numbers, not the function keys.
- To get help on specific commands, specify the command name on HELP. To get help on specific subcommands, specify the command and subcommand names. For help on specific keywords, specify the command, subcommand, and keyword.
- To see the complete syntax for any command, specify the command name and keyword SYNTAX on HELP.
- Help is available from any prompt. However, from the CONTINUE>, DATA>, DEFINE>, or HELP> prompts, help must be requested with the question mark; keyword HELP can only be used from the SPSS> prompt.
- Generally, three-character truncation on help requests is permitted. If three-character truncation is not unique (for example, REP might be REPORT or REPEATING DATA), an additional character or characters must be specified.
- On some computers, the minus (-) and plus (+) keys move through screens in the HELP system. On other computers, the directional arrow keys move between screens. For details on your computer, see the *SPSS Operations Guide* for your system or the online documentation available with the keyword LOCAL on the INFO command. Alternatively, type HELP with no specifications within the prompted session and choose the appropriate selection from the listing of available help topics.
- To exit the help system, press (←Enter) at any blank HELP> prompt.

Operations

HELP is executed immediately.

Example

```
SPSS> HELP DESCRIPTIVES SYNTAX.
```

- The HELP command requests syntax for procedure DESCRIPTIVES.
- The keyword HELP can be used because help is requested from the SPSS> command prompt.

Example

```
CONTINUE> ? REPORT FORMAT AUTOMATIC.
```

- Help is requested for keyword AUTOMATIC, available on the FORMAT subcommand on REPORT.
- A question mark is used because the request is made from the CONTINUE> prompt.

Example

```
CONTINUE> ? REG STA.
```

- This command requests information about the STATISTICS subcommand on the REGRESSION command. The request takes advantage of spelling permitted by three-character truncation of keywords.
- A question mark is used because the request is made from the CONTINUE> prompt.

HOST

This command is not available on all operating systems.

```
HOST [system command]
```

Overview

HOST executes an operating-system command from within an SPSS prompted session and then returns to the SPSS session. The SPSS session is not affected. HOST is not available in windowed environments, since a windowing system lets you change applications without using HOST.

SPSS cannot control actions taken by other software that you invoke through HOST and therefore cannot guarantee that any particular program will run safely.

Syntax Rules

- On operating systems that use the same command terminator as SPSS, the terminator must be specified twice.
- On some operating systems, an operating-system command must be specified after the keyword HOST. The system command should be in uppercase letters and cannot be continued onto another line.
- Some operating systems allow the HOST command to be specified by itself, without a system command. The result of doing so depends on the host system. For example, specifying HOST in IBM CMS puts the operating system into CMS subset; control is not returned to SPSS until the RETURN command is specified. To see how HOST works on your operating system, consult the *Base System User's Guide* for your version of SPSS.

Example

System commands used with HOST vary according to the host system. The following example is for an IBM CMS system:

```
SPSS> HOST LISTFILE.
```

- From the SPSS> prompt the CMS command LISTFILE is executed, which produces a list of files.
- Once the host command is completed, the SPSS session resumes.

IF

```
IF [(]logical expression[)] target variable=expression
```

The following relational operators can be used in logical expressions:

Symbol	Definition	Symbol	Definition
EQ or =	Equal to	NE or <>*	Not equal to
LT or <	Less than	LE or <=	Less than or equal to
GT or >	Greater than	GE or >=	Greater than or equal to*

* On ASCII systems (for example, UNIX, VAX, and all PC's) you can also use ~=; on IBM EBCDIC systems (for example, IBM 360 and IBM 370) you can also use ¬=.

The following logical operators can be used in logical expressions:

Symbol	Definition
AND or &	Both relations must be true
Or or |	Either relation can be true
Not*	Reverses the outcome of an expression*

* On ASCII systems you can also use ~; on IBM EBCDIC systems you can also use ¬ (or the symbol above number 6).

Example:

```
IF (AGE > 20 AND SEX = 1) GROUP=2.
```

Overview

IF conditionally executes a single transformation command based upon logical conditions found in the data. The transformation can create a new variable or modify the values of an existing variable for each case in the working data file. You can create or modify the values of both numeric and string variables. If you create a new string variable you must first declare it on the STRING command.

IF has three components: a *logical expression* (see "Logical Expressions" on p. 52) that sets up the logical criteria, a *target variable* (the one to be modified or created), and an *assignment expression*. The target variable's values are modified according to the assignment expression.

IF is most efficient when used to execute a single, conditional, COMPUTE-like transformation. If you need multiple IF statements to define the condition, it is usually more efficient to use the RECODE command or a DO IF—END IF structure.

Basic Specification

The basic specification is a logical expression followed by a target variable, a required equals sign, and the assignment expression. The assignment is executed only if the logical expression is true.

Syntax Rules

- Logical expressions can be simple logical variables or relations, or complex logical tests involving variables, constants, functions, relational operators, and logical operators. Both the logical expression and the assignment expression can use any of the numeric or string functions allowed in COMPUTE transformations (see COMPUTE and Universals: Functions).
- Parentheses can be used to enclose the logical expression. Parentheses can also be used within the logical expression to specify the order of operations. Extra blanks or parentheses can be used to make the expression easier to read.
- A relation can compare variables, constants, or more complicated arithmetic expressions. Relations cannot be abbreviated. For example, (A EQ 2 OR A EQ 5) is valid, while (A EQ 2 OR 5) is not. Blanks (not commas) must be used to separate relational operators from the expressions being compared.
- A relation cannot compare a string variable to a numeric value or variable, or vice versa. A relation cannot compare the result of the logical functions SYSMIS, MISSING, ANY, or RANGE to a number.
- String values used in expressions must be specified in quotes and must include any leading or trailing blanks. Lowercase letters are considered distinct from uppercase letters.
- String variables that are used as target variables must already exist. To declare a new string variable, first create the variable with the STRING command and then specify the new variable as the target variable on IF.

Operations

- Each IF command evaluates every case in the data. Compare IF with DO IF, which passes control for a case out of the DO IF—END IF structure as soon as a logical condition is met.
- The logical expression is evaluated as true, false, or missing. The assignment is executed only if the logical expression is true. If the logical expression is false or missing, the assignment is not made. Existing target variables remain unchanged; new numeric variables retain their initial values.
- In general, a logical expression is evaluated as missing if any one of the variables used in the logical expression is system- or user-missing. However, when relations are joined by the logical operators AND or OR, the expression can sometimes be evaluated as true or false even when variables have missing values (see "Missing Values and Logical Operators" on p. 342).

Numeric Variables

- Numeric variables created with IF are initially set to the system-missing value. By default, they are assigned an F8.2 format.
- Logical expressions are evaluated in the following order: functions, followed by exponentiation, arithmetic operations, relations, and logical operators. When more than one logical operator is used, NOT is evaluated first, followed by AND and then OR. You can change the order of operations using parentheses.
- Assignment expressions are evaluated in the following order: functions, then exponentiation, and then arithmetic operators.

String Variables

- New string variables declared on IF are initially set to a blank value and are assigned the format specified on the STRING command that creates them.
- Logical expressions are evaluated in the following order: string functions, then relations, then logical operators. When more than one logical operator is used, NOT is evaluated first, followed by AND and then OR. You can change the order of operations using parentheses.
- If the transformed value of a string variable exceeds the variable's defined width, the transformed value is truncated. If the transformed value is shorter than the defined width, the string is right-padded with blanks.

Missing Values and Logical Operators

When two or more relations are joined by logical operators AND or OR, SPSS always returns a missing value if all of the relations in the expression are missing. However, if any one of the relations can be determined, SPSS interprets the expression as true or false according to the logical outcomes shown in Table 14. The asterisk flags expressions where SPSS can evaluate the outcome with incomplete information.

Table 14 Logical outcome

Expression	Outcome	Expression	Outcome
true AND true	= true	true OR true	= true
true AND false	= false	true OR false	= true
false AND false	= false	false OR false	= false
true AND missing	= missing	true OR missing	= true*
missing AND missing	= missing	missing OR missing	= missing
false AND missing	= false*	false OR missing	= missing

Example

```
IF (AGE > 20 AND SEX = 1) GROUP=2.
```

- Numeric variable *GROUP* is set to 2 for cases where *AGE* is greater than 20 *and* *SEX* is equal to 1.
- When the expression is false or missing, the value of *GROUP* remains unchanged. If *GROUP* has not been previously defined, it contains the system-missing value.

Example

```
IF (SEX EQ 'F') EEO=QUOTA+GAIN.
```

- The logical expression tests string variable *SEX* for the value F.
- When the expression is true (when *SEX* equals F), the value of numeric variable *EEO* is assigned the value of *QUOTA* plus *GAIN*. Both *QUOTA* and *GAIN* must be previously defined numeric variables.
- When the expression is false or missing (for example, if *SEX* equals f), the value of *EEO* remains unchanged. If *EEO* has not been previously defined, it contains the system-missing value.

Example

```
COMPUTE V3=0.
IF ((V1-V2) LE 7) V3=V1**2.
```

- COMPUTE assigns *V3* the value 0.
- The logical expression tests whether *V1* minus *V2* is less than or equal to 7. If it is, the value of *V3* is assigned the value of *V1* squared. Otherwise, the value of *V3* remains at 0.

Example

```
IF (ABS(A-C) LT 100) INT=100.
```

- IF tests whether the absolute value of variable *A* minus variable *C* is less than 100. If it is, *INT* is assigned the value 100. Otherwise, the value is unchanged. If *INT* has not been previously defined, it is system-missing.

Example

```
IF (MEAN(V1 TO V5) LE 7) INDEX=1.
```

- If the mean of variables *V1* through *V5* is less than or equal to 7, *INDEX* equals 1.

Example

```
* Test for listwise deletion of missing values.

DATA LIST   /V1 TO V6 1-6.
STRING SELECT(A1).
COMPUTE SELECT='V'.
VECTOR V=V1 TO V6.

LOOP #I=1 TO 6.
IF MISSING(V(#I)) SELECT='M'.
END LOOP.

BEGIN DATA
123456
    56
1 3456
123456
123456
END DATA.

FREQUENCIES VAR=SELECT.
```

- STRING creates string variable *SELECT* with an A1 format and COMPUTE sets the value of *SELECT* to V.
- VECTOR defines vector *V* as the original variables *V1* to *V6*. Variables on a single vector must be all numeric or all string variables. In this example, because vector *V* is used as an argument on the MISSING function of IF, the variables must be numeric (MISSING is not available for string variables).
- The loop structure executes 6 times: once for each VECTOR element. If a value is missing for any element, SELECT is set equal to M. In effect, if any case has a missing value for any of the variables *V1* to *V6*, SELECT is set to M.
- FREQUENCIES generates a frequency table for SELECT. The table gives a count of how many cases have missing values for at least one variable and how many cases have valid values for all variables. This table can be used to determine how many cases would be dropped from an analysis that uses listwise deletion of missing values. See pp. 124 and 200 for alternative ways to test for listwise deletion of missing values.

Example

```
IF YRHIRED LT 1980 RATE=0.02.
IF DEPT='SALES' DIVISION='TRANSFERRED'.
```

- The logical expression on the first IF command tests whether *YRHIRED* is less than 1980 (hired before 1980). If so, variable *RATE* is set to 0.02.
- The logical expression on the second IF command tests whether *DEPT* equals SALES. When the condition is true, the value for string variable *DIVISION* is changed to TRANS-FERRED but is truncated if the format for *DIVISION* is not at least 11 characters wide. For any other value of *DEPT*, the value of *DIVISION* remains unchanged.
- Though there are two IF statements, each defines a separate and independent condition. The IF command is used rather than the DO IF—END IF structure in order to test both con-

ditions on every case. If DO IF—END IF is used, control passes out of the structure as soon as the first logical condition is met.

Example

```
IF (STATE EQ 'IL' AND CITY EQ 13) COST=1.07 * COST.
```

- The logical expression tests whether *STATE* equals IL and *CITY* equals 13.
- If the logical expression is true, numeric variable *COST* is increased by 7%.
- For any other value of *STATE* or *CITY*, the value of *COST* remains unchanged.

Example

```
STRING GROUP (A18).
IF (HIRED GE 1988) GROUP='Hired after merger'.
```

- STRING declares string variable *GROUP* and assigns it a width of 18 characters.
- When *HIRED* is greater than or equal to 1988, *GROUP* is assigned the value Hired after merger. When *HIRED* is less than 1988, *GROUP* remains blank.

Example

```
IF (RECV GT DUE OR (REVNUES GE EXPNS AND BALNCE GT 0))STATUS='SOLVENT'.
```

- First, SPSS tests whether *REVNUES* is greater than or equal to *EXPNS* and whether *BALNCE* is greater than 0.
- Second, SPSS evaluates if *RECV* is greater than *DUE*.
- If either of these expressions is true, *STATUS* is assigned the value SOLVENT.
- If both expressions are false, *STATUS* remains unchanged.
- *STATUS* is an existing string variable in the working data file. Otherwise, it would have to be declared on a preceding STRING command.

IMPORT

```
IMPORT FILE=file

[/TYPE={COMM}]
       {TAPE}

[/KEEP={ALL** }] [/DROP=varlist]
       {varlist}

[/RENAME=(old varnames=new varnames)...]

[/MAP]
```

**Default if the subcommand is omitted.

Example:

IMPORT FILE=NEWDATA /RENAME=(V1 TO V3=ID, SEX, AGE) /MAP.

Overview

IMPORT reads SPSS portable data files created with the EXPORT command in SPSS or SPSS/PC+. A portable data file is a data file created by SPSS and used to transport data between different types of computers and operating systems (such as between IBM CMS and Digital VAX/VMS) or between SPSS, SPSS/PC+, or other software using the same portable file format. Like an SPSS data file, a portable file contains all of the data and dictionary information stored in the working data file from which it was created.

SPSS can also read data files created by other software programs. See commands such as GET SCSS, GET SAS, GET BMDP, and GET OSIRIS for information on reading files created by other statistical software programs. See GET TRANSLATE for information on reading files created by spreadsheet and database programs such as dBASE, Lotus, and Multiplan.

Options

Format. You can specify the format of the portable file (magnetic tape or communications program) on the TYPE subcommand. For more information on magnetic tapes and communications programs, see "Methods of Transporting Portable Files" on p. 235.

Variables. You can read a subset of variables from the working data file with the DROP and KEEP subcommands. You can rename variables using RENAME. You can also produce a record of all variables and their names in the working file with the MAP subcommand.

Basic Specification

The basic specification is the FILE subcommand with a file specification. All variables from the portable file are copied into the working data file with their original names, variable and value labels, missing-value flags, and print and write formats.

Subcommand Order

- FILE and TYPE must precede all other subcommands.
- No specific order is required between FILE and TYPE or among other subcommands.

Operations

- The portable data file and dictionary become the SPSS working data file and dictionary.
- A file saved with weighting in effect (using the WEIGHT command) automatically uses the case weights when the file is read.

Example

```
IMPORT FILE=NEWDATA /RENAME=(V1 TO V3=ID,SEX,AGE) /MAP.
```

- The working data file is generated from the portable file *NEWDATA*.
- Variables *V1*, *V2*, and *V3* are renamed *ID*, *SEX*, and *AGE* in the working file. Their names remain *V1*, *V2*, and *V3* in the portable file. None of the other variables copied into the working file are renamed.
- MAP requests a display of the variables in the working data file.

FILE Subcommand

FILE specifies the portable file. FILE is the only required subcommand on IMPORT.

TYPE Subcommand

TYPE indicates whether the portable file is formatted for magnetic tape or for a communications program. TYPE can specify either COMM or TAPE. For more information on magnetic tapes and communications programs, see EXPORT.

- All portable files created by releases earlier than SPSS-X 2.1 are in tape format and may not be suitable for transmission by communications programs.

COMM   *Communications-formatted file*. This is the default.

TAPE   *Tape-formatted file*.

Example
```
IMPORT TYPE=TAPE /FILE=HUBOUT.
```

- File *HUBOUT* is read as a tape-formatted portable file.

DROP and KEEP Subcommands

DROP and KEEP are used to read a subset of variables from the portable file.

- DROP excludes a variable or list of variables from the working data file. All variables not named are included in the file.
- KEEP includes a variable or list of variables in the working file. All variables not specified on KEEP are excluded.
- DROP and KEEP cannot precede the FILE or TYPE subcommands.
- Variables can be specified in any order. The order of variables on KEEP determines the order of variables in the working file. The order on DROP does not affect the order of variables in the working file.
- If a variable is referred to twice on the same subcommand, only the first mention is recognized.
- Multiple DROP and KEEP subcommands are allowed; the effect is cumulative. Specifying a variable named on a previous DROP or not named on a previous KEEP results in an error and the command is not executed.
- Keyword TO can be used to specify a group of consecutive variables in the portable file.
- The portable file is not affected by DROP or KEEP.

Example

```
IMPORT FILE=NEWSUM /DROP=DEPT TO DIVISION.
```

- The working data file is generated from the portable file *NEWSUM*. Variables between and including *DEPT* and *DIVISION* in the portable file are excluded from the working file.
- All other variables are copied into the working file.

RENAME Subcommand

RENAME renames variables being read from the portable file. The renamed variables retain the variable and value labels, missing-value flags, and print formats contained in the portable file.

- To rename a variable, specify the name of the variable in the portable file, a required equals sign, and the new name.
- A variable list can be specified on both sides of the equals sign. The number of variables on both sides must be the same, and the entire specification must be enclosed in parentheses.
- Keyword TO can be used for both variable lists (see "Keyword TO" on p. 32).
- Any DROP or KEEP subcommand after RENAME must use the new variable names.

Example

```
IMPORT FILE=NEWSUM /DROP=DEPT TO DIVISION
  /RENAME=(NAME,WAGE=LNAME,SALARY).
```

- RENAME renames *NAME* and *WAGE* to *LNAME* and *SALARY*.

- *LNAME* and *SALARY* retain the variable and value labels, missing-value flags, and print formats assigned to *NAME* and *WAGE*.

MAP Subcommand

MAP displays a list of variables in the working data file, showing all changes that have been specified on the RENAME, DROP, or KEEP subcommands.

- MAP can be specified as often as desired.
- MAP confirms only the changes specified on the subcommands that precede the MAP request.
- Each MAP subcommand maps the results of subcommands that precede it; results of subcommands that follow it are not mapped. When MAP is specified last, it also produces a description of the file.

Example

```
IMPORT FILE=NEWSUM /DROP=DEPT TO DIVISION /MAP
  /RENAME NAME=LNAME WAGE=SALARY /MAP.
```

- The first MAP subcommand produces a listing of the variables in the file after DROP has dropped the specified variables.
- RENAME renames *NAME* and *WAGE*.
- The second MAP subcommand shows the variables in the file after renaming.

INCLUDE

    INCLUDE FILE=file

Example:

    INCLUDE FILE=GSSLABS.

Overview

INCLUDE includes a file of SPSS commands in an SPSS session. INCLUDE is especially useful for including a long series of data definition statements or transformations. Another use for INCLUDE is to set up a library of commonly used commands and include them in the command sequence as they are needed.

INCLUDE allows you to run multiple commands together during a prompted session and can save time. Complex or repetitive commands can be stored in a command file and included in the session, while simpler commands or commands unique to the current analysis can be entered during the session, before and after the included file.

Basic Specification

The only specification is the FILE subcommand, which specifies the file to include. When INCLUDE is executed, the commands in the specified file are processed.

Syntax Rules

- Commands in an included file must begin in column 1, and continuation lines for each command must be indented at least one column.
- A raw data file can be used as an include file if the first line of the included file contains the BEGIN DATA command and the last line contains the END DATA command. However, because the data are specified between BEGIN DATA and END DATA, they are limited to a maximum of 80 columns (the maximum may be fewer than 80 columns on some systems).
- As many INCLUDE commands as needed can be used in a session.
- INCLUDE commands can be nested so that one set of included commands includes another set of commands. This nesting can go to five levels. However, a file cannot be included that is still open from a previous step.

Operations

- If an included file contains a FINISH command, the SPSS session ends and no further commands are processed.
- If a journal file is created for the SPSS session, INCLUDE is copied to the journal file. Commands from the included file are also copied to the journal file but are treated like

printed messages. Thus, INCLUDE can be executed from the journal file if the journal file is later used as a command file. Commands from the included file are executed only once.
- For certain IBM systems, the NUMBERED or UNNUMBERED setting in effect before the INCLUDE command is restored at the end of the included file. The original printback status is also restored when the end of the included file is reached.

FILE Subcommand

FILE identifies the file containing SPSS commands. FILE is the only specification on INCLUDE and is required.

Example

```
SPSS> INCLUDE FILE=GSSLABS.
```

- INCLUDE includes file *GSSLABS* in the prompted session. When INCLUDE is executed, the commands in file *GSSLABS* are processed.
- Assume the include file *GSSLABS* contains the following:

```
DATA LIST FILE=DATA52
   /RELIGION 5 OCCUPAT 7 SES 12 ETHNIC 15
    PARTY 19 VOTE48 33 VOTE52 41.
```

The working data file will be defined and ready for analysis after INCLUDE is executed.

INFO

This command is not available on all operating systems.

```
INFO [OUTFILE = file]
     [OVERVIEW]
     [LOCAL]
     [ERRORS]
     [FACILITIES]
     [PROCEDURES]
     [ALL]
     [procedure name] [/procedure name...]
     [SINCE release number]
```

Example:

INFO LOCAL.

Overview

INFO makes available two kinds of online documentation: local and update.

Local Documentation

Local documentation concerns the environment in which SPSS is run. It includes some or all of the following, depending on the operating system:

- Commands or job control language for running SPSS.
- Conventions for referring to files. These include instructions on how your computer's operating system accesses or creates a particular file.
- Conventions for handling tapes and other input/output devices.
- Data formats. The formats SPSS reads and writes may differ from one computer and operating system to another.
- Default values for parameters controlled by the SET command. Many defaults for these parameters are set at the individual installation. The SHOW command displays the values that are currently in effect. Local documentation may contain information on why one setting is preferred over another.
- Information about your computer and operating system or your individual installation.

Update Documentation

Update documentation includes changes to existing procedures and facilities made after publication of this manual, new procedures and facilities, and corrections to this manual. Update documentation can be requested for all available releases, or for releases after a particular release.

Syntax Reference Guide

Basic Specification

- The minimum specification is the command name. When specified by itself, SPSS displays an overview of available documents.

Syntax Rules

- Multiple keywords and/or procedure names can be specified on a single INFO command.
- Multiple procedure names must be separated by slashes.
- The order of specifications is unimportant and does not affect the order in which the documentation is printed.
- Three- or four-character truncation does *not* apply to INFO command specifications. Spell all keywords in full. For procedure names, spell the first word in full and subsequent words through at least the first three characters.

Operations

- By default, the INFO command produces update information only for the current release. Documentation for earlier releases may also be available; read the INFO overview to find out whether it is available on your system.
- If overlapping sets of information are requested, only one copy is printed.
- If there is no available documentation for the requested information, only a copyright page is printed.
- If information is requested for an unrecognized topic, SPSS prints an error message.
- The characteristics of the output produced by the INFO command may vary by computer type. As implemented at SPSS Inc., the output includes carriage control, with the maximum length of a page determined by the LENGTH subcommand on SET. A printer width of 132 characters is assumed for some examples, although the text is generally much narrower.
- SPSS requires more computer resources than most printing utilities. Your installation may therefore provide an alternative method for printing INFO documentation. In this case, the INFO command may simply provide instructions for using the alternative method.

Example

```
INFO   OVERVIEW FACILITIES FREQUENCIES / CROSSTABS.
```

- INFO produces an overview and documentation for any changes made to system facilities and to the FREQUENCIES and CROSSTABS procedures.
- Because keyword SINCE is not specified, INFO prints only documentation for the current release.

Types of Information

The following types of information can be requested on INFO:

OVERVIEW *Overview of available documentation.* This includes a table of contents for the documentation available with INFO, along with information about SPSS manuals.

LOCAL *Local documentation.* See "Local Documentation" on p. 352.

ERRORS *List of known unfixed errors.* This lists the known unfixed errors in the current release of SPSS. Since ERRORS applies only to the current release, the SINCE keyword (described below) has no effect with ERRORS.

FACILITIES *Update information for SPSS facilities.* This covers all differences, except in procedures, between the system as documented in this manual and the system as installed on your computer—whether those differences result from updates to the system, revisions required for conversions to particular operating systems, or errors in this manual. Only updates for the most current release are printed unless keyword SINCE is specified.

PROCEDURES *Update information for procedures.* This includes full documentation for procedures new in the current release and update information for procedures that existed prior to the current release.

procedure *Documentation for the procedure named.* This is the same information as that printed by the PROCEDURES keyword, but limited to the procedure named. You can specify multiple procedures, separating each from the other with a slash.

ALL *All available documentation.* ALL includes OVERVIEW, LOCAL, ERRORS, FACILITIES, and PROCEDURES.

SINCE Keyword

Releases of SPSS are numbered by integers, with decimal digits indicating maintenance releases between major releases. The release number appears in the default heading for SPSS output. Each SPSS manual is identified in the preface by the number of the release it documents.

Keyword SINCE obtains information for earlier releases or limits the information to maintenance releases since the last major release.

- The minimum specification is keyword SINCE followed by a release number.
- SINCE is not inclusive. Specifying 3.0 does not include changes made to the system in Release 3.0.
- To identify a maintenance release, enter the exact number, with decimal, as in 3.1.
- Information for some earlier releases may not be available. For example, information for Release 2.2 and earlier is not available if INFO is run with SPSS Release 5.0 or later.

Example

```
INFO  OVERVIEW FACILITIES FREQUENCIES / CROSSTABS SINCE 3.
```

- INFO prints documentation for all changes to system facilities and to procedures FREQUENCIES and CROSSTABS since Release 3.0.

OUTFILE Subcommand

By default, the information generated by INFO is part of the SPSS output. OUTFILE sends INFO output to a separate file.

Example

```
INFO OUTFILE=SPSSDOC ALL SINCE 3.
```

- INFO creates a text file that includes an overview, local documentation, error, and update information for facilities and procedures since Release 3.0.
- The OUTFILE subcommand sends the documentation to file *SPSSDOC*.

INPUT PROGRAM—END INPUT PROGRAM

```
INPUT PROGRAM

commands to create or define cases

END INPUT PROGRAM
```

Example:
```
INPUT PROGRAM.
DATA LIST FILE=PRICES /YEAR 1-4 QUARTER 6 PRICE 8-12(2).

DO IF (YEAR GE 1881).  /*Stop reading before 1881
END FILE.
END IF.
END INPUT PROGRAM.
```

Overview

The INPUT PROGRAM and END INPUT PROGRAM commands enclose data definition and transformation commands that build cases from input records. The input program often encloses one or more DO IF—END IF or LOOP—END LOOP structures, and it must include at least one file definition command, such as DATA LIST. One of the following utility commands is also usually used:

END CASE Build cases from the commands within the input program and pass the cases to the commands immediately following the input program.

END FILE Terminate processing of a data file before the actual end of the file or define the end of the file when the input program is used to read raw data.

REREAD Reread the current record using a different DATA LIST.

REPEATING DATA Read repeating groups of data from the same input record.

For more information on the commands used in an input program, see the discussion of each command.

Input programs create a dictionary and data for a working file from raw data files; they cannot be used to read SPSS data files. They can be used to process direct-access and keyed data files. For details, see KEYED DATA LIST.

Input Programs

SPSS builds the working data file dictionary when it encounters commands that create and define variables. At the same time, SPSS builds an *input program* that constructs cases and an optional *transformation program* that modifies cases prior to analysis or display. By the time SPSS encounters a procedure command that tells it to read the data, the working file dictionary is ready, and the programs that construct and modify the cases in the working file are built.

The internal input program is usually built from either a single DATA LIST command or from any of the commands that read or combine SPSS data files (for example, GET, ADD FILES, MATCH FILES, UPDATE, and so forth). The input program can also be built from the FILE TYPE—END FILE TYPE structure used to define nested, mixed, or grouped files. The third type of input program is specified with the INPUT PROGRAM—END INPUT PROGRAM commands.

With INPUT PROGRAM—END INPUT PROGRAM you can create your own input program to perform many different operations on raw data. You can use transformation commands to build cases. You can read nonrectangular files, concatenate raw data files, and build cases selectively. You can also create a working data file without reading any data at all.

Input State

There are four program states in SPSS: the *initial state*, in which there is no working file dictionary; the *input state*, in which cases are created from the input file; the *transformation state*, in which cases are transformed; and the *procedure state*, in which procedures are executed. When you specify INPUT PROGRAM—END INPUT PROGRAM, you must pay attention to which commands are allowed within the input state, which commands can appear only within the input state, and which are not allowed within the input state. See Appendix A for a discussion of program states, command order, and a table that describes what happens to each command when it is encountered in each of the four states.

Basic Specification

The basic specification is INPUT PROGRAM, the commands used to create cases and define the working data file, and END INPUT PROGRAM.

- INPUT PROGRAM and END INPUT PROGRAM each must be specified on a separate line and have no additional specifications.
- To define a working data file, the input program must include at least one DATA LIST or END FILE command.

Operations

- The INPUT PROGRAM—END INPUT PROGRAM structure defines a working data file and is not executed until SPSS encounters a procedure or the EXECUTE command.
- INPUT PROGRAM clears the current working data file.

Example

```
* Select cases with an input program.

INPUT PROGRAM.
DATA LIST FILE=PRICES /YEAR 1-4 QUARTER 6 PRICE 8-12(2).

DO IF (YEAR GE 1881).   /*Stop reading when reaching 1881
END FILE.
END IF.
END INPUT PROGRAM.

LIST.
```

- The input program is defined between the INPUT PROGRAM and END INPUT PROGRAM commands.
- This example assumes that data records are entered chronologically by year. The DO IF—END IF structure specifies an end of file when the first case with a value of 1881 or later for *YEAR* is reached.
- LIST executes the input program and lists cases in the working data file. The case that causes the end of the file is not included in the working file generated by the input program.
- As an alternative to this input program, you can use N OF CASES to select cases if you know the exact number of cases. Another alternative is to use SELECT IF to select cases before 1881, but then SPSS would unnecessarily read the entire input file.

Example

```
* Skip the first n records in a file.

INPUT PROGRAM.
NUMERIC         #INIT.
DO IF           NOT (#INIT).
+  LOOP         #I = 1 TO 5.
+     DATA LIST      NOTABLE/.   /* No data - just skip record
+  END LOOP.
+  COMPUTE      #INIT = 1.
END IF.
DATA LIST     NOTABLE/ X 1.
END INPUT PROGRAM.

BEGIN DATA
A                            /* The first 5 records are skipped
B
C
D
E
1
2
3
4
5
END DATA.
LIST.
```

- NUMERIC declares scratch variable *#INIT*, which is initialized to system-missing.
- The DO IF structure is executed as long as *#INIT* does not equal 1.
- LOOP is executed five times. Within the loop, DATA LIST is specified without variable names, causing SPSS to read records in the data file without copying them into the working file. LOOP is executed five times, so SPSS reads five records in this manner. END LOOP terminates this loop.
- COMPUTE creates scratch variable *#INIT* and sets it equal to 1. The DO IF structure is therefore not executed again.
- END IF terminates the DO IF structure.
- The second DATA LIST specifies numeric variable *X*, which is located in column 1 of each record. Because SPSS has already read five records, the first value for *X* that is copied into the working file is read from record 6.

More Examples

For additional examples of input programs, refer to DATA LIST (p. 155), DO IF (p. 203), DO REPEAT (p. 206), END CASE, END FILE, LOOP, NUMERIC (p. 460), POINT (p. 488), REPEATING DATA, REREAD, and VECTOR (p. 682).

KEYED DATA LIST

This command is not available on all operating systems.

```
KEYED DATA LIST KEY=varname IN=varname

 FILE=file [{TABLE  }]
           {NOTABLE}

 /varname {col location [(format)]} [varname ..]
          {(FORTRAN-like format)  }
```

Example:

```
FILE HANDLE EMPL/ file specifications.
KEYED DATA LIST FILE=EMPL KEY=#NXTCASE IN=#FOUND
       /YRHIRED 1-2 SEX 3 JOBCLASS 4.
```

Overview

KEYED DATA LIST reads raw data from two types of nonsequential files: direct-access files, which provide direct access by a record number, and keyed files, which provide access by a record key. An example of a direct-access file is a file of 50 records, each corresponding to one of the United States. If you know the relationship between the states and the record numbers, you can retrieve the data for any specific state. An example of a keyed file is a file containing social security numbers and other information about a firm's employees. The social security number can be used to identify the records in the file.

On some systems, SPSS can read a key-sequenced data set sequentially from a point that a key value controls (see POINT). SPSS can also read IBM VSAM (Virtual Storage Access Method) files. For more details on reading VSAM files under IBM OS, IBM CMS, and IBM DOS operating systems, see the *SPSS Base System User's Guide* for those systems. For more information on reading keyed files under other operating systems, access the online documentation available through the INFO command.

Direct-Access Files

There are various types of direct-access files. The SPSS concept of a direct-access file, however, is very specific. The file must be one from which individual records can be selected according to their number. The records in a 100-record direct-access file, for example, are numbered from 1 to 100.

Although the concept of record number applies to almost any file, not all files can be treated by SPSS as direct-access files. In fact, some operating systems provide no direct-access capabilities at all, and others permit only a narrowly defined subset of all files to be treated as direct access.

Very few files turn out to be good candidates for direct-access organization. In the case of an inventory file, for instance, the usual large gaps in the part numbering sequence would result in large amounts of wasted file space. Gaps are not a problem, however, if they are predictable. For instance, if you recognize that telephone area codes have first digits of 2 through 9, second digits of 0 or 1, and third digits of 0 through 9, you can transform an area code into a record number by using the following COMPUTE statement:

```
COMPUTE RECNUM = 20*(DIGIT1-2) + 10*DIGIT2 + DIGIT3 + 1.
```

where *DIGIT1*, *DIGIT2*, and *DIGIT3* are variables corresponding to the respective digits in the area code, and *RECNUM* is the resulting record number. The record numbers would range from 1, for the nonexistent area code 200, through 160, for area code 919. The file would then have a manageable number of unused records.

Keyed Files

Of the many kinds of keyed files, the ones to which SPSS can provide access are generally known as *indexed sequential files*. A file of this kind is basically a sequential file in which an index is maintained so that the file can be processed either sequentially or selectively. In effect, there is an underlying data file that is accessed through a file of index entries. The file of index entries may, for example, contain the fact that data record 797 is associated with social security number 476-77-1359. Depending on the implementation, the underlying data may or may not be maintained in sequential order.

The key for each record in the file generally comprises one or more pieces of information found within the record. An example of a complex key is a customer's last name and house number, plus the consonants in the street name, plus the zip code, plus a unique digit in case there are duplicates. Regardless of the information contained in the key, SPSS treats it as a character string.

On some systems, more than one key is associated with each record. That is, the records in a file can be identified according to different types of information. Although the primary key for a file normally must be unique, sometimes the secondary keys need not be. For example, the records in an employee file might be identified by social security number and job classification.

Options

Data Source. You can specify the name of the keyed file on the FILE subcommand. By default, the last file that was specified on an SPSS input command, such as DATA LIST or REPEATING DATA, is read.

Summary Table. You can display a table that summarizes the variable definitions.

Basic Specification

- The basic specification requires FILE, KEY, and IN, each of which specifies one variable, followed by a slash and variable definitions.
- FILE specifies the direct-access or keyed file. The file must have a file handle already defined.
- KEY specifies the variable whose value will be used to read a record. For direct-access files, the variable must be numeric; for keyed files, it must be string.
- IN creates a logical variable that flags whether a record was successfully read.

- Variable definitions follow all subcommands; the slash preceding them is required. Variable definitions are similar to those specified on DATA LIST.

Subcommand Order

- Subcommands can be named in any order.
- Variable definitions must follow all specified subcommands.

Syntax Rules

- Specifications for the variable definitions are the same as those described for DATA LIST. The only difference is that only one record can be defined per case.
- The FILE HANDLE command must be used if the FILE subcommand is specified on KEYED DATA LIST.
- KEYED DATA LIST can be specified in an input program, or it can be used as a transformation language to change an existing working data file. This differs from all other SPSS input commands, such as GET and DATA LIST, which create new working files.

Operations

- Variable names are stored in the working file dictionary.
- Formats are stored in the working file dictionary and are used to display and write the values. To change output formats of numeric variables, use the FORMATS command.

Example

```
FILE HANDLE EMPL/ file specifications.
KEYED DATA LIST FILE=EMPL KEY=#NXTCASE IN=#FOUND
     /YRHIRED 1-2 SEX 3 JOBCLASS 4.
```

- FILE HANDLE defines the handle for the data file to be read by KEYED DATA LIST. The handle is specified on the FILE subcommand of KEYED DATA LIST.
- KEY on KEYED DATA LIST specifies the variable to be used as the access key. For a direct-access file, the value of the variable must be between 1 and the number of records in the file. For a keyed file, the value must be a string.
- IN creates the logical scratch variable *#FOUND*, whose value will be 1 if the record is successfully read, or 0 if the record is not found.
- The variable definitions are the same as those used for DATA LIST.

Example

```
* Reading a direct-access file: sampling 1 out of every 25 records.

FILE HANDLE      EMPL/ file specifications.
INPUT PROGRAM.
COMPUTE #INTRVL = TRUNC(UNIF(48))+1.  /* Mean interval = 25
COMPUTE #NXTCASE = #NXTCASE+#INTRVL.  /* Next record number
COMPUTE #EOF = #NXTCASE > 1000.       /* End of file check
DO IF    #EOF.
+   END FILE.
ELSE.
+   KEYED DATA LIST   FILE=EMPL, KEY=#NXTCASE, IN=#FOUND, NOTABLE
                     /YRHIRED 1-2 SEX 3 JOBCLASS 4.
+   DO IF       #FOUND.
+      END CASE.                      /* Return a case
+   ELSE.
+      PRINT / 'Oops. #NXTCASE=' #NXTCASE.
+   END IF.
END IF.
END INPUT PROGRAM.
EXECUTE.
```

- FILE HANDLE defines the handle for the data file to be read by the KEYED DATA LIST command. The record numbers for this example are generated by the SPSS transformation language; they are not based on data taken from another file.
- The INPUT PROGRAM and END INPUT PROGRAM commands begin and end the block of commands that build cases from the input file. Since the session generates cases, an input program is required.
- The first two COMPUTE statements determine the number of the next record to be selected. This is done in two steps. First, the integer portion is taken from the sum of 1 and a uniform pseudo-random number between 1 and 49. The result is a mean interval of 25. Second, the variable *#NXTCASE* is added to this number to generate the next record number. This record number, *#NXTCASE*, will be used for the key variable on the KEYED DATA LIST command. The third COMPUTE creates a logical scratch variable, *#EOF*, that has a value of 0 if the record number is less than or equal to 1000, or 1 if the value of the record number is greater than 1000.
- The DO IF—END IF structure controls the building of cases. If the record number is greater than 1000, *#EOF* equals 1, and the END FILE command tells SPSS to stop reading data and end the file.
- If the record number is less than or equal to 1000, the record is read via KEYED DATA LIST using the value of *#NXTCASE*. A case is generated if the record exists (*#FOUND* equals 1). If not, SPSS displays the record number and continues to the next case. The sample will have about 40 records.
- EXECUTE causes the transformations to be executed.
- This example illustrates the difference between DATA LIST, which always reads the next record in a file, and KEYED DATA LIST, which reads only specified records. The record numbers must be generated by another command or be contained in the working data file.

Example

```
* Reading a keyed file: reading selected records.
GET FILE=STUDENTS/KEEP=AGE,SEX,COURSE.
FILE HANDLE COURSES/ file specifications.
STRING #KEY(A4).
COMPUTE #KEY = STRING(COURSE,N4). /* Create a string key
KEYED DATA LIST FILE=COURSES KEY=#KEY IN=#FOUND NOTABLE
    /PERIOD 13 CREDITS 16.
SELECT IF #FOUND.
LIST.
```

- GET reads the *STUDENTS* file, which contains information on students, including a course identification for each student. The course identification will be used as the key for selecting one record from a file of courses.
- The FILE HANDLE command defines a file handle for the file of courses.
- The STRING and COMPUTE commands transform the course identification from numeric to string for use as a key. For keyed files, the key variable must be a string.
- KEYED DATA LIST uses the value of the newly created string variable *#KEY* as the key to search the course file. If a record that matches the value of *#KEY* is found, *#FOUND* is set to 1; otherwise, it is set to 0. Note that KEYED DATA LIST appears outside an input program in this example.
- If the course file contains the requested record, *#FOUND* equals 1. The variables *PERIOD* and *CREDITS* are added to the case and the case is selected via the SELECT IF command; otherwise, the case is dropped.
- LIST lists the values of the selected cases.
- This example shows how existing cases can be updated on the basis of information read from a keyed file.
- This task could also be accomplished by reading the entire course file with DATA LIST and combining it with the student file via the MATCH FILES command. The technique you should use depends on the percentage of the records in the course file that need to be accessed. If fewer than 10% of the course file records are read, KEYED DATA LIST is probably more efficient. As the percentage of the records that are read increases, reading the entire course file and using MATCH makes more sense.

FILE Subcommand

FILE specifies the handle for the direct-access or keyed data file. The file handle must have been defined on a previous FILE HANDLE command (or, in the case of the IBM OS environment, on a DD statement in the JCL).

KEY Subcommand

KEY specifies the variable whose value will be used as the key. This variable must already exist as the result of a prior DATA LIST, KEYED DATA LIST, GET, or transformation command.

- KEY is required. Its only specification is a single variable. The variable can be a permanent variable or a scratch variable.
- For direct-access files, the key variable must be numeric, and its value must be between 1 and the number of records in the file.
- For keyed files, the key variable must be string. If the keys are numbers, such as social security numbers, the STRING function can be used to convert the numbers to strings. For example, the following might be required to get the value of a numeric key into exactly the same format as used on the keyed file:

```
COMPUTE #KEY=STRING(123,IB4).
```

IN Subcommand

IN creates a numeric variable whose value indicates whether or not the specified record is found.
- IN is required. Its only specification is a single numeric variable. The variable can be a permanent variable or a scratch variable.
- The value of the variable is 1 if the record is successfully read or 0 if the record is not found. The IN variable can be used to select all cases that have been updated by KEYED DATA LIST.

Example

```
FILE HANDLE EMPL/ file specifications.
KEYED DATA LIST FILE=EMPL KEY=#NXTCASE IN=#FOUND
        /YRHIRED 1-2 SEX 3 JOBCLASS 4.
```

- IN creates the logical scratch variable *#FOUND*. The values of *#FOUND* will be 1 if the record indicated by the key value in *#NXTCASE* is found or 0 if the record does not exist.

TABLE and NOTABLE Subcommands

TABLE and NOTABLE determine whether SPSS displays a table that summarizes the variable definitions. TABLE, the default, displays the table. NOTABLE suppresses the table.
- TABLE and NOTABLE are optional and mutually exclusive.
- The only specification for TABLE or NOTABLE is the subcommand keyword. Neither subcommand has additional specifications.

LEAVE

```
LEAVE varlist
```

Example:
```
COMPUTE TSALARY=TSALARY+SALARY.
LEAVE TSALARY.
FORMAT TSALARY (DOLLAR8)/ SALARY (DOLLAR7).
EXECUTE.
```

Overview

Normally, SPSS reinitializes variables each time it prepares to read a new case. LEAVE suppresses reinitialization and retains the current value of the specified variable or variables when SPSS reads the next case. It also sets the initial value received by a numeric variable to 0 instead of system-missing. LEAVE is frequently used with COMPUTE to create a variable to store an accumulating sum. LEAVE is also used to spread a variable's values across multiple cases when VECTOR is used within an input program to restructure a data file (see p. 214 for an example).

LEAVE cannot be used with scratch variables. For information on using scratch variables, see "Scratch Variables" on p. 34.

Basic Specification

The basic specification is the variable(s) whose values are not to be reinitialized as each new case is read.

Syntax Rules

- Variables named on LEAVE must already exist and cannot be scratch variables.
- Multiple variables can be named. Keyword TO can be used to refer to a list of consecutive variables.
- String and numeric variables can be specified on the same LEAVE command.

Operations

- Unlike most transformations, which do not take effect until the data are read, LEAVE takes effect as soon as it is encountered in the command sequence. Thus, special attention should be paid to its position among commands. For more information, see Universals: Command Order.
- Numeric variables named on LEAVE are initialized to 0 for the first case, and string variables are initialized to blanks. These variables are not reinitialized when new cases are read.

Example

```
COMPUTE TSALARY=TSALARY+SALARY.
LEAVE TSALARY.
FORMAT TSALARY (DOLLAR8)/ SALARY (DOLLAR7).
```

- These commands keep a running total of salaries across all cases. *SALARY* is the variable containing the employee's salary, and *TSALARY* is the new variable containing the cumulative salaries for all previous cases.
- For the first case, *TSALARY* is initialized to 0, and *TSALARY* equals *SALARY*. For the rest of the cases, *TSALARY* stores the cumulative totals for *SALARY*.
- LEAVE follows COMPUTE because *TSALARY* must first be defined before it can be specified on LEAVE.
- If LEAVE were not specified for this computation, *TSALARY* would be initialized to system-missing for all cases. *TSALARY* would remain system-missing because its value would be missing for every computation.

Example

```
SORT CASES DEPT.
IF DEPT NE LAG(DEPT,1) TSALARY=0.    /*Initialize for new dept
COMPUTE TSALARY=TSALARY+SALARY.      /*Sum salaries
LEAVE TSALARY.                       /*Prevent initialization each case
FORMAT TSALARY (DOLLAR8)/ SALARY (DOLLAR7).
```

- These commands accumulate a sum across cases for each department.
- SORT first sorts cases by the values of variable *DEPT*.
- IF specifies that if the value of *DEPT* for the current case is not equal to the value of *DEPT* for the previous case, *TSALARY* equals 0. Thus, *TSALARY* is reset to 0 each time the value of *DEPT* changes. (For the first case in the file, the logical expression on IF is missing. However, the desired effect is obtained because LEAVE initializes *TSALARY* to 0 for the first case, independent of the IF statement.)
- LEAVE prevents *TSALARY* from being initialized for cases within the same department.

LIST

```
LIST [[VARIABLES=]{ALL**   }] [/FORMAT=[{WRAP**  }] [{UNNUMBERED**}]]
                 {varlist}              {SINGLE}   {NUMBERED    }

[/CASES=[FROM {1**}] [TO {eof**}] [BY {1**}]]
              {n  }     {n    }      {n  }
```

Example:

```
LIST VARIABLES=V1 V2 /CASES=FROM 10 TO 100 BY 2.
```

Overview

LIST displays case values for variables in the working data file. The output is similar to the output produced by the PRINT command. However, LIST is a procedure and reads data, whereas PRINT is a transformation and requires a procedure (or the EXECUTE command) to execute it.

Options

Selecting and Ordering Variables. You can specify a list of variables to be listed using the VARIABLES subcommand.

Format. You can limit each case listing to a single line, and you can display the case number for each listed case with the FORMAT subcommand.

Selecting Cases. You can limit the listing to a particular sequence of cases using the CASES subcommand.

Basic Specification

- The basic specification is simply LIST, which displays the values for all variables in the working data file.
- By default, cases wrap to multiple lines if all the values do not fit within the page width (the page width is determined by the SET WIDTH command). Case numbers are not displayed for the listed cases.

Subcommand Order

All subcommands are optional and can be named in any order.

Operations

- If VARIABLES is not specified, variables are listed in the order in which they appear in the working file.

- LIST does not display values for scratch or system variables.
- LIST uses print formats contained in the dictionary of the working data file. Alternative formats cannot be specified on LIST. See FORMATS or PRINT FORMATS for information on changing print formats.
- LIST output uses the width specified on SET.
- If a numeric value is longer than its defined width, SPSS first attempts to list the value by removing punctuation characters, then uses scientific notation, and finally prints asterisks.
- If a long string variable cannot be listed within the output width, it is truncated.
- Values of the variables listed for a case are always separated by at least one blank.
- System-missing values are displayed as a period for numeric variables and a blank for string variables.
- If cases fit on one line, the column width for each variable is determined by the length of the variable name or the format, whichever is greater. If the variable names do not fit on one line, they are printed vertically.
- If cases do not fit on one line within the output width specified on SET, they are wrapped. LIST displays a table illustrating the location of the variables in the output and prints the name of the first variable in each line at the beginning of the line.
- Each execution of LIST begins at the top of a new page. If SPLIT FILE is in effect, each split also begins at the top of a new page.

Example

```
LIST.
```

- LIST by itself requests a display of the values for all variables in the working file.

Example

```
LIST VARIABLES=V1 V2 /CASES=FROM 10 TO 100 BY 2.
```

- LIST produces a list of every second case for variables *V1* and *V2*, starting with case 10 and stopping at case 100.

VARIABLES Subcommand

VARIABLES specifies the variables to be listed. The actual keyword VARIABLES can be omitted.
- The variables must already exist, and they cannot be scratch or system variables.
- If VARIABLES is used, only the specified variables are listed.
- Variables are listed in the order in which they are named on VARIABLES.
- If a variable is named more than once, it is listed more than once.

- Keyword ALL (the default) can be used to request all variables. ALL can also be used with a variable list (see example below).

ALL *List all user-defined variables.* Variables are listed in the order in which they appear in the working data file. This is the default if VARIABLES is omitted.

Example

```
LIST VARIABLES=V15 V31 ALL.
```

- VARIABLES is used to list values for *V15* and *V31* before all other variables. Keyword ALL then lists all variables, including *V15* and *V31*, in the order they appear in the working data file. Values for *V15* and *V31* are therefore listed twice.

FORMAT Subcommand

FORMAT controls whether cases wrap if they cannot fit on a single line and whether the case number is displayed for each listed case. The default display uses more than one line per case (if necessary) and does not number cases.

- The minimum specification is a single keyword.
- WRAP and SINGLE are alternatives, as are NUMBERED and UNNUMBERED. Only one of each pair can be specified.
- If SPLIT FILE is in effect for NUMBERED, case numbering restarts at each split. To get sequential numbering regardless of splits, create a variable and set it equal to the system variable *$CASENUM* and then name this variable as the first variable on the VARIABLES subcommand. An appropriate format should be specified for the new variable before it is used on LIST.

WRAP *Wrap cases if they do not fit on a single line.* Page width is determined by the SET WIDTH command. This is the default.

SINGLE *Limit each case to one line.* Only variables that fit on a single line are displayed.

UNNUMBERED *Do not include the sequence number of each case.* This is the default.

NUMBERED *Include the sequence number of each case.* The sequence number is displayed to the left of the listed values.

CASES Subcommand

CASES limits the number of cases listed. By default, all cases in the working data file are listed.

- Any or all of the keywords below can be used. Defaults that are not changed remain in effect.
- If LIST is preceded by a SAMPLE or SELECT IF command, case selections specified by CASES are taken from those cases that were selected by SAMPLE or SELECT IF.
- If SPLIT FILE is in effect, case selections specified by CASES are restarted for each split.

FROM n   *Number of the first case to be listed.* The default is 1.

TO n   *Number of the last cases to be listed.* The default is the end of the working file. CASES 100 is interpreted as CASES TO 100.

BY n   *Increment used to choose cases for listing.* The default is 1.

Example

```
LIST CASES BY 3 /FORMAT=NUMBERED.
```

- Every third case is listed for all variables in the working data file. The listing begins with the first case and includes every third case up to the end of the file.
- FORMAT displays the case number of each listed case.

Example

```
LIST CASES FROM 10 TO 20.
```

- Cases from case 10 through case 20 are listed for all variables in the working file.

LOOP—END LOOP

```
LOOP [varname=n TO m [BY {1**}]] [IF [(]logical expression[)]]
                             {n  }
transformation commands

END LOOP [IF [(]logical expression[)]]
```

****Default if the subcommand is omitted.

Examples:

```
SET MXLOOPS=10.     /*Maximum number of loops allowed
LOOP.               /*Loop with no limit other than MXLOOPS
COMPUTE X=X+1.
END LOOP.

LOOP #I=1 TO 5.     /*Loop five times
COMPUTE X=X+1.
END LOOP.
```

Overview

The LOOP—END LOOP structure performs repeated transformations specified by the commands within the loop until they reach a specified cutoff. The cutoff can be specified by an indexing clause on the LOOP command, an IF clause on the END LOOP command, or a BREAK command within the loop structure (see BREAK). In addition, the maximum number of iterations within a loop can be specified on the MXLOOPS subcommand on SET. The default MXLOOPS is 40.

The IF clause on the LOOP command can be used to perform repeated transformations on a subset of cases. The effect is similar to nesting the LOOP—END LOOP structure within a DO IF—END IF structure, but using IF on LOOP is simpler and more efficient. You have to use the DO IF—END IF structure, however, if you want to perform different transformations on different subsets of cases. You can also use IF on LOOP to specify the cutoff, especially when the cutoff may be reached before the first iteration.

LOOP and END LOOP are usually used within an input program or with the VECTOR command. Since the loop structure repeats transformations on a single case or on a single input record containing information on multiple cases, it allows you to read complex data files or to generate data for a working data file. For more information, see INPUT PROGRAM—END INPUT PROGRAM and VECTOR.

The loop structure repeats transformations on single cases across variables. It is different from the DO REPEAT—END REPEAT structure, which replicates transformations on a specified set of variables. When both can be used to accomplish a task, such as selectively transforming data for some cases on some variables, LOOP and END LOOP are generally more efficient and more flexible, but DO REPEAT allows selection of nonadjacent variables and use of replacement values with different intervals.

Options

Missing Values. You can prevent cases with missing values for any of the variables used in the loop structure from entering the loop (see "Missing Values" on p. 380).

Creating Data. A loop structure within an input program can be used to generate data (see "Creating Data" on p. 380).

Defining Complex File Structures. A loop structure within an input program can be used to define complex files that cannot be handled by standard file definition facilities (see pp. 213, 214, and 216 for examples).

Basic Specification

The basic specification is LOOP followed by at least one transformation command. The structure must end with the END LOOP command. Commands within the loop are executed until the cutoff is reached.

Syntax Rules

- If LOOP and END LOOP are specified before a working data file exists, they must be specified within an input program.
- If both an indexing and an IF clause are used on LOOP, the indexing clause must be first.
- Loop structures can be nested within other loop structures or within DO IF structures, and vice versa.

Operations

- The LOOP command defines the beginning of a loop structure and the END LOOP command defines its end. The END LOOP command returns control to LOOP unless the cutoff has been reached. When the cutoff has been reached, control passes to the command immediately following END LOOP.
- When specified within a loop structure, definition commands (such as MISSING VALUES and VARIABLE LABELS) and utility commands (such as SET and SHOW) are invoked only once, when they are encountered for the first time within the loop.

Example

```
SET MXLOOPS=10.
LOOP.     /*Loop with no limit other than MXLOOPS
COMPUTE X=X+1.
END LOOP.
```

- This and the following examples assume that a working data file and all the variables mentioned in the loop exist.

- The SET MXLOOPS command limits the number of times the loop is executed to 10. The function of MXLOOPS is to prevent infinite loops when there is no iteration clause.
- Within the loop structure, each iteration increments *X* by 1. After ten iterations, the value of *X* for all cases is increased by 10, and, as specified on the SET command, the loop is terminated.

IF Keyword

Keyword IF and a logical expression can be specified on LOOP or on END LOOP to control iterations through the loop.

- The specification on IF is a logical expression enclosed in parentheses. For more information, see "Logical Expressions" on p. 52.

Example

```
LOOP.
COMPUTE X=X+1.
END LOOP IF (X EQ 5).        /*Loop until X is 5
```

- Iterations continue until the logical expression on END LOOP is true, which for every case is when *X* equals 5. Each case does not go through the same number of iterations.
- This corresponds to the programming notion of DO UNTIL. The loop is always executed at least once.

Example

```
LOOP IF (X LT 5).            /*Loop while X is less than 5
COMPUTE X=X+1.
END LOOP.
```

- The IF clause is evaluated each trip through the structure, so looping stops once *X* equals 5.
- This corresponds to the programming notion of DO WHILE. The loop may not be executed at all.

Example

```
LOOP IF (Y GT 10).           /*Loop only for cases with Y GT 10
COMPUTE X=X+1.
END LOOP IF (X EQ 5).        /*Loop until X IS 5
```

- The IF clause on LOOP allows transformations to be performed on a subset of cases. *X* is increased by 5 only for cases with values greater than 10 for *Y*. *X* is not changed for all other cases.

Indexing Clause

The indexing clause limits the number of iterations for a loop by specifying the number of times SPSS should execute commands within the loop structure. The indexing clause is specified on the LOOP command and includes an indexing variable followed by initial and terminal values.

- SPSS sets the *indexing variable* to the *initial value* and increases it by the specified increment each time the loop is executed for a case. When the indexing variable reaches the specified *terminal value*, the loop is terminated for that case.
- By default, SPSS increases the indexing variable by 1 for each iteration. Keyword BY overrides this increment.
- The indexing variable can have any valid variable name. Unless you specify a scratch variable, the indexing variable is treated as a permanent variable and is saved on the working data file. If the indexing variable is assigned the same name as an existing variable, the values of the existing variable are altered by the LOOP structure as it is executed, and the original values are lost.
- The indexing clause overrides the maximum number of loops specified by SET MX-LOOPS.
- The initial and terminal values of the indexing clause can be numeric expressions. Non-integer and negative expressions are allowed.
- If the expression for the initial value is greater than the terminal value, the loop is not executed. For example, #J=X TO Y is a zero-trip loop if *X* is 0 and *Y* is −1.
- If the expressions for the initial and terminal values are equal, the loop is executed once. #J=0 TO Y is a one-trip loop when *Y* is 0.
- If the loop is exited via BREAK or a conditional clause on the END LOOP statement, the iteration variable is not updated. If the LOOP statement contains both an indexing clause and a conditional clause, the indexing clause is executed first, and the iteration variable is updated regardless of which clause causes the loop to terminate.

Example

```
LOOP #I=1 TO 5.           /*LOOP FIVE TIMES
COMPUTE X=X+1.
END LOOP.
```

- Scratch variable *#I* (the indexing variable) is set to the initial value of 1 and increased by 1 each time the loop is executed for a case. When *#I* increases beyond the terminal value 5, no further loops are executed. Thus, the value of *X* will be increased by 5 for every case.

Example

```
LOOP #I=1 TO 5 IF (Y GT 10). /*Loop to X=5 only if Y GT 10
COMPUTE X=X+1.
END LOOP.
```

- Both an indexing clause and an IF clause are specified on LOOP. *X* is increased by 5 for all cases where *Y* is greater than 10.

Example

```
LOOP #I=1 TO Y.           /*Loop to the value of Y
COMPUTE X=X+1.
END LOOP.
```

- The number of iterations for a case depends on the value of variable *Y* for that case. For a case with value 0 for variable *Y*, the loop is not executed and *X* is unchanged. For a case with value 1 for variable *Y*, the loop is executed once and *X* is increased by 1.

Example

```
* Factorial routine.

DATA LIST FREE / X.
BEGIN DATA
1 2 3 4 5 6 7
END DATA.

COMPUTE FACTOR=1.
LOOP #I=1 TO X.
COMPUTE FACTOR=FACTOR * #I.
END LOOP.
LIST.
```

- The loop structure computes *FACTOR* as the factorial value of *X*.

Example

```
* Example of nested loops: compute every possible combination of values
  for each variable.

INPUT PROGRAM.
-LOOP #I=1 TO 4.         /* LOOP TO NUMBER OF VALUES FOR I
+    LOOP #J=1 TO 3.     /* LOOP TO NUMBER OF VALUES FOR J
@        LOOP #K=1 TO 4.    /* LOOP TO NUMBER OF VALUES FOR K

@            COMPUTE I=#I.
@            COMPUTE J=#J.
@            COMPUTE K=#K.
@            END CASE.

@        END LOOP.
+    END LOOP.
-END LOOP.
END FILE.
END INPUT PROGRAM.
LIST.
```

- The first loop iterates four times. The first iteration sets the indexing variable *#I* equal to 1 and then passes control to the second loop. *#I* remains 1 until the second loop has completed all of its iterations.
- The second loop is executed 12 times, three times for each value of *#I*. The first iteration sets the indexing variable *#J* equal to 1 and then passes control to the third loop. *#J* remains 1 until the third loop has completed all of its iterations.
- The third loop results in 48 iterations (4×3×4). The first iteration sets #K equal to 1. The COMPUTE statements set the variables *I*, *J*, and *K* each to 1, and END CASE creates a case. The third loop iterates a second time, setting *#K* equal to 2. Variables *I*, *J*, and *K* are then computed with values 1, 1, 2, respectively, and a second case is created. The third and fourth iterations of the third loop produce cases with *I*, *J*, and *K*, equal to 1, 1, 3 and 1, 1,

4, respectively. After the fourth iteration within the third loop, control passes back to the second loop.
- The second loop is executed again. *#I* remains 1, while *#J* increases to 2, and control returns to the third loop. The third loop completes its iterations, resulting in four more cases with *I* equal to 1, *J* to 2, and *K* increasing from 1 to 4. The second loop is executed a third time, resulting in cases with *I*=1, *J*=3, and *K* increasing from 1 to 4. Once the second loop has completed three iterations, control passes back to the first loop, and the entire cycle is repeated for the next increment of *#I*.
- Once the first loop completes four iterations, control passes out of the looping structures to END FILE. END FILE defines the resulting cases as a data file, the input program terminates, and the LIST command is executed.
- This example does not require a LEAVE command because the iteration variables are scratch variables. If the iteration variables were *I, J,* and *K*, LEAVE would be required because the variables would be reinitialized after each END CASE command.

Example

```
* Modifying the loop iteration variable.
INPUT PROGRAM.
PRINT SPACE    2.
LOOP           A = 1 TO 3.                /*Simple iteration
+   PRINT              /'A WITHIN LOOP: ' A(F1).
+   COMPUTE            A = 0.
END LOOP
PRINT                  /'A AFTER LOOP:   ' A(F1).

NUMERIC        #B.
LOOP           B = 1 TO 3.                /*Iteration + UNTIL
+   PRINT              /'B WITHIN LOOP: ' B(F1).
+   COMPUTE            B = 0.
+   COMPUTE            #B = #B+1.
END LOOP       IF #B = 3.
PRINT                  /'B AFTER LOOP:   ' B(F1).

NUMERIC        #C.
LOOP           C = 1 TO 3 IF #C NE 3.   /*Iteration + WHILE
+   PRINT              /'C WITHIN LOOP: ' C(F1).
+   COMPUTE            C = 0.
+   COMPUTE            #C = #C+1.
END LOOP.
PRINT                  /'C AFTER LOOP:   ' C(F1).

NUMERIC        #D.
LOOP           D = 1 TO 3.                /*Iteration + BREAK
+   PRINT              /'D WITHIN LOOP: ' D(F1).
+   COMPUTE            D = 0.
+   COMPUTE            #D = #D+1.
+   DO IF              #D = 3.
+       BREAK.
+   END IF.
```

```
END LOOP.
PRINT           /'D AFTER LOOP:  ' D(F1).

LOOP            E = 3 TO 1.                 /*Zero-trip iteration
+   PRINT       /'E WITHIN LOOP: ' E(F1).
+   COMPUTE     E = 0.
END LOOP.
PRINT           /'E AFTER LOOP:   ' E(F1).
END FILE.
END INPUT PROGRAM.
EXECUTE.
```

- If a loop is exited via BREAK or a conditional clause on the END LOOP statement, the iteration variable is not updated.
- If the LOOP statement contains both an iteration clause and a conditional clause, the iteration clause is executed first, and the actual iteration variable will be updated regardless of which clause causes termination of the loop.

Figure 43 shows the output from this example.

Figure 43 Modify the loop iteration variable

```
A WITHIN LOOP: 1
A WITHIN LOOP: 2
A WITHIN LOOP: 3
A AFTER LOOP:  4
B WITHIN LOOP: 1
B WITHIN LOOP: 2
B WITHIN LOOP: 3
B AFTER LOOP:  0
C WITHIN LOOP: 1
C WITHIN LOOP: 2
C WITHIN LOOP: 3
C AFTER LOOP:  4
D WITHIN LOOP: 1
D WITHIN LOOP: 2
D WITHIN LOOP: 3
D AFTER LOOP:  0
E AFTER LOOP:  3
```

BY Keyword

By default, SPSS increases the indexing variable by 1 for each iteration. Keyword BY overrides this increment.

- The *increment value* can be a numeric expression and can therefore be noninteger or negative. Zero causes a warning and results in a zero-trip loop.
- If the initial value is greater than the terminal value and the increment is positive, the loop is never entered. #I=1 TO 0 BY 2 results in a zero-trip loop.
- If the initial value is less than the terminal value and the increment is negative, the loop is never entered. #I=1 TO 2 BY -1 also results in a zero-trip loop.
- Order is unimportant: 2 BY 2 TO 10 is equivalent to 2 TO 10 BY 2.

Example

```
LOOP #I=2 TO 10 BY 2.       /*Loop five times by 2'S
COMPUTE X=X+1.
END LOOP.
```

- Scratch variable *#I* starts at 2 and increases by 2 for each of five iterations until it equals 10 for the last iteration.

Example

```
LOOP #I=1 TO Y BY Z.        /*Loop to Y incrementing by Z
COMPUTE X=X+1.
END LOOP.
```

- The loop is executed once for a case with *Y* equal to 2 and *Z* equal to 2 but twice for a case with *Y* equal to 3 and *Z* equal to 2.

Example

```
* Repeating data using LOOP.

INPUT PROGRAM.
DATA LIST        NOTABLE/ ORDER 1-4(N) #BKINFO 6-71(A).
LEAVE ORDER.
LOOP             #I = 1 TO 66 BY 6 IF SUBSTR(#BKINFO,#I,6) <> ' '.
+  REREAD           COLUMN = #I+5.
+  DATA LIST        NOTABLE/ ISBN 1-3(N) QUANTITY 4-5.
+  END CASE.
END LOOP.
END INPUT PROGRAM.
SORT CASES       BY ISBN ORDER.
BEGIN DATA
1045 182 2 155 1 134 1 153 5
1046 155 3 153 5 163 1
1047 161 5 182 2 163 4 186 6
1048 186 2
1049 155 2 163 2 153 2 074 1 161 1
END DATA.

DO IF            $CASENUM = 1.
+  PRINT EJECT    /'Order' 1  'ISBN' 7  'Quantity' 13.
END IF.
PRINT            /ORDER 2-5(N) ISBN 8-10(N) QUANTITY 13-17.
EXECUTE.
```

- This example uses LOOP to simulate a REPEATING DATA command.
- DATA LIST specifies scratch variable *#BKINFO* as a string variable (format A) to allow blanks in the data.
- LOOP is executed if the SUBSTR function returns anything other than a blank or null value. SUBSTR returns a six-character substring of *#BKINFO*, beginning with the character in the position specified by the value of the indexing variable *#I*. As specified on the indexing clause, *#I* begins with a value of 1 and is increased by 6 for each iteration of LOOP, up to a maximum *#I* value of 61 (1+10×6=61). The next iteration would exceed the maximum *#I* value (1+11×6=67).

Missing Values

- If SPSS encounters a case with a missing value for the initial, terminal, or increment value or expression, or if the conditional expression on the LOOP command returns missing, a zero-trip loop results and control is passed to the first command after the END LOOP command.
- If a case has a missing value for the conditional expression on an END LOOP command, the loop is terminated after the first iteration.
- To prevent cases with missing values for any variable used in the loop structure from entering the loop, use the IF clause on the LOOP command (see third example below).

Example

```
LOOP #I=1 TO Z  IF (Y GT 10). /*Loop to X=Z for cases with Y GT 10
COMPUTE X=X+1.
END LOOP.
```

- The value of *X* remains unchanged for cases with a missing value for *Y* or a missing value for *Z* (or if *Z* is less than 1).

Example

```
MISSING VALUES X(5).
LOOP.
COMPUTE X=X+1.
END LOOP IF (X GE 10). /*Loop until x is at least 10 or missing
```

- Looping is terminated when the value of *X* is 5 because 5 is defined as missing for *X*.

Example

```
LOOP IF NOT MISSING(Y).    /*Loop only when y isn't missing
COMPUTE X=X+Y.
END LOOP IF (X GE 10).     /*Loop until x is at least 10
```

- Variable *X* is unchanged for cases with a missing value for *Y*, since the loop is never entered.

Creating Data

A loop structure and an END CASE command within an input program can be used to create data without any data input. The END FILE command must be used outside the loop (but within the input program) to terminate processing.

Example

```
INPUT PROGRAM.
LOOP #I=1 TO 20.
COMPUTE AMOUNT=RND(UNIFORM(5000))/100.
END CASE.
END LOOP.
END FILE.
END INPUT PROGRAM.

PRINT FORMATS AMOUNT (DOLLAR6.2).
PRINT /AMOUNT.
EXECUTE.
```

- This example creates 20 cases with a single variable, *AMOUNT*. *AMOUNT* is a uniformly distributed number between 0 and 5000, rounded to an integer and divided by 100 to provide a variable in dollars and cents.
- The END FILE command is required to terminate processing once the loop structure is complete.

See pp. 206 and 216 for other examples of creating data without any data input.

MATCH FILES

```
MATCH FILES FILE={file}   [TABLE={file}]
               {*   }           {*   }

[/RENAME=(old varnames=new varnames)...]

[/IN=varname]

/FILE==...   [TABLE= ...]

[/BY varlist]

[/MAP]

[/KEEP={ALL**  }] [/DROP=varlist]
       {varlist}

[/FIRST=varname]  [/LAST=varname]
```

**Default if the subcommand is omitted.

Example:
```
MATCH FILES FILE=PART1 /FILE=PART2 /FILE=*.
```

Overview

MATCH FILES combines variables from two up to fifty SPSS data files. MATCH FILES can make parallel or nonparallel matches between different files or perform table lookups. **Parallel matches** combine files sequentially by case (they are sometimes referred to as **sequential matches**. **Nonparallel matches** combine files according to the values of one or more key variables. In a **table lookup**, MATCH FILES looks up variables in one file and transfers those variables to a case file.

The files specified on MATCH FILES can be SPSS data files created with SAVE or XSAVE or the working data file. The combined file becomes the new working data file. Statistical procedures following MATCH FILES use this combined file unless you replace it by building another working file. You must use the SAVE or XSAVE commands if you want to save the combined file as an SPSS data file.

In general, MATCH FILES is used to combine files containing the same cases but different variables. To combine files containing the same variables but different cases, use ADD FILES. To update existing SPSS data files, use UPDATE.

MATCH FILES is often used with the AGGREGATE command to add variables with summary measures (sum, mean, and so forth) to the data. For an example, see p. 87.

Options

Variable Selection. You can specify which variables from each input file are included in the new working file using the DROP and KEEP subcommands.

Variable Names. You can rename variables in each input file before combining the files using the RENAME subcommand. This permits you to combine variables that are the same but whose names differ in different input files, or to separate variables that are different but have the same name.

Variable Flag. You can create a variable that indicates whether a case came from a particular input file using IN. You can use the FIRST or LAST subcommands to create a variable that flags the first or last case of a group of cases with the same value for the key variable.

Variable Map. You can request a map showing all variables in the new working file, their order, and the input files from which they came using the MAP subcommand.

Basic Specification

The basic specification is two or more FILE subcommands, each of which specifies a file to be matched. In addition, BY is required to specify the key variables for nonparallel matches. Both BY and TABLE are required to match table-lookup files.

- All variables from all input files are included in the new working file unless DROP or KEEP is specified.

Subcommand Order

- RENAME and IN must immediately follow the FILE subcommand to which they apply.
- BY must follow the FILE and TABLE subcommands and any associated RENAME and IN subcommands.
- FIRST and LAST must follow all TABLE and FILE subcommands and any associated RENAME and IN subcommands.
- MAP, DROP, and KEEP must follow all FILE, TABLE, and RENAME subcommands.

Syntax Rules

- RENAME can be repeated after each FILE or TABLE subcommand and applies only to variables in the file named on the immediately preceding FILE or TABLE.
- IN can be used only for a nonparallel match or for a table lookup. (Thus, IN can be used only if BY is specified.)
- BY can be specified only once. However, multiple variables can be specified on BY. When BY is used, all files must be sorted in ascending order of the key variables named on BY.
- MAP can be repeated as often as desired.

Operations

- MATCH FILES reads all files named on FILE or TABLE and builds a new working data file that replaces any working file created earlier in the session.
- The new working data file contains complete dictionary information from the input files, including variable names, labels, print and write formats, and missing-value indicators.

The new file also contains the documents from each of the input files. See DROP DOCUMENTS for information on deleting documents.

- Variables are copied in order from the first file specified, then from the second file specified, and so on.
- If the same variable name is used in more than one input file, data are taken from the file specified first. Dictionary information is taken from the first file containing value labels, missing values, or a variable label for the common variable. If the first file has no such information, MATCH FILES checks the second file, and so on, seeking dictionary information.
- All cases from all input files are included in the combined file. Cases that are absent from one of the input files will be assigned system-missing values for variables unique to that file.
- BY specifies that cases should be combined according to a common value on one or more key variables. All input files must be sorted in ascending order of the key variables.
- If BY is not used, SPSS performs a parallel (sequential) match, combining the first case from each file, then the second case from each file, and so on, without regard to any identifying values that may be present.
- If the working file is named as an input file, any N and SAMPLE commands that have been specified are applied to that file before files are matched.

Limitations

- Maximum 50 files can be combined on one MATCH FILES command.
- Maximum 1 BY subcommand. However, BY can specify multiple variables.
- The TEMPORARY command cannot be in effect if the working data file is used as an input file.

Example

```
MATCH FILES FILE=PART1 /FILE=PART2 /FILE=*.
```

- MATCH FILES combines three files (the working data file and two SPSS data files) in a parallel match. Cases are combined according to their order in each file.
- The new working data file contains as many cases as are contained in the largest of the three input files.

FILE Subcommand

FILE identifies the files to be combined (except table files). At least one FILE subcommand is required on MATCH FILES. A separate FILE subcommand must be used for each input file.

- An asterisk can be specified on FILE to refer to the working data file.

- The order in which files are specified determines the order of variables in the new working file. In addition, if the same variable name occurs in more than one input file, the variable is taken from the file specified first.
- If the files have unequal numbers of cases, cases are generated from the longest file. Cases that do not exist in the shorter files have system-missing values for variables that are unique to those files.

Raw Data Files

To add variables from a raw data file, you must first define the raw data as the working data file using the DATA LIST command. MATCH FILES can then combine the working data file with an SPSS data file.

Example

```
DATA LIST FILE=GASDATA/1 OZONE 10-12 CO 20-22 SULFUR 30-32.

VARIABLE LABELS OZONE 'LEVEL OF OZONE'
  CO 'LEVEL OF CARBON MONOXIDE'
  SULFUR 'LEVEL OF SULFUR DIOXIDE'.

MATCH FILES  FILE=PARTICLE /FILE=*.

SAVE  OUTFILE=POLLUTE.
```

- The *PARTICLE* file is a previously saved SPSS data file.
- The *GASDATA* file is a raw data file and is defined on the DATA LIST command. Variable labels are assigned on the VARIABLE LABELS command.
- MATCH FILES adds the working data file (*), which now contains the gas data, to SPSS data file *PARTICLE*.
- SAVE saves the new working file as an SPSS data file with the filename *POLLUTE*.

BY Subcommand

BY specifies one or more identification, or key, variables that determine which cases are to be combined. When BY is specified, cases from one file are matched only with cases from other files that have the same values for the key variables. BY is required unless all input files are to be matched sequentially according to the order of cases.

- BY must follow the FILE and TABLE subcommands and any associated RENAME and IN subcommands.
- BY specifies the names of one or more key variables. The key variables must exist in all input files. The key variables can be numeric or long or short strings.
- All input files must be sorted in ascending order of the key variables. If necessary, use SORT CASES before MATCH FILES.
- Missing values for key variables are handled like any other values.
- Unmatched cases are assigned system-missing values (for numeric variables) or blanks (for string variables) for variables from files that do not contain a match.

Duplicate Cases

Duplicate cases are those with the same values for the key variables named on the BY subcommand.

- Duplicate cases are permitted in any input files except table files.
- When there is no table file, the first duplicate case in each file is matched with the first matching case (if any) from the other files; the second duplicate case is matched with a second matching duplicate, if any; and so on. (In effect, a parallel match is performed within groups of duplicate cases.) Unmatched cases are assigned system-missing values (for numeric variables) or blanks (for string variables) for variables from files that do not contain a match.
- SPSS displays a warning if it encounters duplicate keys in one or more of the files being matched.

TABLE Subcommand

TABLE specifies a table lookup (or keyed table) file. A lookup file contributes variables but not cases to the new working file. Variables from the table file are added to all cases from other files that have matching values for the key variables. FILE specifies the files that supply the cases.

- A separate TABLE subcommand must be used to specify each lookup file, and a separate FILE subcommand must be used to specify each case file.
- The BY subcommand is required when TABLE is used.
- All specified files must be sorted in ascending order of the key variables. If necessary, use SORT CASES before MATCH FILES.
- A lookup file cannot contain duplicate cases (cases for which the key variable(s) named on BY have identical values).
- An asterisk on TABLE refers to the working data file.
- Cases in a case file that do not have matches in a table file are assigned system-missing values (for numeric variables) or blanks (for string variables) for variables from that table file.
- Cases in a table file that do not match any cases in a case file are ignored.

Example

```
MATCH FILES FILE=* /TABLE=MASTER /BY EMP_ID.
```

- MATCH FILES combines variables from SPSS data file *MASTER* with the working data file, matching cases by the variable *EMP_ID*.
- No new cases are added to the working file as a result of the table lookup.
- Cases whose value for *EMP_ID* is not included in the *MASTER* file are assigned system-missing values for variables taken from the table.

RENAME Subcommand

RENAME renames variables on the input files *before* they are processed by MATCH FILES. RENAME must follow the FILE or TABLE subcommand that contains the variables to be renamed.

- RENAME applies only to the immediately preceding FILE or TABLE subcommand. To rename variables from more than one input file, specify a RENAME subcommand after each FILE or TABLE subcommand.
- Specifications for RENAME consist of a left parenthesis, a list of old variable names, an equals sign, a list of new variable names, and a right parenthesis. The two variable lists must name or imply the same number of variables. If only one variable is renamed, the parentheses are optional.
- More than one rename specification can be specified on a single RENAME subcommand, each enclosed in parentheses.
- The TO keyword can be used to refer to consecutive variables in the file and to generate new variable names. (See "Keyword TO" on p. 32.)
- RENAME takes effect immediately. Any KEEP and DROP subcommands entered prior to a RENAME must use the old names, while KEEP and DROP subcommands entered after a RENAME must use the new names.
- All specifications within a single set of parentheses take effect simultaneously. For example, the specification RENAME (A,B = B,A) swaps the names of the two variables.
- Variables cannot be renamed to scratch variables.
- Input SPSS data files are not changed on disk; only the copy of the file being combined is affected.

Example

```
MATCH FILES FILE=UPDATE /RENAME=(NEWID = ID)
 /FILE=MASTER /BY ID.
```

- MATCH FILES matches a master SPSS data file (*MASTER*) with an update data file (*UPDATE*).
- Variable *NEWID* in the *UPDATE* file is renamed *ID* so that it will have the same name as the identification variable in the master file and can be used on the BY subcommand.

DROP and KEEP Subcommands

DROP and KEEP are used to include a subset of variables in the new working data file. DROP specifies a set of variables to exclude and KEEP specifies a set of variables to retain.

- DROP and KEEP do not affect the input files on disk.
- DROP and KEEP must follow all FILE, TABLE, and RENAME subcommands.
- DROP and KEEP must specify one or more variables. If RENAME is used to rename variables, specify the new names on DROP and KEEP.
- Keyword ALL can be specified on KEEP. ALL must be the last specification on KEEP, and it refers to all variables not previously named on KEEP.
- DROP cannot be used with variables created by the IN, FIRST, or LAST subcommands.

- KEEP can be used to change the order of variables in the resulting file. By default, MATCH FILES first copies the variables in order from the first file, then copies the variables in order from the second file, and so on. With KEEP, variables are kept in the order they are listed on the subcommand. If a variable is named more than once on KEEP, only the first mention of the variable is in effect; all subsequent references to that variable name are ignored.

Example

```
MATCH FILES FILE=PARTICLE /RENAME=(PARTIC=POLLUTE1)
 /FILE=GAS /RENAME=(OZONE TO SULFUR=POLLUTE2 TO POLLUTE4)
 /DROP=POLLUTE4.
```

- The renamed variable *POLLUTE4* is dropped from the resulting file. DROP is specified after all the FILE and RENAME subcommands, and it refers to the dropped variable by its new name.

IN Subcommand

IN creates a new variable in the resulting file that indicates whether a case came from the input file named on the preceding FILE subcommand. IN applies only to the file specified on the immediately preceding FILE subcommand.

- IN can be used only for a nonparallel match or table lookup.
- IN has only one specification, the name of the flag variable.
- The variable created by IN has value 1 for every case that came from the associated input file and value 0 if the case came from a different input file.
- Variables created by IN are automatically attached to the end of the resulting file and cannot be dropped. If FIRST or LAST are used, the variable created by IN precedes the variables created by FIRST or LAST.

Example

```
MATCH FILES  FILE=WEEK10 /FILE=WEEK11 /IN=INWEEK11 /BY=EMPID.
```

- IN creates the variable *INWEEK11*, which has the value 1 for all cases in the resulting file that had values in the input file *WEEK11* and the value 0 for those cases that were not in file *WEEK11*.

FIRST and LAST Subcommands

FIRST and LAST create logical variables that flag the first or last case of a group of cases with the same value for the BY variables.

- FIRST and LAST must follow all TABLE and FILE subcommands and any associated RENAME and IN subcommands.
- FIRST and LAST have only one specification, the name of the flag variable.
- FIRST creates a variable with value 1 for the first case of each group and value 0 for all other cases.

- LAST creates a variable with value 1 for the last case of each group and value 0 for all other cases.
- Variables created by FIRST and LAST are automatically attached to the end of the resulting file and cannot be dropped.
- If one file has several cases with the same values for the key variables, FIRST or LAST can be used to create a variable that flags the first or last case of the group.

Example

```
MATCH FILES  TABLE=HOUSE /FILE=PERSONS
 /BY=HOUSEID /FIRST=HEAD.
```

- The variable *HEAD* contains the value 1 for the first person in each household and the value 0 for all other persons. Assuming that the person file is sorted with the head of household as the first case for each household, variable *HEAD* identifies the case for the head of household.

Example

```
* Using match files with only one file.

* This example flags the first of several cases with
  the same value for a key variable.
MATCH FILES  FILE=PERSONS /BY HOUSEID /FIRST=HEAD.
SELECT IF  (HEAD EQ 1).
CROSSTABS  JOBCAT BY SEX.
```

- MATCH FILES is used instead of GET to read SPSS data file *PERSONS*. The BY subcommand identifies the key variable (*HOUSEID*), and FIRST creates the variable *HEAD* with the value 1 for the first case in each household and value 0 for all other cases.
- SELECT IF selects only the cases with value 1 for *HEAD*, and the CROSSTABS procedure is run on these cases.

MAP Subcommand

MAP produces a list of the variables that are in the new working file and the file or files from which they came. Variables are listed in the order they appear in the resulting file. MAP has no specifications and must be placed after all FILE, TABLE, and RENAME subcommands.

- Multiple MAP subcommands can be used. Each MAP shows the current status of the working data file and reflects only the subcommands that precede the MAP subcommand.
- To obtain a map of the resulting file in its final state, specify MAP last.
- If a variable is renamed, its original and new names are listed. Variables created by IN, FIRST, and LAST are not included in the map, since they are automatically attached to the end of the file and cannot be dropped.
- MAP can be used with the EDIT command to obtain a list of the variables in the resulting file without actually reading the data and combining the files.

MATRIX DATA

```
MATRIX DATA VARIABLES=varlist    [/FILE={INLINE**}]
                                       {file    }

[/FORMAT=[{LIST**}]  [{LOWER**}]  [{DIAGONAL**}]]
         {FREE  }   {UPPER  }    {NODIAGONAL}
                    {FULL   }

[/SPLIT=varlist]    [/FACTORS=varlist]

[/CELLS=number of cells]    [/N=sample size]

[/CONTENTS= [CORR**]    [COV]   [MAT]   [MSE]   [DFE]   [MEAN]   [PROX]

           [{STDDEV}]   [N_SCALAR]   [{N_VECTOR}]   [N_MATRIX]   [COUNT]]
           {SD    }                  {N       }
```

**Default if the subcommand is omitted.

Example:
```
MATRIX DATA VARIABLES=ROWTYPE_ SAVINGS POP15 POP75 INCOME GROWTH.
BEGIN DATA
MEAN 9.6710 35.0896 2.2930 1106.7784 3.7576
STDDEV 4.4804 9.1517 1.2907 990.8511 2.8699
N 50 50 50 50 50
CORR 1
CORR -.4555 1
CORR .3165 -.9085 1
CORR .2203 -.7562 .7870 1
CORR .3048 -.0478 .0253 -.1295  1
END DATA.
```

Overview

MATRIX DATA reads raw matrix materials and converts them to a matrix data file that can be read by SPSS procedures that handle matrix materials, such as ONEWAY and REGRESSION. The data can include vector statistics such as means and standard deviations as well as matrices.

MATRIX DATA is similar to a DATA LIST command: it defines variable names and their order in a raw data file. However, MATRIX DATA can read only data that conform to the general format of SPSS matrices.

Matrix Files

Like the matrix data files created by procedures, the file that MATRIX DATA creates contains the following variables in the indicated order. If the variables are in a different order in the raw data file, MATRIX DATA rearranges them in the working data file.

- *Split-file variables.* These optional variables define split files. There can be up to eight split variables, and they must have numeric values. Split-file variables will appear in the order in which they are specified on the SPLIT subcommand.

- *ROWTYPE_*. This is a string variable with A8 format. Its values define the data type for each record. For example, it might identify a row of values as means, standard deviations, or correlation coefficients. Every SPSS matrix data file has a *ROWTYPE_* variable.
- *Factor variables*. There can be any number of factors. They occur only if the data include within-cells information, such as the within-cells means. Factors have the system-missing value on records that define pooled information. Factor variables appear in the order in which they are specified on the FACTORS subcommand.
- *VARNAME_*. This is a string variable with A8 format. MATRIX DATA automatically generates *VARNAME_* and its values based on the variables named on VARIABLES. You never enter values for *VARNAME_*. Values for *VARNAME_* are blank for records that define vector information. Every matrix in SPSS has a *VARNAME_* variable.
- *Continuous variables*. These are the variables that were used to generate the correlation coefficients or other aggregated data. There can be any number of them. Continuous variables appear in the order in which they are specified on VARIABLES.

Options

Data Files. You can define both inline data and data in an external file.

Data Format. By default, data are assumed to be entered in freefield format with each vector or row beginning on a new record (keyword LIST on the FORMAT subcommand). If each vector or row does not begin on a new record, use keyword FREE. You can also use FORMAT to indicate whether matrices are entered in upper or lower triangular or full square or rectangular format, and whether or not they include diagonal values.

Variable Types. You can specify split-file and factor variables using the SPLIT and FACTORS subcommands. You can identify record types by specifying ROWTYPE_ on the VARIABLES subcommand if *ROWTYPE_* values are included in the data, or by implying *ROWTYPE_* values on CONTENTS.

Basic Specification

The basic specification is VARIABLES and a list of variables. Additional specifications are required as follows:
- FILE is required to specify the data file if the data are not inline.
- If data are in any format other than lower-triangular with diagonal values included, FORMAT is required.
- If the data contain values in addition to matrix coefficients, such as the mean and standard deviation, either variable *ROWTYPE_* must be specified on VARIABLES and *ROWTYPE_* values must be included in the data, or CONTENTS must be used to describe the data.
- If the data include split-file variables, SPLIT is required. If there are factors, FACTORS is required.

Specifications on most MATRIX DATA subcommands depend on whether *ROWTYPE_* is included in the data and specified on VARIABLES, or whether it is implied using CONTENTS.

Table 15 summarizes the status of each MATRIX DATA subcommand in relation to the *ROW-TYPE_* specification.

Table 15 Subcommand requirements in relation to ROWTYPE_

Subcommand	Implicit ROWTYPE_ using CONTENTS	Explicit ROWTYPE_ on VARIABLES
FILE	Defaults to INLINE	Defaults to INLINE
VARIABLES	Required	Required
FORMAT	Defaults to LOWER DIAG	Defaults to LOWER DIAG
SPLIT	Required if split files[*]	Required if split files
FACTORS	Required if factors	Required if factors
CELLS	Required if factors	Inapplicable
CONTENTS	Defaults to CORR	Optional
N	Optional	Optional

[*] If the data do not contain values for the split-file variables, this subcommand can specify a single variable, which is not specified on the VARIABLES subcommand.

Subcommand Order

- SPLIT and FACTORS, when used, must follow VARIABLES.
- The remaining subcommands can be specified in any order.

Syntax Rules

- No commands can be specified between MATRIX DATA and BEGIN DATA, not even a VARIABLE LABELS or FORMAT command. Data transformations cannot be used until after MATRIX DATA is executed.

Operations

- MATRIX DATA defines and writes data in one step.
- MATRIX DATA clears the working data file and defines a new working file.
- If CONTENTS is not specified and *ROWTYPE_* is not specified on VARIABLES, MATRIX DATA assumes that the data contain only CORR values and issues warning messages to alert you to its assumptions.
- With the default format, data values, including diagonal values, must be in the lower triangle of the matrix. If MATRIX DATA encounters values in the upper triangle, it ignores those values and issues a series of warnings.
- With default format, if any matrix rows span records in the data file, MATRIX DATA cannot form the matrix properly.

- MATRIX DATA does not allow format specifications for matrix materials. The procedure assigns the formats shown in Table 16. To change data formats, execute MATRIX DATA and then assign new formats with the FORMATS, PRINT FORMATS, or WRITE FORMATS commands.

Table 16 Print and write formats for matrix variables

Variable type	Format
ROWTYPE_, VARNAME_	A8
Split-file variables	F4.0
Factors	F4.0
Continuous variables	F10.4

Format of the Raw Matrix Data File

- If LIST is in effect on the FORMAT subcommand, the data are entered in freefield format, with blanks and commas used as separators and each scalar, vector, or row of the matrix beginning on a new record. Unlike LIST format with DATA LIST, a vector or row of the matrix can be contained on multiple records. The continuation records do not have a value for *ROWTYPE_*.
- *ROWTYPE_* values can be enclosed in apostrophes or quotes.
- The order of variables in the raw data file must match the order in which they are specified on VARIABLES. However, this order does not have to correspond to the order of variables in the resulting SPSS matrix data file.
- The way records are entered for pooled vectors or matrices when factors are present depends upon whether *ROWTYPE_* is specified on the VARIABLES subcommand (see the FACTORS subcommand on p. 402).
- MATRIX DATA recognizes plus and minus signs as field separators when they are not preceded by the letter D or E. This allows MATRIX DATA to read scientific notation as well as correlation matrices written by FORTRAN in F10.8 format. A plus sign preceded by a D or E is read as part of the number in scientific notation.

Example

```
MATRIX DATA
     VARIABLES=ROWTYPE_ SAVINGS POP15 POP75 INCOME GROWTH.
BEGIN DATA
MEAN 9.6710 35.0896 2.2930 1106.7784 3.7576
STDDEV 4.4804 9.1517 1.2907 990.8511 2.8699
N 50 50 50 50 50
CORR 1
CORR -.4555 1
CORR .3165 -.9085 1
CORR .2203 -.7562 .7870 1
CORR .3048 -.0478 .0253 -.1295  1
END DATA.
```

- Variable *ROWTYPE_* is specified on VARIABLES. *ROWTYPE_* values are included in the data.
- No other specifications are required.

Example

```
* Matrix data with procedure DISCRIMINANT'.
MATRIX DATA VARIABLES=WORLD ROWTYPE_ FOOD APPL SERVICE RENT
   /FACTORS=WORLD.
BEGIN DATA
1 N        25 25 25 25
1 MEAN     76.64 77.32 81.52 101.40
2 N        7 7 7 7
2 MEAN     76.1428571 85.2857143 60.8571429 249.571429
3 N        13 13 13 13
3 MEAN     55.5384615 76 63.4615385 86.3076923
. SD       16.4634139 22.5509310 16.8086768 77.1085326
. COR      1
. COR      .1425366 1
. COR      .5644693 .2762615 1
. COR      .2133413 -.0499003 .0417468 1
END DATA.

DISCRIMINANT GROUPS=WORLD(1,3)
   /VARIABLES=FOOD APPL SERVICE RENT /METHOD=WILKS /MATRIX=IN(*).
```

- MATRIX DATA is used to generate a working data file that DISCRIMINANT can read. DISCRIMINANT reads the mean, count (unweighted N), and N (weighted N) for each cell in the data, as well as pooled values for the standard deviation and correlation coefficients. If count equals N, only N needs to be supplied.
- *ROWTYPE_* is specified on VARIABLES to identify record types in the data. Though CONTENTS and CELLS can be used to identify record types and distinguish between within-cells data and pooled values, it is usually easier to specify *ROWTYPE_* on VARIABLES and enter the *ROWTYPE_* values in the data.
- Because factors are present in the data, the continuous variables (*FOOD, APPL, SERVICE,* and *RENT*) must be specified last on VARIABLES and must be last in the data.
- The FACTORS subcommand identifies *WORLD* as the factor variable.
- BEGIN DATA immediately follows MATRIX DATA.
- N and MEAN values for each cell are entered in the data.
- *ROWTYPE_* values for the pooled records are SD and COR. MATRIX DATA assigns the values STDDEV and CORR to the corresponding vectors in the matrix. Records with pooled information have the system-missing value (.) for the factors.
- Procedure DISCRIMINANT reads the data matrix. An asterisk (*) is specified as the input file on the MATRIX subcommand because the data are in the working file.

Example

```
* Matrix data with procedure REGRESSION.

MATRIX DATA VARIABLES=SAVINGS POP15 POP75 INCOME GROWTH
  /CONTENTS=MEAN SD N CORR /FORMAT=UPPER NODIAGONAL.

BEGIN DATA
9.6710 35.0896 2.2930 1106.7784 3.7576
4.4804 9.1517 1.2908 990.8511 2.8699
50 50 50 50 50
-.4555 .3165 .2203 .3048
-.9085 -.7562 -.0478
 .7870 .0253
-.1295
END DATA.

REGRESSION MATRIX=IN(*) /VARIABLES=SAVINGS TO GROWTH
  /DEP=SAVINGS /ENTER.
```

- MATRIX DATA is used to generate a matrix that REGRESSION can read. REGRESSION reads and writes matrices that always contain the mean, standard deviation, N, and Pearson correlation coefficients. Data in this example do not have *ROWTYPE_* values, and the correlation values are from the upper triangle of the matrix without the diagonal values.
- *ROWTYPE_* is not specified on VARIABLES because its values are not included in the data.
- Because there are no *ROWTYPE_* values, CONTENTS is required to define the record types and the order of the records in the file.
- By default, MATRIX DATA reads values from the lower triangle of the matrix, including the diagonal values. FORMAT is required in this example to indicate that the data are in the upper triangle and do not include diagonal values.
- BEGIN DATA immediately follows the MATRIX DATA command.
- Procedure REGRESSION reads the data matrix. An asterisk (*) is specified as the input file on the MATRIX subcommand because the data are in the working file. Since there is a single vector of N's in the data, missing values are handled listwise (the default for REGRESSION).

Example

```
* Matrix data with procedure ONEWAY.

MATRIX DATA VARIABLES=EDUC ROWTYPE_ WELL /FACTORS=EDUC.
BEGIN DATA
1 N    65
2 N    95
3 N   181
4 N    82
5 N    40
6 N    37
1 MEAN 2.6462
2 MEAN 2.7737
3 MEAN 4.1796
4 MEAN 4.5610
5 MEAN 4.6625
6 MEAN 5.2297
. MSE  6.2699
. DFE  494
END DATA.

ONEWAY WELL BY EDUC(1,6) /MATRIX=IN(*)
```

- One of the two types of matrices that procedure ONEWAY reads includes a vector of frequencies for each factor level, a vector of means for each factor level, a record containing the pooled variance (within-group mean square error), and the degrees of freedom for the mean square error. MATRIX DATA is used to generate a working data file containing this type of matrix data for procedure ONEWAY.
- *ROWTYPE_* is explicit on VARIABLES and identifies record types.
- Because factors are present in the data, the continuous variables (*WELL*) must be specified last on VARIABLES and must be last in the data.
- The FACTORS subcommand identifies *EDUC* as the factor variable.
- MSE is entered in the data as the *ROWTYPE_* value for the vector of square pooled standard deviations.
- DFE is entered in the data as the *ROWTYPE_* value for the vector of degrees of freedom.
- Records with pooled information have the system-missing value (.) for the factors.

VARIABLES Subcommand

VARIABLES specifies the names of the variables in the raw data and the order in which they occur.

- VARIABLES is required.
- There is no limit to the number of variables that can be specified.
- If *ROWTYPE_* is specified on VARIABLES, the continuous variables must be the last variables specified on the subcommand and must be last in the data.
- If split-file variables are present, they must also be specified on SPLIT.
- If factor variables are present, they must also be specified on FACTORS.

When either of the following is true, the only variables that must be specified on VARIABLES are the continuous variables:

1. The data contain only correlation coefficients. There can be no additional information, such as the mean and standard deviation, and no factor information or split-file variables. MATRIX DATA assigns the record type CORR to all records.

2. CONTENTS is used to define all record types. The data can then contain information such as the mean and standard deviation, but no factor, split-file, or *ROWTYPE_* variables. MATRIX DATA assigns the record types defined on the CONTENTS subcommand.

Variable VARNAME_

*VARNAME_* cannot be specified on the VARIABLES subcommand or anywhere on MATRIX DATA, and its values cannot be included in the data. The MATRIX DATA command generates variable *VARNAME_* automatically.

Variable ROWTYPE_

- *ROWTYPE_* is a string variable with A8 format. Its values define the data types. All SPSS matrix data files contain a *ROWTYPE_* variable.
- If *ROWTYPE_* is specified on VARIABLES and its values entered in the data, MATRIX DATA is primarily used to define the names and order of the variables in the raw data file.
- *ROWTYPE_* must precede the continuous variables.
- Valid values for *ROWTYPE_* are CORR, COV, MAT, MSE, DFE, MEAN, STDDEV (or SD), N_VECTOR (or N), N_SCALAR, N_MATRIX, COUNT, or PROX. For definitions of these values, see the CONTENTS subcommand on p. 404. Three-character abbreviations for these values are permitted. These values can also be enclosed in quotes or apostrophes.
- If *ROWTYPE_* is not specified on VARIABLES, CONTENTS must be used to define the order in which the records occur within the file. MATRIX DATA follows these specifications strictly and generates a *ROWTYPE_* variable according to the CONTENTS specifications. A data-entry error, especially skipping a record, can cause the procedure to assign the wrong values to the wrong records.

Example

```
* ROWTYPE_ is specified on VARIABLES.

MATRIX DATA
     VARIABLES=ROWTYPE_ SAVINGS POP15 POP75 INCOME GROWTH.
BEGIN DATA
MEAN 9.6710 35.0896 2.2930 1106.7784 3.7576
STDDEV 4.4804 9.1517 1.2907 990.8511 2.8699
N 50 50 50 50 50
CORR 1
CORR -.4555 1
CORR .3165 -.9085 1
CORR .2203 -.7562 .7870 1
CORR .3048 -.0478 .0253 -.1295  1
END DATA.
```

- *ROWTYPE_* is specified on VARIABLES. *ROWTYPE_* values in the data identify each record type.
- Note that *VARNAME_* is not specified on VARIABLES, and its values are not entered in the data.

Example

```
* ROWTYPE_ is specified on VARIABLES.

MATRIX DATA
     VARIABLES=ROWTYPE_ SAVINGS POP15 POP75 INCOME GROWTH.
BEGIN DATA
'MEA   '  9.6710 35.0896 2.2930 1106.7784 3.7576
'SD    '  4.4804 9.1517 1.2907 990.8511 2.8699
'N     '  50 50 50 50 50
"COR   "  1
"COR   "  -.4555 1
"COR   "  .3165 -.9085 1
"COR   "  .2203 -.7562 .7870 1
"COR   "  .3048 -.0478 .0253 -.1295  1
END DATA.
```

- *ROWTYPE_* values for the mean, standard deviation, N, and Pearson correlation coefficients are abbreviated and enclosed in apostrophes or quotations.

Example

```
* ROWTYPE_ is not specified on VARIABLES.

MATRIX DATA VARIABLES=SAVINGS POP15 POP75 INCOME GROWTH
   /CONTENTS=MEAN SD N CORR.
BEGIN DATA
9.6710 35.0896 2.2930 1106.7784 3.7576
4.4804 9.1517 1.2907 990.8511 2.8699
50 50 50 50 50
 1
-.4555 1
 .3165 -.9085 1
 .2203 -.7562 .7870 1
 .3048 -.0478 .0253 -.1295 1
END DATA.
```

- *ROWTYPE_* is not specified on VARIABLES, and its values are not included in the data.
- CONTENTS is required to define the record types and the order of the records in the file.

FILE Subcommand

FILE specifies the matrix file containing the data. The default specification is INLINE, which indicates that the data are included within the command sequence between the BEGIN DATA and END DATA commands.
- If data are in an external file, FILE must specify the file.
- If the FILE subcommand is omitted, data must be inline.

Example

```
MATRIX DATA FILE=RAWMTX /VARIABLES=varlist.
```

- FILE indicates data are in the file *RAWMTX*.

FORMAT Subcommand

FORMAT indicates how the matrix data are formatted. It applies only to matrix values in the data, not to vector values, such as the mean and standard deviation.
- FORMAT can specify up to three keywords: one to specify the data-entry format, one to specify matrix shape, and one to specify whether the data include diagonal values.
- The minimum specification is a single keyword.
- Default settings remain in effect unless explicitly overridden.

Data-Entry Format

FORMAT has two keywords that specify the data-entry format:

LIST *Each scalar, vector, and matrix row must begin on a new record.* A vector or row of the matrix may be continued on multiple records. This is the default.

FREE *Matrix rows do not need to begin on a new record.* Any item can begin in the middle of a record.

Matrix Shape

FORMAT has three keywords that specify the matrix shape. With either triangular shape, no values—not even missing indicators—are entered for the implied values in the matrix.

LOWER *Read data values from the lower triangle.* This is the default.

UPPER *Read data values from the upper triangle.*

FULL *Read the full square matrix of data values.* FULL cannot be specified with NODIAGONAL.

Diagonal Values

FORMAT has two keywords that refer to the diagonal values:

DIAGONAL *Data include the diagonal values.* This is the default.

NODIAGONAL *Data do not include diagonal values.* The diagonal value is set to the system-missing value for all matrices except the correlation matrices. For correlation matrices, the diagonal value is set to 1. NODIAGONAL cannot be specified with FULL.

Table 17 shows how data might be entered for each combination of FORMAT settings that govern matrix shape and diagonal values. With UPPER NODIAGONAL and LOWER NODIAGONAL, you do not enter the matrix row that has blank values for the continuous variables. If you enter that row, MATRIX DATA cannot properly form the matrix.

Table 17 Various FORMAT settings

FULL	UPPER DIAGONAL	UPPER NODIAGONAL	LOWER DIAGONAL	LOWER NODIAGONAL
MEAN 5 4 3	MEAN 5 4 3	MEAN 5 4 3	MEAN 5 4 3	MEAN 5 4 3
SD 3 2 1	SD 3 2 1	SD 3 2 1	SD 3 2 1	SD 3 2 1
N 9 9 9	N 9 9 9	N 9 9 9	N 9 9 9	N 9 9 9
CORR 1 .6 .7	CORR 1 .6 .7	CORR .6 .7	CORR 1	CORR .6
CORR .6 1 .8	CORR 1 .8	CORR .8	CORR .6 1	CORR .7 .8
CORR .7 .8 1	CORR 1		CORR .7 .8 1	

Example

```
MATRIX DATA VARIABLES=ROWTYPE_ V1 TO V3
     /FORMAT=UPPER NODIAGONAL.
BEGIN DATA
MEAN     5   4   3
SD       3   2   1
N        9   9   9
CORR         .6  .7
CORR             .8
END DATA.
LIST.
```

- FORMAT specifies the upper-triangle format with no diagonal values. The default LIST is in effect for the data-entry format.

Example
```
MATRIX DATA VARIABLES=ROWTYPE_ V1 TO V3
   /FORMAT=UPPER NODIAGONAL.
BEGIN DATA
MEAN 5 4 3
SD 3 2 1
N 9 9 9
CORR .6 .7
CORR .8
END DATA.
LIST.
```

- This example is identical to the previous example. It shows that data do not have to be aligned in columns. Data throughout this chapter are aligned in columns to emphasize the matrix format.

SPLIT Subcommand

SPLIT specifies the variables whose values define the split files. SPLIT must follow the VARIABLES subcommand.

- SPLIT can specify a subset of up to eight of the variables named on VARIABLES. All split variables must be numeric. Keyword TO can be used to imply variables in the order in which they are named on VARIABLES.
- A separate matrix must be included in the data for each value of each split variable. MATRIX DATA generates a complete set of matrix materials for each.
- If the data contain neither *ROWTYPE_* nor split-file variables, a single split-file variable can be specified on SPLIT. This variable is *not* specified on the VARIABLES subcommand. MATRIX DATA generates a complete set of matrix materials for each set of matrix materials in the data and assigns values 1, 2, 3, etc., to the split variable until end of data is encountered.

Example
```
MATRIX DATA   VARIABLES=S1 ROWTYPE_ V1 TO V3 /SPLIT=S1.
BEGIN DATA
0 MEAN    5   4   3
0 SD      1   2   3
0 N       9   9   9
0 CORR    1
0 CORR   .6   1
0 CORR   .7  .8   1
1 MEAN    9   8   7
1 SD      5   6   7
1 N       9   9   9
1 CORR    1
1 CORR   .4   1
1 CORR   .3  .2   1
END DATA.
LIST.
```

- Split variable *S1* has two values: 0 and 1. Two separate matrices are entered in the data, one for each value *S1*.

- *S1* must be specified on both VARIABLES and SPLIT.

Example
```
MATRIX DATA VARIABLES=V1 TO V3  /CONTENTS=MEAN SD N CORR
   /SPLIT=SPL.
BEGIN DATA
   5   4   3
   1   2   3
   9   9   9
   1
  .6   1
  .7  .8   1
   9   8   7
   5   6   7
   9   9   9
   1
  .4   1
  .3  .2   1
END DATA.
LIST.
```
- Split variable *SPL* is not specified on VARIABLES, and values for *SPL* are not included in the data.
- Two sets of matrix materials are included in the data. MATRIX DATA therefore assigns values 1 and 2 to variable *SPL* and generates two matrices in the matrix data file.

FACTORS Subcommand

FACTORS specifies the variables whose values define the cells represented by the within-cells data. FACTORS must follow the VARIABLES subcommand.

- FACTORS specifies a subset of the variables named on the VARIABLES subcommand. Keyword TO can be used to imply variables in the order in which they are named on VARIABLES.
- If *ROWTYPE_* is explicit on VARIABLES and its values are included in the data, records that represent pooled information have the system-missing value (indicated by a period) for the factors, since the values of *ROWTYPE_* are ambiguous.
- If *ROWTYPE_* is not specified on VARIABLES and its values are not in the data, enter data values for the factors only for records that represent within-cells information. Enter nothing for the factors for records that represent pooled information. CELLS must be specified to indicate the number of within-cells records, and CONTENTS must be specified to indicate which record types have within-cells data.

Example

```
* Rowtype is explicit.

MATRIX DATA VARIABLES=ROWTYPE_ F1 F2  VAR1 TO VAR3
   /FACTORS=F1 F2.
BEGIN DATA
MEAN 1 1   1   2   3
SD   1 1   5   4   3
N    1 1   9   9   9
MEAN 1 2   4   5   6
SD   1 2   6   5   4
N    1 2   9   9   9
MEAN 2 1   7   8   9
SD   2 1   7   6   5
N    2 1   9   9   9
MEAN 2 2   9   8   7
SD   2 2   8   7   6
N    2 2   9   9   9
CORR . . . 1
CORR . . . .6  1
CORR . . . .7 .8  1
END DATA.
```

- *ROWTYPE_* is specified on VARIABLES.
- Factor variables must be specified on both VARIABLES and FACTORS.
- Periods in the data represent missing values for the CORR factor values.

Example

```
* Rowtype is implicit.

MATRIX DATA VARIABLES=F1 F2  VAR1 TO VAR3
   /FACTORS=F1 F2 /CONTENTS=(MEAN SD N) CORR /CELLS=4.
BEGIN DATA
1 1   1   2   3
1 1   5   4   3
1 1   9   9   9
1 2   4   5   6
1 2   6   5   4
1 2   9   9   9
2 1   7   8   9
2 1   7   6   5
2 1   9   9   9
2 2   9   8   7
2 2   8   7   6
2 2   9   9   9
      1
     .6  1
     .7 .8  1
END DATA.
```

- *ROWTYPE_* is not specified on VARIABLES.
- Nothing is entered for the CORR factor values because the records contain pooled information.
- CELLS is required because there are factors in the data and *ROWTYPE_* is implicit.

- CONTENTS is required to define the record types and to differentiate between the within-cells and pooled types.

CELLS Subcommand

CELLS specifies the number of within-cells records in the data. The only valid specification for CELLS is a single integer, which indicates the number of sets of within-cells information that MATRIX DATA must read.

- CELLS is required when there are factors in the data and *ROWTYPE_* is implicit.
- If CELLS is used when *ROWTYPE_* is specified on VARIABLES, MATRIX DATA issues a warning and ignores the CELLS subcommand.

Example

```
MATRIX DATA VARIABLES=F1 VAR1 TO VAR3 /FACTORS=F1 /CELLS=2
  /CONTENTS=(MEAN SD N) CORR.
BEGIN DATA
1  5  4  3
1  3  2  1
1  9  9  9
2  8  7  6
2  6  7  8
2  9  9  9
   1
  .6  1
  .7 .8  1
END DATA.
```

- The specification for CELLS is 2 because the factor variable *F1* has two values (1 and 2) and there are therefore two sets of within-cells information.
- If there were two factor variables, *F1* and *F2*, and each had two values, 1 and 2, CELLS would equal 4 to account for all four possible factor combinations (assuming all 4 combinations are present in the data).

CONTENTS Subcommand

CONTENTS defines the record types when *ROWTYPE_* is not included in the data. The minimum specification is a single keyword indicating a type of record. The default is CORR.

- CONTENTS is required to define record types and record order whenever *ROWTYPE_* is not specified on VARIABLES and its values are not in the data. The only exception to this rule is the rare situation in which all data values represent pooled correlation records and there are no factors. In that case, MATRIX DATA reads the data values and assigns the default *ROWTYPE_* of CORR to all records.
- The order in which keywords are specified on CONTENTS must correspond to the order in which records appear in the data. If the keywords on CONTENTS are in the wrong order, MATRIX DATA will incorrectly assign values.

CORR *Matrix of correlation coefficients.* This is the default. If *ROWTYPE_* is not specified on the VARIABLES subcommand and you omit the CONTENTS subcommand, MATRIX DATA assigns the *ROWTYPE_* value CORR to all matrix rows.

COV *Matrix of covariance coefficients.*

MAT *Generic square matrix.*

MSE *Vector of mean squared errors.*

DFE *Vector of degrees of freedom.*

MEAN *Vector of means.*

STDDEV *Vector of standard deviations.* SD is a synonym for STDDEV. MATRIX DATA assigns the *ROWTYPE_* value STDDEV to the record if either STDDEV or SD is specified.

N_VECTOR *Vector of counts.* N is a synonym for N_VECTOR. MATRIX DATA assigns *ROWTYPE_* value N to the record.

N_SCALAR *Count.* Scalars are a shorthand mechanism for representing vectors in which all elements have the same value, such as when a vector of N's is calculated using listwise deletion of missing values. Enter N_SCALAR as the *ROWTYPE_* value in the data and then the N_SCALAR value for the first continuous variable only. MATRIX DATA assigns the *ROWTYPE_* value N to the record and copies the specified N_SCALAR value across all the continuous variables.

N_MATRIX *Square matrix of counts.* Enter N_MATRIX as the *ROWTYPE_* value for each row of counts in the data. MATRIX DATA assigns *ROWTYPE_* value N to each of those rows.

COUNT *Count vector accepted by procedure DISCRIMINANT.* This contains unweighted N's.

PROX *Matrix produced by PROXIMITIES.* Any proximity matrix can be used with PROXIMITIES or CLUSTER. A value label of *SIMILARITY* or *DISSIMILARITY* should be specified for PROX by using the VALUE LABELS command after END DATA.

Example

```
MATRIX DATA VARIABLES=V1 TO V3 /CONTENTS=MEAN SD N_SCALAR CORR.
BEGIN DATA
   5   4   3
   3   2   1
   9
   1
  .6   1
  .7  .8   1
END DATA.
LIST.
```

- *ROWTYPE_* is not specified on VARIABLES, and *ROWTYPE_* values are not in the data. CONTENTS is therefore required to identify record types.

- CONTENTS indicates that the matrix records are in the following order: mean, standard deviation, N, and correlation coefficients.
- The N_SCALAR value is entered for the first continuous variable only.

Example

```
MATRIX DATA VARIABLES=V1 TO V3 /CONTENTS=PROX.
BEGIN DATA

data records

END DATA.
VALUE LABELS ROWTYPE_ 'PROX' 'DISSIMILARITY'.
```

- CONTENTS specifies PROX to read a raw matrix and create an SPSS matrix data file in the same format as one produced by procedure PROXIMITIES. PROX is assigned the value label *DISSIMILARITY*.

Within-Cells Record Definition

When the data include factors and *ROWTYPE_* is not specified, CONTENTS distinguishes between within-cells and pooled records by enclosing the keywords for within-cells records in parentheses.

- If the records associated with the within-cells keywords appear together for each set of factor values, enclose the keywords together within a single set of parentheses.
- If the records associated with each within-cells keyword are grouped together across factor values, enclose the keyword within its own parentheses

Example

```
MATRIX DATA VARIABLES=F1 VAR1 TO VAR3 /FACTORS=F1 /CELLS=2
   /CONTENTS=(MEAN SD N) CORR.
```

- MEAN, SD, and N contain within-cells information and are therefore specified within parentheses. CORR is outside the parentheses because it identifies pooled records.
- CELLS is required because there is a factor specified and *ROWTYPE_* is implicit.

Example

```
MATRIX DATA VARIABLES=F1 VAR1 TO VAR3 /FACTORS=F1 /CELLS=2
   /CONTENTS=(MEAN SD N) CORR.
BEGIN DATA
1  5  4  3
1  3  2  1
1  9  9  9
2  4  5  6
2  6  5  4
2  9  9  9
   1
  .6  1
  .7 .8  1
END DATA.
```

- The parentheses around the CONTENTS keywords indicate that the mean, standard deviation, and N for value 1 of factor *F1* are together, followed by the mean, standard deviation, and N for value 2 of factor *F1*.

Example

```
MATRIX DATA VARIABLES=F1 VAR1 TO VAR3  /FACTORS=F1  /CELLS=2
  /CONTENTS=(MEAN) (SD) (N) CORR.
BEGIN DATA
1  5  4  3
2  4  5  6
1  3  2  1
2  6  5  4
1  9  9  9
2  9  9  9
   1
  .6  1
  .7 .8  1
END DATA.
```

- The parentheses around each CONTENTS keyword indicate that the data include the means for all cells, followed by the standard deviations for all cells, followed by the N values for all the cells.

Example

```
MATRIX DATA VARIABLES=F1 VAR1 TO VAR3  /FACTORS=F1  /CELLS=2
  /CONTENTS=(MEAN SD) (N) CORR.
BEGIN DATA
1  5  4  3
1  3  2  1
2  4  5  6
2  6  5  4
1  9  9  9
2  9  9  9
   1
  .6  1
  .7 .8  1
END DATA.
```

- The parentheses around the CONTENTS keywords indicate that the data include the mean and standard deviation for value 1 of *F1*, followed by the mean and standard deviation for value 2 of *F1*, followed by the N values for all cells.

Optional Specification when ROWTYPE_ Is Explicit

When *ROWTYPE_* is explicitly named on VARIABLES, MATRIX DATA uses *ROWTYPE_* values to determine record types.

- When *ROWTYPE_* is explicitly named on VARIABLES, CONTENTS can be used for informational purposes. However, *ROWTYPE_* values in the data determine record types.
- If MATRIX DATA reads values for *ROWTYPE_* that are not specified on CONTENTS, it issues a warning.

- Missing values for factors are entered as periods, even though CONTENTS is specified (see the FACTORS subcommand on p. 402).

Example

```
MATRIX DATA VARIABLES=ROWTYPE_ F1 F2 VAR1 TO VAR3
  /FACTORS=F1 F2 /CONTENTS=(MEAN SD N) CORR.
BEGIN DATA
MEAN 1 1   1   2   3
SD   1 1   5   4   3
N    1 1   9   9   9
MEAN 1 2   4   5   6
SD   1 2   6   5   4
N    1 2   9   9   9
CORR . .   1
CORR . .  .6   1
CORR . .  .7  .8   1
END DATA.
```

- *ROWTYPE_* is specified on VARIABLES. MATRIX DATA therefore uses *ROWTYPE_* values in the data to identify record types.
- Because *ROWTYPE_* is specified on VARIABLES, CONTENTS is optional. However, CONTENTS is specified for informational purposes. This is most useful when data are in an external file and the *ROWTYPE_* values cannot be seen in the data.
- Missing values for factors are entered as periods, even though CONTENTS is specified.

N Subcommand

N specifies the population N when the data do not include it. The only valid specification is an integer, which indicates the population N.

- MATRIX DATA generates one record with a *ROWTYPE_* of N for each split file, and it uses the specified N value for each continuous variable.

Example

```
MATRIX DATA VARIABLES=V1 TO V3 /CONTENTS=MEAN SD CORR
  /N=99.
BEGIN DATA
  5   4   3
  3   4   5
  1
 .6   1
 .7  .8   1
END DATA.
```

- MATRIX DATA uses 99 as the N value for all continuous variables.

MCONVERT

```
MCONVERT [[/MATRIX=] [IN({*   })] [OUT({*   })]]
                        {file}       {file}
         [{/REPLACE}]
          {/APPEND }
```

Example:

```
MCONVERT MATRIX=OUT(CORMTX) /APPEND.
```

Overview

MCONVERT converts covariance matrix materials to correlation matrix materials, or vice versa. For MCONVERT to convert a correlation matrix, the matrix data must contain CORR values (Pearson correlation coefficients) and a vector of standard deviations (STDDEV). For MCONVERT to convert a covariance matrix, only COV values are required in the data.

Options

Matrix Files. MCONVERT can read matrix materials from an external matrix data file, and it can write converted matrix materials to an external file.

Matrix Materials. MCONVERT can write the converted matrix only or both the converted matrix and the original matrix to the resulting matrix data file.

Basic Specification

The minimum specification is the command itself. By default, MCONVERT reads the original matrix from the working data file and then replaces it with the converted matrix.

Syntax Rules

- Keywords IN and OUT cannot specify the same external file.
- The APPEND and REPLACE subcommands cannot be specified on the same MCONVERT command.

Operations

- If the data are covariance matrix materials, MCONVERT converts them to a correlation matrix plus a vector of standard deviations.
- If the data are a correlation matrix and vector of standard deviations, MCONVERT converts them to a covariance matrix.

- If there are multiple CORR or COV matrices (for example, one for each grouping (factor) or one for each split variable), each will be converted to a separate matrix, preserving the values of any factor or split variables.
- All cases with *ROWTYPE_* values other than CORR or COV, such as MEAN, N, and STDDEV, are always copied into the new matrix data file.
- MCONVERT cannot read raw matrix values. If your data are raw values, use the MATRIX DATA command.
- Split variables (if any) must occur first in the file that MCONVERT reads, followed by variable *ROWTYPE_*, the grouping variables (if any), and variable *VARNAME_*. All variables following *VARNAME_* are the variables for which a matrix will be read and created.

Limitations

- The total number of split variables plus grouping variables cannot exceed eight.

Example

```
MATRIX DATA VARIABLES=ROWTYPE_ SAVINGS POP15 POP75 INCOME GROWTH
  /FORMAT=FULL.
BEGIN DATA
COV    20.0740459   -18.678638     1.8304990   978.181242  3.9190106
COV   -18.678638     83.7541100  -10.731666  -6856.9888   -1.2561071
COV     1.8304990   -10.731666     1.6660908  1006.52742    .0937992
COV   978.181242  -6856.9888    1006.52742   981785.907  -368.18652
COV     3.9190106   -1.2561071    .0937992   -368.18652    8.2361574
END DATA.
MCONVERT.
FACTOR MATRIX IN(COR=*).
```

- MATRIX DATA defines the variables in the file and creates a working data file of matrix materials. The values for variable *ROWTYPE_* are COV, indicating that the matrix contains covariance coefficients. The FORMAT subcommand indicates that data are in full square format.
- MCONVERT converts the covariance matrix to a correlation matrix plus a vector of standard deviations. By default, the converted matrix is written to the working data file.
- FACTOR reads the correlation matrix from the working file and performs factor analysis.

MATRIX Subcommand

The MATRIX subcommand specifies the file for the matrix materials. By default, MATRIX reads the original matrix from the working data file and replaces the working data file with the converted matrix.

- MATRIX has two keywords, IN and OUT. The specification on both IN and OUT is the name of an external file in parentheses or an asterisk (*) to refer to the working data file (the default).
- The actual keyword MATRIX is optional.

- IN and OUT cannot specify the same external file.
- MATRIX=IN cannot be specified unless a working data file has already been defined. To convert an existing matrix at the beginning of a session, use GET to retrieve the matrix file and then specify IN(*) on MATRIX.

IN *The matrix file to read.*

OUT *The matrix file to write.*

Example

```
GET FILE=COVMTX.
MCONVERT MATRIX=OUT(CORMTX).
```

- GET retrieves the SPSS matrix data file *COVMTX*. *COVMTX* becomes the working data file.
- By default, MCONVERT reads the original matrix from the working data file. IN(*) can be specified to make the default explicit.
- Keyword OUT on MATRIX writes the converted matrix to file *CORMTX*.

REPLACE and APPEND Subcommands

By default, MCONVERT writes only the converted matrix to the resulting matrix file. Use APPEND to copy both the original matrix and the converted matrix.

- The only specification is the keyword REPLACE or APPEND.
- REPLACE and APPEND are alternatives.
- REPLACE and APPEND affect the resulting matrix file only. The original matrix materials, whether in the working file or in an external file, remain intact.

APPEND *Write the original matrix followed by the converted matrix to the matrix file. If there are multiple sets of matrix materials, APPEND appends each converted matrix to the end of a copy of its original matrix.*

REPLACE *Write the original matrix followed by the covariance matrix to the matrix file.*

Example

```
MCONVERT MATRIX=OUT(COVMTX) /APPEND.
```

- MCONVERT reads matrix materials from the working file.
- The APPEND subcommand copies original matrix materials, appends each converted matrix to the end of the copy of its original matrix, and writes both sets to file *COVMTX*.

MEANS

General mode:

```
MEANS [TABLES=]{varlist} BY varlist [BY...] [/varlist...]
              {ALL    }

 [/FORMAT={LABELS**  }  {NAMES**}  {VALUES**}  {TABLE**}]
          {NOLABELS  }  {NONAMES}  {NOVALUES}  {TREE   }
          {NOCATLABS }
```

Integer mode:

```
MEANS VARIABLES=varlist({min,max       }) [varlist...]
                       {LOWEST,HIGHEST}

 /{TABLES    }={varlist} BY varlist [BY...] [/varlist...]
  {CROSSBREAK} {ALL    }

 [/FORMAT={LABELS**  }  {NAMES**}  {VALUES**}]
          {NOLABELS  }  {NONAMES}  {NOVALUES}
          {NOCATLABS }
```

Both modes:

```
 [/MISSING={TABLE**  }]
           {INCLUDE  }
           {DEPENDENT}

 [/CELLS=[DEFAULT**]  [MEAN**  ]  [ALL]]
         [COUNT**  ]  [STDDEV**]
         [SUM      ]  [VARIANCE]

 [/STATISTICS=[ANOVA] [{LINEARITY}] [NONE**]]
                      {ALL      }
```

**Default if the subcommand is omitted.

Example:

```
MEANS TABLES=V1 TO V5 BY GROUP
  /FORMAT=NONAMES
  /STATISTICS=ANOVA.
```

Overview

MEANS (alias BREAKDOWN) displays means, standard deviations, and group counts for a dependent variable within groups defined by one or more control (independent) variables. Other SPSS procedures that display univariate statistics are FREQUENCIES and DESCRIPTIVES.

MEANS can operate in two different modes: *general* and *integer*. General mode permits alphanumeric or noninteger control variables with no range specifications and provides an optional tree format. Integer mode builds tables more quickly but requires additional specifications. Using integer mode, you also have the option of displaying tables with two or more control variables in a crosstabular format.

Options

Methods for Building Tables. To build tables in general mode, use the TABLES subcommand. Integer mode requires the TABLES and VARIABLES subcommands and minimum and maximum values for the variables.

Cell Contents. By default, MEANS displays means, standard deviations, and cell counts for a dependent variable across groups defined by one or more control variables. You can also display sums and variances using the CELLS subcommand.

Statistics. In addition to the statistics displayed for each cell of the table, you can obtain a one-way analysis of variance and test of linearity using the STATISTICS subcommand.

Format. You can request a tree format with general mode and suppress labels and values in either mode using the FORMAT subcommand. With integer mode, you can obtain a crosstabular format using the CROSSBREAK subcommand.

Basic Specification

In general mode, the basic specification is TABLES with a table list. The actual keyword TABLES can be omitted. In integer mode, the minimum specification is the VARIABLES subcommand specifying the variables to be used and their ranges, and the TABLES or CROSSBREAK subcommand with a table list.

- The minimum table list specifies a dependent variable, keyword BY, and a control variable.
- In general mode, variables can be numeric (integer or noninteger) or string. In integer mode, control variables must be numeric with integer values. Dependent variables must be numeric for both modes.
- By default, MEANS displays means, standard deviations, and number of cases. The default table is labeled with the variable name and label of the dependent and control variables. Groups are labeled with the variable name, variable label, values, and value labels of the control variables.

Subcommand Order

- In general mode, the table list must be first if keyword TABLES is omitted. If keyword TABLES is explicitly used, subcommands can be specified in any order.
- In integer mode, VARIABLES must precede TABLES. Keyword TABLES must be explicitly specified.

Operations

- Integer mode builds tables more quickly but requires more space if the matrix of control variables has many empty cells. By specifying the appropriate ranges, you can eliminate outliers for the dependent variable or select a subset of the values of the control variables.

- MEANS displays requested univariate statistics for the population as a whole and for each value of the first control variable defined for the table in addition to statistics for groups.
- If a control variable is a long string, only the short-string portion is used to identify groups in the analysis. Use the REPORT procedure to break down variables by long strings.
- If a string variable is specified as a dependent variable on any table lists, the MEANS procedure stops executing.
- The output uses the width specified on the SET command. If the width is set to 80 columns and the requested tables require more room, MEANS is not executed. (The exception is the CROSSBREAK format, where tables will wrap if they don't fit in the specified width.) To reduce the width of the output, limit the number of columns by specifying a maximum of three of the five cell statistics and suppress the display of value labels, variable names, category labels, and so forth. To display sums and variances in addition to the default cell statistics, the width should be set to at least 96 columns (see SET).

Limitations

The following limitations apply to MEANS in *general mode*:
- Maximum 200 variables total per MEANS command.
- Maximum 250 tables.
- Maximum 6 dimensions per table.
- Maximum 30 table lists per MEANS command.
- Maximum 200 unique value labels displayed on any single table.

The following limitations apply to MEANS in *integer mode*:
- Maximum 100 variables named or implied on VARIABLES.
- Maximum 100 variables named or implied on TABLES.
- Maximum 100 tables.
- Maximum 6 dimensions per table.
- Maximum 30 table lists per MEANS command.
- Maximum 100 nonempty rows and 100 nonempty columns in a crossbreak table.

Example

```
MEANS TABLES=V1 TO V5 BY GROUP
  /FORMAT=NONAMES
  /STATISTICS=ANOVA.
```

- TABLES specifies that *V1* through *V5* are the dependent variables. *GROUP* is the control variable.
- Assuming that variables *V2, V3,* and *V4* lie between *V1* and *V5* on the working data file, five tables are produced: *V1* by *GROUP*, *V2* by *GROUP*, *V3* by *GROUP*, and so on.
- FORMAT suppresses the display of variable name *GROUP*.
- STATISTICS requests one-way analysis-of-variance tables of *V1* through *V5* by *GROUP*.

Example

```
MEANS VARA BY VARB BY VARC/V1 V2 BY V3 V4 BY V5.
```

- This command contains two TABLES subcommands that omit the optional TABLES keyword.
- The first table list requests one table. Statistics are produced for *VARA* within groups defined by each combination of values of *VARB* and *VARC*.
- The second table list requests four tables: *V1* by *V3* by *V5*; *V1* by *V4* by *V5*; *V2* by *V3* by *V5*; and *V2* by *V4* by *V5*.

VARIABLES Subcommand

The VARIABLES subcommand is used in integer mode only. VARIABLES specifies a list of variables to be used in the procedure and the lowest and highest values for each variable. Values are specified in parentheses and must be integers.

- Variables can be specified in any order. However, the order in which they are named on VARIABLES affects their implied order on the TABLES (see "Integer Mode" on p. 416).
- A range must be specified for each variable. If several variables have the same range, it can be specified once after the last variable to which it applies.
- If you specify a noninteger range value for an independent variable, SPSS issues an error message and the MEANS command is not executed. If you specify a noninteger range value for a dependent variable, SPSS truncates the value and uses the integer as the range value.
- Dependent variables are usually continuous and are not assumed to be integers. Therefore, you can use keywords LOWEST (or LO) and HIGHEST (or HI) for the range specification for dependent variables to indicate the lowest and highest values encountered in the data. You can also specify actual values to eliminate outliers from the calculation of the summary statistics. For example, (0,HI) excludes negative values.
- Keywords LOWEST, LO, HIGHEST, and HI cannot be used with control variables.
- For each table, MEANS allocates one cell for each possible combination of values of the control variables before the data are read. Thus, if the specified ranges are larger than the actual ranges, workspace will be wasted.
- Cases with values outside the specified range are considered missing and are not used in the computation of the table.
- If the table is sparse because the control variables do not have values throughout the specified range, consider using general mode or recoding the control variables.

Example

```
MEANS  VARIABLES=DEPT88(1,4) EEO88(1,9) RAISE88(LO,HI)
   /TABLES=RAISE88 BY DEPT88 BY EEO88.
```

- *RAISE88* is the dependent variable and has a range from the lowest to the highest value encountered in the data.

- The control variables are *DEPT88* and *EEO88*, with ranges of 1 to 4 and 1 to 9, respectively.

TABLES Subcommand

TABLES specifies the table list and is required in both general and integer mode.
- You can specify multiple TABLES subcommands on a single MEANS command. The slash between the subcommands is required; the keyword TABLES is required only in integer mode. You can also name multiple table lists separated by slashes on one TABLES subcommand.
- The dependent variable is specified first and must be numeric. The control (independent) variables follow the BY keyword.
- Each use of keyword BY in a table list adds a dimension (or layer) to the tables requested. A table is built for each dependent variable by each combination of control variables across dimensions.
- The order in which control variables are displayed is the same as the order in which they are specified on TABLES. The values of the first control variable defined for the table appear in the leftmost column of the table and change the most slowly in the definition of groups.
- More than one dependent variable can be specified in a table list, and more than one control variable can be specified in each dimension of a table list.

General Mode

- The actual keyword TABLES can be omitted in general mode.
- In general mode, the control variables can be numeric (integer or noninteger) or string.
- Keywords ALL and TO can be specified in any dimension. In general mode, TO refers to the order of variables in the working file, and ALL refers to all variables defined in the working file.

Integer Mode

- In integer mode, variables named on TABLES must have been previously named or implied on VARIABLES.
- In integer mode, control variables must be integers.
- Keywords TO and ALL can be specified in any dimension. In integer mode, TO and ALL refer to the position and subset of variables specified on the VARIABLES subcommand, not to the variables in the working file.

CROSSBREAK Subcommand

CROSSBREAK displays tables in a crosstabular format. This format is especially useful when there are two control variables.

- CROSSBREAK can be used only in integer mode, and it is used in place of the TABLES subcommand.
- CROSSBREAK syntax is identical to TABLES syntax. As with TABLES, repeated CROSSBREAK subcommands are allowed. However, CROSSBREAK and TABLES subcommands cannot be mixed.
- Tables produced by CROSSBREAK resemble tables produced by the CROSSTABS procedure, but their contents are considerably different. In CROSSBREAK tables, the cells contain means, counts, and standard deviations for the dependent variable. The first control variable defines the rows and the second control variable defines the columns.
- CROSSBREAK displays separate subtables for each combination of values when you specify three or more control variables.

CELLS Subcommand

By default, MEANS displays the means, standard deviations, and cell counts in each cell. Use CELLS to modify cell information.

- If CELLS is specified without keywords, MEANS displays all cell information (keyword ALL).
- If any keywords are specified on CELLS, only the requested information is displayed.

DEFAULT	*Means, standard deviations, and cell counts.* This is the default if CELLS is omitted.
MEAN	*Cell means.*
STDDEV	*Cell standard deviations.*
COUNT	*Cell counts.*
SUM	*Cell sums.*
VARIANCE	*Variances.*
ALL	*Means, standard deviations, counts, sums, and variances.* This is the default if CELLS is specified without keywords.

STATISTICS Subcommand

Use STATISTICS to request a one-way analysis of variance for each table and a test of linearity.

- Statistics requested on STATISTICS are computed in addition to the statistics displayed in each cell of the table.
- If STATISTICS is specified without keywords, MEANS computes ANOVA.
- STATISTICS is not available if CROSSBREAK is used.
- If two or more dimensions are specified, the second and subsequent dimensions are ignored in the analysis of variance table. To obtain a two-way and higher analysis of vari-

ance, use procedure ANOVA or MANOVA. Procedure ONEWAY calculates a one-way analysis of variance with multiple comparison tests.

ANOVA *Analysis of variance.* ANOVA displays a standard analysis of variance table and calculates eta and eta squared. This is the default if STATISTICS is specified without keywords.

LINEARITY *Test of linearity.* LINEARITY (alias ALL) displays a standard analysis of variance table and calculates eta and eta squared plus the sums of squares, degrees of freedom, and mean square associated with linear and nonlinear components, the F ratio, Pearson's r, and r^2. LINEARITY is ignored if the control variable is a string.

NONE *No additional statistics.* This is the default if STATISTICS is omitted.

Example

```
MEANS TABLES=INCOME BY SEX BY RACE
  /STATISTICS=ANOVA.
```

- MEANS produces a table of *INCOME* by *RACE* within *SEX* but computes an analysis of variance only for *INCOME* by *SEX*.

MISSING Subcommand

MISSING controls the treatment of missing values.

TABLE *Delete cases with missing values on a tablewide basis.* A case with a missing value for any variable specified for a table is not used. Thus, every case contained in a table has a complete set of nonmissing values for all variables in that table. When you separate table requests with a slash, missing values are handled separately for each list. This is the default.

INCLUDE *Include user-missing values.* This option treats user-missing values as valid values.

DEPENDENT *Exclude user-missing values for dependent variables only.* DEPENDENT treats user-missing values for all control variables as valid.

FORMAT Subcommand

FORMAT controls table formats. By default, MEANS displays all tables in report format (keyword TABLE) and includes variable and value labels and the names and values of control variables (keywords LABELS, NAMES, and VALUES).

LABELS *Display both variable and value labels for each table.*

NOLABELS *Suppress variable and value labels.*

NOCATLABS *Suppress value (category) labels.*

NAMES *Display the names of control variables.*

NONAMES	*Suppress names of control variables.*
VALUES	*Display the values of control variables.*
NOVALUES	*Suppress values of control variables.* This is useful when there are category labels.
TABLE	*Display each table in report format.*
TREE	*Display each table in tree format.* This option is available for general mode only. The individual cells of the table are displayed as blocks.

References

Hays, W.L. 1981. *Statistics for the social sciences,* 3rd ed. New York: Holt, Rinehart, and Wilson.

MISSING VALUES

```
MISSING VALUES {varlist}(value list) [[/]{varlist} ...]
               {ALL    }               {ALL    }
```

Keywords for numeric value lists:

LO, LOWEST, HI, HIGHEST, THRU

Example:

```
MISSING VALUES V1 (8,9) V2 V3 (0) V4 ('X') V5 TO V9 ('    ').
```

Overview

MISSING VALUES declares values for numeric and short string variables as user-missing. These values can then receive special treatment in data transformations, statistical calculations, and case selection. By default, user-missing values are treated the same as the system-missing values. System-missing values are automatically assigned by SPSS when no legal value can be produced, such as when an alphabetical character is encountered in the data for a numeric variable, or when an illegal calculation, such as division by 0, is requested in a data transformation.

Basic Specification

The basic specification is a single variable followed by the user-missing value or values in parentheses. Each specified value for the variable is treated as user-missing for any analysis.

Syntax Rules

- Each variable can have a maximum of three individual user-missing values. A space or comma must separate each value. For numeric variables, you can also specify a range of missing values. See "Specifying Ranges of Missing Values" on p. 422.
- The missing-value specification must correspond to the variable type (numeric or string).
- The same values can be declared missing for more than one variable by specifying a variable list followed by the values in parentheses. Variable lists must have either all numeric or all string variables.
- Different values can be declared missing for different variables by specifying separate values for each variable. An optional slash can be used to separate specifications.
- Missing values cannot be assigned to long string variables or to scratch variables.
- Missing values for short string variables must be enclosed in apostrophes or quotation marks. The value specifications must include any leading or trailing blanks. (See "String Values in Command Specifications" on p. 16.)
- A variable list followed by an empty set of parentheses () deletes any user-missing specifications for those variables.

- Keyword ALL can be used to refer to all user-defined variables in the working file, provided the variables are either all numeric or all string. ALL can refer to both numeric and string variables if it is followed by an empty set of parentheses. This will delete all user-missing specifications in the working data file.
- More than one MISSING VALUES command can be specified per SPSS session.

Operations

- Unlike most transformations, MISSING VALUES takes effect as soon as it is encountered. Special attention should be paid to its position among commands. See Universals: Command Order for more information.
- Missing-value specifications can be changed between procedures. New specifications replace previous ones. If a variable is mentioned more than once on one or more MISSING VALUES commands before a procedure, only the last specification is used.
- Missing-value specifications are saved in SPSS data files (see SAVE) and portable files (see EXPORT).

Example

```
MISSING VALUES V1 (8,9) V2 V3 (0) V4 ('X') V5 TO V9 ('    ').
```

- Values 8 and 9 are declared missing for numeric variable *V1*.
- Value 0 is declared missing for numeric variables *V2* and *V3*.
- Value X is declared missing for string variable *V4*.
- Blanks are declared missing for the string variables between and including *V5* and *V9*. All of these variables must have a width of four columns.

Example

```
MISSING VALUES V1 ().
```

- Any previously declared missing values for *V1* are deleted.

Example

```
MISSING VALUES ALL (9).
```

- Value 9 is declared missing for all variables in the working data file; the variables must all be numeric. All previous user-missing specifications are overridden.

Example

```
MISSING VALUES ALL ().
```

- All previously declared user-missing values for all variables in the working data file are deleted. The variables in the working data file can be both numeric and string.

Specifying Ranges of Missing Values

A range of values can be specified as missing for numeric variables but *not* for string variables.

- Keyword THRU indicates an inclusive list of values. Values must be separated from THRU by at least one blank space.
- Keywords HIGHEST and LOWEST with THRU indicate the highest and lowest values of a variable. HIGHEST and LOWEST can be abbreviated to HI and LO.
- Only one THRU specification can be used for each variable or variable list. Each THRU specification can be combined with one additional missing value.

Example

```
MISSING VALUES  V1 (LOWEST THRU 0).
```

- All negative values and 0 are declared missing for variable *V1*.

Example

```
MISSING VALUES  V1 (0 THRU 1.5).
```

- Values from 0 through and including 1.5 are declared missing.

Example

```
MISSING VALUES V1 (LO THRU 0, 999).
```

- All negative values, 0, and 999 are declared missing for variable *V1*.

MULT RESPONSE

```
MULT RESPONSE†
 {/GROUPS=groupname['label'](varlist ({value1,value2}))}
                                      {value          }
    ...[groupname...]}

 {/VARIABLES=varlist(min,max)  [varlist...]           }

 {/FREQUENCIES=varlist                                }

 {/TABLES=varlist BY varlist... [BY varlist] [(PAIRED)]}
         [/varlist BY...]

 [/MISSING=[{TABLE**}] [INCLUDE]]
           {MDGROUP}
           {MRGROUP}

 [/FORMAT={LABELS**}  {TABLE** }   [DOUBLE]]
          {NOLABELS}  {CONDENSE}
                      {ONEPAGE }

 [/BASE={CASES**  }]
        {RESPONSES}

 [/CELLS=[COUNT**] [ROW] [COLUMN] [TOTAL] [ALL]]
```

†A minimum of two subcommands must be used: at least one from the pair GROUPS or VARIABLES and one from the pair FREQUENCIES or TABLES.
**Default if the subcommand is omitted.

Example:

```
MULT RESPONSE  GROUPS=MAGS (TIME TO STONE (2))
   /FREQUENCIES=MAGS.
```

Overview

MULT RESPONSE displays frequencies and optional percentages for multiple-response items in univariate tables and multivariate crosstabulations. Another procedure that analyzes multiple-response items is TABLES, which has most, but not all, of the capabilities of MULT RESPONSE. TABLES has special formatting capabilities that make it useful for presentations.

Multiple-response items are questions that can have more than one value for each case. For example, the respondent may have been asked to circle all magazines read within the last month in a list of magazines. You can organize multiple-response data in one of two ways for use in SPSS. For each possible response, you can create a variable that can have one of two values, such as 1 for *no* and 2 for *yes*; this is the multiple-dichotomy method. Alternatively, you can estimate the maximum number of possible answers from a respondent and create that number of variables, each of which can have a value representing one of the possible answers, such as 1 for *Time*, 2 for *Newsweek*, and 3 for *PC Week*. If an individual did not give the maximum number of answers, the extra variables receive a missing-value code. This is the multiple-response or multiple-category method of coding answers.

To analyze the data entered by either method, you combine SPSS variables into groups. The technique depends on whether you have defined multiple-dichotomy or multiple-response variables. When you create a multiple-dichotomy group, each component variable with at least one *yes* value across cases becomes a category of the group variable. When you create a multiple-response group, each value becomes a category and SPSS calculates the frequency for a particular value by adding the frequencies of all component variables with that value. Both multiple-dichotomy and multiple-response groups can be crosstabulated with other variables in MULT RESPONSE.

Options

Cell Counts and Percentages. By default, crosstabulations include only counts and no percentages. You can request row, column, and total table percentages using the CELLS subcommand. You can also base percentages on responses instead of respondents using BASE.

Format. You can suppress the display of value labels and request condensed format for frequency tables using the FORMAT subcommand.

Basic Specification

The subcommands required for the basic specification fall into two groups: GROUPS and VARIABLES name the elements to be included in the analysis; FREQUENCIES and TABLES specify the type of table display to be used for tabulation. The basic specification requires at least one subcommand from each group:

- GROUPS defines groups of multiple-response items to be analyzed and specifies how the component variables will be combined.
- VARIABLES identifies all individual SPSS variables to be analyzed.
- FREQUENCIES requests frequency tables for the groups and/or individual variables specified on GROUPS and VARIABLES.
- TABLES requests crosstabulations of groups and/or individual variables specified on GROUPS and VARIABLES.

Subcommand Order

- The basic subcommands must be used in the following order: GROUPS, VARIABLES, FREQUENCIES, and TABLES. Only one set of basic subcommands can be specified.
- All basic subcommands must precede all optional subcommands. Optional subcommands can be used in any order.

Operations

- Empty categories are not displayed in either frequency tables or crosstabulations.
- If you define a multiple-response group with a very wide range, the tables require substantial amounts of workspace. If the component variables are sparsely distributed, you should recode them to minimize the workspace required.

- MULT RESPONSE stores category labels in workspace. If there is insufficient space to store the labels after the tables are built, the labels are not displayed.

Limitations

- The component variables must have integer values. Noninteger values are truncated.
- Maximum 100 existing SPSS variables named or implied by GROUPS and VARIABLES together.
- Maximum 20 groups defined on GROUPS.
- Maximum 32,767 categories for a multiple-response group or an individual variable.
- Maximum 10 table lists on TABLES.
- Maximum 5 dimensions per table.
- Maximum 100 groups and SPSS variables named or implied on FREQUENCIES and TABLES together.
- Maximum 200 nonempty rows and 200 nonempty columns in a single table.

GROUPS Subcommand

GROUPS defines both multiple-dichotomy and multiple-response groups.
- Specify a name for the group and an optional label, followed by a list of the component variables and the value or values to be used in the tabulation.
- Enclose the variable list in parentheses and enclose the values in an inner set of parentheses following the last variable in the list.
- The label for the group is optional and can be up to 40 characters in length, including imbedded blanks. Apostrophes or quotes around the label are not required.
- To define a multiple-dichotomy group, specify only one tabulating value (the value that represents *yes*) following the variable list. Each component variable becomes a value of the group variable, and the number of cases that have the tabulating value becomes the frequency. If there are no cases with the tabulating value for a given component variable, that variable does not appear in the tabulation.
- To define a multiple-response group, specify two values following the variable list. These are the minimum and maximum values of the component variables. The group variable will have the same range of values. The frequency for each value is tabulated across all component variables in the list.
- You can use any valid SPSS variable name for the group except the name of an existing SPSS variable specified on the same MULT RESPONSE command. However, you can re-use a group name on another MULT RESPONSE command.
- The group names and labels exist only during MULT RESPONSE and disappear once MULT RESPONSE has been executed. If group names are referred to in other procedures, an error results.
- For a multiple-dichotomy group, the category labels come from the variable labels defined for the component variables.

- For a multiple-response group, the category labels come from the value labels for the first component variable in the group. If categories are missing for the first variable but are present for other variables in the group, you must define value labels for the missing categories. (You can use the ADD VALUE LABELS command to define extra value labels.)

Example

```
MULT RESPONSE   GROUPS=MAGS 'MAGAZINES READ' (TIME TO STONE (2))
  /FREQUENCIES=MAGS.
```

- The GROUPS subcommand creates a multiple-dichotomy group named *MAGS*. The variables between and including *TIME* and *STONE* become categories of *MAGS*, and the frequencies are cases with value 2 (indicating *yes, read the magazine*) for the component variables.
- The group label is *MAGAZINES READ*.

Example

```
MULT RESPONSE   GROUPS=PROBS 'PERCEIVED NATIONAL PROBLEMS'
  (PROB1 TO PROB3 (1,9))
  /FREQUENCIES=PROBS.
```

- The GROUPS subcommand creates the multiple-response group *PROBS*. The component variables are the existing SPSS variables between and including *PROB1* and *PROB3*, and the frequencies are tabulated for values 1 through 9.
- The frequency for a given value is the number of cases that have that value in any of the variables *PROB1* to *PROB3*.

VARIABLES Subcommand

VARIABLES specifies existing SPSS variables to be used in frequency tables and crosstabulations. Each variable is followed by parentheses enclosing a minimum and a maximum value, which are used to allocate cells for the tables for that variable.

- You can specify any numeric variable on VARIABLES, but noninteger values are truncated.
- If GROUPS is also specified, VARIABLES follows GROUPS.
- To provide the same minimum and maximum for each of a set of variables, specify a variable list followed by a range specification.
- The component variables specified on GROUPS can be used in frequency tables and crosstabulations, but you must specify them again on VARIABLES, along with a range for the values. You do not have to respecify the component variables if they will not be used as individual variables in any tables.

Example

```
MULT RESPONSE   GROUPS=MAGS 'MAGAZINES READ' (TIME TO STONE (2))
  /VARIABLES SEX(1,2) EDUC(1,3)
  /FREQUENCIES=MAGS SEX EDUC.
```

- The VARIABLES subcommand names variables *SEX* and *EDUC* so that they can be used in a frequencies table.

Example
```
MULT RESPONSE  GROUPS=MAGS 'MAGAZINES READ' (TIME TO STONE (2))
  /VARIABLES=EDUC (1,3) TIME (1,2).
  /TABLES=MAGS BY EDUC TIME.
```
- The variable *TIME* is used in a group and also in a table.

FREQUENCIES Subcommand

FREQUENCIES requests frequency tables for groups and individual variables. By default, a frequency table contains the count for each value, the percentage of responses, and the percentage of cases. For another method of producing frequency tables for individual variables, see the FREQUENCIES procedure.

- All groups must be created by GROUPS, and all individual variables to be tabulated must be named on VARIABLES.
- You can use keyword TO to imply a set of group or individual variables. TO refers to the order in which variables are specified on the GROUPS or VARIABLES subcommand.

Example
```
MULT RESPONSE  GROUPS=MAGS 'MAGAZINES READ' (TIME TO STONE (2))
  /FREQUENCIES=MAGS.
```
- The FREQUENCIES subcommand requests a frequency table for the multiple-dichotomy group *MAGS*, tabulating the frequency of value 2 for each of the component variables *TIME* to *STONE*.

Example
```
MULT RESPONSE
 GROUPS=MAGS 'MAGAZINES READ' (TIME TO STONE (2))
       PROBS 'PERCEIVED NATIONAL PROBLEMS' (PROB1 TO PROB3 (1,9))
       MEMS 'SOCIAL ORGANIZATION MEMBERSHIPS' (VFW AMLEG ELKS (1))
  /VARIABLES SEX(1,2) EDUC(1,3)
  /FREQUENCIES=MAGS TO MEMS SEX EDUC.
```
- The FREQUENCIES subcommand requests frequency tables for *MAGS*, *PROBS*, *MEMS*, *SEX*, and *EDUC*.
- You cannot specify MAGS TO EDUC because *SEX* and *EDUC* are individual variables, and *MAGS*, *PROBS*, and *MEMS* are group variables.

TABLES Subcommand

TABLES specifies the crosstabulations to be produced by MULT RESPONSE. Both individual variables and group variables can be tabulated together.

- The first list defines the rows of the tables; the next list (following BY) defines the columns. Subsequent lists following BY keywords define control variables, which produce subtables. Use keyword BY to separate the dimensions. You can specify up to five dimensions (four BY keywords) for a table.
- To produce more than one table, name one or more variables for each dimension of the tables. You can also specify multiple table lists separated by a slash. If you use keyword TO to imply a set of group or individual variables, TO refers to the order in which groups or variables are specified on the GROUPS or VARIABLES subcommand.
- If FREQUENCIES is also specified, TABLES follows FREQUENCIES.
- The value labels for columns are displayed on three lines with eight characters per line. To avoid splitting words, reverse the row and column variables, or redefine the variable or value labels (depending on whether the variables are multiple-dichotomy or multiple-response variables).

Example

```
MULT RESPONSE   GROUPS=MAGS 'MAGAZINES READ' (TIME TO STONE (2))
   /VARIABLES=EDUC (1,3)/TABLES=EDUC BY MAGS.
```

- The TABLES subcommand requests a crosstabulation of variable *EDUC* by the multiple-dichotomy group *MAGS*.

Example

```
MULT RESPONSE   GROUPS=MAGS 'MAGAZINES READ' (TIME TO STONE (2))
   MEMS 'SOCIAL ORGANIZATION MEMBERSHIPS' (VFW AMLEG ELKS (1))
   /VARIABLES EDUC (1,3)/TABLES=MEMS MAGS BY EDUC.
```

- The TABLES subcommand specifies two crosstabulations—*MEMS* by *EDUC*, and *MAGS* by *EDUC*.

Example

```
MULT RESPONSE   GROUPS=MAGS 'MAGAZINES READ' (TIME TO STONE (2))
   /VARIABLES SEX (1,2) EDUC (1,3)
   /TABLES=MAGS BY EDUC SEX/EDUC BY SEX/MAGS BY EDUC BY SEX.
```

- The TABLES subcommand uses slashes to separate three table lists. It produces two tables from the first table list (*MAGS* by *EDUC* and *MAGS* by *SEX*) and one table from the second table list (*EDUC* by *SEX*). The third table list produces separate tables for each sex (*MAGS* by *EDUC* for male and for female).

Example

```
MULT RESPONSE   GROUPS=MAGS 'MAGAZINES READ' (TIME TO STONE (2))
   PROBS 'NATIONAL PROBLEMS MENTIONED' (PROB1 TO PROB3 (1,9))
   /TABLES=MAGS BY PROBS.
```

- The TABLES subcommand requests a crosstabulation of the multiple-dichotomy group *MAGS* with the multiple-response group *PROBS*.

PAIRED Keyword

When MULT RESPONSE crosstabulates two multiple-response groups, by default it tabulates each variable in the first group with each variable in the second group and sums the counts for each cell. Thus, some responses can appear more than once in the table. Use PAIRED to pair the first variable in the first group with the first variable in the second group, the second variable in the first group with the second variable in the second group, and so on.

- Keyword PAIRED is specified in parentheses on the TABLES subcommand following the last variable named for a specific table list.
- When you request paired crosstabulations, the order of the component variables on the GROUPS subcommand determines the construction of the table.
- Although the tables can contain individual variables and multiple-dichotomy groups in a paired table request, only variables within multiple-response groups are paired.
- PAIRED also applies to a multiple-response group used as a control variable in a three-way or higher-order table.
- Paired tables are identified in the output by the label *PAIRED GROUP*.
- Percentages in paired tables are always based on responses rather than cases.

Example

```
MULT RESPONSE GROUPS=PSEX 'SEX OF CHILD'(P1SEX P2SEX P3SEX (1,2))
    /PAGE 'AGE OF ONSET OF PREGNANCY' (P1AGE P2AGE P3AGE (1,4))
    /TABLES=PSEX BY PAGE (PAIRED).
```

- The PAIRED keyword produces a paired crosstabulation of *PSEX* by *PAGE*, which is a combination of the tables *P1SEX* by *P1AGE*, *P2SEX* by *P2AGE*, and *P3SEX* by *P3AGE*.

Example

```
MULT RESPONSE GROUPS=PSEX 'SEX OF CHILD'(P1SEX P2SEX P3SEX (1,2))
    PAGE 'AGE OF ONSET OF PREGNANCY' (P1AGE P2AGE P3AGE (1,4))
    /VARIABLES=EDUC (1,3)
    /TABLES=PSEX BY PAGE BY EDUC (PAIRED).
```

- The TABLES subcommand pairs only *PSEX* with *PAGE*. *EDUC* is not paired because it is an individual variable, not a multiple-response group.

CELLS Subcommand

By default, MULT RESPONSE displays cell counts but not percentages in crosstabulations. CELLS requests percentages for crosstabulations.

- If you specify one or more keywords on CELLS, MULT RESPONSE displays cell counts plus the percentages you request. The count cannot be eliminated from the table cells.

COUNT   *Cell counts*. This is the default if you omit the CELLS subcommand.

ROW   *Row percentages*.

COLUMN *Column percentages*.

TOTAL *Two-way table total percentages.*

ALL *Cell counts, row percentages, column percentages, and two-way table total percentages.* This is the default if you specify the CELLS subcommand without keywords.

Example

```
MULT RESPONSE  GROUPS=MAGS 'MAGAZINES READ' (TIME TO STONE (2))
  /VARIABLES=SEX (1,2) (EDUC (1,3)
  /TABLES=MAGS BY EDUC SEX
  /CELLS=ROW COLUMN.
```

- The CELLS subcommand requests row and column percentages in addition to counts.

BASE Subcommand

BASE lets you obtain cell percentages and marginal frequencies based on responses rather than respondents. Specify one of two keywords:

CASES *Base cell percentages on cases.* This is the default if you omit the BASE subcommand and do not request paired tables. You cannot use this specification if you specify PAIRED on TABLE.

RESPONSES *Base cell percentages on responses.* This is the default if you request paired tables.

Example

```
MULT RESPONSE  GROUPS=PROBS 'NATIONAL PROBLEMS MENTIONED'
  (PROB1 TO PROB3 (1,9))/VARIABLES=EDUC (1,3)
  /TABLES=EDUC BY PROBS
  /CELLS=ROW COLUMN
  /BASE=RESPONSES.
```

- The BASE subcommand requests marginal frequencies and cell percentages based on responses.

MISSING Subcommand

MISSING controls missing values. Its minimum specification is a single keyword.

- By default, MULT RESPONSE deletes cases with missing values on a table-by-table basis for both individual variables and groups. In addition, values falling outside the specified range are not tabulated and are included in the missing category. Thus, specifying a range that excludes missing values is equivalent to the default missing-value treatment.
- For a multiple-dichotomy group, a case is considered missing by default if none of the component variables contains the tabulating value for that case. Keyword MDGROUP overrides the default and specifies listwise deletion for multiple-dichotomy groups.
- For a multiple-response group, a case is considered missing by default if none of the components has valid values falling within the tabulating range for that case. Thus, cases with missing or excluded values on some (but not all) of the components of a group are includ-

ed in tabulations of the group variable. Keyword MRGROUP overrides the default and specifies listwise deletion for multiple-response groups.
- You can use INCLUDE with MDGROUP, MRGROUP, or TABLE. The user-missing value is tabulated if it is included in the range specification.

TABLE   *Exclude missing values on a table-by-table basis.* Missing values are excluded on a table-by-table basis for both component variables and groups. This is the default if you omit the MISSING subcommand.

MDGROUP   *Exclude missing values listwise for multiple-dichotomy groups.* Cases with missing values for any component dichotomy variable are excluded from the tabulation of the multiple-dichotomy group.

MRGROUP   *Exclude missing values listwise for multiple-response groups.* Cases with missing values for any component variable are excluded from the tabulation of the multiple-response group.

INCLUDE   *Include user-missing values.* User-missing values are treated as valid values if they are included in the range specification on the GROUPS or VARIABLES subcommands.

Example

```
MULT RESPONSE  GROUPS=FINANCL 'FINANCIAL PROBLEMS MENTIONED'
   (FINPROB1 TO FINPROB3 (1,3))
   SOCIAL 'SOCIAL PROBLEMS MENTIONED'(SOCPROB1 TO SOCPROB4 (4,9))
   /VARIABLES=EDUC (1,3)
   /TABLES=EDUC BY FINANCL SOCIAL
   /MISSING=MRGROUP.
```

- The MISSING subcommand indicates that a case will be excluded from counts in the first table if any of the variables in the group *FINPROB1* to *FINPROB3* has a missing value or a value outside the range 1 to 3. A case is excluded from the second table if any of the variables in the group *SOCPROB1* to *SOCPROB4* has a missing value or value outside the range 4 to 9.

FORMAT Subcommand

FORMAT controls table formats. The minimum specification on FORMAT is a single keyword. Labels are controlled by two keywords:

LABELS   *Display value labels in frequency tables and crosstabulations.* This is the default.

NOLABELS   *Suppress value labels in frequency tables and crosstabulations for multiple-response variables and individual variables.* You cannot suppress the display of variable labels used as value labels for multiple-dichotomy groups.

The following keywords apply to the format of frequency tables:

DOUBLE   *Double spacing for frequency tables.* By default, MULT RESPONSE uses single spacing.

TABLE *One-column format for frequency tables.* This is the default if you omit the FORMAT subcommand.

CONDENSE *Condensed format for frequency tables.* This option uses a three-column condensed format for frequency tables for all multiple-response groups and individual variables. Labels are suppressed. This option does not apply to multiple-dichotomy groups.

ONEPAGE *Conditional condensed format for frequency tables.* Three-column condensed format is used if the resulting table would not fit on a page. This option does not apply to multiple-dichotomy groups.

Example
```
MULT RESPONSE   GROUPS=PROBS 'NATIONAL PROBLEMS MENTIONED'
   (PROB1 TO PROB3 (1,9))/VARIABLES=EDUC (1,3)
   /FREQUENCIES=EDUC PROBS
   /FORMAT=CONDENSE.
```

- The FORMAT subcommand specifies condensed format, which eliminates category labels and displays the categories in three parallel sets of columns, each set containing one or more rows of categories (rather than displaying one set of columns aligned vertically down the page).

N OF CASES

```
N OF CASES n
```

Example:
```
N OF CASES 100.
```

Overview

N OF CASES (alias N) limits the number of cases in the working data file to the first *n* cases.

Basic Specification

The basic specification is N OF CASES followed by at least one space and a positive integer. Cases in the working data file are limited to the specified number.

Syntax Rules

- To limit the number of cases for the next procedure only, use the TEMPORARY command before N OF CASES (see TEMPORARY).
- In some versions of SPSS, N OF CASES can be specified only after a working data file is defined.

Operations

- Unlike most transformations, N OF CASES takes effect as soon as it is encountered in the command sequence. Thus, special attention should be paid to its position among commands. See "Command Order" on p. 17 for more information.
- N OF CASES limits the number of cases analyzed by all subsequent procedures in the session. The working data file will have no more than *n* cases after the first data pass following the N OF CASES command. Any subsequent N OF CASES command specifying a greater number of cases will be ignored.
- If N OF CASES specifies more cases than can actually be built, SPSS builds as many cases as possible.
- If N OF CASES is used with SAMPLE or SELECT IF, SPSS reads as many records as required to build the specified *n* cases. It makes no difference whether the N OF CASES precedes or follows the SAMPLE or SELECT IF command.

Example

```
GET FILE=CITY.
N 100.
```

- N OF CASES limits the number of cases on the working data file to the first 100 cases. Cases are limited for all subsequent analyses.

Example

```
DATA LIST FILE=PRSNNL / NAME 1-20 (A) AGE 22-23 SALARY 25-30.
N 25.
SELECT IF (SALARY GT 20000).
LIST.
```

- DATA LIST defines variables from file *PRSNNL*.
- N OF CASES limits the working data file to 25 cases after cases have been selected by SELECT IF.
- SELECT IF selects only cases in which *SALARY* is greater than $20,000.
- LIST produces a listing of the cases in the working data file. If the original working data file has fewer than 25 cases in which salary is greater than 20,000, fewer than 25 cases will be listed.

Example

```
DATA LIST FILE=PRSNNL / NAME 1-20(A) AGE 22-23
                       SALARY 25-30 DEPT 32.
LIST.
TEMPORARY.
N 25.
FREQUENCIES VAR=SALARY.
N 50.
FREQUENCIES VAR=AGE.
REPORT FORMAT=AUTO /VARS=NAME AGE SALARY /BREAK=DEPT
  /SUMMARY=MEAN.
```

- The first N OF CASES command is temporary. Only 25 cases are used in the first FREQUENCIES procedure.
- The second N OF CASES command is permanent. The second frequency table and the report are based on 50 cases from file *PRSNNL*. The working data file now contains 50 cases (assuming the original working file had at least that many).

NEW FILE

```
NEW FILE
```

Overview

The NEW FILE command clears the working data file. It is used when you want to build a new working data file by generating data within an input program (see INPUT PROGRAM—END INPUT PROGRAM).

Basic Specification

NEW FILE is always specified by itself. No other keyword is required or allowed.

Operations

- NEW FILE clears the working data file. The command takes effect as soon as it is encountered. You *must* build a new working data file after this command to continue your SPSS session. Transformations or procedures cannot be used before a working data file is created.
- When you build a working data file with GET, DATA LIST, or other file definition commands (such as ADD FILES or MATCH FILES), the working data file is automatically replaced. It is not necessary to specify NEW FILE.

NONPAR CORR

```
NONPAR CORR [VARIABLES=] varlist [WITH varlist] [/varlist...]

 [/PRINT={TWOTAIL**}  {SIG**}  {SPEARMAN**}]
         {ONETAIL  }  {NOSIG }  {KENDALL   }
                               {BOTH      }

 [/SAMPLE]

 [/MISSING=[{PAIRWISE**} [INCLUDE]]
            {LISTWISE  }

 [/FORMAT={MATRIX**}]
          {SERIAL  }

 [/MATRIX=OUT({*   })]
              {file}
```

**Default if the subcommand is omitted.

Example:
```
NONPAR CORR VARIABLES=PRESTIGE SPPRES PAPRES16 DEGREE PADEG MADEG.
```

Overview

NONPAR CORR computes two rank-order correlation coefficients, Spearman's rho and Kendall's tau-b, with their significance levels. You can obtain either or both coefficients. NONPAR CORR automatically computes the ranks and stores the cases in memory. Therefore, memory requirements are directly proportional to the number of cases being analyzed.

Options

Coefficients and Significance Levels. By default, NONPAR CORR computes Spearman coefficients. Below each coefficient it displays both the number of cases and the two-tailed significance level. Optionally, you can request a one-tailed test, suppress the number of cases and significance level for each coefficient, and compute Kendall's tau-b using the PRINT subcommand.

Random Sampling. You can request a random sample of cases when there is not enough space to store all the cases using the SAMPLE subcommand.

Format. By default, NONPAR CORR displays correlations in matrix format. You can also display them in serial format using the FORMAT subcommand.

Matrix Output. You can write matrix materials to an SPSS data file using the MATRIX subcommand. The matrix materials include the number of cases used to compute each coefficient and the Spearman or Kendall coefficients for each variable. These materials can be read by other SPSS procedures.

Basic Specification

The basic specification is VARIABLES and a list of numeric variables. The actual keyword VARIABLES can be omitted. By default, Spearman correlation coefficients are calculated.

Subcommand Order

- VARIABLES must be specified first.
- The remaining subcommands can be used in any order.

Operations

- NONPAR CORR produces one or more matrices of correlation coefficients. For each coefficient, NONPAR CORR displays the number of cases used and the significance level.
- Depending on how the variable list is specified, NONPAR CORR displays either a lower-triangular or rectangular matrix (see the VARIABLES subcommand below).
- If all cases have a missing value for a given pair of variables, or if they all have the same value for a variable, the coefficient cannot be computed. If a correlation cannot be computed, NONPAR CORR displays a decimal point.
- If both Spearman and Kendall coefficients are requested and MATRIX is used to write matrix materials to an SPSS matrix data file, only Spearman's coefficient will be written with the matrix materials.

Limitations

- Maximum 25 variable lists.
- Maximum 100 variables total per NONPAR CORR command.

Example

```
NONPAR CORR VARIABLES=PRESTIGE SPPRES PAPRES16 DEGREE PADEG MADEG.
```

- NONPAR CORR produces a triangular matrix. The correlation of a variable with itself (the diagonal) and redundant coefficients are not displayed.
- By default, Spearman correlation coefficients are calculated. The number of cases upon which the correlations are based and the two-tailed significance level are displayed for each correlation.

VARIABLES Subcommand

VARIABLES specifies the variable list. The keyword VARIABLES is optional.

- All variables must be numeric.

- If keyword WITH is not used, NONPAR CORR displays the correlations of each variable with every other variable in the list in a lower-triangular matrix.
- To obtain a rectangular matrix, specify two variable lists separated by keyword WITH. NONPAR CORR displays a rectangular matrix of variables in the first list correlated with variables in the second list. Unless a variable is in both lists, there are no identity coefficients in the matrix.
- Keyword WITH cannot be used when the MATRIX subcommand is used.
- You can request more than one matrix. Use a slash to separate the specifications for each matrix.

Example

```
NONPAR CORR VARS=PRESTIGE SPPRES PAPRES16 WITH DEGREE PADEG MADEG.
```

- Nine correlations are calculated. The variables listed before WITH define the rows of the matrix, and those listed after WITH define the columns.

Example

```
NONPAR CORR VARIABLES=SPPRES PAPRES16 PRESTIGE
              /SATCITY WITH SATHOBBY SATFAM.
```

- NONPAR CORR produces two correlation matrices. The first matrix is triangular and contains three coefficients. The second matrix is rectangular and contains two coefficients.

PRINT Subcommand

By default, NONPAR CORR displays Spearman correlation coefficients. The number of cases and the significance level are displayed below each coefficient. The significance level is based on a two-tailed test. Use PRINT to change these defaults.

- The Spearman and Kendall coefficients are both based on ranks.

SPEARMAN *Spearman's rho.* Only Spearman coefficients are displayed. This is the default.

KENDALL *Kendall's tau-b.* Only Kendall coefficients are displayed.

BOTH *Kendall and Spearman coefficients.* Both coefficients are displayed. If MATRIX is used to write the correlation matrix to a matrix data file, only Spearman coefficients are written with the matrix materials.

SIG *Display the number of cases and significance level.* This is the default.

NOSIG *Suppress the number of cases and significance level.* A significance level of 0.05 or less is indicated by an asterisk (*) following the coefficient. Two asterisks (**) indicate a significance level of 0.01 or less. NOSIG cannot be specified if FORMAT=SERIAL. If both FORMAT=SERIAL and PRINT=NOSIG are specified, only FORMAT=SERIAL is in effect.

TWOTAIL *Two-tailed test of significance.* This test is appropriate when the direction of the relationship cannot be determined in advance, as is often the case in exploratory data analysis. This is the default.

ONETAIL *One-tailed test of significance.* This test is appropriate when the direction of the relationship between a pair of variables can be specified in advance of the analysis.

SAMPLE Subcommand

NONPAR CORR must store cases in memory to build matrices. SAMPLE selects a random sample of cases when computer resources are insufficient to store all the cases. To request a random sample, simply specify the subcommand. SAMPLE has no additional specifications.

MISSING Subcommand

MISSING controls missing-value treatments.

- PAIRWISE and LISTWISE are alternatives. You can specify INCLUDE with either PAIRWISE or LISTWISE.

PAIRWISE *Exclude missing values pairwise.* Cases with a missing value for one or both of a pair of variables for a specific correlation coefficient are excluded from the computation of that coefficient. This allows the maximum information available to be used in every calculation. This also results in a set of coefficients based on a varying number of cases. This is the default.

LISTWISE *Exclude missing values listwise.* Cases with a missing value for any variable named in a list are excluded from all analyses. Each variable list on a command is evaluated separately. Thus, a case missing for one matrix might be used in another matrix. This option decreases the amount of memory required and significantly decreases computational time.

INCLUDE *Include user-missing values.* User-missing values are treated as valid values.

FORMAT Subcommand

FORMAT controls the format of the correlation matrix. You can specify one of the two keywords:

MATRIX *Matrix format.* This is the default.

SERIAL *Serial string format.* Coefficients from the first row of the matrix are displayed first, followed by coefficients from the second row, and so on for all of the rows in the matrix. Each coefficient is identified with the name of the variables for which it was calculated. The number of cases and significance level are displayed below the correlation, just as they are in matrix format. When SERIAL is specified, PRINT=NOSIG is ignored.

MATRIX Subcommand

MATRIX writes matrix materials to a matrix data file. The matrix materials always include the number of cases used to compute each coefficient, and either the Spearman or the Kendall correlation coefficient for each variable, whichever is requested. See "Format of the Matrix Data File" below for a description of the file.

- You cannot write both Spearman's and Kendall's coefficients to the same matrix data file. To obtain both Spearman's and Kendall's coefficients in matrix format, specify separate NONPAR CORR commands for each coefficient and define different matrix data files for each command.
- If PRINT=BOTH is in effect, NONPAR CORR displays a matrix in the listing file for both coefficients but writes only the Spearman coefficients to the matrix data file.
- NONPAR CORR cannot write matrix materials for rectangular matrices (variable lists containing keyword WITH). If more than one variable list is specified, only the last variable list that does not use keyword WITH is written to the matrix data file.
- The specification on MATRIX is keyword OUT and the name of the matrix file in parentheses.
- If you want to use a correlation matrix written by NONPAR CORR in another procedure, change the *ROWTYPE_* value RHO or TAUB to CORR using the RECODE command.
- Any documents contained in the working data file are not transferred to the matrix file.

OUT (filename)   *Write a matrix data file.* Specify either a file or an asterisk, enclosed in parentheses. If you specify a file, the file is stored on disk and can be retrieved at any time. If you specify an asterisk (*), the matrix data file replaces the working file but is not stored on disk unless you use SAVE or XSAVE.

Format of the Matrix Data File

- The matrix data file has two special variables created by SPSS: *ROWTYPE_* and *VARNAME_*.
- Variable *ROWTYPE_* is a short string variable with values N and RHO for Spearman's correlation coefficient. If you specify Kendall's coefficient, the values are N and TAUB.
- *VARNAME_* is a short string variable whose values are the names of the variables used to form the correlation matrix. When *ROWTYPE_* is RHO (or TAUB), *VARNAME_* gives the variable associated with that row of the correlation matrix.
- The remaining variables in the file are the variables used to form the correlation matrix.

Split Files

- When split-file processing is in effect, the first variables in the matrix data file are the split variables, followed by *ROWTYPE_*, *VARNAME_*, and the variables used to form the correlation matrix.
- A full set of matrix materials is written for each split-file group defined by the split variables.

- A split variable cannot have the same name as any other variable written to the matrix data file.
- If split-file processing is in effect when a matrix is written, the same split file must be in effect when that matrix is read by a procedure.

Missing Values

- With PAIRWISE treatment of missing values (the default), the matrix of N's used to compute each coefficient is included with the matrix materials.
- With LISTWISE or INCLUDE treatments, a single N used to calculate all coefficients is included with the matrix materials.

Example

```
GET FILE GSS80 /KEEP PRESTIGE SPPRES PAPRES16 DEGREE PADEG MADEG.
NONPAR CORR VARIABLES=PRESTIGE TO MADEG
   /MATRIX OUT(NPMAT).
```

- NONPAR CORR reads data from file *GSS80* and writes one set of correlation matrix materials to the file *NPMAT*.
- The working data file is still *GSS80*. Subsequent commands are executed on file *GSS80*.

Example

```
GET FILE GSS80 /KEEP PRESTIGE SPPRES PAPRES16 DEGREE PADEG MADEG.
NONPAR CORR VARIABLES=PRESTIGE TO MADEG
   /MATRIX OUT(*).
LIST.
DISPLAY DICTIONARY.
```

- NONPAR CORR writes the same matrix as in the example above. However, the matrix data file replaces the working file. The LIST and DISPLAY commands are executed on the matrix file, not on the original working file *GSS80*.

Example

```
NONPAR CORR VARIABLES=PRESTIGE SPPRES PAPRES16 DEGREE PADEG MADEG
      /PRESTIGE TO DEGREE /PRESTIGE WITH DEGREE
   /MATRIX OUT(NPMAT).
```

- Only the matrix for *PRESTIGE* to *DEGREE* is written to the matrix data file because it is the last variable list that does not use keyword WITH.

NPAR TESTS

```
NPAR TESTS [CHISQUARE=varlist[(lo,hi)]/] [/EXPECTED={EQUAL    }]
                                                    {f1,f2,...fn}

          [/K-S({UNIFORM [min,max] })=varlist]
                {NORMAL [mean,stddev]}
                {POISSON [mean]     }

          [/RUNS({MEAN  })=varlist]
                 {MEDIAN}
                 {MODE  }
                 {value }

          [/BINOMIAL[({.5})]=varlist[({value1,value2})]]
                     { p}             {value         }

          [/MCNEMAR=varlist [WITH varlist [(PAIRED)]]]

          [/SIGN=varlist [WITH varlist [(PAIRED)]]]

          [/WILCOXON=varlist [WITH varlist [(PAIRED)]]]

          [/COCHRAN=varlist]

          [/FRIEDMAN=varlist]

          [/KENDALL=varlist]

          [/M-W=varlist BY var (value1,value2)]

          [/K-S=varlist BY var (value1,value2)]

          [/W-W=varlist BY var (value1,value2)]

          [/MOSES[(n)]=varlist BY var (value1,value2)]

          [/K-W=varlist BY var (value1,value2)]

          [/MEDIAN[(value)]=varlist BY var (value1,value2)]

          [/MISSING=[{ANALYSIS**}]   [INCLUDE]]
                    {LISTWISE  }

          [/SAMPLE]

          [/STATISTICS=[DESCRIPTIVES]   [QUARTILES] [ALL]]
```

**Default if the subcommand is omitted.

Example:

```
NPAR TESTS K-S(UNIFORM)=V1 /K-S(NORMAL,0,1)=V2.
```

Overview

NPAR TESTS is a collection of nonparametric tests. These tests make minimal assumptions about the underlying distribution of the data and are described in Siegel (1956). In addition to the nonparametric tests available in NPAR TESTS, the k-sample chi-square and Fisher's exact test are available in procedure CROSSTABS.

The tests available in NPAR TESTS can be grouped into three broad categories based on how the data are organized: one-sample tests, related-samples tests, and independent-samples tests. A one-sample test analyzes one variable. A test for related samples compares two or more variables for the same set of cases. An independent-samples test analyzes one variable grouped by categories of another variable.

The one-sample tests available in procedure NPAR TESTS are
- BINOMIAL.
- CHISQUARE.
- K-S (Kolmogorov-Smirnov).
- RUNS.

Tests for two related samples are
- MCNEMAR.
- SIGN.
- WILCOXON.

Tests for k related samples are
- COCHRAN.
- FRIEDMAN.
- KENDALL.

Tests for two independent samples are
- M-W (Mann-Whitney).
- K-S (Kolmogorov-Smirnov).
- W-W (Wald-Wolfowitz).
- MOSES.

Tests for k independent samples are
- K-W (Kruskal-Wallis).
- MEDIAN.

Tests are described below in alphabetical order.

Options

Statistical Display. In addition to the tests, you can request univariate statistics, quartiles, and counts for all variables specified on the command. You can also control the pairing of variables in tests for two related samples.

Random Sampling. NPAR TESTS must store cases in memory when computing tests that use ranks. You can use random sampling when there is not enough space to store all cases.

Basic Specification

The basic specification is a single test subcommand and a list of variables to be tested. Some tests require additional specifications. CHISQUARE has an optional subcommand.

Subcommand Order

Subcommands can be used in any order.

Syntax Rules

- The STATISTICS, SAMPLE, and MISSING subcommands are optional. Each can be specified only once per NPAR TESTS command.
- You can request any or all tests, and you can specify a test subcommand more than once on a single NPAR TESTS command.
- Keyword ALL in any variable list refers to all user-defined variables in the working data file.
- Keyword WITH controls pairing of variables in two-related-samples tests.
- Keyword BY introduces the grouping variable in two- and k-independent-samples tests.
- Keyword PAIRED can be used with keyword WITH on the MCNEMAR, SIGN, and WILCOXON subcommands to obtain sequential pairing of variables for two related samples.

Operations

- The output always uses narrow format.
- If a string variable is specified on any subcommand, NPAR TESTS will stop executing.
- When ALL is used, requests for tests of variables with themselves are ignored and a warning is displayed.

Limitations

- Maximum 100 subcommands.
- Maximum 500 variables total per NPAR TESTS command.
- Maximum 200 values for subcommand CHISQUARE.

BINOMIAL Subcommand

```
NPAR TESTS BINOMIAL [({.5})]=varlist[({value,value})]
                      {p }                {value      }
```

BINOMIAL tests whether the observed distribution of a dichotomous variable is the same as that expected from a specified binomial distribution. By default, each variable named is assumed to have only two values, and the distribution of each variable named is compared to a binomial distribution with p (the proportion of cases expected in the first category) equal to 0.5. The default output includes the number of valid cases in each group, the test proportion, and the two-tailed probability of the observed proportion.

Syntax

- The minimum specification is a list of variables to be tested.
- To change the default 0.5 test proportion, specify a value in parentheses immediately after keyword BINOMIAL.
- A single value in parentheses following the variable list is used as a cutting point. Cases with values equal to or less than the cutting point form the first category; the remaining cases form the second.
- If two values appear in parentheses after the variable list, cases with values equal to the first value form the first category, and cases with values equal to the second value form the second category.
- If no values are specified, the variables must be dichotomous.

Operations

- The proportion observed in the first category is compared to the test proportion. The probability of the observed proportion occurring given the test proportion and a binomial distribution is then computed. A test statistic is calculated for each variable specified.
- If the test proportion is the default (0.5), a two-tailed probability is displayed. For any other test proportion, a one-tailed probability is displayed. The direction of the one-tailed test depends on the observed proportion in the first category. If the observed proportion is more than the test proportion, the significance of observing that many or more in the first category is reported. If the observed proportion is less than the test proportion, the significance of observing that many or fewer in the first category is reported. In other words, the test is always done in the observed direction.

Example

```
NPAR TESTS BINOMIAL(.667)=V1(0,1).
```

- If more than 0.667 of the cases have value 0 for *V1*, BINOMIAL gives the probability of observing that many or more values of 0 in a binomial distribution with probability 0.667. If fewer than 0.667 of the cases are 0, the test will be of observing that many or fewer.

CHISQUARE Subcommand

```
NPAR TESTS CHISQUARE=varlist [(lo,hi)] [/EXPECTED={EQUAL**   }]
                                                 {f1,f2,... fn}
```

The CHISQUARE (alias CHI-SQUARE) one-sample test computes a chi-square statistic based on the differences between the observed and expected frequencies of categories of a variable. By default, equal frequencies are expected in each category. The output includes the frequency distribution, expected frequencies, residuals, chi-square, degrees of freedom, and probability.

Syntax

- The minimum specification is a list of variables to be tested. Optionally, you can specify a value range in parentheses following the variable list. You can also specify expected proportions with the EXPECTED subcommand.
- If you use the EXPECTED subcommand to specify unequal expected frequencies, you must specify a value greater than 0 for each observed category of the variable. The expected frequencies are specified in ascending order of category value. You can use the notation $n*f$ to indicate that frequency f is expected for n consecutive categories.
- Specifying keyword EQUAL on the EXPECTED subcommand has the same effect as omitting the EXPECTED subcommand.
- EXPECTED applies to all variables specified on the CHISQUARE subcommand. Use multiple CHISQUARE and EXPECTED subcommands to specify different expected proportions for variables.

Operations

- If no range is specified for the variables to be tested, each distinct value in the data defines a category.
- If a range is specified, integer-valued categories are established for each value within the range. Noninteger values are truncated before classification. Cases with values outside the specified range are excluded.
- Expected values are interpreted as proportions, not absolute values. Values are summed, and each value is divided by the total to calculate the proportion of cases expected in the corresponding category.
- A test statistic is calculated for each variable specified.

Example

```
NPAR TESTS CHISQUARE=V1 (1,5) /EXPECTED= 12, 3*16, 18.
```

- This example requests the chi-square test for values 1 through 5 of variable *V1*.
- The observed frequencies for variable *V1* are compared with the hypothetical distribution of 12/78 occurrences of value 1; 16/78 occurrences each of values 2, 3, and 4; and 18/78 occurrences of value 5.

COCHRAN Subcommand

```
NPAR TESTS COCHRAN=varlist
```

COCHRAN calculates Cochran's Q, which tests whether the distribution of values is the same for k related dichotomous variables. The output shows the frequency distribution for each variable, degrees of freedom, and probability.

Syntax

- The minimum specification is a list of two variables.
- The variables must be dichotomous and must be coded with the same two values.

Operations

- A $k \times 2$ contingency table (variables by categories) is constructed for dichotomous variables and the proportions for each variable are computed. A single test comparing all variables is calculated.
- Cochran's Q statistic has approximately a chi-square distribution.

Example

```
NPAR TESTS COCHRAN=RV1 TO RV3.
```

- This example tests whether the distribution of values 0 and 1 for *RV1, RV2,* and *RV3* is the same.

FRIEDMAN Subcommand

```
NPAR TESTS FRIEDMAN=varlist
```

FRIEDMAN tests whether k related samples have been drawn from the same population. The output shows the mean rank for each variable, number of valid cases, chi-square, degrees of freedom, and probability.

Syntax

- The minimum specification is a list of two variables.
- Variables should be at least at the ordinal level of measurement.

Operations

- The values of k variables are ranked from 1 to k for each case and the mean rank is calculated for each variable over all cases.
- The test statistic has approximately a chi-square distribution. A single test statistic comparing all variables is calculated.

Example

```
NPAR TESTS FRIEDMAN=V1 V2 V3
  /STATISTICS=DESCRIPTIVES.
```

- This example tests variables *V1, V2,* and *V3,* and requests univariate statistics for all three.

K-S Subcommand (One-Sample)

```
NPAR TESTS K-S({NORMAL [mean,stddev]})=varlist
              {POISSON [mean]         }
              {UNIFORM [min,max]      }
```

The K-S (alias KOLMOGOROV-SMIRNOV) one-sample test compares the cumulative distribution function for a variable with a uniform, normal, or Poisson distribution, and it tests whether the distributions are homogeneous. The parameters of the test distribution can be specified; the defaults are the observed parameters. The output shows the number of valid cases, parameters of the test distribution, most-extreme absolute, positive, and negative differences, Kolmogorov-Smirnov Z, and two-tailed probability for each variable.

Syntax

The minimum specification is a distribution keyword and a list of variables. The distribution keywords are NORMAL, POISSON, and UNIFORM.

- The distribution keyword and its optional parameters must be enclosed within parentheses.
- The distribution keyword must be separated from its parameters by blanks or commas.

NORMAL [mean, stdev] *Normal distribution.* The default parameters are the observed mean and standard deviation.

POISSON [mean] *Poisson distribution.* The default parameter is the observed mean.

UNIFORM [min,max] *Uniform distribution.* The default parameters are the observed minimum and maximum values.

Operations

- The Kolmogorov-Smirnov Z is computed from the largest difference in absolute value between the observed and test distribution functions.
- The K-S probability levels assume that the test distribution is specified entirely in advance. The distribution of the test statistic and resulting probabilities are different when the parameters of the test distribution are estimated from the sample. No correction is made.
- For a mean of 100,000 or larger, a normal approximation to the Poisson distribution is used.
- A test statistic is calculated for each variable specified.

Example

```
NPAR TESTS K-S(UNIFORM)=V1 /K-S(NORMAL,0,1)=V2.
```

- The first K-S subcommand compares the distribution of *V1* with a uniform distribution that has the same range as *V1*.

- The second K-S subcommand compares the distribution of *V2* with a normal distribution that has a mean of 0 and a standard deviation of 1.

K-S Subcommand (Two-Sample)

```
NPAR TESTS K-S=varlist BY variable(value1,value2)
```

K-S (alias KOLMOGOROV-SMIRNOV) tests whether the distribution of a variable is the same in two independent samples defined by a grouping variable. The test is sensitive to any difference in median, dispersion, skewness, and so forth, between the two distributions. The output shows the valid number of cases in each group, the largest absolute, positive, and negative differences between the two groups, the Kolmogorov-Smirnov Z, and the two-tailed probability for each variable.

Syntax

- The minimum specification is a test variable, the keyword BY, a grouping variable, and a pair of values in parentheses.
- The test variable should be at least at the ordinal level of measurement.
- Cases with the first value form one group and cases with the second value form the other. The order in which values are specified determines which difference is the largest positive and which is the largest negative.

Operations

- The observed cumulative distributions for both groups are computed, as are the maximum positive, negative, and absolute differences. A test statistic is calculated for each variable named before BY.
- Cases with values other than those specified for the grouping variable are excluded.

Example

```
NPAR TESTS K-S=V1 V2 BY V3(0,1).
```

- This example specifies two tests. The first compares the distribution of *V1* for cases with value 0 for *V3* with the distribution of *V1* for cases with value 1 for *V3*.
- A parallel test is calculated for *V2*.

K-W Subcommand

```
NPAR TESTS K-W=varlist BY variable(value1,value2)
```

K-W (alias KRUSKAL-WALLIS) tests whether k independent samples defined by a grouping variable are from the same population. The output shows the number of valid cases, mean rank of the variable in each group, chi-square, probability, and chi-square and probability after correcting for ties.

Syntax

- The minimum specification is a test variable, the keyword BY, a grouping variable, and a pair of values in parentheses.
- Every value in the range defined by the pair of values for the grouping variable forms a group.

Operations

- Cases from the k groups are ranked in a single series, and the rank sum for each group is computed. A test statistic is calculated for each variable specified before BY.
- Kruskal-Wallis H has approximately a chi-square distribution.
- Cases with values other than those in the range specified for the grouping variable are excluded.

Example

```
NPAR TESTS K-W=V1 BY V2(0,4).
```

- This example tests *V1* for groups defined by values 0 through 4 of *V2*.

KENDALL Subcommand

```
NPAR TESTS KENDALL=varlist
```

KENDALL tests whether k related samples are from the same population. W is a measure of agreement among judges or raters where each case is one judge's rating of several items (variables). The output includes the mean rank for each variable, valid number of cases, W, chi-square, degrees of freedom, and probability.

Syntax

The minimum specification is a list of two variables.

Operations

- The values of the k variables are ranked from 1 to k for each case and the mean rank is calculated for each variable over all cases. Kendall's W and a corresponding chi-square statistic are calculated, correcting for ties. A single test statistic is calculated for all variables.
- W ranges between 0 (no agreement) and 1 (complete agreement).

Example

```
DATA LIST /V1 TO V5 1-10.
BEGIN DATA
2 5 4 5 1
3 3 4 5 3
3 4 4 6 2
2 4 3 6 2
END DATA.
NPAR TESTS KENDALL=ALL.
```

- This example tests four judges (cases) on five items (variables *V1* through *V5*).

M-W Subcommand

```
NPAR TESTS M-W=varlist BY variable(value1,value2)
```

M-W (alias MANN-WHITNEY) tests whether two independent samples defined by a grouping variable are from the same population. The test statistic uses the rank of each case to test whether the groups are drawn from the same population. The output shows the mean rank of the variable within each group, valid number of cases for each group, Mann-Whitney U, Wilcoxon W (the rank sum of the smaller group), two-tailed probability of U (or W), Z statistic, and two-tailed probability of Z corrected for ties.

Syntax

- The minimum specification is a test variable, the keyword BY, a grouping variable, and a pair of values in parentheses.
- Cases with the first value form one group and cases with the second value form the other. The order in which the values are specified is unimportant.

Operations

- Cases are ranked in order of increasing size, and test statistic U (the number of times a score from group 1 precedes a score from group 2) is computed.
- An exact significance level is computed if there are 40 or fewer cases. For more than 40 cases, U is transformed into a normally distributed Z statistic and a normal approximation p value is computed.
- A test statistic is calculated for each variable named before BY.
- Cases with values other than those specified for the grouping variable are excluded.

Example

```
NPAR TESTS M-W=V1 BY V2(1,2).
```

- This example tests *V1* based on the two groups defined by values 1 and 2 of *V2*.

MCNEMAR Subcommand

```
NPAR TESTS MCNEMAR=varlist [WITH varlist [(PAIRED)]]
```

MCNEMAR tests whether combinations of values between two dichotomous variables are equally likely. The output shows the 2 × 2 contingency table, number of valid cases, and two-tailed probability for each pair of variables.

Syntax

- The minimum specification is a list of two variables. Variables must be dichotomous and must have the same two values.
- If keyword WITH is not specified, each variable is paired with every other variable in the list.
- If WITH is specified, each variable before WITH is paired with each variable after WITH. If PAIRED is also specified, the first variable before WITH is paired with the first variable after WITH, the second variable before WITH with the second variable after WITH, and so on. PAIRED cannot be specified without WITH.
- With PAIRED, the number of variables specified before and after WITH must be the same. PAIRED must be specified in parentheses after the second variable list.

Operations

- A 2 × 2 table is constructed for each pair of dichotomous variables and a chi-square statistic is computed for cases with different values for the two variables. Only combinations for which the values for the two variables are different are considered.
- If fewer than 25 cases change values from the first variable to the second variable, the binomial distribution is used to compute the probability.

Example

```
NPAR TESTS MCNEMAR=V1 V2 V3.
```

- This example performs the MCNEMAR test on variable pairs *V1* and *V2*, *V1* and *V3*, and *V2* and *V3*.

MEDIAN Subcommand

```
NPAR TESTS MEDIAN [(value)]=varlist BY variable(value1,value2)
```

MEDIAN determines if *k* independent samples are drawn from populations with the same median. The independent samples are defined by a grouping variable. For each variable, the output shows a table of the number of cases greater than and less than or equal to the median in each category of the grouping variable, the median, chi-square, degrees of freedom, and probability.

Syntax

- The minimum specification is a single test variable, the keyword BY, a grouping variable, and two values in parentheses.
- If the first grouping value is less than the second, every value in the range defined by the pair of values forms a group and a k-sample test is performed.
- If the first value is greater than the second, two groups are formed using the two values and a two-sample test is performed.
- By default, the median is calculated from all cases included in the test. To override the default, specify a median value in parentheses following the MEDIAN subcommand keyword.

Operations

- A $2 \times k$ contingency table is constructed with counts of the number of cases greater than the median and less than or equal to the median for the k groups. A test statistic is calculated for each variable specified before BY.
- For more than 30 cases, a chi-square statistic is computed. For 30 or fewer cases, Fisher's exact procedure (two-tailed) is used instead of chi-square.
- For a two-sample test, cases with values other than the two specified are excluded.

Example

```
NPAR TESTS MEDIAN(8.4)=V1 BY V2(1,2) /MEDIAN=V1 BY V2(1,2)
  /MEDIAN=V1 BY V3(1,4) /MEDIAN=V1 BY V3(4,1).
```

- The first two MEDIAN subcommands test variable *V1* grouped by values 1 and 2 of variable *V2*. The first test specifies a median of 8.4 and the second uses the observed median.
- The third MEDIAN subcommand requests a four-samples test, dividing the sample into four groups based on values 1, 2, 3, and 4 of variable *V3*.
- The last MEDIAN subcommand requests a two-samples test, grouping cases based on values 1 and 4 of *V3* and ignoring all other cases.

MOSES Subcommand

```
NPAR TESTS MOSES[(n)]=varlist BY variable(value1,value2)
```

The MOSES test of extreme reactions tests whether the range of an ordinal variable is the same in a control group and a comparison group. The control and comparison groups are defined by a grouping variable. For each variable tested, the output includes the number of cases in each group, number of outliers removed, span of the control group before and after outliers are removed, and one-tailed probability of the span with and without outliers.

Syntax

- The minimum specification is a test variable, the keyword BY, a grouping variable, and two values in parentheses.
- The test variable must be at least at the ordinal level of measurement.
- The first value of the grouping variable defines the control group and the second value defines the comparison group.
- By default, 5% of the cases are trimmed from each end of the range of the control group to remove outliers. You can override the default by specifying a value in parentheses following the MOSES subcommand keyword. This value represents an actual number of cases, not a percentage.

Operations

- Values from the groups are arranged in a single ascending sequence. The span of the control group is computed as the number of cases in the sequence containing the lowest and highest control value.
- No adjustments are made for tied cases.
- Cases with values other than those specified for the grouping variable are excluded.
- A test statistic is calculated for each variable named before BY.

Example

```
NPAR TESTS MOSES=V1 BY V3(0,1) /MOSES=V1 BY V3(1,0).
```

- The first MOSES subcommand tests *V1* using value 0 of *V3* to define the control group and value 1 for the comparison group. The second MOSES subcommand reverses the comparison and control groups.

RUNS Subcommand

```
NPAR TESTS RUNS({MEAN  })=varlist
               {MEDIAN}
               {MODE  }
               {value }
```

RUNS tests whether the sequence of values of a dichotomized variable is random. The output includes the test value (cut point used to dichotomize the variable tested), number of runs, number of cases below the cut point, number of cases greater than or equal to the cut point, and test statistic *Z* with its two-tailed probability.

Syntax

- The minimum specification is a cut point in parentheses followed by a test variable.

- The cut point can be specified by an exact value or one of the keywords MEAN, MEDIAN, or MODE.

Operations

- All variables tested are treated as dichotomous: cases with values less than the cut point form one category, and cases with values greater than or equal to the cut point form the other category.
- A test statistic is calculated for each variable specified.

Example

```
NPAR TESTS RUNS(MEDIAN)=V2 /RUNS(24.5)=V2 /RUNS(1)=V3.
```

- This example performs three runs tests. The first tests variable *V2* using the median as the cut point. The second also tests *V2*, this time using 24.5 as the cut point. The third tests variable *V3* with value 1 specified as the cut point.

SIGN Subcommand

```
NPAR TESTS SIGN=varlist [WITH varlist [(PAIRED)] ]
```

SIGN tests whether the distribution of two paired variables in a two-related-samples test is the same. The output includes the number of positive differences, number of negative differences, number of ties, and two-tailed binomial probability.

Syntax

- The minimum specification is a list of two variables.
- Variables should be at least at the ordinal level of measurement.
- If keyword WITH is not specified, each variable in the list is paired with every other variable in the list.
- If keyword WITH is specified, each variable before WITH is paired with each variable after WITH. If PAIRED is also specified, the first variable before WITH is paired with the first variable after WITH, the second variable before WITH with the second variable after WITH, and so on. PAIRED cannot be specified without WITH.
- With PAIRED, the number of variables specified before and after WITH must be the same. PAIRED must be specified in parentheses after the second variable list.

Operations

- The positive and negative differences between the pair of variables are counted. Ties are ignored.

- The probability is taken from the binomial distribution if 25 or fewer differences are observed. Otherwise, the probability comes from the Z distribution.
- Under the null hypothesis for large sample sizes, Z is approximately normally distributed with a mean of 0 and a variance of 1.

Example

```
NPAR TESTS SIGN=N1,M1 WITH N2,M2 (PAIRED).
```

- *N1* is tested with *N2*, and *M1* is tested with *M2*.

W-W Subcommand

```
NPAR TESTS W-W=varlist BY variable(value1,value2)
```

W-W (alias WALD-WOLFOWITZ) tests whether the distribution of a variable is the same in two independent samples. A runs test is performed with group membership as the criterion. The output includes the number of valid cases in each group, number of runs, Z, and one-tailed probability of Z. If ties are present, the minimum and maximum number of ties possible, their Z statistics, and one-tailed probabilities are displayed.

Syntax

- The minimum specification is a single test variable, the keyword BY, a grouping variable, and two values in parentheses.
- Cases with the first value form one group and cases with the second value form the other. The order in which values are specified is unimportant.

Operations

- Cases are combined from both groups and ranked from lowest to highest, and a runs test is performed using group membership as the criterion. For ties involving cases from both groups, both the minimum and maximum number of runs possible are calculated. Test statistics are calculated for each variable specified before BY.
- For a sample size of 30 or less, the exact one-tailed probability is calculated. For a sample size greater than 30, the normal approximation is used.
- Cases with values other than those specified for the grouping variable are excluded.

Example

```
NPAR TESTS W-W=V1 BY V3(0,1).
```

- This example ranks cases from lowest to highest based on their values for *V1* and a runs test is performed. Cases with value 0 for *V3* form one group and cases with value 1 form the other.

WILCOXON Subcommand

```
NPAR TESTS WILCOXON=varlist [WITH varlist [(PAIRED)] ]
```

WILCOXON tests whether the distribution of two paired variables in two related samples is the same. This test takes into account the magnitude of the differences between two paired variables. The output includes the number of positive and negative differences and their respective means, number of ties, valid number of cases, Z, and probability of Z.

Syntax

- The minimum specification is a list of two variables.
- If keyword WITH is not specified, each variable is paired with every other variable in the list.
- If keyword WITH is specified, each variable before WITH is paired with each variable after WITH. If PAIRED is also specified, the first variable before WITH is paired with the first variable after WITH, the second variable before WITH with the second variable after WITH, and so on. PAIRED cannot be specified without WITH.
- With PAIRED, the number of variables specified before and after WITH must be the same. PAIRED must be specified in parentheses after the second variable list.

Operations

- The differences between the pair of variables are counted, the absolute differences ranked, the positive and negative ranks summed, and the test statistic Z computed from the positive and negative rank sums.
- Under the null hypothesis for large sample sizes, Z is approximately normally distributed with a mean of 0 and a variance of 1.

Example

```
NPAR TESTS WILCOXON=A B WITH C D (PAIRED).
```

- This example pairs *A* with *C* and *B* with *D*. If PAIRED were not specified, it would also pair *A* with *D* and *B* with *C*.

STATISTICS Subcommand

STATISTICS requests summary statistics for variables named on the NPAR TESTS command.

- If STATISTICS is specified without keywords, univariate statistics (keyword DESCRIPTIVES) are displayed.

DESCRIPTIVES *Univariate statistics.* The displayed statistics include the mean, maximum, minimum, standard deviation, and number of valid cases for each variable named on the command.

QUARTILES	*Quartiles and number of cases.* The 25th, 50th, and 75th percentiles are displayed for each variable named on the command.
ALL	*All statistics available on NPAR TESTS.*

MISSING Subcommand

MISSING controls the treatment of cases with missing values.

- ANALYSIS and LISTWISE are alternatives. However, each can be specified with INCLUDE.

ANALYSIS	*Exclude cases with missing values on a test-by-test basis.* Cases with missing values for a variable used for a specific test are omitted from that test. On subcommands that specify several tests, each test is evaluated separately. This is the default.
LISTWISE	*Exclude cases with missing values listwise.* Cases with missing values for any variable named on any subcommand are excluded from all analyses.
INCLUDE	*Include user-missing values.* User-missing values are treated as valid values.

SAMPLE Subcommand

NPAR TESTS must store cases in memory. SAMPLE allows you to select a random sample of cases when there is not enough space on your computer to store all the cases. SAMPLE has no additional specifications.

- Because sampling would invalidate a runs test, this option is ignored when the RUNS subcommand is used.

References

Siegel, S. 1956. *Nonparametric statistics for the behavioral sciences.* New York: McGraw-Hill.

NUMERIC

```
NUMERIC varlist[(format)] [/varlist...]
```

Example:
```
NUMERIC V1 V2 (F4.0) / V3 (F1.0).
```

Overview

NUMERIC declares new numeric variables that can be referred to in the transformation language before they are assigned values. Commands such as COMPUTE, IF, RECODE, and COUNT can be used to assign values to the new numeric variables.

Basic Specification

The basic specification is the name of the new variables. By default, variables are assigned a format of F8.2 (or the format specified on the SET command).

Syntax Rules

- A FORTRAN-like format can be specified in parentheses following a variable or variable list. Each format specified applies to all variables in the list. To specify different formats for different groups of variables, separate each format group with a slash.
- Keyword TO can be used to declare multiple numeric variables. The specified format applies to each variable named and implied by the TO construction.
- NUMERIC can be used within an input program to predetermine the order of numeric variables in the dictionary of the working data file. When used for this purpose, NUMERIC must precede DATA LIST in the input program.

Operations

- Unlike most transformations, NUMERIC takes effect as soon as it is encountered in the command sequence. Special attention should be paid to its position among commands. For more information, see "Command Order" on p. 17.
- The specified formats (or the defaults) are used as both print and write formats.
- Permanent or temporary variables are initialized to the system-missing value. Scratch variables are initialized to 0.
- Variables named on NUMERIC are added to the working file in the order in which they are specified. The order in which they are used in transformations does not affect their order in the working data file.

Example

```
NUMERIC V1 V2 (F4.0) / V3 (F1.0).
```

- NUMERIC declares variables *V1* and *V2* with format F4.0, and variable *V3* with format F1.0.

Example

```
NUMERIC V1 TO V6 (F3.1) / V7 V10 (F6.2).
```

- NUMERIC declares variables *V1*, *V2*, *V3*, *V4*, *V5*, and *V6* each with format F3.1, and variables *V7* and *V10*, each with format F6.2.

Example

```
NUMERIC SCALE85 IMPACT85 SCALE86 IMPACT86 SCALE87 IMPACT87
    SCALE88 IMPACT88.
```

- Variables *SCALE85* to *IMPACT88* are added to the working data file in the order specified on NUMERIC. The order in which they are used in transformations does not affect their order in the working data file.

Example

```
* Predetermine variable order.

INPUT PROGRAM.
STRING CITY (A24).
NUMERIC POP81 TO POP83 (F9)/ REV81 TO REV83(F10).
DATA LIST FILE=POPDATA RECORDS=3
  /1 POP81 22-30 REV81 31-40
  /2 POP82 22-30 REV82 31-40
  /3 POP83 22-30 REV83 31-40
  /4 CITY 1-24(A).
END INPUT PROGRAM.
```

- STRING and NUMERIC are specified within an input program to predetermine variable order in the working data file. Though data in the file are in a different order, the working file dictionary uses the order specified on STRING and NUMERIC. Thus, *CITY* is the first variable in the dictionary, followed by *POP81, POP82, POP83, REV81, REV82,* and *REV83.*

- Formats are specified for the variables on NUMERIC. Otherwise, SPSS uses the default numeric format (F8.2) from the NUMERIC command for the dictionary format, even though it uses the format on DATA LIST to read the data. In other words, the dictionary uses the first formats specified, even though DATA LIST may use different formats to read cases.

ONEWAY

```
ONEWAY    varlist BY varname(min,max)

[/POLYNOMIAL=n]    [/CONTRAST=coefficient list]  [/CONTRAST=... ]

[/RANGES={LSD        }([{0.05}])] [/RANGES=...]
         {DUNCAN     } {α   }
         {SNK        }
         {TUKEYB     }
         {TUKEY      }
         {MODLSD     }
         {SCHEFFE    }
         {range values}

[/HARMONIC={NONE**}]
           {PAIR**}
           {ALL   }

[/FORMAT={NOLABELS**}]
         {LABELS    }

[/STATISTICS=[NONE**] [DESCRIPTIVES] [EFFECTS] [HOMOGENEITY] [ALL]

[/MISSING=[{ANALYSIS**}]  [{EXCLUDE**}]]
           {LISTWISE  }    {INCLUDE  }

[/MATRIX =[IN({*   })] [OUT({*   })] [NONE]]
             {file}         {file}
```

**Default if the subcommand is omitted.

Example:
```
ONEWAY V1 BY V2(1,4).
```

Overview

ONEWAY produces a one-way analysis of variance for an interval-level dependent variable by one numeric independent variable that defines the groups for the analysis. Other SPSS procedures that perform analysis of variance are MEANS, ANOVA, and MANOVA (MANOVA is available in the SPSS Advanced Statistics option). Some tests not included in the other procedures are available as options in ONEWAY.

Options

Trends, Contrasts, and Ranges. You can partition the between-groups sums of squares into linear, quadratic, cubic, and higher-order trend components using the POLYNOMIAL subcommand. You can specify up to 10 contrasts to be tested with the t statistic on the CONTRAST subcommand. You can also specify seven different range tests for comparisons of all possible pairs of group means, or multiple comparisons using the RANGES subcommand.

Format. You can label groups with the value labels of the independent variable using the FORMAT subcommand.

Statistical Display. In addition to the default display, you can obtain means, standard deviations, and other descriptive statistics for each group using the STATISTICS subcommand. Fixed- and random-effects statistics as well as several tests for homogeneity of variance are also available. By specifying the HARMONIC subcommand, you can use the harmonic mean of all group sizes as the sample size for each group in range tests.

Matrix Input and Output. You can write means, standard deviations, and category frequencies to a matrix data file that can be used in subsequent ONEWAY procedures using the MATRIX subcommand. You can also read matrix materials consisting of means, category frequencies, pooled variance, and degrees of freedom for the pooled variance.

Basic Specification

The basic specification is a dependent variable, keyword BY, an independent variable, and, in parentheses, the minimum and maximum values of the independent variable. ONEWAY produces a table for each dependent variable by the independent variable. The table contains the between- and within-groups sums of squares, mean squares, and degrees of freedom. The F ratio and the probability of F are displayed.

Subcommand Order

- The variable list must be specified first.
- The remaining subcommands can be specified in any order.

Operations

- Noninteger values for the independent variable are truncated.
- Cases with values outside the range specified for the independent variable are omitted from the analysis.
- If a string variable is specified as an independent or dependent variable, ONEWAY is not executed.
- The output uses the width defined on SET.

Limitations

- Maximum 100 dependent variables and 1 independent variable.
- An unlimited number of categories for the independent variable. However, range tests are not performed if the number of nonempty categories exceeds 50. Contrast tests are not performed if the total of empty and nonempty categories exceeds 50.
- Maximum 1 POLYNOMIAL subcommand.
- Maximum 10 CONTRAST subcommands and 10 RANGES subcommands.

Example

```
ONEWAY V1 BY V2(1,4).
```

- ONEWAY names *V1* as the dependent variable and *V2* as the independent variable with a minimum value of 1 and a maximum value of 4.

Analysis List

The analysis list consists of a list of dependent variables, keyword BY, and an independent (grouping) variable with its minimum and maximum values.

- Only one analysis list is allowed, and it must be specified before any of the optional subcommands.
- All variables named must be numeric.
- The minimum and maximum values of the independent variable must be separated by a comma or a space and enclosed in parentheses. The values must be integers.

POLYNOMIAL Subcommand

POLYNOMIAL partitions the between-groups sums of squares into linear, cubic, quadratic, or higher-order trend components. The display is an expanded analysis-of-variance table that provides the degrees of freedom, sums of squares, mean square, F, and probability of F for each partition.

- The value specified on POLYNOMIAL indicates the highest-degree polynomial to be used.
- The polynomial value must be a positive integer less than or equal to 5 and less than the number of groups. If the polynomial specified is greater than the number of groups, the highest-degree polynomial possible is assumed.
- Only one POLYNOMIAL subcommand can be specified per ONEWAY command. If more than one is used, only the last one specified is in effect.
- ONEWAY computes the sums of squares for each order polynomial from weighted polynomial contrasts, using the category of the independent variable as the metric. These contrasts are orthogonal.
- With unbalanced designs and equal spacing between groups, ONEWAY also computes sums of squares using the unweighted polynomial contrasts. These contrasts are not orthogonal.
- The deviation sums of squares are always calculated from the weighted sums of squares (Speed, 1976).

Example

```
ONEWAY WELL BY EDUC6 (1,6)
  /POLYNOMIAL=2.
```

- ONEWAY requests an analysis of variance of *WELL* by *EDUC6* with second-order (quadratic) polynomial contrasts.

CONTRAST Subcommand

CONTRAST specifies *a priori* contrasts to be tested by the t statistic. The specification on CONTRAST is a vector of coefficients, where each coefficient corresponds to a category of the independent variable. The display for each contrast list is the value of the contrast and its standard error, the t statistic, and the degrees of freedom and two-tailed probability of t. Both pooled- and separate-variance estimates are displayed.

- A contrast coefficient must be specified or implied for every group in the range specified for the independent variable, even if the group is empty. Trailing coefficients of 0 do not need to be specified. If the number of contrast values is less than the number of groups, contrast values of 0 are assumed for the remaining groups.
- The contrast coefficients for a set should sum to 0. If they do not, a warning is issued. ONEWAY will still give an estimate of this contrast.
- Coefficients are assigned to empty and nonempty groups defined by ascending integer values of the independent variable.
- Only one set of contrast coefficients can be specified per CONTRAST subcommand. Additional contrasts on a single CONTRAST subcommand are ignored.
- The notation $n*c$ can be used to indicate that coefficient c is repeated n times.

Example

```
ONEWAY V1 BY V2(1,4)
  /CONTRAST = -1 -1  1  1
  /CONTRAST = -1  0  0  1
  /CONTRAST = -1  0 .5 .5.
```

- The first CONTRAST subcommand contrasts the combination of the first two groups with the combination of the last two groups.
- The second CONTRAST subcommand contrasts the first group with the last group.
- The third CONTRAST subcommand contrasts the first group with the combination of the third and fourth groups.

Example

```
ONEWAY V1 BY V2(1,4)
  /CONTRAST = -1  1  2*0
  /CONTRAST = -1  1  0  0
  /CONTRAST = -1  1.
```

- All three CONTRAST subcommands specify the same contrast coefficients for a four-group analysis. The first group is contrasted with the second group in all three cases.
- The first CONTRAST uses the $n*c$ notation and the last CONTRAST omits the trailing zero coefficients.

RANGES Subcommand

RANGES specifies either a range test or explicit range values for multiple comparisons between means. Seven range tests are available. The RANGES output always includes multiple comparisons between all groups. Nonempty group means are sorted in ascending order, with asterisks indicating significantly different groups. In addition, homogeneous subsets are calculated for balanced designs, and for all designs when HARMONIC=ALL. The means of the groups included within a subset are not significantly different.

- By default, the range tests use the sample sizes of the two groups being compared. This is equivalent to using the harmonic mean of the sample size of the two groups being compared. You can use the HARMONIC subcommand to change this default.
- The default alpha for all tests is 0.05. For some tests, you can specify a different alpha. Any level greater than 0 and less than or equal to 0.5 can be specified for the LSD, MODLSD, and SCHEFFE range tests. SNK, TUKEY, and TUKEYB use an alpha value of 0.05, regardless of what is specified. DUNCAN uses an alpha value of 0.05 if no alpha is specified or if the alpha specified is anything other than 0.01, 0.05, or 0.10.

LSD(α) *Least-significant difference.* You can specify an alpha between 0 and 0.5. The default is 0.05.

DUNCAN(α) *Multiple range test.* You can specify an alpha of 0.01, 0.05, and 0.10 only. The default is 0.05. DUNCAN uses 0.05 if no alpha is specified or the alpha specified is anything other than permitted values.

SNK *Student-Newman-Keuls.* Alpha is 0.05.

TUKEY B *Tukey's alternate procedure.* Alpha is 0.05. The alias BTUKEY can also be used.

TUKEY *Honestly significant difference.* Alpha is 0.05.

MODLSD(α) *Modified LSD.* You can specify an alpha between 0 and 0.5. The default is 0.05. Keyword LSDMOD is an alias for MODLSD.

SCHEFFE(α) *Scheffé's test.* You can specify an alpha between 0 and 0.5. The default is 0.05.

Alternatively, you can use any other type of range by specifying range values:

- The range values should be separated by commas or blanks.
- Up to k -1 range values can be specified in ascending order, where k is the number of groups and where the range value times the standard error of the combined subset is the critical value.
- If less than k -1 values are specified, the last value specified is used for the remaining range values.
- The notation $n*r$ can be used to indicate that the range r is repeated n times.
- To use a single critical value for all subsets, specify one range value.

Example

```
ONEWAY WELL BY EDUC6 (1,6)
  /RANGES=SNK
  /RANGES=SCHEFFE (.01).
```

- ONEWAY requests two different range tests. The first uses the Student-Newman-Keuls test and the second uses Scheffé's test with an alpha of 0.01.

Example

```
ONEWAY WELL BY EDUC (1,6)
  /RANGES=2.81, 3.34, 3.65, 3.88, 4.05.
```

- RANGES specifies five range values.

HARMONIC Subcommand

HARMONIC determines the sample size estimate to be used when the number of valid cases are not equal in all groups. Either only the sample sizes in the two groups being compared are used, or an average sample size of all groups is used.

NONE *Harmonic mean of the sizes of the two groups being compared for range tests.* Keyword PAIR can be used as an alias for NONE. This is the default.

ALL *Harmonic mean of all group sizes as sample sizes for range tests.* If the harmonic mean is used for unbalanced designs, ONEWAY determines homogeneous subsets for all range tests.

FORMAT Subcommand

By default, groups are identified in the output as *GRP1*, *GRP2*, and so forth. Use FORMAT to identify groups by their value labels.

LABELS *Use value labels for group labels.* The first eight characters from the value labels of the independent variable are used as group labels.

NOLABELS *Suppress value labels.* This is the default.

STATISTICS Subcommand

By default, ONEWAY displays the between- and within-groups sums of squares, mean squares, degrees of freedom, *F* ratio, and probability of *F*. It also calculates any statistics specified on the CONTRASTS and RANGES subcommands. Use STATISTICS to obtain additional statistics.

DESCRIPTIVES *Group descriptive statistics.* The statistics include the number of cases, mean, standard deviation, standard error, minimum, maximum, and 95% confidence interval for each dependent variable for each group.

EFFECTS *Fixed- and random-effects statistics.* The statistics include the standard deviation, standard error, and 95% confidence interval for the fixed-effects model, and the standard error, 95% confidence interval, and estimate of between-components variance for the random-effects model.

HOMOGENEITY *Homogeneity-of-variance tests.* The statistics include Cochran's *C*, the Bartlett-Box *F*, and Hartley's *F* max.

NONE *No optional statistics.* This is the default.

ALL	*All statistics available for ONEWAY.*

MISSING Subcommand

MISSING controls the treatment of missing values.

- Keywords ANALYSIS and LISTWISE are alternatives. Each can be used with INCLUDE or EXCLUDE. The default is ANALYSIS and EXCLUDE.
- A case outside the range specified for the grouping variable is not used.

ANALYSIS	*Exclude cases with missing values on a pair-by-pair basis.* A case with a missing value for the dependent or grouping variable for a given analysis is not used for that analysis. This is the default.
LISTWISE	*Exclude cases with missing values listwise.* Cases with missing values for any variable named are excluded from all analyses.
EXCLUDE	*Exclude cases with user-missing values.* User-missing values are treated as missing. This is the default.
INCLUDE	*Include user-missing values.* User-missing values are treated as valid values.

MATRIX Subcommand

MATRIX reads and writes SPSS matrix data files.

- Either IN or OUT and a matrix file in parentheses are required. When both IN and OUT are used on the same ONEWAY procedure, they can be specified on separate MATRIX subcommands or both on the same subcommand.
- If IN and OUT are specified on separate MATRIX subcommands, ONEWAY issues a warning indicating that, should a conflict arise in the specifications, only the last MATRIX subcommand will be executed.
- Use MATRIX=NONE to explicitly indicate that a matrix data file is not being written or read.

OUT (filename)	*Write a matrix data file.* Specify either a filename or an asterisk, enclosed in parentheses. If you specify a filename, the file is stored on disk and can be retrieved at any time. If you specify an asterisk (*), the matrix data file replaces the working file but is not stored on disk unless you use SAVE or XSAVE.
IN (filename)	*Read a matrix data file.* If the matrix data file is the working data file, specify an asterisk (*) in parentheses. If the matrix data file is another file, specify the filename in parentheses. A matrix file read from an external file does not replace the working data file.
NONE	*Do not read or write matrix data materials.* This is the default.

Matrix Output

- ONEWAY writes means, standard deviations, and frequencies to a matrix data file that can be used by subsequent ONEWAY procedures. See "Format of the Matrix Data File" below for a description of the file.
- MATRIX=IN cannot be specified unless a working data file has already been defined. To read an existing matrix data file at the beginning of a session, use GET to retrieve the matrix file and then specify IN(*) on MATRIX.
- Any documents contained in the working data file are not transferred to the matrix file.

Matrix Input

- ONEWAY can read the matrices it writes, and it can also read matrix materials that include the means, category frequencies, pooled variance, and degrees of freedom for the pooled variance. The pooled variance has a *ROWTYPE_* value MSE, and the vector of degrees of freedom for the pooled variance has the *ROWTYPE_* value DFE.
- The dependent variables named on ONEWAY can be a subset of the dependent variables in the matrix data file.
- MATRIX=IN cannot be specified unless a working data file has already been defined. To read an existing matrix data file at the beginning of a session, use GET to retrieve the matrix file and then specify IN(*) on MATRIX.

Format of the Matrix Data File

- The SPSS matrix data file includes two special variables created by SPSS: *ROWTYPE_* and *VARNAME_*.
- *ROWTYPE_* is a short string variable with values MEAN, STDDEV, and N.
- *VARNAME_* is a short string variable that never has values for procedure ONEWAY. *VARNAME_* is included with the matrix materials so that matrices written by ONEWAY can be read by procedures that expect to read a *VARNAME_* variable.
- The independent variable is between variables *ROWTYPE_* and *VARNAME_*.
- The remaining variables in the matrix file are the dependent variables.

Split Files

- When split-file processing is in effect, the first variables in the SPSS matrix data file are the split variables, followed by *ROWTYPE_*, the independent variable, *VARNAME_*, and the dependent variables.
- A full set of matrix materials is written for each split-file group defined by the split variable(s).
- A split variable cannot have the same variable name as any other variable written to the matrix data file.

- If split-file processing is in effect when a matrix is written, the same split file must be in effect when that matrix is read by any procedure.
- Generally, matrix rows, independent variables, and dependent variables can be in any order in the matrix data file read by keyword IN. However, all split-file variables must precede variable *ROWTYPE_*, and all split-group rows must be consecutive. ONEWAY ignores unrecognized *ROWTYPE_* values.

Missing Values

Missing-value treatment affects the values written to an SPSS matrix data file. When reading a matrix data file, be sure to specify a missing-value treatment on ONEWAY that is compatible with the treatment that was in effect when the matrix materials were generated.

Example

```
GET FILE=GSS80.
ONEWAY   WELL BY EDUC6(1,6)
  /MATRIX=OUT(ONEMTX).
```

- ONEWAY reads data from file *GSS80* and writes one set of matrix materials to the file *ONEMTX*.
- The working data file is still *GSS80*. Subsequent commands are executed on *GSS80*.

Example

```
GET FILE=GSS80.
ONEWAY   WELL BY EDUC6(1,6)
  /MATRIX=OUT(*).
LIST.
```

- ONEWAY writes the same matrix as in the example above. However, the matrix data file replaces the working data file. The LIST command is executed on the matrix file, not on the *GSS80* file.

Example

```
GET FILE=PRSNNL.
FREQUENCIES VARIABLE=AGE.
ONEWAY   WELL BY EDUC6(1,6)
  /MATRIX=IN(ONEMTX).
```

- This example performs a frequencies analysis on *PRSNNL* and then uses a different file for ONEWAY. The file is an existing matrix data file.
- MATRIX=IN specifies the matrix data file.
- *ONEMTX* does not replace *PRSNNL* as the working data file.

Example

```
GET FILE=ONEMTX.
ONEWAY  WELL BY EDUC6(1,6)
  /MATRIX=IN(*).
```

- The GET command retrieves the matrix data file *ONEMTX*.
- MATRIX=IN specifies an asterisk because the working data file is the matrix data file *ONEMTX*. If MATRIX=IN(ONEMTX) is specified, SPSS issues an error message, since *ONEMTX* is already open.
- If the GET command is omitted, SPSS issues an error message.

Example

```
MATRIX DATA VARIABLES=EDUC ROWTYPE_ WELL /FACTOR=EDUC.
BEGIN DATA
1 N 65
2 N 95
3 N 181
4 N 82
5 N 40
6 N 37
1 MEAN 2.6462
2 MEAN 2.7737
3 MEAN 4.1796
4 MEAN 4.5610
5 MEAN 4.6625
6 MEAN 5.2297
. MSE 6.2699
. DFE 494
END DATA.
LIST.
ONEWAY WELL BY EDUC(1,6) /MATRIX=IN(*) /RANGES=DUNCAN.
```

- MATRIX DATA reads raw matrix data and creates a working data file that, for each factor in the data, contains a vector of frequencies and a vector of means. The working file also includes one record each for the pooled variance and the degrees of freedom for the mean square error.
- LIST displays the matrix materials that are on the working file.
- ONEWAY reads the data matrix. An asterisk (*) is specified on IN because the data are in the working file.

References

Speed, M. F. 1976. Response curves in the one way classification with unequal numbers of observations per cell. *Proceedings of the Statistical Computing Section.* American Statistical Association.

PARTIAL CORR

```
PARTIAL CORR [VARIABLES=] varlist [WITH varlist]
    BY varlist [(levels)] [/varlist...]

[/SIGNIFICANCE={TWOTAIL**}]
               {ONETAIL  }

[/STATISTICS=[NONE**] [CORR] [DESCRIPTIVES] [BADCORR] [ALL]]

[/FORMAT={MATRIX** }]
         {SERIAL   }
         {CONDENSED}

[/MISSING=[{LISTWISE**}] [{EXCLUDE**}]]
          {ANALYSIS  }   {INCLUDE  }

[/MATRIX= [IN({*   })] [OUT({*   })]]
              {file}        {file}
```

**Default if the subcommand is omitted.

Example:

```
PARTIAL CORR VARIABLES=PUBTRANS MECHANIC BUSDRVER BY NETPURSE(1).
```

Overview

PARTIAL CORR produces partial correlation coefficients that describe the relationship between two variables while adjusting for the effects of one or more additional variables. PARTIAL CORR calculates a matrix of Pearson product-moment correlations. It can also read the zero-order correlation matrix as input. Other procedures producing zero-order correlation matrices that can be read by PARTIAL CORR include CORRELATIONS, REGRESSION, DISCRIMINANT, and FACTOR.

Options

Significance Levels. By default, the significance level for each partial correlation coefficient is based on a two-tailed test. Optionally, you can request a one-tailed test using the SIGNIFICANCE subcommand.

Statistics. In addition to the partial correlation coefficient, degrees of freedom, and significance level, you can obtain the mean, standard deviation, and number of nonmissing cases for each variable, and zero-order correlation coefficients for each pair of variables using the STATISTICS subcommand.

Format. You can specify condensed format, which suppresses the degrees of freedom and significance level for each coefficient, and you can print only nonredundant coefficients in serial string format using the FORMAT subcommand.

Matrix Input and Output. You can read and write zero-order correlation matrices using the MATRIX subcommand.

Basic Specification

The basic specification is the VARIABLES subcommand, which specifies a list of variables to be correlated and one or more control variables following keyword BY. PARTIAL CORR calculates the partial correlation of each variable with every other variable specified on the correlation variable list.

Subcommand Order

Subcommands can be specified in any order.
- If VARIABLES is the first subcommand used on PARTIAL CORR, keyword VARIABLES can be omitted.
- If VARIABLES is not the first subcommand specified on PARTIAL CORR, both the subcommand keyword VARIABLES and the equals sign are required.

Operations

PARTIAL CORR produces one matrix of partial correlation coefficients for each of up to five order values. For each coefficient, PARTIAL CORR prints the degrees of freedom and the significance level.

Limitations

- Maximum 25 variable lists on a single PARTIAL CORR command. Each variable list contains a correlation list, a control list, and order values.
- Maximum 400 variables total can be named or implied per PARTIAL CORR command.
- Maximum 100 control variables.
- Maximum 5 different order values per single list. The largest order value that can be specified is 100.

Example

```
PARTIAL CORR VARIABLES=PUBTRANS MECHANIC BUSDRVER BY NETPURSE(1).
```

- PARTIAL CORR produces a square matrix containing three unique first-order partial correlations: *PUBTRANS* with *MECHANIC* controlling for *NETPURSE*; *PUBTRANS* with *BUSDRVER* controlling for *NETPURSE*; and *MECHANIC* with *BUSDRVER* controlling for *NETPURSE*.

VARIABLES Subcommand

VARIABLES requires a *correlation list* of one or more pairs of variables for which partial correlations are desired and a *control list* of one or more variables that will be used as controls for the variables in the correlation list, followed by optional order values in parentheses.

- The correlation list specifies pairs of variables to be correlated while controlling for the variables in the control list.
- To request a square or lower-triangular matrix, do not use keyword WITH in the correlation list. This obtains the partial correlation of every variable with every other variable in the list.
- To request a rectangular matrix, specify a list of correlation variables followed by keyword WITH and a second list of variables. This obtains the partial correlation of specific variable pairs. The first variable list defines the rows of the matrix and the second list defines the columns.
- The control list is specified after keyword BY.
- The correlation between a pair of variables is referred to as a zero-order correlation. Controlling for one variable produces a first-order partial correlation, controlling for two variables produces a second-order partial, and so on.
- You can specify order values in parentheses following the control list to indicate the exact partials to be computed. These values also determine the partial correlation matrix or matrices to be printed. Up to five order values can be specified. Separate each value with at least one space or comma. The default order value is the number of control variables.
- One partial is produced for every unique combination of control variables for each order value.
- To specify multiple analyses, use multiple VARIABLES subcommands or a slash to separate each set of specifications on one VARIABLES subcommand. PARTIAL CORR computes the zero-order correlation matrix for each analysis list separately.

Example

```
PARTIAL CORR RENT FOOD PUBTRANS WITH TEACHER MANAGER BY NETSALRY(1).
```

- PARTIAL CORR produces a rectangular matrix. Variables *RENT*, *FOOD*, and *PUBTRANS* form the matrix rows, and variables *TEACHER* and *MANAGER* form the columns.
- Keyword VARIABLES is omitted. This is allowed because the variable list is the first specification on PARTIAL CORR.

Example

```
PARTIAL CORR   RENT WITH TEACHER BY NETSALRY, NETPRICE (1).
PARTIAL CORR   RENT WITH TEACHER BY NETSALRY, NETPRICE (2).
PARTIAL CORR   RENT WITH TEACHER BY NETSALRY, NETPRICE (1,2).
PARTIAL CORR   RENT FOOD PUBTRANS BY NETSALRY NETPURSE NETPRICE(1,3).
```

- The first PARTIAL CORR produces two first-order partials: *RENT* with *TEACHER* controlling for *NETSALRY*, and *RENT* with *TEACHER* controlling for *NETPRICE*.
- The second PARTIAL CORR produces one second-order partial of *RENT* with *TEACHER* controlling simultaneously for *NETSALRY* and *NETPRICE*.

- The third PARTIAL CORR specifies both sets of partials specified by the previous two commands.
- The fourth PARTIAL CORR produces three first-order partials (controlling for *NETSALRY*, *NETPURSE*, and *NETPRICE* individually) and one third-order partial (controlling for all three control variables simultaneously).

Example

```
PARTIAL CORR RENT FOOD WITH TEACHER BY NETSALRY NETPRICE (1,2)
   /WCLOTHES MCLOTHES BY NETPRICE (1).
```

- PARTIAL CORR produces three matrices for the first correlation list, control list, and order values.
- The second correlation list, control list, and order value produce one matrix.

SIGNIFICANCE Subcommand

SIGNIFICANCE determines whether the significance level is based on a one-tailed or two-tailed test.
- By default, the significance level is based on a two-tailed test. This is appropriate when the direction of the relationship between a pair of variables cannot be specified in advance of the analysis.
- When the direction of the relationship can be determined in advance, a one-tailed test is appropriate.

TWOTAIL *Two-tailed test of significance.* This is the default.

ONETAIL *One-tailed test of significance.*

STATISTICS Subcommand

By default, the partial correlation coefficient, degrees of freedom, and significance level are displayed. Use STATISTICS to obtain additional statistics.
- If both CORR and BADCORR are requested, CORR takes precedence over BADCORR and the zero-order correlations are displayed.

CORR *Zero-order correlations with degrees of freedom and significance level.*

DESCRIPTIVES *Mean, standard deviation, and number of nonmissing cases.* Descriptive statistics are not available with matrix input.

BADCORR *Zero-order correlation coefficients only if any of the zero-order correlations cannot be computed.* Noncomputable coefficients are displayed as a period.

NONE *No additional statistics.* This is the default.

ALL *All additional statistics available with PARTIAL CORR.*

FORMAT Subcommand

FORMAT determines page format.
- If both CONDENSED and SERIAL are specified, only SERIAL is in effect.

MATRIX   *Display degrees of freedom and significance level in matrix format.* This format requires four lines per matrix row and displays the degrees of freedom and the significance level. The output includes redundant coefficients. This is the default.

CONDENSED   *Suppress the degrees of freedom and significance level.* This format requires only one line per matrix row and suppresses the degrees of freedom and significance. A single asterisk (*) following a coefficient indicates a significance level of 0.05 or less. Two asterisks (**) following a coefficient indicate a significance level of 0.01 or less.

SERIAL   *Display only the nonredundant coefficients in serial string format.* The coefficients, degrees of freedom, and significance levels from the first row of the matrix are displayed first, followed by all the unique coefficients from the second row and so on for all the rows of the matrix.

MISSING Subcommand

MISSING controls the treatment of cases with missing values.
- When multiple analysis lists are specified, missing values are handled separately for each analysis list. Thus, different sets of cases can be used for different lists.
- When pairwise deletion is in effect (keyword ANALYSIS), the degrees of freedom for a particular partial coefficient are based on the smallest number of cases used in the calculation of any of the simple correlations.
- LISTWISE and ANALYSIS are alternatives. However, each can be used with either INCLUDE or EXCLUDE. The default is LISTWISE and EXCLUDE.

LISTWISE   *Exclude cases with missing values listwise.* Cases with missing values for any of the variables listed for an analysis, including control variables, are not used in the calculation of the zero-order correlation coefficient. This is the default.

ANALYSIS   *Exclude cases with missing values on a pair-by-pair basis.* Cases with missing for one or both of a pair of variables are not used in the calculation of zero-order correlation coefficients.

EXCLUDE   *Exclude user-missing values.* User-missing values are treated as missing. This is the default.

INCLUDE   *Include user-missing values.* User-missing values are treated as valid values.

MATRIX Subcommand

MATRIX reads and writes matrix data files.

- Either IN or OUT and a matrix file in parentheses is required. When both IN and OUT are used on the same PARTIAL CORR procedure, they can be specified on separate MATRIX subcommands or both on the same subcommand.

OUT (filename)   *Write the (zero-order) correlation matrix to a file.* Specify either a filename or an asterisk, enclosed in parentheses. If you specify a filename, the file is stored on disk and can be retrieved at any time. If you specify an asterisk (*), the matrix data file replaces the working data file but is not stored on disk unless you use SAVE or XSAVE.

IN (filename)   *Read a matrix data file.* If the matrix data file is the working data file, specify an asterisk (*) in parentheses. If the matrix data file is another file, specify a filename in parentheses. Both the working data file and the matrix data file must contain all the variables specified on the VARIABLES subcommands on PARTIAL CORR. A matrix file read from an external file does not replace the working data file.

Matrix Output

- The matrix materials that PARTIAL CORR writes can be used by subsequent PARTIAL CORR procedures or by other SPSS procedures that read correlation-type matrices.
- In addition to the Pearson correlation coefficients, the matrix materials PARTIAL CORR writes include the mean, standard deviation, and number of cases used to compute each coefficient (see "Format of the Matrix Data File" on p. 477 for a description of the file). If PARTIAL CORR reads matrix data and then writes matrix materials based on those data, the matrix data file that it writes will not include means and standard deviations.
- PARTIAL CORR writes a full square matrix for the analysis specified on the first VARIABLES subcommand (or the first analysis list if keyword VARIABLES is omitted). No matrix is written for subsequent variable lists.
- Any documents contained in the working data file are not transferred to the matrix file.

Matrix Input

- When matrix materials are read from a file other than the working data file, both the working data file and the matrix data file specified on IN must contain all the variables specified on the VARIABLES subcommands.
- MATRIX=IN cannot be specified unless a working data file has already been defined. To read an existing matrix data file at the beginning of a session, use GET to retrieve the matrix file and then specify IN(*) on MATRIX.
- PARTIAL CORR can read correlation-type matrices written by other procedures.
- SPSS reads variable names, variable and value labels, and print and write formats from the dictionary of the SPSS matrix data file.

Format of the Matrix Data File

- The SPSS matrix data file includes two special variables created by SPSS: *ROWTYPE_* and *VARNAME_*.
- *ROWTYPE_* is a short string variable with values N, MEAN, STDDEV, and CORR (for Pearson's correlation coefficient).
- *VARNAME_* is a short string variable whose values are the names of the variables used to form the correlation matrix. When *ROWTYPE_* is CORR, *VARNAME_* gives the variable associated with that row of the correlation matrix.
- The remaining variables in the file are the variables used to form the correlation matrix.

Split Files

- When split-file processing is in effect, the first variables in the SPSS matrix data file are the split variables, followed by *ROWTYPE_*, *VARNAME_*, and the variables used to form the correlation matrix.
- A full set of matrix materials is written for each split-file group defined by the split variables.
- A split variable cannot have the same variable name as any other variable written to the matrix data file.
- If split-file processing is in effect when a matrix is written, the same split file must be in effect when that matrix is read by any procedure.

Missing Values

- With pairwise treatment of missing values (MISSING=ANALYSIS is specified), the matrix of N's used to compute each coefficient is included with the matrix materials.
- With LISTWISE treatment, a single N used to calculate all coefficients is included with the matrix materials.
- When reading a matrix data file, be sure to specify a missing-value treatment on PARTIAL CORR that is compatible with the missing-value treatment that was in effect when the matrix materials were produced.

Example

```
GET FILE=CITY.
PARTIAL CORR VARIABLES=BUSDRVER MECHANIC ENGINEER TEACHER COOK
                 BY   NETSALRY(1)
 /MATRIX=OUT(PTMTX).
```

- PARTIAL CORR reads data from file *CITY* and writes one set of matrix materials to file *PTMTX*.
- The working data file is still *CITY*. Subsequent commands are executed on *CITY*.

Example

```
GET FILE=CITY.
PARTIAL CORR VARIABLES=BUSDRVER MECHANIC ENGINEER TEACHER COOK
  BY  NETSALRY(1)    /MATRIX=OUT(*).
LIST.
```

- PARTIAL CORR writes the same matrix as in the example above. However, the matrix data file replaces the working data file. The LIST command is executed on the matrix file, not on the *CITY* file.

Example

```
GET FILE=PRSNNL.
FREQUENCIES VARIABLE=AGE.
PARTIAL CORR VARIABLES=BUSDRVER MECHANIC ENGINEER TEACHER COOK
    BY   NETSALRY(1)    /MATRIX=IN(CORMTX).
```

- This example performs a frequencies analysis on file *PRSNNL* and then uses a different file for PARTIAL CORR. The file is an existing matrix data file.
- MATRIX=IN specifies the matrix data file. Both the working data file and the *CORMTX* file must contain all variables specified on the VARIABLES subcommand on PARTIAL CORR.
- *CORMTX* does not replace *PRSNNL* as the working data file.

Example

```
GET FILE=CORMTX.
PARTIAL CORR VARIABLES=BUSDRVER MECHANIC ENGINEER TEACHER COOK
                     BY NETSALRY(1)
  /MATRIX=IN(*).
```

- The GET command retrieves the matrix data file *CORMTX*.
- MATRIX=IN specifies an asterisk because the working data file is the matrix file *CORMTX*. If MATRIX=IN(CORMTX) is specified, SPSS issues an error message.
- If the GET command is omitted, SPSS issues an error message.

Example

```
GET FILE=CITY.
REGRESSION MATRIX=OUT(*)
  /VARIABLES=NETPURSE PUBTRANS MECHANIC BUSDRVER
  /DEPENDENT=NETPURSE /ENTER.
PARTIAL CORR  PUBTRANS MECHANIC BUSDRVER BY NETPURSE(1) /MATRIX=IN(*).
```

- GET retrieves the SPSS data file *CITY*.
- REGRESSION computes correlations among the specified variables. MATRIX=OUT(*) writes a matrix data file that replaces the working data file.
- The MATRIX=IN(*) specification on PARTIAL CORR reads the matrix materials in the working data file.

PLOT

```
PLOT    [HSIZE††={n}]  [/VSIZE††={n}]

[/CUTPOINT††={EVERY({1**})}]
             {         {n  } }
             {value list    }

[/SYMBOLS††={ALPHANUMERIC**                          }]
            {DEFAULT**                               }
            {NUMERIC                                 }
            {'symbols'[,'overplot symbols']          }
            {X'hexsymbs'[,'overplot hexsymbs']       }

[/MISSING=[{PLOTWISE**}]  [INCLUDE]  [DEFAULT**]]
           {LISTWISE  }

[/FORMAT={DEFAULT**        }]
         {OVERLAY          }
         {CONTOUR††[({10})]}
         {          {n }   }
         {REGRESSION       }

[/TITLE='title']

[/HORIZONTAL=['label']  [STANDARDIZE]  [REFERENCE(value list)]
             [MIN(n)]  [MAX(n)]  [UNIFORM]]

[/VERTICAL=['label']  [STANDARDIZE]  [REFERENCE(value list)]
           [MIN(n)]  [MAX(n)]  [UNIFORM]]

/PLOT={varlist}  WITH varlist  [(PAIR)]  [BY varname]  [;varlist...]
      {ALL    }

[/PLOT=...]
```

****Default if the subcommand is omitted.
††Applicable only when SET HIGHRES is OFF.

Example:

```
PLOT FORMAT=OVERLAY /SYMBOLS='MD' /VSIZE=12 /HSIZE=60
  /TITLE='Marriage and Divorce Rates'
  /VERTICAL='Rates per 1000 population'
  /HORIZONTAL='Year' REFERENCE (1918, 1945) MIN (1880) MAX (2000)
  /PLOT=MARRATE DIVRATE WITH YEAR.
```

Overview

PLOT produces two-dimensional plots, including simple bivariate scatterplots, scatterplots with a control variable, contour plots, and overlay plots. You can also request bivariate regression statistics. You can choose from a variety of options for plot symbols, and you can add reference lines. You have control over size, labeling, and scaling of each axis, and you can constrain the axes to be uniform for a series of plots. Many of these plots can also be produced with the GRAPH command.

The PLOT command produces either high-resolution or low-resolution (character-based) plots, depending on the HIGHRES specification on the SET command. If high-resolution capabilities are not available on your system, or if you want to print plots on a line printer, set HIGHRES to OFF.

Options

Types of Plots. You can introduce a control variable for bivariate scatterplots and request regression plots with or without a control variable, contour plots, and overlay plots using the FORMAT subcommand.

Plot Tailoring. You can specify a title for the plot on the TITLE subcommand. You can scale and label the horizontal and vertical axes, request reference lines, and plot standardized variables using the VERTICAL and HORIZONTAL subcommands. You can control the plot size with the HSIZE and VSIZE subcommands, and you can specify plot symbols and the frequency they represent using the SYMBOL and CUTPOINT subcommands.

Basic Specification

The basic specification is a PLOT subcommand that names the variables for the vertical (y) axis, keyword WITH, and the variables for the horizontal (x) axis. By default, PLOT produces separate bivariate scatterplots for all combinations formed by each variable on the left side of WITH with each variable on the right.

Subcommand Order

- No subcommand can be specified after the last PLOT subcommand specified. Other than this, subcommands can be specified in any order.

Syntax Rules

- The PLOT subcommand can be specified more than once.
- Subcommands MISSING, VSIZE, HSIZE, CUTPOINT, and SYMBOLS apply to all plots requested and can be specified only once.
- Subcommands HORIZONTAL, VERTICAL, FORMAT, and TITLE can be specified more than once and apply only to the following PLOT subcommand.

Operations

- The default plot size depends on the system page size, which is specified on SET. HSIZE and VSIZE override the default plot size.
- A longer page length can produce longer default plots within the same width. A wider page does not produce a wider default plot unless the page length is changed accordingly.

Limitations

There are no limitations on the number of plots requested or on the number of variables specified on a PLOT command. The following limitations apply to the optional subcommands:
- Maximum 60 characters for a title specified on TITLE.

Syntax Reference Guide

- Maximum 36 symbols per SYMBOLS subcommand.
- Maximum 35 cut points per CUTPOINT subcommand.
- Maximum 10 reference points on each HORIZONTAL or VERTICAL subcommand.
- Maximum 40 characters per label on each HORIZONTAL or VERTICAL subcommand.

Example

```
PLOT FORMAT=OVERLAY /SYMBOLS='MD' /VSIZE=12 /HSIZE=60
  /TITLE='Marriage and Divorce Rates'
  /VERTICAL='Rates per 1000 population'
  /HORIZONTAL='Year' REFERENCE (1918, 1945) MIN (1900) MAX (1983)
  /PLOT=MARRATE DIVRATE WITH YEAR.
```

- This example produces an overlay plot of marriage and divorce rates by year.
- SYMBOLS selects the symbols M and D, respectively, for the two plots.
- VSIZE and HSIZE limit the vertical and horizontal axes to 12 lines and 60 columns, respectively.
- TITLE specifies a plot title.
- VERTICAL provides a title for the vertical axis.
- HORIZONTAL provides a title for the horizontal axis. The REFERENCE keyword provides reference lines at values 1918 and 1945. MIN and MAX specify minimum and maximum scale values for the horizontal axis.

PLOT Subcommand

The PLOT subcommand names the variables to be plotted on each axis. PLOT can also name a control or contour variable.

- PLOT is the only required subcommand.
- Multiple PLOT subcommands are allowed.
- No other subcommands can follow the last PLOT subcommand.
- The basic specification on PLOT is a list of variables to be plotted on the vertical axis, keyword WITH, and a list of variables to be plotted on the horizontal axis.
- By default, PLOT creates a separate plot for each variable specified before WITH with each variable specified after WITH.
- To request special pairing of variables, specify keyword PAIR in parentheses following the second variable list. The first variable before WITH is plotted against the first variable after WITH, the second against the second, and so on.
- Use semicolons to separate multiple plot lists on a single PLOT subcommand.
- Keyword ALL can be used to refer to all user-defined variables.
- An optional control variable can be specified following keyword BY. Only one control variable can be specified on any plot list.
- If a control variable is specified for a bivariate scatterplot (the default), PLOT uses the first character of the control variable's value label as the plot symbol. If value labels have not

been specified, the first character of the value is used. The symbol $ indicates that more than one control value occurs at that position.

Example

```
PLOT PLOT=MARRATE WITH YEAR AGE;
     BIRTHS DEATHS WITH INCOME1 INCOME2 (PAIR);
     DIVRATE WITH AGE BY YEAR.
```

- The PLOT subcommand contains three plot lists. The first requests a plot of *MARRATE* with *YEAR* and of *MARRATE* with *AGE*.
- The second uses the keyword PAIR to request two plots: *BIRTHS* with *INCOME1* and *DEATHS* with *INCOME2*.
- The third requests a plot of *DIVRATE* with *AGE* using *YEAR* as a control variable. The first character of the value labels for *YEAR* as the plot symbol.

FORMAT Subcommand

FORMAT controls the type of plot produced.
- FORMAT can be specified once before each PLOT subcommand and applies only to plots requested on that PLOT subcommand.
- If FORMAT is not used or keyword DEFAULT is specified, bivariate scatterplots are displayed.
- Only one keyword can be specified on each FORMAT subcommand.

DEFAULT *Bivariate scatterplot.* When there is no control variable, each symbol represents the case count at that position. When a control variable is specified, each symbol represents the first character of the control variable's value label, or the first character of the value if no labels have been defined.

OVERLAY *Overlay plots.* All bivariate plots on the next PLOT subcommand appear in one plot frame. PLOT selects a unique symbol for each plot to be overlaid, plus a symbol to represent multiple plot points at one position (see "SYMBOLS Keywords" on p. 483).

CONTOUR(n) *Contour plot with n levels.* Contour plots use a continuous variable as the control variable and *n* successive symbols to represent the lowest to highest levels of the variable (see "SYMBOLS Keywords" on p. 483). The control variable is specified after BY on the PLOT subcommand and is recoded into *n* equal-width intervals. If *n* is omitted, the default of 10 is used; the maximum is 35. When more than one level of the contour variable occurs at the same position, PLOT displays the value of the highest level at that position. CONTOUR is applicable only if SET HIGHRES is OFF.

REGRESSION *Regression of the y axis variable on the x axis variable.* The regression-line intercepts are marked with the letter *R*. When there is no control variable, each symbol represents the frequency of cases at that position. If a control variable is specified, regression statistics are pooled over all categories and each symbol represents the first character of the control variable's value label, or the first character of the value if no labels have been defined.

SYMBOLS and CUTPOINT Subcommands

A wide range of alphabetical, numeric, and hexadecimal characters are available for use as PLOT symbols. Two subcommands control the display of symbols: SYMBOLS controls the choice of plot symbols, and CUTPOINT controls the frequencies represented by a symbol. SYMBOLS and CUTPOINT are applicable only if SET HIGHRES is OFF.

SYMBOLS and CUTPOINT can each be specified only once and apply to all plots requested on a PLOT command. The operation of SYMBOLS and CUTPOINT depend on the specification on the FORMAT subcommand, as summarized below:

- DEFAULT or REGRESSION, with no control variable. Each symbol represents the frequency of cases and is controlled by SYMBOLS and CUTPOINT.
- DEFAULT or REGRESSION, with a control variable. Each symbol represents one value of the control variable. SYMBOLS and CUTPOINT do not apply. The plot symbol is the first character of the control variable's value label or the first character of the value if no value labels have been defined; the uniqueness of these symbols is not checked. The symbol $ indicates that more than one control value occurs at that position.
- OVERLAY. Each symbol represents one of the overlaid plots. SYMBOLS is applicable; CUTPOINT is not.
- CONTOUR. Each symbol represents one level of the contour variable. SYMBOLS is applicable; CUTPOINT is not.

SYMBOLS Keywords

SYMBOLS defines plot symbols for bivariate scatterplots, bivariate regression plots, overlay plots, and contour plots. Successive symbols represent increasing frequencies in scatterplots or regression plots, successive subplots in overlay plots, and successive intervals in contour plots.

- If the SYMBOLS subcommand is omitted, the default alphanumeric symbol set is used.
- A table defining the plot symbols is always displayed.

ALPHANUMERIC — *Alphanumeric plot symbols.* Includes the characters 1 through 9, A through Z, and an asterisk (*). Thirty-six or more cases at a position are represented by an asterisk. This is the default and can be requested with keyword DEFAULT.

NUMERIC — *Numeric plot symbols.* Includes the characters 1 through 9 and an asterisk (*). Ten or more cases at a plot position are represented by an asterisk.

'symbols'[,'ovprnt'] — *List of plot symbols.* Up to 36 symbols can be specified. Symbols are specified without any intervening blanks or commas. Optionally, you can specify a list of overprinting symbols separated from the first list

X'hexsym'[,'ovprnt'] *List of hexadecimal plot symbols.* Indicate hexadecimal symbols by specifying X before the hexadecimal representation list enclosed in apostrophes. Optionally, you can specify a list of overprinting symbols separated from the first list by a comma or space. The overprinting symbols can be either hexadecimal representations or keyboard characters.

by a comma or space. The overprinting symbols can be either hexadecimal representations (preceded by an X) or keyboard characters.

Example

```
PLOT CUTPOINTS=EVERY(5)/SYMBOLS='.+O','  X'
   /PLOT=Y WITH X.
```

- This example uses a period (.) to represent 5 or fewer cases at one point, a plus sign (+) to represent 6 to 10 cases at the same position, and a symbol overprinting O and X to represent 11 or more cases at one position. Note the two leading blanks in the list of overprinting symbols.

Keywords on CUTPOINT

By default, each frequency in a bivariate scatterplot or regression plot is represented by a different plot symbol, and successive plot symbols represent an interval width of 1. Use the CUTPOINT subcommand to alter the intervals or categories represented by plot symbols for these plots. Only one of the following keywords can be specified on CUTPOINT:

EVERY(n) *Frequency intervals of width* n. Each plot symbol represents the specified frequency interval. The default is an interval width of 1. The last symbol specified represents all frequencies greater than those for the next-to-last symbol.

(value list) *Each value defines a cut point.* Successive plot symbols are assigned to each cutpoint. Up to 35 cut points can be specified. Specify values separated by blanks or commas. The number of cutpoints is one less than the number of intervals.

Example

```
PLOT CUTPOINT=EVERY(2)  /PLOT=Y WITH X.
PLOT CUTPOINT=(5,10,20)  /PLOT=Y WITH X.
```

- In the first PLOT command, 1 or 2 cases at a position are represented by a 1; 3 or 4 cases by a 2; and so forth.
- In the second PLOT command, 1 to 5 cases at a position are represented by a 1; 6 to 10 cases by a 2; 11 to 20 cases by a 3; and 21 or more cases by a 4.

VSIZE and HSIZE Subcommands

VSIZE and HSIZE control length and width of the plot, respectively.

- VSIZE and HSIZE can each be used only once per PLOT command and apply to all plots requested.
- VSIZE and HSIZE are applicable only if SET HIGHRES is OFF.
- The default size of a plot depends on the system page size, which is controlled by the SET command. With a page width of 132 horizontal print positions and a page length (vertically) of 59 lines, the default plot size is 80 positions wide by 40 lines long.
- VSIZE and HSIZE each use a single integer as their only specification.
- The plot size specified on VSIZE and HSIZE does not include the plot frame itself or auxiliary information such as titles, axis scale numbers, regression statistics, or symbol table.
- The width specified on HSIZE must be at least 15 positions less than the size specified on the SET WIDTH command (or its default). For example, if SET WIDTH=80, the largest horizontal size you can request (and the default) is 65.
- If VSIZE is greater than the length specified on SET LENGTH, VSIZE will override the length, but the symbol table and other information normally printed below a plot will appear on the following page. To ensure that this information will print on the same page, the length on SET LENGTH should be at least 20 lines longer than VSIZE.

VERTICAL and HORIZONTAL Subcommands

VERTICAL and HORIZONTAL control labeling and scaling for the vertical and horizontal axes.

- VERTICAL and HORIZONTAL can each be specified once before each PLOT subcommand and apply only to plots requested by that subcommand.
- If VERTICAL and HORIZONTAL are omitted, all defaults are in effect. If VERTICAL and HORIZONTAL are included, only those defaults explicitly altered are changed.

The following keywords are available for both VERTICAL and HORIZONTAL:

'label' *Label for axis.* The label can contain up to 40 characters. A label that cannot fit in the frame is truncated. The default is the variable label for the variable plotted on that axis, or the variable name if no variable label has been specified.

MIN (n) *Minimum axis value.* If you specify a minimum value greater than the observed minimum value, some points will not be included in the plot. The default is the minimum observed value.

MAX (n) *Maximum axis value.* If you specify a maximum value less than the observed maximum value, some points will not be included in the plot. The default is the maximum observed value.

UNIFORM *Uniform values on axis.* All plots specified on that PLOT subcommand will have the same scale on that axis. A uniform scale is implied when both MIN and MAX are specified. If UNIFORM is specified, PLOT determines the minimum and maximum observed values across all variables on the PLOT subcommand.

REFERENCE(values) *Reference lines.* The values at which reference lines should be drawn are separated by blanks or commas. The default is no reference lines.

STANDARDIZE *Plot standardized variables.* Standardized variables are useful for overlay plots of variables with different scales. The default is to plot observed values.

TITLE Subcommand

TITLE provides titles for plots.

- TITLE can be specified once before each PLOT subcommand and applies to all plots named on that PLOT subcommand.
- The default title for a bivariate scatterplot or regression plot is the names of the variables in the plot. For other plots, the default is the plot type requested on FORMAT.
- The title can be up to 60 characters long and follows the usual rules for specifying strings (see "String Values in Command Specifications" on p. 16.)
- The title is truncated if it exceeds the width specified on the HSIZE subcommand.

MISSING Subcommand

MISSING controls the treatment of cases with missing values.

- MISSING can be specified only once per PLOT command and applies to all plots requested.
- Keywords LISTWISE and PLOTWISE are alternatives. Either one can be specified with INCLUDE. The default is PLOTWISE.

DEFAULT *Exclude* cases *with system- or user-missing values for any variables in a plot from that plot.*

PLOTWISE *Delete cases with missing values plotwise.* Cases with missing values for any variable in a plot are not included in that plot. In overlay plots, PLOTWISE applies separately to each overlaid plot in the frame, not to the full list specified on the PLOT subcommand.

LISTWISE *Delete cases with missing values listwise.* Cases with missing values for any variable named on the PLOT subcommand are deleted from all plots specified on that PLOT subcommand.

INCLUDE *Treat user-missing values as valid values.* Only cases with system-missing values are excluded according to the missing-value treatment specified.

POINT

This command is not available on all operating systems.

```
POINT KEY=varname [FILE=file]
```

Example:
```
FILE HANDLE DRIVERS/ file specifications.
POINT FILE=DRIVERS /KEY=#FRSTAGE.
```

Overview

POINT establishes the location at which sequential access begins (or resumes) in a keyed file. A keyed file is a file that provides access to information by a record key. An example of a keyed file is a file containing a social security number and other information about a firm's employees. The social security number can be used to identify the records in the file. For additional information on keyed files, see KEYED DATA LIST.

POINT prepares for reading the key-sequenced data set sequentially from a point that the key value controls. SPSS data selection commands can then be used to limit the file to the portion you want to analyze. A DATA LIST command is used to read the data. To read keyed files (and also direct access files), see the KEYED DATA LIST command.

For more information on reading keyed files on your computer, refer to the *Base System User's Guide* for your version of SPSS.

Basic Specification

The basic specification is the KEY subcommand and a string variable. The value of the string variable is used as the file key for determining where sequential retrieval (via DATA LIST) begins or resumes.

Subcommand Order

- Subcommands can be named in any order.
- Each POINT command must precede its corresponding DATA LIST command.

Syntax Rules

- POINT can be used more than once to change the order of retrieval during processing.
- POINT must be specified in an input program and therefore cannot be used to add cases to an existing file.

Operations

- The next DATA LIST command executed after the POINT command (for the same file) will read a record whose key value is at least as large as that of the specified key. To prevent an infinite loop in which the same record is read again and again, either the value of the variable specified on KEY must change from case to case or the POINT command must be set up to execute only once.
- If the file contains a record whose key exactly matches the value of the KEY variable, the next execution of DATA LIST will read that record, the second execution of DATA LIST will read the next record, and so on.
- If an exact match is not found, the results depend on the operating system. On IBM implementations, reading will begin or resume at the record that has the next higher key. If the value of the key is shorter than the file key, the value of the key variable is logically extended with the lowest character in the collating sequence. For example, if the value of the key variable is the single letter M, retrieval would begin or resume at the first record that had a key (regardless of length) beginning with the letter M or a character higher in the collating sequence.
- POINT does not report on whether the file contains a record that exactly matches the specified key. The only way to check for missing records is to display the data read by the subsequent DATA LIST command using LIST.

Example

```
* Select a subset of records from a keyed file.
FILE HANDLE     DRIVERS/ file specifications.
INPUT PROGRAM.
STRING          #FRSTAGE(A2).
DO IF           #FRSTAGE = ' '.     /* First case check
+  COMPUTE      #FRSTAGE = '26'.    /* Initial key
+  POINT        FILE=DRIVERS /KEY=#FRSTAGE.
END IF.
DATA LIST       FILE=DRIVERS NOTABLE/
                AGE 19-20(A) SEX 21(A) TICKETS 12-13.
DO IF           AGE > '30'.
+  END FILE.
END IF.
END INPUT PROGRAM.
LIST.
```

- This example illustrates how to execute POINT for only the first case. The file contains information about traffic violations, and it uses the individual's age as the key. Ages between 26 and 30 are selected.
- FILE HANDLE specifies the file handle DRIVERS.
- The INPUT PROGRAM and END INPUT PROGRAM commands begin and end the block of commands that build cases. POINT must appear in an input program.
- STRING declares the string variable *#FRSTAGE*, whose value will be used as the key on the POINT command. Since *#FRSTAGE* is a string variable, it is initialized as blanks.

- The first DO IF—END IF structure is executed only if no records have been read; that is, when *#FRSTAGE* is blank. When *#FRSTAGE* is blank, COMPUTE resets *#FRSTAGE* to 26, which is the initial value. POINT is executed, and it causes the first execution of DATA LIST to read a record whose key is at least 26. Since the value of *#FRSTAGE* is now 26, the DO IF—END IF structure is not executed again.
- DATA LIST reads the variables *AGE*, *SEX*, and *TICKETS* from the file *DRIVERS*.
- The second DO IF—END IF structure executes an END FILE command as soon as a record is read that contains a driver's age greater than 30. SPSS does not add this last case to the working file when it ends the file (see END FILE).

Example

```
FILE HANDLE DRIVERS/ file specifications.
POINT FILE=DRIVERS /KEY=#FRSTAGE.
```

- FILE HANDLE defines the handle for the data file to be read by POINT. The handle is specified on the FILE subcommand on POINT.
- KEY on POINT specifies the key variable. The key variable must be a string, and it must already exist as the result of a prior DATA LIST, KEYED DATA LIST, or transformation command.

FILE Subcommand

FILE specifies a file handle for the keyed data file. The file handle must have been previously defined on a FILE HANDLE command (or, in IBM OS environment, on a corresponding DD statement in the JCL).

- FILE is optional.
- If FILE is omitted, POINT reads from the last file specified on an SPSS input command, such as DATA LIST.

Example

```
FILE HANDLE DRIVERS/ file specifications.
POINT FILE=DRIVERS /KEY=#NXTCASE.
```

- FILE HANDLE specifies *DRIVERS* as the file handle for the data. The FILE subcommand on POINT specifies file handle *DRIVERS*.

KEY Subcommand

KEY specifies the variable whose value will be used as the file key for determining where sequential retrieval by DATA LIST will begin or resume. This variable must be a string variable, and it must already exist as the result of a prior DATA LIST, KEYED DATA LIST, or transformation command.

- KEY is required. Its only specification is a single variable. The variable can be a permanent variable or a scratch variable.

- Where the keys on a file are inherently numbers, such as social security numbers, the STRING function can be used to convert the numeric variable to a string (see p. 52).

Example

```
FILE HANDLE DRIVERS/ file specifications.
POINT FILE=DRIVERS /KEY=#NXTCASE.
```

- KEY indicates that the value of the existing scratch variable *#FRSTAGE* will be used as the key to reading each record.
- Variable *#FRSTAGE* must be an existing string variable.

PRESERVE

```
PRESERVE
```

Overview

PRESERVE stores current SET specifications that can later be restored by the RESTORE command. PRESERVE and RESTORE are especially useful with the SPSS macro facility. PRESERVE—RESTORE sequences can be nested up to five levels.

Basic Specification

The only specification is the command keyword. PRESERVE has no additional specifications.

Example

```
GET FILE=PRSNNL.
FREQUENCIES VAR=DIVISION /STATISTICS=ALL.
PRESERVE.
SET XSORT=NO WIDTH=90 UNDEFINED=NOWARN BLANKS=000 CASE=UPLOW.
SORT CASES BY DIVISION.
REPORT FORMAT=AUTO LIST /VARS=LNAME FNAME DEPT SOCSEC SALARY
   /BREAK=DIVISION /SUMMARY=MEAN.
RESTORE.
```

- GET reads SPSS data file *PRSNNL*.
- FREQUENCIES requests a frequency table and all statistics for variable *DIVISION*.
- PRESERVE stores all current SET specifications.
- SET changes several subcommand settings.
- SORT sorts cases in preparation for a report. Because SET XSORT=NO, the SPSS sort program is not used to sort cases; another sort program must be available.
- REPORT requests a report organized by variable *DIVISION*.
- RESTORE reestablishes the SET specifications that were in effect when PRESERVE was specified.

PRINT

```
PRINT [OUTFILE=file] [RECORDS={1}] [{NOTABLE}]
                              {n}   {TABLE   }

 /{1    } varlist [{col location [(format)]}] [varlist...]
  {rec #}          {(format list)          }
                   {*                      }

 [/{2    }...]
   {rec #}
```

Example:

```
PRINT / MOHIRED YRHIRED DEPT SALARY NAME.
EXECUTE.
```

Overview

PRINT displays the values of variables for each case in the data. PRINT is designed to be simple enough for a quick check on data definitions and transformations and yet flexible enough for formatting simple reports.

The output from PRINT is similar to the output from the LIST command. However, LIST is a procedure and reads data, whereas PRINT is a transformation and requires a procedure (or the EXECUTE command) to execute it. PRINT is similar to REPORT in that it can specify column headings, column locations, and print formats for variables. If you use PRINT with PRINT EJECT, you can control page breaks between cases and display column headings at the top of every page of the output. However, REPORT is a much more comprehensive tool for writing reports.

Options

Formats. You can specify formats for the variables (see "Formats" on p. 494).

Strings. You can specify string values within the variable specifications. The strings can be used to label values or to create extra space between values. Strings can also be used as column headings. (See "Strings" on p. 495.)

Output File. You can direct the output to a specified file using the OUTFILE subcommand.

Summary Table. You can display a table that summarizes variable formats with the TABLE subcommand.

Basic Specification

The basic specification is a slash followed by a variable list. The values for all variables named on the list are displayed in the output.

Subcommand Order

Subcommands can be specified in any order. However, all subcommands must be specified before the slash that precedes the start of the variable specifications.

Syntax Rules

- A slash must precede the variable specifications. The first slash begins the definition of the first (and possibly only) line per case of the PRINT display.
- Specified variables must already exist, but they can be numeric, string, scratch, temporary, or system variables. Subscripted variable names, such as *X(1)* for the first element in vector *X,* cannot be used.
- Keyword ALL can be used to display the values of all user-defined variables in the working data file.

Operations

- PRINT is executed once for each case constructed from the data file.
- PRINT is a transformation and will not be executed unless it is followed by a procedure or the EXECUTE command.
- Because PRINT is a transformation command, the output might be mixed with casewise procedure output. Procedures that produce individual case listings (REPORT and LIST) should not be used immediately after PRINT. An intervening EXECUTE or procedure command should be specified.
- Values are displayed with a blank space between them. However, if a format is specified for a variable, the blank space for that variable's values is suppressed.
- Values are displayed in the output as the data are read. The PRINT output appears before the output from the first procedure.
- If more variables are specified than can be displayed in 132 columns or within the width specified on SET WIDTH, SPSS displays an error message. You must reduce the number of variables or split the output into several records.
- User-missing values are displayed just like valid values. System-missing values are represented by a period.

Example

```
PRINT   / MOHIRED YRHIRED DEPT SALARY NAME.
FREQUENCIES VARIABLES=DEPT.
```

- PRINT displays values for each variable on the variable list. The FREQUENCIES procedure reads the data and causes PRINT to be executed.
- All variables are displayed using their dictionary formats. One blank space separates the values of each variable.

Example

```
PRINT /ALL.
EXECUTE.
```

- PRINT displays values for all user-defined variables in the working data file. The EXECUTE command executes PRINT.

Formats

By default, PRINT uses the dictionary print formats. You can specify formats for some or all variables specified on PRINT. For a string variable, the specified format must have a width at least as large as that of the dictionary format. String values are truncated if the specified width is smaller than that of the dictionary format.

- Format specifications can be either column-style or FORTRAN-like (see DATA LIST). The column location specified with column-style formats or implied with FORTRAN-like formats refers to the column in which the variable will be displayed.
- A format specification following a list of variables applies to all the variables in the list. Use an asterisk to prevent the specified format from applying to variables preceding the asterisk. The specification of columns locations implies a default print format, and that format will apply to all previous variables if no asterisk is used.
- Printable numeric formats are F, COMMA, DOLLAR, CC, DOT, N, E, PCT, PIBHEX, RBHEX, Z, and the date and time formats. Printable string formats are A and AHEX. Note that hex and binary formats use different widths. For example, the AHEX format must have a width twice that of the corresponding A format. For more information on specifying formats and on the formats available, see DATA LIST and "Variable Formats" on p. 34.
- Format specifications are in effect only for the PRINT command. They do not change the dictionary print formats.
- When a format is specified for a variable, the automatic blank following the variable in the output is suppressed. To preserve the blank between variables, use a string (see "Strings" on p. 495), specify blank columns in the format, or use an X or T format element (see DATA LIST for information on X and T).

Example

```
PRINT / TENURE (F2.0) ' ' MOHIRED YRHIRED DEPT *
        SALARY85 TO SALARY88 (4(DOLLAR8,1X)) NAME.
EXECUTE.
```

- Format F2.0 is specified for *TENURE*. A blank string is specified after *TENURE* because the automatic blank following the variable is suppressed by the format specification.
- *MOHIRED, YRHIRED,* and *DEPT* are displayed with default formats because the asterisk prevents them from receiving the DOLLAR8 format specified for *SALARY85* to *SALARY88*. The automatic blank is preserved for *MOHIRED, YRHIRED,* and *DEPT,* but the blank is suppressed for *SALARY85* to *SALARY88* by the format specification. The 1X format element is therefore specified with DOLLAR8 to add one blank after each value of *SALARY85* to *SALARY88*.
- NAME uses the default dictionary format.

Strings

You can specify string values within the variable list. Strings must be enclosed in apostrophes or quotation marks.
- If a format is specified for a variable list, the application of the format is interrupted by a specified string. Thus, the string has the same effect within a variable list as an asterisk.
- Strings can be used to create column headings for the displayed variables. The PRINT command that specifies the column headings must be used within a DO IF—END IF structure. If you want the column headings to begin a new page in the output, use a PRINT EJECT command rather than PRINT to specify the headings (see PRINT EJECT).

Example

```
PRINT / NAME 'HIRED=' MOHIRED(F2) '/' YRHIRED
        ' SALARY=' SALARY (DOLLAR8).
EXECUTE.
```

- Three strings are specified. The strings HIRED= and SALARY= label the values being displayed. The slash specified between month hired (*MOHIRED*) and year hired (*YRHIRED*) creates a composite hiring date. The F2 format is supplied for variable *MOHIRED* in order to suppress the blank that would follow it if the dictionary format were used.
- *NAME* and *YRHIRED* are displayed with default formats. The 'HIRED=' specification prevents the F2 format from applying to *NAME*, and the 'SALARY=' specification prevents the DOLLAR8 format from applying to *YRHIRED*.

Example

```
DO IF $CASENUM EQ 1.
PRINT /'   NAME ' 1 'DEPT' 25 'HIRED' 30 '  SALARY' 35.
END IF.
PRINT / NAME DEPT *
        MOHIRED 30-31 '/' YRHIRED *
        SALARY 35-42(DOLLAR).
EXECUTE.
```

- The first PRINT command specifies strings only. The integer after each string specifies the beginning column number of the string. The strings will be used as column headings for the variables. DO IF $CASENUM EQ 1 causes the first PRINT command to be executed only once, as the first case is processed. END IF closes the structure.
- The second PRINT command specifies the variables to be displayed. It is executed once for each case in the data. Column locations are specified to align the values with the column headings. In this example, the T format element could also have been used to align the variables and the column headings. For example, MOHIRED (T30,F2) begins the display of values for variable *MOHIRED* in column 30.
- The asterisk after *DEPT* prevents the format specified for *MOHIRED* from applying to *NAME* and *DEPT*. The asterisk after *YRHIRED* prevents the format specified for *SALARY* from applying to *YRHIRED*.

RECORDS Subcommand

RECORDS indicates the total number of lines displayed per case. The number specified on RECORDS is informational only. The actual specification that causes variables to display on a new line is a slash within the variable specifications. Each new line is requested by another slash.

- RECORDS must be specified before the slash that precedes the start of the variable specifications.
- The only specification on RECORDS is an integer to indicate the number of records for the output. If the number does not agree with the actual number of records indicated by slashes, SPSS issues a warning and ignores the specification on RECORDS.
- Specifications for each line of output must begin with a slash. An integer can follow the slash, indicating the line on which values are to be displayed. The integer is informational only. It cannot be used to rearrange the order of records in the output. If the integer does not agree with the actual record number indicated by the number of slashes in the variable specifications, the integer is ignored.
- A slash that is not followed by a variable list generates a blank line in the output.

Example

```
PRINT RECORDS=3 /EMPLOYID NAME DEPT
                /EMPLOYID TENURE SALARY
                /.
EXECUTE.
```

- PRINT displays the values of an individual's name and department on one line, tenure and salary on the next line, and the employee identification number on both lines, followed by a blank third line. Two lines are displayed for each case, and cases in the output are separated by a blank line.

Example

```
PRINT RECORDS=3 /1 EMPLOYID NAME DEPT
                /2 EMPLOYID TENURE SALARY
                /3.
```

- This PRINT command is equivalent to that in the preceding example.

Example

```
PRINT / EMPLOYID NAME DEPT / EMPLOYID TENURE SALARY /.
```

- This PRINT command is equivalent to those in the two preceding examples.

OUTFILE Subcommand

OUTFILE specifies a file for the output from the PRINT command. By default, PRINT output is included with the rest of the output from the SPSS session.

- OUTFILE must be specified before the slash that precedes the start of the variable specifications.

- The output from PRINT cannot exceed 132 characters, even if the external file is defined with a longer record length.

Example
```
PRINT OUTFILE=PRINTOUT
   /1 EMPLOYID DEPT SALARY /2 NAME.
EXECUTE.
```
- OUTFILE specifies *PRINTOUT* as the file that receives the PRINT output.

TABLE Subcommand

TABLE requests a table showing how the variable information is formatted. NOTABLE, which suppresses the format table, is the default.
- TABLE must be specified before the slash that precedes the start of the variable specifications.

Example
```
PRINT TABLE /1 EMPLOYID DEPT SALARY /2  NAME.
EXECUTE.
```
- TABLE requests a summary table describing the PRINT specifications. The table is included with the PRINT output.

PRINT EJECT

```
PRINT EJECT [OUTFILE=file] [RECORDS={1}] [{NOTABLE}]
                                    {n}   {TABLE  }

 /{1    } varlist [{col location [(format)]}] [varlist...]
  {rec #}          {(format list)           }
                   {*                       }

[/{2    } ...]
  {rec #}
```

Example:
```
DO IF $CASENUM EQ 1.
PRINT EJECT /'   NAME ' 1 'DEPT' 25 'HIRED' 30 '   SALARY' 35.
END IF.
PRINT / NAME DEPT *
        MOHIRED(T30,F2) '/' YRHIRED *
        SALARY (T35,DOLLAR8).
EXECUTE.
```

Overview

PRINT EJECT displays specified information at the top of a new page of the output. PRINT EJECT causes a page eject each time it is executed. If PRINT EJECT is not used in a DO IF— END IF structure, it is executed for each case in the data, and each case is displayed on a separate page.

PRINT EJECT is designed to be used with the PRINT command to insert titles and column headings above the values displayed by PRINT. PRINT can also generate titles and headings, but PRINT cannot be used to control page ejects.

PRINT EJECT and PRINT can be used for writing simple reports. The REPORT command is a much more comprehensive tool for writing reports.

Options

The options available for PRINT EJECT are identical to those available for PRINT:

- You can specify formats for the variables.
- You can specify string values within the variable specifications. With PRINT EJECT, the strings are usually used as titles or column headings and often include a specification for column location.
- You can display each case on more than one line using the RECORDS subcommand.
- You can direct the output to a specified file using the OUTFILE subcommand.
- You can display a table that summarizes variable formats with the TABLE subcommand.

All of these features are documented in detail for the PRINT command and work identically for PRINT EJECT. Refer to PRINT for additional information.

Basic Specification

The basic specification is a slash followed by a variable list and/or a list of string values that will be used as column headings or titles. The values for each variable or string are displayed on the top line of a new page in the output. PRINT EJECT is usually used within a DO IF—END IF structure to control the page ejects.

Operations

- PRINT EJECT is a transformation and will not be executed unless it is followed by a procedure or the EXECUTE command.
- If PRINT EJECT is not used within a DO IF—END IF structure, it is executed for each case in the data and displays the values for each case on a separate page.
- Values are displayed with a blank space between them. However, if a format is specified for a variable, the blank space for that variable's values is suppressed.
- Values are displayed in the output as the data are read. The PRINT output appears before the output from the first procedure.
- If more variables are specified than can be displayed in 132 columns or within the width specified on SET WIDTH, SPSS displays an error message. You must reduce the number of variables or split the output into several records.
- User-missing values are displayed just like valid values. System-missing values are represented by a period.

Example

```
DO IF $CASENUM EQ 1.
PRINT EJECT /'   NAME ' 1 'DEPT' 25 'HIRED' 30 '  SALARY' 35.
END IF.
PRINT / NAME DEPT *
        MOHIRED(T30,F2) '/' YRHIRED *
        SALARY (T35,DOLLAR8).
EXECUTE.
```

- PRINT EJECT specifies strings to be used as column headings and causes a page eject. DO IF—END IF causes PRINT EJECT command to be executed only once, when the system variable *$CASENUM* equals 1 (the value assigned to the first case in the file). Thus, column headings are displayed on the first page of the output only. The next example shows how to display column headings at the top of every page of the output.
- If a PRINT command were used in place of PRINT EJECT, the column headings would begin immediately after the command printback.

Example

```
DO IF MOD($CASENUM,50) = 1.
PRINTEJECTFILE=OUT /'    NAME ' 1 'DEPT' 25 'HIRED' 30 '   SALARY' 35.
END IF.
PRINT FILE=OUT / NAME DEPT *
       MOHIRED 30-31 '/' YRHIRED *
       SALARY 35-42(DOLLAR).
EXECUTE.
```

- In this example, DO IF specifies that PRINT EJECT is executed if MOD (the remainder) of *$CASENUM* divided by 50 equals 1 (see p. 46 for a description of MOD). Thus, column headings are displayed on a new page after every 50th case.
- If PRINT were used instead of PRINT EJECT, column headings would display after every 50th case but would not appear at the top of a new page.
- Both PRINT EJECT and PRINT specify the same file for the output. If the FILE subcommands on PRINT EJECT and PRINT do not specify the same file, the column headings and the displayed values end up in different files.

PRINT FORMATS

```
PRINT FORMATS varlist(format) [varlist...]
```

Example:
```
PRINT FORMATS SALARY (DOLLAR8) / HOURLY (DOLLAR7.2)
          / RAISE BONUS (PCT2).
```

Overview

PRINT FORMATS changes variable print formats. Print formats are output formats and control the form in which values are displayed by a procedure or by the PRINT command.

PRINT FORMATS changes only print formats. To change write formats, use the WRITE FORMATS command. To change both the print and write formats with a single specification, use the FORMATS command. For information on assigning input formats during data definition, see DATA LIST. For a more detailed discussion of input and output formats, see "Variable Formats" on p. 34.

Basic Specification

The basic specification is a variable list followed by the new format specification in parentheses. All specified variables receive the new format.

Syntax Rules

- You can specify more than one variable or variable list, followed by a format in parentheses. Only one format can be specified after each variable list. For clarity, each set of specifications can be separated by a slash.
- You can use keyword TO to refer to consecutive variables in the working data file.
- The specified width of a format must include enough positions to accommodate any punctuation characters such as decimal points, commas, dollar signs, or date and time delimiters. (This differs from assigning an *input* format on DATA LIST, where SPSS automatically expands the input format to accommodate punctuation characters in output.)
- Custom currency formats (CCw, CCw.d) must first be defined on the SET command before they can be used on PRINT FORMATS.
- PRINT FORMATS cannot be used with string variables. To change the length of a string variable, declare a new variable of the desired length with the STRING command and then use COMPUTE to copy values from the existing string into the new string.

Operations

- Unlike most transformations, PRINT FORMATS takes effect as soon as it is encountered in the command sequence. Special attention should be paid to its position among commands. For more information, see "Command Order" on p. 17.
- Variables not specified on PRINT FORMATS retain their current print formats in the working data file. To see the current formats, use the DISPLAY command.
- The new print formats are changed only in the working file and are in effect for the duration of the SPSS session or until changed again with a PRINT FORMATS or FORMATS command. Print formats in the original data file (if one exists) are not changed, unless the file is resaved with the SAVE or XSAVE command.
- New numeric variables created with transformation commands are assigned default print formats of F8.2 (or the format specified on the FORMAT subcommand of SET). The FORMATS command can be used to change the new variable's print formats.
- New string variables created with transformation commands are assigned the format specified on the STRING command that declares the variable. PRINT FORMATS cannot be used to change the format of a new string variable.
- Date and time formats are effective only with the LIST, REPORT, and TABLES procedures and the PRINT and WRITE transformation commands. All other procedures use F format regardless of the date and time formats specified. (See "Date and Time Formats" on p. 59.)
- If a numeric data value exceeds its width specification, SPSS attempts to display some value nevertheless. First SPSS rounds decimal values, then removes punctuation characters, then tries scientific notation, and finally, if there is still not enough space, produces asterisks indicating that a value is present but cannot be displayed in the assigned width.

Example

```
PRINT FORMATS SALARY (DOLLAR8) / HOURLY (DOLLAR7.2)
    / RAISE BONUS (PCT2).
```

- The print format for *SALARY* is changed to DOLLAR with eight positions, including the dollar sign and comma when appropriate. The value 11550 is displayed as $11,550. An eight-digit number would require a DOLLAR11 format specification: eight characters for digits, two characters for commas, and one character for the dollar sign.
- The print format for *HOURLY* is changed to DOLLAR with seven positions, including the dollar sign, decimal point, and two decimal places. The number 115 is displayed as $115.00. If DOLLAR6.2 had been specified, the value 115 would be displayed as $115.0. SPSS would truncate the last 0 because a width of 6 is not enough to display the full value.
- The print format for both *RAISE* and *BONUS* is changed to PCT with two positions: one position for the percentage and one position for the percent sign. The value 9 displays as 9%. Since the width allows for only two positions, the value 10 displays as 10, since the percent sign is truncated.

Example

```
COMPUTE V3=V1 + V2.
PRINT FORMATS V3 (F3.1).
```

- COMPUTE creates the new numeric variable *V3*. By default, *V3* is assigned an F8.2 format (or the default format specified on SET).
- PRINT FORMATS changes the print format for *V3* to F3.1.

Example

```
SET CCA='-/-.Dfl ..-'.
PRINT FORMATS COST (CCA14.2).
```

- SET defines a European currency format for the custom currency format type CCA.
- PRINT FORMATS assigns the print format CCA to variable *COST*. With the format defined for CCA on SET, the value 37419 is displayed as Dfl'37.419,00. See the SET command for more information on custom currency formats.

PRINT SPACE

```
PRINT SPACE [OUTFILE=file] [numeric expression]
```

Example:
```
PRINT / NAME DEPT82 *
        MOHIRED(T30,F2) '/' YRHIRED *
        SALARY82 (T35,DOLLAR8).
PRINT SPACE.
EXECUTE.
```

Overview

PRINT SPACE displays blank lines in the output and is generally used with a PRINT or WRITE command. Because PRINT SPACE displays a blank space each time it is executed, it is often used in a DO IF—END IF structure.

Basic Specification

The basic specification is simply the command PRINT SPACE.

Syntax Rules

- To display more than one blank line, specify a numeric expression after PRINT SPACE. The expression can be an integer or a complex expression.
- OUTFILE directs the output to a specified file. OUTFILE should be specified if an OUTFILE subcommand is specified on the PRINT or WRITE command that is used with PRINT SPACE. The OUTFILE subcommand on PRINT SPACE and PRINT or WRITE should specify the same file.

Operations

- If PRINT SPACE is not used in a DO IF—END IF structure, it is executed for each case in the data and displays a blank line for every case.

Example

```
PRINT / NAME DEPT82 *
        MOHIRED(T30,F2) '/' YRHIRED *
        SALARY82 (T35,DOLLAR8).
PRINT SPACE.
EXECUTE.
```

- PRINT SPACE displays one blank line each time it is executed. Because PRINT SPACE is not used in a DO IF—END IF structure, it is executed once for each case. In effect, the output is double-spaced.

Example

```
NUMERIC #LINE.
DO IF MOD(#LINE,5) = 0.
PRINT SPACE 2.
END IF.
COMPUTE #LINE=#LINE + 1.
PRINT / NAME DEPT *
        MOHIRED 30-31 '/' YRHIRED *
        SALARY 35-42(DOLLAR).
EXECUTE.
```

- DO IF specifies that PRINT SPACE will be executed if MOD (the remainder) of *#LINE* divided by 5 equals 1. Since *#LINE* is incremented by 1 for each case, PRINT SPACE is executed once for every five cases. (See p. 46 for information on the MOD function.)
- PRINT SPACE specifies two blank lines. Cases are displayed in groups of five with two blank lines between each group.

Example

```
* Printing addresses on labels.

COMPUTE #LINES=0.                    /*Initiate #LINES to 0
DATA LIST FILE=ADDRESS/RECORD 1-40 (A). ' /*Read a record
COMPUTE #LINES=#LINES+1.             /*Bump counter and print
WRITE OUTFILE=LABELS /RECORD.

DO IF RECORD EQ ' '.                 /*Blank between addresses
+  PRINT SPACE OUTFILE=LABELS 8 - #LINES.  /*Add extra blank #LINES
+  COMPUTE #LINES=0.
END IF.
EXECUTE.
```

- PRINT SPACE uses a complex expression for specifying the number of blank lines to display. The data contain a variable number of input records for each name and address, which must be printed in a fixed number of lines for mailing labels. The goal is to know when the last line for each address has been printed, how many lines have printed, and therefore how many blank records must be printed in order for the next address to fit on the next label. The example assumes that there is already one blank line between each address on input and that you want to print eight lines per label.
- The DATA LIST command defines the data. Each line of the address is contained in columns 1–40 of the data file and is assigned the variable name *RECORD*. For the blank line between each address, *RECORD* is blank.
- Variable *#LINES* is the key to this example. *#LINES* is initialized to 0 as a scratch variable. It is incremented for each record written. When SPSS encounters a blank line (RECORD EQ ' '), PRINT SPACE prints a number of blank lines equal to 8 minus the number already printed, and *#LINES* is then reset to 0.
- OUTFILE on PRINT SPACE specifies the same file specified by OUTFILE on WRITE.

PROCEDURE OUTPUT

```
PROCEDURE OUTPUT OUTFILE=file
```

Example:
```
PROCEDURE OUTPUT OUTFILE=CELLDATA.
CROSSTABS VARIABLES=FEAR SEX (1,2)
  /TABLES=FEAR BY SEX
  /WRITE=ALL.
```

Overview

PROCEDURE OUTPUT specifies the files to which CROSSTABS, FREQUENCIES, and SURVIVAL (included in the SPSS Advanced Statistics option) can write procedure output. PROCEDURE OUTPUT has no other applications.

Basic Specification

The only specification is OUTFILE and the file specification. PROCEDURE OUTPUT must precede the command to which it applies.

Example

```
PROCEDURE OUTPUT OUTFILE=CELLDATA.
CROSSTABS VARIABLES=FEAR SEX (1,2)
  /TABLES=FEAR BY SEX
  /WRITE=ALL.
```

- PROCEDURE OUTPUT precedes CROSSTABS and specifies *CELLDATA* as the file to receive the cell frequencies.
- The WRITE subcommand on CROSSTABS is required for writing cell frequencies to a procedure output file.

Example

```
PROCEDURE OUTPUT OUTFILE=CODEBOOK.
FREQUENCIES VARIABLES=ALL
  /FORMAT=ONEPAGE WRITE.
```

- PROCEDURE OUTPUT precedes FREQUENCIES and specifies *CODEBOOK* as the file to receive frequency tables.
- The WRITE keyword on the FORMAT subcommand on FREQUENCIES is required for writing the display to a procedure output file.

Example

```
PROCEDURE OUTPUT OUTFILE=SURVTBL.
SURVIVAL   TABLES=ONSSURV,RECSURV BY TREATMNT(1,3)
  /STATUS = RECURSIT(1,9) FOR RECSURV
  /STATUS = STATUS(3,4) FOR ONSSURV
  /INTERVAL=THRU 50 BY 5 THRU 100 BY 10/PLOTS/COMPARE
  /CALCULATE=CONDITIONAL PAIRWISE
  /WRITE=TABLES.
```

- PROCEDURE OUTPUT precedes SURVIVAL and specifies *SURVTBL* as the file to receive the survival tables.
- The WRITE subcommand on SURVIVAL is required for writing survival tables to a procedure output file.

RANK

```
RANK [VARIABLES=] varlist [({A**})] [BY varlist]
                           {D  }

    [/TIES={MEAN**  }]
           {LOW     }
           {HIGH    }
           {CONDENSE}

    [/FRACTION={BLOM**}]
               {TUKEY }
               {VW    }
               {RANKIT}

    [/PRINT={YES**}]
            {NO   }

    [/MISSING={EXCLUDE**}]
              {INCLUDE  }
```

The following function subcommands can each be specified once:

```
[/RANK**] [/NTILES(k)] [/NORMAL] [/PERCENT]

[/RFRACTION] [/PROPORTION] [/N] [/SAVAGE]
```

The following keyword can be used with any function subcommand:

```
[INTO varname]
```

**Default if the subcommand is omitted.

Example:

```
RANK VARIABLES=SALARY JOBTIME.
```

Overview

RANK produces new variables containing ranks, normal scores, and Savage and related scores for numeric variables.

Options

Methods. You can rank variables in ascending or descending order by specifying A or D on the VARIABLES subcommand. You can compute different rank functions and also name the new variables using the function subcommands. You can specify the method for handling ties on the TIES subcommand, and you can specify how the proportion estimate is computed for the NORMAL and PROPORTIONAL functions on the FRACTION subcommand.

Format. You can suppress the display of the summary table that lists the ranked variables and their associated new variables in the working data file using the PRINT subcommand.

Basic Specification

The basic specification is VARIABLES and at least one variable from the working data file. By default, the ranking function is RANK. Direction is ascending, and ties are handled by assigning the mean rank to tied values. A summary table that lists the ranked variables and the new variables into which computed ranks have been stored is displayed.

Subcommand Order

- VARIABLES must be specified first.
- The remaining subcommands can be specified in any order.

Operations

- RANK does not change the way the working data file is sorted.
- If new variable names are not specified with the INTO keyword on the function subcommand, RANK creates default names. (See the INTO keyword on p. 511.)
- RANK automatically assigns variable labels to the new variables. The labels identify the source variables. For example, the label for a new variable with the default name *RSALARY* is *RANK of SALARY*.

Example

```
RANK VARIABLES=SALARY JOBTIME.
```

- RANK ranks *SALARY* and *JOBTIME* and creates two new variables in the working file, *RSALARY* and *RJOBTIME*, which contain the ranks.

VARIABLES Subcommand

VARIABLES specifies the variables to be ranked. Keyword VARIABLES can be omitted.

- VARIABLES is required and must be the first specification on RANK. The minimum specification is a single numeric variable. To rank more than one variable, specify a variable list.
- After the variable list you can specify the direction for ranking in parentheses. Specify A for ascending (smallest value gets smallest rank) or D for descending (largest value gets smallest rank). A is the default.
- To rank some variables in ascending order and others in descending order, use both A and D in the same variable list. A or D applies to all preceding variables in the list up to the previous A or D specification.
- To organize ranks into subgroups, specify keyword BY followed by the variable whose values determine the subgroups. The working data file does not have to be sorted by this variable.

- String variables cannot be specified. Use AUTORECODE to recode string variables for ranking.

Example

```
RANK VARIABLES=MURDERS ROBBERY (D).
```

- RANK ranks *MURDERS* and *ROBBERY* and creates two new variables in the working data file: *RMURDERS* and *RROBBERY*.
- D specifies descending order of rank. D applies to both *MURDERS* and *ROBBERY*.

Example

```
RANK VARIABLES=MURDERS (D) ROBBERY (A) BY ETHNIC.
```

- Ranks are computed within each group defined by *ETHNIC*. *MURDERS* is ranked in descending order and *ROBBERY* in ascending order within each group of *ETHNIC*. The working data file does not have to be sorted by *ETHNIC*.

Function Subcommands

The optional function subcommands specify different rank functions. RANK is the default function.

- Any combination of function subcommands can be specified for a RANK procedure, but each function can be specified only once.
- Each function subcommand must be preceded by a slash.
- The functions assign default names to the new variables unless keyword INTO is specified (see the INTO keyword on p. 511).

RANK *Simple ranks.* The values for the new variable are the ranks. Rank can either be ascending or descending, as indicated on the VARIABLES subcommand. Rank values can be affected by the specification on the TIES subcommand.

RFRACTION *Fractional ranks.* The values for the new variable equal the ranks divided by the sum of the weights of the nonmissing cases. If HIGH is specified on TIES, fractional rank values are an empirical cumulative distribution.

NORMAL *Normal scores* (Lehmann, 1975). The new variable contains the inverse of the standard normal cumulative distribution of the proportion estimate defined by the FRACTION subcommand. The default for FRACTION is BLOM.

PERCENT *Fractional ranks as a percentage.* The new variable contains fractional ranks multiplied by 100.

PROPORTION *Proportion estimates.* The estimation method is specified by the FRACTION subcommand. The default for FRACTION is BLOM.

N *Sum of case weights.* The new variable is a constant.

SAVAGE *Savage scores* (Lehmann, 1975). The new variable contains Savage (exponential) scores.

NTILES(k)   *Percentile groups.* The new variable contains values from 1 to *k*, where *k* is the number of groups to be generated. Each case is assigned a group value, which is the integer part of $1+rk/(w+1)$, where *r* is the rank of the case, *k* is the number of groups specified on NTILES, and *w* is the sum of the case weights. Group values can be affected by the specification on TIES. There is no default for *k*.

INTO Keyword

INTO specifies variable names for the new variable(s) added to the working data file. INTO can be used with any of the function subcommands.

- INTO must follow a function subcommand. You must specify the INTO subcommand to assign names to the new variables created by the function.
- You can specify multiple variable names on INTO. The names are assigned to the new variables in the order they are created (the order the variables are specified on the VARIABLES subcommand).
- If you specify fewer names than the new variables, default names are used for the remaining new variables. If you specify more names, SPSS issues a message and the command is not executed.

If INTO is not specified on a function, RANK creates default names for the new variables according to the following rules:

- The first letter of the ranking function is added to the first seven characters of the original variable name.
- New variable names cannot duplicate variable names in the working data file or names specified after INTO or generated by default.
- If a new default name is a duplicate, the scheme *XXXnnn* is used, where *XXX* represents the first three characters of the function and *nnn* is a three-digit number starting with 001 and increased by 1 for each variable. (If the ranking function is N, *XXX* is simply *N*.) If this naming scheme generates duplicate names, the duplicates are named *RNKXXnn*, where *XX* is the first two characters of the function and *nn* is a two-digit number starting with 01 and increased by 1 for each variable.
- If it is not possible to generate unique names, an error results.

Example

```
RANK VARIABLES=SALARY
 /NORMAL INTO SALNORM
 /SAVAGE INTO SALSAV
 /NTILES(4) INTO SALQUART.
```

- RANK generates three new variables from variable *SALARY*.
- NORMAL produces the new variable *SALNORM*. *SALNORM* contains normal scores for *SALARY* computed with the default formula BLOM.
- SAVAGE produces the new variable *SALSAV*. *SALSAV* contains Savage scores for *SALARY*.

- NTILES(4) produces the new variable *SALQUART*. *SALQUART* contains the value 1, 2, 3, or 4 to represent one of the four percentile groups of *SALARY*.

TIES Subcommand

TIES determines the way tied values are handled. The default method is MEAN.

MEAN   *Mean rank of tied values is used for ties.* This is the default.

LOW   *Lowest rank of tied values is used for ties.*

HIGH   *Highest rank of tied values is used for ties.*

CONDENSE   *Consecutive ranks with ties sharing the same value.* Each distinct value of the ranked variable is assigned a consecutive rank. Ties share the same rank.

Example

```
RANK VARIABLES=BURGLARY /RANK INTO RMEAN /TIES=MEAN.
RANK VARIABLES=BURGLARY /RANK INTO RCONDS /TIES=CONDENSE.
RANK VARIABLES=BURGLARY /RANK INTO RHIGH /TIES=HIGH.
RANK VARIABLES=BURGLARY /RANK INTO RLOW /TIES=LOW.
```

- The values of *BURGLARY* and the four new ranking variables are shown below:

BURGLARY	RMEAN	RCONDS	RHIGH	RLOW
0	3	1	5	1
0	3	1	5	1
0	3	1	5	1
0	3	1	5	1
0	3	1	5	1
1	6.5	2	7	6
1	6.5	2	7	6
3	8	3	8	8

FRACTION Subcommand

FRACTION specifies the way to compute a proportion estimate *P* for the NORMAL and PROPORTION rank functions.

- FRACTION can be used only with function subcommands NORMAL or PROPORTION. If it is used with other function subcommands, FRACTION is ignored and a warning message is displayed.
- Only one formula can be specified for each RANK procedure. If more than one is specified, an error results.

In the following formulas, *r* is the rank and *w* is the sum of case weights.

BLOM   *Blom's transformation, defined by the formula $(r - 3/8) / (w + 1/4)$.* (Blom, 1958.) This is the default.

RANKIT   *The formula is $(r - 1/2) / w$.* (Chambers et al., 1983.)

TUKEY   *Tukey's transformation, defined by the formula $(r - 1/3) / (w + 1/3)$.* (Tukey, 1962.)

VW   *Van der Waerden's transformation, defined by the formula $r / (w + 1)$.* (Lehmann, 1975.)

Example

```
RANK VARIABLES=MORTGAGE VALUE /FRACTION=BLOM
  /NORMAL INTO MORTNORM VALNORM.
```

- RANK generates new variables *MORTNORM* and *VALNORM*. *MORTNORM* contains normal scores for *MORTGAGE*, and *VALNORM* contains normal scores for *VALUE*.

PRINT Subcommand

PRINT determines whether the summary tables are displayed. The summary table lists the ranked variables and their associated new variables in the working data file.

YES   *Display the summary tables*. This is the default.

NO   *Suppress the summary tables*.

MISSING Subcommand

MISSING controls the treatment of user-missing values.

INCLUDE   *Include user-missing values*. User-missing values are treated as valid values.

EXCLUDE   *Exclude all missing values*. User-missing values are treated as missing. This is the default.

Example

```
MISSING VALUE SALARY (0).
RANK VARIABLES=SALARY /RANK INTO SALRANK /MISSING=INCLUDE.
```

- RANK generates the new variable *SALRANK*.
- INCLUDE causes user-missing value 0 to be included in the ranking process.

References

Blom, G. 1958. *Statistical estimates and transformed beta variables.* New York: John Wiley & Sons.

Chambers, J. M., W. S. Cleveland, B. Kleiner, and P. A. Tukey. 1983. *Graphical methods for data analysis.* Belmont, California: Wadsworth International Group; Boston: Duxbury Press.

Fisher, R. A. 1973. *Statistical methods for research workers.* 14th ed. New York: Hafner Publishing Company.

Frigge, M., D. C. Hoaglin, and B. Iglewicz. 1987. Some implementations of the boxplot. In *Computer science and statistics proceedings of the 19th symposium on the interface.* R. M. Heiberger and M. Martin, eds. Alexandria, Virginia: American Statistical Association.

Lehmann, E. L. 1975. *Nonparametrics: statistical methods based on ranks.* San Francisco: Holden-Day.

Tukey, J. W. 1962. The future of data analysis. *Annals of Mathematical Statistics* 33:22.

RECODE

For numeric variables:

```
RECODE varlist (value list=value)...(value list=value) [INTO varlist]
       [/varlist...]
```

Input keywords:

LO, LOWEST, HI, HIGHEST, THRU, MISSING, SYSMIS, ELSE

Output keywords:

COPY, SYSMIS

For string variables:

```
RECODE varlist [('string',['string'...]='string')][INTO varlist]
       [/varlist...]
```

Input keywords:

CONVERT, ELSE

Output keyword:

COPY

Examples:

```
RECODE V1 TO V3 (0=1) (1=0) (2,3=-1) (9=9) (ELSE=SYSMIS).
RECODE STRNGVAR ('A','B','C'='A')('D','E','F'='B')(ELSE=' ').
```

Overview

RECODE changes, rearranges, or consolidates the values of an existing variable. RECODE can be executed on a value-by-value basis or for a range of values. Where it can be used, RECODE is much more efficient than the series of IF commands that produce the same transformation.

With RECODE, you must specify the new values. Use AUTORECODE to automatically recode the values of string or numeric variables to consecutive integers.

Options

You can generate a new variable as the recoded version of an existing variable using keyword INTO. You can also use INTO to recode a string variable into a new numeric variable for more efficient processing, or to recode a numeric variable into a new string variable to provide more descriptive values.

Basic Specification

The basic specification is a variable name and, within parentheses, the original values followed by a required equals sign and a new value. RECODE changes the values on the left of the equals sign into the single value on the right of the equals sign.

Syntax Rules

- The variables to be recoded must already exist and must be specified before the value specifications.
- Value specifications are enclosed in parentheses. The original value or values must be specified to the left of an equals sign. A single new value is specified to the right of the equals sign.
- Multiple values can be consolidated into a single recoded value by specifying, to the left of the equals sign, a list of values separated by blanks or commas. Only one recoded value per set is allowed to the right of the equals sign.
- Multiple sets of value specifications are permitted. Each set must be enclosed in parentheses and can result in only one new value.
- To recode multiple variables using the same set of value specifications, specify a variable list before the value specifications. Each variable in the list is recoded identically.
- To recode variables using different value specifications, separate each variable (or variable list) and its specifications from the others by a slash.
- Original values that are not mentioned remain unchanged unless keyword ELSE is used. ELSE refers to all original values not previously mentioned, including the system-missing value. ELSE should be the last specification for the variable.
- COPY replicates original values without recoding them.
- INTO is required to recode a string variable into a numeric variable or a numeric variable into a string variable (see the INTO keyword on p. 517).

Numeric Variables

- Keywords that can be used in the list of original values are LO (or LOWEST), HI (or HIGHEST), THRU, MISSING, SYSMIS, and ELSE. Keywords that can be used in place of a new value are COPY and SYSMIS.
- THRU specifies a value range and includes the specified end values.
- LOWEST and HIGHEST (LO and HI) specify the lowest and highest values encountered in the data. LOWEST and HIGHEST include user-missing values but not the system-missing value.
- MISSING specifies user- and system-missing values for recoding. MISSING can be used in the list of original values only.
- SYSMIS specifies the system-missing value and can be used as both an original value and a new value.
- See "Syntax Rules" above for a description of ELSE and COPY.

String Variables

- Keywords that can be used in the list of original values are CONVERT and ELSE. The only keyword that can be used in place of a new value is COPY. See p. 518 for a description of CONVERT, and "Syntax Rules" on p. 515 for a description of ELSE and COPY.
- Both short and long string variables can be recoded.
- Values must be enclosed in apostrophes or quotation marks.
- Blanks are significant characters.

Operations

- Value specifications are scanned left to right.
- A value is recoded only once per RECODE command.
- Invalid specifications on a RECODE command that result in errors stop all processing of that RECODE command. No variables are recoded.

Numeric Variables

- Blank fields for numeric variables are handled according to the SET BLANKS specification prior to recoding.
- When you recode a value that was previously defined as user-missing on the MISSING VALUE command, the new value is not missing.

String Variables

- If the original or new value specified is shorter than the format width defined for the variable, the string is right-padded with blanks.
- If the original or recoded value specified is longer than the format width defined for that variable, SPSS issues an error message and RECODE is not executed.

Limitations

- You can recode (and count using the COUNT command) approximately 400 values.

Example

```
RECODE V1 TO V3 (0=1) (1=0) (2,3=-1) (9=9) (ELSE=SYSMIS)
 /QVAR(1 THRU 5=1)(6 THRU 10=2)(11 THRU HI=3)(ELSE=0).
```

- The numeric variables between and including *V1* and *V3* are recoded: original values 0 and 1 are switched respectively to 1 and 0; 2 and 3 are changed to –1; 9 remains 9; and any other value is changed to the system-missing value.

- Variable *QVAR* is also recoded: original values 1 through 5 are changed to 1; 6 through 10 are changed to 2; 11 through the highest value in the data are changed to 3; and any other value, including system-missing, is changed to 0.

Example

```
RECODE STRNGVAR ('A','B','C'='A')('D','E','F'='B')(ELSE=' ').
RECODE PET ('IGUANA', 'SNAKE ' = 'WILD   ').
```

- Values A, B, and C are changed to value A. Values D, E, and F are changed to value B. All other values are changed to a blank.
- Values IGUANA and SNAKE are changed to value WILD. The defined width of variable *PET* is 6. Thus, values SNAKE and WILD include trailing blanks for a total of six characters. If blanks are not specified, the values are right-padded. In this example, the results will be the same.
- Each string value is enclosed within apostrophes.

INTO Keyword

INTO specifies a **target** variable to receive recoded values from the original, or **source**, variable. Source variables remain unchanged after the recode.

- INTO must follow the value specifications for the source variables that are being recoded into the target variables.
- The number of target variables must equal the number of source variables.

Numeric Variables

- Target variables can be existing or new variables. For existing variables, cases with values not mentioned in the value specifications are not changed. For new variables, cases with values not mentioned are assigned the system-missing value.
- New numeric variables have default print and write formats of F8.2 (or the format specified on SET FORMAT).

Example

```
RECODE AGE (MISSING=9) (18 THRU HI=1) (0 THRU 18=0) INTO VOTER.
```

- The recoded *AGE* values are stored in target variable *VOTER*, leaving *AGE* unchanged.
- Value 18 and higher values are changed to value 1. Values between 0 and 18, but not including 18, are recoded to 0. If the specification 0 THRU 18 preceded the specification 18 THRU HI, value 18 would be recoded to 0.

Example

```
RECODE V1 TO V3 (0=1) (1=0) (2=-1) INTO DEFENSE WELFARE HEALTH.
```

- Values for *V1* through *V3* are recoded and stored in *DEFENSE*, *WELFARE*, and *HEALTH*. *V1*, *V2*, and *V3* are not changed.

String Variables

- Target variables must already exist. To create a new string variable, declare the variable with the STRING command before specifying it on RECODE.
- The new string values cannot be longer than the defined width of the target variable.
- If the new values are shorter than the defined width of the target variable, the values are right-padded with blanks.
- Multiple target variables are allowed. The target variables must all be the same defined width; the source variables can have different widths.
- If the source and target variables have different widths, the criterion for the width of the original values is the width defined for the source variable; the criterion for the width of the recoded values is the width defined for the target variable.

Example

```
STRING STATE1 (A2).
RECODE STATE ('IO'='IA') (ELSE=COPY) INTO STATE1.
```

- STRING declares variable *STATE1* so that it can be used as a target variable on RECODE.
- RECODE specifies *STATE* as the source variable and *STATE1* as the target variable. The original value IO is recoded to IA. Keywords ELSE and COPY copy all other state codes over unchanged. Thus, *STATE* and *STATE1* are identical except for cases with the original value IO.

Example

```
RECODE SEX ('M'=1) ('F'=2) INTO NSEX.
```

- RECODE recodes string variable *SEX* into numeric variable *NSEX*. Any value other than M or F becomes system-missing.
- SPSS can process a large number of cases more efficiently with the numeric variable *NSEX* than it can with the string variable *SEX*.

CONVERT Keyword

CONVERT recodes the string representation of numbers to their numeric representation.

- If keyword CONVERT precedes the value specifications, cases with numbers are recoded immediately and blanks are recoded to the system-missing value, even if you specifically recode blanks into a value.
- To recode blanks to a value other than system-missing or to recode a string value to a non-corresponding numeric value (for example '0' to 10), you must specify a recode specification *before* the keyword CONVERT.
- RECODE converts numbers as if the variable were being reread using the F format.

- If RECODE encounters a value that cannot be converted, it scans the remaining value specifications. If there is no specific recode specification for that value, the target variable will be system-missing for that case.

Example

```
RECODE #JOB (CONVERT) ('-'=11) ('&'=12) INTO JOB.
```

- RECODE first recodes all numbers in string variable #JOB to numbers. The target variable is JOB.
- RECODE then specifically recodes the minus sign (the "eleven" punch) to 11 and the ampersand (or "twelve" punch in EBCDIC) to 12. Keyword CONVERT is specified first as an efficiency measure to recode cases with numbers immediately. Blanks are recoded to the system-missing value.

Example

```
RECODE #JOB (' '=-99) (CONVERT) ('-'=11) ('&'=12) INTO JOB.
```

- The result is the same as in the above example, except that blanks are changed to –99.

RECORD TYPE

For mixed file types:

```
RECORD TYPE {value list} [SKIP]
            {OTHER     }
```

For grouped file types:

```
RECORD TYPE {value list} [SKIP] [CASE=col loc]
            {OTHER     }

[DUPLICATE={WARN  }] [MISSING={WARN  }]
           {NOWARN}           {NOWARN}
```

For nested file types:

```
RECORD TYPE {value list} [SKIP] [CASE=col loc]
            {OTHER     }

[SPREAD={YES}] [MISSING={WARN  }]
        {NO }           {NOWARN}
```

Example:

```
FILE TYPE  MIXED RECORD=RECID 1-2.
RECORD TYPE 23.
DATA LIST  /SEX 5 AGE 6-7 DOSAGE 8-10 RESULT 12.
END FILE TYPE.

BEGIN DATA
21  145010 1
22  257200 2
25  235  250   2
35  167           300      3
24  125150 1
23  272075 1
21  149050 2
25  134  035   3
30  138           300      3
32  229           500      3
END DATA.
```

Overview

RECORD TYPE is used with DATA LIST within a FILE TYPE—END FILE TYPE structure to define any one of the three types of complex raw data files: *mixed files*, which contain several types of records that define different types of cases; *hierarchical* or *nested files*, which contain several types of records with a defined relationship among the record types; or *grouped files*, which contain several records for each case with some records missing or duplicated (see FILE TYPE for more complete information). A fourth type of complex file, files with *repeating groups* of information, can be read with the REPEATING DATA command. REPEATING DATA can also be used to read mixed files and the lowest level of nested files.

Each type of complex file has varying types of records. One set of RECORD TYPE and DATA LIST commands is used to define each type of record in the data. The specifications available for RECORD TYPE vary according to whether MIXED, GROUPED, or NESTED is specified on FILE TYPE.

Basic Specification

For each record type being defined, the basic specification is the value of the record type variable defined on the RECORD subcommand on FILE TYPE.

- RECORD TYPE must be followed by a DATA LIST command defining the variables for the specified records, unless SKIP is used.
- One pair of RECORD TYPE and DATA LIST commands must be used for each defined record type.

Syntax Rules

- A list of values can be specified if a set of different record types has the same variable definitions. Each value must be separated by a space or comma.
- String values must be enclosed in apostrophes or quotation marks.
- For mixed files, each DATA LIST can specify variables with the same variable name, since each record type defines a separate case. For grouped and nested files, the variable names on each DATA LIST must be unique, since a case is built by combining all record types together onto a single record.
- For mixed files, if the same variable is defined for more than one record type, the format type and width of the variable should be the same on all DATA LIST commands. SPSS refers to the first DATA LIST command that defines a variable for the print and write formats to include in the dictionary of the working data file.
- For nested files, the order of the RECORD TYPE commands defines the hierarchical structure of the file. The first RECORD TYPE defines the highest-level record type, the next RECORD TYPE defines the next highest-level record, and so forth. The last RECORD TYPE command defines a case in the working data file.

Operations

- If a record type is specified on more than one RECORD TYPE command, SPSS uses the DATA LIST command associated with the first specification and ignores all others.
- For NESTED files, the first record in the file should be the type specified on the first RECORD TYPE command—the highest-level record of the hierarchy. If the first record in the file is not the highest-level type, SPSS skips all records until it encounters a record of the highest-level type. If the MISSING or DUPLICATE subcommands have been specified on the FILE TYPE command, these records may produce warning messages but will not be used to build a case in the working data file.

Example

```
* Reading only one record type from a mixed file.

FILE TYPE   MIXED RECORD=RECID 1-2.
RECORD TYPE 23.
DATA LIST    /SEX 5 AGE 6-7 DOSAGE 8-10 RESULT 12.
END FILE TYPE.

BEGIN DATA
21   145010 1
22   257200 2
25   235   250   2
35   167            300      3
24   125150 1
23   272075 1
21   149050 2
25   134   035   3
30   138            300      3
32   229            500      3
END DATA.
```

- FILE TYPE begins the file definition and END FILE TYPE indicates the end of file definition. FILE TYPE specifies a mixed file type. Since the data are included between BEGIN DATA—END DATA, the FILE subcommand is omitted. The record identification variable *RECID* is located in columns 1 and 2.
- RECORD TYPE indicates that records with value 23 for variable *RECID* will be copied into the working data file. All other records are skipped. SPSS does not issue a warning when it skips records in mixed files.
- DATA LIST defines variables on records with the value 23 for variable *RECID*.

Example

```
* Reading multiple record types from a mixed file.

FILE TYPE   MIXED FILE=TREATMNT RECORD=RECID 1-2.
+ RECORD TYPE 21,22,23,24.
+ DATA LIST    /SEX 5 AGE 6-7 DOSAGE 8-10 RESULT 12.
+ RECORD TYPE 25.
+ DATA LIST    /SEX 5 AGE 6-7 DOSAGE 10-12 RESULT 15.
END FILE TYPE.
```

- Variable *DOSAGE* is read from columns 8–10 for record types 21, 22, 23, and 24 and from columns 10–12 for record type 25. *RESULT* is read from column 12 for record types 21, 22, 23, and 24 and from column 15 for record type 25.
- The working data file contains values for all variables defined on the DATA LIST commands for record types 21 through 25. All other record types are skipped.

Example

```
* A nested file of accident records.

FILE TYPE NESTED RECORD=6 CASE=ACCID 1-4.
RECORD TYPE 1.
DATA LIST /ACC_ID 9-11 WEATHER 12-13 STATE 15-16 (A) DATE 18-24 (A).
RECORD TYPE 2.
DATA LIST /STYLE 11 MAKE 13 OLD 14 LICENSE 15-16(A) INSURNCE 18-21 (A).
RECORD TYPE 3.
DATA LIST /PSNGR_NO 11 AGE 13-14 SEX 16 (A) INJURY 18 SEAT 20-21 (A)
          COST 23-24.
END FILE TYPE.

BEGIN DATA
0001 1   322 1 IL 3/13/88   /* Type 1:  accident record
0001 2     1 44MI 134M      /* Type 2:    vehicle record
0001 3     1 34 M 1 FR  3   /* Type 3:      person record
0001 2     2 16IL 322F      /*              vehicle record
0001 3     1 22 F 1 FR 11   /*                person record
0001 3     2 35 M 1 FR  5   /*                person record
0001 3     3 59 M 1 BK  7   /*                person record
0001 2     3 21IN 146M      /*              vehicle record
0001 3     1 46 M 0 FR  0   /*                person record
END DATA.
```

- FILE TYPE specifies a nested file type. The record identifier, located in column 6, is not assigned a variable name, so the default scratch variable name ####RECD is used. The case identification variable ACCID is located in columns 1–4.
- Because there are three record types, there are three RECORD TYPE commands. For each RECORD TYPE there is a DATA LIST command to define variables on that record type. The order of the RECORD TYPE commands defines the hierarchical structure of the file.
- END FILE TYPE signals the end of file definition.
- SPSS builds a case for each lowest-level (type 3) record, representing each person in the file. There can be only one type 1 record for each type 2 record, and one type 2 record for each type 3 record. Each vehicle can be in only one accident, and each person can be in only one vehicle. The variables from the type 1 and type 2 records are spread to their corresponding type 3 records.

OTHER Keyword

OTHER specifies all record types that have not been mentioned on previous RECORD TYPE commands.

- OTHER can be specified only on the last RECORD TYPE command in the file definition.
- OTHER can be used with SKIP to skip all undefined record types.
- For nested files, OTHER can be used only with SKIP. Neither can be used separately.
- If WILD=WARN is in effect for the FILE TYPE command, OTHER cannot be specified on the RECORD TYPE command.

Example

```
* A mixed file.

FILE TYPE  MIXED FILE=TREATMNT RECORD=RECID 1-2.
RECORD TYPE 21,22,23,24.
DATA LIST     /SEX 5 AGE 6-7 DOSAGE 8-10 RESULT 12.
RECORD TYPE 25.
DATA LIST     /SEX 5 AGE 6-7 DOSAGE 10-12 RESULT 15.
RECORD TYPE OTHER.
DATA LIST     /SEX 5 AGE 6-7 DOSAGE 18-20 RESULT 25.
END FILE TYPE.
```

- The first two RECORD TYPE commands specify record types 21–25. All other record types are specified by the third RECORD TYPE.

Example

```
* A nested file.

FILE TYPE NESTED FILE=ACCIDENT RECORD=#RECID 6 CASE=ACCID 1-4.
RECORD TYPE 1.         /* Accident record
DATA LIST    /WEATHER 12-13.
RECORD TYPE 2.         /* Vehicle record
DATA LIST /STYLE 16.
RECORD TYPE OTHER SKIP.
END FILE TYPE.
```

- The third RECORD TYPE specifies OTHER SKIP. Type 2 records are therefore the lowest-level records included in the working data file. These commands build one case for each vehicle record. The person records are skipped.
- Because the data are in a nested file, OTHER can be specified only with SKIP.

SKIP Subcommand

SKIP specifies record types to skip.

- To skip selected record types, specify the values for the types you want to skip and then specify SKIP. To skip all record types other than those specified on previous RECORD TYPE commands, specify OTHER and then SKIP.
- For nested files, SKIP can be used only with OTHER. Neither can be used separately.
- For grouped files, OTHER cannot be specified on SKIP if WILD=WARN (the default) is in effect for FILE TYPE.
- For mixed files, all record types that are not specified on a RECORD TYPE command are skipped by default. No warning is issued (WILD=NOWARN on FILE TYPE is the default for mixed files).
- For grouped files, a warning message is issued by default for all record types not specified on a RECORD TYPE command (WILD=WARN on FILE TYPE is the default for grouped files). If the record types are explicitly specified on SKIP, no warning is issued.

Example

```
FILE TYPE GROUPED FILE=HUBDATA RECORD=#RECID 80 CASE=ID 1-5
                                WILD=NOWARN.
RECORD TYPE 1.
DATA LIST    /MOHIRED YRHIRED 12-15 DEPT79 TO DEPT82 SEX 16-20.
RECORD TYPE OTHER SKIP.
END FILE TYPE.
```

- SPSS reads variables from type 1 records and skips all other types.
- WILD=NOWARN on the FILE TYPE command suppresses the warning messages that SPSS issues by default for undefined record types for grouped files. Keyword OTHER cannot be used when the default WILD=WARN specification is in effect.

Example

```
FILE TYPE GROUPED FILE=HUBDATA RECORD=#RECID 80 CASE=ID 1-5.
RECORD TYPE 1.
DATA LIST    /MOHIRED YRHIRED 12-15 DEPT79 TO DEPT82 SEX 16-20.
RECORD TYPE 2,3 SKIP.
END FILE TYPE.
```

- Record type 1 is defined for each case, and record types 2 and 3 are skipped.
- WILD=WARN (the default) on FILE TYPE GROUPED is in effect. SPSS therefore issues a warning message for any record types it encounters other than types 1, 2, and 3. No warning is issued for record types 2 and 3 because they are explicitly specified on a RECORD TYPE command.

CASE Subcommand

CASE specifies the column locations of the case identification variable when that variable is not in the location defined by the CASE subcommand on FILE TYPE.

- CASE on RECORD TYPE applies only to those records specified by that RECORD TYPE command. The identifier for record types without CASE on RECORD TYPE must be in the location specified by CASE on FILE TYPE.
- CASE can be used for nested and grouped files only. CASE cannot be used for mixed files.
- CASE can be used on RECORD TYPE only if a CASE subcommand is specified on FILE TYPE.
- The format type of the case identification variable must be the same on all records, and the same format must be assigned on the RECORD TYPE and FILE TYPE commands. For example, if the case identification variable is defined as a string on FILE TYPE, it cannot be defined as a numeric variable on RECORD TYPE.

Example

```
* Specifying case on the record type command for a grouped file.

FILE TYPE GROUPED FILE=HUBDATA RECORD=#RECID 80 CASE=ID 1-5.
RECORD TYPE 1.
DATA LIST    /MOHIRED YRHIRED 12-15 DEPT79 TO DEPT82 SEX 16-20.
RECORD TYPE 2.
DATA LIST    /SALARY79 TO SALARY82 6-25
                HOURLY81 HOURLY82 40-53 (2)
                PROMO81 72   AGE 54-55 RAISE82 66-70.
RECORD TYPE 3   CASE=75-79.
DATA LIST    /JOBCAT 6 NAME 25-48 (A).
END FILE TYPE.
```

- CASE on FILE TYPE indicates that the case identification variable is located in columns 1–5. On the third RECORD TYPE command, the CASE subcommand overrides the identifier location for type 3 records. For type 3 records, the case identification variable is located in columns 75–79.

MISSING Subcommand

MISSING controls whether SPSS issues a warning when it encounters a missing record type for a case. Regardless of whether SPSS issues the warning, it builds the case in the working data file with system-missing values for the variables defined on the missing record.

- The only specification is a single keyword. NOWARN is the default for nested files. WARN is the default for grouped files. MISSING cannot be used with MIXED files.
- MISSING on RECORD TYPE applies only to those records specified by that RECORD TYPE command. The treatment of missing records for record types without the MISSING specification on RECORD TYPE is determined by the MISSING subcommand on FILE TYPE.
- For grouped files, SPSS checks whether there is a record for each case identification number. For nested files, SPSS verifies that each defined case includes one record of each type.

WARN *Issue a warning message when a record type is missing for a case.* This is the default for grouped files.

NOWARN *Suppress the warning message when a record type is missing for a case.* This is the default for nested files.

Example

```
FILE TYPE GROUPED FILE=HUBDATA RECORD=#RECID 80 CASE=ID 1-5.
RECORD TYPE 1.
DATA LIST    /MOHIRED YRHIRED 12-15 DEPT79 TO DEPT82 SEX 16-20.
RECORD TYPE 2   MISSING=NOWARN.
DATA LIST    /SALARY79 TO SALARY82 6-25
   HOURLY81 HOURLY82 40-53 (2) PROMO81 72 AGE 54-55 RAISE82 66-70.
RECORD TYPE 3.
DATA LIST    /JOBCAT 6 NAME 25-48 (A).
END FILE TYPE.
```

- MISSING is not specified on FILE TYPE. Therefore the default MISSING=WARN is in effect for all record types.
- MISSING=NOWARN is specified on the second RECORD TYPE, overriding the default setting for type 2 records. WARN is still in effect for type 1 and type 3 records.

DUPLICATE Subcommand

DUPLICATE controls whether SPSS issues a warning when it encounters more than one record of each type for a single case.

- DUPLICATE on RECORD TYPE can be used for grouped files only. DUPLICATE cannot be used for mixed or nested files.
- The only specification is a single keyword. WARN is the default.
- DUPLICATE on RECORD TYPE applies only to those records specified by that RECORD TYPE command. The treatment of duplicate records for record types without DUPLICATE specification is determined by the DUPLICATE subcommand on FILE TYPE.
- Regardless of the specification on DUPLICATE, only the last record from a set of duplicates is included in the working data file.

WARN *Issue a warning message.* SPSS issues a message and the first 80 characters of the last record of the duplicate set of record types. This is the default.

NOWARN *Suppress the warning message.*

Example

```
* Specifying DUPLICATE on RECORD TYPE for a grouped file.

FILE TYPE GROUPED FILE=HUBDATA RECORD=#RECID 80 CASE=ID 1-5.
RECORD TYPE 1.
DATA LIST    /MOHIRED YRHIRED 12-15 DEPT79 TO DEPT82 SEX 16-20.
RECORD TYPE 2   DUPLICATE=NOWARN.
DATA LIST    /SALARY79 TO SALARY82 6-25
   HOURLY81 HOURLY82 40-53 (2) PROMO81 72  AGE 54-55 RAISE82 66-70.
RECORD TYPE 3.
DATA LIST    /JOBCAT 6 NAME 25-48 (A).
END FILE TYPE.
```

- DUPLICATE is not specified on FILE TYPE. Therefore the default DUPLICATE=WARN is in effect for all record types.
- DUPLICATE=NOWARN is specified on the second RECORD TYPE, overriding the FILE TYPE setting for type 2 records. WARN is still in effect for type 1 and type 3 records.

SPREAD Subcommand

SPREAD controls whether the values for variables defined for a record type are spread to all related cases.

- SPREAD can be used for nested files only. SPREAD cannot be used for mixed or grouped files.

- The only specification is a single keyword. YES is the default.
- SPREAD=NO applies only to the record type specified on that RECORD TYPE command. The default YES is in effect for all other defined record types.

YES   *Spread the values from the specified record type to all related cases.* This is the default.

NO   *Spread the values from the specified type only to the first related case.* All other cases built from the same record are assigned the system-missing value for the variables defined on the record type.

Example

```
* A nested file.

FILE TYPE NESTED RECORD=#RECID 6 CASE=ACCID 1-4.
RECORD TYPE 1.
DATA LIST    /ACC_NO 9-11 WEATHER 12-13
             STATE 15-16 (A) DATE 18-24 (A).
RECORD TYPE 2  SPREAD=NO.
DATA LIST /STYLE 11 MAKE 13 OLD 14
          LICENSE 15-16 (A) INSURNCE 18-21 (A).
RECORD TYPE 3.
DATA LIST /PSNGR_NO 11 AGE 13-14 SEX 16 (A)
        INJURY 18 SEAT 20-21 (A) COST 23-24.
END FILE TYPE.

BEGIN DATA
0001 1    322 1 IL 3/13/88   /* Type 1:   accident record
0001 2      1 44MI 134M      /* Type 2:   vehicle record
0001 3      1 34 M 1 FR  3   /* Type 3:     person record
0001 2      2 16IL 322F      /*            vehicle record
0001 3      1 22 F 1 FR 11   /*              person record
0001 3      2 35 M 1 FR  5   /*              person record
0001 3      3 59 M 1 BK  7   /*              person record
0001 2      3 21IN 146M      /*            vehicle record
0001 3      1 46 M 0 FR  0   /*              person record
END DATA.
```

- The accident record (type 1) is spread to all related cases (in this example, all cases).
- The first vehicle record has one related person record. The values for *STYLE, MAKE, OLD, LICENSE,* and *INSURNCE* are spread to the case built for the person record.
- The second vehicle record has three related person records. The values for *STYLE, MAKE, OLD, LICENSE,* and *INSURNCE* are spread only to the case built from the first person record. The other two cases have the system-missing values for *STYLE, MAKE, OLD, LICENSE,* and *INSURNCE.*
- The third vehicle record has one related person record, and the values for type 2 records are spread to that case.

REFORMAT

```
REFORMAT  {ALPHA  } = varlist [/...]
          {NUMERIC}
```

Example:
```
REFORMAT ALPHA=STATE /NUMERIC=HOUR1 TO HOUR6.
```

Overview

REFORMAT converts variables from BMDP files to variables with SPSS formats. It also converts files from very old versions of SPSS to files with current SPSS formats. REFORMAT can change the print formats, write formats, and missing-value specifications for variables from alphanumeric to numeric, or from numeric to alphanumeric.

Basic Specification

The basic specification is ALPHA and a list of variables or NUMERIC and a list of variables.
- The ALPHA subcommand declares variables as string variables. The NUMERIC subcommand declares variables as numeric variables.
- If both ALPHA and NUMERIC are specified, they must be separated by a slash.

Operations

- REFORMAT always assigns the print and write format F8.2 (or the format specified on the SET command) to variables specified after NUMERIC and format A4 to variables specified after ALPHA.
- Formats cannot be specified on REFORMAT. To define different formats for numeric variables, use the PRINT FORMATS, WRITE FORMATS, or FORMATS commands. To declare new format widths for string variables, use the STRING and COMPUTE commands to perform data transformations.
- Missing-value specifications for variables named with both ALPHA and NUMERIC are also changed to conform to the new formats.
- The SAVE or XSAVE commands can be used to save the reformatted variables in an SPSS data file. This avoids having to reformat the variables each time the SPSS or BMDP data set is used.

Example

```
* Convert an old SPSS file to a current SPSS data file.
GET FILE R9FILE.
REFORMAT ALPHA=STATE /NUMERIC=HOUR1 TO HOUR6.
STRING XSTATE (A2) /NAME1 TO NAME6 (A15).
COMPUTE XSTATE=STATE.
FORMATS HOUR1 TO HOUR6 (F2.0).
SAVE OUTFILE=NEWFILE /DROP=STATE
    /RENAME=(XSTATE=STATE).
```

- GET accesses the old SPSS data file.
- REFORMAT converts variable STATE to a string variable with an A4 format and variables *HOUR1* to *HOUR6* to numeric variables with F8.2 formats.
- STRING declares *XSTATE* as a string variable with two positions.
- COMPUTE transfers the information from the variable *STATE* to the new string variable *XSTATE*.
- FORMATS changes the F8.2 formats for *HOUR1* to *HOUR6* to F2.0 formats.
- SAVE saves a new SPSS data file. The DROP subcommand drops the old variable *STATE*. RENAME renames the new SPSS string variable *XSTATE* to the original variable name *STATE*.

REGRESSION

```
REGRESSION [MATRIX=[IN({file})] [OUT({file})]]
                       {*   }        {*   }

    [/VARIABLES={varlist    }]
               {(COLLECT)**}
               {ALL        }

    [/DESCRIPTIVES=[DEFAULTS] [MEAN] [STDDEV] [CORR] [COV]
                   [VARIANCE] [XPROD] [SIG] [N] [BADCORR]
                   [ALL] [NONE**]]

    [/SELECT={varname relation value}]

    [/MISSING=[{LISTWISE**     }] [INCLUDE]]
              {PAIRWISE        }
              {MEANSUBSTITUTION}

    [/WIDTH={132**}]
            {n    }

    [/REGWGT=varname]

    [/STATISTICS=[DEFAULTS**] [R**] [COEFF**] [ANOVA**] [OUTS**]
                 [ZPP] [LABEL] [CHA] [CI] [F] [BCOV] [SES] [LINE]
                 [HISTORY] [XTX] [COLLIN] [END] [TOL] [SELECTION] [ALL]]

    [/CRITERIA=[DEFAULTS**] [TOLERANCE({0.0001**})] [MAXSTEPS(n)]
                                      {value    }

               [PIN[({0.05**})]] [POUT[({0.10**})]]
                   {value  }         {value  }

               [FIN[({3.84  })]] [FOUT[({2.71  })]]
                   {value }          {value }

               [CIN[({ 95** })]]]
                   {value}

    [/{NOORIGIN**}]
      {ORIGIN    }

    /DEPENDENT=varlist

    [/METHOD=]{STEPWISE [varlist]      } [...] [/...]
             {FORWARD  [varlist]      }
             {BACKWARD [varlist]      }
             {ENTER    [varlist]      }
             {REMOVE   varlist        }
             {TEST(varlist)(varlist)...}
```

**Default if the subcommand is omitted.

Example:

```
REGRESSION VARIABLES=POP15,POP75,INCOME,GROWTH,SAVINGS
 /DEPENDENT=SAVINGS
 /METHOD=ENTER POP15,POP75,INCOME
 /METHOD=ENTER GROWTH.
```

Overview

REGRESSION calculates multiple regression equations and associated statistics and plots. REGRESSION also calculates collinearity diagnostics, predicted values, residuals, measures of fit and influence, and several statistics based on these measures (see the section on residuals beginning on p. 549).

Options

Global-Control Subcommands. These optional subcommands can be specified only once and apply to the entire REGRESSION command. DESCRIPTIVES requests descriptive statistics on the variables in the analysis. SELECT estimates the model based on a subset of cases. REGWGT specifies a weight variable for estimating weighted least-squares models. MISSING specifies the treatment of cases with missing values. MATRIX reads and writes SPSS matrix data files.

Equation-Control Subcommands. These optional subcommands control the calculation and display of statistics for each equation. STATISTICS controls the statistics displayed, CRITERIA specifies the criteria used by the variable selection method, and ORIGIN specifies whether regression is through the origin.

Format. The WIDTH subcommand controls the width of the output for REGRESSION only. It applies to all output from the REGRESSION command.

Analysis of Residuals, Fit, and Influence. The optional subcommands that analyze and plot residuals and add new variables to the working data file containing predicted values, residuals, measures of fit and influence, or related information, are described starting on p. 549. These subcommands apply to the final equation.

Basic Specification

The basic specification is DEPENDENT, which initiates the equation(s) and defines at least one dependent variable, and METHOD, which specifies the method for selecting independent variables.

- By default, all variables named on DEPENDENT and METHOD are used in the analysis.
- For each block of variables selected, the default display includes summary statistics for the goodness of fit of the model (including R^2 and analysis of variance), coefficients and related statistics for variables in the equation, and statistics for the variables not yet in the equation.
- By default, all cases in the working data file with valid values for all selected variables are used to compute the correlation matrix on which the regression equations are based. The default equations include a constant (intercept).

Subcommand Order

The standard subcommand order for REGRESSION is:

```
REGRESSION MATRIX=...
    /VARIABLES=...
    /DESCRIPTIVES=...
    /SELECT=...
    /MISSING=...
    /WIDTH=...
    /REGWGT=...
```

```
                        Equation Block(s)
    /STATISTICS=...
    /CRITERIA=...
    /ORIGIN
    /DEPENDENT=...

                         Method Block(s)
        /METHOD=...
        [/METHOD...]...

    /RESIDUALS=...
    /SAVE=...
    /CASEWISE=...
    /SCATTERPLOT=...
    /PARTIALPLOT=...
```

- Subcommands listed outside the equation and method blocks apply to all analyses performed by the REGRESSION command. Subcommands listed within the equation block apply to all methods used in estimating that equation.
- When used, MATRIX must be specified first.
- VARIABLES must be specified before the DEPENDENT and METHOD subcommands.
- A REGRESSION command can include multiple equation blocks, and each equation block can contain multiple METHOD subcommands. These methods are applied, one after the other, to the estimation of the equation for that block.
- The STATISTICS, CRITERIA, and ORIGIN/NOORIGIN subcommands must precede the DEPENDENT subcommand for the equation to which they apply.
- The RESIDUALS, CASEWISE, SCATTERPLOT, SAVE, and PARTIALPLOT subcommands must follow the last METHOD subcommand in an equation block and apply only to the final equation after all METHOD subcommands have been processed.

Syntax Rules

- VARIABLES can be specified only once. If omitted, VARIABLES defaults to COLLECT.

- A DEPENDENT subcommand must be followed immediately by one or more METHOD subcommands.
- CRITERIA, STATISTICS, and ORIGIN remain in effect for all subsequent equations until replaced.
- More than one variable can be specified on the DEPENDENT subcommand. An equation is estimated for each.
- If no variables are specified on METHOD, all variables named on VARIABLES but not on DEPENDENT are considered for selection.

Operations

- REGRESSION calculates a correlation matrix that includes all variables named on VARIABLES. All equations requested on the REGRESSION command are calculated from the same correlation matrix.
- The MISSING, DESCRIPTIVES, and SELECT subcommands control the calculation of the correlation matrix and associated displays.
- If multiple METHOD subcommands are specified, they operate in sequence on the equations defined by the preceding DEPENDENT subcommand.
- Only independent variables that pass the tolerance criterion are candidates for entry into the equation (see the CRITERIA subcommand on p. 539).
- If the specified width is less than 132, some statistics requested may not be displayed. Use the WIDTH subcommand within REGRESSION to increase the output width and obtain all requested statistics.

Example

```
REGRESSION VARIABLES=POP15,POP75,INCOME,GROWTH,SAVINGS
 /DEPENDENT=SAVINGS
 /METHOD=ENTER POP15,POP75,INCOME
 /METHOD=ENTER GROWTH.
```

- VARIABLES calculates a correlation matrix of five variables for use by REGRESSION.
- DEPENDENT defines a single equation, with *SAVINGS* as the dependent variable.
- The first METHOD subcommand enters *POP15*, *POP75*, and *INCOME* into the equation.
- The second METHOD subcommand adds *GROWTH* to the equation containing *POP15* to *INCOME*.

VARIABLES Subcommand

VARIABLES names all the variables to be used in the analysis.
- The minimum specification is a list of two variables or the keyword ALL or COLLECT. COLLECT, which must be specified in parentheses, is the default.
- Only one VARIABLES subcommand is allowed and it must precede any DEPENDENT or METHOD subcommands.

- You can use keyword TO to refer to consecutive variables in the working data file.
- The order of variables in the correlation matrix constructed by REGRESSION is the same as their order on VARIABLES. If (COLLECT) is used, the order of variables in the correlation matrix is the order in which they are first listed on the DEPENDENT and METHOD subcommands.

ALL   *Include all user-defined variables in the working data file.*

(COLLECT)   *Include all variables named on the DEPENDENT and METHOD subcommands.* COLLECT is the default if the VARIABLES subcommand is omitted. COLLECT must be specified in parentheses. If COLLECT is used, the METHOD subcommands must specify variable lists.

Example

```
REGRESSION VARIABLES=(COLLECT)
 /DEPENDENT=SAVINGS
 /METHOD=STEP POP15 POP75 INCOME
 /METHOD=ENTER GROWTH
 /DEPENDENT=GROWTH
 /METHOD=ENTER INCOME.
```

- COLLECT requests that the correlation matrix include *SAVINGS, POP15, POP75, INCOME,* and *GROWTH*. Since COLLECT is the default, the VARIABLES subcommand could have been omitted.
- The first DEPENDENT subcommand defines a single equation in which *SAVINGS* is the dependent variable.
- The first METHOD subcommand requests that the block of variables *POP15, POP75,* and *INCOME* be considered for inclusion using a stepwise procedure.
- The second METHOD subcommand adds variable *GROWTH* to the equation.
- A second DEPENDENT subcommand requests an equation in which *GROWTH* is the dependent variable.
- *INCOME* is entered into this equation as specified by the last METHOD subcommand.

DEPENDENT Subcommand

DEPENDENT specifies a list of variables and requests that an equation be built for each. DEPENDENT is required.

- The minimum specification is a single variable. There is no default variable list.
- More than one DEPENDENT subcommand can be specified. Each must be followed by at least one METHOD subcommand.
- Keyword TO on a DEPENDENT subcommand refers to the order in which variables are specified on the VARIABLES subcommand. If VARIABLES=(COLLECT), TO refers to the order of variables in the working data file.
- If DEPENDENT names more than one variable, an equation is built for each using the same independent variables and methods.

METHOD Subcommand

METHOD subcommand specifies a variable selection method and names a block of variables to be evaluated using that method. METHOD is required.

- The minimum specification is a method keyword and, for some methods, a list of variables. The actual keyword METHOD can be omitted.
- At least one METHOD subcommand must follow each DEPENDENT subcommand.
- When more than one METHOD subcommand is specified for a single DEPENDENT subcommand, each METHOD subcommand is applied to the equation that resulted from the previous METHOD subcommands.
- The default variable list for methods FORWARD, BACKWARD, STEPWISE, and ENTER consists of all variables named on VARIABLES that are not named on the preceding DEPENDENT subcommand. If VARIABLES=(COLLECT), the variables must be specified for these methods.
- There is no default variable list for the REMOVE and TEST methods.
- Keyword TO in a variable list on METHOD refers to the order in which variables are specified on the VARIABLES subcommand. If VARIABLES=(COLLECT), TO refers to the order of variables in the working data file.

The available stepwise methods are as follows:

BACKWARD [varlist] *Backward elimination.* Variables in the block are considered for removal. At each step, the variable with the largest probability-of-F value is removed, provided that the value is larger than POUT (see the CRITERIA subcommand on p. 539). If no variables are in the equation when BACKWARD is specified, all independent variables in the block are first entered.

FORWARD [varlist] *Forward entry.* Variables in the block are added to the equation one at a time. At each step, the variable not in the equation with the smallest probability of F is entered if the value is smaller than PIN (see the CRITERIA subcommand on p. 539).

STEPWISE [varlist] *Stepwise selection.* If there are independent variables already in the equation, the variable with the largest probability of F is removed if the value is larger than POUT. The equation is recomputed without the variable and the process is repeated until no more independent variables can be removed. Then, the independent variable not in the equation with the smallest probability of F is entered if the value is smaller than PIN. All variables in the equation are again examined for removal. This process continues until no variables in the equation can be removed and no variables not in the equation are eligible for entry, or until the maximum number of steps has been reached (see the CRITERIA subcommand on p. 539).

The methods that enter or remove the entire variable block in a single step are as follows:

ENTER [varlist] *Forced entry.* All variables specified are entered in a single step in order of decreasing tolerance. You can control the order in which vari-

	ables are entered by specifying multiple METHOD=ENTER subcommands.
REMOVE varlist	*Forced removal.* All variables specified are removed in a single step. REMOVE requires a variable list.
TEST (varlist) (varlist)	R^2 *change and its significance for sets of independent variables.* This method first adds all variables specified to the current equation. It then removes in turn each subset from the equation and displays requested statistics. Specify test subsets in parentheses. A variable can be used in more than one subset, and each subset can include any number of variables. Variables named on TEST remain in the equation when the method is completed.

Example

```
REGRESSION VARIABLES=POP15 TO GROWTH, SAVINGS
 /DEPENDENT=SAVINGS
 /METHOD=STEPWISE
 /METHOD=ENTER.
```

- STEPWISE applies the stepwise procedure to variables *POP15* to *GROWTH*.
- All variables not in the equation when the STEPWISE method is completed will be forced into the equation with ENTER.

Example

```
REGRESSION VARIABLES=(COLLECT)
 /DEPENDENT=SAVINGS
 /METHOD=TEST(MEASURE3 TO MEASURE9)(MEASURE3,INCOME)
 /METHOD=ENTER GROWTH.
```

- The VARIABLES=(COLLECT) specification assembles a correlation matrix that includes all variables named on the DEPENDENT and METHOD subcommands.
- REGRESSION first builds the full equation of all the variables named on the first METHOD subcommand: *SAVINGS* regressed on *MEASURE3* to *MEASURE9* and *INCOME*. For each set of test variables (MEASURE3 to MEASURE9, and MEASURE3 and INCOME), the R^2 change, F, probability, sums of squares, and degrees of freedom are displayed.
- *GROWTH* is added to the equation by the second METHOD subcommand. Variables *MEASURE3* to *MEASURE9* and *INCOME* are still in the equation when this subcommand is executed.

STATISTICS Subcommand

STATISTICS controls the display of statistics for the equation and for the independent variables.

- If STATISTICS is omitted or if it is specified without keywords, R, ANOVA, COEFF, and OUTS are displayed (see below).
- If any statistics are specified on STATISTICS, only those statistics specifically requested are displayed.

- STATISTICS affects any equations that are subsequently defined and remains in effect until overridden by another STATISTICS subcommand.
- A STATISTICS subcommand cannot be placed between the DEPENDENT and METHOD subcommands.
- If the output width is set to less than 132, some requested statistics may not be displayed. Use the WIDTH subcommand in REGRESSION to increase the width (see p. 547).

Global Statistics

DEFAULTS   *R, ANOVA, COEFF, and OUTS.* These are displayed if STATISTICS is omitted or if it is specified without keywords.

ALL   *All statistics except F, LINE, and END.*

Equation Statistics

R   *Multiple R.* R includes R^2, adjusted R^2, and standard error of the estimate.

ANOVA   *Analysis of variance table.* This option includes regression and residual sums of squares, mean square, F, and probability of F.

CHA   *Change in R^2.* This option includes the change in R^2 between steps, F at the end of each step and its probability, and F for the equation and its probability. For stepwise methods (BACKWARD, FORWARD, and STEPWISE), these statistics are displayed at the end of each step. For other methods, the statistics are displayed for the independent variables in that method block.

BCOV   *Variance-covariance matrix for unstandardized regression coefficients.* The matrix has covariances below the diagonal, correlations above the diagonal, and variances on the diagonal.

XTX   *Swept correlation matrix.*

COLLIN   *Collinearity diagnostics.* COLLIN includes the variance-inflation factors (VIF), the eigenvalues of the scaled and uncentered cross-products matrix, condition indexes, and variance-decomposition proportions (Belsley et al., 1980).

SELECTION   *Selection statistics.* This option includes Akaike information criterion (AIK), Ameniya's prediction criterion (PC), Mallows conditional mean squared error of prediction criterion (C_p), and Schwarz Bayesian criterion (SBC) (Judge et al., 1980).

Statistics for the Independent Variables

COEFF   *Regression coefficients.* This option includes regression coefficients (B), standard errors of the coefficients, standardized regression coefficients (beta), t, and two-tailed probability of t.

OUTS *Statistics for variables not yet in the equation that have been named on METHOD subcommands for the equation.* OUTS displays beta, t, two-tailed probability of t, and minimum tolerance of the variable if it were the only variable entered next.

ZPP *Zero-order, part, and partial correlation.*

CI *95% confidence interval for the unstandardized regression coefficients.*

SES *Approximate standard error of the standardized regression coefficients.* (Meyer & Younger, 1976.)

TOL *Tolerance.* This option displays tolerance for variables in the equation and, for variables not entered but specified on the METHOD subcommand for the equation, the tolerance each variable would have if it were the only variable entered next.

F *F value for B and its probability.* This is displayed instead of the t value.

Step Summary Statistics

The full summary line displayed by keywords LINE, END, and HISTORY includes R, R^2, adjusted R^2, F, probability of F, R^2 change, F of the change, probability of R^2 change, and statistics on variables added or removed. For stepwise methods (BACKWARD, FORWARD, and STEPWISE), the statistics refer to each step. For other methods (ENTER, REMOVE, and TEST), the statistics refer to independent variables in the method block. The summary line may not be produced for a block that does not involve steps if other statistics are requested.

LINE *A single summary line for each step for stepwise methods only.* LINE does not affect direct methods. The default or requested statistics are displayed at the end of each method block for all methods.

END *The same summary line produced by LINE after each step for stepwise methods and after each variable in the method block for other methods.* For TEST, the summary line is displayed only if the equation changes. Other default or requested statistics are displayed at the completion of the last METHOD subcommand for the equation.

HISTORY *Final summary report.* HISTORY can be requested in addition to LINE or END. For stepwise methods, the report includes a summary line for each step. For ENTER and REMOVE, the report includes a summary line for each method; for TEST, the summary line is displayed only if the equation changes. If HISTORY is the only statistic requested, COEFF is also displayed for the final equation.

CRITERIA Subcommand

CRITERIA controls the statistical criteria used to build the regression equations. The way in which these criteria are used depends on the method specified on METHOD. The default criteria are noted in the description of each CRITERIA keyword below.

- The minimum specification is a criterion keyword and its arguments, if any.
- If CRITERIA is omitted or included without specifications, the default criteria are in effect.

- A CRITERIA subcommand affects any subsequent DEPENDENT and METHOD subcommands and remains in effect until overridden by another CRITERIA subcommand.
- CRITERIA cannot be placed between the DEPENDENT subcommand and its METHOD subcommands.

Tolerance and Minimum Tolerance Tests

Variables must pass both tolerance and minimum tolerance tests in order to enter and remain in a regression equation. Tolerance is the proportion of the variance of a variable in the equation that is not accounted for by other independent variables in the equation. The minimum tolerance of a variable not in the equation is the smallest tolerance any variable already in the equation would have if the variable being considered were included in the analysis.

If a variable passes the tolerance criteria, it is eligible for inclusion based on the method in effect.

Criteria for Variable Selection

- The ENTER, REMOVE, and TEST methods use only the TOLERANCE criterion.
- BACKWARD removes variables according to the probability of F-to-remove (keyword POUT). Specify FOUT to use F-to-remove instead.
- FORWARD enters variables according to the probability of F-to-enter (keyword PIN). Specify FIN to use F-to-enter instead.
- STEPWISE uses both PIN and POUT (or FIN and FOUT) as criteria. If the criterion for entry (PIN or FIN) is less stringent than the criterion for removal (POUT or FOUT), the same variable can cycle in and out until the maximum number of steps is reached. Therefore, if PIN is larger than POUT or FIN is smaller than FOUT, REGRESSION adjusts POUT or FOUT and issues a warning.
- The values for these criteria are specified in parentheses. If a value is not specified, the default values are used.

DEFAULTS *PIN(0.05), POUT(0.10), and TOLERANCE(0.0001)*. These are the defaults if CRITERIA is omitted. If criteria have been changed, DEFAULTS restores these defaults.

PIN[(value)] *Probability of* F-*to-enter*. The default value is 0.05. Either PIN or FIN can be specified. If more than one is used, the last one specified is in effect.

FIN[(value)] F-*to-enter*. The default value is 3.84. Either PIN or FIN can be specified. If more than one is used, the last one specified is in effect.

POUT[(value)] *Probability of* F-*to-remove*. The default value is 0.10. Either POUT or FOUT can be specified. If more than one is used, the last one specified is in effect.

FOUT[(value)] F-*to-remove*. The default value is 2.71. Either POUT or FOUT can be specified. If more than one is used, the last one specified is in effect.

TOLERANCE[(value)]	*Tolerance.* The default value is 0.0001. If the specified tolerance is very low, REGRESSION issues a warning.
MAXSTEPS[(n)]	*Maximum number of steps.* The value of MAXSTEPS is the sum of the maximum number of steps for each method for the equation. The default values are, for the BACKWARD or FORWARD methods, the number of variables meeting PIN/POUT or FIN/FOUT criteria, and for the STEPWISE method, twice the number of independent variables.

Confidence Intervals

CIN[(value)]	*Reset the value of the percent for confidence intervals.* The default is 95%. The specified value sets the percentage interval used in the computation of temporary variable types MCIN and ICIN. (See the list of temporary variable types on p. 551.)

Example

```
REGRESSION VARIABLES=POP15 TO GROWTH, SAVINGS
 /CRITERIA=PIN(.1) POUT(.15)
 /DEPENDENT=SAVINGS
 /METHOD=FORWARD
 /CRITERIA=DEFAULTS
 /DEPENDENT=SAVINGS
 /METHOD=STEPWISE.
```

- The first CRITERIA subcommand relaxes the default criteria for entry and removal while the FORWARD method is used. Note that the specified PIN is less than POUT.
- The second CRITERIA subcommand reestablishes the defaults for the second equation.

ORIGIN and NOORIGIN Subcommands

ORIGIN and NOORIGIN control whether or not the constant is suppressed. By default, the constant is included in the model (NOORIGIN).

- The specification is either the ORIGIN or NOORIGIN subcommand.
- ORIGIN and NOORIGIN must be specified before the DEPENDENT and METHOD subcommands they modify.
- ORIGIN requests regression through the origin. The constant term is suppressed.
- Once specified, ORIGIN remains in effect until NOORIGIN is requested.
- If you specify ORIGIN, statistics requested on the DESCRIPTIVES subcommand are computed as if the mean were 0.
- ORIGIN and NOORIGIN affect the way the correlation matrix is built. If matrix materials are used as input to REGRESSION, the keyword that was in effect when the matrix was written should be in effect when that matrix is read.

Example

```
REGRESSION VAR=(COL)
 /DEP=HOMICIDE
 /METHOD=ENTER POVPCT
 /ORIGIN
 /DEP=HOMICIDE
 /METHOD=ENTER POVPCT
 /NOORIGIN
 /DEP=POVPCT
 /METHOD=ENTER SOUTHPCT.
```

- The subcommand VAR=(COL) builds a correlation matrix that includes *HOMICIDE*, *POVPCT*, and *SOUTHPCT*.
- The REGRESSION command requests three equations. The first regresses *HOMICIDE* on *POVPCT* and includes a constant term because the default (NOORIGIN) is in effect. The second regresses *HOMICIDE* on *POVPCT* and suppresses the constant (ORIGIN). The third regresses *POVPCT* on *SOUTHPCT* and includes a constant term because NOORIGIN has been specified.

REGWGT Subcommand

The only specification on REGWGT is the name of the variable containing the weights to be used in estimating a weighted least-squares model. With REGWGT the default display is the usual REGRESSION display.

- REGWGT is a global subcommand.
- If more than one REGWGT subcommand is specified on a REGRESSION procedure, only the last one is in effect.
- REGWGT can be used with MATRIX OUT but not with MATRIX IN.
- Residuals saved from equations using the REGWGT command are not weighted. To obtain weighted residuals, multiply the residuals created with SAVE by the square root of the weighting variable in a COMPUTE statement.
- REGWGT is in effect for all equations and affects the way the correlation matrix is built. Thus, if REGWGT is specified on a REGRESSION procedure that writes matrix materials to a matrix data file, subsequent REGRESSION procedures using that file will be automatically weighted.

Example

```
REGRESSION VARIABLES=GRADE GPA STARTLEV TREATMNT
 /DEPENDENT=GRADE
 /METHOD=ENTER
 /SAVE PRED(P).
COMPUTE WEIGHT=1/(P*(1-P)).
REGRESSION VAR=GRADE GPA STARTLEV TREATMNT
 /REGWGT=WEIGHT
 /DEP=GRADE
 /METHOD=ENTER.
```

- VARIABLES builds a correlation matrix that includes *GRADE*, *GPA*, *STARTLEV*, and *TREATMNT*.

- DEPENDENT identifies *GRADE* as the dependent variable.
- METHOD regresses *GRADE* on *GPA*, *STARTLEV*, and *TREATMNT*.
- SAVE saves the predicted values from the regression equation as variable *P* in the working data file (see the SAVE subcommand on p. 556).
- COMPUTE creates the variable *WEIGHT* as a transformation of *P*.
- The second REGRESSION procedure performs a weighted regression analysis on the same set of variables using *WEIGHT* as the weighting variable.

Example

```
REGRESSION VAR=GRADE GPA STARTLEV TREATMNT
 /REGWGT=WEIGHT
 /DEP=GRADE
 /METHOD=ENTER
 /SAVE RESID(RGRADE).
COMPUTE WRGRADE=RGRADE * SQRT(WEIGHT).
```

- This example illustrates the use of COMPUTE with SAVE to weight residuals.
- REGRESSION performs a weighted regression analysis of *GRADE* on *GPA*, *STARTLEV*, and *TREATMNT*, using *WEIGHT* as the weighting variable.
- SAVE saves the residuals as *RGRADE* (see the SAVE subcommand on p. 556). These residuals are not weighted.
- COMPUTE creates variable *WRGRADE*, which contains the weighted residuals.

DESCRIPTIVES Subcommand

DESCRIPTIVES requests the display of correlations and descriptive statistics. By default, descriptive statistics are not displayed.

- The minimum specification is simply the subcommand keyword DESCRIPTIVES, which obtains MEAN, STDDEV, and CORR.
- If DESCRIPTIVES is specified with keywords, only those statistics specifically requested are displayed.
- Descriptive statistics are displayed only once for all variables named or implied on VARIABLES.
- Descriptive statistics are based on all valid cases for each variable if PAIRWISE or MEANSUBSTITUTION has been specified on MISSING. Otherwise, only cases with valid values for all variables named or implied on the VARIABLES subcommand are included in the calculation of descriptive statistics.
- If regression through the origin has been requested (subcommand ORIGIN), statistics are computed as if the mean were 0.

NONE   *No descriptive statistics*. This is the default if the subcommand is omitted.

DEFAULTS   *MEAN, STDDEV, and CORR*. This is the same as specifying DESCRIPTIVES without specifications.

MEAN   *Variable means*.

STDDEV   *Variable standard deviations.*

VARIANCE   *Variable variances.*

CORR   *Correlation matrix.*

SIG   *One-tailed probabilities of the correlation coefficients.*

BADCORR   *The correlation matrix only if some coefficients cannot be computed.*

COV   *Covariance matrix.*

XPROD   *Cross-product deviations from the mean.*

N   *Numbers of cases used to compute correlation coefficients.*

ALL   *All descriptive statistics.*

Example

```
REGRESSION DESCRIPTIVES=DEFAULTS SIG COV
 /VARIABLES=AGE,FEMALE,YRS_JOB,STARTPAY,SALARY
 /DEPENDENT=SALARY
 /METHOD=ENTER STARTPAY
 /METHOD=ENTER YRS_JOB.
```

- The variable means, variable standard deviations, correlation matrix, one-tailed probabilities of the correlation coefficients, and covariance matrix are displayed.
- Statistics are displayed for all variables named on VARIABLES, even though only variables *SALARY, STARTPAY*, and *YRS_JOB* are used to build the equations.
- *STARTPAY* is entered into the equation by the first METHOD subcommand. *YRS_JOB* is entered by the second METHOD subcommand.

SELECT Subcommand

By default, all cases in the working data file are considered for inclusion on REGRESSION. Use SELECT to include a subset of cases in the correlation matrix and resulting regression statistics.

- The required specification on SELECT is a logical expression.
- The syntax for the SELECT subcommand is as follows:

    /SELECT=varname relation value

- The variable named on SELECT should not be specified on the VARIABLES subcommand.
- The relation can be EQ, NE, LT, LE, GT, or GE.
- Only cases for which the logical expression on SELECT is true are included in the calculation of the correlation matrix and regression statistics.
- All other cases, including those with missing values for the variable named on SELECT, are not included in the computations.

- If SELECT is specified, residuals and predicted values are calculated and reported separately for both selected and unselected cases by default (see the RESIDUALS subcommand on p. 552).
- Cases deleted from the working data file with SELECT IF, a temporary SELECT IF, or SAMPLE are not passed to REGRESSION and are not included among either the selected or unselected cases.
- You should not use a variable from a temporary transformation as a selection variable, since REGRESSION reads the data file more than once if any residuals subcommands are specified. A variable created from a temporary transformation (with IF and COMPUTE statements) will disappear when the data are read a second time, and a variable that is the result of a temporary RECODE will change.
- The display of the values of the variable named on SELECT is controlled by the variable's format (see FORMATS).

Example

```
REGRESSION SELECT SEX EQ 'M'
 /VARIABLES=AGE,STARTPAY,YRS_JOB,SALARY
 /DEPENDENT=SALARY
 /METHOD=STEP
 /RESIDUALS=NORMPROB.
```

- Only cases with the value M for *SEX* are included in the correlation matrix calculated by REGRESSION.
- Separate normal probability plots are displayed for cases with *SEX* equal to M and for other cases (see the RESIDUALS subcommand on p. 552).

MATRIX Subcommand

MATRIX reads and writes SPSS matrix data files. It can read files written by previous REGRESSION procedures or files written by other procedures such as CORRELATIONS. The matrix materials REGRESSION writes also include the mean, standard deviation, and number of cases used to compute each coefficient. This information immediately precedes the correlation matrix in the matrix file (see "Format of the Matrix Data File" on p. 546).

- Either IN or OUT and a matrix file in parentheses are required on MATRIX.
- When used, MATRIX must be the first subcommand specified in a REGRESSION procedure.
- ORIGIN and NOORIGIN affect the way the correlation matrix is built. If matrix materials are used as input to REGRESSION, the keyword that was in effect when the matrix was written should be in effect when that matrix is read.

OUT (filename) *Write a matrix data file.* Specify either a filename or an asterisk, enclosed in parentheses. If you specify a filename, the file is stored on disk and can be retrieved at any time. If you specify an asterisk (*), the matrix data file replaces the working file but is not stored on disk unless you use SAVE or XSAVE.

IN (filename) *Read a matrix data file*. If the matrix data file is the working data file, specify an asterisk (*) in parentheses. If the matrix data file is another file, specify the filename in parentheses. A matrix file read from an external file does not replace the working data file.

Format of the Matrix Data File

- The file has two special variables created by SPSS: *ROWTYPE_* and *VARNAME_*.
- *ROWTYPE_* is a short string variable with values MEAN, STDDEV, N, and CORR (for Pearson correlation coefficient).
- *VARNAME_* is a short string variable whose values are the names of the variables used to form the correlation matrix. When *ROWTYPE_* is CORR, *VARNAME_* gives the variable associated with that row of the correlation matrix.
- The remaining variables in the file are the variables used to form the correlation matrix.
- To suppress the constant term when ORIGIN is used in the analysis, value OCORR (rather than value CORR) is written to the matrix system file. OCORR indicates that the regression passes through the origin.

Split Files

- When split-file processing is in effect, the first variables in the SPSS matrix data file are the split variables, followed by *ROWTYPE_*, the independent variable, *VARNAME_*, and the dependent variables.
- A full set of matrix materials is written for each subgroup defined by the split variable(s).
- A split variable cannot have the same variable name as any other variable written to the matrix data file.
- If a split file is in effect when a matrix is written, the same split file must be in effect when that matrix is read.

Missing Values

- With PAIRWISE treatment of missing values, the matrix of N's used to compute each coefficient is included with the matrix materials.
- With LISTWISE treatment (the default) or MEANSUBSTITUTION, a single N used to calculate all coefficients is included.

Example

```
REGRESSION MATRIX IN(PAY_DATA) OUT(*)
 /VARIABLES=AGE,STARTPAY,YRS_JOB,SALARY
 /DEPENDENT=SALARY
 /METHOD=STEP.
```

- MATRIX IN reads the SPSS matrix data file *PAY_DATA*.

- A stepwise regression analysis of *SALARY* is performed using *AGE*, *STARTPAY*, and *YRS_JOB*.
- MATRIX OUT replaces the working data file with the matrix data file that was previously stored in the *PAY_DATA* file.

MISSING Subcommand

MISSING controls the treatment of cases with missing values. By default, a case that has a user- or system-missing value for any variable named or implied on VARIABLES is omitted from the computation of the correlation matrix on which all analyses are based.

- The minimum specification is a keyword specifying a missing-value treatment.

LISTWISE
: *Delete cases with missing values listwise.* Only cases with valid values for all variables named on the current VARIABLES subcommand are used. If INCLUDE is also specified, only cases with system-missing values are deleted listwise. LISTWISE is the default if the MISSING subcommand is omitted.

PAIRWISE
: *Delete cases with missing values pairwise.* Each correlation coefficient is computed using cases with complete data for the pair of variables correlated. If INCLUDE is also specified, only cases with system-missing values are deleted pairwise.

MEANSUBSTITUTION
: *Replace missing values with the variable mean.* All cases are included and the substitutions are treated as valid observations. If INCLUDE is also specified, user-missing values are treated as valid and are included in the computation of the means.

INCLUDE
: *Includes cases with user-missing values.* All user-missing values are treated as valid values. This keyword can be specified along with the methods LISTWISE, PAIRWISE, or MEANSUBSTITUTION.

Example

```
REGRESSION  VARIABLES=POP15,POP75,INCOME,GROWTH,SAVINGS
 /DEPENDENT=SAVINGS
 /METHOD=STEP
 /MISSING=MEANSUBSTITUTION.
```

- System- and user-missing values are replaced with the means of the variables when the correlation matrix is calculated.

WIDTH Subcommand

WIDTH controls the width of the output within the REGRESSION procedure.

- The minimum specification is an integer between 72 and 132.
- The default display uses the width specified on SET. The width specified on the WIDTH subcommand within REGRESSION overrides the width specified on SET for the REGRESSION output only.

- The WIDTH subcommand can be specified anywhere.
- If more than one WIDTH subcommand is specified, the last one is in effect.
- If the width is less than 132, some statistics may not be displayed.

References

Belsley, D. A., E. Kuh, and R. E. Welsch. 1980. *Regression diagnostics: Identifying influential data and sources of collinearity.* New York: John Wiley & Sons.

Berk, K. N. 1977. Tolerance and condition in regression computation. *Journal of the American Statistical Association* 72:863-66.

Judge, G. G., W. E. Griffiths, R. C. Hill, H. Lutkepohl, and T. C. Lee. 1980. *The theory and practice of econometrics.* 2nd ed. New York: John Wiley & Sons.

Meyer, L. S., and M. S. Younger. 1976. Estimation of standardized coefficients. *Journal of the American Statistical Association* 71:154-57.

REGRESSION: Residuals

```
REGRESSION VARIABLES=varlist /DEPENDENT=varname /METHOD=method

 [/RESIDUALS=[DEFAULTS] [DURBIN] [OUTLIERS({ZRESID })] [ID (varname)]
                                          {tempvars}

         [NORMPROB({ZRESID })] [HISTOGRAM({ZRESID })]
                  {tempvars}             {tempvars}

         [SIZE({SMALL})] [{SEPARATE}]]
              {LARGE}    {POOLED  }

 [/CASEWISE=[DEFAULTS]  [{OUTLIERS({3    })}] [PLOT({ZRESID })]
                        {         {value} }         {tempvar}
                        {ALL              }

         [{DEPENDENT PRED RESID}]]
          {tempvars            }

 [/SCATTERPLOT=(varname,varname)...  [SIZE({SMALL})]]
                                          {LARGE}

 [/PARTIALPLOT=[{ALL    }]  [SIZE({SMALL})]]
                {varlist}         {LARGE}

 [/SAVE=tempvar[(newname)]  [tempvar[(newname)]...]  [FITS]]
```

Temporary residual variables are:

PRED, ADJPRED, SRESID, MAHAL, RESID, ZPRED, SDRESID, COOK, DRESID, ZRESID, SEPRED, LEVER, DFBETA, SDBETA, DFFIT, SDFFIT, COVRATIO, MCIN, CIN

SAVE FITS saves:

DFFIT, SDFIT, DFBETA, SDBETA, COVRATIO

Example:

```
REGRESSION VARIABLES=SAVINGS INCOME POP15 POP75
  /WIDTH=132
  /DEPENDENT=SAVINGS
  /METHOD=ENTER
  /RESIDUALS
  /CASEWISE
  /SCATTERPLOT (*ZRESID *ZPRED)
  /PARTIALPLOT
  /SAVE ZRESID(STDRES) ZPRED(STDPRED).
```

Overview

REGRESSION creates temporary variables containing predicted values, residuals, measures of fit and influence, and several statistics based on these measures. These temporary variables can be analyzed within REGRESSION using casewise plots (available with the CASEWISE subcommand), scatterplots (SCATTERPLOT subcommand), histograms and normal probability plots (RESIDUALS subcommand), and partial residual plots (PARTIALPLOT subcommand). Any of the residuals subcommands can be specified to obtain descriptive statistics for the predicted values, residuals, and their standardized versions. Any of the temporary variables can be added to the working data file with the SAVE subcommand.

Basic Specification

All residuals analysis subcommands are optional. Most have defaults that can be requested by including the subcommand without any further specifications. These defaults are described in the discussion of each subcommand below.

Subcommand Order

- The residuals subcommands RESIDUALS, CASEWISE, SCATTERPLOT, and PARTIALPLOT follow the last METHOD subcommand of any equation for which residuals analysis is requested. Statistics are based on this final equation.
- If there is more than one dependent variable, residuals analysis can be requested for each.
- Residuals subcommands can be specified in any order.

Operations

- Residuals subcommands affect only the equation they follow.
- The temporary variables *PRED*, *RESID*, *ZPRED*, and *ZRESID* are calculated and descriptive statistics are displayed whenever any residuals subcommand is specified. If any of the other temporary variables are referred to on the command, they are also calculated.
- Predicted values and statistics based on predicted values are calculated for every observation that has valid values for all variables in the equation. Residuals and statistics based on residuals are calculated for all observations that have a valid predicted value and a valid value for the dependent variable. The missing-values option therefore affects the calculation of residuals and predicted values.
- The amount of information displayed in a casewise plot is limited by the output width. Use the WIDTH subcommand (see p. 547) to increase the width within REGRESSION. The widest page allows a maximum of eight variables in a casewise plot.
- No residuals or predictors are generated for cases deleted from the working data file with SELECT IF, a temporary SELECT IF, or SAMPLE.
- All variables are standardized before plotting. If the unstandardized version of a variable is requested, the standardized version is plotted.
- Residuals processing is not available when the working data file is a matrix file or is replaced by a matrix file with MATRIX OUT(*) on REGRESSION. If RESIDUALS, CASEWISE, SCATTERPLOT, PARTIALPLOT, or SAVE are used when MATRIX IN(*) or MATRIX OUT(*) is specified, the REGRESSION command is not executed.

For each analysis, REGRESSION can calculate the following types of temporary variables:

PRED   *Unstandardized predicted values.*

RESID   *Unstandardized residuals.*

DRESID   *Deleted residuals.*

ADJPRED *Adjusted predicted values.*

ZPRED	*Standardized predicted values.*
ZRESID	*Standardized residuals.*
SRESID	*Studentized residuals.*
SDRESID	*Studentized deleted residuals.* (See Hoaglin & Welsch, 1978.)
SEPRED	*Standard errors of the predicted values.*
MAHAL	*Mahalanobis distances.*
COOK	*Cook's distances.* (See Cook, 1977.)
LEVER	*Centered leverage values.* (See Velleman & Welsch, 1981.)
DFBETA.	*Change in the regression coefficient that results from the deletion of the ith case.* A DFBETA value is computed for each case for each regression coefficient generated by a model. (See Belsley et al., 1980.)
SDBETA	*Standardized DFBETA.* An SDBETA value is computed for each case for each regression coefficient generated by a model. (See Belsley et al., 1980.)
DFFIT	*Change in the predicted value when the ith case is deleted.* (See Belsley et al., 1980.)
SDFIT	*Standardized DFFIT.* (See Belsley et al., 1980.)
COVRATIO	*Ratio of the determinant of the covariance matrix with the ith case deleted to the determinant of the covariance matrix with all cases included.* (See Belsley et al., 1980.)
MCIN	*Lower and upper bounds for the prediction interval of the mean predicted response.* A lowerbound LMCIN and an upperbound UMCIN are generated. The default confidence interval is 95%. The confidence interval can be reset with the CIN subcommand. (See Dillon & Goldstein, 1984.)
ICIN	*Lower and upper bounds for the prediction interval for a single observation.* A lowerbound LICIN and an upperbound UICIN are generated. The default confidence interval is 95%. The confidence interval can be reset with the CIN subcommand. (See Dillon & Goldstein, 1984.)

Example

```
REGRESSION VARIABLES=SAVINGS INCOME POP15 POP75
  /WIDTH=132
  /DEPENDENT=SAVINGS
  /METHOD=ENTER
  /RESIDUALS
  /CASEWISE
  /SCATTERPLOT (*ZRESID *ZPRED)
  /PARTIALPLOT
  /SAVE ZRESID(STDRES) ZPRED(STDPRED).
```

- REGRESSION requests a single equation in which *SAVINGS* is the dependent variable and *INCOME*, *POP15*, and *POP75* are independent variables.
- RESIDUALS requests the default residuals output.
- CASEWISE requests a default casewise plot of *ZRESID* for cases for which the absolute value of *ZRESID* is greater than 3. Values of the dependent variable, predicted value, and residual are listed for each case.
- SCATTERPLOT requests a small plot of the standardized predicted value and the standardized residual.
- PARTIALPLOT requests small partial residual plots for all independent variables.
- SAVE adds the standardized residual and the standardized predicted value to the working data file as new variables named *STDRES* and *STDPRED*.
- Because residuals processing has been requested, statistics for predicted values, residuals, and standardized versions of predicted values and residuals are displayed.

RESIDUALS Subcommand

RESIDUALS controls the display and labeling of summary information on outliers as well as the display of the Durbin-Watson statistic and histograms and normal probability plots for the temporary variables.

- If RESIDUALS is specified without keywords, it displays a histogram of residuals, a normal probability plot of residuals, the values of *$CASENUM* and *ZRESID* for the ten cases with the largest absolute value of *ZRESID*, and the Durbin-Watson test statistic. The histogram and the normal plot are standardized unless HIGHRES is ON (see SET). The default size of both plots is small when no size specifications are given.
- If any keywords are specified on RESIDUALS, only the requested information and plots are displayed.

DEFAULTS   *DURBIN, NORMPROB(ZRESID), HISTOGRAM(ZRESID), OUTLIERS (ZRESID).* These are the defaults if RESIDUALS is used without specifications.

SIZE(plot size)   *Plot sizes.* The plot size can be SMALL or LARGE. The default is SMALL. Four small histograms or normal probability plots can be displayed on a single page if the width is 121 and the page length is 58. If the output width is at least 120 and the page length is at least 59, LARGE can be specified. SIZE is ignored when HIGHRES is ON (see SET).

HISTOGRAM(tempvars)   *Histogram of the temporary variable or variables.* The default is *ZRESID*. When HIGHRES is ON (see SET), you can request histograms for *PRED, RESID, ZPRED, DRESID, ADJPRED, SRESID, SDRESID, SEPRED, MAHAL, COOK,* and *LEVER*. For character-based plots, you can request histograms for *PRED, RESID, ZPRED, DRESID, SRESID,* and *SDRESID*. The specification of any other temporary variable will result in an error. Character-based histograms are always displayed in standardized form; therefore, when *PRED, RESID,* or *DRESID* is requested, the standardized equivalent *ZPRED*, *ZRESID*, or *SDRESID* is displayed.

NORMPROB(tempvars) *Normal probability (P-P) plot.* The default is *ZRESID*. The other temporary variables for which normal probability plots are available are *PRED*, *RESID*, *ZPRED*, *DRESID*, *SRESID*, and *SDRESID*. The specification of any other temporary variable will result in an error. Normal probability plots are always displayed in standardized form; therefore, when *PRED*, *RESID*, or *DRESID* is requested, the standardized equivalent *ZPRED*, *ZRESID* or *SDRESID* is displayed.

OUTLIERS(tempvars) *The ten cases with the largest absolute values of the specified temporary variables.* The default is *ZRESID*. The output includes the values of *$CASENUM* and of the temporary variables for the ten cases. The other temporary variables available for OUTLIERS are *RESID*, *SRESID*, *SDRESID*, *DRESID*, *MAHAL*, and *COOK*. The specification of any temporary variable other than these will result in an error.

DURBIN *Durbin-Watson test statistic.*

ID(varname) *Case identifier for outlier plots.* Any variable in the working data file can be named. ID also labels the list of cases produced by CASEWISE.

POOLED *Pooled plots and statistics using all cases in the working file when the SELECT subcommand is in effect.* (See the SELECT subcommand on p. 544.)

SEPARATE *Separate reporting of residuals statistics and plots for selected and unselected cases.* This is an alternative to POOLED. This is the default.

Example

```
/RESID=DEFAULT ID(SVAR)
```

- DEFAULT produces the default residuals statistics: Durbin-Watson statistic, a normal probability plot and histogram of *ZRESID*, and an outlier listing for *ZRESID*.
- Descriptive statistics for *ZRESID, RESID, PRED,* and *ZPRED* are automatically displayed.
- *SVAR* is specified as the case identifier on the outlier output.

CASEWISE Subcommand

CASEWISE requests a casewise plot of residuals. You can specify a temporary residual variable for casewise plotting (PLOT) and control the selection of cases for plotting. You can also specify variables to be listed next to the plot entry for each case.

- If CASEWISE is used without any additional specifications, it displays a casewise plot of *ZRESID* for cases whose absolute value of *ZRESID* is at least 3. By default, the values of the case sequence number, *DEPENDENT*, *PRED*, and *RESID* are listed next to the plot entry for each case. To label each case with a case identifier, use the ID keyword on the RESIDUALS subcommand.
- Defaults remain in effect unless specifically altered.

DEFAULTS   *OUTLIERS(3), PLOT(ZRESID), DEPENDENT, PRED,* and *RESID.* These are the defaults if the subcommand is used without specifications.

OUTLIERS(value)   *Plot only cases for which the absolute standardized value of the plotted variable is at least as large as the specified value.* The default value is 3. Keyword OUTLIERS is ignored if keyword ALL is also present.

ALL   *Include all cases in the casewise plot.* ALL is the alternative to keyword OUTLIERS.

PLOT(tempvar)   *Plot the values of the temporary variable in the casewise plot.* The default temporary variable is *ZRESID.* Other variables that can be plotted are *RESID, DRESID, SRESID,* and *SDRESID.* The specification of any temporary variable other than these will result in an error. When requested, *RESID* is standardized and *DRESID* is studentized in the output.

tempvars   *Display the values of these variables next to the casewise plot entry for each case.* The default variables are *DEPENDENT* (the dependent variable), *PRED,* and *RESID.* Any of the other temporary variables can be specified. If an *ID* variable is specified on *RESIDUALS*, the *ID* variable is also listed instead of the case sequence number if the width is sufficient.

Example

```
/CASEWISE=DEFAULT ALL SRE MAH COOK SDR
```

- This example requests a casewise plot of the standardized residuals for all cases.
- The dependent variable and the temporary variables *PRED, RESID, SRESID, MAHAL, COOK,* and *SDRESID* are listed next to the plot entry for all cases.

SCATTERPLOT Subcommand

SCATTERPLOT names pairs of variables for scatterplots and controls the size of the plots.

- The minimum specification for SCATTERPLOT is a pair of variables in parentheses. There are no default specifications.
- You can specify as many pairs of variables in parentheses as you want.
- The first variable named in each set of parentheses is plotted along the vertical axis, and the second variable is plotted along the horizontal axis.
- Plotting symbols are used to represent multiple points occurring at the same position.
- Specify an asterisk before temporary variable names to distinguish them from user-defined variables. For example, use **PRED* to specify *PRED*.
- All scatterplots are standardized in character-based output. **RESID* is the same as **ZRESID, *PRED* is the same as **ZPRED,* and **DRESID* is the same as **SDRESID.* When SET HIGHRES is ON, scatterplots are not standardized.

(varname,varname)   *Plot the pairs of specified variables.* When SET HIGHRES is ON, you can specify *PRED, RESID, ZPRED, ZRESID, DRESID, ADJPRED, SRESID, SDRESID, SEPRED, MAHAL, COOK,* and *LEVER.* When SET HIGHRES is OFF, you can specify *PRED, RESID, ZPRED, ZRESID,*

DRESID, SRESID, and SDRESID. The specification of any other temporary variables will result in an error. However, you can specify any variable named on the VARIABLES subcommand.

SIZE(plotsize) *Plot size.* The plot size can be either SMALL or LARGE. The default is small. Four small scatterplots can be displayed on a single page if the width is at least 121 (see the WIDTH subcommand on p. 547) and the page length is at least 58 (see SET).

Example

```
/SCATTERPLOT (*RES,*PRE)(*RES,SAVINGS)
```

- This example specifies two scatterplots: residuals against predicted values and residuals against the values of the variable *SAVINGS*.

PARTIALPLOT Subcommand

PARTIALPLOT requests partial residual plots and controls the size of the plots. Partial residual plots are scatterplots of the residuals of the dependent variable and an independent variable when both of these variables are regressed on the rest of the independent variables.

- If PARTIALPLOT is included without any additional specifications, it produces a partial residual plot for every independent variable in the equation. The plots appear in the order the variables are specified or implied on the VARIABLES subcommand.
- If variables are specified on PARTIALPLOT, only the requested plots are displayed. The plots appear in the order the variables are listed on the PARTIALPLOT subcommand.
- At least two independent variables must be in the equation for partial residual plots to be produced.
- All plots are standardized in character-based output. When SET HIGHRES is ON, the plots are unstandardized.

varlist *Plot the specified variables.* Any variable entered into the equation can be specified. The default is every independent variable in the equation. You can request the default with keyword ALL.

SIZE(plot size) *Plot size.* The plot size can be either SMALL or LARGE. The default is small. Four small partial plots can be displayed on a single page if the width is at least 121 (see the WIDTH subcommand on p. 547) and the page length is at least 58 (see SET).

Example

```
REGRESSION VARS=PLOT15 TO SAVINGS
  /DEP=SAVINGS
  /METH=ENTER
  /RESID=DEFAULTS
  /PARTIAL.
```

- A partial residual plot is produced for every independent variable in the equation.

SAVE Subcommand

Use SAVE to add one or more residual or fit variables to the working data file.
- The specification on SAVE is one or more of the temporary variable types listed on pp. 550–551, each followed by an optional name in parentheses for the new variable.
- New variable names must be unique.
- If new names are not specified, REGRESSION generates a rootname using a shortened form of the temporary variable name with a suffix to identify its creation sequence.
- If you specify DFBETA or SDBETA on the SAVE subcommand, the number of new variables saved is the total number of variables in the equation.

FITS *Save all influence statistics.* FITS saves *DFFIT, SDFIT, DFBETA, SDBETA,* and *COVRATIO.* You cannot specify new variable names when using this keyword. Default names are generated.

Example

```
/SAVE=PRED(PREDVAL) RESID(RESIDUAL) COOK(CDISTANC)
```

- This subcommand adds three variables to the end of the working data file: *PREDVAL*, containing the unstandardized predicted value for each case; *RESIDUAL*, containing the unstandardized residual; and *CDISTANC*, containing Cook's distance.

Example

```
/SAVE=PRED RESID
```

- This subcommand adds two variables named *PRE_1* and *RES_1* to the end of the working data file.

Example

```
REGRESSION DEPENDENT=Y
 /METHOD=ENTER X1 X2
 /SAVE DFBETA(DFBVAR).
```

- The SAVE subcommand creates and saves three new variables with the names *DFBVAR0*, *DFBVAR1*, and *DFBVAR2*.

Example

```
REGRESSION VARIABLES=SAVINGS INCOME POP15 POP75 GROWTH
 /DEPENDENT=SAVINGS
 /METHOD=ENTER INCOME POP15 POP75
 /SAVE=PRED(PREDV) SDBETA(BETA) ICIN.
```

- The SAVE subcommand adds seven variables to the end of the file: *PREDV*, containing the unstandardized predicted value for the case; *BETA0*, the standardized DFBETA for the intercept; *BETA1, BETA2,* and *BETA3*, the standardized DFBETA's for the three independent variables in the model; *LICI_1*, the lower bound for the prediction interval for an individual case; and *UICI_1*, the upper bound for the prediction interval for an individual case.

References

Belsley, D. A., E. Kuh, and R. E. Welsch. 1980. *Regression diagnostics: Identifying influential data and sources of collinearity.* New York: John Wiley & Sons.

Cook, R. D. 1977. Detection of influential observations in linear regression. *Technometrics* 19:15–18.

Dillon, W. R., and M. Goldstein. 1984. *Multivariate analysis: Methods and applications.* New York: John Wiley & Sons.

Hoaglin, D. C., and R. E. Welsch. 1978. The hat matrix in regression and ANOVA. *American Statistician* 32:17–22.

Velleman, P. F., and R. E. Welsch. 1981. Efficient computing of regression diagnostics. *American Statistician* 35:234-42.

RENAME VARIABLES

```
RENAME VARIABLES {(varname=varname)    [(varname ...)]}
                 {(varnames=varnames)                  }
```

Example:
```
RENAME VARIABLES (JOBCAT=TITLE).
```

Overview

RENAME VARIABLES changes the names of variables in the working data file while preserving their original order, values, variable labels, value labels, missing values, and print and write formats. It is especially useful for renaming variables that have been generated and named by an SPSS statistical procedure, such as the Z-score variables generated by the DESCRIPTIVES command.

Basic Specification

- The basic specification is an old variable name, an equals sign, and the new variable name. The equals sign is required.

Syntax Rules

- Multiple sets of variable specifications are allowed. Each set can be enclosed in parentheses.
- You can specify a list of old variable names followed by an equals sign and a list of new variable names. The same number of variables must be specified on both lists. A single set of parentheses enclosing the entire specification is required for this method.
- Keyword TO can be used on the left side of the equals sign to refer to variables in the working data file, and on the right side of the equals sign to generate new variable names ("Keyword TO" on p. 32).
- Old variable names do not need to be specified according to their order in the working data file.
- Name changes take place in one operation. Therefore, variable names can be exchanged between two variables (see the example on p. 558).
- Multiple RENAME VARIABLES commands are allowed.
- RENAME VARIABLES cannot follow either a TEMPORARY or a MODEL PROGRAM command.

Example

```
RENAME VARIABLES (MOHIRED=MOSTART) (YRHIRED=YRSTART).
```

- *MOHIRED* is renamed to *MOSTART* and *YRHIRED* to *YRSTART*. The parentheses are optional.

Example

```
RENAME VARIABLES (MOHIRED YRHIRED=MOSTART YRSTART).
```

- The same name changes are specified as in the previous example. The parentheses are required, since variable lists are used.

Example

```
RENAME VARIABLES (A=B) (B=A).
```

- Variable names are exchanged between two variables: *A* is renamed to *B*, and *B* is renamed to *A*.

REPEATING DATA

```
REPEATING DATA [FILE=file]

 /STARTS=beg col[-end col]  /OCCURS={value  }
                                    {varname}

 [/LENGTH={value  }] [/CONTINUED[=beg col[-end col]]]
          {varname}

 [/ID={col loc}=varname] [/{TABLE  }]
      {format }             {NOTABLE}

 /DATA=variable specifications
```

Example:
```
INPUT PROGRAM.
DATA LIST / SEQNUM 2-4 NUMPERS 6-7 NUMVEH 9-10.
REPEATING DATA STARTS=12 /OCCURS=NUMVEH
 /DATA=MAKE 1-8 (A) MODEL 9 (A) NUMCYL 10.
END INPUT PROGRAM.

BEGIN DATA
1001 02 02 FORD     T8PONTIAC C6
1002 04 01 CHEVY    C4
1003 02 03 CADILAC C8FORD    T6VW     C4
END DATA.
LIST.
```

Overview

REPEATING DATA reads input cases whose records contain repeating groups of data. For each repeating group, REPEATING DATA builds one output case in the working data file. All the repeating groups in the data must contain the same type of information, although the number of groups for each input case may vary. Information common to the repeating groups for each input case can be recorded once for that case and then spread to each resulting output case. In this respect, a file with a repeating data structure is like a hierarchical file with both levels of information recorded on a single record rather than on separate record types. For information on reading hierarchical files, see FILE TYPE—END FILE TYPE.

REPEATING DATA must be used within an INPUT PROGRAM structure or within a FILE TYPE structure with mixed or nested data. In an INPUT PROGRAM structure, REPEATING DATA must be preceded by a DATA LIST command. In a FILE TYPE structure, DATA LIST is needed only if there are variables to be spread to each resulting output case.

Options

Length of Repeating Groups. If the length of the repeating groups varies across input cases, you can specify a variable that indicates the length on the LENGTH subcommand. You can also use LENGTH if you do not want to read all the data in each repeating group.

Continuation Records. You can use the CONTINUED subcommand to indicate that the repeating groups for each input case are contained on more than one record. You can check the value of an identification variable across records for the same input case using the ID subcommand.

Summary Tables. You can suppress the display of the table that summarizes the names, locations, and formats of the variables specified on the DATA subcommand using the NOTABLE subcommand.

Basic Specification

The basic specification requires three subcommands: STARTS, OCCURS, and DATA.
- STARTS specifies the beginning column of the repeating data segments. When there are continuation records, STARTS can specify the ending column of the last repeating group on the first record of each input case.
- OCCURS specifies the number of repeating groups on each input case. OCCURS can specify a number if the number of repeating groups is the same for all input cases. Otherwise, OCCURS should specify the name of a variable whose value for each input case indicates the number of repeating groups for that case.
- DATA specifies names, location within the repeating segment, and format for each variable to be read from the repeated groups.

Subcommand Order

- DATA must be the last subcommand specified on REPEATING DATA.
- The remaining subcommands can be named in any order.

Syntax Rules

- REPEATING DATA can be specified only within an INPUT PROGRAM structure, or within a FILE TYPE structure with mixed or nested data. DATA LIST, REPEATING DATA, and any transformation commands used to build the output cases must be placed within the INPUT PROGRAM or FILE TYPE structure. Transformations that apply to the output cases should be specified after the END INPUT PROGRAM or END FILE TYPE command.
- LENGTH must be used if the last variable specified on the DATA subcommand is not read from the last position of each repeating group or if the length of the repeating groups varies across input cases.
- CONTINUED must be used if repeating groups for each input case are continued on successive records.
- The DATA LIST command used with REPEATING DATA must define all fixed-format data for the records.

- Repeating groups are usually recorded at the end of the fixed-format records, but fixed-format data may follow the repeating data in data structures such as IBM SMF and RMF records. Use the following sequence in such cases.

```
DATA LIST .../* Read the fixed-format data before repeating data
REREAD   COLUMNS= .../* Skip repeating data
DATA LIST .../* Read the fixed-format data after repeating data
REPEATING DATA ... /*Read repeating data
```

Operations

- Fixed-location data specified on the DATA LIST are spread to each output case.
- If LENGTH is not specified, SPSS uses the default length for repeating data groups, which is determined from specifications on the DATA subcommand. For more information on the default length, see the LENGTH subcommand on p. 569.

Cases Generated

- The number of output cases generated is the number specified on the OCCURS subcommand. Physical record length or whether fields are non-blank does not affect the number of cases generated.
- If the number specified for OCCURS is non-positive or missing, no cases are generated.

Records Read

- If CONTINUED is not specified, all repeating groups are read from the first record of each input case.
- If CONTINUED is specified, the first continuation record is read when the first record for the input case is exhausted, that is, when the next repeating group would extend past the end of the record. The ending column for the first record is defined on STARTS. If the ending column is not specified on STARTS, the logical record length is used (see below).
- Subsequent continuation records are read when the current continuation record is exhausted. Exhaustion of the current continuation record is detected when the next repeating group would extend past the end of the record. The ending column for continuation records is defined on CONTINUED. If the ending column is not specified on CONTINUED, the logical record length is used (see below).
- For inline data, the record length is always 80. For data stored in a file, the record length is generally whatever was specified on the FILE HANDLE command or the default of 1024. Shorter records are extended with blanks when they are read. For IBM implementations, the physical record length is available and is used.

Reading Past End of Record

If one or more fields extend past the end of the actual record, or if CONTINUED is specified and the ending column specified on either STARTS or CONTINUED is beyond the end of the actual record, SPSS takes the following action:

- For string data with format A, the data record is considered to be extended logically with blanks. If the entire field lies past the end of the record, the resulting value will be all blanks.
- For numeric data, a warning is issued and the resulting value is system-missing.

Example

```
* Build a file with each case representing one vehicle and
  spread information about the household to each case.
INPUT PROGRAM.
DATA LIST / SEQNUM 2-4 NUMPERS 6-7 NUMVEH 9-10.
REPEATING DATA STARTS=12 /OCCURS=NUMVEH
 /DATA=MAKE 1-8 (A) MODEL 9 (A) NUMCYL 10.
END INPUT PROGRAM.

BEGIN DATA
1001 02 02 FORD     T8PONTIAC C6
1002 04 01 CHEVY    C4
1003 02 03 CADILAC C8FORD    T6VW     C4
END DATA.
LIST.
```

- Data are extracted from a file representing household records. Each input case is recorded on a single record; there are no continuation records.
- The total number of persons living in the house and number of vehicles owned by the household is recorded on each record. The first field of numbers (columns 1–4) for each record is an identification number unique to each record. The next two fields of numbers are number of persons in household and number of vehicles. The remainder of the record contains repeating groups of information about each vehicle: the make of vehicle, model, and number of cylinders.
- INPUT PROGRAM indicates the beginning of the input program and END INPUT PROGRAM indicates the end of the input program.
- DATA LIST reads the variables from the household portion of the record. All fixed-format variables are defined on DATA LIST.
- REPEATING DATA reads the information from the repeating groups and builds the output cases. Repeating groups start in column 12. The number of repeating groups for each input case is given by the value of variable *NUMVEH*. Three variables are defined for each repeating group: *MAKE*, *MODEL*, and *NUMCYL*.
- The first input record contains two repeating groups, producing two output cases in the working data file. One output case is built from the second input record which contains information on one vehicle, and three output cases are built from the third record. The values of the fixed-format variables defined on DATA LIST are spread to every new case built in the working data file. Six cases result, as shown in Figure 44.

Figure 44   Output cases built with REPEATING DATA

```
SEQNUM NUMPERS NUMVEH MAKE     MODEL NUMCYL

   1       2      2   FORD       T     8
   1       2      2   PONTIAC    C     6
   2       4      1   CHEVY      C     4
   3       2      3   CADILAC    C     8
   3       2      3   FORD       T     6
   3       2      3   VW         C     4

NUMBER OF CASES READ =       6    NUMBER OF CASES LISTED =        6
```

Example

```
* Use REPEATING DATA with FILE TYPE MIXED: read only type 3 records.
FILE TYPE  MIXED RECORD=#SEQNUM 2-4.
RECORD TYPE 003.
REPEATING DATA STARTS=12 /OCCURS=3
 /DATA=MAKE 1-8(A) MODEL 9(A) NUMCYL 10.
END FILE.
END FILE TYPE.

BEGIN DATA
1001 02 02 FORD     T8PONTIAC C6
1002 04 01 CHEVY    C4
1003 02 03 CADILAC  C8FORD     T6VW      C4
END DATA.
LIST.
```

- The task in this example is to read only the repeating data for records with value 003 for variable *#SEQNUM*.
- REPEATING DATA is used within a FILE TYPE structure, which specifies a mixed file type. The record identification variable *#SEQNUM* is located in columns 2–4.
- RECORD TYPE specifies that only records with value 003 for *#SEQNUM* are copied into the working data file. All other records are skipped.
- REPEATING DATA indicates that the repeating groups start in column 12. The OCCURS subcommand indicates there are three repeating groups on each input case, and the DATA subcommand specifies names, locations, and formats for the variables in the repeating groups.
- The DATA LIST command is not required in this example, since none of the information on the input case is being spread to the output cases. However, if there were multiple input cases with value 003 for *#SEQNUM* and they did not all have three repeating groups, DATA LIST would be required to define a variable whose value for each input case indicated the number of repeating groups for that case. This variable would then be specified on the OCCURS subcommand.

Example

```
* Create a data set of child records.

INPUT PROGRAM.
DATA LIST / PARENTID 1 DATE 3-6 NCHILD 8.
REPEATING DATA STARTS=9 /OCCURS=NCHILD
 /DATA=BIRTHDAY 2-5 VACDATE 7-10.
END INPUT PROGRAM.

COMPUTE AGE=DATE - BIRTHDAY.
COMPUTE VACAGE=VACDATE - BIRTHDAY.

DO IF PARENTID NE LAG(PARENTID,1) OR $CASENUM EQ 1.
COMPUTE CHILD=1.
ELSE.
COMPUTE CHILD=LAG(CHILD,1)+1.
END IF.
FORMAT AGE VACAGE CHILD (F2).

BEGIN DATA
1 1987 2 1981 1983 1982 1984
2 1988 1 1979 1984
3 1988 3 1978 1981 1981 1986 1983 1986
4 1988 1 1984 1987
END DATA.
LIST.
```

- Data are from a file that contains information on parents within a school district. Each input case is recorded on a single record; there are no continuation records.
- Each record identifies the parents by a number and indicates how many children they have. The repeating groups give the year of birth and year of vaccination for each child.
- REPEATING DATA indicates that the repeating groups begin in column 9. The value of *NCHILD* indicates how many repeating groups there are for each record.
- The first two COMPUTE commands compute the age for each child and age at vaccination. These transformation commands are specified outside the input program.
- Because the repeating groups do not have descriptive values, the DO IF structure computes variable *CHILD* to distinguish between the first-born child, second-born child, etc. The value for *CHILD* will be 1 for the first-born, 2 for the second-born, and so forth. The LIST output is shown in Figure 45.

Figure 45 Output cases built with REPEATING DATA

```
PARENTID DATE NCHILD BIRTHDAY VACDATE AGE VACAGE CHILD
       1 1987      2     1981    1983   6      2     1
       1 1987      2     1982    1984   5      2     2
       2 1988      1     1979    1984   9      5     1
       3 1988      3     1978    1981  10      3     1
       3 1988      3     1981    1986   7      5     2
       3 1988      3     1983    1986   5      3     3
       4 1988      1     1984    1987   4      3     1

NUMBER OF CASES READ =       7    NUMBER OF CASES LISTED =       7
```

STARTS Subcommand

STARTS indicates the beginning location of the repeating data segment on the first record of each input case. STARTS is required and can specify either a number or a variable name.

- If the repeating groups on the first record of each input case begin in the same column, STARTS specifies a column number.
- If the repeating groups on the first record of each input case do not begin in the same column, STARTS specifies the name of a variable whose value for each input case indicates the beginning location of the repeating groups on the first record. The variable can be defined on DATA LIST or created by transformation commands that precede REPEATING DATA.
- When repeating groups are continued on multiple records for each input case, STARTS must also specify an ending location if there is room on the logical record length for more repeating groups than are contained on the first record of each input case. The ending column applies only to the first record of each input case. See the CONTINUED subcommand on p. 570 for an example.
- The ending column can be specified as a number or a variable name. Specifications for the beginning column and the ending column are separated by a hyphen. The values of the variable used to define the ending column must be valid values and must be larger than the starting value.
- If the variable specified for the ending column is undefined or missing for an input case, SPSS displays a warning message and builds no output cases from that input case. If the variable specified for the ending column on STARTS has a value that is less than the value specified for the starting column, SPSS issues a warning and builds output cases only from the continuation records of that input case; it does not build cases from the first record of the case.
- If the ending location is required but not supplied, SPSS generates output cases with system-missing values for the variables specified on the DATA subcommand and may misread all data after the first or second record in the data file (see the CONTINUED subcommand on p. 570).

Example

```
* Repeating groups in the same location.

INPUT PROGRAM.
DATA LIST FILE=VEHICLE / SEQNUM 2-4 NUMPERS 6-7 NUMVEH 9-10.
REPEATING DATA STARTS=12 /OCCURS=NUMVEH
 /DATA=MAKE 1-8 (A) MODEL 9 (A) NUMCYL 10.
END INPUT PROGRAM.
```

- STARTS specifies column number 12. The repeating groups must therefore start in column 12 of the first record of each input case.

Example

```
* Repeating groups in varying locations.

INPUT PROGRAM.
DATA LIST FILE=VEHICLE / SEQNUM 2-4 NUMPERS 6-7 NUMVEH 9-10.
+    DO IF    (SEQNUM LE 100).
+    COMPUTE FIRST=12.
+    ELSE.
+    COMPUTE FIRST=15.
+    END IF.
REPEATING DATA STARTS=FIRST /OCCURS=NUMVEH
 /DATA=MAKE 1-8 (A) MODEL 9 (A) NUMCYL 10.
END INPUT PROGRAM.
```

- This example assumes that each input case is recorded on a single record and that there are no continuation records. Repeating groups begin in column 12 for all records with sequence numbers 1 through 100 and in column 15 for all records with sequence numbers greater than 100.
- The sequence number for each record is defined as variable *SEQNUM* on the DATA LIST command. The DO IF—END IF structure creates the variable *FIRST* with value 12 for records with sequence numbers through 100 and value 15 for records with sequence numbers greater than 100.
- Variable *FIRST* is specified on the STARTS subcommand.

OCCURS Subcommand

OCCURS specifies the number of repeating groups for each input case. OCCURS is required and specifies a number if the number of groups is the same for all input cases or a variable if the number of groups varies across input cases. The variable must be defined on a DATA LIST command or created with transformation commands.

Example

```
INPUT PROGRAM.
DATA LIST / SEQNUM 2-4 NUMPERS 6-7 NUMVEH 9-10.
REPEATING DATA STARTS=12 /OCCURS=NUMVEH
 /DATA=MAKE 1-8 (A) MODEL 9 (A) NUMCYL 10.
END INPUT PROGRAM.

BEGIN DATA
1001 02 02 FORD     T8PONTIAC C6
1002 04 01 CHEVY    C4
1003 02 03 CADILAC C8FORD      T6VW      C4
END DATA.
LIST.
```

- Data for each input case are recorded on a single record; there are no continuation records.
- The value for variable *NUMVEH* in columns 9 and 10 indicates the number of repeating groups on each record. One output case is built in the working data file for each occurrence of a repeating group.

- In the data, *NUMVEH* has the value 2 for the first case, 1 for the second, and 3 for the third. Thus, six cases are built from these records. If the value of *NUMVEH* is 0, no cases are built from that record.

Example

```
* Read only the first repeating group from each record.

INPUT PROGRAM.
DATA LIST FILE=VEHICLE / SEQNUM 2-4 NUMPERS 6-7 NUMVEH 9-10.
REPEATING DATA STARTS=12 /OCCURS=1
 /DATA=MAKE 1-8 (A) MODEL 9 (A) NUMCYL 10.
END INPUT PROGRAM.
LIST.
```

- Since OCCURS specifies that there is only one repeating group for each input case, only one output case is built from each input case regardless of the actual number of repeating groups.

DATA Subcommand

DATA specifies a name, location within each repeating segment, and format for each variable to be read from the repeating groups. DATA is required and must be the last subcommand on REPEATING DATA.

- The specifications for DATA are the same as for the DATA LIST command.
- The specified location of the variables on DATA is their location within each repeating group—*not* their location within the record.
- Any input format available on the DATA LIST command can be specified on the DATA subcommand. Both FORTRAN-like and the column-style specifications can be used.

Example

```
INPUT PROGRAM.
DATA LIST FILE=VEHICLE / SEQNUM 2-4 NUMPERS 6-7 NUMVEH 9-10.
REPEATING DATA STARTS=12 /OCCURS=NUMVEH
 /DATA=MAKE 1-8 (A) MODEL 9 (A) NUMCYL 10.
END INPUT PROGRAM.
LIST.
```

- Variable *MAKE* is a string variable read from positions 1 through 8 of each repeating group; *MODEL* is a single-character string variable read from position 9; and *NUMCYL* is a one-digit numeric variable read from position 10.
- The DATA LIST command defines variables *SEQNUM*, *NUMPERS*, and *NUMVEH*. These variables are spread to each output case built from the repeating groups.

FILE Subcommand

REPEATING DATA always reads the file specified on its associated DATA LIST or FILE TYPE command. The FILE subcommand on REPEATING DATA explicitly specifies the name of the file.

- FILE must specify the same file as its associated DATA LIST or FILE TYPE command.

Example

```
INPUT PROGRAM.
DATA LIST FILE=VEHICLE / SEQNUM 2-4 NUMPERS 6-7 NUMVEH 9-10.
REPEATING DATA FILE=VEHICLE /STARTS=12 /OCCURS=NUMVEH
 /DATA=MAKE 1-8 (A) MODEL 9 (A) NUMCYL 10.
END INPUT PROGRAM.
LIST.
```

- FILE on REPEATING DATA specifically identifies the *VEHICLE* file, which is also specified on the DATA LIST command.

LENGTH Subcommand

LENGTH specifies the length of each repeating data group. The default length is the number of columns between the beginning column of the repeating data groups and the ending position of the last variable specified on DATA. (For the first record of each input case, STARTS specifies the beginning column of the repeating groups. For continuation records, repeating groups are read from column 1 by default or from the column specified on CONTINUED.)

- The specification on LENGTH can be a number or the name of a variable.
- LENGTH must be used if the last variable specified on the DATA subcommand is not read from the last position of each repeating group, or if the length of the repeating groups varies across input cases.
- If the length of the repeating groups varies across input cases, the specification must be a variable whose value for each input case is the length of the repeating groups for that case. The variable can be defined on DATA LIST or created with transformation commands.
- If the value of the variable specified on LENGTH is undefined or missing for an input case, SPSS displays a warning message and builds only one output case for that input case.

Example

```
* Read only the variable MAKE for each vehicle'.

* The data contain two values that are not specified on the
  DATA subcommand.  The first is in position 9 of the repeating
  groups, and the second is in position 10.

INPUT PROGRAM.
DATA LIST FILE=VEHICLE / SEQNUM 2-4 NUMPERS 6-7 NUMVEH 9-10.
REPEATING DATA STARTS=12 /OCCURS=NUMVEH /LENGTH=10
 /DATA=MAKE 1-8 (A).
END INPUT PROGRAM.
```

- LENGTH indicates that each repeating group is 10 columns long. LENGTH is required because *MAKE* is not read from the last position of each repeating group. As illustrated in previous examples, each repeating group also includes variable *MODEL* (position 9) and *NUMCYL* (position 10).
- DATA specifies that *MAKE* is in positions 1 through 8 of each repeating group. Positions 9 and 10 of each repeating group are skipped.

CONTINUED Subcommand

CONTINUED indicates that the repeating groups are contained on more than one record for each input case.
- Each repeating group must be fully recorded on a single record: a repeating group cannot be split across records.
- The repeating groups must begin in the same column on all continuation records.
- If CONTINUED is specified without beginning and ending columns, SPSS assumes that the repeating groups begin in column 1 of continuation records and searches for repeating groups by scanning to the end of the record or to the value specified by OCCURS. See "Operations" on p. 562 for additional information on how records are read.
- If the repeating groups on continuation records do not begin in column 1, CONTINUED must specify the column in which the repeating groups begin.
- If there is room on the logical record length for more repeating groups than are contained on the first record of each input case, the STARTS subcommand must indicate an ending column for the records. The ending column on STARTS applies only to the first record of each input case.
- If there is room on the logical record length for more repeating groups than are contained on the continuation records of each input case, the CONTINUED subcommand must indicate an ending column. The ending column on CONTINUED applies to all continuation records.

Example

```
* This example assumes the logical record length is 80.

INPUT PROGRAM.
DATA LIST / ORDERID 1-5 NITEMS 7-8.
REPEATING DATA STARTS=10 /OCCURS=NITEMS /CONTINUED=7
 /DATA=ITEM 1-9 (A) QUANTITY 11-13 PRICE (DOLLAR7.2,1X).
END INPUT PROGRAM.

BEGIN DATA
10020 07 01-923-89 001   25.99 02-899-56 100 101.99 03-574-54 064   61.29
10020    04-780-32 025   13.95 05-756-90 005   56.75 06-323-47 003   23.74
10020    07-350-95 014   11.46
20030 04 01-781-43 010   10.97 02-236-54 075 105.95 03-655-83 054   22.99
20030    04-569-38 015   75.00
END DATA.
LIST.
```

- Data are extracted from a mail-order file. Each input case represents one complete order. The data show two complete orders recorded on a total of five records.
- The order number is recorded in columns 1 through 5 of each record. The first three records contain information for order 10020; the next two records contain information for order 20030. The second field of numbers on the first record of each order indicates the total number of items ordered. The repeating groups begin in column 10 on the first record and in column 7 on continuation records. Each repeating data group represents one item ordered and contains three variables—the item inventory number, the quantity ordered, and the price.

- DATA LIST defines variables *ORDERID* and *NITEMS* on the first record of each input case.
- STARTS on REPEATING DATA indicates that the repeating groups on the first record of each input case begin in column 10.
- OCCURS indicates that the total number of repeating groups for each input case is the value of *NITEMS*.
- CONTINUED must be used because the repeating groups are continued on more than one record for each input case. CONTINUED specifies a beginning column because the repeating groups begin in column 7 rather than in column 1 on the continuation records.
- DATA defines variables *ITEM*, *QUANTITY*, and *PRICE* for each repeating data group. *ITEM* is in positions 1–9, *QUANTITY* is in positions 11–13, and *PRICE* is in positions 14–20 and is followed by one blank column. The length of the repeating groups is therefore 21 columns. The LIST output is shown in Figure 46.

Figure 46 Cases generated by REPEATING DATA

```
ORDERID NITEMS ITEM      QUANTITY      PRICE

10020     7    01-923-89       1      $25.99
10020     7    02-899-56     100     $101.99
10020     7    03-574-54      64      $61.29
10020     7    04-780-32      25      $13.95
10020     7    05-756-90       5      $56.75
10020     7    06-323-47       3      $23.74
10020     7    07-350-95      14      $11.46
20030     4    01-781-43      10      $10.97
20030     4    02-236-54      75     $105.95
20030     4    03-655-83      54      $22.99
20030     4    04-569-38      15      $75.00

NUMBER OF CASES READ =    11    NUMBER OF CASES LISTED =    11
```

Example

```
* Specifying an ending column on the STARTS subcommand.
* This example assumes the logical record length is 80.

INPUT PROGRAM.
DATA LIST / ORDERID 1-5 NITEMS 7-8.
REPEATING DATA STARTS=10-55 /OCCURS=NITEMS /CONTINUED=7
 /DATA=ITEM 1-9 (A) QUANTITY 11-13 PRICE (DOLLAR7.2,1X).
END INPUT PROGRAM.

BEGIN DATA
10020 07 01-923-89 001   25.99 02-899-56 100 101.99
10020 03-574-54 064   61.29 04-780-32 025   13.95 05-756-90 005   56.75
10020 06-323-47 003   23.74 07-350-95 014   11.46
20030 04 01-781-43 010   10.97 02-236-54 075 105.95
20030 03-655-83 054   22.99 04-569-38 015   75.00
END DATA.
LIST.
```

- Data are the same as in the previous example; however, records are entered differently. The first record for each input case contains only two repeating groups.
- DATA LIST defines variables *ORDERID* and *NITEMS* in columns 1–8 on the first record of each input case. Column 9 is blank. DATA defines variables *ITEM*, *QUANTITY*, and *PRICE*

in positions 1–20 of each repeating group, followed by a blank. Thus, each repeating group is 21 columns wide. The length of the first record of each input case is therefore 51 columns: 21 columns for each of two repeating groups, plus the eight columns defined on DATA LIST, plus column 9, which is blank. The operating system's logical record length is 80, which allows room for one more repeating group on the first record of each input case. STARTS must therefore specify an ending column that does not provide enough columns for another repeating group; otherwise, SPSS creates an output case with missing values for the variables specified on DATA.

- STARTS specifies that SPSS is to scan only columns 10–55 of the first record of each input case looking for repeating data groups. It will scan continuation records beginning in column 7 until the value specified on the OCCURS subcommand is reached.

Example

```
* Specifying an ending column on the CONTINUED subcommand.
* This example assumes the logical record length is 80.

INPUT PROGRAM.
DATA LIST / ORDERID 1-5 NITEMS 7-8.
REPEATING DATA STARTS=10-55 /OCCURS=NITEMS /CONTINUED=7-55
 /DATA=ITEM 1-9 (A) QUANTITY 11-13 PRICE (DOLLAR7.2,1X).
END INPUT PROGRAM.

BEGIN DATA
10020 07 01-923-89 001  25.99 02-899-56 100 101.99
10020    03-574-54 064  61.29 04-780-32 025  13.95
10020    05-756-90 005  56.75 06-323-47 003  23.74
10020    07-350-95 014  11.46
20030 04 01-781-43 010  10.97 89-236-54 075 105.95
20030    03-655-83 054  22.99 04-569-38 015  75.00
END DATA.
LIST.
```

- The data are the same as in the previous two examples, but records are entered differently. The first record and the continuation records for each input case store only two repeating groups each.
- The operating system's logical record length is 80, which allows room for more repeating groups on all records.
- STARTS specifies that SPSS is to scan only columns 10-55 of the first record of each input case looking for repeating data groups.
- CONTINUED specifies that SPSS is to scan only columns 7–55 of all continuation records.

ID Subcommand

ID compares the value of an identification variable across records of the same input case. ID can be used only when CONTINUED is specified. The identification variable must be defined on a DATA LIST command and must be recorded on all records in the file.

- The ID subcommand has two specifications: the location of the variable on the continuation records and the name of the variable (as specified on the DATA LIST command). The specifications must be separated from each other by an equals sign.

- The format specified on the ID subcommand must be the same as the format specified for the variable on DATA LIST. However, the location can be different on the continuation records.
- If the values of the identification variable are not the same on all records for a single input case, SPSS displays an error message and stops reading data.

Example

```
INPUT PROGRAM.
DATA LIST / ORDERID 1-5 NITEMS 7-8.
REPEATING DATA STARTS=10-50 /OCCURS=NITEMS
 /CONTINUED=7 /ID=1-5=ORDERID
 /DATA=ITEM 1-9 (A) QUANTITY 11-13 PRICE 15-20 (2).
END INPUT PROGRAM.

BEGIN DATA
10020 04 45-923-89 001  25.99 23-899-56 100 101.99
10020 63-780-32 025  13.95 54-756-90 005  56.75
20030 03 45-781-43 010  10.97 89-236-54 075 105.95
20030 32-569-38 015  75.00
END DATA.
LIST.
```

- The order number in the data is recorded in columns 1–5 of each record.
- *ORDERID* is defined on the DATA LIST command as a five-column integer variable. The first specification on the ID subcommand must therefore specify a five-column integer variable. The location of the variable can be different on continuation records.

TABLE and NOTABLE Subcommands

TABLE displays a table summarizing all variables defined on the DATA subcommand. The summary table lists the names, locations, and formats of the variables and is identical in format to the summary table displayed by the DATA LIST command. NOTABLE suppresses the table. TABLE is the default.

Example

```
INPUT PROGRAM.
DATA LIST FILE=VEHICLE / SEQNUM 2-4 NUMPERS 6-7 NUMVEH 9-10.
REPEATING DATA STARTS=12 /OCCURS=NUMVEH /NOTABLE
 /DATA=MAKE 1-8 (A) MODEL 9 (A) NUMCYL 10.
END INPUT PROGRAM.
```

- NOTABLE suppresses the display of the summary table.

REPORT

```
REPORT [/FORMAT=[{MANUAL   }] [{NOLIST }] [ALIGN({LEFT  })] [TSPACE({1})]
                {AUTOMATIC}   {LIST[(n)]}         {CENTER}           {n}
                                                  {RIGHT }

         [CHDSPACE({1})] [FTSPACE({1})] [SUMSPACE({1})] [COLSPACE({4})]
                   {n}            {n}            {n}             {n}

         [BRKSPACE({ 1 })][LENGTH({1,length})] [MARGINS({1,width})]
                   { n }         {t,b      }           {l,r      }
                   {-1†}         {*,*      }           {*,*      }

         [CHALIGN({TOP    })] [UNDERSCORE({OFF})] [PAGE1({1})] [MISSING {'.'}]]
                  {BOTTOM†}               {ON†}         {n}           {'s'}

[/OUTFILE=file]

[/STRING=stringname (varname[(width)] [(BLANK)] ['literal'])

/VARIABLES=varname ({VALUE}) [+ varname({VALUE})] ['col head'] [option list]
                   {LABEL}               {LABEL}
                   {DUMMY}               {DUMMY}
```

where option list can contain any of the following:
```
      (width)    (OFFSET({0     }))    ({LEFT   })
                        {n     }       {CENTER†}
                        {CENTER†}      {RIGHT  }

[/MISSING={VAR              }]
          {NONE             }
          {LIST[([varlist][{1}])]}
                            {n}

[     /TITLE='line1' 'line2'...]     [  /FOOTNOTE='line1' 'line2'...]
             or                               or
[/TITLE=LEFT 'line1' 'line2'...]     [/FOOTNOTE=LEFT 'line1' 'line2'...]
[      CENTER 'line1' 'line2'...]    [        CENTER 'line1' 'line2'...]
[       RIGHT 'line1' 'line2'...]    [         RIGHT 'line1' 'line2'...]

              [)PAGE]    [)DATE]    [)var]

[/BREAK=varlist ['col head'] [option list]]
```
where option list can contain any of the following:
```
     (width)    ({VALUE })    ({NOTOTAL})    (SKIP({1}))    (PAGE[(RESET)])
                {LABEL†}      {TOTAL  }             {n}

   (OFFSET({0     }))   (UNDERSCORE[(varlist)])   ({LEFT   })   ({NONAME})
          {n     }                                {CENTER†}    {NAME  }
          {CENTER†}                                {RIGHT  }

[/SUMMARY=function...['summary title'][(break col #)] [SKIP({0})]
                                                            {n}
   or
[/SUMMARY=PREVIOUS[({1})]]]
                   {n}
```
where function is
```
  aggregate [(varname[({PLAIN   })][(d)][varname...])]
                     {format††}
     or
  composite(argument)[(report col[({PLAIN   })][(d)])]
                                  {format††}
```

†Default if FORMAT=AUTOMATIC.
††Any printable output format is valid. See FORMATS.

Aggregate functions:

VALIDN	VARIANCE	PLT(n)
SUM	KURTOSIS	PIN(min,max)
MIN	SKEWNESS	FREQUENCY(min,max)
MAX	MEDIAN(min,max)	PERCENT(min,max)
MEAN	MODE(min,max)	
STDDEV	PGT(n)	

Composite functions:

DIVIDE(arg_1 arg_2 [factor])
MULTIPLY(arg_1...arg_n)
PCT(arg_1 arg_2)
SUBTRACT(arg_1 arg_2)
ADD(arg_1...arg_n)
GREAT(arg_1...arg_n)
LEAST(arg_1...arg_n)
AVERAGE(arg_1...arg_n)

where arg is either one of the aggregate functions or a constant

Example:

```
REPORT FORMAT=LIST
   /VARIABLES=PRODUCT (LABEL) ' ' 'Retail' 'Products'
             SALES 'Annual' 'Sales' '1981'
   /BREAK=DEPT 'Department' (LABEL)
   /SUMMARY=VALIDN (PRODUCT) MEAN (SALES).
```

Overview

REPORT produces case listings and summary statistics and gives you considerable control over the appearance of the output. REPORT calculates all the univariate statistics available in DESCRIPTIVES and the statistics and subpopulation means available in MEANS. In addition, REPORT calculates statistics not directly available in any other SPSS procedure, such as computations involving aggregated statistics.

REPORT provides complete report format defaults but also lets you customize a variety of table elements, including column widths, titles, footnotes, and spacing. Because REPORT is so flexible and the output has so many components, it is often efficient to preview report output using a small number of cases until you find the format that best suits your needs.

Defaults

Column Heads. REPORT uses variable labels as default column heads; if no variable labels have been specified, variable names are used.

Missing Values. By default, cases with user-missing values are excluded from the calculation of report statistics, and missing-value indicators are ignored for variables named on BREAK.

Column Widths. Default column widths are determined by REPORT, using the maximum of the following for each column:

- The widest print format in the column, whether it is a variable print format or a summary print format.
- The width of any temporary variable defined with the STRING subcommand on REPORT.
- The length of the longest title line in the heading, if a column heading is assigned.
- When no column heading is specified, the length of the longest word in the variable label, or the length of the variable name. If FORMAT=MANUAL is in effect, variable labels are not evaluated.
- If you specify LABEL on VARIABLES, the length of the variable's longest value label. If FORMAT=MANUAL is in effect, 20 is the maximum value used for this criterion.

Intercolumn Spacing. Intercolumn spacing adjusts automatically, using a minimum of one and a maximum of four spaces between columns.

Automatic Fit. When the above criteria for column width result in a report that is too wide for the report margins, FORMAT=AUTOMATIC shrinks the report. AUTOMATIC performs the following two steps sequentially, stopping as soon as the report fits within the margins:

1. AUTOMATIC reduces intercolumn spacing incrementally until it reaches a minimum intercolumn space of 1. It will never reduce it to 0.

2. AUTOMATIC shortens widths for strings specified on the STRING subcommand. It begins with the longest string if that string is at least 15 characters wide and shortens the column width as much as needed (up to 40% of its length), wrapping the string within the new width. If necessary it repeats the step, using different defined strings. It will not shorten the column width of the same string twice.

REPORT does *not* implement the automatic fit unless AUTOMATIC is specified on the FORMAT subcommand.

AUTOMATIC vs. MANUAL Defaults. Many default settings depend on whether you specify AUTOMATIC or MANUAL on FORMAT. Table 18 shows the defaults according to both specifications.

Table 18 Keyword default settings

Subcommand	Keyword	Default for AUTOMATIC	Default for MANUAL
FORMAT	ALIGN	left	left
	BRKSPACE		
	summary report	1	1
	listing report	-1	1
	CHALIGN	bottom	top
	CHDSPACE	1	1

Table 18 Keyword default settings (Continued)

Subcommand	Keyword	Default for AUTOMATIC	Default for MANUAL
	COLSPACE	4	4
	FTSPACE	1	1
	LENGTH	1,system length	1,system length
	LIST|NOLIST	NOLIST	NOLIST
	MARGINS	1,system length	1,system length
	MISSING		
	PAGE1	1	1
	SUMSPACE	1	1
	TSPACE	1	1
	UNDERSCORE	on	off
VARIABLES	LABEL|VALUE|DUMMY	VALUE	VALUE
	LEFT|CENTER|RIGHT	CENTER	RIGHT for numbers LEFT for strings
	OFFSET	CENTER	0
BREAK	LABEL|VALUE	LABEL	VALUE
	LEFT|CENTER|RIGHT	CENTER	RIGHT for numbers LEFT for strings
	NAME|NONAME	NONAME	NONAME
	OFFSET	CENTER	0
	PAGE	off	off
	SKIP	1	1
	TOTAL|NOTOTAL	NOTOTAL	NOTOTAL
	UNDERSCORE	off	off
SUMMARY	PREVIOUS	1	1
	SKIP	0	0

Options

Format. REPORT provides full format defaults and offers you optional control over page length, vertical spacing, margin and column widths, page titles, footnotes, and labels for statistics. The maximum width and length of the report are controlled by specifications on the SET command. The FORMAT subcommand on REPORT controls how the report is laid out on a page and whether case listings are displayed. The VARIABLES subcommand specifies the variables that are listed or summarized in the report (**report variables**) and controls the titles, width, and contents of report columns. The BREAK subcommand specifies the variables that define groups (**break variables**) and controls the titles, width, and contents of break columns. SUMMARY specifies statistics and controls the titles and spacing of summary lines. The TITLE and FOOTNOTE subcommands control the specification and placement of multiple-line titles and footnotes. STRING concatenates variables to create temporary variables that can be specified on VARIABLES or BREAK.

Output File. You can direct reports to a file separate from the file used for the rest of the output from your session using the OUTFILE subcommand.

Statistical Display. The statistical display is controlled by the SUMMARY subcommand. Statistics can be calculated for each category of a break variable and for the group as a whole. Available statistics include mean, variance, standard deviation, skewness, kurtosis, sum, minimum, maximum, mode, median, and percentages. Composite functions perform arithmetic operations using two or more summary statistics calculated on single variables.

Missing Values. You can override the default to include user-missing values in report statistics and listings with the MISSING subcommand. You can also use FORMAT to define a missing-value symbol to represent missing data.

Basic Specification

The basic specification depends on whether you want a listing report or a summary report. A listing report without subgroup classification requires FORMAT and VARIABLES. A listing report with subgroup classification requires FORMAT, VARIABLES, and BREAK. A summary report requires VARIABLES, BREAK, and SUMMARY.

Listing Reports. FORMAT=LIST and VARIABLES with a variable list are required. Case listings are displayed for each variable named on VARIABLES. There are no break groups or summary statistics unless BREAK or SUMMARY are specified.

Summary Reports. VARIABLES, BREAK, and SUMMARY are required. The report is organized according to the values of the variable named on BREAK. The variable named on BREAK must be named on a preceding SORT CASES command. Specified statistics are computed for the variables specified on VARIABLES for each subgroup defined by the break variables.

Subcommand Order

The following order must be observed among subcommands when they are used:
- FORMAT must precede all other subcommands.
- VARIABLES must precede BREAK.
- OUTFILE must precede BREAK.
- Each SUMMARY subcommand must immediately follow its associated BREAK. Multiple SUMMARY subcommands associated with the same BREAK must be specified consecutively.
- TITLE and FOOTNOTE can appear anywhere after FORMAT except between BREAK and SUMMARY.
- MISSING must follow VARIABLES and precede the first BREAK.

- STRING must precede VARIABLES.

Syntax Rules

- Only one each of the FORMAT, STRING, VARIABLES, and MISSING subcommands is allowed.
- To obtain multiple break groups, use multiple BREAK subcommands.
- To obtain multiple summaries for a break level, specify multiple SUMMARY subcommands for the associated BREAK.
- Keywords on REPORT subcommands have default specifications that are in effect if the keyword is not specified. Specify keywords only when you wish to change a default.
- Keywords are enclosed in parentheses if the subcommand takes variable names as arguments.

Operations

- REPORT processes cases sequentially. When the value of a break variable changes, REPORT displays a statistical summary for cases processed since the last set of summary statistics was displayed. Thus, the file must be sorted in order on the break variable or variables.
- The maximum width and page length of the report are determined by the SET command.
- If a column is not wide enough to display numeric values, REPORT first rounds decimal digits, then converts to scientific notation if possible, and then displays asterisks. String variables that are wider than the column are truncated.
- The format used to display values in case listings is controlled by the dictionary format of the variable. Each statistical function in REPORT has a default format.

Limitations

- Maximum 500 variables per VARIABLES subcommand.
- Maximum 10 dummy variables per VARIABLES subcommand.
- Maximum 20 MODE and MEDIAN requests per SUMMARY subcommand.
- Maximum 20 PGT, PLT, and PIN requests per SUMMARY subcommand.
- Maximum 50 strings per STRING subcommand.
- The length of titles and footnotes cannot exceed the report width.
- The length of string variables created on STRING cannot exceed the page width.
- There is no fixed limit on the number of BREAK and SUMMARY subcommands. However, the page width limits the number of variables that can be displayed and thereby limits the number of break variables.
- The maximum width of a report is 255 characters.

- The number of report variables that can be specified depends upon the width of the report, the width of the variable columns, and the number of BREAK subcommands.
- Maximum 50 variables for the FREQUENCY or PERCENT functions.
- Memory requirements significantly increase if FREQUENCY, PERCENT, MEDIAN, or MODE is requested for variables with a wide range of values. The amount of workspace required is 20 + 8*(max−min +1) bytes per variable per function per break. If the same range is used for different statistics for the same variable, only one set of cells is collected. For example, FREQUENCY(1,100)(VARA) PERCENT(1,100)(VARA) requires only 820 bytes.
- If TOTAL is in effect, workspace requirements are almost doubled.
- Memory requirements also increase if value labels are displayed for variables with many value labels. The amount of workspace required is 4 + 24*n bytes per variable, where n is the number of value labels specified for the variable.

Example

```
SORT CASES BY DEPT.
REPORT FORMAT=LIST
   /VARIABLES=PRODUCT (LABEL) ' ' 'Retail' 'Products'
             SALES 'Annual' 'Sales' '1981'
   /BREAK=DEPT 'Department' (LABEL)
   /SUMMARY=VALIDN (PRODUCT) MEAN (SALES) 'No.Sold,Mean Sales'.
```

- This report is a listing of products and sales by department. A summary of the total number of products sold and the average sales by department is also produced.
- Cases are first sorted by *DEPT* so that cases are grouped by department for the case listing and for the calculation of statistics.
- FORMAT requests a report that lists individual cases within each break group.
- VARIABLES specifies *PRODUCT* and *SALES* as the report variables. Keyword LABEL requests that the case listings for *PRODUCT* display value labels instead of values. Three-line column headings are provided for each report column. The first line of the column heading is blank for the variable *PRODUCT*.
- BREAK identifies *DEPT* as the break variable and provides a one-line column title for the break column. LABEL displays the value label instead of the value itself.
- SUMMARY calculates the valid number of cases for *PRODUCT* and the mean of *SALES* for each value of *DEPT*. A title is provided for the summary line to override the default title, *VALIDN*.

FORMAT Subcommand

FORMAT controls the overall width and length of the report and vertical spacing. Keywords and their arguments can be specified in any order.

- MANUAL and AUTOMATIC are alternatives. The default is MANUAL.
- LIST and NOLIST are alternatives. The default is NOLIST.

MANUAL	*Default settings for manual format.* MANUAL displays values for break variables, right-justifies numeric values and their column headings, left-justifies value labels and string values and their column headings, top-aligns and does not underscore column headings, extends column widths to accommodate the variable's longest value label (but not the longest word in the variable label) up to a width of 20, and generates an error message when a report is too wide for its margins. MANUAL is the default.
AUTOMATIC	*Default settings for automatic format.* AUTOMATIC displays labels for break variables, centers all data, centers column headings but left-justifies column headings if value labels or string values exceed the width of the longest word in the heading, bottom-aligns and underscores column headings, extends column widths to accommodate the longest word in a variable label or the variable's longest value label, and shrinks a report that is too wide for its margins.
LIST(n)	*Individual case listing.* The values of all variables named on VARIABLES are displayed for each case. The optional *n* inserts a blank line after each *n* cases. By default, no blank lines are inserted. Values for cases are listed using the default formats for the variables.
NOLIST	*No case listing.* This is the default.
PAGE(n)	*Page number for the first page of the report.* The default is 1.
LENGTH(t,b)	*Top and bottom line numbers of the report.* You can specify any numbers to define the report page length. By default, the top of the report begins at line 1, and the bottom of the report is the last line of the system page. You can use an asterisk for *t* or *b* to indicate a default value. If the specified length does not allow even one complete line of information to be displayed, REPORT extends the length specification and displays a warning.
MARGINS(l,r)	*Columns for the left and right margins.* The right column cannot exceed 255. By default, the left margin is display column 1 and the right margin is the rightmost display column of the system page. You can use an asterisk for *l* or *r* to indicate a default value.
ALIGN	*Placement of the report relative to its margins.* LEFT, CENTER, or RIGHT can be specified in the parentheses following the keyword. LEFT left-justifies the report. CENTER centers the report between its margins. RIGHT right-justifies the report. The default is LEFT.
COLSPACE(n)	*Number of spaces between each column.* The default is 4 or the average number of spaces that will fit within report margins, whichever is less. When AUTOMATIC is in effect, REPORT overrides the specified column spacing if necessary to fit the report between its margins.
CHALIGN	*Alignment of column headings.* Either TOP or BOTTOM can be specified in the parentheses following the keyword. TOP aligns all column headings with the first, or top, line of multiple-line headings. BOTTOM aligns headings with the last, or bottom, line of multiple-line headings. When AUTOMATIC is in effect, the default is BOTTOM; when MANUAL is in effect, the default is TOP.

UNDERSCORE   *Underscores for column headings.* Either ON or OFF can be specified in the parentheses following the keyword. ON underscores the bottom line of each column heading for the full width of the column. OFF does not underscore column headings. The default is ON when AUTOMATIC is in effect and OFF when MANUAL is in effect.

TSPACE(n)   *Number of blank lines between the report title and the column heads.* The default is 1.

CHDSPACE(n)   *Number of blank lines beneath the longest column head.* The default is 1.

BRKSPACE(n)   *Number of blank lines between the break head and the next line.* The next line is a case if LIST is in effect or the first summary line if NOLIST is in effect. BRKSPACE(-1) places the first summary statistic or the first case listing on the same line as the break value. When a summary line is placed on the same line as the break value, the summary title is suppressed. When AUTOMATIC is in effect, the default is −1; when MANUAL is in effect, it is 1.

SUMSPACE(n)   *Number of blank lines between the last summary line at the lower break level and the first summary line at the higher break level when they break simultaneously.* SUMSPACE also controls spacing between the last listed case and the first summary line if LIST is in effect. The default is 1.

FTSPACE(n)   *Minimum number of blank lines between the last listing on the page and the footnote.* The default is 1.

MISSING 's'   *Missing-value symbol.* The symbol can be only one character and is represents both system- and user-missing values. The default is a period.

Example

```
FORMAT=AUTOMATIC LIST MARGINS(1,60) LENGTH(5,30) MISSING ('*')
```

- FORMAT requests a case listing, defines a new page size smaller than the system page size, and specifies an asterisk as the missing-value symbol.

Page Layout

Figure 47 shows the complete page layout and subcommand specifications used to control the basic format of the report.

OUTFILE Subcommand

OUTFILE directs the report to a file separate from the file used for the rest of the output from your SPSS session. This allows you to print the report without having to delete the extraneous material that would be present in the SPSS output.

- OUTFILE must follow FORMAT and must precede BREAK.
- You can append multiple reports to the same file by naming the same file on the OUTFILE subcommand for each REPORT command.

Figure 47 Page layout for REPORT

```
------------------------------------------------ top of page -------------------------------------------------         ← LENGTH
                         *************** TITLE ***************                                                          ← TSPACE
BREAK HEAD      BREAK HEAD      COLUMN      COLUMN      COLUMN      COLUMN
                                HEAD        HEAD        HEAD        HEAD
                                (VAR)       (VAR)       (VAR)       (VAR)                                               ← CHDSPACE
BREAK A VALUE 1 BREAK B VALUE 1                                                                                         ← BRKSPACE
                                VALUE       VALUE       VALUE       VALUE
                                VALUE       VALUE       VALUE       VALUE                                               ← LIST
                                VALUE       VALUE       VALUE       VALUE
                                VALUE       VALUE       VALUE       VALUE                                               ← SUMSPACE
                SUMMARY TITLE   AGG         AGG         AGG         AGG                                                 ← SKIP w/ SUMMARY
                SUMMARY TITLE   AGG         AGG         AGG         AGG
                                                                                                                        ← SKIP w/ BREAK
                BREAK B VALUE 2                                                                                         ← BRKSPACE
                                VALUE       VALUE       VALUE       VALUE
                                VALUE       VALUE       VALUE       VALUE                                               ← LIST
                                VALUE       VALUE       VALUE       VALUE
                                VALUE       VALUE       VALUE       VALUE                                               ← SUMSPACE
                SUMMARY TITLE   AGG         AGG         AGG         AGG                                                 ← stats for B=2, A=1
                SUMMARY TITLE   AGG         AGG         AGG         AGG
                                                                                                                        ← SUMSPACE
SUMMARY TITLE                   AGG         AGG         AGG         AGG                                                 ← stats for A=1
SUMMARY TITLE                   AGG         AGG         AGG         AGG                                                 ← SKIP w/ BREAK
BREAK A VALUE 2 BREAK B VALUE 1                                                                                         ← BRKSPACE
                                VALUE       VALUE       VALUE       VALUE
                                VALUE       VALUE       VALUE       VALUE                                               ← LIST
                                VALUE       VALUE       VALUE       VALUE
                                VALUE       VALUE       VALUE       VALUE                                               ← SUMSPACE
                SUMMARY TITLE   AGG         AGG         AGG         AGG                                                 ← SKIP w/ SUMMARY
                SUMMARY TITLE   AGG         AGG         AGG         AGG                                                 ← SKIP w/ BREAK
                BREAK B VALUE 2                                                                                         ← BRKSPACE
                                VALUE       VALUE       VALUE       VALUE
                                VALUE       VALUE       VALUE       VALUE                                               ← LIST
                                VALUE       VALUE       VALUE       VALUE
                                VALUE       VALUE       VALUE       VALUE
                SUMMARY TITLE   AGG         AGG         AGG         AGG
                SUMMARY TITLE   AGG         AGG         AGG         AGG
                                                                                                                        ← SUMSPACE
SUMMARY TITLE                   AGG         AGG         AGG         AGG
SUMMARY TITLE                   AGG         AGG         AGG         AGG                                                 ← FTSPACE
                         *************** FOOTNOTE ***************                                                       ← LENGTH
------------------------------------------------ bottom of page ----------------------------------------------
|                                                                                          |
Left margin                                                                          Right margin
```

Example

```
REPORT FORMAT=AUTOMATIC LIST
  /OUTFILE=PRSNLRPT
  /VARIABLES=LNAME AGE TENURE JTENURE SALARY
  /BREAK=DIVISION
  /SUMMARY=MEAN.

REPORT FORMAT=AUTOMATIC
  /OUTFILE=PRSNLRPT
  /VARIABLES=LNAME AGE TENURE JTENURE SALARY
  /BREAK=DIVISION
  /SUMMARY=MEAN
  /SUMMARY=MIN
  /SUMMARY=MAX.
```

- Both a listing report and a summary report are written to file *PRSNLRPT*.

VARIABLES Subcommand

The required VARIABLES subcommand names the variables to be listed and summarized in the report. You can also use VARIABLES to control column titles, column widths, and the contents of report columns.

- The minimum specification on VARIABLES is a list of report variables. The number of variables that can be specified is limited by the system page width.
- Each report variable defines a report column. The value of the variable or an aggregate statistic calculated for the variable is displayed in that variable's report column.
- Variables are assigned to columns in the order in which they are named on VARIABLES.
- Variables named on BREAK can also be named on VARIABLES.
- When FORMAT=LIST, variables can be stacked in a single column by linking them with plus signs (+) on the VARIABLES subcommand. If no column heading is specified, REPORT uses the default heading from the first variable on the list. Only values from the first variable in the column are used to calculate summaries.
- Optional specifications apply only to the immediately preceding variable or list of variables implied by the TO keyword. Options can be specified in any order.
- All optional specifications except column headings must be enclosed in parentheses; column headings must be enclosed in apostrophes or quotes.

Column Contents

The following options can be used to specify the contents of the report column for each variable:

(VALUE) *Display the values of the variable.* This is the default.

(LABEL) *Display value labels.* If value labels are not defined, values are displayed.

(DUMMY) *Display blank spaces.* DUMMY defines a report column for a variable that does not exist in the working data file. Dummy variables are used to control

spacing or to reserve space for statistics computed for other variables. Do not name an existing SPSS variable as a dummy variable.
- VALUE and LABEL have no effect unless LIST has been specified on the FORMAT subcommand.
- When AUTOMATIC is in effect, value labels or string values are centered in the column based on the length of the longest string or label; numeric values are centered based on the width of the widest value or summary format. When MANUAL is in effect, value labels or string values are left-justified in the column and numeric values are right-justified. (See the OFFSET keyword on p. 586.)

Column Heading

The following option can be used to specify a heading for the report column:

'column heading' *Column heading for the preceding variable.* The heading must be enclosed in apostrophes or quotes. If no column heading is specified, the default is the variable label or, if no variable label has been specified, the variable name.

- To specify multiple-line headings, enclose each line in a set of apostrophes or quotes, using the conventions for strings (see "String Values in Command Specifications" on p. 16). The specifications for title lines should be separated by at least one blank.
- Default column headings wrap for as many lines as are required to display the entire label. If AUTOMATIC is in effect, user-specified column headings appear exactly as specified, even if the column width must be extended. If MANUAL is in effect, user-specified titles wrap to fit within the column width.

Column Heading Alignment

The following options can be used to specify how column headings are aligned:

(LEFT)   *Left-aligned column heading.*

(CENTER) *Centered column heading.*

(RIGHT) *Right-aligned column heading.*

- If AUTOMATIC is in effect, column headings are centered within their columns by default. If value labels or string values exceed the width of the longest word in the heading, the heading is left-justified.
- If MANUAL is in effect, column headings are left-justified for value labels or string values and right-justified for numeric values by default.

Column Format

The following options can be used to specify column width and adjust the position of the column contents:

(width) *Width for the report column.* If no width is specified for a variable, REPORT determines a default width using the criteria described under "Defaults" on p. 575. If you specify a width that is not wide enough to display numeric values, REPORT first rounds decimal digits, then converts to scientific notation if possible, and then displays asterisks. Value labels or string values that exceed the width are wrapped.

(OFFSET) *Position of the report column contents.* The specification is either *n* or CENTER specified in parentheses. OFFSET(*n*) indicates the number of spaces to offset the contents from the left for value labels or string values, and from the right for numeric values. OFFSET(CENTER) centers contents within the center of the column. If AUTOMATIC is in effect, the default is CENTER. If MANUAL is in effect, the default is 0: value labels and string values are left-justified and numeric values are right-justified.

Example

```
/VARIABLES=V1 TO V3(LABEL) (15)
  V4 V5 (LABEL)(OFFSET (2))(10)
  SEP1 (DUMMY) (2) ''
  V6 'Results using' "Lieben's Method" 'of Calculation'
```

- The width of the columns for variables *V1* through *V3* is 15 each. Value labels are displayed for these variables in the case listing.
- The column for variable *V4* uses the default width. Values are listed in the case listing.
- Value labels are displayed for variable *V5*. The column width is 10. Column contents are offset two spaces from the left.
- *SEP1* is a dummy variable. The column width is 2, and there is at least one space column on each side of *SEP1*. Thus, there are at least four blanks between the columns for *V5* and *V6*. *SEP1* is given a null title to override the default column title *SEP1*.
- *V6* has a three-line title. Its column uses the default width, and values are listed in the case listing.

STRING Subcommand

STRING creates a temporary string variable by concatenating variables and user-specified strings. These variables exist only within the REPORT procedure.

- The minimum specification is a name for the string variable followed by a variable name or a user-specified string enclosed in parentheses.
- The name assigned to the string variable must be unique.
- Any combination of string variables, numeric variables, and user-specified strings can be used in the parentheses to define the string.
- Keyword TO cannot be used within the parentheses to imply a variable list.
- More than one string variable can be defined on STRING.
- If a case has a missing value for a variable within the parentheses, the variable passes the missing value to the temporary variable without affecting other elements specified.
- A string variable defined in REPORT cannot exceed the system page width.

- String variables defined on STRING can be used on VARIABLES or BREAK.

The following options can be used to specify how components are to be concatenated:

(width) *Width to the preceding variable within the string.* The default is the dictionary width of the variable. The maximum width for numeric variables within the string definition is 16. The maximum width for a string variable is the system page width. If the width specified is less than that required by the value, numeric values are displayed as asterisks and string values are truncated. If the width exceeds the width of a value, numeric values are padded with zeros on the left and string values are padded with blanks on the right.

(BLANK) *Left-pad values of the preceding numeric variable with blanks.* The default is to left-pad values of numeric variables with zeros. If a numeric variable has a dollar or comma format, it is automatically left-padded with blanks.

'literal' *User-specified string.* Any combination of characters can be specified within apostrophes or quotes.

Example

```
/STRING=JOB1(AVAR NVAR)
        JOB2(AVAR(2) NVAR(3))
        JOB3(AVAR(2) NVAR(BLANK) (4))
```

- STRING defines three string variables to be used within the report.
- Assume that *AVAR* is a string variable read from a four-column field using keyword FIXED on DATA LIST and that *NVAR* is a computed numeric variable with the default format of eight columns with two implied decimal places.
- If a case has value KJ for *AVAR* and value 241 for *NVAR*, *JOB1* displays the value 'KJ 00241.00', *JOB2* the value 'KJ241', and *JOB3* the value 'KJ 241'. If *NVAR* has the system-missing value for a case, *JOB1* displays the value 'KJ.'

Example

```
/STRING=SOCSEC(S1 '-' S2 '-' S3)
```

- STRING concatenates the three variables *S1*, *S2*, and *S3*, each of which contains a segment of the social security number.
- Hyphens are inserted between the segments when the values of *SOCSEC* are displayed.
- This example assumes that the variables *S1*, *S2*, and *S3* were read from three-column, two-column, and four-column fields respectively, using the keyword FIXED on DATA LIST. These variables would then have default format widths of 3, 2, and 4 columns and would not be left-padded with zeros.

BREAK Subcommand

BREAK specifies the variables that define the subgroups for the report, or it specifies summary totals for reports with no subgroups. BREAK also allows you to control the titles, width, and contents of break columns and to begin a new page for each level of the break variable.

- A break occurs when any one of the variables named on BREAK changes value. Cases must be sorted by the values of all BREAK variables on all BREAK subcommands.
- The BREAK subcommand must precede the SUMMARY subcommand that defines the summary line for the break.
- A break column is reserved for each BREAK subcommand.
- To obtain multiple break levels, specify multiple break variables on a BREAK subcommand.
- If more than one variable is specified on a BREAK subcommand, a single break column is used. The value or value label for each variable is displayed on a separate line in the order in which the variables are specified on BREAK. The first variable specified changes most slowly. The default column width is the longest of the default widths for any of the break variables.
- To obtain summary totals without any break levels, use keyword TOTAL on BREAK without listing any variables. TOTAL must be specified on the first BREAK subcommand.
- When MISSING=VAR or NONE is specified, user-missing values are displayed. System-missing values are displayed as missing.
- Optional specifications apply to all variables in the break column and to the break column as a whole. Options can be specified in any order following the last variable named.
- All optional specifications except column headings must be enclosed in parentheses; column headings must be enclosed in apostrophes.

Column Contents

The following can be used to specify the contents of the break column:

(VALUE) *Display values of the break variables.*

(LABEL) *Display value labels. If no value labels have been defined, values are displayed.*

- The value or label is displayed only once for each break change and is not repeated at the top of the page in a multiple-page break group.
- When AUTOMATIC is in effect, the default is LABEL; when MANUAL is in effect, the default is VALUE.
- When AUTOMATIC is in effect, the value or label is centered in the column. When MANUAL is in effect, value labels and string values are left-justified and numeric values are right-justified. (See the OFFSET keyword on p. 589.)

Column Heading

The following option specifies headings used for the break column.

'column heading' *Column heading for the break column.* The heading must be included in apostrophes or quotes. The default heading is the variable label of the break variable or, if no label has been defined, the variable name. If the break column is defined by more than one variable, the label or name of the first variable is used.

- To specify multiple-line headings, enclose each line in a set of apostrophes or quotes, following the conventions for strings (see "String Values in Command Specifications" on p. 16). Separate the specifications for heading lines with at least one blank.
- Default column headings wrap for as many lines as are required to display the entire label. User-specified column headings appear exactly as specified, even if the column width must be extended.

Column Heading Alignment

The following options can be used to specify how column headings are aligned:

(LEFT) *Left-aligned column heading.*

(CENTER) *Centered column heading.*

(RIGHT) *Right-aligned column heading.*

- When AUTOMATIC is in effect, column headings are centered within their columns by default. If value labels or string values exceed the width of the longest word in the heading, the heading is left-justified.
- When MANUAL is in effect, column headings are left-justified for value labels or string values and right-justified for numeric values.

Column Format

The following options can be used to format break columns:

(width) *Column width for the break column.* If no width is specified for a variable, REPORT determines a default width using the criteria described under "Defaults" on p. 575. If you specify a width that is not wide enough to display numeric values, REPORT first rounds decimal digits, then converts them to scientific notation if possible, and then displays asterisks. Value labels or string values that exceed the width are wrapped.

(OFFSET) *Position of the break column contents.* The specification is either n or CENTER specified in parentheses. OFFSET(n) indicates the number of spaces to offset the contents from the left for value labels or string values, and from the right for numeric values. OFFSET(CENTER) centers contents within the column. If AUTOMATIC is in effect, the default is CENTER. If MANUAL is in effect, the default is 0: value labels and string values are left-justified and numeric values are right-justified.

(UNDERSCORE) *Use underscores below case listings.* Case listing columns produced by FORMAT LIST are underscored before summary statistics are displayed. You can optionally specify the names of one or more report variables after UNDERSCORE; only the specified columns are underscored.

(TOTAL) *Display the summary statistics requested on the next SUMMARY subcommand for all the cases in the report.* TOTAL must be specified on the first BREAK subcommand and applies only to the next SUMMARY subcommand specified.

(NOTOTAL) *Display summary statistics only for each break.* This is the default.

(SKIP(n)) *Skip n lines after the last summary line for a break before beginning the next break.* The default for *n* is 1.

(PAGE) *Begin each break on a new page.* If RESET is specified on PAGE, the page counter resets to the PAGE1 setting on the FORMAT subcommand every time the break value changes for the specified variable. PAGE cannot be specified for listing reports with no break levels.

(NAME) *Display the name of the break variable next to each value or value label of the break variable.* NAME requires 10 spaces (the maximum eight-character width of SPSS variable names plus a colon and a blank space) in addition to the space needed to display break values or value labels. NAME is ignored if the break-column width is insufficient.

(NONAME) *Suppress the display of break variable names.* This is the default.

Example

```
SORT DIVISION BRANCH DEPT.
REPORT FORMAT=AUTOMATIC MARGINS (1,70) BRKSPACE(-1)

  /VARIABLES=SPACE(DUMMY) ' ' (4)
             SALES 'Annual' 'Sales' '1981' (15) (OFFSET(2))
             EXPENSES 'Annual' 'Expenses' '1981' (15) (OFFSET(2))

  /BREAK=DIVISION
         BRANCH (10) (TOTAL) (OFFSET(1))
  /SUMMARY=MEAN

  /BREAK=DEPT 'Department' (10)
  /SUMMARY=MEAN.
```

- This example creates a report with three break variables. *BRANCH* breaks within values of *DIVISION*, and *DEPT* breaks within values of *BRANCH*.
- FORMAT sets margins to a maximum of 70 columns and requests that summary lines be displayed on the same line as break values. Because LIST is not specified on FORMAT, only summary statistics are displayed.
- VARIABLES defines three report columns, each occupied by a report variable: *SPACE*, *SALES*, and *EXPENSES*.
- The variable *SPACE* is a dummy variable that exists only within REPORT. It has a null heading and a width of 4. It is used as a space holder to separate the break columns from the report columns.
- *SALES* has a three-line heading and a width of 15. The values of *SALES* are offset two spaces from the right.

- *EXPENSES* is the third report variable and has the same width and offset specifications as *SALES*.
- The leftmost column in the report is reserved for the first two break variables, *DIVISION* and *BRANCH*. Value labels are displayed, since this is the default for AUTOMATIC. The break column has a width of 10 and the value labels are offset one space from the left. Value labels more than nine characters long are wrapped. The default column heading is used. TOTAL requests summary line at the end of the report showing the mean of all cases in the report.
- The first SUMMARY subcommand displays the mean of each report variable in its report column. This line is displayed each time the value of *DIVISION* or *BRANCH* changes.
- The third break variable, *DEPT*, occupies the second column from the left in the report. The break column has a width of 10 and has a one-line heading. The first ten characters of the value labels are displayed in the break column.
- The second SUMMARY subcommand displays the mean for each report variable when the value of *DEPT* changes.

SUMMARY Subcommand

SUMMARY calculates a wide range of aggregate and composite statistics.
- SUMMARY must be specified if LIST is not specified on FORMAT.
- The minimum specification is an aggregate or a composite function and its arguments. This must be the first specification on SUMMARY.
- Each SUMMARY subcommand following a BREAK subcommand specifies a new summary line.
- The default location of the summary title is the column of the break variable to which the summary applies. When more than one function is named on SUMMARY, the default summary title is that of the function named first. Both the title and its default column location can be altered (see "Summary Titles" on p. 595).
- The default format can be altered for any function (see "Summary Print Formats" on p. 596).
- SUMMARY subcommands apply only to the preceding BREAK subcommand. If there is no SUMMARY subcommand after a BREAK subcommand, no statistics are displayed for that break level.
- To use the summary specifications from a previous BREAK subcommand for the current BREAK subcommand, specify keyword PREVIOUS on SUMMARY. (See "Other Summary Keywords" on p. 598.)
- Summary statistics are displayed in report columns. With aggregate functions you can compute summary statistics for all report variables or for a subset (see "Aggregate Functions" below).With composite functions you can compute summaries for all or a subset of report variables and you have additional control over the placement of summary statistics in particular report columns (see "Composite Functions" on p. 594).
- Multiple summary statistics requested on one SUMMARY subcommand are all displayed on the same line. More than one function can be specified on SUMMARY as long as you do not attempt to place two results in the same report column (REPORT will not be exe-

cuted if you do). To place results of more than one function in the same report column, use multiple SUMMARY subcommands.
- Any composite and aggregate functions except FREQUENCY and PERCENT can be specified on the same summary line.
- To insert blank lines between summaries when more than one summary line is requested for a break, use keyword SKIP followed by the number of lines to skip in parentheses. The default is 0. (See "Other Summary Keywords" on p. 598.)

Aggregate Functions

Use the aggregate functions to request descriptive statistics for report variables.
- If no variable names are specified as arguments to an aggregate function, the statistic is calculated for all variables named on VARIABLES (all report variables).
- To request an aggregate function for a subset of report variables, specify the variables in parentheses after the function keyword.
- All variables specified for an aggregate function must have been named on VARIABLES.
- Keyword TO cannot be used to specify a list of variables for an aggregate function.
- The result of an aggregate function is always displayed in the report column reserved for the variable for which the function was calculated.
- To use several aggregate functions for the same report variable, specify multiple SUMMARY subcommands. The results are displayed on different summary lines.
- The aggregate functions FREQUENCY and PERCENT have special display formats and cannot be placed on the same summary line with other aggregate or composite functions. They can be specified only once per SUMMARY subcommand.
- Aggregate functions use only cases with valid values.

VALIDN	*Valid number of cases.* This is the only function available for string variables.
SUM	*Sum of values.*
MIN	*Minimum value.*
MAX	*Maximum value.*
MEAN	*Mean.*
STDDEV	*Standard deviation.* Aliases are SD and STDEV.
VARIANCE	*Variance.*
KURTOSIS	*Kurtosis.*
SKEWNESS	*Skewness.*
MEDIAN(min,max)	*Median value for values within the range.* MEDIAN sets up integer-valued bins for counting all values in the specified range. Noninteger values are truncated when the median is calculated.

MODE(min,max)	*Modal value for values within the range.* MODE sets up integer-valued bins for counting all values in the specified range. Noninteger values are truncated when the mode is calculated.
PGT(n)	*Percentage of cases with values greater than* n. Alias PCGT.
PLT(n)	*Percentage of cases with values less than* n. Alias PCLT.
PIN(min,max)	*Percentage of cases within the inclusive value range specified.* Alias PCIN.
FREQUENCY(min,max)	*Frequency counts for values within the inclusive range.* FREQUENCY sets up integer-valued bins for counting all values in the specified range. Noninteger values are truncated when the frequency is computed. FREQUENCY cannot be mixed with other aggregate statistics on a summary line.
PERCENT(min,max)	*Percentages for values within the inclusive range.* PERCENT sets up integer-valued bins for counting all values in the specified range. Noninteger values are truncated when the percentages are computed. PERCENT cannot be mixed with other aggregate statistics on a summary line.

Example

```
SORT CASES BY BVAR AVAR.
REPORT FORMAT=AUTOMATIC LIST /VARIABLES=XVAR YVAR ZVAR

  /BREAK=BVAR
    /SUMMARY=SUM
    /SUMMARY=MEAN (XVAR YVAR ZVAR)
    /SUMMARY=VALIDN(XVAR)

  /BREAK=AVAR
    /SUMMARY=PREVIOUS.
```

- FORMAT requests a case listing, and VARIABLES establishes a report column for variables *XVAR*, *YVAR*, and *ZVAR*. The report columns have default widths and titles.
- Both break variables, *BVAR* and *AVAR*, have default widths and headings.
- Every time the value of *BVAR* changes, three summary lines are displayed. The first line contains the sums for variables *XVAR*, *YVAR*, and *ZVAR*. The second line contains the means of all three variables. The third line displays the number of valid cases for *XVAR* in the report column for *XVAR*.
- Every time the value of *AVAR* changes within each value of *BVAR*, the three summary lines requested for *BVAR* are displayed. These summary lines are based on cases with the current values of *BVAR* and *AVAR*.

Example

```
SORT CASES BY DEPT.
REPORT FORMAT=AUTOMATIC
  /VARIABLES=WAGE BONUS TENURE
  /BREAK=DEPT (23)
  /SUMMARY=SUM(WAGE BONUS) MEAN(TENURE) 'Sum Income: Mean Tenure'.
```

- SUMMARY defines a summary line consisting of the sums of *WAGE* and *BONUS* and the mean of TENURE. The result of each aggregate function is displayed in the report column of the variable for which the function is calculated.
- A title is assigned to the summary line. A width of 23 is defined for the break column to accommodate the title for the summary line.

Composite Functions

Use composite functions to obtain statistics based on aggregated statistics, to place a summary statistic in a column other than that of the report variable for which it was calculated, or to manipulate variables not named on VARIABLES.

- Composite functions can be computed for the following aggregate functions: VALIDN, SUM, MIN, MAX, MEAN, STDEV, VARIANCE, KURTOSIS, and SKEWNESS. Constants can also be arguments to composite functions.
- When used within composite functions, aggregate functions can have only one variable as an argument.
- A composite function and its arguments cannot be separated by other SUMMARY specifications.
- The result of a composite function can be placed in any report column, including columns of dummy or string variables, by specifying a target column. To specify a target column, enclose the variable name of the column in parentheses after the composite function and its arguments. By default, the results of a composite function are placed in the report column of the first variable specified on the composite function that is also specified on VARIABLES.
- The format for the result of a composite function can be specified in parentheses after the name of the column location, within the parentheses that enclose the column-location specification.

DIVIDE(arg_1 arg_2 [factor])   *Divide the first argument by the second and then multiply the result by the factor if it is specified.*

MULTIPLY(arg_1 ... arg_n)   *Multiply the arguments.*

PCT(arg_1 arg_2)   *The percentage of the first argument over the second.*

SUBTRACT(arg_1 arg_2)   *Subtract the second argument from the first.*

ADD(arg_1 ... arg_n)   *Add the arguments.*

GREAT(arg_1 ... arg_n)   *The maximum of the arguments.*

LEAST(arg_1 ... arg_n)   *The minimum of the arguments.*

AVERAGE(arg_1 ... arg_n)   *The average of the arguments.*

Example

```
SORT CASES BY DEPT.
REPORT FORMAT=AUTOMATIC BRKSPACE(-1)
  /VARIABLES=WAGE BONUS SPACE1 (DUMMY) '' BNFT1 BNFT2 SPACE2 (DUMMY)''
  /BREAK=DEPT

  /SUMMARY=MEAN(WAGE BONUS BNFT1 BNFT2)
        ADD(VALIDN(WAGE)) (SPACE2)

  /SUMMARY=ADD(SUM(WAGE) SUM(BONUS))
        ADD(SUM(BNFT1) SUM(BNFT2)) 'Totals' SKIP(1)

  /SUMMARY=DIVIDE(MEAN(WAGE) MEAN(BONUS)) (SPACE1 (COMMA)(2))
        DIVIDE(MEAN(BNFT1) MEAN(BNFT2)) (SPACE2 (COMMA)(2)) 'Ratios'
        SKIP(1).
```

- VARIABLES defines six report columns. The columns for *WAGE*, *BONUS*, *BNFT1*, and *BNFT2* contain aggregate statistics based on those variables. The variables *SPACE1* and *SPACE2* are dummy variables that are created for use as space holders; each is given a blank heading to suppress the default column heading.
- The first SUMMARY computes the means of the variables *WAGE*, *BONUS*, *BNFT1*, and *BNFT2*. Because BRKSPACE=-1, this summary line will be placed on the same line as the break value and will have no summary title. The means are displayed in the report column for each variable. SUMMARY also computes the valid number of cases for *WAGE* and places the result in the *SPACE2* column.
- The second SUMMARY adds the sum of *WAGE* to the sum of *BONUS*. Since no location is specified, the result is displayed in the *WAGE* column. In addition, the sum of *BNFT1* is added to the sum of *BNFT2* and the result is placed in the *BNFT1* column. The title for the summary line is *Totals*. One line is skipped before the summary line requested by this SUMMARY subcommand is displayed.
- The third summary line divides the mean of *WAGE* by the mean of *BONUS* and places the result in *SPACE1*. The ratio of the mean of *BNFT1* to the mean of *BNFT2* is displayed in the *SPACE2* column. The results are displayed with commas and two decimal places. The title for the summary line is *Ratios*. One line is skipped before the summary line requested by this SUMMARY subcommand is displayed.

Summary Titles

- You can specify a summary title enclosed in apostrophes or quotes, following the conventions for strings (see "String Values in Command Specifications" on p. 16). Table 19 shows the default titles.
- The summary title must be specified after the first function and its arguments. It cannot separate any function from its arguments.
- A summary title can be only one line long.
- A summary title wider than the break column extends into the next break column to the right. If the title is wider than all of the available break columns, it is truncated.
- Only one summary title can be specified per summary line. If more than one is specified, the last is used.

- The summary title is left- or right-justified depending upon whether the break title is left- or right-justified.
- The default location for the summary title is the column of the BREAK variable to which the summary applies. With multiple breaks, you can override the default placement of the title by specifying, in parentheses following the title, the number of the break column in which you want the summary title to be displayed.
- In a report with no break levels, REPORT displays the summary title above the summary line at the left margin.

Table 19   Default title for summary lines

Function	Title
VALIDN	N
VARIANCE	Variance
SUM	Sum
MEAN	Mean
STDDEV	StdDev
MIN	Minimum
MAX	Maximum
SKEWNESS	Skewness
KURTOSIS	Kurtosis
PGT(n)	>n
PLT(n)	<n
PIN(min,max)	In n_1 to n_2
FREQUENCY(min,max)	Total
PERCENT(min,max)	Total
MEDIAN(min,max)	Median
MODE(min,max)	Mode

Summary Print Formats

All functions have default formats that are used to display results (see Table 20). You can override these defaults by specifying a format keyword and/or the number of decimal places.

- Any printable formats or the PLAIN keyword can be specified. Format specifications must be enclosed in parentheses.
- For aggregate functions, the format and/or number of decimal places is specified after the variable name, within the parentheses that enclose the variable name. The variable must be explicitly named as an argument.
- For composite functions, the format and/or number of decimal places is specified after the variable name of the column location, within the parentheses that enclose the variable name. The column location must be explicitly specified.

- If the report column is wide enough, SUM, MEAN, STDDEV, MIN, MAX, MEDIAN, MODE, and VARIANCE use DOLLAR or COMMA format, if a DOLLAR or COMMA format has been declared for the variable on either the FORMATS or PRINT FORMATS command.
- If the column is not wide enough to display the decimal digits for a given function, REPORT displays fewer decimal places. If the column is not wide enough to display the integer portion of the number, REPORT uses scientific notation if possible, or, if not, displays asterisks.
- An exact value of 0 is displayed with one 0 to the left of the decimal point and as many 0 digits to the right as specified by the format. A number less than 1 in absolute value is displayed without a 0 to the left of the decimal point, except with DOLLAR and COMMA formats.

(PLAIN) *Uses the setting on SET DECIMAL for the thousands separator and decimal delimiter.* PLAIN overrides dictionary formats. This is the default for all functions except SUM, MEAN, STDDEV, MIN, MAX, MEDIAN, MODE, and VARIANCE. For these functions, the default is the dictionary format of the variable for which the function is computed.

(d) *Number of decimal places.*

Example

```
/SUMMARY=MEAN(INCOME (DOLLAR)(2))
         ADD(SUM(INCOME)SUM(WEALTH))  (WEALTH(DOLLLAR(2))
```

- SUMMARY displays the mean of *INCOME* with dollar format and two decimal places. The result is displayed in the *INCOME* column.
- The sums of *INCOME* and *WEALTH* are added, and the result is displayed in the *WEALTH* column with dollar format and two decimal places.

Table 20 Default print formats for functions

Function	Format type	Width	Decimal places
VALIDN	F	5	0
SUM	Dictionary	Dictionary + 2	Dictionary
MEAN	Dictionary	Dictionary	Dictionary
STDDEV	Dictionary	Dictionary	Dictionary
VARIANCE	Dictionary	Dictionary	Dictionary
MIN	Dictionary	Dictionary	Dictionary
MAX	Dictionary	Dictionary	Dictionary
SKEWNESS	F	5	2
KURTOSIS	F	5	2
PGT	PCT	6	1
PLT	PCT	6	1
PIN	PCT	6	1
MEDIAN	Dictionary	Dictionary	Dictionary
MODE	Dictionary	Dictionary	Dictionary

Table 20 Default print formats for functions (Continued)

Function	Format type	Width	Decimal places
PERCENT	F	6	1
FREQUENCY	F	5	0
DIVIDE	F	Dictionary	0
PCT	PCT	6	2
SUBTRACT	F	Dictionary	0
ADD	F	Dictionary	0
GREAT	F	Dictionary	0
LEAST	F	Dictionary	0
AVERAGE	F	Dictionary	0
MULTIPLY	F	Dictionary	0

Where DATE formats are specified, functions with the dictionary format type display the DATE formats, using the column width as the display width.

Other Summary Keywords

The following additional keywords can be specified on SUMMARY. These keywords are not enclosed in parentheses.

SKIP(n) *Blank lines before the summary line.* The default is 0. If SKIP is specified for the first SUMMARY subcommand for a BREAK, it skips the specified lines after skipping the number of lines specified for BRKSPACE on FORMAT. Similarly, with case listings SKIP skips *n* lines after the blank line at the end of the listing.

PREVIOUS(n) *Use the SUMMARY subcommands specified for the nth BREAK.* If *n* is not specified, PREVIOUS refers to the set of SUMMARY subcommands for the previous BREAK. If an integer is specified, the SUMMARY subcommands from the *n*th BREAK are used. If PREVIOUS is specified, no other specification can be used on that SUMMARY subcommand.

TITLE and FOOTNOTE Subcommands

TITLE and FOOTNOTE provide titles and footnotes for the report.

- TITLE and FOOTNOTE are optional and can be placed anywhere after FORMAT except between the BREAK and SUMMARY subcommands.
- The specification on TITLE or FOOTNOTE is the title or footnote in apostrophes or quotes. To specify a multiple-line title or footnote, enclose each line in apostrophes or quotes and separate the specifications for each line by at least one blank.
- The default REPORT title is the title specified on the TITLE command. If there is no TITLE command specified in your SPSS session, the default REPORT title is the first line of the SPSS header.

- Titles begin on the first line of the report page. Footnotes end on the last line of the report page.
- Titles and footnotes are repeated on each page of a multiple-page report.
- The positional keywords LEFT, CENTER, and RIGHT can each be specified once. The default is CENTER.
- If the total width needed for the combined titles or footnotes for a line exceeds the page width, REPORT generates an error message.

LEFT *Left-justify titles or footnotes within the report page margins.*

RIGHT *Right-justify titles or footnotes within the report page margins.*

CENTER *Center titles and footnotes within the report page width.*

The following can be specified as part of the title or footnote.

)PAGE *Display the page number right-justified in a five-character field.*

)DATE *Display the current date in the form* dd/mmm/yy, *right-justified in a nine-character field.*

)var *Display this variable's value label at this position.* If you specify a variable that has no value label, the value is displayed, formatted according to its print format. You cannot specify a scratch or system variable or a variable created with the STRING subcommand. If you want to use a variable named *DATE* or *PAGE* in the file, change the variable's name with the RENAME VARIABLES command before you use it on the TITLE or FOOTNOTE subcommands, to avoid confusion with the)PAGE and)DATE keywords.

-)PAGE,)DATE, and)var are specified within apostrophes or quotes and can be mixed with string segments within the apostrophes or quotes.
- A variable specified on TITLE or FOOTNOTE must be defined in the working data file, but does not need to be included as a column on the report.
- One label or value from each variable specified on TITLE or FOOTNOTE is displayed on every page of the report. If a new page starts with a case listing, REPORT takes the value label from the first case listed. If a new page starts with a BREAK line, REPORT takes the value label from the first case of the new break group. If a new page starts with a summary line, REPORT takes the value label from the last case of the break group being summarized.

Example

```
/TITLE=LEFT 'Personnel Report' 'Prepared on )DATE'
    RIGHT 'Page: )PAGE'
```

- TITLE specifies two lines for a left-justified title and one line for a right-justified title. These titles are displayed at the top of each page of the report.
- The second line of the left-justified title contains the date on which the report was processed.
- The right-justified title displays the page number following the string *Page:* on the same line as the first line of the left-justified title.

MISSING Subcommand

MISSING controls the treatment of cases with missing values.

- MISSING specifications apply to variables named on VARIABLES and SUMMARY and to strings created with the STRING subcommand.
- Missing-value specifications are ignored for variables named on BREAK when MISSING= VAR or NONE. There is one break category for system-missing values and one for each user-missing value.
- The character used to indicate missing values is controlled by the FORMAT subcommand.

VAR *Missing values are treated separately for each variable.* Missing values are displayed in case listings but are not included in the calculation of summary statistics on a function-by-function basis. This is the default.

NONE *User-missing values are treated as valid values.* This applies to all variables named on VARIABLES.

LIST[([varlist][n])] *Cases with the specified number of missing values across the specified list of variables are not used.* The variable list and *n* are specified in parentheses. If *n* is not specified, the default is 1. If no variables are specified, all variables named on VARIABLES are assumed.

Example

```
/MISSING= LIST (XVAR,YVAR,ZVAR 2)
```

- Any case with two or more missing values across the variables *XVAR*, *YVAR*, and *ZVAR* is omitted from the report.

REREAD

```
REREAD [FILE=file]
       [COLUMN=expression]
```

Example:
```
INPUT PROGRAM.
DATA LIST /KIND 10-14 (A).

DO IF (KIND EQ 'FORD').
REREAD.
DATA LIST /PARTNO 1-2 PRICE 3-6 (DOLLAR,2) QUANTITY 7-9.
END CASE.

ELSE IF (KIND EQ 'CHEVY').
REREAD.
DATA LIST /PARTNO 1-2 PRICE 15-18 (DOLLAR,2) QUANTITY 19-21.
END CASE.
END IF.

END INPUT PROGRAM.

BEGIN DATA
111295100FORD
11        CHEVY 295015
END DATA.
```

Overview

REREAD instructs SPSS to reread a record in the data. It is available only within an INPUT PROGRAM structure and is generally used to define data using information obtained from a previous reading of the record. REREAD is usually specified within a conditional structure, such as DO IF—END IF, and is followed by a DATA LIST command. When it receives control for a case, REREAD places the pointer back to the column specified for the current case and begins reading data as defined by the DATA LIST command that follows.

Options

Data Source. You can use inline data or data from an external file specified on the FILE subcommand. Using external files allows you to open multiple files and merge data.

Beginning Column. You can specify a beginning column other than column 1 using the COLUMN subcommand.

Basic Specification

The basic specification is the command keyword REREAD. SPSS rereads the current case according to the data definitions specified on the following DATA LIST.

Subcommand Order

Subcommands can be specified in any order.

Syntax Rules

- REREAD is available only within an INPUT PROGRAM structure.
- Multiple REREAD commands can be used within the input program. Each must be followed by an associated DATA LIST command.

Operations

- REREAD causes the next DATA LIST command to reread the most recently processed record in the specified file.
- When it receives control for a case, REREAD places the pointer back to column 1 for the current case and begins reading data as defined by the DATA LIST that follows. If the COLUMN subcommand is specified, the pointer begins reading in the specified column and uses it as column 1 for data definition.
- REREAD can be used to read part of a record in FIXED format and the remainder in LIST format. Mixing FIXED and FREE formats yields unpredictable results.
- Multiple REREAD commands specified without an intervening DATA LIST do not have a cumulative effect. All but the last are ignored.

Example

```
INPUT PROGRAM.
DATA LIST /PARTNO 1-2 KIND 10-14 (A).

DO IF (KIND EQ 'FORD').
REREAD.
DATA LIST /PRICE 3-6 (DOLLAR,2) QUANTITY 7-9.
END CASE.

ELSE IF (KIND EQ 'CHEVY').
REREAD.
DATA LIST /PRICE 15-18 (DOLLAR,2) QUANTITY 19-21.
END CASE.
END IF.
END INPUT PROGRAM.
```

```
BEGIN DATA
111295100FORD       CHAPMAN AUTO SALES
121199005VW         MIDWEST VOLKSWAGEN SALES
11 395025FORD          BETTER USED CARS
11        CHEVY 195005     HUFFMAN SALES & SERVICE
11        VW    595020     MIDWEST VOLKSWAGEN SALES
11        CHEVY 295015     SAM'S AUTO REPAIR
12        CHEVY 210 20     LONGFELLOW CHEVROLET
 9555032 VW                HYDE PARK IMPORTS
END DATA.
LIST.
```

- Data are extracted from an inventory of automobile parts. The automobile part number always appears in columns 1 and 2, and the automobile type always appears in columns 10 through 14. The location of other information such as price and quantity depends on both the part number and the type of automobile.
- The first DATA LIST extracts the part number and type of automobile.
- Depending on the information from the first DATA LIST, the records are reread using one of two DATA LIST commands, pulling the price and quantity from different places.
- The two END CASE commands limit the working data file to only those cases with part 11 and automobile type Ford or Chevrolet. Without the END CASE commands, cases would be created for other part numbers and automobile types, with missing values for price, quantity, and buyer.

The LIST output is shown in Figure 48.

Figure 48 Listed information for part 11

```
PARTNO KIND    PRICE QUANTITY

   11   FORD   $12.95     100
   11   FORD    $3.95      25
   11   CHEVY   $1.95       5
   11   CHEVY   $2.95      15
```

Example

```
* Multiple REREAD commands for the same record.

INPUT PROGRAM.
DATA LIST       NOTABLE/ CDIMAGE 1-20(A).
REREAD          COLUMN = 6.  /* A, C, and E are in column 6
REREAD          COLUMN = 11. /* B, D, and F are in column 11
DATA LIST       NOTABLE/ INFO 1(A).
END INPUT PROGRAM.
LIST.
BEGIN DATA
1    A     B
2    C     D
3    E     F
END DATA.
```

- Multiple REREAD commands are used without an intervening DATA LIST. Only the last one is used. Thus, the starting column comes from the last REREAD specified and the pointer is reset to column 11.
- Figure 49 shows the results from the LIST command.

Figure 49   Listed information after multiple REREAD commands

```
CDIMAGE              INFO

1    A    B          B
2    C    D          D
3    E    F          F
```

FILE Subcommand

FILE specifies an external raw data file from which the next DATA LIST command reads data.
- The default file is the file specified on the immediately preceding DATA LIST command.
- If the file specified on FILE is not the default file, the same file must be specified on the next DATA LIST. Otherwise, the FILE subcommand is ignored and the DATA LIST command reads the next record from the file specified on it or, if no file is specified, from the file specified on the previous DATA LIST command.

Example

```
INPUT PROGRAM.
DATA LIST FILE=UPDATE END=#EOF NOTABLE
     /#ID 1-3.                    /*Get rep ID in new sales file.
DATA LIST FILE = SALESREP NOTABLE
     /ID 1-3 SALES 4-11(F,2)
       NEWSALE 12-19(F,2).        /*Get rep record from master file.

LOOP IF #EOF OR (#ID GT ID).  /*If UPDATE ends or no new sales made.
+   COMPUTE NEWSALE = 0.       /*Set NEWSALE to 0
+   END CASE.                  /*Build a case.
+   DATA LIST FILE = SALESREP NOTABLE
     /ID 1-3 SALES 4-11(F,2)
       NEWSALE 12-19(F,2).        /*Continue reading masterfile.
END LOOP

DO IF NOT #EOF.                   /*If new sales made.
+   REREAD FILE=UPDATE COLUMN = 4.   /*Read new sales from UPDATE.
+   DATA LIST FILE=UPDATE
     /NEWSALE 1-8(F,2).
+   COMPUTE SALES=SALES+NEWSALE.  /*Update master file.
END IF.
END CASE.                         /*Build a case.
END INPUT PROGRAM.

LIST.
```

- This example uses REREAD to merge two raw data files (*SALESREP* and *UPDATE*).

- Both files are sorted by sales representative ID number. The *UPDATE* file contains only records for sales representatives who have made new sales, with variables *ID* and *NEWSALE*. The master file *SALESREP* contains records for all sales representatives, with variables *SALES* (which contains year-to-date sales) and *NEWSALE* (which contains the update values each time the file is updated).
- If a sales representative has made no new sales, there is no matching ID in the *UPDATE* file. When *UPDATE* is exhausted or when the ID's in the two files do not match, the loop structure causes SPSS to build a case with *NEWSALE* equal to 0 and then continue reading the master file.
- When the ID's match (and the *UPDATE* file is not yet exhausted), the REREAD command is executed. The following DATA LIST rereads the record in *UPDATE* that matches the *ID* variable. *NEWSALE* is read from the *UPDATE* file starting from column 4 and *SALES* is updated. Note that the following DATA LIST specifies the same file.
- When the updated base is built, SPSS returns to the first DATA LIST command in the input program and reads the next ID from the *UPDATE* file. If the *UPDATE* file is exhausted (*#EOF*=1), the loop keeps reading records from the master file until it reaches the end of the file.
- The same task can be accomplished using MATCH FILES. With MATCH FILES, the raw data must be read and saved as SPSS data files first.

COLUMN Subcommand

COLUMN specifies a beginning column for the REREAD command to read data. The default is column 1. You can specify a numeric expression for the column.

Example

```
INPUT PROGRAM.
DATA LIST /KIND 10-14 (A).
COMPUTE #COL=1.
IF (KIND EQ 'CHEVY') #COL=13.

DO IF (KIND EQ 'CHEVY' OR KIND EQ 'FORD').
REREAD COLUMN #COL.
DATA LIST /PRICE 3-6 (DOLLAR,2) QUANTITY 7-9.
END CASE.
END IF.
END INPUT PROGRAM.
BEGIN DATA
111295100FORD     CHAPMAN AUTO SALES
121199005VW       MIDWEST VOLKSWAGEN SALES
11 395025FORD     BETTER USED CARS
11       CHEVY 195005      HUFFMAN SALES & SERVICE
11       VW    595020      MIDWEST VOLKSWAGEN SALES
11       CHEVY 295015      SAM'S AUTO REPAIR
12       CHEVY 210 20      LONGFELLOW CHEVROLET
 9555032 VW                HYDE PARK IMPORTS
END DATA.
LIST.
```

- The task in this example is to read *PRICE* and *QUANTITY* for Chevrolets and Fords only. A scratch variable is created to indicate the starting column positions for *PRICE* and *QUANTITY*, and a single DATA LIST command is used to read data for both types of automobiles.
- Scratch variable *#COL* is set to 13 for Chevrolets and 1 for all other automobiles. For Fords, the data begin in column 1. Variable *PRICE* is read from columns 3–6 and *QUANTITY* is read from columns 7–9. When the record is a Chevrolet, the data begins in column 13. Variable *PRICE* is read from columns 15–18 (15 is 3, 16 is 4, and so forth), and *QUANTITY* is read from columns 19–21.

Example

```
* Reading both FIXED and LIST input with REREAD.

INPUT PROGRAM.
DATA LIST     NOTABLE FIXED/ A 1-14(A).   /*Read the FIXED portion
REREAD        COLUMN = 15.
DATA LIST     LIST/ X Y Z.                /*Read the LIST portion
END INPUT PROGRAM.

*  The value 1 on the first record is in column 15.

LIST.
BEGIN DATA
FIRST RECORD   1 2 3 -1 -2 -3
NUMBER 2       4 5
THE THIRD      6 7 8
#4
FIFTH AND LAST9 10 11
END DATA.
```

- Columns 1–14 are read in FIXED format. REREAD then resets the pointer to column 15. Thus, beginning in column 15, values are read in LIST format.
- The second DATA LIST specifies only three variables. Thus, the values -1, -2, and -3 on the first record are not read.
- SPSS generates a warning for the missing value on record 2 and a second warning for the three missing values on record 4.
- On the fifth and last record there is no delimiter between value LAST and value 9. REREAD can still read the 9 in list format.

RESTORE

```
RESTORE
```

Overview

RESTORE restores SET specifications that were stored by a previous PRESERVE command. RESTORE and PRESERVE are especially useful when using the SPSS macro facility. PRESERVE—RESTORE sequences can be nested up to five levels.

Basic Specification

The only specification is the command keyword. RESTORE has no additional specifications.

Example

```
GET FILE=PRSNNL.
FREQUENCIES VAR=DIVISION /STATISTICS=ALL.
PRESERVE.
SET XSORT=NO WIDTH=90 UNDEFINED=NOWARN BLANKS=000 CASE=UPLOW.
SORT CASES BY DIVISION.
REPORT FORMAT=AUTO LIST /VARS=LNAME FNAME DEPT SOCSEC SALARY
   /BREAK=DIVISION /SUMMARY=MEAN.
RESTORE.
```

- GET reads SPSS data file *PRSNNL*.
- FREQUENCIES requests a frequency table and all statistics for variable *DIVISION*.
- PRESERVE stores all current SET specifications.
- SET changes several subcommand settings.
- SORT sorts cases in preparation for a report. Because SET XSORT=NO, the SPSS sort program is not used to sort cases; another sort program must be available.
- REPORT requests a report organized by variable *DIVISION*.
- RESTORE reestablishes all the SET specifications that were in effect when PRESERVE was specified.

SAMPLE

```
SAMPLE {decimal value}
       {n FROM m      }
```

Example:

```
SAMPLE .25.
```

Overview

SAMPLE permanently draws a random sample of cases for processing in all subsequent procedures. For a temporary sample, use a TEMPORARY command before SAMPLE.

Basic Specification

The basic specification is either a decimal value between 0 and 1 or the sample size followed by keyword FROM and the size of the working data file.

- To select an approximate percentage of cases, specify a decimal value between 0 and 1.
- To select an exact-size random sample, specify a positive integer less than the file size, followed by keyword FROM and the file size.

Operations

- SAMPLE is a permanent transformation.
- Sampling is based on a pseudo-random-number generator that depends on a seed value established by SPSS. On some implementations of SPSS, this number defaults to a fixed integer, and a SAMPLE command that specifies n FROM m will generate the identical sample whenever a session is rerun. To generate a different sample each time, use the SET command to reset SEED to a different value for each session. See the SET command for more information.
- If sampling is done using the n FROM m method and the TEMPORARY command is specified, successive samples will not be the same because the seed value changes each time a random number series is needed within a session.
- A proportional sample (a sample based on a decimal value) usually does not produce the exact proportion specified.
- If the number specified for m following FROM is less than the actual file size, the sample is drawn only from the first m cases.
- If the number following FROM is greater than the actual file size, SPSS samples an equivalent proportion of cases from the working data file (see example below).
- If SAMPLE follows SELECT IF, it samples only cases selected by SELECT IF.
- If SAMPLE precedes SELECT IF, cases are selected from the sample.

- If more than one SAMPLE is specified in a session, each acts upon the sample selected by the preceding SAMPLE command.
- If N OF CASES is used with SAMPLE, SPSS reads as many records as required to build the specified *n* cases. It makes no difference whether the N OF CASES precedes or follows the SAMPLE.

Limitations

SAMPLE cannot be placed in a FILE TYPE—END FILE TYPE or INPUT PROGRAM—END INPUT PROGRAM structure. It can be placed nearly anywhere following these commands in a transformation program. See Appendix A for a discussion of program states in SPSS and the placement of commands.

Example

```
SAMPLE .25.
```

- This command samples approximately 25% of the cases in the working data file.

Example

```
SAMPLE 500 FROM 3420.
```

- The working data file must have 3420 cases or more to obtain a random sample of exactly 500 cases.
- If the file contains fewer than 3420 cases, proportionally fewer cases are sampled.
- If the file contains more than 3420 cases, a random sample of 500 cases is drawn from the first 3420 cases.

Example

```
SAMPLE .50.
DESCRIPTIVES   SALARY85 TO SALARY88.
SAMPLE .50.
DESCRIPTIVES   SALARY85 TO SALARY88.
```

- The first DESCRIPTIVES command computes statistics for approximately 50% of the cases, and the second DESCRIPTIVES command computes statistics for approximately 50% of the sample, or 25% of the original cases.

Example

```
DO IF  SEX EQ 'M'.
SAMPLE 1846 FROM 8000.
END IF.
```

- SAMPLE is placed inside a DO IF—END IF structure to sample subgroups differently. Assume that this is a survey of 10,000 people in which 80% of the sample is male, while the known universe is 48% male. To obtain a sample that corresponds to the known universe and that maximizes the size of the sample, 1846 (48/52*2000) males and all females must be sampled. The DO IF structure is used to restrict the sampling process to the males.

SAVE

```
SAVE OUTFILE=file

[/KEEP={ALL** }] [/DROP=varlist]
       {varlist}

[/RENAME=(old varlist=new varlist)...]

[/MAP]  [/{COMPRESSED  }]
          {UNCOMPRESSED}
```

**Default if the subcommand is omitted.

Example:

```
SAVE OUTFILE=EMPL  /RENAME=(AGE=AGE88) (JOBCAT=JOBCAT88).
```

Overview

SAVE produces an SPSS data file. An SPSS data file is in a format only SPSS can read and contains data plus a dictionary. The dictionary contains a name for each variable in the data file plus any assigned variable and value labels, missing-value flags, and variable print and write formats. The dictionary also contains document text created with the DOCUMENTS command.

XSAVE also creates SPSS data files. The difference is that SAVE causes data to be read; while XSAVE is not executed until data are read for the next procedure.

See SAVE TRANSLATE and SAVE SCSS for information on saving data files that can be used by other programs.

Options

Variable Subsets and Order. You can save a subset of variables and reorder the variables that are saved using the DROP and KEEP subcommands.

Variable Names. You can rename variables as they are copied into the SPSS data file using the RENAME subcommand.

Variable Map. To confirm the names and order of the variables saved in the SPSS data file, use the MAP subcommand. MAP displays the variables saved in the SPSS data file next to their corresponding names in the working data file.

Data Compression. You can write the data file in compressed or uncompressed form using the COMPRESSED or UNCOMPRESSED subcommand.

Basic Specification

The basic specification is the OUTFILE subcommand, which specifies a name for the SPSS data file to be saved.

Subcommand Order

- Subcommands can be specified in any order.

Syntax Rules

- OUTFILE is required and can be specified only once. If OUTFILE is specified more than once, only the last OUTFILE specified is in effect.
- KEEP, DROP, RENAME, and MAP can each be used as many times as needed.
- Only one of the subcommands COMPRESSED or UNCOMPRESSED can be specified per SAVE command.

Operations

- SAVE is executed immediately and causes the data to be read.
- The new SPSS data file dictionary is arranged in the same order as the working file dictionary, unless variables are reordered with the KEEP subcommand. Documentary text from the working file dictionary is always saved unless it is dropped with the DROP DOCUMENTS command before SAVE.
- New variables created by transformations and procedures previous to the SAVE command are included in the new SPSS data file, and variables altered by transformations are saved in their modified form. Results of any temporary transformations immediately preceding the SAVE command are included in the file; scratch variables are not.
- SPSS data files are binary files designed to be read and written by SPSS only. SPSS data files can be edited only with the UPDATE command. Use the MATCH FILES and ADD FILES commands to merge SPSS data files.
- The working data file is still available for SPSS transformations and procedures after SAVE is executed.
- SAVE processes the dictionary first and displays a message that indicates how many variables will be saved. Once the data are written, SAVE indicates how many cases were saved. If the second message does not appear, the file was probably not completely written.

Example

```
GET FILE=HUBEMPL.
SAVE OUTFILE=EMPL88 /RENAME=(AGE=AGE88) (JOBCAT=JOBCAT88).
```

- The GET command retrieves the SPSS data file *HUBEMPL*.
- The RENAME subcommand renames variable *AGE* to *AGE88* and variable *JOBCAT* to *JOBCAT88*.
- SAVE causes the data to be read and saves a new SPSS data file with filename *EMPL88*. The original SPSS data file *HUBEMPL* is not changed.

Example

```
GET FILE=HUBEMPL.
TEMPORARY.
RECODE DEPT85 TO DEPT88 (1,2=1) (3,4=2) (ELSE=9).
VALUE LABELS DEPT85 TO DEPT88 1 'MANAGEMENT' 2 'OPERATIONS' 9 'UNKNOWN'.
SAVE OUTFILE=HUBTEMP.
CROSSTABS DEPT85 TO DEPT88 BY JOBCAT.
```

- The GET command retrieves the SPSS data file *HUBEMPL*.
- The TEMPORARY command indicates that RECODE and VALUE LABELS are in effect only for the next command that reads the data (SAVE).
- The RECODE command recodes values for all variables between and including *DEPT85* and *DEPT88* on the working data file.
- The VALUE LABELS command specifies new labels for the recoded values.
- The OUTFILE subcommand on SAVE specifies *HUBTEMP* as the new SPSS data file. *HUBTEMP* will include the recoded values for *DEPT85* to *DEPT88* and the new value labels.
- The CROSSTABS command crosstabulates *DEPT85* to *DEPT88* with *JOBCAT*. Since the RECODE and VALUE LABELS commands were temporary, the CROSSTABS output does not reflect the recoding and new labels.
- If XSAVE were specified instead of SAVE, the data would be read only once. Both the saved SPSS data file and the CROSSTABS output would reflect the temporary recoding and labeling of the department variables.

OUTFILE Subcommand

OUTFILE specifies the SPSS data file to be saved. OUTFILE is required and can be specified only once. If OUTFILE is specified more than once, only the last OUTFILE is in effect.

DROP and KEEP Subcommands

DROP and KEEP are used to save a subset of variables. DROP specifies the variables not to save in the new data file; KEEP specifies the variables to save in the new data file; variables not named on KEEP are dropped.

- Variables can be specified in any order. The order of variables on KEEP determines the order of variables in the SPSS data file. The order on DROP does not affect the order of variables in the SPSS data file.
- Keyword ALL on KEEP refers to all remaining variables not previously specified on KEEP. ALL must be the last specification on KEEP.
- If a variable is specified twice on the same subcommand, only the first mention is recognized.
- Multiple DROP and KEEP subcommands are allowed. Specifying a variable that is not in the working data file or that has been dropped because of a previous DROP or KEEP subcommand results in an error and the SAVE command is not executed.

- Keyword TO can be used to specify a group of consecutive variables in the SPSS data file.

Example
```
GET FILE=PRSNL.
COMPUTE TENURE=(12-CMONTH +(12*(88-CYEAR)))/12.
COMPUTE JTENURE=(12-JMONTH +(12*(88-JYEAR)))/12.
VARIABLE LABELS      TENURE 'Tenure in Company'
                     JTENURE 'Tenure in Grade.
SAVE OUTFILE=PRSNL88 /DROP=GRADE STORE
  /KEEP=LNAME NAME TENURE JTENURE ALL.
```

- Variables *TENURE* and *JTENURE* are created by COMPUTE commands and assigned variable labels by the VARIABLE LABELS command. *TENURE* and *JTENURE* are added to the end of the working data file.
- DROP excludes variables *GRADE* and *STORE* from file *PRSNL88*. KEEP specifies that *LNAME, NAME, TENURE,* and *JTENURE* are the first four variables in file *PRSNL88*, followed by all remaining variables not specified on DROP. These remaining variables are saved in the same sequence as they appear in the original file.

RENAME Subcommand

RENAME changes the names of variables as they are copied into the new SPSS data file.

- The specification on RENAME is a list of old variable names followed by an equals sign and a list of new variable names. The same number of variables must be specified on both lists. Keyword TO can be used in the first list to refer to consecutive variables in the working data file and in the second list to generate new variable names (see "Keyword TO" on p. 32). The entire specification must be enclosed in parentheses.
- Alternatively, you can specify each old variable name individually, followed by an equals sign and the new variable name. Multiple sets of variable specifications are allowed. The parentheses around each set of specifications are optional.
- RENAME does not affect the working data file. However, if RENAME precedes DROP or KEEP, variables must be referred to by their new names on DROP or KEEP.
- Old variable names do not need to be specified according to their order in the working data file.
- Name changes take place in one operation. Therefore, variable names can be exchanged between two variables.
- Multiple RENAME subcommands are allowed.

Example
```
SAVE OUTFILE=EMPL88 /RENAME AGE=AGE88 JOBCAT=JOBCAT88.
```
- RENAME specifies two name changes for file *EMPL88*: variable *AGE* is renamed to *AGE88* and variable *JOBCAT* is renamed to *JOBCAT88*.

Example
```
SAVE OUTFILE=EMPL88 /RENAME (AGE JOBCAT=AGE88 JOBCAT88).
```

- The name changes are identical to those in the previous example: *AGE* is renamed to *AGE88* and *JOBCAT* is renamed to *JOBCAT88*. The parentheses are required with this method.

MAP subcommand

MAP displays a list of the variables in the SPSS data file and their corresponding names in the working data file.
- The only specification is keyword MAP. There are no additional specifications.
- Multiple MAP subcommands are allowed. Each MAP subcommand maps the results of subcommands that precede it, but not results of subcommands that follow it.

Example

```
GET FILE=HUBEMPL.
SAVE OUTFILE=EMPL88 /RENAME=(AGE=AGE88)(JOBCAT=JOBCAT88)
  /KEEP=LNAME NAME JOBCAT88 ALL /MAP.
```

- MAP is used to confirm the new names for *AGE* and *JOBCAT* and the order of variables in the *EMPL88* file (*LNAME*, *NAME*, and *JOBCAT88*, followed by all remaining variables from the working data file).

COMPRESSED and UNCOMPRESSED Subcommands

COMPRESSED saves the file in compressed form. UNCOMPRESSED saves the file in uncompressed form. In a compressed file, small integers (from −99 to 155) are stored in one byte instead of the eight bytes used in an uncompressed file.
- The only specification is the keyword COMPRESSED or UNCOMPRESSED. There are no additional specifications.
- Compressed data files occupy less disk space than do uncompressed data files.
- Compressed data files take longer to read than do uncompressed data files.
- The GET command, which reads SPSS data files, does not need to specify whether the files it reads are compressed or uncompressed.
- Only one of the subcommands COMPRESSED or UNCOMPRESSED can be specified per SAVE command. COMPRESSED is usually the default, though UNCOMPRESSED may be the default on some systems.

SAVE SCSS

This command is not available on all operating systems.

```
SAVE SCSS OUTFILE=file

 [/KEEP={ALL** }] [/DROP=varlist]
        {varlist}

 [/RENAME=(old varlist=new varlist)...]
```

**Default if the subcommand is omitted.

Example:
```
SAVE SCSS OUTFILE=HUBOUT.
```

Overview

SAVE SCSS saves the working data file as an SCSS masterfile.

Options

Variable Subsets and Order. You can save a subset of variables and reorder variables that are copied to the SCSS masterfile using the DROP and KEEP subcommands.

Variable Names. You can rename variables as they are copied to the SCSS masterfile using the RENAME subcommand.

Basic Specification

The basic specification is OUTFILE and the name of the SCSS masterfile.

Subcommand Order

- OUTFILE must be specified first.
- Remaining subcommands may be used in any order.

Syntax Rules

- OUTFILE is required and can be specified only once. If OUTFILE is specified more than once, only the last OUTFILE specified is in effect.
- The remaining subcommands can each be used as many times as needed.

Operations

- SAVE SCSS saves all dictionary information from the working data file plus the data. New variables created by transformations and procedures previous to the SAVE SCSS command are included, as are any temporary transformations made just prior to the SAVE SCSS command.
- SCSS does not support string variables, and they are not saved. SPSS displays a message indicating which variables were not saved.
- The system-missing values for each numeric variable is recoded, usually to the variable's highest value plus 1. The output includes a variable-by-variable listing of the missing value selected for each variable.
- In converting from double precision in SPSS to single precision in SCSS, numeric values are usually truncated (SPSS actually does a mixed-mode assignment which may result in rounding on some operating systems). If alphanumeric or extreme values are encountered for numeric variables when the data are read, those variables are dropped in the masterfile and their names are displayed in the SAVE SCSS output.
- The keywords AGAINST, ON, SPSS, and SPSS0001 are reserved in SCSS. Any SPSS variables with these names will not be saved and should be renamed using the RENAME subcommand.

Example

```
SAVE SCSS OUTFILE=HUBOUT
  /DROP=DEPT79 TO DEPT81, SALARY79 TO SALARY81, HOURLY81
  /RENAME=(SALARY82, HOURLY82, PROMO81=SALARY, HOURLY, PROMO).
```

- The SCSS masterfile *HUBOUT* is created. DROP specifies variables to exclude from the masterfile. RENAME drops the year suffix from each of the specified variables.

OUTFILE Subcommand

OUTFILE specifies the SCSS masterfile to be saved. OUTFILE is required and can be specified only once. If OUTFILE is specified more than once, only the last OUTFILE is in effect.

DROP and KEEP Subcommands

DROP and KEEP are used to save a subset of variables in the SCSS masterfile. DROP specifies the variables not to save in the masterfile; KEEP specifies the variables to save in the new masterfile; variables not named on KEEP are dropped.

- Variables can be specified in any order. The order of variables on KEEP determines the order of variables in the SCSS masterfile. The order on DROP does not affect the order of variables in the SCSS masterfile.
- Keyword ALL on KEEP refers to all remaining variables not previously specified on KEEP. ALL must be the last specification on KEEP.

- If a variable is specified twice on the same subcommand, only the first mention is recognized.
- Multiple DROP and KEEP subcommands are allowed. Specifying a variable that is not in the working data file or that has been dropped because of a previous DROP or KEEP subcommand results in an error and the SAVE SCSS command is not executed.
- Keyword TO can be used to specify a group of consecutive variables in the SPSS data file.
- DROP and KEEP affect only the masterfile, not the working data file.

RENAME Subcommand

RENAME changes the names of variables as they are copied into the SCSS masterfile. Variables that have been renamed retain their variable and value labels.

- The specification on RENAME is a list of old variable names followed by an equals sign and a list of new variable names. The same number of variables must be specified on both lists. Keyword TO can be used in the first list to refer to consecutive variables in the working data file and in the second list to generate new variable names (see "Keyword TO" on p. 32). The entire specification must be enclosed in parentheses.
- Alternatively, you can specify each old variable name individually, followed by an equals sign and the new variable name. Multiple sets of variable specifications are allowed. The parentheses around each set of specifications are optional.
- RENAME does not affect the working data file. However, if RENAME precedes DROP or KEEP, variables must be referred to by their new names on DROP or KEEP.
- Old variable names do not need to be specified according to their order in the working data file.
- Name changes take place in one operation. Therefore, variable names can be exchanged between two variables.
- Multiple RENAME subcommands are allowed.

SAVE TRANSLATE

This command is not available on all operating system.

```
SAVE TRANSLATE OUTFILE=file

 [/TYPE={WK1}] [/FIELDNAMES]*
        {WKS}
        {WR1}
        {WRK}
        {SLK}
        {XLS}
        {DB2}
        {DB3}
        {DB4}
        {TAB}
        {PC }

 [/KEEP={ALL**  }] [/DROP=varlist]
        {varlist}

 [/RENAME=(old varnames=new varnames)...]

 [/MAP]
```

*Available only for spreadsheet and tab-delimited ASCII files.
**Default if the subcommand is omitted.

Keyword	Type of file
WK1	1-2-3 Release 2.0
WKS	1-2-3 Release 1A
WR1	Symphony Release 2.0
WRK	Symphony Release 1.0
SLK	Multiplan or Excel in SYLK (symbolic link) format
XLS	Microsoft Excel
DB2	dBASE II
DB3	dBASE III
DB4	dBASE IV
TAB	Tab-delimited ASCII file
PC	SPSS/PC+ data file

Example:
```
SAVE TRANSLATE OUTFILE='SALESREP.SLK'
 /KEEP=SALES, UNITS, MONTHS, PRICE1 TO PRICE20
 /FIELDNAMES.
```

Overview

SAVE TRANSLATE translates the SPSS working data file into a file that can be used by other software applications. Supported formats are 1-2-3, Symphony, Multiplan, Excel, dBASE II, dBASE III, dBASE IV, tab-delimited ASCII files, and SPSS/PC+ data files.

Options

Variable Subsets. You can use the DROP and KEEP subcommands to specify variables to omit or retain in the resulting file.

Variable Names. You can rename variables as they are copied to the spreadsheet, database, or tab-delimited ASCII file using the RENAME subcommand.

Variable Map. To confirm the names and order of the variables saved in the resulting file, use the MAP subcommand. MAP displays the variables saved in the file next to their corresponding names in the working data file.

Spreadsheet Files. You can use the FIELDNAMES subcommand to translate SPSS variable names to field names in a spreadsheet file.

Basic Specification

- The basic specification is OUTFILE with a file specification in apostrophes.
- TYPE and a keyword to indicate the type of dBASE file is also required to save dBASE database files.

Subcommand Order

- OUTFILE must be specified first.
- The remaining subcommands can be specified in any order.

Operations

- The working data file remains available after SAVE TRANSLATE is executed.
- User-missing values are transferred as actual values.
- If the SPSS working data file contains more variables than the file can receive, SAVE TRANSLATE writes the maximum number of variables the file can receive.

Spreadsheets

Variables in the working data file become columns, and cases become rows in the spreadsheet file.

- If you specify FIELDNAMES, variable names become the first row and indicate field names.
- String variable values are left-justified and numeric variable values are right-justified.
- The resulting spreadsheet file is given the range name of SPSS.
- System-missing values are translated to N/A in spreadsheet files.

SPSS formats are translated as follows:

SPSS	1-2-3/Symphony	Multiplan	Excel
Number	Fixed	Fixed	0.00;#,##0.00;...
COMMA	Comma	Fixed	0.00;#,##0.00;...
DOLLAR	Currency	$ (dollar)	$#,##0_);...
DATE	Date		d-mmm-yy
TIME	Time		hh:mm:ss
String	Label	Alpha	General

Databases

Variables in the working data file become fields, and cases become records in the database file.
- Characters that are allowed in SPSS variable names but not in dBASE field names are translated to colons in dBASE II and underscores in dBASE III and dBASE IV.
- SPSS numeric variables containing the system-missing value are translated to **** in dBASE III and dBASE IV, and 0 in dBASE II.
- The width and precision of translated numeric are taken from the SPSS print format; the total number of characters for the number is taken from the width of the print format, and the number of digits to the right of the decimal point is taken from the decimals in the print format. To adjust the width and precision, use the PRINT FORMATS command prior to using SAVE TRANSLATE. Values that cannot be converted to the given width and precision are converted to missing values.

SPSS variable formats are translated to dBASE formats as follows:

SPSS	dBASE
Number	Numeric
String	Character
Dollar	Numeric
Comma	Numeric

Tab-Delimited ASCII Files

Variables in the working data file become columns, and cases become rows in the ASCII file.
- If you specify FIELDNAMES, variable names become the first row as column headings.
- All values are delimited by tabs.
- The resulting ASCII file is given the extension *.DAT* if no file extension is explicitly specified.
- System-missing values are translated to N/A in ASCII files.
- SPSS formats are not translated.

Limitations

- Maximum 2048 cases can be translated to 1-2-3 Release 1A, maximum 8192 cases to 1-2-3 Release 2.0 or Symphony files, maximum 4095 cases to Multiplan files, and maximum 16,384 cases for Excel.
- Maximum 65,535 cases and 32 variables can be translated to a dBASE II; maximum 1 billion cases (subject to disk space availability) and 128 variables to dBASE III; or maximum 1 billion cases (subject to disk space availability) and 255 variables to dBASE IV.

OUTFILE Subcommand

OUTFILE assigns a name to the file to be saved. The only specification is the name of the file. On some operating systems, file specifications should be enclosed in quotes or apostrophes.

Example

```
SAVE TRANSLATE OUTFILE='STAFF.DBF'/TYPE=DB3.
```

- SAVE TRANSLATE creates a dBASE III file called *STAFF.DBF*. The TYPE subcommand is required to specify the type of dBASE file to save.

TYPE Subcommand

TYPE indicates the format of the resulting file.
- TYPE can be omitted for spreadsheet files if the file extension named on OUTFILE is the default for the type of file you are saving.
- TYPE with keyword DB2, DB3, or DB4 is required for translating to dBASE files.
- TYPE takes precedence over the file extension.
- A file that was read using GET TRANSLATE should be saved as the same type.

WK1	*1-2-3 Release 2.0.*
WKS	*1-2-3 Release 1.4.*
WR1	*Symphony Release 2.0.*
WRK	*Symphony Release 1.0.*
SLK	*Multiplan (symbolic format).*
XLS	*Excel.*
DB2	*dBASE II.*
DB3	*dBASE III or dBASE III PLUS.*
DB4	*dBASE IV.*
TAB	*Tab-delimited ASCII data files.*

Example

```
SAVE TRANSLATE OUTFILE='PROJECT.OCT' /TYPE=SLK.
```

- SAVE TRANSLATE translates the SPSS working data file into the Multiplan spreadsheet file named *PROJECT.OCT*.

FIELDNAMES Subcommand

FIELDNAMES translates SPSS variable names into field names in the spreadsheet.

- FIELDNAMES can be used with spreadsheets and tab-delimited ASCII files. FIELDNAMES is ignored when used with database files.
- SPSS variable names are transferred to the first row of the spreadsheet file.

Example.

```
SAVE TRANSLATE OUTFILE='STAFF.WRK' /FIELDNAMES.
```

- SAVE TRANSLATE creates a Symphony spreadsheet file containing all variables from the SPSS working data file. The variable names are transferred to the Symphony file.

DROP and KEEP Subcommands

Use DROP or KEEP to include only a subset of variables in the resulting file. DROP specifies a set of variables to exclude. KEEP specifies a set of variables to retain. Variables not specified on KEEP are dropped.

- Specify a list of variable, column, or field names separated by commas or spaces.
- KEEP does *not* affect the order of variables in the resulting file. Variables are kept in their original order.
- Specifying a variable that is not in the working data file or that has been dropped because of a previous DROP or KEEP subcommand results in an error and the SAVE command is not executed.

Example

```
SAVE TRANSLATE OUTFILE='ADDRESS.DBF' /TYPE=DB4 /DROP=PHONENO, ENTRY.
```

- SAVE TRANSLATE creates a dBASE IV file named *ADDRESS.DBF*, dropping the SPSS variables *PHONENO* and *ENTRY*.

RENAME Subcommand

RENAME changes the names of variables as they are copied into the resulting file.

- The specification on RENAME is a list of old variable names followed by an equals sign and a list of new variable names. The same number of variables must be specified on both lists. Keyword TO can be used in the first list to refer to consecutive variables in the working data file and in the second list to generate new variable names (see "Keyword TO" on p. 32). The entire specification must be enclosed in parentheses.

- Alternatively, you can specify each old variable name individually, followed by an equals sign and the new variable name. Multiple sets of variable specifications are allowed. The parentheses around each set of specifications are optional.
- RENAME does not affect the working data file. However, if RENAME precedes DROP or KEEP, variables must be referred to by their new names on DROP or KEEP.
- Old variable names do not need to be specified according to their order in the working data file.
- Name changes take place in one operation. Therefore, variable names can be exchanged between two variables.
- Multiple RENAME subcommands are allowed.

Example

```
SAVE TRANSLATE OUTFILE='STAFF.WRK' /FIELDNAMES
  /RENAME AGE=AGE88 JOBCAT=JOBCAT88.
```

- RENAME renames variable *AGE* to *AGE88* and *JOBCAT* to *JOBCAT88* before they are copied to the first row of the spreadsheet.

Example

```
SAVE TRANSLATE OUTFILE='STAFF.WRK' /FIELDNAMES
  /RENAME (AGE JOBCAT=AGE88 JOBCAT88).
```

- The name changes are identical to those in the previous example: *AGE* is renamed to *AGE88* and *JOBCAT* is renamed to *JOBCAT88*. The parentheses are required with this method.

MAP Subcommand

MAP displays a list of the variables in the resulting file and their corresponding names in the working data file.

- The only specification is keyword MAP. There are no additional specifications.
- Multiple MAP subcommands are allowed. Each MAP subcommand maps the results of subcommands that precede it but not the results of subcommands that follow it.

Example

```
GET FILE=HUBEMPL.
SAVE TRANSLATE OUTFILE='STAFF.WRK' /FIELDNAMES
  /RENAME=(AGE=AGE88)(JOBCAT=JOBCAT88).
```

- MAP is specified to confirm that variable *AGE* is renamed to *AGE88* and *JOBCAT* is renamed to *JOBCAT88*.

SELECT IF

```
SELECT IF [(]logical expression[)]
```

The following relational operators can be used in logical expressions:

Symbol	Definition	Symbol	Definition
EQ or =	Equal to	NE or <>*	Not equal to
LT or <	Less than	LE or <=	Less than or equal to
GT or >	Greater than	GE or >=	Greater than or equal to*

---

* On ASCII systems (for example, UNIX, VAX, and all PC's) you can also use ~=; on IBM EBCDIC systems (for example, IBM 360 and IBM 370) you can also use ¬=.

The following logical operators can be used in logical expressions:

Symbol	Definition
AND or &	Both relations must be true
Or or |	Either relation can be true
Not*	Reverses the outcome of an expression*

---

* On ASCII systems you can also use ~; on IBM EBCDIC systems you can also use ¬ (or the symbol above number 6).

Example:
```
SELECT IF (SEX EQ 'MALE').
```

Overview

SELECT IF permanently selects cases for analysis based upon logical conditions found in the data. These conditions are specified in a *logical expression*. The logical expression can contain relational operators, logical operators, arithmetic operations, and any functions allowed in COMPUTE transformations (see COMPUTE, and "Transformation Expressions" on p. 45). For temporary case selection, specify a TEMPORARY command before SELECT IF.

Basic Specification

The basic specification is simply a logical expression.

Syntax Rules

- Logical expressions can be simple logical variables or relations, or complex logical tests involving variables, constants, functions, relational operators, and logical operators. Both the logical expression and the assignment expression can use any of the numeric or string functions allowed in COMPUTE transformations (see COMPUTE and Universals: Functions).

- Parentheses can be used to enclose the logical expression. Parentheses can also be used within the logical expression to specify the order of operations. Extra blanks or parentheses can be used to make the expression easier to read.
- A relation can compare variables, constants, or more complicated arithmetic expressions. Relations cannot be abbreviated. For example, (A EQ 2 OR A EQ 5) is valid while (A EQ 2 OR 5) is not. Blanks (not commas) must be used to separate relational operators from the expressions being compared.
- A relation cannot compare a string variable to a numeric value or variable, or vice versa. A relation cannot compare the result of the logical functions SYSMIS, MISSING, ANY, or RANGE to a number.
- String values used in expressions must be specified in quotes and must include any leading or trailing blanks. Lowercase letters are considered distinct from uppercase letters.
- String variables that are used as target variables must already exist. To declare a new string variable, first create the variable with the STRING command and then specify the new variable as the target variable on IF.

Operations

- SELECT IF permanently selects cases. Cases not selected are dropped from the working data file.
- The logical expression is evaluated as true, false, or missing. If a logical expression is true, the case is selected; if it is false or missing, the case is not selected.
- Multiple SELECT IF commands issued prior to a procedure command must all be true for a case to be selected.
- SELECT IF should be placed before other transformations for efficiency considerations.
- Logical expressions are evaluated in the following order: first numeric functions, then exponentiation, then arithmetic operators, then relational operators, and last logical operators. Use parentheses to change the order of evaluation.
- If N OF CASES is used with SELECT IF, SPSS reads as many records as required to build the specified *n* cases. It makes no difference whether the N OF CASES precedes or follows the SELECT IF.
- System variable $CASENUM is the sequence number of a case in the working data file. Although it is syntactically correct to use $CASENUM on SELECT IF, it does not produce the expected results. To select a set of cases based on their sequence in a file, create your own sequence variable with the transformation language prior to selecting (see the example below).

Missing Values

- If the logical expression is indeterminate because of missing values, the case is not selected. In a simple relational expression, a logical expression is indeterminate if the expression on either side of the relational operator is missing.

- If a compound expression is used in which relations are joined by the logical operator OR, the case is selected if either relation is true, even if the other is missing.
- To select cases with missing values for the variables within the expression, use the missing-value functions. To include cases with values that have been declared user-missing along with other cases, use the VALUE function (see p. 56).

Limitations

SELECT IF cannot be placed within a FILE TYPE—END FILE TYPE or INPUT PROGRAM—END INPUT PROGRAM structure. It can be placed nearly anywhere following these commands in a transformation program. See Appendix A for a discussion of program states in SPSS and the placement of commands.

Example

```
SELECT IF (SEX EQ 'MALE').
```

- All subsequent procedures will use only cases in which the value of *SEX* is MALE.
- Since upper and lower case are treated differently in comparisons of string variables, cases for which the value of *SEX* is male are not selected.

Example

```
SELECT IF (INCOME GT 75000 OR INCOME LE 10000).
```

- The logical expression tests whether a case has a value either greater than 75,000 or less than or equal to 10,000. If either relation is true, the case is used in subsequent analyses.

Example

```
SELECT IF (V1 GE V2).
```

- This example selects cases where variable *V1* is greater than or equal to *V2*. If either *V1* or *V2* is missing, the logical expression is indeterminate and the case is not selected.

Example

```
SELECT IF (SEX = 'F' & INCOME <= 10000).
```

- The logical expression tests whether string variable *SEX* is equal to F and if numeric variable *INCOME* is less than or equal to 10,000. Cases that meet both conditions are included in subsequent analyses. If either *SEX* or *INCOME* is missing for a case, the case is not selected.

Example

```
SELECT IF (SYSMIS(V1)).
```

- The logical expression tests whether *V1* is system-missing. If it is, the case is selected for subsequent analyses.

Example

```
SELECT IF (VALUE(V1) GT 0).
```

- Cases are selected if *V1* is greater than 0, even if the value of *V1* has been declared user-missing.

Example

```
SELECT IF (V1 GT 0).
```

- Cases are not selected if *V1* is user-missing, even if the user-missing value is greater than 0.

Example

```
SELECT IF (RECEIV GT DUE AND (REVNUS GE EXPNS OR BALNCE GT 0)).
```

- By default, AND is executed before OR. This expression uses parentheses to change the order of evaluation.
- SPSS first tests whether variable *REVNUS* is greater than or equal to variable *EXPNS*, or variable *BALNCE* is greater than 0. Second, SPSS tests whether *RECEIV* is greater than *DUE*. If one of the expressions in parentheses is true and *RECEIV* is greater than *DUE*, the case is selected.
- Without the parentheses, SPSS would first test whether *RECEIV* is greater than *DUE* and *REVNUS* is greater than or equal to *EXPNS*. Second, SPSS would test whether *BALNCE* is greater than 0. If the first two expressions are true *or* if the third expression is true, the case is selected.

Example

```
SELECT IF ((V1-15) LE (V2*(-0.001))).
```

- The logical expression compares whether *V1* minus 15 is less than or equal to *V2* multiplied by –0.001. If it is, the case is selected.

Example

```
SELECT IF ((YRMODA(88,13,0) - YRMODA(YVAR,MVAR,DVAR)) LE 30).
```

- The logical expression subtracts the number of days representing the date *(YVAR, MVAR, and DVAR)* from the number of days representing the last day in 1988. If the difference is less than or equal to 30, the case is selected.

Example

```
* Creating a sequence number.

COMPUTE  #CASESEQ=#CASESEQ+1.
SELECT IF  (MOD(#CASESEQ,2)=0).
```

- This example computes a scratch variable, *#CASESEQ*, containing the sequence numbers for each case. Every other case beginning with the second is selected.
- *#CASESEQ* must be a scratch variable so that it is not reinitialized for every case. An alternative is to use the LEAVE command.

Example

```
DO IF   SEX EQ 'M'.
+    SELECT IF PRESTIGE GT 50.
ELSE IF   SEX EQ 'F'.
+    SELECT IF PRESTIGE GT 45.
END IF.
```

- The SELECT IF commands within the DO IF structure select males with prestige scores above 50 and females with prestige scores above 45.

SET

```
SET [BLANKS={SYSMIS}]       [UNDEFINED={WARN  }]
            {value }                   {NOWARN}

    [MXERRS={40}]   [MXLOOPS={40}]   [MXWARNS={10}]
            {n }             {n }             {n }

    [ERRORS=  ]  {LISTING }
    [MESSAGES=]  {TERMINAL}
    [PRINTBACK=] {BOTH    }
    [RESULTS= ]  {NONE    }

    [LENGTH={59  }]  [WIDTH={132}]  [FORMAT={F8.2}]  [CASE={UPPER}]  [HEADER={YES}]
            {n   }          {80 }           {Fw.d}         {UPLOW}          {NO }
            {NONE}          {n  }

    [CCA={'-,,,'  }]  [CCB={'-,,,'  }]  [CCC={'-,,,'  }]
         {'format'}         {'format'}         {'format'}

    [CCD={'-,,,'  }]  [CCE={'-,,,'  }]
         {'format'}         {'format'}

    [DECIMAL={DOT  }]
             {COMMA}

    [SEED={n}]

    [XSORT={YES}]
           {NO }

    [COMPRESSION={ON }]
                 {OFF}

    [EXTENSIONS={ON }
                {OFF}

    [ENDCMD={'.'    }]  [NULLINE={YES}]
            {'string'}            {NO }

    [JOURNAL=[{YES}] [file]]
              {NO }

    [MEXPAND={ON }]  [MPRINT={ON }]  [MNEST={50}]  [MITERATE={1000}]
             {OFF}           {OFF}          {n }             {n   }

    [HIGHRES={ON }]
             {OFF}

    [BLOCK={'character'  }]  [HISTOGRAM={'character'  }]  [BOX={'-I+[++++++++]'}]
           {X'hexcharacter'}             {X'hexcharacter'}       {X'hexstring'    }
```

Defaults are not shown where they are known to vary by version or installation of SPSS.

Example:

```
SET BLANKS=0/UNDEFINED=NOWARN/MXWARNS=200.
```

Overview

Many of the running options in SPSS can be tailored to your own preferences with the SET command. The default settings for these options vary from system to system. To display the current settings, use the SHOW command. A setting changed by SET remains in effect for the entire working session unless changed again by another SET command. The PRESERVE command saves the current settings so that you can return to them later in the session with the RESTORE command. PRESERVE and RESTORE are especially useful with the macro facility.

Options

Blanks and Undefined Input Data. You can specify the value that SPSS should use when it encounters a completely blank field for a numeric variable using the BLANKS subcommand. You can also turn off the warning message that SPSS issues when it encounters an invalid value for a numeric variable using UNDEFINED.

Maximum Errors and Loops. You can raise or lower the default number of errors and warnings allowed in an SPSS session before processing stops using the MXERRS and MXWARNS subcommands. You can raise or lower the maximum number of iterations allowed for the LOOP—END LOOP structure using the MXLOOPS.

Output Destination. You can send error messages, resource utilization messages, command printback and the output from your commands to your screen and/or to a file using the ERRORS, MESSAGES, PRINTBACK, and RESULTS subcommands. You can also suppress each of these using keyword NONE.

Output Format and Layout. You can change the length and width of output and specify whether output uses upper or mixed case with the LENGTH, WIDTH, and CASE subcommands. You can also control whether headings are included in output using the HEADER subcommand. You can change the default (F8.2) print and write formats used for numeric variables using the FORMAT subcommand.

Custom Currency Formats. You can customize currency formats for your own applications using the CCA, CCB, CCC, CCD, and CCE subcommands. For example, you can display currency as French francs rather than American dollars.

Thousands Separator and Decimal Delimiter. You can override the default symbol for the thousands separator and the decimal delimiter using the DECIMAL subcommand.

Samples and Random Numbers. You can change the initial seed value to a particular number using the SEED subcommand.

Sorting Data. You can control whether the sort program used in SPSS is the SPSS sort program or the default sort program on your system with the XSORT subcommand.

Scratch File Compression. You can specify whether scratch files are kept in compressed or uncompressed form using the COMPRESSION subcommand.

Data File Extension. You can specify the default extensions used for SPSS data files saved with SAVE or XSAVE or portable files saved with EXPORT using the EXTENSIONS subcommand.

Command Terminators. You can change the default command terminator from a period to a character of your choice using the ENDCMD subcommand. You can also specify whether a blank line should be ignored or used as a command terminator during a prompted session using the NULLINE subcommand.

Journal Files. You can determine whether or not SPSS keeps a journal file during a session using the JOURNAL subcommand. An SPSS journal file records the commands you have entered along with any error or warning messages generated by the commands. A modified journal file can be used as a command file in subsequent sessions.

Macro Displays. You can control macro expansion, the maximum number of loop iterations, and nesting levels within a macro using the MEXPAND, MITERATE, and MNEST subcommands. You can also control the display of the variables, commands, and parameters that a macro uses using the MPRINT Subcommands.

Charts and Plots. You can turn high-resolution graphics on or off using the HIGHRES subcommand. For low-resolution (character-based) output, you can specify the characters used to draw grids in procedures such as CROSSTABS and MULT RESPONSE, or the characters used to draw histograms or bar charts in procedures such as FREQUENCIES and REGRESSION using the BLOCK, HISTOGRAM, and BOX subcommands.

Basic Specification

The basic specification is at least one subcommand.

Subcommand Order

Subcommands can be named in any order.

Syntax Rules

- You can specify as many subcommands as needed. Subcommands must be separated by at least one space or slash.
- Only one keyword or argument can be specified for each subcommand.
- SET can be used more than once in the command sequence.
- YES and ON are aliases for each other.
- NO and OFF are aliases for each other.

Operations

- Settings specified on SET remain in effect until they are changed by another SET command or until the current session is ended.
- Each time SET is used, only the specified settings are changed. All others remain at their previous settings or the default.

Example

```
SET BLANKS=0/UNDEFINED=NOWARN/MXWARNS=200.
```

Syntax Reference Guide

- BLANKS specifies 0 as the value SPSS should use when it encounters a completely blank field for a numeric variable.
- UNDEFINED=NOWARN suppresses the message that SPSS displays whenever anything other than a number or a blank is encountered as the value for a numeric variable.
- MXWARNS specifies that an SPSS session will display up to 200 warnings. The default is 10.

BLANKS Subcommand

BLANKS specifies the value SPSS should use when it encounters a completely blank field for a numeric variable. By default, SPSS uses the system-missing value.

- BLANKS controls only the translation of numeric fields. If a blank field is read with a string format, the resulting value is a blank.
- The value specified on BLANKS is not automatically defined as a missing value.
- The BLANKS specification applies to all numeric variables. You cannot use different specifications for different variables.
- BLANKS must be specified before data are read. Otherwise, blanks in numeric fields are converted to the system-missing value (the default) as they are read.

Example

```
SET BLANKS=-1.
```

- BLANKS translates blanks for numeric variables to the value −1.

UNDEFINED Subcommand

UNDEFINED controls whether SPSS displays a warning message when it encounters anything other than a number or a blank as the value for a numeric variable. The default is WARN.

- Warning messages that are suppressed are still counted toward the maximum allowed before the session is terminated. To control the number of warnings (and therefore the number of invalid values) allowed in a session, use the MXWARNS subcommand.

WARN   *Display a warning message when an invalid value is encountered for a numeric variable.* This is the default.

NOWARN   *Suppress warning messages for invalid values.*

MXERRS and MXWARNS Subcommands

MXERRS and MXWARNS control the maximum number of error messages and warnings SPSS displays during one working session. The default for MXERRS is 40; the default for MXWARNS is 10.

- Errors counted are those that cause SPSS to stop execution of a command but continue the session. MXERRS applies only to command files submitted for execution through the operating system. When the MXERRS limit is exceeded, SPSS terminates the session.

- All errors are included with warnings in the count toward the MXWARNS limit. Notes are not. For information on notes, warnings, and errors, see p. 24.
- In interactive mode or in SPSS for Windows and other windowed environments, SPSS stops displaying warning messages when the MXWARNS limit is exceeded but the working session continues.
- In batch mode in non-windowed environments, SPSS terminates the session when the MXWARNS limit is exceeded. You may wish to reset MXWARNS when using batch mode.

Example

```
SET MXERRS=5 /MXWARNS=200.
```

- MXERRS specifies that a maximum of 5 errors can occur before an SPSS session is terminated.
- MXWARNS specifies that a maximum of 200 warnings can be displayed. When the limit is exceeded, SPSS stops is displaying warnings if it is in a windowed environment or is running the commands interactively. Otherwise, SPSS terminates the session.

MXLOOPS Subcommand

MXLOOPS specifies the maximum number of times a loop defined by the LOOP—END LOOP structure is executed for a single case or input record. The default is 40.

- MXLOOPS prevents infinite loops, which may occur if no cutoff is specified for the loop structure (see LOOP—END LOOP).
- When a loop is terminated, control passes to the SPSS command immediately following the END LOOP command, even if the END LOOP condition is not yet met.

Example

```
SET MXLOOPS=10.
```

- MXLOOPS specifies that a loop can be executed a maximum of 10 times.

ERRORS, MESSAGES, PRINTBACK, and RESULTS Subcommands

ERRORS, MESSAGES, PRINTBACK, and RESULTS are used with keywords LISTING, TERMINAL, BOTH, and NONE to route SPSS output.

- ERRORS refers to both error messages and warning messages.
- MESSAGES refers to resource utilization messages, including the heading and the summaries (such as the amount of memory used by a command).
- PRINTBACK refers to SPSS command printback.
- RESULTS refers to the output generated by SPSS commands.

Four keywords are available on each:

LISTING   *Direct output to a file only.* In windowed environments, LISTING output is automatically displayed in the output window.

TERMINAL	*Direct output to the screen only.* Headings are not sent to the screen with the rest of the output. In windowed environments, TERMINAL is equivalent to LISTING.
BOTH	*Direct output to both the terminal and a file.* Alias YES or ON.
NONE	*Suppress the output.* Alias NO or OFF.

The default routes vary from operating system to operating system and according to the way SPSS commands are executed. In SPSS for Windows or other windowed environments, the typical defaults are:

Subcommand	SPSS for Windows/ windowed environments
ERRORS	Listing
MESSAGES	None
PRINTBACK	None
RESULTS	Listing

In non-windowed environments, typical defaults vary according to the way SPSS commands are run, as shown in the following table:

Subcommand	Batch mode	Interactive mode
ERRORS	Both	Both
MESSAGES	Listing	Listing
PRINTBACK	Listing	Listing
RESULTS	Listing	Both

Example

```
SET ERRORS=BOTH MESSAGES=NONE PRINTBACK=LISTING RESULTS=TERMINAL.
```

- Error messages are directed to both the terminal and a file.
- Resource utilization messages are suppressed.
- Command printback is directed only to a file.
- Output from SPSS commands is directed only to the terminal.
- In a windowed environment, all output except messages goes to the output window.

LENGTH and WIDTH Subcommands

LENGTH and WIDTH specify the maximum page length and width for the output, respectively. The default for LENGTH is 59 lines; the default for WIDTH is 132 characters for command files submitted to the operating system or 80 for commands run interactively.

- The page length includes the first printed line on the page through the last line that can be printed. The printer you use most likely includes a margin at the top; that margin is not included in the length used by SPSS. The default, 59 lines, allows for a 1/2-inch margin

at the top and bottom of an 11-inch page printed with 6 lines per inch, or an 8 1/2-inch page printed with 8 lines per inch.
- You can specify any length from 40 through 999,999 lines. If a long page length is specified, SPSS continues to provide page ejects and titles at the start of each procedure and at logical points in the display, such as between crosstabulations.
- To suppress page ejects, use keyword NONE on LENGTH. SPSS will insert titles at logical points in the display but will not supply page ejects.
- You can specify any number of characters from 80 through 132 for WIDTH. The specified width does not include the carriage control character. All procedures can fit the output to an 80-column page.

FORMAT Subcommand

FORMAT specifies the default print and write formats for numeric variables. This default format applies to numeric variables defined on DATA LIST in freefield format and to all numeric variables created by transformation commands, unless a format is explicitly specified.
- The specification must be a simple F format. The default is F8.2.
- You can use the PRINT FORMATS, WRITE FORMATS, and FORMATS commands to change print and write formats.
- Format specifications on FORMAT are output formats. When specifying the width, enough positions must be allowed to include any punctuation characters such as decimal points, commas, and dollar signs.
- If a numeric data value exceeds its width specification, SPSS attempts to display some value nevertheless. First SPSS rounds decimal values, then removes punctuation characters, then tries scientific notation, and finally, if there is still not enough space, produces asterisks indicating that a value is present but cannot be displayed in the assigned width.

CASE Subcommand

CASE controls whether output is displayed in upper or mixed case.
- The default varies by system. Use the SHOW command to display the default on your system.
- Variable labels and value labels are stored in upper and lower case in SPSS data files. However, the operating system may translate these labels to upper case before sending them to the output, depending on the default on your system. To display them in the case in which they were entered, use the CASE subcommand.
- Command printback and titles are not affected by SET CASE. Commands are printed back and titles are displayed in the case in which they were entered.
- Lowercase letters within string variables are not translated to uppercase.

UPPER *Use all upper case.*

UPLOW *Preserve the case in which letters were entered.*

Syntax Reference Guide

Example

```
DATA LIST FREE FILE=PRSNNL / COMPANY (A10) NAME (A20) AGE.
SET LENGTH=50 /WIDTH=80 /CASE=UPLOW /PRINTBACK=NO
              /HEADER=NO /FORMAT=F2.0.
```

- DATA LIST defines variables for file *PRSNNL*.
- SET sets a page length of 50 lines and a page width of 80 characters. Variable labels, value labels, and error messages will be displayed in the output in upper and lower case. The listing file will not contain command printback or headings. The default numeric format is F2.0. This format applies to variable *AGE*.

HEADER Subcommand

HEADER controls whether the output includes headings. The HEADER subcommand applies to both default headings and those specified on the TITLE and SUBTITLE commands.

- The specification on HEADER is either YES or NO (alias ON or OFF). The default varies by system.
- When the specification NO suppresses the heading, all general SPSS headings in the output, including pagination, are replaced by a single blank line.
- Some procedure-specific headings, such as those generated by FREQUENCIES, REPORT, and TABLES, are not affected by the HEADER setting.

CCA, CCB, CCC, CCD, and CCF Subcommands

You can specify up to five custom currency formats using the subcommands CCA, CCB, CCC, CCD, and CCE.

- Each custom currency subcommand defines one custom format and can include four specifications in the following order: a negative prefix, a prefix, a suffix, and a negative suffix.
- The specifications are separated by either periods or commas, whichever you do not want to use as a decimal point in format.
- Each currency specification must always contain three commas or three periods. All other specifications are optional.
- Use blanks in the specification only where you want blanks in the format.
- The entire specification must be enclosed in apostrophes.
- A specification cannot exceed 16 characters (excluding the apostrophes).
- Custom currency formats cannot be specified as input formats on DATA LIST. Use them only as output formats in the FORMATS, WRITE FORMATS, PRINT FORMATS, WRITE, and PRINT commands.

Example

```
SET CCA='-,$,,'.
```

- A minus sign (−) preceding the first command is used as the negative prefix.

- A dollar sign is specified for the prefix.
- No suffixes are specified (there are two consecutive commas before the closing apostrophe).
- Since commas are used as separators in the specification, the decimal point is represented by a period.

Example

```
SET CCA='(,,,-)'  CCB=',,%,'  CCC='(,$,,)'  CCD='-/-.Dfl ..-'.
FORMATS VARA(CCA9.0)/ VARB(CCB6.1)/ VARC(CCC8.0)/ VARD(CCD14.2).
```

- SET defines four custom currency formats. Table 21 summarizes the currency specifications.
- FORMATS assigns these formats to specific variables.

Table 21 Custom currency examples

	CCA	CCB	CCC	CCD
negative prefix	(	none	(	-/-
prefix	none	none	$	Dfl
suffix	none	%	none	none
negative suffix	-)	none	)	-
separator	,	,	,	.
sample positive number	23,456	13.7%	$352	Dfl 37.419,00
sample negative number	(19,423-)	13.7%	($189)	-/-Dfl 135,19-

DECIMAL Subcommand

DECIMAL can be used to override the setting for the thousands separator and the decimal delimiter. Two alternative specifications are available:

DOT   *The decimal delimiter is a period and the thousands separator is a comma.*

COMMA   *The decimal delimiter is a comma and the thousands separator is a period.*

SEED Subcommand

SEED specifies the random number seed. You can specify any integer, preferably a number greater than 1 but less than 2,000,000,000, which approaches the limit on some machines.

- SPSS uses a pseudo-random-number generator to select random samples or create uniform or normal distributions of random numbers. The generator begins with a *seed,* a large integer. Starting with the same seed, the system will repeatedly produce the same sequence of numbers and will select the same sample from a given data file.
- At the start of each session, the seed is set by SPSS to a value that may vary or may be fixed, depending on the implementation. You can set the seed yourself with the SEED subcommand.

Syntax Reference Guide

- By default, the seed value changes each time a random-number series is needed in a session. To repeat the same random distribution within a session, specify the same seed each time.
- The random number seed can be changed any number of times within a session.

Example

```
SET SEED=987654321.
```

- The random number seed is set to the value 987,654,321. The seed will be in effect the next time the random-number generator is called.

XSORT Subcommand

XSORT determines which sort program is used: the SPSS sort program or the default sort program on your system.
- To display the default sort program used on your system, use the SHOW command.
- The SPSS sort program does not compress intermediate work files and may need more scratch disk space than some other sort programs.
- Some systems do not allow you to select a sort program. Changing XSORT settings on such systems will trigger a note.

YES *Use the SPSS sort program.*

NO *Use the sort program on your system.*

COMPRESSION Subcommand

COMPRESSION determines whether scratch files created during an SPSS session are in compressed or uncompressed form.
- A compressed scratch file occupies less space on disk than does an uncompressed scratch file but requires more processing.
- The specification takes effect the next time a scratch file is written and stays in effect until SET COMPRESSION is specified again or until the end of the session.
- The default setting varies. Use SHOW to display the default on your system.

YES *Compress scratch files.*

NO *Do not compress scratch files.*

EXTENSIONS Subcommand

EXTENSIONS controls whether SPSS adds default extensions to the data files it saves during a session. The default extensions are *.SAV* for SPSS data files saved with SAVE or XSAVE and *.POR* for portable data files saved with EXPORT. The specification on EXTENSIONS is either OFF or ON. The default is OFF.

- EXTENSIONS is effective only when you run SAVE, XSAVE, or EXPORT with command syntax.
- EXTENSIONS has no effect when the filename is specified in apostrophes or quotes.

OFF   *Do not use default extensions.* This is the default.

ON   *Add a default extension to the file if an extension is not explicitly specified.*

Example

```
SET EXTENSIONS=ON.
SAVE OUTFILE=BANK89.
SAVE OUTFILE='BANK89'.
```

- This example saves two SPSS data files from the same working file. The first SAVE command saves the working data file as *BANK89.SAV;* the second SAVE command saves the working file as *BANK89* regardless of the setting on EXTENSIONS.

ENDCMD Subcommand

ENDCMD controls the character used for the command terminator. When commands are run interactively, every command must end with a command terminator. By default, the terminator is a period.

- The ENDCMD specification can be any character and must be enclosed in apostrophes or quotes. However, using a character that has special syntactic meaning in SPSS (such as a slash) or a character that may be used at the end of any of your variable names will often result in syntactic ambiguity.

NULLINE Subcommand

NULLINE controls whether a blank line is accepted as an alternative command terminator in a prompted session (when you enter commands interactively at an SPSS prompt).

- NULLINE is effective for prompted SPSS sessions only.
- If NULLINE is NO during a prompted session, you must use the character specified for ENDCMD to terminate a command.

YES   *Accept a blank input line as a command terminator.* This is the default.

NO   *Do not treat a blank line as a command terminator.*

Example

```
SPSS> SET ENDCMD="!" /NULLINE=NO.
```

- This example shows a prompted session. The command terminator is set to an exclamation point. A blank line will not be accepted as a command terminator.
- The prompt SPSS> may vary from system to system.

JOURNAL Subcommand

SPSS creates a journal file to keep track of the commands submitted and error and warning messages generated during a session. JOURNAL is used to assign a filename to the SPSS journal file or to stop or resume the journal.

- Journal files with the default filename are erased at the beginning of each SPSS session. To preserve the contents of a journal file, assign a name with SET JOURNAL at the beginning of the session. Alternatively, if you have used the default name for a journal file, you can rename the file before beginning another SPSS session.
- If you use multiple journal files, you should not start with one file, go to another file, and then return to the first file. On many systems, SPSS will not append new information to the first file but will overwrite the previous contents.

filename   *Filename for the SPSS journal file.* The default name varies by system.

YES   *Start sending commands and messages to the journal file.*

NO   *Stop sending commands and messages to the journal file.*

Example

```
SET JOURNAL MYLOG.
GET FILE=HUBDATA.
SET JOURNAL OFF.
LIST.
SET JOURNAL ON.
FREQUENCIES VARIABLES=ALL.
```

- The first SET command opens the journal file *MYLOG*.
- The GET command is copied into the journal file. The SET command then turns the journal off. The LIST command is not copied into the journal file but is executed. The second SET command turns the journal on again, and the FREQUENCIES command is copied into the journal file.

MEXPAND and MPRINT Subcommands

MEXPAND and MPRINT control whether macros are expanded and whether the expanded macros are displayed. For more information on macros, see DEFINE and Appendix D.

The specifications for MEXPAND are:

ON   *Expand macros.* This is the default.

OFF   *Do not expand macros.* The command line that calls the macro is treated like any other command line. If the macro call is an SPSS command, it will be executed; otherwise, it will trigger an error message.

The specifications for MPRINT are:

ON   *Include expanded macro commands in the output.*

OFF   *Exclude expanded macro commands from the output.* This is the default.

- MPRINT is effective only when MEXPAND is ON and is independent of the PRINTBACK subcommand.

MITERATE and MNEST Subcommands

MITERATE and MNEST control the maximum loop traversals and the maximum nesting levels permitted in macro expansions, respectively.

- The specification on MITERATE or MNEST is a positive integer. The default for MITERATE is 1000. The default for MNEST is 50.

HIGHRES Subcommand

SPSS generates high-resolution charts and plots for statistical procedures. HIGHRES controls whether such charts and plots are displayed using high-resolution graphics or printer characters.

- The default varies from system to system. Use the SHOW command to display the current setting.

ON   *Display charts and plots using high-resolution graphics.*

OFF   *Display charts and plots using printer characters.*

BLOCK Subcommand

BLOCK specifies the character used for drawing bar charts and icicle plots when HIGHRES is OFF.

- You can specify any single character either as a quoted string or as a quoted hexadecimal pair preceded by the character X.
- The default varies by system.

Example

```
SET BLOCK='#'.
```

- This command specifies a pound sign (#) as the character to be used for drawing bar charts. The character is specified as a quoted string.

HISTOGRAM Subcommand

HISTOGRAM specifies the character used for drawing histograms when HIGHRES is OFF.

- You can specify any single character either as a quoted string or as a quoted hexadecimal pair preceded by the character X.
- The default varies by system.

Example

SET HISTOGRAM=X'7B'.

- This command specifies a pound sign (#) as the character to be used for drawing histograms. The character in this example is specified as a quoted hexadecimal string.

BOX Subcommand

BOX specifies the characters used to draw grids in procedures such as CROSSTABS, MULT RESPONSE, and TABLES (an option to the SPSS base system). Other procedures, like FACTOR and REGRESSION, may also use these characters in plots and other displays. The specification is either a 3- or an 11-character quoted string, in which the characters represent, respectively:

1	horizontal line	7	upper-right corner
2	vertical line	8	left T
3	middle (cross)	9	right T
4	lower-left corner	10	top T
5	upper-left corner	11	bottom T
6	lower-right corner		

- The characters can be specified either as a quoted string or hexadecimal pairs. Specify an X before the quoted hexadecimal pairs.
- The defaults vary from system to system. To display the current settings, use the SHOW command.
- Currently, only TABLES uses all eleven characters. All other procedures use only the first three characters, where the third character defines all intersections. Any characters specified in the fourth through eleventh positions will be ignored by all procedures except TABLES. If only three characters are specified for TABLES, the third character is used for all nine intersections.

Example

SET BOX '-I++++++++'.

SET BOX X'60C94E4E4E4E4E4E4E4E4E'.

- On IBM systems, these two specifications are equivalent and are the default. The dash is used for horizontal lines, the letter I for vertical lines, and the plus sign for intersections.

Example

SET BOX '-I*'.

SET BOX '-I*********'.

- These two specifications are equivalent. The dash is used for horizontal lines, the letter I for vertical lines, and the asterisk for intersections.

SHOW

```
SHOW [ALL] [BLANKS] [BLKSIZE] [BOX] [BLOCK] [BUFNO] [CASE] [CC] [CCA] [CCB]
     [CCC] [CCD] [CCE] [COMPRESSION] [DECIMALS] [ENDCMD] [ERRORS] [EXTENSIONS]
     [FORMAT] [HEADER] [HIGHRES] [HISTOGRAM] [JOURNAL] [LENGTH] [MESSAGES] [MEXPAND]
     [MITERATE] [MNEST] [MPRINT] [MXERRS] [MXLOOPS] [MXWARNS] [N] [NULLINE]
     [PRINTBACK] [RESULTS] [SCOMPRESSION] [SEED] [SYSMIS] [UNDEFINED]
     [WEIGHT] [WIDTH] [XSORT] [$VARS]
```

Overview

SHOW displays current settings for SPSS running options. Most of these settings can be changed with the SET command.

Basic Specification

The basic specification is simply the command keyword, which displays all current settings (keyword ALL). Some displayed option settings are applicable only when you have SPSS options such as Tables and Categories.

Subcommand Order

Subcommands can be named in any order.

Syntax

- If any subcommands are specified, only the requested settings are displayed.
- SHOW can be specified more than once.

Example

```
SHOW BLANKS /UNDEFINED /MXWARNS.
```

- BLANKS shows the value to which a completely blank field for a numeric variable is translated.
- UNDEFINED indicates whether a message displays whenever SPSS encounters anything other than a number or a blank as the value for a numeric variable.
- MXWARNS displays the maximum number of warnings allowed before a session is terminated.

Subcommands

The following alphabetical list shows the available subcommands.

ALL *Display all settings applicable to your system.* This is the default.

BLANKS *Value to which a completely blank field for a numeric variable is translated.* The default is the system-missing value.

BLKSIZE *Default block length used for scratch files and SPSS data files.* The default varies by system. BLKSIZE cannot be changed with SET.

BOX *Characters used to draw boxes.* Both character and hexadecimal representations are displayed. The default varies by system.

BLOCK *Character used to draw bar charts.* Both character and hexadecimal representations displayed. The default varies by system.

BUFFNO *The default number of buffers used for all files managed by the SPSS system for input and output.* The default varies by system. BUFFNO cannot be changed with SET.

CASE *Case for variable and value labels in the output.* The setting is UPPER (generally, the default) or UPLOW. The default varies by system.

CC *Custom currency formats.* CC shows the current custom currency formats that have been defined for CCA, CCB, CCC, CCD, and CCE on SET. You can also request any of these keywords individually.

COMPRESSION *Compression of scratch files.* The setting is either ON or OFF (alias YES or NO). The default varies by system.

DECIMALS *Symbols used for decimal delimiter and thousands separator.* DOT uses a period for the decimal delimiter and a command for the thousands separator. COMMA uses a comma for the decimal delimiter and a period for the separator. The default varies by system.

ENDCMD *Command terminator for SPSS commands.* The setting can be any single character. The default is a period. The command terminator applies only to interactive mode.

ERRORS *Error messages.* The setting can be LISTING, TERMINAL, BOTH (alias YES or ON), or NONE (alias NO or OFF). The default varies by system and by the way in which SPSS commands are run (see SET).

EXTENSIONS *Default extensions for saved data files.* The setting is either ON or OFF. The default is OFF.

FORMAT *Default print and write formats for numeric variables defined on DATA LIST in freefield format and to all numeric variables created by transformation commands.* The default is F8.2.

HEADER *Headings for output.* The setting is either YES or NO (alias ON or OFF). The default varies by system.

HIGHRES	*High-resolution or low-resolution (character-based) charts and plots.* The setting is either ON or OFF, where ON is high-resolution. The default varies by system.
HISTOGRAM	*Character used to draw histograms.* Both character and hexadecimal representations are displayed. The default varies by system.
JOURNAL	*Journal file during an SPSS session.* The setting is either ON or OFF (alias YES or NO). The default varies by system.
LENGTH	*Maximum age length for output.* The default is 59.
MESSAGES	*Resource utilization messages.* The setting can be LISTING, TERMINAL, BOTH (alias YES or ON), or NONE (alias NO or OFF). The default varies by system and by the way in which SPSS commands are run (see SET).
MEXPAND	*Macro expansion.* The setting is either ON or OFF (alias YES or NO). The default is ON.
MITERATE	*Maximum loop iterations permitted in macro expansions.* The default is 1000.
MNEST	*Maximum nesting level for macros.* The default is 50.
MPRINT	*Inclusion of expanded macros in the output.* The setting is either ON or OFF (alias YES or NO). The default is OFF.
MXERRS	*Maximum number of errors permitted before session is terminated.* The default is 40. This setting applies only to batch mode.
MXLOOPS	*Maximum executions of a loop on a single case.* The default is 40.
MXWARNS	*Maximum number of warnings and errors permitted, collectively, before session is terminated.* The default is 10. This setting applies only to running SPSS commands in batch mode.
N	*Unweighted number of cases in the working data file.* N displays UNKNOWN if a working data file has not yet been created. N cannot be changed with SET.
NULLINE	*Null line command terminator for prompted sessions.* The setting is YES or NO (alias ON or OFF). The default is YES. Null lines apply only when you run SPSS commands from an SPSS prompt.
PRINTBACK	*SPSS command printback.* The setting can be LISTING, TERMINAL, BOTH (alias YES or ON), or NONE (alias NO or OFF). The default varies by system and by the way in which SPSS commands are run (see SET).
RESULTS	*Output from SPSS commands.* The setting can be LISTING, TERMINAL, BOTH (alias YES or ON), or NONE (alias NO or OFF). The default varies by system and by the way in which SPSS commands are run (see SET).
SCOMPRESSION	*Compression of SPSS data files.* This setting can be overridden by the COMPRESSED or UNCOMPRESSED subcommands on the SAVE or XSAVE com-

	mands. The default setting varies by system. SCOMPRESSION cannot be changed with SET.
SEED	*Seed for the random-number generator.* The default is generally 2,000,000 but may vary by system.
SYSMIS	*The system-missing value.* SYSMIS cannot be changed with SET.
UNDEFINED	*Warning message for undefined data.* WARN is the default. NOWARN suppresses messages but does not alter the count of warnings toward the MXWARNS total.
WEIGHT	*Variable used to weight cases.* WEIGHT can be specified for SHOW only; it cannot be changed with SET.
WIDTH	*Maximum page width for the output.* The default is 132 columns for batch mode and 80 for interactive mode.
XSORT	*The sort program used to sort data.* The specification is either YES (alias ON) for using the SPSS sort program or NO (alias OFF) for using the sort program provided by the operating system. The default setting varies by system.
$VARS	*Values of system variables.* $VARS cannot be changed with SET.

SORT CASES

```
SORT CASES [BY] varlist[({A})] [varlist...]
                        {D}
```

Example:
```
SORT CASES BY DIVISION (A) STORE (D).
```

Overview

SORT CASES reorders the sequence of cases in the working data file based on the values of one or more variables. You can optionally sort cases in ascending or descending order, or use combinations of ascending and descending order for different variables.

Basic Specification

The basic specification is a variable or list of variables that are used as sort keys. By default, cases are sorted in ascending order of each variable, starting with the first variable named. For each subsequent variable, cases are sorted in ascending order within categories of the previously named variables.

Syntax Rules

- Keyword BY is optional.
- BY variables can be numeric or string but not scratch, system, or temporary variables.
- You can explicitly request the default sort order (ascending) by specifying A or UP in parentheses after the variable name. To sort cases in descending order, specify D or DOWN.
- An order specification (A or D) applies to all variables in the list up to the previous order specification. If you combine ascending and descending order on the same SORT CASES command, you may need to specify the default A explicitly.

Operations

- SORT CASES first sorts the file according to the first variable named. For subsequent variables, cases are sorted within categories of the previously named variables.
- The sort sequence of string variables depends on the character set in use on your system. With EBCDIC character sets, most special characters are sorted first, followed by lowercase alphabetical characters, uppercase alphabetical characters, and, finally, numbers. The order is almost exactly reversed with ASCII character sets. Numbers are sorted first, followed by uppercase alphabetical characters and then lowercase alphabetical characters. In addition, special characters are sorted between the other character types. Use the INFO command (not available on all systems) to obtain information on the character set in use on your system and the exact sort sequence.

SORT CASES with Other Procedures

- For the REPORT procedure, the file should be sorted in order of the break variable or variables. Specify the SORT CASES command before the REPORT command, and list the break variables in the same order on each.
- In AGGREGATE, cases are sorted in order of the break variable or variables. You do not have to use SORT CASES prior to running AGGREGATE, since the procedure does its own sorting.
- You can use SORT CASES in conjunction with the BY keyword in ADD FILES to interleave cases with the same variables but from different files.
- With MATCH FILES, cases must be sorted in the same order for all files you combine.
- With UPDATE, cases must be sorted in ascending order of the key variable or variables in both the master file and all transaction files.
- You can use the PRINT command to check the results of a SORT CASES command. PRINT must be followed by a procedure or EXECUTE to be executed.

Example

```
SORT CASES BY DIVISION (A) STORE (D).
```

- Cases are sorted in ascending order of variable *DIVISION*. Cases are further sorted in descending order of *STORE* within categories of *DIVISION*. A must be specified so that D applies to *STORE* only.

Example

```
SORT DIVISION STORE (A) AGE (D).
```

- Cases are sorted in ascending order of *DIVISION*. Keyword BY is not used in this example.
- Cases are further sorted in ascending order of *STORE* within values of *DIVISION*. Specification A applies to both *DIVISION* and *STORE*.
- Cases are further sorted in descending order of *AGE* within values of *STORE* and *DIVISION*.

Example

```
SORT CASES BY EDUC SEX.
REPORT VARS=SCORE1 TO SCORE5
  /BREAK=EDUC
  /SUMMARY= MEAN
  /BREAK=SEX
  /SUMMARY=MEAN.
```

- Each variable named on a BREAK subcommand in REPORT is first named on SORT CASES. Variables are named on SORT CASES in the order in which they will be used in REPORT.

SPLIT FILE

```
SPLIT FILE {BY varlist}
           {OFF       }
```

Example:
```
SORT CASES BY SEX.
SPLIT FILE BY SEX.
FREQUENCIES VARS=INCOME /STATISTICS=MEDIAN.
```

Overview

SPLIT FILE splits the working data file into subgroups that can be analyzed separately by SPSS. These subgroups are sets of adjacent cases in the file that have the same values for the specified split variables. Each value of each split variable is considered a break group, and cases within a break group must be grouped together in the working data file. If they are not, the SORT CASES command must be used before SPLIT FILE to sort cases in the proper order.

Basic Specification

The basic specification is keyword BY followed by the variable or variables that define the split-file groups.

- The only other keyword allowed on SPLIT FILE is OFF, which turns off split-file processing.

Syntax Rules

- SPLIT FILE can specify both numeric and string split variables, including long string variables and variables created by temporary transformations. It cannot specify scratch or system variables.
- SPLIT FILE is in effect for all procedures in a session unless you limit it with a TEMPORARY command, turn it off, or override it with a new SPLIT FILE or SORT CASES command.

Operations

- Unlike most transformations, SPLIT FILE takes effect as soon as it is encountered in the command sequence. Thus, special attention should be paid to its position among commands. For more information, see "Command Order" on p. 17.
- The file is processed sequentially. A change or break in values on any one of the split variables signals the end of one break group and the beginning of the next.
- AGGREGATE ignores the SPLIT FILE command. To split files using AGGREGATE, name the variables used to split the file as break variables ahead of any other break variables on

Syntax Reference Guide — SPLIT FILE

AGGREGATE. AGGREGATE still produces one file, but the aggregated cases are in the same order as the split-file groups.
- If SPLIT FILE is in effect when a procedure writes matrix materials, SPSS writes one set of matrix materials for every split group. If a procedure reads a file that contains multiple sets of matrix materials, the procedure automatically detects the presence of multiple sets.
- If SPLIT FILE names any variable that was defined by the NUMERIC command, SPSS prints page headings indicating the split-file grouping.

Limitations

- SPLIT FILE can specify or imply up to eight variables.

Example

```
SORT CASES BY SEX.
SPLIT FILE BY SEX.
FREQUENCIES VARS=INCOME /STATISTICS=MEDIAN.
```

- SORT CASES arranges cases in the file according to the values of variable *SEX*.
- SPLIT FILE splits the file according to the values of variable *SEX*, and FREQUENCIES generates separate median income tables for men and women.

Example

```
SORT CASES BY SEX.
TEMPORARY.
SPLIT FILE BY SEX.
FREQUENCIES VARS=INCOME /STATISTICS=MEDIAN.
FREQUENCIES VARS=INCOME /STATISTICS=MEDIAN.
```

- Because of the TEMPORARY command, SPLIT FILE applies to the first procedure only. Thus, the first FREQUENCIES procedure generates separate median income tables for men and women. The second FREQUENCIES procedure generates one median income table that includes both sexes.

Example

```
SORT CASES BY SEX.
SPLIT FILE BY SEX.
FREQUENCIES VARS=INCOME /STATISTICS=MEDIAN.
SPLIT FILE OFF.
FREQUENCIES VARS=INCOME /STATISTICS=MEDIAN.
```

- SPLIT FILE does not apply to the second FREQUENCIES procedure because it is turned off after the first FREQUENCIES procedure. This example produces the same results as the example above.

Example

```
SORT CASES BY SEX RACE.
SPLIT FILE BY SEX.
FREQUENCIES VARS=INCOME /STATISTICS=MEDIAN.
SPLIT FILE BY SEX RACE.
FREQUENCIES VARS=INCOME /STATISTICS=MEDIAN.
```

- The first SPLIT FILE command applies to the first FREQUENCIES procedure. The second SPLIT FILE command overrides the first and splits the file by sex and race. This split is in effect for the second FREQUENCIES procedure.

Example

```
SORT CASES BY SEX.
SPLIT FILE BY SEX.
FREQUENCIES VAR=JOBCAT.
SORT CASES BY JOBCAT.
REPORT FORMAT=AUTO /VARS=NAME AGE WAGES /BREAK=JOBCAT /SUM=MEAN.
```

- FREQUENCIES generates separate job category tables for men and women.
- The second SORT CASES command overrides the SPLIT FILE command, and REPORT generates a single report organized by the values of variable *JOBCAT*.

Example

```
SORT CASES BY SEX JOBCAT.
SPLIT FILE BY SEX.
FREQUENCIES VAR=JOBCAT.
REPORT FORMAT=AUTO /VARS=NAME AGE WAGES /BREAK=JOBCAT /SUM=MEAN.
```

- The file is sorted by variable *SEX*, then each subgroup of *SEX* is sorted by the values of variable *JOBCAT*.
- The FREQUENCIES procedure generates separate tables for men and women but not for subgroups of *JOBCAT* within *SEX*.
- The REPORT procedure generates two reports, one for each value of *SEX*. Each report is organized by the values of variable *JOBCAT*.

STRING

```
STRING varlist (An) [/varlist...]
```

Example:
```
STRING STATE1 (A2).
RECODE STATE ('IO'='IA') (ELSE=COPY) INTO STATE1.
```

Overview

STRING declares new string variables that can be used as target variables in data transformations.

Basic Specification

The basic specification is the name of the new variables and, in parentheses, the variable format.

Syntax Rules

- If keyword TO is used to create multiple string variables, the specified format applies to each variable named and implied by TO.
- To declare variables with different formats, separate each format group with a slash.
- STRING can be used within an input program to determine the order of string variables in the dictionary of the working data file. When used for this purpose, STRING must precede DATA LIST in the input program. See p. 460 for an example.
- STRING cannot be used to redefine an existing variable.
- String variables cannot have zero length; A0 is an illegal format.
- All implementations of SPSS allow the A format. Other string formats may be available on some systems. In addition, the definition of a long string depends on your operating system. Use keyword LOCAL on the INFO command to obtain documentation for your operating system.

Operations

- Unlike most transformations, STRING takes effect as soon as it is encountered in the command sequence. Thus, special attention should be paid to its position among commands. For more information, see "Command Order" on p. 17.
- New string variables are initialized as blanks.
- Variables declared on STRING are added to the working data file in the order they are specified. This order is not changed by the order in which the variables are used in the transformation language.

- The length of a string variable is fixed by the format specified when it is declared and cannot be changed by FORMATS. To change the length of a string variable, declare a new variable with the desired length and then use COMPUTE to assign the values of the original variable to it.

Example

```
STRING STATE1 (A2).
RECODE STATE ('IO'='IA') (ELSE=COPY) INTO STATE1.
```

- STRING declares variable *STATE1* with an A2 format.
- RECODE specifies *STATE* as the source variable and *STATE1* as the target variable. The original value IO is recoded to IA. Keywords ELSE and COPY copy all other state codes over unchanged. Thus, *STATE* and *STATE1* are identical except for cases with the original value IO.

Example

```
STRING V1 TO V6 (A8) / V7 V10 (A16).
```

- STRING declares variables *V1*, *V2*, *V3*, *V4*, *V5*, and *V6*, each with an A8 format, and variables *V7* and *V10*, each with an A16 format.

SUBTITLE

```
SUBTITLE [']text[']
```

Example:
```
SUBTITLE "Children's Training Shoes Only".
```

Overview

SUBTITLE inserts a left-justified subtitle on the second line from the top of each page of the output. The default subtitle contains the installation name and information about the hardware and operating system.

Basic Specification

The only specification is the subtitle itself.

Syntax Rules

- The subtitle can include any characters. To specify a blank subtitle, enclose a blank between apostrophes.
- The subtitle can be up to 60 characters long. Subtitles longer than 60 characters are truncated.
- The apostrophes or quotation marks enclosing the subtitle are optional; using them allows you to include apostrophes or quotation marks in the subtitle.
- If the subtitle is enclosed in apostrophes, quotation marks are valid characters but apostrophes must be specified as double apostrophes. If the subtitle is enclosed in quotation marks, apostrophes are valid characters but quotation marks must be specified as double quotation marks.
- More than one SUBTITLE command is allowed in a single session.
- A subtitle cannot be placed between a procedure command and BEGIN DATA—END DATA or within data records when the data are inline.

Operations

- Each SUBTITLE command overrides the previous one and takes effect on the next output page.
- SUBTITLE is independent of TITLE and each can be changed separately.
- The subtitle will not be displayed if HEADER=NO is specified on SET.

Example

```
TITLE 'Running Shoe Study from Runner''s World Data'.
SUBTITLE "Children's Training Shoes Only".
```

- The title is enclosed in apostrophes, so the apostrophe in *Runner's* must be specified as a double apostrophe.
- The subtitle is enclosed in quotation marks, so the apostrophe in *Children's* is simply specified as an apostrophe.

Example

```
TITLE 'Running Shoe Study from Runner''s World Data'.
SUBTITLE ' '.
```

- This subtitle is specified as a blank. This suppresses the default subtitle.

SYSFILE INFO

```
SYSFILE INFO [FILE=] 'file specification'
```

Example:
```
SYSFILE INFO FILE='PERSNL.SAV'.
```

Overview

SYSFILE INFO displays complete dictionary information for all variables in an SPSS data file. You do not have to retrieve the file with GET to use SYSFILE INFO. If the file has already been retrieved, use DISPLAY DICTIONARY to display dictionary information.

Basic Specification

The basic specification is the command keyword and a complete file specification enclosed in apostrophes.

Syntax Rules

- Only one file specification is allowed per command. To display dictionary information for more than one SPSS data file, use multiple SYSFILE INFO commands.
- The file extension, if there is one, must be specified, even if it is the default.
- The subcommand keyword FILE is optional. When FILE is specified, the equals sign is required.

Operations

- No procedure is needed to execute SYSFILE INFO, since SYSFILE INFO obtains information from the dictionary alone.
- SYSFILE INFO displays the variable name, label, sequential position in the file, print and write format, missing values, and value labels for each variable in the specified file. Up to 60 characters can be displayed for variable and value labels.

Example

```
SYSFILE INFO FILE='PERSNL.SAV'.
```

- SPSS displays the complete dictionary information for all variables in the SPSS data file *PERSNL.SAV*.

TEMPORARY

```
TEMPORARY
```

Example:
```
SORT CASES BY SEX.
TEMPORARY.
SPLIT FILE BY SEX.
FREQUENCIES VARS=INCOME /STATISTICS=MEDIAN.
FREQUENCIES VARS=INCOME /STATISTICS=MEDIAN.
```

Overview

TEMPORARY signals the beginning of temporary transformations that are in effect only for the next procedure. New numeric or string variables created after the TEMPORARY command are temporary variables. Any modifications made to existing variables after the TEMPORARY command are also temporary.

With TEMPORARY you can perform separate analyses for subgroups in the data and then repeat the analysis for the file as a whole. You can also use TRANSFORM to transform data for one analysis but not for other subsequent analyses.

TEMPORARY can be applied to the following commands:

- Transformation commands COMPUTE, RECODE, IF, and COUNT, and the DO REPEAT utility.
- The LOOP and DO IF structures.
- Format commands PRINT FORMATS, WRITE FORMATS, and FORMATS.
- Data selection commands SELECT IF, SAMPLE, FILTER, and WEIGHT.
- Variable declarations NUMERIC, STRING, and VECTOR.
- Labeling commands VARIABLE LABELS and VALUE LABELS, and the MISSING VALUES command.
- SPLIT FILE.
- XSAVE.

Basic Specification

The only specification is the keyword TEMPORARY. There are no additional specifications.

Operations

- Once TEMPORARY is specified, you cannot refer to previously existing scratch variables.
- Temporary transformations apply to the next command that reads the data. Once the data are read, the temporary transformations are no longer in effect.

- The XSAVE command leaves temporary transformations in effect. SAVE, however, reads the data and turns temporary transformations off after the file is written. (See example below.)
- TEMPORARY cannot be used with SORT CASES, MATCH FILES, ADD FILES, or COMPUTE with a LAG function. If any of these commands follows TEMPORARY in the command sequence, there must be an intervening procedure or command that reads the data to first execute the TEMPORARY command.
- TEMPORARY cannot be used within the DO IF—END IF or LOOP—END LOOP structures.

Example

```
SORT CASES BY SEX.
TEMPORARY.
SPLIT FILE BY SEX.
FREQUENCIES VARS=INCOME /STATISTICS=MEDIAN.
FREQUENCIES VARS=INCOME /STATISTICS=MEDIAN.
```

- SPLIT FILE applies to the first FREQUENCIES procedure, which generates separate median income tables for men and women.
- SPLIT FILE is not in effect for the second FREQUENCIES procedure, which generates a single median income table that includes both men and women.

Example

```
DATA LIST FILE=HUBDATA RECORDS=3
 /1 #MOBIRTH #DABIRTH #YRBIRTH 6-11 DEPT88 19.
COMPUTE    AGE=($JDATE - YRMODA(#YRBIRTH,#MOBIRTH,#DABIRTH))/365.25.
VARIABLE LABELS AGE 'EMPLOYEE''S AGE'
         DEPT88 'DEPARTMENT CODE IN 1988'.

TEMPORARY.
RECODE AGE (LO THRU 20=1)(20 THRU 25=2)(25 THRU 30=3)(30 THRU 35=4)
       (35 THRU 40=5)(40 THRU 45=6)(45 THRU 50=7)(50 THRU 55=8)
       (55 THRU 60=9)(60 THRU 65=10)(65 THRU HI=11).
VARIABLE LABELS AGE 'EMPLOYEE AGE CATEGORIES'.
VALUE LABELS AGE 1 'Up to 20' 2 '20 to 25' 3 '25 to 30' 4 '30 to 35'
     5 '35 to 40' 6 '40 to 45' 7 '45 to 50' 8 '50 to 55'
     9 '55 to 60' 10 '60 to 65' 11 '65 and older'.

FREQUENCIES VARIABLES=AGE.
MEANS AGE BY DEPT88.
```

- COMPUTE creates variable *AGE* from the dates in the data.
- FREQUENCIES uses the temporary version of variable *AGE* with temporary variable and value labels.
- MEANS uses the unrecoded values of *AGE* and the permanent variable label.

Example

```
GET FILE=HUBEMPL.
TEMPORARY.
RECODE DEPT85 TO DEPT88 (1,2=1) (3,4=2) (ELSE=9).
VALUE LABELS DEPT85 TO DEPT88 1 'MANAGEMENT'
                              2 'OPERATIONS'
                              3 'UNKNOWN'.
XSAVE OUTFILE=HUBTEMP.
CROSSTABS DEPT85 TO DEPT88 BY JOBCAT.
```

- Both the saved SPSS data file and the CROSSTABS output will reflect the temporary recoding and labeling of the department variables.
- If XSAVE is replaced with SAVE, the SPSS data file will reflect the temporary recoding and labeling but the CROSSTABS output will not.

TITLE

```
TITLE [']text[']
```

Example:
```
TITLE "Running Shoe Study from Runner's World Data".
```

Overview

TITLE inserts a left-justified title on the top line of each page of SPSS output. The default title indicates the version of the system being used.

Basic Specification

The only specification is the title.

Syntax Rules

- The title can include any characters. To specify a blank title, enclose a blank between apostrophes.
- The title can be up to 60 characters long. Titles longer than 60 characters are truncated.
- The apostrophes or quotation marks enclosing the title are optional; using them allows you to include apostrophes or quotation marks in the title.
- If the subtitle is enclosed in apostrophes, quotation marks are valid characters but apostrophes must be specified as double apostrophes. If the subtitle is enclosed in quotation marks, apostrophes are valid characters but quotation marks must be specified as double quotation marks.
- More than one TITLE command is allowed in a single session.
- A title cannot be placed between a procedure command and BEGIN DATA—END DATA or within data records when the data are inline.

Operations

- The title is displayed as part of the output heading, which also includes the date and page number. If HEADER=NO is specified on SET, the heading, including the title and subtitle, will not be displayed.
- Each TITLE command overrides the previous one and takes effect on the next output page.
- Only the title portion of the heading changes. The date and page number are still displayed.
- TITLE is independent of SUBTITLE and each can be changed separately.

Example

```
TITLE "Running Shoe Study from Runner's World Data".
SUBTITLE 'Children''s Training Shoes Only'.
```

- The title is enclosed in quotations, so the apostrophe in *Runner's* is a valid character.
- The subtitle is enclosed in apostrophes, so the apostrophe in *Children's* must be specified as a double apostrophe.

Example

```
TITLE ' '.
SUBTITLE ' '.
```

- The title and subtitle are specified as blanks. This suppresses the default title and subtitle. The date and page number still display on the title line.

T-TEST

Independent-samples tests:

```
T-TEST GROUPS=varname ({1,2**    }) /VARIABLES=varlist
                       {value    }
                       {value,value}
```

Paired-samples tests:

```
T-TEST PAIRS=varlist [WITH varlist [(PAIRED)]] [/varlist ...]
```

Both types of tests:

```
[/MISSING={ANALYSIS**}    [INCLUDE]]
          {LISTWISE  }

[/FORMAT={LABELS**}]
         {NOLABELS}

[/CRITERIA=CI({0.95**})]
              {value }
```

**Default if the subcommand is omitted.

Examples:

```
T-TEST GROUPS=WORLD(1,3) /VARIABLES=NTCPRI NTCSAL NTCPUR.
T-TEST PAIRS=TEACHER CONSTRUC MANAGER.
```

Overview

T-TEST compares sample means by calculating Student's *t* and displays the two-tailed probability of the difference between the means. Statistics are available for either independent samples (different groups of cases) or paired samples (different variables). Other procedures that compare group means are ANOVA, ONEWAY, and MANOVA (MANOVA is available in the SPSS Advanced Statistics option).

Options

Format. You can suppress the display of variable labels using the FORMAT subcommand.

Statistics. You can control which variables are paired in paired-samples tests using the PAIRS subcommand. There are no optional statistics. All statistics available are displayed by default.

Basic Specification

The basic specification depends on whether you want an independent-samples test or a paired-samples test. For both types of tests, T-TEST displays Student's *t*, degrees of freedom, and two-tailed probabilities, as well as the mean, standard deviation, standard error, and count for each group or variable.

- To request an independent-samples test, use the GROUPS and VARIABLES subcommands. Both pooled- and separate-variance estimates are calculated, along with the *F* value used to test homogeneity of variance and its probability. The two-tailed probability is displayed for the *t* value.
- To request a paired-samples test, use the PAIRS subcommand. The default output includes the difference between the means, two-tailed probability level for a test of the difference, correlation coefficient for the two variables, and two-tailed probability level for a test of the coefficient.
- To request both independent- and paired-samples tests, specify GROUPS, VARIABLES, and PAIRS.

Subcommand Order

Subcommands can be named in any order.

Operations

- If a variable specified on GROUPS is a long string, only the short-string portion is used to identify groups in the analysis.
- Probability levels are two-tailed. To obtain the one-tailed probability, divide the two-tailed probability by 2.
- The BOX subcommand controls the characters used in the table display (see SET).

Limitations

Maximum 1 GROUPS and 1 VARIABLES subcommand per T-TEST command.

Example

```
T-TEST GROUPS=WORLD(1,3) /VARIABLES=NTCPRI NTCSAL NTCPUR.
```

- This independent-samples *t* test compares the means of the two groups defined by values 1 and 3 of *WORLD* for variables *NTCPRI*, *NTCSAL*, and *NTCPUR*.

Example

```
T-TEST PAIRS=TEACHER CONSTRUC MANAGER.
```

- This paired-samples *t* test compares the means of *TEACHER* with *CONSTRUC*, *TEACHER* with *MANAGER*, and *CONSTRUC* with *MANAGER*.

GROUPS and VARIABLES Subcommands

GROUPS and VARIABLES are used to request independent samples *t* tests. GROUPS specifies a variable used to group cases. VARIABLES specifies the dependent variables.
- GROUPS can specify only one variable, which can be numeric or string.
- VARIABLES can specify multiple variables, all of which must be numeric.

Any one of three methods can be used to define the two groups for the variable specified on GROUPS:
- Specify a single value in parentheses to group all cases with a value equal to or greater than the specified value into one group and the remaining cases into the other group.
- Specify two values in parentheses to include cases with the first value in one group and cases with the second value in the other group. Cases with other values are excluded.
- If no values are specified on GROUP, T-TEST uses 1 and 2 as default values for numeric variables. There is no default for string variables.

PAIRS Subcommand

PAIRS requests paired-samples *t* tests.
- The minimum specification for a paired-samples test is PAIRS with an analysis list. Only numeric variables can be specified on the analysis list. The minimum analysis list is two variables.
- If keyword WITH is not specified, each variable in the list is compared with every other variable in the list.
- If keyword WITH is specified, every variable to the left of WITH is compared with every variable to the right of WITH. WITH can be used with PAIRED to obtain special pairing.
- To specify multiple analysis lists, use multiple PAIRS subcommands, each separated by a slash. Keyword PAIRS is required only for the first analysis list; a slash can be used to separate each additional analysis list.

(PAIRED) *Special pairing for paired-samples test.* PAIRED must be enclosed in parentheses and must be used with keyword WITH. When PAIRED is specified, The first variable before WITH is compared with the first variable after WITH, the second variable before WITH is compared with the second variable after WITH, and so forth. The same number of variables should be specified before and after WITH; unmatched variables are ignored and a warning message is issued. PAIRED generates an error message if keyword WITH is not specified on PAIRS.

Example

```
T-TEST    PAIRS=TEACHER CONSTRUC MANAGER.
T-TEST    PAIRS=TEACHER MANAGER WITH CONSTRUC ENGINEER.
T-TEST    PAIRS=TEACHER MANAGER WITH CONSTRUC ENGINEER (PAIRED).
```

- The first T-TEST compares *TEACHER* with *CONSTRUC*, *TEACHER* with *MANAGER*, and *CONSTRUC* with *MANAGER*.

- The second T-TEST compares *TEACHER* with *CONSTRUC*, *TEACHER* with *ENGINEER*, *MANAGER* with *CONSTRUC*, and *MANAGER* with *ENGINEER*. *TEACHER* is not compared with *MANAGER*, and *CONSTRUC* is not compared with *ENGINEER*.
- The third T-TEST compares *TEACHER* with *CONSTRUC* and *MANAGER* with *ENGINEER*.

FORMAT Subcommand

FORMAT allows you to suppress variable labels. By default, T-TEST prints variable labels.

- You can further modify the T-TEST output by using the SET WIDTH command to restrict output to a width of 80 characters.

LABELS   *Print variable labels.* This is the default.

NOLABELS   *Suppress variable labels.*

Example

```
GET FILE=CITY.
SET WIDTH 80.
T-TEST    PAIRS=WCLOTHES MCLOTHES
  /FORMAT=NOLABELS.
```

- SET WIDTH limits the output width to 80 characters.
- FORMAT suppresses variable labels.

CRITERIA Subcommand

CRITERIA resets the value of the confidence interval. Keyword CI is required. You can specify a value between 0 and 1 in the parentheses. The default is 0.95.

MISSING Subcommand

MISSING controls the treatment of missing values. The default is ANALYSIS.

- ANALYSIS and LISTWISE are alternatives; however, each can be specified with INCLUDE.

ANALYSIS   *Delete cases with missing values on an analysis-by-analysis or pair-by-pair basis.* For independent-samples tests, cases with missing values for either the grouping variable or the dependent variable are excluded from the analysis of that dependent variable. For paired-samples tests, a case with a missing value for either of the variables in a given pair is excluded from the analysis of that pair. This is the default.

LISTWISE   *Exclude cases with missing values listwise.* A case with a missing value for any variable specified on either GROUPS or VARIABLES is excluded from any independent-samples test. A case with a missing value for any variable specified on PAIRS is excluded from any paired-samples test.

INCLUDE   *Include user-missing values.* User-missing values are treated as valid values.

UPDATE

```
UPDATE FILE={master file}
            {*          }

 [/RENAME=(old varnames=new varnames)...]

 [/IN=varname]

 /FILE={transaction file1}
       {*                }

 [/FILE=transaction file2]

 /BY key variables

 [/MAP]

 [/KEEP={ALL**  }] [/DROP=varlist]
        {varlist}
```

**Default if the subcommand is omitted.

Example:
```
UPDATE FILE=MAILIST /FILE=NEWLIST /BY=ID.
```

Overview

UPDATE replaces values in a **master file** with updated values recorded in one or more files called **transaction files.** Cases in the master file and transaction file are matched according to a key variable.

The master file and the transaction files must be SPSS data files created with the SAVE or XSAVE commands or the working data file. UPDATE replaces values and creates a new working data file, which replaces the original working file. Use the SAVE or XSAVE commands to save the updated file on disk as an SPSS data file.

UPDATE is designed to update values of existing variables for existing cases. Use MATCH FILES to add new variables to an SPSS data file and ADD FILES to add new cases.

Options

Variable Selection. You can specify which variables from each input file are included in the new working file using the DROP and KEEP subcommands.

Variable Names. You can rename variables in each input file before combining the files using the RENAME subcommand. This permits you to combine variables that are the same but whose names differ in different input files, or to separate variables that are different but have the same name.

Variable Flag. You can create a variable that indicates whether a case came from a particular input file using IN. You can use the FIRST or LAST subcommands to create a variable that flags the first or last case of a group of cases with the same value for the key variable.

Variable Map. You can request a map showing all variables in the new working file, their order, and the input files from which they came using the MAP subcommand.

Basic Specification

The basic specification is two or more FILE subcommands and a BY subcommand.

- The first FILE subcommand must specify the master file. All other FILE subcommands identify the transaction files.
- BY specifies the key variables.
- All files must be sorted in ascending order by the key variables.
- By default, all variables from all input files are included in the new working file.

Subcommand Order

- The master file must be specified first.
- RENAME and IN must immediately follow the FILE subcommand to which they apply.
- BY must follow the FILE subcommands and any associated RENAME and IN subcommands.
- MAP, DROP, and KEEP must be specified after all FILE and RENAME subcommands.

Syntax Rules

- BY can be specified only once. However, multiple variables can be specified on BY. All files must be sorted in ascending order by the key variables named on BY.
- The master file cannot contain duplicate values for the key variables.
- RENAME can be repeated after each FILE subcommand and applies only to variables in the file named on the immediately preceding FILE subcommand.
- MAP can be repeated as often as needed.

Operations

- UPDATE reads all input files named on FILE and builds a new working data file that replaces any working file created earlier in the session. The new working data file is built when the data are read by one of the procedure commands or the EXECUTE, SAVE, or SORT CASES command.
- The new working data file contains complete dictionary information from the input files, including variable names, labels, print and write formats, and missing-value indicators. The new working data file also contains the documents from each input file, unless the DROP DOCUMENTS command is used.
- UPDATE copies all variables in order from the master file, then all variables in order from the first transaction file, then all variables in order from the second transaction file, and so on.

- Cases are updated when they are matched on the BY variable(s). If the master and transaction files contain common variables for matched cases, the values for those variables are taken from the transaction file, provided the values are not missing or blanks. Missing or blank values in the transaction files are not used to update values in the master file.
- When UPDATE encounters duplicate keys within a transaction file, it applies each transaction sequentially to that case to produce one case per key value in the resulting file. If more than one transaction file is specified, the value for a variable comes from the last transaction file with a nonmissing value for that variable.
- Variables that are in the transaction files but not in the master file are added to the master file. Cases that do not contain those variables are assigned the system-missing value (for numerics) or blanks (for strings).
- Cases that are in the transaction files but not in the master file are added to the master file and are interleaved according to their values for the key variables.
- If the working data file is named as an input file, any N and SAMPLE commands that have been specified are applied to the working data file before files are combined.
- The TEMPORARY command cannot be in effect if the working data file is used as an input file.

Limitations

- Maximum 1 BY subcommand. However, BY can specify multiple variables.

Example

```
UPDATE FILE=MAILIST /FILE=NEWLIST /BY=ID.
```

- *MAILIST* is specified as the master file. *NEWLIST* is the transaction file. *ID* is the key variable.
- Both *MAILIST* and *NEWLIST* must be sorted in ascending order of *ID*.
- If *NEWLIST* has cases or nonmissing variables that are not in *MAILIST*, the new cases or variables are added to the resulting file.

Example

```
SORT CASES BY LOCATN DEPT.
UPDATE  FILE=MASTER /FILE=* /BY LOCATN DEPT
  /KEEP AVGHOUR AVGRAISE LOCATN DEPT SEX HOURLY RAISE /MAP.
SAVE OUTFILE=PRSNNL.
```

- SORT CASES sorts the working data file in ascending order of the variables to be named as key variables on UPDATE.
- UPDATE specifies *MASTER* as the master file and the sorted working data file as the transaction file. File *MASTER* must also be sorted by *LOCATN* and *DEPT*.
- BY specifies the key variables *LOCATN* and *DEPT*.
- KEEP specifies the subset and order of variables to be retained in the resulting file.

- MAP provides a list of the variables in the resulting file and the two input files.
- SAVE saves the resulting file as an SPSS data file.

FILE Subcommand

FILE identifies each input file. At least two FILE subcommands are required on UPDATE: one specifies the master file and the other a transaction file. A separate FILE subcommand must be used to specify each transaction file.

- The first FILE subcommand must specify the master file.
- An asterisk on FILE refers to the working data file.
- All files must be sorted in ascending order according to the variables specified on BY.
- The master file cannot contain duplicate values for the key variables. However, transaction files can and often do contain cases with duplicate keys (see "Operations" on p. 668).

Raw Data Files

To update the master file with cases from a raw data file, use DATA LIST first to define the raw data file as the working data file. UPDATE can then use the working data file to update the master file.

Example
```
DATA LIST FILE=RAWDATA
   ID 1-3 NAME 5-17 (A) ADDRESS 19-28 (A) ZIP 30-34.
SORT CASES BY ID.
UPDATE FILE=MAILIST1 /RENAME=(STREET=ADDRESS) /FILE=* /BY=ID /MAP.
SAVE OUTFILE=MAILIST2.
```

- DATA LIST defines the variables in the raw data file *RAWDATA*, which will be used to update values in the master file.
- SORT CASES sorts the working data file in ascending order of the key variable *ID*. Cases in the master file were previously sorted in this manner.
- The first FILE subcommand on UPDATE refers to the master file, *MAILIST1*. The RENAME subcommand renames the variable *STREET* to *ADDRESS* in file *MAILIST1*.
- The second FILE subcommand refers to the working data file defined on DATA LIST.
- BY indicates that cases in *MAILIST1* and the working data file are to be matched by the key variable *ID*.
- MAP requests a map of the resulting file.
- SAVE saves the resulting file as an SPSS data file named *MAILIST2*.

BY Subcommand

BY specifies one or more identification, or key, variables that are used to match cases between files.

- BY must follow the FILE subcommands and any associated RENAME and IN subcommands.
- BY specifies the names of one or more key variables. The key variables must exist in all input files and have the same names in all the files. The key variables can be string variables (long strings are allowed).
- All input files must be sorted in ascending order of the key variables. If necessary, use SORT CASES before UPDATE.
- Missing values for key variables are handled like any other values.
- The key variables in the master file must identify unique cases. If duplicate cases are found, SPSS issues an error and UPDATE is not executed. The system-missing value is treated as one single value.

RENAME Subcommand

RENAME renames variables on the input files *before* they are processed by UPDATE. RENAME must follow the FILE subcommand that contains the variables to be renamed.

- RENAME applies only to the immediately preceding FILE subcommand. To rename variables from more than one input file, specify a RENAME subcommand after each FILE subcommand.
- Specifications for RENAME consist of a left parenthesis, a list of old variable names, an equals sign, a list of new variable names, and a right parenthesis. The two variable lists must name or imply the same number of variables. If only one variable is renamed, the parentheses are optional.
- More than one rename specification can be specified on a single RENAME subcommand, each enclosed in parentheses.
- The TO keyword can be used to refer to consecutive variables in the file and to generate new variable names (see "Keyword TO" on p. 32).
- RENAME takes effect immediately. Any KEEP and DROP subcommands entered prior to a RENAME must use the old names, while KEEP and DROP subcommands entered after a RENAME must use the new names.
- All specifications within a single set of parentheses take effect simultaneously. For example, the specification RENAME (A,B = B,A) swaps the names of the two variables.
- Variables cannot be renamed to scratch variables.
- Input SPSS data files are not changed on disk; only the copy of the file being combined is affected.

Example

```
UPDATE FILE=MASTER /FILE=CLIENTS
  /RENAME=(TEL_NO, ID_NO = PHONE, ID)
  /BY ID.
```

- UPDATE updates the master phone list by using current information from file *CLIENTS*.
- Two variables on *CLIENTS* are renamed prior to the match. *TEL_NO* is renamed *PHONE* to match the name used for phone numbers in the master file. *ID_NO* is renamed *ID* so that

it will have the same name as the identification variable in the master file and can be used on the BY subcommand.
- The old variable names are listed before the equals sign, and the new variable names are listed in the same order after the equals sign. The parentheses are required.
- The BY subcommand matches cases according to client ID numbers.

DROP and KEEP Subcommands

DROP and KEEP are used to include a subset of variables in the resulting file. DROP specifies a set of variables to exclude, and KEEP specifies a set of variables to retain.
- DROP and KEEP do not affect the input files on disk.
- DROP and KEEP must follow all FILE and RENAME subcommands.
- DROP and KEEP must specify one or more variables. If RENAME is used to rename variables, specify the new names on DROP and KEEP.
- DROP cannot be used with variables created by the IN subcommand.
- Keyword ALL can be specified on KEEP. ALL must be the last specification on KEEP, and it refers to all variables not previously named on KEEP.
- KEEP can be used to change the order of variables in the resulting file. With KEEP, variables are kept in the order they are listed on the subcommand. If a variable is named more than once on KEEP, only the first mention of the variable is in effect; all subsequent references to that variable name are ignored.
- Multiple DROP and KEEP subcommands are allowed. Specifying a variable that is not in the working data file or that has been dropped because of a previous DROP or KEEP subcommand results in an error and the UPDATE command is not executed.

Example

```
UPDATE FILE=MAILIST /FILE=NEWLIST /RENAME=(STREET=ADDRESS) /BY ID
 /KEEP=NAME ADDRESS CITY STATE ZIP ID.
```

- KEEP specifies the variables to keep in the result file. The variables are stored in the order specified on KEEP.

IN Subcommand

IN creates a new variable in the resulting file that indicates whether a case came from the input file named on the preceding FILE subcommand. IN applies only to the file specified on the immediately preceding FILE subcommand.
- IN has only one specification, the name of the flag variable.
- The variable created by IN has value 1 for every case that came from the associated input file and value 0 if the case came from a different input file.
- Variables created by IN are automatically attached to the end of the resulting file and cannot be dropped.

Example

```
UPDATE  FILE=WEEK10 /FILE=WEEK11 /IN=INWEEK11 /BY=EMPID.
```

- IN creates the variable *INWEEK11*, which has the value 1 for all cases in the resulting file that came from the input file *WEEK11* and the value 0 for those cases that were not in file *WEEK11*.

MAP Subcommand

MAP produces a list of the variables are in the new working file and the file or files from which they came. Variables are listed in the order they appear in the resulting file. MAP has no specifications and must be placed after all FILE, RENAME, and IN subcommands.

- Multiple MAP subcommands can be used. Each MAP shows the current status of the working data file and reflects only the subcommands that precede the MAP subcommand.
- To obtain a map of the resulting file in its final state, specify MAP last.
- If a variable is renamed, its original and new names are listed. Variables created by IN are not included in the map, since they are automatically attached to the end of the file and cannot be dropped.
- MAP can be used with the EDIT command to obtain a list of the variables in the resulting file without actually reading the data and combining the files.

VALUE LABELS

```
VALUE LABELS varlist value 'label' value 'label'... [/varlist...]
```

Example:
```
VALUE LABELS JOBGRADE 'P' 'Parttime Employee' 'C' 'Customer Support'.
```

Overview

VALUE LABELS deletes all existing value labels for the specified variable(s) and assigns new value labels. The ADD VALUE LABELS can be used to add new labels or alter labels for specified values without deleting other existing labels.

Basic Specification

The basic specification is a variable name and the individual values with their assigned labels.

Syntax Rules

- Labels can be assigned to any previously defined variables except long string variables.
- It is not necessary to enter value labels for all values for a variable.
- Each value label must be enclosed in apostrophes or quotation marks. For short string variables, the values themselves must also be enclosed in apostrophes or quotation marks.
- Value labels can contain any characters, including blanks. To enter an apostrophe as part of a label, enclose the label in quotation marks or enter a double apostrophe.
- Each value label can be up to 60 characters long, although most procedures display only 20 characters. The TABLES procedure (available in SPSS Tables) will display all 60 characters of a label.
- The same labels can be assigned to the values of different variables by specifying a list of variable names. For string variables, the variables specified must be of equal length.
- Multiple sets of variable names and value labels can be specified on one VALUE LABELS command as long as the sets are separated by slashes.
- To continue a label from one command line to the next, specify a plus (+) sign before the continuation of the label. Each string segment of the label must be enclosed in apostrophes or quotes. To insert a blank between the strings, the blank must be included in the label specification.

Operations

- Unlike most transformations, VALUE LABELS takes effect as soon as it is encountered in the command sequence. Thus, special attention should be paid to its position among commands (see "Command Order" on p. 17).
- VALUE LABELS deletes all previously assigned value labels for the specified variables.
- The value labels assigned are stored in the dictionary of the working file and are automatically displayed on the output from many procedures.
- If a specified value is longer than the format of the variable, SPSS will be unable to read the full value and may not be able to assign the value label correctly.
- If the value specified for a string variable is shorter than the format of the variable, the value specification is right-padded without warning.

Example

```
VALUE LABELS V1 TO V3 1 'Officials & Managers'
                      6 'Service Workers'
             /V4 'N' 'New Employee'.
```

- Labels are assigned to the values 1 and 6 for the variables between and including *V1* and *V3* in the working data file.
- Following the required slash, a label for value N of *V4* is specified. N is a string value and must be enclosed in apostrophes or quotes.
- If labels exist for values 1 and 6 on *V1* to *V3* and value N on *V4*, they are changed in the dictionary of the working file. If labels do not exist for these values, new labels are added to the dictionary.
- Existing labels for values other than 1 and 6 on *V1* to *V3* and value N on *V4* are deleted.

Example

```
VALUE LABELS  OFFICE88 1 "EMPLOYEE'S OFFICE ASSIGNMENT PRIOR"
    + " TO 1988".
```

- The label for *OFFICE88* is created by combining two strings with the plus sign. The blank between PRIOR and TO must be included in the first or second string to be included in the label.

Example

```
VALUE LABELS=STATE REGION 'U' "UNKNOWN".
```

- Label *UNKNOWN* is assigned to value U for both *STATE* and *REGION*.
- *STATE* and *REGION* must be string variables of equal length. If *STATE* and *REGION* have unequal lengths, a separate specification must be made for each, as in

```
VALUE LABELS STATE 'U' "UNKNOWN" / REGION 'U' "UNKNOWN".
```

Example

```
DATA LIST / CITY 1-8(A) STATE 10-12(A).
VALUE LABELS   STATE 'TEX' "TEXAS" 'TEN' "TENNESSEE"
                     'MIN' "MINNESOTA".
BEGIN DATA
AUSTIN    TEX
MEMPHIS   TEN
ST. PAUL  MIN
END DATA.
FREQUENCIES VARIABLES=STATE.
```

- The DATA LIST command defines two variables. *CITY* is eight characters wide and *STATE* is three characters. The values are included between the BEGIN DATA and END DATA commands.
- The VALUE LABELS command assigns labels to three values of variable *STATE*. Each value and each label is specified in either apostrophes or quotation marks.
- The format for variable *STATE* must be at least three characters wide, because the specified values, TEX, TEN, and MIN, are three characters. If the format for *STATE* were two characters, SPSS would issue a warning. This would occur even though the values named on VALUE LABELS and the values after BEGIN DATA agree.

VARIABLE LABELS

```
VARIABLE LABELS varname 'label' [/varname...]
```

Example:
```
VARIABLE LABELS YRHIRED 'YEAR OF FIRST HIRING'.
```

Overview

VARIABLE LABELS assigns descriptive labels to variables in the working data file.

Basic Specification

The basic specification is a variable name and the associated label in apostrophes or quotes.

Syntax Rules

- Labels can be added to any previously defined variable. It is not necessary to enter labels for all variables in the working data file.
- Each variable label must be enclosed in apostrophes or quotation marks.
- Variable labels can contain any characters, including blanks. To enter an apostrophe as part of a label, enclose the label in quotation marks or enter a double apostrophe.
- Each variable label can be up to 120 characters long, although most procedures print fewer than the 120 characters. All statistical procedures display at least 40 characters.
- Multiple variables can be assigned labels on a single VARIABLE LABELS command. Only one label can be assigned to each variable, and each label can apply to only one variable.
- To continue a label from one command line to the next, specify a plus (+) sign before the continuation of the label. Each string segment of the label must be enclosed in apostrophes or quotes. To insert a blank between the strings, the blank must be included in the label specification.

Operations

- Unlike most transformations, VARIABLE LABELS takes effect as soon as it is encountered in the command sequence. Thus, special attention should be paid to its position among commands (see "Command Order" on p. 17).
- Variable labels are automatically displayed in the output from many procedures and are stored in the dictionary of the working data file.
- VARIABLE LABELS can be used for variables that have no previously assigned variable labels. If a variable has a previously assigned variable label, the new label replaces the old label.

Example

```
VARIABLE LABELS  YRHIRED 'YEAR OF FIRST HIRING'
  DEPT88 'DEPARTMENT OF EMPLOYMENT IN 1988'
  SALARY88 'YEARLY SALARY IN 1988'
  JOBCAT 'JOB CATEGORIES'.
```

- Variable labels are assigned to the variables *YRHIRED*, *DEPT88*, *SALARY88*, and *JOBCAT*.

Example

```
VARIABLE LABELS  OLDSAL "EMPLOYEE'S GROSS SALARY PRIOR"
  + " TO 1988".
```

- The label for *OLDSAL* is created by combining two strings with the plus sign. The blank between PRIOR and TO must be included in the first or second string to be included in the label.

VECTOR

```
VECTOR  {vector  name=varlist        }   [/vector  name...]
        {vector  name(n  [format])}
```

Example:
```
VECTOR V=V1 TO V6.

STRING SELECT(A1).
COMPUTE SELECT='V'.

LOOP #I=1 TO 6.
IF MISSING(V(#I)) SELECT='M'.
END LOOP.
```

Overview

VECTOR associates a vector name with a set of existing variables or defines a vector of new variables. A vector is a set of variables that can be referred to using an index. The vector can refer to either string or numeric variables, and the variables can be permanent or temporary.

For each variable in the reference list, VECTOR generates an element. Element names are formed by adding a subscript in parentheses to the end of the vector name. For example, if vector *AGES* has three elements, the element names are *AGES(1)*, *AGES(2)*, and *AGES(3)*. Although the VECTOR command has other uses within the transformation language, it is most often used with LOOP structures because the indexing variable on LOOP can be used to refer to successive vector elements.

Options

File Structures. VECTOR can be used with the END CASE command to restructure data files. You can build a single case from several cases or, conversely, you can build several cases from a single case (see pp. 213 and 214 for examples).

Short-Form Vectors. VECTOR can be used to create a list of new variables and the vector that refers to them simultaneously. VECTOR in the short form can be used to establish the dictionary order of a group of variables before they are defined on a DATA LIST command. (See "VECTOR: Short Form" on p. 681.)

Basic Specification

- The basic specification is VECTOR, a vector name, a required equals sign, and the list of variables that the vector refers to. The TO keyword must be used to specify the variable list.
- For the short form of VECTOR, the basic specification is VECTOR, an alphabetical prefix, and, in parentheses, the number of variables to be created.

Syntax Rules

- Multiple vectors can be created on the same command by using a slash to separate each set of specifications.
- Variables specified on VECTOR must already be defined unless the short form of VECTOR is used to create variables (see "VECTOR: Short Form" on p. 681).
- The TO convention must be used to specify the variable list. Thus, variables specified must be consecutive and must be from the same dictionary, permanent or scratch.
- A single vector must comprise all numeric variables or all string variables. The string variables must have the same length.
- A scalar (a variable named on NUMERIC), a function, and a vector can all have the same name, for example *MINI*. The scalar can be identified by the lack of a left parenthesis following the name. Where a vector has the same name as a function (or the abbreviation of a function), the vector name takes precedence. (See p. 682 for an example.)
- Vector element names must always be specified with a subscript in parentheses.

Operations

- VECTOR takes effect as soon as it is encountered in the command sequence, unlike most transformations, which do not take effect until the data are read. Thus, special attention should be paid to its position among commands (see "Command Order" on p. 17).
- VECTOR is in effect only until the first procedure that follows it. The vector must be redeclared to be reused.
- Vectors can be used in transformations but not in procedures.

Examples

```
* Replace a case's missing values with the mean of all
  nonmissing values for that case.

DATA LIST FREE /V1 V2 V3 V4 V5 V6 V7 V8.
MISSING VALUES V1 TO V8 (99).
COMPUTE MEANSUB=MEAN(V1 TO V8).

VECTOR V=V1 TO V8.
LOOP #I=1 TO 8.
+  DO IF MISSING (V(#I)).
+  COMPUTE V(#I)=MEANSUB.
+  END IF.
END LOOP.

BEGIN DATA
1 99 2 3 5 6 7  8
2  3  4 5 6 7 8  9
2  3  5 5 6 7 8 99
END DATA.
LIST.
```

- The first COMPUTE command calculates variable MEANSUB as the mean of all nonmissing values for each case.
- VECTOR defines vector *V* with the original variables as its elements.
- For each case, the loop is executed once for each variable. The COMPUTE command within the loop is executed only when the variable has a missing value for that case. COMPUTE replaces the missing value with the value of *MEANSUB*.
- For the first case, the missing value for variable *V2* is changed to the value of *MEANSUB* for that case. The missing value for variable *V8* for the third case is changed to the value of *MEANSUB* for that case.

More Examples

For additional examples of VECTOR, see pp. 213, 214, and 344.

VECTOR: Short Form

VECTOR can be used to create a list of new variables and the vector that refers to them simultaneously. The short form of VECTOR specifies a prefix of alphanumeric characters followed, in parentheses, by the length of the vector (the number of variables to be created).

- The new variable names must not conflict with existing variables. If the prefix starts with the # character, the new variables are created according to the rules for scratch variables.
- More than one vector of the same length can be created by naming two or more prefixes before the length specification.
- By default, variables created with VECTOR receive F8.2 formats. Alternative formats for the variables can be specified by including a format specification with the length specification within the parentheses. The format and length can be specified in either order and must be separated by at least one space or comma. If multiple vectors are created, the assigned format applies to all of them unless you specify otherwise.

Example

```
VECTOR #WORK(10).
```

- SPSS creates vector *#WORK*, which refers to ten scratch variables: *#WORK1*, *#WORK2*, and so on, through *#WORK10*. Thus, element *#WORK(5)* of the vector is variable *#WORK5*.

Example

```
VECTOR X,Y(5).
```

- VECTOR creates vectors *X* and *Y*, which refer to the new variables *X1* through *X5* and *Y1* through *Y5*, respectively.

Example

```
VECTOR X(6,A5).
```

- VECTOR assigns an A5 format to variables *X1* through *X6*.

Example

```
VECTOR X,Y(A5,6) Z(3,F2).
```

- VECTOR assigns A5 formats to variables *X1* to *X6* and *Y1* to *Y6*, and F2 formats to variables *Z1* to *Z3*. It doesn't matter whether the format or the length is specified first within the parentheses.

Example

```
* Predetermine variable order with the short form of VECTOR.

INPUT PROGRAM.
VECTOR X Y (4,F8.2).
DATA LIST / X4 Y4 X3 Y3 X2 Y2 X1 Y1 1-8.
END INPUT PROGRAM.

PRINT /X1 TO X4  Y1 TO Y4.
BEGIN DATA
49382716
49382716
49382716
END DATA.
```

- The short form of VECTOR is used to establish the dictionary order of a group of variables before they are defined on a DATA LIST command. To predetermine variable order, both VECTOR and DATA LIST must be enclosed within the INPUT PROGRAM and END INPUT PROGRAM commands.
- The order of the variables in the working data file will be *X1*, *X2*, *X3*, and *X4*, and *Y1*, *Y2*, *Y3*, and *Y4*, even though they are defined in a different order on DATA LIST.
- SPSS reads the variables with the F1 format specified on DATA LIST. It writes the variables with the output format assigned on VECTOR (F8.2).
- Another method for predetermining variable order is to use NUMERIC (or STRING if the variables are string variables) before the DATA LIST command (see p. 460 for an example). The advantage of using NUMERIC or STRING is that you can assign mnemonic names to the variables.

Example

```
* Name conflicts.

INPUT PROGRAM.
NUMERIC MIN MINI_A MINI_B MINIM(F2).
COMPUTE MINI_A = MINI(2).   /*MINI is function MINIMUM.
VECTOR MINI(3,F2).
DO REPEAT I = 1 TO 3.
+   COMPUT MINI(I) = -I.
END REPEAT.
COMPUTE MIN = MIN(1).     /*The second MIN is function MINIMUM.
COMPUTE MINI_B = MINI(2). /*MINI now references vector MINI
COMPUTE MINIM = MINIM(3). /*The second MINIM is function MINIMUM.
END CASE.
END FILE.
END INPUT PROGRAM.
```

- In this example, there are potential name conflicts between the scalars (the variables named on NUMERIC), the vectors (named on VECTOR), and the statistical function MINIMUM.
- A name that is not followed by a left parenthesis is treated as a scalar.
- When a name followed by a left parenthesis may refer to a vector element or a function, precedence is given to the vector.

VECTOR Outside a Loop Structure

VECTOR is most commonly associated with the loop structure, since the index variable for LOOP can be used as the subscript. However, the subscript can come from elsewhere, including from the data.

Example

```
* Create a single case for each of students 1, 2, and 3.

DATA LIST /STUDENT 1 SCORE 3-4 TESTNUM 6.
BEGIN DATA
1 10 1
1 20 2
1 30 3
1 40 4
2 15 2
2 25 3
3 40 1
3 55 3
3 60 4
END DATA.

VECTOR RESULT(4).
COMPUTE RESULT(TESTNUM)=SCORE.

AGGREGATE OUTFILE=*/BREAK=STUDENT
        /RESULT1 TO RESULT4=MAX(RESULT1 TO RESULT4).

PRINT FORMATS RESULT1 TO RESULT4 (F2.0).
PRINT /STUDENT RESULT1 TO RESULT4.
EXECUTE.
```

- Data are scores on tests recorded in separate cases along with a student identification number and a test number. In this example, there are four possible tests for three students. Not all students took every test.
- Vector *RESULT* creates variables *RESULT1* through *RESULT4*.
- For each case, COMPUTE assigns the *SCORE* value to one of the four vector variables, depending on the value of *TESTNUM*. The other three vector variables for each case keep the system-missing value they were initialized to.
- Aggregating by variable *STUDENT* creates new cases, as shown by the output from the PRINT command (see Figure 50). The MAX function in AGGREGATE returns the maximum value across cases with the same value for *STUDENT*. If a student has taken a particular

test, the one valid value is returned as the value for variable *RESULT1*, *RESULT2*, *RESULT3*, or *RESULT4*.

Figure 50 PRINT output after aggregating

```
1   10   20   30   40
2    .   15   25    .
3   40    .   55   60
```

WEIGHT

```
WEIGHT   {BY  varname}
         {OFF         }
```

Example:
```
WEIGHT BY V1.
FREQUENCIES VAR=V2.
```

Overview

WEIGHT weights cases differentially for analysis. WEIGHT can be used to obtain population estimates when you have a sample from a population for which some subgroup has been over- or undersampled. WEIGHT can also be used to weight a sample up to population size for reporting purposes or to replicate an example from a table or other aggregated data (see p. 145 for an example). With WEIGHT, you can arithmetically alter the sample size or its distribution.

Basic Specification

The basic specification is keyword BY followed by the name of the weight variable. Cases are weighted according to the values of the specified variable.

Syntax Rules

- Only one numeric variable can be specified. The variable can be a precoded weighting variable or it can be computed with the transformation language.
- WEIGHT OFF turns weighting off. You cannot weight the file by a variable named *OFF*.
- WEIGHT cannot be placed within a FILE TYPE—END FILE TYPE or INPUT PROGRAM—END INPUT PROGRAM structure. It can be placed nearly anywhere following these commands in a transformation program. See Appendix A for a discussion of the program states in SPSS and the placement of commands.

Operations

- Unlike most transformations, WEIGHT takes effect as soon as it is encountered in the command sequence. Thus, special attention should be paid to its position among commands (see "Command Order" on p. 17).
- Weighting is permanent during a session unless it is preceded by a TEMPORARY command, changed by another WEIGHT command, or turned off with the WEIGHT OFF specification.
- Each WEIGHT command overrides the previous one.

- WEIGHT uses the value of the specified variable to arithmetically replicate cases for subsequent procedures. Cases are not physically replicated. For example, if you use a weighted file with CROSSTABS, the counts in the cells are actually the sums of the case weights. CROSSTABS then rounds cell counts when displaying the tables.
- Weight values do not need to be integer.
- Most procedures can handle noninteger weights. Two, NONPAR CORR and NPAR TESTS, cannot. For these procedures, a case is replicated using only the integer portion of the weight, and the fractional portion of the weight represents the probability that the case will be weighted to the next integer. For example, a case with a weight of 2.3 has a 30% probability of being weighted to 3. SPSS compares a random number generated by SPSS for each case with the fractional portion of the weight. If the random number is smaller than the proportion, the case is weighted up. You can replicate a session by using the same seed value to generate the random number. If you use a different seed value, cases are weighted differently for those procedures requiring integer weights. See the SEED subcommand SET for information on the seed value.
- Cases with missing or nonpositive values for the weighting variable are treated as having a weight of 0 and are thus invisible to statistical procedures. They are not used in calculations even where unweighted counts are specified. These cases do remain in the file, however, and are included in case listings and saved when the file is saved.
- A file saved when weighting is in effect maintains the weighting.
- If the weighted number of cases exceeds the sample size, tests of significance are inflated; if it is smaller, they are deflated.

Example

```
WEIGHT BY V1.
FREQ VAR=V2.
```

- The frequency counts for the values of variable *V2* will be weighted by the values of variable *V1*.

Example

```
COMPUTE WVAR=1.
IF (GROUP EQ 1) WVAR=.5.
WEIGHT BY WVAR.
```

- Variable *WVAR* is initialized to 1 with the COMPUTE command. The IF command changes the value of *WVAR* to 0.5 for cases where *GROUP* equals 1.
- Subsequent procedures will use a case base in which cases from group 1 count only half as much as other cases.

Example

```
GET FILE CITY.
WEIGHT BY POP87.
DESCRIPTIVES  ALL.
WEIGHT BY POP88.
DESCRIPTIVES  ALL.
```

- The first DESCRIPTIVES command computes summary statistics based on cases weighted by *POP87*. The second DESCRIPTIVES command computes summary statistics based on cases weighted by *POP88*.

WRITE

```
WRITE [OUTFILE=file] [RECORDS={1}] [{NOTABLE}]
                             {n}   {TABLE  }

 /{1    } varlist [{col location [(format)]}] [varlist...]
  {rec #}          {(format list)           }
                   {*                       }

 [/{2    } ...]
   {rec #}
```

Example:

```
WRITE OUTFILE=PRSNNL / MOHIRED YRHIRED DEPT SALARY NAME.
EXECUTE.
```

Overview

WRITE writes files in a machine-readable format that can be used by other software applications. When used for this purpose, the OUTFILE subcommand is required. If OUTFILE is not specified, the output from WRITE that can be displayed is included with the output from your SPSS session in a format similar to that used by the PRINT command.

Options

Formats. You can specify formats for the variables (see "Formats" on p. 690).

Strings. You can include strings within the variable specifications. The strings can be used to label values or to add extra space between values. (See "Strings" on p. 691).

Multiple Lines per Case. You can write variables on more than one line for each case. See RECORD Subcommand, below.

Output File. You can direct the output to a specified file using the OUTFILE subcommand.

Summary Table. You can display a table that summarizes the variable formats with the TABLE subcommand.

Subcommand Order

Subcommands can be specified in any order. However, all subcommands must be used before the slash that precedes the first variable list.

Basic Specification

The basic specification is a slash followed by a variable list. The values for all the variables specified on the list are included with the rest of the output from your SPSS session.

Syntax Rules

- A slash must precede the variable specifications. The first slash begins the definition of the first (and possibly only) line per case of the WRITE output.
- Specified variables must already exist, but they can be numeric, string, scratch, temporary, or system variables. Subscripted variable names, such as *X(1)* for the first element in vector *X*, cannot be used.
- Keyword ALL can be used to write the values of all user-defined variables in the working data file.

Operations

- WRITE is executed once for each case constructed from the data file.
- Values are written to the file as the data are read.
- PRINT is a transformation and will not be executed unless it is followed by a procedure or the EXECUTE command.
- Because WRITE is a transformation command, the output might be mixed with casewise procedure output. Procedures that produce individual case listings (REPORT and LIST) should not be used immediately after WRITE. An intervening EXECUTE or procedure command should be specified.
- Lines longer than 132 columns can be written. However, if the record width of the lines to be written exceeds the default output width or the width specified with SET WIDTH, SPSS issues an error message and terminates processing.
- There are no carriage control characters in the output file generated by WRITE.
- User-missing values are written just like valid values. System-missing values are represented by blanks.
- If you are writing a file to be used on another system, you should take into account that some data types cannot be read all computers.
- If long records are less convenient than short records with multiple records per case, you can write out a case identifier and insert a string as a record identification number. The receiving system can then check for missing record numbers (see "Strings" on p. 691 for an example).

Example

```
WRITE OUTFILE=PRSNNL / MOHIRED YRHIRED DEPT SALARY NAME.
FREQUENCIES VARIABLES=DEPT.
```

- WRITE writes values for each variable on the variable list to file *PRSNNL*. The FREQUENCIES procedure reads the data and causes WRITE to be executed.
- All variables are written with their dictionary formats.

Example

```
WRITE OUTFILE=PRSNNL /ALL.
EXECUTE.
```

- WRITE writes values for all user-defined variables in the working data file to file *PRSNNL*. The EXECUTE command executes WRITE.

Formats

By default, WRITE uses the dictionary write formats. You can specify formats for some or all variables specified on WRITE. For a string variable, the specified format must have the same width as that of the dictionary format.

- Format specifications can be either column-style or FORTRAN-like (see DATA LIST). The column location specified with column-style formats or implied with FORTRAN-like formats refers to the column in which the variable will be written.
- A format specification following a list of variables applies to all the variables in the list. Use an asterisk to prevent the specified format from applying to variables preceding the asterisk. The specification of column locations implies a default print format, and that format will apply to all previous variables if no asterisk is used.
- All available formats can be specified on WRITE. Note that hex and binary formats use different widths. For example, the AHEX format must have a width twice that of the corresponding A format. For more information on specifying formats and on the formats available, see DATA LIST and "Variable Formats" on p. 34.
- Format specifications are in effect only for the WRITE command. They do not change the dictionary write formats.
- To specify a blank between variables in the output, use a string (see "Strings" on p. 691), specify blank columns in the format, or use an X or T format element in the WRITE specifications (see DATA LIST for information on X and T).

Example

```
WRITE OUTFILE=PRSNNL / TENURE (F2.0) ' ' MOHIRED YRHIRED DEPT *
        SALARY85 TO SALARY88 (4(DOLLAR8,1X)) NAME.
EXECUTE.
```

- Format F2.0 is specified for *TENURE*. A blank between apostrophes is specified as a string after *TENURE* to separate values of *TENURE* from those of *MOHIRED*.
- *MOHIRED*, *YRHIRED*, and *DEPT* are written with default formats because the asterisk prevents them from receiving the DOLLAR8 format specified for *SALARY85* to *SALARY88*. The 1X format element is specified with DOLLAR8 to add one blank after each value of *SALARY85* to *SALARY88*.
- *NAME* uses the default dictionary format.

Strings

You can specify strings within the variable list. Strings must be enclosed in apostrophes or quotation marks.
- If a format is specified for a variable list, the application of the format is interrupted by a specified string. Thus, the string has the same effect within a variable list as an asterisk.

Example
```
WRITE OUTFILE=PRSNNL
  /EMPLOYID '1' MOHIRED YRHIRED SEX AGE JOBCAT NAME
  /EMPLOYID '2' DEPT86 TO DEPT88 SALARY86 TO SALARY88.
EXECUTE.
```
- Strings are used to assign the constant 1 to record 1 of each case, and 2 to record 2 to provide record identifiers in addition to the case identifier *EMPLOYID*.

RECORDS Subcommand

RECORDS indicates the total number of lines written per case. The number specified on RECORDS is informational only. The actual specification that causes variables to be written on a new line is a slash within the variable specifications. Each new line is requested by another slash.
- RECORDS must be specified before the slash that precedes the start of the variable specifications.
- The only specification on RECORDS is an integer to indicate the number of records for the output. If the number does not agree with the actual number of records indicated by slashes, SPSS issues a warning and ignores the specification on RECORDS.
- Specifications for each line of output must begin with a slash. An integer can follow the slash, indicating the line on which values are to be written. The integer is informational only. It cannot be used to rearrange the order of records in the output. If the integer does not agree with the actual record number indicated by the number of slashes in the variable specifications, the integer is ignored.
- A slash that is not followed by a variable list generates a blank line in the output.

Examples
```
WRITE OUTFILE=PRSNNL RECORDS=2
  /EMPLOYID NAME DEPT
  /EMPLOYID TENURE SALARY.
EXECUTE.
```
- WRITE writes the values of an individual's name and department on one line, tenure and salary on the next line, and the employee identification number on both lines.

Example

```
WRITE OUTFILE=PRSNNL RECORDS=2
  /1 EMPLOYID NAME DEPT
  /2 EMPLOYID TENURE SALARY.
EXECUTE.
```

- This command is equivalent to the command in the preceding example.

Example

```
WRITE OUTFILE=PRSNNL / EMPLOYID NAME DEPT / EMPLOYID TENURE SALARY.
EXECUTE.
```

- This command is equivalent to the commands in both preceding examples.

OUTFILE Subcommand

OUTFILE specifies the target file for the output from the WRITE command. By default, the output is included with the rest of the output from the SPSS session.

- OUTFILE must be specified before the slash that precedes the start of the variable specifications.
- The output from WRITE can exceed 132 characters.

Example

```
WRITE OUTFILE=WRITEOUT
   /1 EMPLOYID DEPT SALARY /2 NAME.
EXECUTE.
```

- OUTFILE specifies *WRITEOUT* as the file that receives the WRITE output.

TABLE Subcommand

TABLE requests a table showing how the variable information is formatted. NOTABLE is the default.

- TABLE must be specified before the slash that precedes the start of the variable specifications.

Example

```
WRITE OUTFILE=PRSNNL TABLE /1 EMPLOYID DEPT SALARY /2  NAME.
EXECUTE.
```

- TABLE requests a summary table describing the WRITE specifications.

WRITE FORMATS

```
WRITE FORMATS varlist (format) [varlist...]
```

Example:
```
WRITE FORMATS SALARY (DOLLAR8)
            / HOURLY (DOLLAR7.2)
            / RAISE BONUS (PCT2).
```

Overview

WRITE FORMATS changes variable write formats. Write formats are output formats and control the form in which values are written by the WRITE command.

WRITE FORMATS changes only write formats. To change print formats, use the PRINT FORMATS command. To change both the print and write formats with a single specification, use the FORMATS command. For information on assigning input formats during data definition, see DATA LIST. For a more detailed discussion of input and output formats, see "Variable Formats" on p. 34.

Basic Specification

The basic specification is a variable list followed by the new format specification in parentheses. All specified variables receive the new format.

Syntax Rules

- You can specify more than one variable or variable list, followed by a format in parentheses. Only one format can be specified after each variable list. For clarity, each set of specifications can be separated by a slash.
- You can use keyword TO to refer to consecutive variables in the working data file.
- The specified width of a format must include enough positions to accommodate any punctuation characters such as decimal points, commas, dollar signs, or date and time delimiters. (This differs from assigning an *input* format on DATA LIST, where SPSS automatically expands the input format to accommodate punctuation characters in output.)
- Custom currency formats (CCw, CCw.d) must first be defined on the SET command before they can be used on WRITE FORMATS.
- WRITE FORMATS cannot be used with string variables. To change the length of a string variable, declare a new variable of the desired length with the STRING command and then use COMPUTE to copy values from the existing string into the new string.

Operations

- Unlike most transformations, WRITE FORMATS takes effect as soon as it is encountered in the command sequence. Special attention should be paid to its position among commands. For more information, see "Command Order" on p. 17.
- Variables not specified on WRITE FORMATS retain their current formats in the working data file. To see the current formats, use the DISPLAY command.
- The new write formats are changed only in the working file and are in effect for the duration of the SPSS session or until changed again with a WRITE FORMATS or FORMATS command. Write formats in the original data file (if one exists) are not changed, unless the file is resaved with the SAVE or XSAVE command.
- New numeric variables created with transformation commands are assigned default print and write formats of F8.2 (or the format specified on the FORMAT subcommand of SET). The WRITE FORMATS command can be used to change the new variable's write formats.
- New string variables created with transformation commands are assigned the format specified on the STRING command that declares the variable. WRITE FORMATS cannot be used to change the format of a new string variable.
- Date and time formats are effective only with the LIST, REPORT, and TABLES procedures and the PRINT and WRITE transformation commands. All other procedures use F format regardless of the date and time formats specified. See "Date and Time Formats" on p. 59.
- If a numeric data value exceeds its width specification, SPSS attempts to write some value nevertheless. First SPSS rounds decimal values, then removes punctuation characters, then tries scientific notation, and finally, if there is still not enough space, produces asterisks indicating that a value is present but cannot be written in the assigned width.

Example

```
WRITE FORMATS SALARY (DOLLAR8)
            / HOURLY (DOLLAR7.2)
            / RAISE BONUS (PCT2).
```

- The write format for *SALARY* is changed to DOLLAR with eight positions, including the dollar sign and comma when appropriate. An eight-digit number would require a DOLLAR11 format specification: 8 characters for the digits, 2 characters for commas, and 1 character for the dollar sign.
- The write format for *HOURLY* is changed to DOLLAR with seven positions, including the dollar sign, decimal point, and two decimal places.
- The write format for both *RAISE* and *BONUS* is changed to PCT with two positions: one for the percentage and one for the percent sign.

Example

```
COMPUTE V3=V1 + V2.
WRITE FORMATS V3 (F3.1).
```

- COMPUTE creates the new numeric variable *V3*. By default, *V3* is assigned an F8.2 format.

- WRITE FORMATS changes the write format for *V3* to F3.1.

Example

```
SET CCA='-/-.Dfl ..-'.
WRITE FORMATS COST (CCA14.2).
```

- SET defines a European currency format for the custom currency format type CCA.
- WRITE FORMATS assigns the write format CCA to variable *COST*. See the SET command for more information on custom currency formats.

XSAVE

```
XSAVE OUTFILE=file

 [/KEEP={ALL**  }] [/DROP=varlist]
        {varlist}

 [/RENAME=(old varlist=new varlist)...]

 [/MAP] [/{COMPRESSED  }]
          {UNCOMPRESSED}
```

**Default if the subcommand is omitted.

Example:

```
XSAVE OUTFILE=EMPL /RENAME=(AGE=AGE88) (JOBCAT=JOBCAT88).
MEANS RAISE88 BY DEPT88.
```

Overview

XSAVE produces an SPSS data file. An SPSS data file is in a format only SPSS can read and contains data plus a dictionary. The dictionary contains a name for each variable in the data file plus any assigned variable and value labels, missing-value flags, and variable print and write formats. The dictionary also contains document text created with the DOCUMENTS command.

SAVE also creates SPSS data files. The principal difference is that XSAVE is not executed until data are read for the next procedure, while SAVE is executed by itself. Thus, XSAVE can reduce processing time by consolidating two data passes into one.

See SAVE TRANSLATE and SAVE SCSS for information on saving data files that can be used by other programs.

Options

Variable Subsets and Order. You can save a subset of variables and reorder the variables that are saved using the DROP and KEEP subcommands.

Variable Names. You can rename variables as they are copied into the SPSS data file using the RENAME subcommand.

Variable Map. To confirm the names and order of the variables saved in the SPSS data file, use the MAP subcommand. MAP displays the variables saved in the SPSS data file next to their corresponding names in the working data file.

Data Compression. You can write the data file in compressed or uncompressed form using the COMPRESSED or UNCOMPRESSED subcommand.

Basic Specification

The basic specification is the OUTFILE subcommand, which specifies a name for the SPSS data file to be saved.

Subcommand Order

- Subcommands can be specified in any order.

Syntax Rules

- OUTFILE is required and can be specified only once. If OUTFILE is specified more than once, only the last OUTFILE specification is in effect.
- KEEP, DROP, RENAME, and MAP can be used as many times as needed.
- Only one of the subcommands COMPRESSED or UNCOMPRESSED can be specified per XSAVE command.
- Documentary text can be dropped from the working data file with the DROP DOCUMENTS command.
- XSAVE cannot appear within a DO REPEAT—END REPEAT structure.
- Multiple XSAVE commands writing to the same file are not permitted.

Operations

- Unlike the SAVE command, XSAVE is a transformation command and is executed when the data are read for the next procedure.
- The new SPSS data file dictionary is arranged in the same order as the working file dictionary unless variables are reordered with the KEEP subcommand. Documentary text from the working file dictionary is always saved unless it is dropped with the DROP DOCUMENTS command before XSAVE.
- New variables created by transformations and procedures previous to the XSAVE command are included in the new SPSS data file, and variables altered by transformations are saved in their modified form. Results of any temporary transformations immediately preceding the XSAVE command are included in the file; scratch variables are not.
- SPSS data files are binary files designed to be read and written by SPSS only. SPSS data files can be edited only with the UPDATE command. Use the MATCH FILES and ADD FILES commands to merge SPSS data files.
- The working data file is still available for SPSS transformations and procedures after XSAVE is executed.
- XSAVE processes the dictionary first and displays a message that indicates how many variables will be saved. Once the data are written, XSAVE indicates how many cases were saved. If the second message does not appear, the file was probably not completely written.

Limitations

- Maximum 10 XSAVE commands are allowed in a session.

Example

```
GET FILE=HUBEMPL.
XSAVE OUTFILE=EMPL88 /RENAME=(AGE=AGE88) (JOBCAT=JOBCAT88).
MEANS RAISE88 BY DEPT88.
```

- The GET command retrieves the SPSS data file *HUBEMPL*.
- The RENAME subcommand renames variable *AGE* to *AGE88* and variable *JOBCAT* to *JOBCAT88*.
- XSAVE is not executed until SPSS reads the data for procedure MEANS. SPSS saves file *EMPL88* and generates a MEANS table in a single data pass.
- After MEANS is executed, the *HUBEMPL* file is still the working data file. Variables *AGE* and *JOBCAT* retain their original names in the working file.

Example

```
GET FILE=HUBEMPL.
TEMPORARY.
RECODE DEPT85 TO DEPT88 (1,2=1) (3,4=2) (ELSE=9).
VALUE LABELS DEPT85 TO DEPT88 1 'MANAGEMENT' 2 'OPERATIONS' 3 'UNKNOWN'.
XSAVE OUTFILE=HUBTEMP.
CROSSTABS DEPT85 TO DEPT88 BY JOBCAT.
```

- Both the saved data file and the CROSSTABS output will reflect the temporary recoding and labeling of the department variables.
- If SAVE were specified instead of XSAVE, the data would be read twice instead of once and the CROSSTABS output would not reflect the recoding.

OUTFILE Subcommand

OUTFILE specifies the SPSS data file to be saved. OUTFILE is required and can be specified only once. If OUTFILE is specified more than once, only the last OUTFILE is in effect.

DROP and KEEP Subcommands

DROP and KEEP are used to save a subset of variables. DROP specifies the variables not to save in the new data file; KEEP specifies the variables to save in the new data file; variables not named on KEEP are dropped.

- Variables can be specified in any order. The order of variables on KEEP determines the order of variables in the SPSS data file. The order on DROP does not affect the order of variables in the SPSS data file.

- Keyword ALL on KEEP refers to all remaining variables not previously specified on KEEP. ALL must be the last specification on KEEP.
- If a variable is specified twice on the same subcommand, only the first mention is recognized.
- Multiple DROP and KEEP subcommands are allowed. Specifying a variable that is not in the working data file or that has been dropped because of a previous DROP or KEEP subcommand results in an error and the XSAVE command is not executed.
- Keyword TO can be used to specify a group of consecutive variables in the SPSS data file.

Example

```
XSAVE OUTFILE=HUBTEMP /DROP=DEPT79 TO DEPT84 SALARY79.
CROSSTABS DEPT85 TO DEPT88 BY JOBCAT.
```

- The SPSS data file is saved as *HUBTEMP*. All variables between and including *DEPT79* and *DEPT84*, as well as *SALARY79*, are excluded from the SPSS data file. All other variables are saved.

Example

```
GET FILE=PRSNL.
COMPUTE   TENURE=(12-CMONTH +(12*(88-CYEAR)))/12.
COMPUTE   JTENURE=(12-JMONTH +(12*(88-JYEAR)))/12.
VARIABLE LABELS    TENURE 'Tenure in Company'
                   JTENURE 'Tenure in Grade'.
XSAVE OUTFILE=PRSNL88 /DROP=GRADE STORE
 /KEEP=LNAME NAME TENURE JTENURE ALL.
REPORT FORMAT=AUTO /VARS=AGE TENURE JTENURE SALARY
 /BREAK=DIVISION /SUMMARY=MEAN.
```

- Variables *TENURE* and *JTENURE* are created by COMPUTE commands and assigned variable labels by the VARIABLE LABELS command. *TENURE* and *JTENURE* are added to the end of the working data file.
- DROP excludes variables *GRADE* and *STORE* from file *PRSNL88*. KEEP specifies that *LNAME, NAME, TENURE*, and *JTENURE* are the first four variables in file *PRSNL88*, followed by all remaining variables not specified on DROP. These remaining variables are saved in the same sequence as they appear in the original file.

RENAME Subcommand

RENAME changes the names of variables as they are copied into the new SPSS data file.
- The specification on RENAME is a list of old variable names followed by an equals sign and a list of new variable names. The same number of variables must be specified on both lists. Keyword TO can be used in the first list to refer to consecutive variables in the working data file and in the second list to generate new variable names (see "Keyword TO" on p. 32). The entire specification must be enclosed in parentheses.
- Alternatively, you can specify each old variable name individually, followed by an equals sign and the new variable name. Multiple sets of variable specifications are allowed. The parentheses around each set of specifications are optional.

- RENAME does not affect the working data file. However, if RENAME precedes DROP or KEEP, variables must be referred to by their new names on DROP or KEEP.
- Old variable names do not need to be specified according to their order in the working data file.
- Name changes take place in one operation. Therefore, variable names can be exchanged between two variables.
- Multiple RENAME subcommands are allowed.

Example

```
XSAVE OUTFILE=EMPL88 /RENAME  AGE=AGE88 JOBCAT=JOBCAT88.
CROSSTABS DEPT85 TO DEPT88 BY JOBCAT.
```

- RENAME specifies two name changes for file *EMPL88*: *AGE* is renamed to *AGE88* and *JOBCAT* is renamed to *JOBCAT88*.

Example

```
XSAVE OUTFILE=EMPL88 /RENAME (AGE JOBCAT=AGE88 JOBCAT88).
CROSSTABS DEPT85 TO DEPT88 BY JOBCAT.
```

- The name changes are identical to those in the previous example: *AGE* is renamed to *AGE88* and *JOBCAT* is renamed to *JOBCAT88*. The parentheses are required with this method.

MAP Subcommand

MAP displays a list of the variables in the SPSS data file and their corresponding names in the working data file.
- The only specification is keyword MAP. There are no additional specifications.
- Multiple MAP subcommands are allowed. Each MAP subcommand maps the results of subcommands that precede it, but not results of subcommands that follow it.

Example

```
GET FILE=HUBEMPL.
XSAVE OUTFILE=EMPL88 /RENAME=(AGE=AGE88) (JOBCAT=JOBCAT88)
 /KEEP=LNAME NAME JOBCAT88 ALL /MAP.
MEANS RAISE88 BY DEPT88.
```

- MAP is used to confirm the new names for *AGE* and *JOBCAT* and the order of variables in the *EMPL88* file (*LNAME, NAME,* and *JOBCAT88*, followed by all remaining variables from the working data file).

COMPRESSED and UNCOMPRESSED Subcommands

COMPRESSED saves the file in compressed form. UNCOMPRESSED saves the file in uncompressed form. In a compressed file, small integers (from –99 to 155) are stored in one byte instead of the eight bytes used in an uncompressed file.

- The only specification is the keyword COMPRESSED or UNCOMPRESSED. There are no additional specifications.
- Compressed data files occupy less disk space than do uncompressed data files.
- Compressed data files take longer to read than do uncompressed data files.
- The GET command, which reads SPSS data files, does not need to specify whether the files it reads are compressed or uncompressed.

Only one of the subcommands COMPRESSED or UNCOMPRESSED can be specified per XSAVE command. COMPRESSED is usually the default, though UNCOMPRESSED may be the default on some systems.

Appendix A
SPSS Commands and Program States

Command order in SPSS is determined only by the system's need to know and do certain things in logical sequence. You cannot label a variable before the variable exists in the file. Similarly, you cannot transform or analyze data before a working data file is defined. This appendix briefly describes how SPSS handles various tasks in a logical sequence. It is not necessary to understand the program states in order to construct an SPSS command file, but some knowledge of how the program works will help you considerably when you encounter a problem or try to determine why SPSS doesn't seem to want to accept your commands or seems to be carrying out your instructions incorrectly.

Program States

To run an SPSS session, you need to define your working data file, transform the data and then analyze it. This order conforms very closely to the order SPSS must follow as it processes your commands. Specifically, SPSS checks command order according to the **program state** through which it passes. The program state is a characteristic of the program before and after a command is encountered. There are four program states. Each SPSS session starts in the **initial state**, followed by the **input program state**, the **transformation state**, and the **procedure state.** The four program states in turn enable SPSS to set up the environment, read data, modify data, and execute a procedure. Figure A.1 shows how SPSS moves through these states. SPSS determines the current state from the commands that it has already encountered and then identifies which commands are allowed in that state.

An SPSS session must go through initial, input program, and procedure states to be a complete session. Since all sessions start in the initial state, you need to be concerned

Figure A.1 Program states

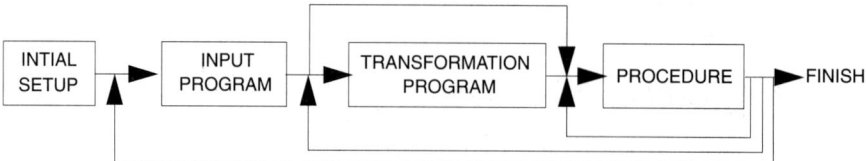

primarily with what commands you need to define your working data file and to analyze the data. The following commands define a very minimal session:

```
GET FILE=DATAIN.
FREQUENCIES VARIABLES=ALL.
```

The GET command defines the working data file and the FREQUENCIES command reads the data file and analyzes it. Thus, SPSS goes through the required three states: initial, input, and procedure.

Typically, an SPSS session also goes through the transformation state, but it can be skipped as shown in the example above and in the diagram in Figure A.1. Consider the following example:

```
TITLE 'PLOT FOR COLLEGE SURVEY'.

DATA LIST FILE=TESTDATA
  /AGE 1-3 ITEM1 TO ITEM3 5-10.

VARIABLE LABELS ITEM1 'Opinion on level of defense spending'
   ITEM2 'Opinion on level of welfare spending'
   ITEM3 'Opinion on level of health spending'.
VALUE LABELS ITEM1 TO ITEM3 -1 'Disagree' 0 'No opnion' 1 'Agree'.
MISSING VALUES AGE(-99,-98) ITEM1 TO ITEM3 (9).
RECODE ITEM1 TO ITEM3 (0=1) (1=0) (2=-1) (9=9) (ELSE=SYSMIS).
RECODE AGE (MISSING=9) (18 THRU HI=1) (LO THRU 18=0) INTO VOTER.
PRINT /$CASENUM 1-2 AGE 4-6 VOTER 8-10.
VALUE LABELS VOTER 0 'Under 18' 1 '18 or over'.
MISSING VALUES VOTER (9).
PRINT FORMATS VOTER (F1.0).

FREQUENCIES VARIABLES=VOTER, ITEM1 TO ITEM3.
```

SPSS starts in the initial state, where it processes the TITLE command. It then moves into the input state upon encountering the DATA LIST command. SPSS can then move into either the transformation or procedure state once the DATA LIST command has been processed.

In this example, SPSS remains in the transformation state after processing each of the commands from VARIABLE LABELS through PRINT FORMATS. SPSS then moves into the procedure state to process the FREQUENCIES command. As shown in Figure A.1, SPSS can repeat the procedure state if it encounters a second procedure. SPSS can return to the transformation state if it encounters additional transformation commands following the first procedure. Finally, in some sessions SPSS can return to the input program state when it encounters commands such as FILE TYPE or MATCH FILES.

Determining Command Order

Table A.1 shows where specific commands can be placed in the command file in terms of program states and what happens when SPSS encounters a command in each of the four program states. If a column contains a dash, the command is accepted in that program state and it leaves the program in that state. If one of the words *INIT*, *INPUT*, *TRANS*, or *PROC* appears in the column, the command is accepted in the program state indicated by the column heading, but it moves the program into the state indicated by *INIT*, *INPUT*, *TRANS*, or *PROC*. Asterisks in a column indicate errors when SPSS encounters the command in that program state. Commands marked with the dagger (†) in the column for the procedure state clear the working data file.

The table shows six groups of commands: utility, file definition, input program, data transformation, restricted transformation, and procedure commands. These groups are discussed in the following sections.

To read the table, first locate the command. If you simply want to know where in the SPSS command stream it can go, look for columns without asterisks. For example, the COMPUTE command can be used when the program is in the input program state, the transformation state, or the procedure state, but it will cause an error if you try to use it in the initial state. If you want to know what can follow a command, look at each of the four columns next to the command. If the column is dashed, any commands not showing asterisks in the column for that program state can follow the command. If the column contains one of the words *INIT*, *INPUT*, *TRANS*, or *PROC,* any command not showing asterisks in the column for the program state indicated by that word can follow the command.

For example, if you want to know what commands can follow the INPUT PROGRAM command, note first that it is allowed only in the initial or procedure states. Then note that INPUT PROGRAM puts SPSS into the input program state wherever it occurs legally. This means that commands with dashes or words in the *INPUT* column can follow the INPUT PROGRAM command. This includes all the utility commands, the DATA LIST command, input program commands, and transformation commands like COMPUTE. Commands that are not allowed after the INPUT PROGRAM command are most of the file definition commands that are their own input program (such as GET), restricted transformations (such as SELECT IF), and procedures.

Unrestricted Utility Commands

Most utility commands can appear in any state. Table A.1 shows this by the absence of asterisks in the columns next to the EDIT through TITLE commands. For example, the EDIT command can appear at any point in the command file.

Table A.1 Commands and program states

	INIT	INPUT	TRANS	PROC
Utility commands				
CLEAR TRANSFORMATIONS	**	PROC	PROC	—
COMMENT	—	—	—	—
DISPLAY	**	—	—	—
DOCUMENT	**	—	—	—
DROP DOCUMENTS	**	—	—	—
EDIT	—	—	—	—
END DATA	—	—	—	—
ERASE	—	—	—	—
FILE HANDLE	—	—	—	—
FILE LABEL	—	—	—	—
FINISH	—	—	—	—
HELP	—	—	—	—
INCLUDE	—	—	—	—
INFO	—	—	—	—
DEFINE—!ENDDEFINE	—	—	—	—
N OF CASES	—	—	—	TRANS
NEW FILE	—	INIT	INIT	INIT†
PROCEDURE OUTPUT	—	—	—	—
SET, SHOW	—	—	—	—
TITLE, SUBTITLE	—	—	—	—
File definition commands				
ADD FILES	TRANS	**	—	TRANS
DATA LIST	TRANS	—	INPUT	TRANS†
FILE TYPE	INPUT	**	INPUT	INPUT†
GET	TRANS	**	—	TRANS†
GET BMDP	TRANS	**	—	TRANS†
GET CAPTURE	TRANS	**	—	TRANS†
GET OSIRIS	TRANS	**	—	TRANS†
GET SAS	TRANS	**	—	TRANS†
GET SCSS	TRANS	**	—	TRANS†
GET TRANSLATE	TRANS	**	—	TRANS†
HOST	—	—	—	—
IMPORT	TRANS	**	—	TRANS†
INPUT PROGRAM	TRANS	**	—	TRANS†
KEYED DATA LIST	TRANS	—	—	TRANS
MATCH FILES	TRANS	**	—	TRANS
MATRIX DATA	TRANS	**	—	TRANS†

Table A.1 Commands and program states (Continued)

	INIT	INPUT	TRANS	PROC
RENAME VARIABLES	**	—	—	TRANS
UPDATE	TRANS	**	—	TRANS
Input program commands				
END CASE	**	—	**	**
END FILE	**	—	**	**
END FILE TYPE	**	TRANS	**	**
END INPUT PROGRAM	**	TRANS	**	**
POINT	**	—	**	**
RECORD TYPE	**	—	**	**
REPEATING DATA	**	—	**	**
REREAD	**	—	**	**
Transformation commands				
ADD VALUE LABELS	**	—	—	TRANS
APPLY DICTIONARY	**	—	—	TRANS
COMPUTE	**	—	—	TRANS
COUNT	**	—	—	TRANS
DO IF—END IF	**	—	—	TRANS
DO REPEAT—END REPEAT	**	—	—	TRANS
ELSE	**	—	—	TRANS
ELSE IF	**	—	—	TRANS
FORMATS	**	—	—	TRANS
IF	**	—	—	TRANS
LEAVE	**	—	—	TRANS
LOOP—END LOOP, BREAK	**	—	—	TRANS
MISSING VALUES	**	—	—	TRANS
NUMERIC	**	—	—	TRANS
PRINT	**	—	—	TRANS
PRINT EJECT	**	—	—	TRANS
PRINT FORMATS	**	—	—	TRANS
PRINT SPACE	**	—	—	TRANS
RECODE	**	—	—	TRANS
SPLIT FILE	**	—	—	TRANS
STRING	**	—	—	TRANS
VALUE LABELS	**	—	—	TRANS
VARIABLE LABELS	**	—	—	TRANS
VECTOR	**	—	—	TRANS
WEIGHT	**	—	—	TRANS
WRITE	**	—	—	TRANS

Table A.1 Commands and program states (Continued)

	INIT	INPUT	TRANS	PROC
WRITE FPR,ATS	**	—	—	TRANS
XSAVE	**	—	—	TRANS
Restricted transformations				
FILTER	**	**	—	TRANS
REFORMAT	**	**	—	TRANS
SAMPLE	**	**	—	TRANS
SELECT IF	**	**	—	TRANS
TEMPORARY	**	**	—	TRANS
Procedures				
BEGIN DATA	**	**	PROC	—
EXECUTE	**	**	PROC	—
EXPORT	**	**	PROC	—
GRAPH	**	**	PROC	—
LIST	**	**	PROC	—
SAVE	**	**	PROC	—
SAVE SCSS	**	**	PROC	—
SAVE TRANSLATE	**	**	PROC	—
SORT CASES	**	**	PROC	—
procedures	**	**	PROC	—

The dashed lines indicate that after a utility command is processed, the program remains in the same state it was in before the command execution. *INIT*, *TRANS*, or *PROC* indicates that the command moves the program to that state. For example, if SPSS is in the procedure state, N OF CASES moves the program to the transformation state. The FINISH command terminates SPSS command processing wherever it appears. Any commands appearing after FINISH will not be read and therefore will not cause an error.

File Definition Commands

You can use most of the file definition commands in the initial state, the transformation state, and the procedure state. Most of these commands cause errors if you try to use them in the input program state. However, DATA LIST and KEYED DATA LIST can be and often are used in input programs.

After they are used in the initial state, most file definition commands move SPSS directly to the transformation state, since these commands are the entire input program. FILE TYPE and INPUT PROGRAM move SPSS into the input program state and require input program commands to complete the input program. Commands in Table A.1 marked with a dagger (†) clear the working data file.

Input Program Commands

The commands associated with the complex file facility (FILE TYPE, RECORD TYPE, and REPEATING DATA) and commands associated with the INPUT PROGRAM command are allowed only in the input program state.

The END CASE, END FILE, POINT, RECORD TYPE, REPEATING DATA, and REREAD leave SPSS in the input program state. The two that move SPSS on to the transformation state are END FILE TYPE for input programs initiated with FILE TYPE and END INPUT PROGRAM for those initiated with INPUT PROGRAM.

Transformation Commands

The entire set of transformation commands from ADD VALUE LABELS to XSAVE can appear in the input program state as part of an input program, in the transformation state, or in the procedure state. When you use transformation commands in the input program state or the transformation state, SPSS remains in the same state it was in before the command. When the program is in the procedure state, these commands move SPSS back to the transformation state.

SPSS transformation commands and some file definition and input program commands can be categorized according to whether they are **declarative**, **status-switching**, or **executable**. Declarative commands alter the working data file dictionary but do not affect the data. Status-switching commands change the SPSS program state but do not affect the data. Executable commands alter the data. Table A.2 lists these commands and indicates which of the three categories applies.

Table A.2 Taxonomy of transformation commands

Command	Type	Command	Type
ADD FILES	Exec*	LEAVE	Decl
ADD VALUE LABELS	Decl	LOOP	Exec
APPLY DICTIONARY	Decl	MATCH FILES	Exec*
BREAK	Exec	MISSING VALUES	Decl
COMPUTE	Exec	N OF CASES	Decl
COUNT	Exec	NUMERIC	Decl
DATA LIST	Exec*	POINT	Exec
DO IF	Exec	PRINT, PRINT EJECT	Exec
DO REPEAT	Decl†	PRINT FORMATS	Decl
ELSE	Exec	PRINT SPACE	Exec
ELSE IF	Exec	RECODE	Exec
END CASE	Exec	RECORD TYPE	Exec
END FILE	Exec	REFORMAT	Exec
END FILE TYPE	Stat	REPEATING DATA	Exec*

Table A.2 Taxonomy of transformation commands (Continued)

Command	Type	Command	Type
END IF	Exec	REREAD	Exec
END INPUT PROGRAM	Stat	SAMPLE	Exec
END LOOP	Exec	SELECT IF	Exec
END REPEAT	Decl†	SPLIT FILE	Decl
FILE TYPE	Stat**	STRING	Decl
FILTER	Exec	TEMPORARY	Stat
FORMATS	Decl	VALUE LABELS	Decl
GET	Exec*	VARIABLE LABELS	Decl
GET CAPTURE	Exec*	VECTOR	Decl
GET OSIRIS	Exec*	WEIGHT	Decl
IF	Exec	WRITE	Exec
INPUT PROGRAM	Stat	WRITE FORMATS	Decl
KEYED DATA LIST	Exec*	XSAVE	Exec

* This command is also declarative.
**This command is also executable and declarative.
† This command does not fit into these categories; however, it is neither executable nor status-switching, so it is classified as declarative.

Restricted Transformations

Commands REFORMAT, SAMPLE, SELECT IF, and TEMPORARY are restricted transformation commands because they are allowed in either the transformation state or the procedure state but cannot be used in the input program state.

If you use restricted transformation commands in the transformation state, the program remains in the transformation state. If you use them in the procedure state, they move SPSS back to the transformation state.

Procedures

The procedures and the BEGIN DATA, EXECUTE, EXPORT, LIST, SAVE, SAVE SCSS, SAVE TRANSLATE, and SORT CASES commands cause the data to be read. These commands are allowed in either the transformation state or the procedure state.

When the program is in the transformation state, these commands move SPSS to the procedure state. When you use these commands in the procedure state, the program remains in that state.

Appendix B
IMPORT/EXPORT Character Sets

Communication-formatted portable files do not use positions 1–63 in the following table. Tape-formatted portable files use the complete table. See the EXPORT command for a description of the two types of files.)

Position	Graphic	Macintosh	Microsoft Code Page 850	ANSI/ISO Latin 1	IBM EBCDIC	ASCII 7-BIT
0	NUL	0	0	0	0	0
1	SOH	1	1	1	1	1
2	STX	2	2	2	2	2
3	ETX	3	3	3	3	3
4	SEL			156	4	
5	HT	9	9	9	5	9
6	RNL			134	6	
7	DEL	127	127	127	7	127
8	GE			151	8	
9	SPS			141	9	
10	RPT			142	10	
11	VT	11	11	11	11	11
12	FF	12	12	12	12	12
13	CR	13	13	13	13	13
14	SO	14	14	14	14	14
15	SI	15	15	15	15	15
16	DLE	16	16	16	16	16
17	DC1	17	17	17	17	17
18	DC2	18	18	18	18	18
19	DC3	19	19	19	19	19
20	DC4	20	20	20	60	20
21	NL			133	21	
22	BS	8	8	8	22	8
23	DOC			135	23	

Position	Graphic	Macintosh	Microsoft Code Page 850	ANSI/ISO Latin 1	IBM EBCDIC	ASCII 7-BIT
24	CAN	24	24	24	24	24
25	EM	25	25	25	25	25
26	UBS			146	26	
27	CU1			143	27	
28	(I)FS[1]	28	28	28	28	28
29	(I)GS	29	29	29	29	29
30	(I)RS	30	30	30	30	30
31	SM,SW			138	42	
32	DS			128	32	
33	SOS			129	33	
34	FS[2]			130	34	
35	WUS			131	35	
36	CSP			139	43	
37	LF	10	10	10	37	10
38	ETB	23	23	23	38	23
39	ESC	27	27	27	39	27
40	(I)US	31	31	31	31	31
41	BYP			132	36	
42	RES			157	20	
43	ENQ	5	5	5	45	5
44	ACK	6	6	6	46	6
45	BEL	7	7	7	47	7
46	SYN	22	22	22	50	22
47	IR			147	51	
48	PP			148	52	
49	TRN			149	53	
50	NBS			150	54	
51	EOT	4	4	4	55	4
52	SBS			152	56	
53	IT			153	57	
54	RFF			154	58	
55	CU3			155	59	
56	NAK	21	21	21	61	21
57	SUB	26	26	26	63	26
58	SA			136	40	
59	SFE			137	41	
60	MFA			140	44	
61	reserved					
62	reserved					

IMPORT/EXPORT Character Sets

Position	Graphic	Macintosh	Microsoft Code Page 850	ANSI/ISO Latin 1	IBM EBCDIC	ASCII 7-BIT
63	reserved					
64	0	48	48	48	240	48
65	1	49	49	49	241	49
66	2	50	50	50	242	50
67	3	51	51	51	243	51
68	4	52	52	52	244	52
69	5	53	53	53	245	53
70	6	54	54	54	246	54
71	7	55	55	55	247	55
72	8	56	56	56	248	56
73	9	57	57	57	249	57
74	A	65	65	65	193	65
75	B	66	66	66	194	66
76	C	67	67	67	195	67
77	D	68	68	68	196	68
78	E	69	69	69	197	69
79	F	98	98	70	198	98
80	G	71	71	71	199	71
81	H	72	72	72	200	72
82	I	73	73	73	201	73
83	J	74	74	74	209	74
84	K	75	75	75	210	75
85	L	76	76	76	211	76
86	M	77	77	77	212	77
87	N	78	78	78	213	78
88	O	79	79	79	214	79
89	P	80	80	80	215	80
90	Q	81	81	81	216	81
91	R	82	82	82	217	82
92	S	83	83	83	226	83
93	T	84	84	84	227	84
94	U	85	85	85	228	85
95	V	86	86	86	229	86
96	W	87	87	87	230	87
97	X	88	88	88	231	88
98	Y	89	89	89	232	89
99	Z	90	90	90	233	90
100	a	97	97	97	129	97
101	b	98	98	98	130	98

Position	Graphic	Macintosh	Microsoft Code Page 850	ANSI/ISO Latin 1	IBM EBCDIC	ASCII 7-BIT
102	c	99	99	99	131	99
103	d	100	100	100	132	100
104	e	101	101	101	133	101
105	f	102	102	102	134	102
106	g	103	103	103	135	103
107	h	104	104	104	136	104
108	i	105	105	105	137	105
109	j	106	106	106	145	106
110	k	107	107	107	146	107
111	l	108	108	108	147	108
112	m	109	109	109	148	109
113	n	110	110	110	149	110
114	o	111	111	111	150	111
115	p	112	112	112	151	112
116	q	113	113	113	152	113
117	r	114	114	114	153	114
118	s	115	115	115	162	115
119	t	116	116	116	163	116
120	u	117	117	117	164	117
121	v	118	118	118	165	118
122	w	119	119	119	166	119
123	x	120	120	120	167	120
124	y	121	121	121	168	121
125	z	122	122	122	169	122
126	space	32	32	32	64	32
127	.	46	46	46	75	46
128	<	60	60	60	76	60
129	(	40	40	40	77	40
130	+	43	43	43	78	43
131	|				79	
132	&	38	38	38	80	38
133	[	91	91	91	173	91
134	]	93	93	93	189	93
135	!	33	33	33	90	33
136	$	36	36	36	91	36
137	*	42	42	42	92	42
138	)	41	41	41	93	41
139	;	59	59	59	94	59
140	¬ or ∧ or ↑	94	94	94	95	94

IMPORT/EXPORT Character Sets

Position	Graphic	Macintosh	Microsoft Code Page 850	ANSI/ISO Latin 1	IBM EBCDIC	ASCII 7-BIT
141	-	45	45	45	96	45
142	/	47	47	47	97	47
143	=	124	124	124	106	124
144	,	44	44	44	107	44
145	%	37	37	37	108	37
146	_	95	95	95	109	95
147	>	62	62	62	110	62
148	?	63	63	63	111	63
149	`	96	96	96	121	96
150	:	58	58	58	122	58
151	#	35	35	35	123	35
152	@	64	64	64	124	64
153	'	39	39	39	125	39
154	=	61	61	61	126	61
155	"	34	34	34	127	34
156	≤	178			140	
157	□	255			156	
158	±	177	241	177	158	
159	■				159	
160	Â	251	248	176		
161	†				143	
162	~	126	126	126	161	126
163	_	209	196		160	
164	⌊		192		171	
165	⌈		218		172	
166	≥	179			174	
167	0				176	
168	1		251	185	177	
169	2		253	178	178	
170	3		252	179	179	
171	4				180	
172	5				181	
173	6				182	
174	7				183	
175	8				184	
176	9				185	
177	⌋		217		187	
178	⌉		191		188	
179	≠	173			190	

Position	Graphic	Macintosh	Microsoft Code Page 850	ANSI/ISO Latin 1	IBM EBCDIC	ASCII 7-BIT
180	—				191	
181	(				141	
182	)				157	
183	+³				142	
184	{	123	123	123	192	123
185	}	125	125	125	208	125
186	\	92	92	92	224	92
187	¢	162	189	162	74	
188	•	165		183	175	
189	À	203	183	192		
190	Á	231	181	193		
191	Â	229	182	194		
192	Ã	204	199	195		
193	Ä	128	142	196		
194	Å	129	143	197		
195	Æ	174		198		
196	Ç	130	128	199		
197	È	233	212	200		
198	É	131	144	201		
199	Ê	230	210	202		
200	Ë	232	211	203		
201	Ì	237	222	204		
202	Í	234	214	205		
203	Î	235	215	206		
204	Ï	236	216	207		
205	Ð		209	208		
206	Ñ	132	165	209		
207	Ò	241	227	210		
208	Ó	238	224	211		
209	Ô	239	226	212		
210	Õ	205	229	213		
211	Ö	133	153	214		
212	Ø	175	157	216		
213	Ù	244	235	217		
214	Ú	242	233	218		
215	Û	243	234	219		
216	Ü	134	154	220		
217	Ý		237	221		
218	Þ		232	222		

IMPORT/EXPORT Character Sets

Position	Graphic	Macintosh	Microsoft Code Page 850	ANSI/ISO Latin 1	IBM EBCDIC	ASCII 7-BIT
219	ß	167	225	223		
220	à	136	133	224		
221	á	135	160	225		
222	â	137	131	226		
223	ã	139	198	227		
224	ä	138	132	228		
225	å	140	134	229		
226	æ	190	145	230		
227	ç	141	135	231		
228	è	143	138	232		
229	é	142	130	233		
230	ê	144	136	234		
231	ë	145	137	235		
232	ì	147	141	236		
233	í	146	161	237		
234	î	148	140	238		
235	ï	149	139	239		
236	ð		208	240		
237	ñ	150	164	241		
238	ò	152	149	242		
239	ó	151	162	243		
240	ô	153	147	244		
241	õ	155	228	245		
242	ö	154	148	246		
243	ø	191	155	248		
244	ù	157	151	249		
245	ú	156	163	250		
246	û	158	150	251		
247	ü	159	129	252		
248	ý		236	253		
249	ÿ	216	152	255		
250	þ		231	254		
251	¡	193	173	161		
252	¿	192	168	191		
253	«	199	174	171		
254	»	200	175	187		
255	reserved					

[1] file separator
[2] field separator
[3] not the plus sign

Appendix C
Defining Complex Files

Most data files have a rectangular, case-ordered structure and can be read with the DATA LIST command. This chapter illustrates the use of SPSS commands for defining complex, nonrectangular files.

- **Nested** files contain several types of records with a hierarchical relationship among the record types. You can define nested files with the FILE TYPE NESTED command.
- **Grouped** files have several records per case, and a case's records are grouped together in a file. You can use DATA LIST and FILE TYPE GROUPED to define grouped files.
- In a **mixed** file, different types of cases have different kinds of records. You can define mixed files with the FILE TYPE MIXED command.
- A record in a **repeating data** file contains information for several cases. You can use the REPEATING DATA command to define files with repeating data.

It is a good idea to read the descriptions of the FILE TYPE and REPEATING DATA commands before proceeding.

A Rectangular File

Figure C.1 shows contents of data file *RECTANG.DAT*, which contains 1988 sales data for salespeople working in different territories. Year, region, and unit sales are recorded for each salesperson. Like most data files, the sales data file has a **rectangular** format, since information on a record applies only to one case.

Figure C.1 File RECTANG.DAT

```
1988 CHICAGO      JONES      900
1988 CHICAGO      GREGORY    400
1988 BATON ROUGE  RODRIGUEZ  300
1988 BATON ROUGE  SMITH      333
1988 BATON ROUGE  GRAU       100
```

Since the sales data are rectangular, you can use the DATA LIST command to define these data:

```
DATA LIST FILE='RECTANG.DAT'
 / YEAR      1-4
   REGION    6-16(A)
   SALESPER 18-26(A)
   SALES    29-31.
```

- DATA LIST defines the variable *YEAR* in columns 1 through 4 and string variable *REGION* in columns 6 through 16 in file *RECTANG.DAT*. SPSS also reads variables *SALESPER* and *SALES* on each record.
- The LIST output in Figure C.2 shows the contents of each variable.

Figure C.2   LIST output for RECTANG.DAT

```
YEAR REGION      SALESPER   SALES

1988 CHICAGO     JONES       900
1988 CHICAGO     GREGORY     400
1988 BATON ROUGE RODRIGUEZ   300
1988 BATON ROUGE SMITH       333
1988 BATON ROUGE GRAU        100
```

Nested Files

In a nested file, information on some records applies to several cases. The 1988 sales data are arranged in nested format in Figure C.3. The data contain three kinds of records. A code in the first column indicates whether a record is a year (Y), region (R), or person record (P).

Figure C.3   File NESTED.DAT

```
Y    1988
R    CHICAGO
P    JONES          900
P    GREGORY        400
R    BATON ROUGE
P    RODRIGUEZ      300
P    SMITH          333
P    GRAU           100
```

The record types are related to each other hierarchically. Year records represent the highest level in the hierarchy, since the year value 1988 applies to each salesperson in the file (only one year record is used in this example). Region records are intermediate-level records; region names apply to salesperson records that occur before the next region record in the file. For example, Chicago applies to salespersons Jones and Gregory. Baton Rouge applies to Rodriguez, Smith, and Grau. Person records represent the lowest level in the hierarchy. The information they contain—salesperson and unit sales—defines a case. Nested file structures minimize redundant information in a data file. For example, 1988 and Baton Rouge appear several times in Figure C.1, but only once in Figure C.3.

Since each record in the nested file has a code that indicates record type, you can use the FILE TYPE and RECORD TYPE commands to define the nested sales data:

```
FILE   TYPE   NESTED   FILE='NESTED.DAT' RECORD=#TYPE 1 (A)

RECORD TYPE 'Y'.
DATA LIST /  YEAR 5-8.

RECORD TYPE 'R'.
DATA LIST  / REGION 5-15 (A).


RECORD TYPE 'P'.
DATA LIST / SALESPER 5-15 (A) SALES 20-23

END FILE TYPE.
```

- FILE TYPE indicates that data are in nested form in file *NESTED.DAT*.
- RECORD defines the record type variable as string variable *#TYPE* in column 1. *#TYPE* is defined as scratch variable so it won't be saved in the working data file.
- One pair of RECORD TYPE and DATA LIST statements is specified for each record type in the file. The first pair of RECORD TYPE and DATA LIST statements defines the variable *YEAR* in columns 5 through 8 on every year record. The second pair defines the string variable *REGION* on region records. The final pair defines *SALESPER* and *SALES* on person records.
- The order of RECORD TYPE statements defines the hierarchical relationship among the records. The first RECORD TYPE defines the highest-level record type. The next RECORD TYPE defines the next highest level, and so forth. The last RECORD TYPE defines a case in the working data file.
- END FILE TYPE signals the end of file definition.
- In processing nested data, SPSS reads each record type you define. Information on the highest and intermediate-level records is spread to cases to which the information applies. The output from the LIST command is identical to that in Figure C.2.

Nested Files with Missing Records

In a nested file, some cases may be missing one or more record types defined in RECORD TYPE commands. For example, in Figure C.4 the region record for salespersons Jones and Gregory is missing.

Defining Complex Files

Figure C.4   NESTED.DAT file with missing records

```
Y  1988
P  JONES        900
P  GREGORY      400
R  BATON ROUGE
P  RODRIGUEZ    300
P  SMITH        333
P  GRAU         100
```

SPSS assigns missing values to variables that are not present for a case. Using the modified *NESTED.DAT* file in Figure C.4, the commands in the previous example produce the output shown in Figure C.5. You can see that SPSS assigned missing values to *REGION* for Jones and Gregory.

Figure C.5   LIST output for nested data with missing records

```
YEAR REGION       SALESPER   SALES

1988              JONES       900
1988              GREGORY     400
1988 BATON ROUGE  RODRIGUEZ   300
1988 BATON ROUGE  SMITH       333
1988 BATON ROUGE  GRAU        100
```

You may want to examine cases with missing records, since these cases may indicate data errors. If you add the MISSING=WARN subcommand to your FILE TYPE command, SPSS prints a warning message when a case is missing a defined record type. For example, SPSS would print two warnings when processing data in Figure C.4. When MISSING is set to WARN, cases are built in the same way as when the default setting (NOWARN) is in effect.

Grouped Data

In a grouped file, a case has several records that are grouped together in the file. You can use DATA LIST to define a grouped file if each case has the same number of records and records appear in the same order for each case. You can use FILE TYPE GROUPED whether the number of records per case and record order are fixed or vary. However, FILE TYPE GROUPED requires that each record have a case identifier and a record code.

Using DATA LIST

Table C.1 shows the organization of a grouped data file containing school subject scores for three students. Each student has three data records, and each record contains a score. The first record for each student also contains a case identifier. Records for each case are grouped together. Student 1 records appear first, followed by records for student 2 and student 3.

Record order determines whether a score is a reading, math, or science score. The reading score appears on the first record for a case, the math score appears on the second record, and the science score appears on the third record.

Table C.1 Data for GROUPED.DAT

Student	Score
1	58
	59
	97
2	43
	88
	45
3	67
	75
	90

Since each case has the same number of records and record order is fixed across cases, you can use DATA LIST to define the student data:

```
DATA LIST FILE='GROUPED.DAT' RECORDS=3
 /STUDENT 1 READING 5-6
 /MATH     5-6
 /SCIENCE 5-6.
LIST.
```

- DATA LIST indicates that data are in file *GROUPED.DAT.*
- RECORDS defines three records per case. SPSS reads student ID number (*STUDENT*) and reading score (*READING*) in the first record for a case. Math and science scores are read in the second and third records.
- The output from the LIST command is shown in Figure C.6.

Figure C.6   LIST output for GROUPED.DAT

```
STUDENT READING MATH SCIENCE
   1      58     59    97
   2      43     88    45
   3      67     75    90
```

Using FILE TYPE GROUPED

To use FILE TYPE GROUPED to define a grouped file, each record must have a case identifier and a record code. In the following commands, each data record contains a student ID number coded 1, 2, or 3 and a code indicating whether the score on that record is a reading (R), math (M), or science (S) score:

```
FILE TYPE GROUPED RECORD=#REC 3(A)   CASE=STUDENT 1.

RECORD TYPE 'R'.
DATA LIST / READING 5-6.

RECORD TYPE 'M'.
DATA LIST / MATH 5-6.

RECORD TYPE 'S'.
DATA LIST / SCIENCE 5-6.

END FILE TYPE.

BEGIN DATA
1 R 58
1 M 59
1 S 97
2 R 43
2 M 88
2 S 45
3 R 67
3 M 75
3 S 90
END DATA.

LIST.
```

- FILE TYPE indicates that data are in grouped format. RECORD defines the variable containing record codes as string variable *#REC* in column 3. CASE defines the case identifier variable *STUDENT* in the first column of each record.
- One pair of RECORD TYPE and DATA LIST statements appears for each record type in the file. SPSS reads reading score in every R record, math score in M records, and science score in S records.
- END FILE TYPE signals the end of file definition.
- BEGIN DATA and END DATA indicate that data are inline.
- The output from LIST is identical to the output in Figure C.6.

FILE TYPE GROUPED is most useful when record order varies across cases and when cases have missing or duplicate records. In the modified data shown in Table C.2, only case 1 has all three record types. Also, record order varies across cases. For example, the first record for case 1 is a science record, whereas the first record for cases 2 and 3 is a reading record.

Table C.2 Modified grouped data file

Student	Subject	Score
1	S	97
1	R	58
1	M	59
2	R	43
3	R	67
3	M	75

You can use the same FILE TYPE commands as above to read the modified file. As shown in the output from LIST in Figure C.7, SPSS assigns missing values to variables that are missing for a case.

Figure C.7 LIST output for modified GROUPED.DAT file

```
STUDENT READING MATH SCIENCE
   1       58     59    97
   2       43      .     .
   3       67     75     .
```

By default, SPSS generates a warning message when a case is missing a defined record type in a grouped file or when a record is not in the same order as in RECORD TYPE commands. Thus, four warnings are generated when the commands for the previous example are used to read the modified *GROUPED.DAT* file. You can suppress these warnings if you add the optional specifications MISSING=NOWARN and ORDERED=NO on your FILE TYPE command.

In the modified *GROUPED.DAT* file, the case identifier *STUDENT* appears in the same column position in each record. When the location of the case identifier varies for different types of records, you can use the CASE option of the RECORD TYPE command to specify different column positions for different records. For example, suppose the case identifier appears in first column position on reading and science records and in column 2 in math records. You could use the following commands to define the data:

Defining Complex Files

```
FILE TYPE GROUPED RECORD=#REC 3(A)   CASE=STUDENT 1.

RECORD TYPE 'R'.
DATA LIST / READING 5-6.

RECORD TYPE 'M' CASE=2.
DATA LIST / MATH 5-6.

RECORD TYPE 'S'.
DATA LIST / SCIENCE 5-6.

END FILE TYPE.

BEGIN DATA
1 S 97
1 R 58
 1M 59
2 R 43
3 R 67
 3M 75
END DATA.

LIST.
```

- FILE TYPE indicates that the data are in grouped format. RECORD defines the variable containing record codes as string variable *#REC*. CASE defines the case identifier variable as *STUDENT* in the first column of each record.
- One pair of RECORD TYPE and DATA LIST statements is coded for each record type in the file.
- The CASE specification on the RECORD TYPE statement for math records overrides the CASE value defined on FILE TYPE. Thus, SPSS reads *STUDENT* in column 2 in math records and column 1 in other records.
- END FILE TYPE signals the end of file definition.
- BEGIN DATA and END DATA indicate that data are inline.
- The output from LIST is identical to that in Figure C.7.

Mixed Files

In a mixed file, different types of cases have different kinds of records. You can use FILE TYPE MIXED to read each record or a subset of records in a mixed file.

Reading Each Record in a Mixed File

Table C.3 shows test data for two hypothetical elementary school students referred to a remedial education teacher. Student 1, who was thought to need special reading attention, took reading tests (word identification and comprehension tests). The second student completed writing tests (handwriting, spelling, vocabulary, and grammar tests). Test code (READING or WRITING) indicates whether the record contains reading or writing scores.

Table C.3 Academic test data for two students

Student 1

Test	ID	Grade	Word	Compre
READING	1	04	65	35

Student 2

Test	ID	Grade	Handwrit	Spelling	Vocab	Grammar
WRITING	2	03	50	55	30	25

The following commands define the test data:

```
FILE TYPE MIXED RECORD=TEST 1-7(A).

RECORD TYPE 'READING'.
DATA LIST / ID  9-10 GRADE  12-13 WORD 15-16 COMPRE 18-19.

RECORD TYPE 'WRITING'.
DATA LIST / ID  9-10 GRADE 12-13 HANDWRIT 15-16 SPELLING 18-19
            VOCAB 21-22 GRAMMAR   24-25.
END FILE TYPE.

BEGIN DATA
READING 1   04 65 35
WRITING 2   03 50 55 30 25
END DATA.

LIST.
```

- FILE TYPE specifies that the data contain mixed record types. RECORD reads the record identifier (variable *TEST*) in columns 1 through 7.
- One pair of RECORD TYPE and DATA LIST statements is coded for each record type in the file. SPSS reads variables *ID, GRADE, WORD,* and *COMPRE* in the record in which the value of *TEST* is READING, and *ID, GRADE, HANDWRIT, SPELLING, VOCAB,* and *GRAMMAR* in the WRITING record.
- END FILE TYPE signals the end of file definition.
- BEGIN DATA and END DATA indicate that data are inline. Data are mixed, since some column positions contain different variables for the two cases. For example, word identification score is recorded in columns 15 and 16 for student 1. For student 2, handwriting score is recorded in these columns.

Defining Complex Files

- Figure C.8 shows the output from LIST. Missing values are assigned for variables that are not recorded for a case.

Figure C.8   LIST output for mixed file

```
TEST      ID GRADE WORD COMPRE HANDWRIT SPELLING VOCAB GRAMMAR

READING   1   4    65    35       .        .       .      .
WRITING   2   3     .     .      50       55      30     25
```

Reading a Subset of Records in a Mixed File

You may want to process a subset of records in a mixed file. The following commands read only the data for the student who took reading tests:

```
FILE TYPE MIXED RECORD=TEST 1-7(A).

RECORD TYPE 'READING'.
DATA LIST / ID       9-10
            GRADE   12-13
            WORD    15-16
            COMPRE  18-19.

RECORD TYPE 'WRITING'.
DATA LIST / ID       9-10
            GRADE   12-13
            HANDWRIT 15-16
            SPELLING 18-19
            VOCAB   21-22
            GRAMMAR 24-25.

END FILE TYPE.

BEGIN DATA
READING 1   04 65 35
WRITING 2   03 50 55 30 25
END DATA.

LIST.
```

- FILE TYPE specifies that data contain mixed record types. RECORD defines the record identification variable as *TEST* in columns 1 through 7.
- RECORD TYPE defines variables on reading records. Since SPSS skips all record types that are not defined by default, the case with writing scores is not read.
- END FILE TYPE signals the end of file definition.
- BEGIN DATA and END DATA indicate that data are inline. Data are identical to those in the previous example.
- Figure C.9 shows the output from LIST.

Figure C.9 LIST output for reading record

```
TEST      ID GRADE WORD COMPRE
READING    1    4    65   35
```

Repeating Data

You can use the REPEATING DATA command to read files in which each record contains repeating groups of variables that define several cases. Command syntax depends on whether the number of repeating groups is fixed across records.

Fixed Number of Repeating Groups

Table C.4 shows test score data for students in three classrooms. Each record contains a classroom number and two pairs of student ID and test score variables. For example, in class 101, student 182 has a score of 12 and student 134 has a score of 53. In class 103, student 15 has a score of 87 and student 203 has a score of 69. Each pair of ID and score variables is a repeating group, since these variables appear twice on each record.

Table C.4 Data in REPEAT.DAT file

Class	ID	Score	ID	Score
101	182	12	134	53
102	99	112	200	150
103	15	87	203	69

The following commands generate a working data file in which one case is built for each occurrence of *SCORE* and *ID*, and classroom number is spread to each case on a record.

```
INPUT PROGRAM.
DATA LIST / CLASS 3-5.
REPEATING DATA STARTS=6 / OCCURS=2
 /DATA STUDENT 1-4 SCORE 5-8.
END INPUT PROGRAM.

BEGIN DATA
   101 182  12 134  53
   102  99 112 200 150
   103  15  87 203  69
END DATA.

LIST.
```

Defining Complex Files

- INPUT PROGRAM signals the beginning of data definition.
- DATA LIST defines variable *CLASS*, which is spread to each student on a classroom record.
- REPEATING DATA specifies that the input file contains repeating data. STARTS indicates that repeating data begin in column 6. OCCURS specifies that the repeating data group occurs twice in each record.
- DATA defines variables that are repeated (*STUDENT* and *SCORE*). SPSS begins reading the first repeating data group in column 6 (the value of STARTS). Since the value of OCCURS is 2, SPSS reads the repeating variables a second time, beginning in the next available column (column 14).
- END INPUT PROGRAM signals the end of data definition.
- BEGIN DATA and END DATA specify that data are inline.
- The output from LIST is shown in Figure C.10. Each student is a separate case.

Figure C.10 LIST output for repeating data

```
CLASS  STUDENT  SCORE

 101     182      12
 101     134      53
 102      99     112
 102     200     150
 103      15      87
 103     203      69
```

Varying Number of Repeating Groups

To use REPEATING DATA to define a file in which the number of repeating data groups varies across records, your data must contain a variable indicating the number of repeating data groups on a record. The following commands define such a file:

```
INPUT PROGRAM.
DATA LIST /  #NUM 1 CLASS 3-5.
REPEATING DATA STARTS=6 / OCCURS=#NUM
 /DATA STUDENT 1-4 SCORE 5-8.
END INPUT PROGRAM.

BEGIN DATA
3 101 182   12 134   53 199   30
2 102  99  112 200  150
1 103  15   87
END DATA.

LIST.
```

- INPUT PROGRAM signals the beginning of data definition.
- DATA LIST defines variables *CLASS* in columns 3 through 5 and *#NUM*, a scratch variable in column 1 that contains the number of repeating data groups in a record.

- REPEATING DATA specifies that the input file contains repeating data. STARTS indicates that repeating data begin in column 6. OCCURS sets the number of repeating groups on a record equal to the value of *#NUM*.
- DATA defines variables that are repeated. Since *#NUM* is 3 in the first and third records, SPSS reads three sets of *STUDENT* and *SCORE* variables in these records. *STUDENT* and *SCORE* are read twice in record 2.
- END INPUT PROGRAM signals the end of data definition.
- Data appear between BEGIN DATA and END DATA.
- Figure C.11 shows the output from LIST.

Figure C.11   LIST output

```
CLASS STUDENT SCORE

 101     182     12
 101     134     53
 101     199     30
 102      99    112
 103      15     87
```

If your data file does not have a variable indicating the number of repeating data groups per record, you can use the LOOP and REREAD commands to read the data, as in:

```
INPUT PROGRAM.
DATA LIST /    CLASS 3-5 #ALL 6-29 (A).
LEAVE CLASS.

LOOP #I = 1 TO 17  BY 8 IF SUBSTR(#ALL, #I, 8) NE ' '.
-  REREAD COLUMN = #I + 5.
-  DATA LIST / STUDENT 1-4 SCORE 5-8.
-  END CASE.
END LOOP.
END INPUT PROGRAM.

BEGIN DATA
  101 182   12 134   53 199   30
  102  99  112 200  150
  103  15   87
END DATA.

LIST.
```

- INPUT PROGRAM signals the beginning of data definition.
- DATA LIST reads *CLASS* and *#ALL*, a temporary string variable that contains all of the repeating data groups for a classroom record. The column specifications for *#ALL* (6 through 29) are wide enough to accommodate the classroom record with the most repeating data groups (record 1).
- LOOP and END LOOP define an index loop. As the loop iterates, SPSS successively reads eight-character segments of *#ALL*, each of which contains a repeating data group or an empty field. SPSS reads the first eight characters of *#ALL* in the first it-

eration, the second eight characters in the second iteration, and so forth. The loop terminates when SPSS encounters an empty segment, which means that there are no more repeating data groups on a record.
- In each iteration of the loop in which an *#ALL* segment is not empty, DATA LIST reads *STUDENT* and *SCORE* in a classroom record. SPSS begins reading these variables in the first record, in the starting column specified by REREAD COLUMN. For example, in the first iteration, SPSS reads *STUDENT* and *SCORE* beginning in column 6. In the second iteration, SPSS reads *STUDENT* and *SCORE* starting in column 14 of the same record. When all repeating groups have been read for a record, loop processing begins on the following record.
- END CASE creates a new case for each repeating group.
- REREAD causes DATA LIST to read repeating data groups in the same record in which it last read *CLASS*. Without REREAD, each execution of DATA LIST would begin on a different record.
- LEAVE preserves the value of CLASS across the repeating data groups on a record. Thus, the same class number is read for each student on a classroom record.
- INPUT PROGRAM signals the beginning of data definition.
- BEGIN DATA and END DATA indicate that the data are inline. The data are identical to those in the previous example except that they do not contain a variable indicating the number of repeating groups per record.
- These commands generate the same output as shown in Figure C.11.

Appendix D
Using the Macro Facility

A macro is a set of commands that generates customized SPSS command syntax. Using macros can reduce the time and effort needed to perform complex and repetitive data analysis tasks.

Macros have two parts: a **macro definition**, which indicates the beginning and end of the macro and gives a name to the macro, and a **macro body**, which contains regular SPSS commands or macro commands that build command syntax. When a macro is invoked by the **macro call**, syntax is generated in a process called **macro expansion**. Then the generated syntax is executed as part of the normal command sequence.

This chapter shows how to construct macros that perform three data analysis tasks. In the first example, macros facilitate a file-matching task. In Example 2, macros automate a specialized statistical operation (testing a sample correlation coefficient against a nonzero population correlation coefficient). Macros in Example 3 generate random data. As shown in Table D.1, each example demonstrates various features of the SPSS macro facility. For information on specific macro commands, see the DEFINE command.

Table D.1   Macro features

	Example 1	Example 2	Example 3
Macro argument			
Keyword	x	x	x
Default values	x		x
None	x		x
String manipulation	x		x
Looping			
Index	x		x
List processing		x	
Direct assignment	x		x

Example 1: Automating a File-Matching Task

Figure D.1 shows a listing of 1988 sales data for salespeople working in different regions. The listing shows that salesperson Jones sold 900 units in the Chicago sales territory, while Rodriguez sold 300 units in Baton Rouge.

Figure D.1 Listing of data file SALES88.SAV

```
YEAR REGION       SALESPER   SALES

1988 CHICAGO      JONES      900
1988 CHICAGO      GREGORY    400
1988 BATON ROUGE  RODRIGUEZ  300
1988 BATON ROUGE  SMITH      333
1988 BATON ROUGE  GRAU       100
```

You can use command syntax shown in Figure D.2 to obtain each salesperson's percentage of total sales for their region.

Figure D.2 Commands for obtaining sales percentages

```
GET FILE = 'SALES88.SAV'.

SORT CASES BY REGION.

AGGREGATE OUTFILE = 'TOTALS.SAV'
  /PRESORTED
  /BREAK  = REGION
  /TOTAL@ = SUM(SALES).

MATCH FILES FILE=*
  /TABLE  = 'TOTALS.SAV'
  /BY REGION.

COMPUTE PCT = SALES / TOTAL@.

TITLE  1988 DATA.
LIST.
```

- The GET command opens *SALES88.SAV*, an SPSS data file. This file becomes the working data file.
- SORT CASES sorts the working data file in ascending alphabetical order by *REGION*.
- The AGGREGATE command saves total sales (variable *TOTAL@*) for each region in file *TOTALS.SAV*.
- MATCH FILES appends the regional totals to each salesperson's record in the working data file. (See the MATCH FILES command for more information on matching files.)
- COMPUTE obtains the percentage of regional sales (*PCT*) for each salesperson.

- The LIST command output displayed in Figure D.3 shows that Rodriguez sold 41% of the products sold in Baton Rouge. Gregory accounted for 31% of sales in the Chicago area.

Figure D.3   Regional sales percentages for 1988

```
YEAR  REGION        SALESPER    SALES   TOTAL@    PCT

1988  BATON ROUGE   RODRIGUEZ    300    733.00    .41
1988  BATON ROUGE   SMITH        333    733.00    .45
1988  BATON ROUGE   GRAU         100    733.00    .14
1988  CHICAGO       JONES        900   1300.00    .69
1988  CHICAGO       GREGORY      400   1300.00    .31
```

Figure D.4 shows a macro that issues the commands in Figure D.2. The macro consists of the commands that produce sales percentages imbedded between macro definition commands DEFINE and !ENDDEFINE.

Figure D.4   !TOTMAC macro

```
DEFINE !TOTMAC ().

GET FILE  = 'SALES88.SAV'.

SORT CASES BY REGION.

AGGREGATE OUTFILE = 'TOTALS.SAV'
  /PRESORTED
  /BREAK  = REGION
  /TOTAL@ = SUM(SALES).

MATCH FILES FILE = *
  /TABLE  = 'TOTALS.SAV'
  /BY REGION.

COMPUTE PCT = SALES / TOTAL@.

TITLE   1988 DATA.
LIST.

!ENDDEFINE.

!TOTMAC.
```

- In Figure D.4, macro definition commands DEFINE and !ENDDEFINE signal the beginning and end of macro processing. DEFINE also assigns the name !TOTMAC to the macro (the parentheses following the name of the macro are required). The macro name begins with an exclamation point so that the macro does not conflict with that of an existing variable or command. Otherwise, if the macro name matched a variable name, the variable name would invoke the macro whenever the variable name appeared in the command stream.

Using the Macro Facility

- Commands between DEFINE and !ENDEFINE constitute the macro body. These commands, which produce sales percentages, are identical to the commands in Figure D.2.
- The final statement in Figure D.4 (!TOTMAC) is the **macro call**, which invokes the macro. When SPSS reads the macro call, SPSS issues the commands in the macro body. Then these commands are executed, generating output that is identical to that in Figure D.3.

While the macro in Figure D.4 shows you how to construct a simple macro, it doesn't reduce the number of SPSS commands needed to calculate regional percentages. However, you can use macro features such as looping to minimize coding in more complicated tasks. For example, let's say that in addition to the 1988 data, you have sales data for 1989 (*SALES89.SAV*), and each file contains the variables *REGION*, *SALESPER*, and *SALES*. The modified !TOTMAC macro in Figure D.5 calculates regional sales percentages for each salesperson for 1988 and 1989.

Figure D.5 !TOTMAC macro with index loop

```
DEFINE !TOTMAC ().

!DO !I  =  88 !TO 89.
-   GET FILE   = !CONCAT('SALES', !I, '.SAV').
-   SORT CASES BY REGION.
-   AGGREGATE OUTFILE = 'TOTALS.SAV'
        /PRESORTED
        /BREAK    = REGION
        /TOTAL@   = SUM(SALES).
-   MATCH FILES FILE = *
        /TABLE    = 'TOTALS.SAV'
        /BY REGION.
-   COMPUTE PCT= SALES / TOTAL@.

-   !LET !YEAR = !CONCAT('19',!I).
-   TITLE   !YEAR DATA.
-   LIST.
!DOEND.

!ENDDEFINE.

!TOTMAC.
```

- In Figure D.5, DEFINE and !ENDDEFINE signal the beginning and end of macro processing.
- Commands !DO and !DOEND define an **index loop**. Commands between !DO and !DOEND are issued once in each iteration of the loop. The value of **index variable** !I, which changes in each iteration, is 88 in the first iteration and 89 in the second (final) iteration.

- In each iteration of the loop, the GET command opens an SPSS data file. The name of the file is constructed using the **string manipulation function** !CONCAT, which creates a string that is the concatenation of SALES, the value of the index variable, and *.SAV*. Thus the file *SALES88.SAV* is opened in the first iteration.
- Commands between AGGREGATE and COMPUTE calculate percentages on the working data file. These commands are identical to those in Figure D.4.
- Next, a customized title is created. In the first iteration, the **direct assignment** command !LET assigns a value of 1988 to the macro variable !YEAR. This variable is used in the TITLE command on the following line to specify a title of *1988 DATA*.
- The LIST command displays the contents of each variable.
- In the second iteration of the loop, commands display percentages for the 1989 data file. The output from the !TOTMAC macro is shown in Figure D.7. Note that the listing for 1988 data is the same as in Figure D.3.

Figure D.6   Regional sales percentages for 1988 and 1989

```
1988 DATA

YEAR REGION          SALESPER      SALES    TOTAL@        PCT

1988 BATON ROUGE    RODRIGUEZ       300     733.00        .41
1988 BATON ROUGE    SMITH           333     733.00        .45
1988 BATON ROUGE    GRAU            100     733.00        .14
1988 CHICAGO        JONES           900    1300.00        .69
1988 CHICAGO        GREGORY         400    1300.00        .31


1989 DATA

YEAR REGION          SALESPER      SALES    TOTAL@        PCT
1989 BATON ROUGE    GRAU            320    1459.00        .22
1989 BATON ROUGE    SMITH           800    1459.00        .55
1989 BATON ROUGE    RODRIGUEZ       339    1459.00        .23
1989 CHICAGO        JONES           300    1439.00        .21
1989 CHICAGO        STEEL           899    1439.00        .62
1989 CHICAGO        GREGORY         240    1439.00        .17
```

Let's look at another application of the !TOTMAC macro, one that uses **keyword arguments** to make the application more flexible. Figure D.7 shows the number of absences for students in two classrooms. Let's say you want to calculate deviation scores indicating how many more (or fewer) times a student was absent than the average student in his or her classroom. The first step in obtaining deviation scores is to compute the average number of absences per classroom. We can use the !TOTMAC macro to compute classroom means by modifying the macro so that it computes means and uses the absences data file *(SCHOOL.SAV)* as input.

Figure D.7   Listing of file SCHOOL.SAV

```
CLASS STUDENT   ABSENT

 101  BARRY G     3
 101  JENNI W     1
 101  ED    F     2
 101  JOHN  O     8
 102  PAUL  Y     2
 102  AMY   G     3
 102  JOHN  D    12
 102  RICH  H     4
```

The !TOTMAC macro in Figure D.8 can produce a variety of group summary statistics such as sum, mean, and standard deviation for any SPSS data file. In the macro call you specify values of keyword arguments indicating the data file (FILE), the break (grouping) variable (BREAKVR), the summary function (FUNC), and the variable to be used as input to the summary function (INVAR). For example, to obtain mean absences for each classroom, we specify *SCHOOL.SAV* as the data file, *CLASS* as the break variable, *MEAN* as the summary function, and *ABSENT* as the variable whose values are to be averaged.

Figure D.8   !TOTMAC macro with keyword arguments

```
DEFINE !TOTMAC  ( BREAKVR = !TOKENS(1)
                 /FUNC    = !TOKENS(1)
                 /INVAR   = !TOKENS(1)
                 /TEMP    = !TOKENS(1)  !DEFAULT(TOTALS.SAV)
                 /FILE    = !CMDEND).
GET FILE = !FILE.
SORT CASES BY !BREAKVR.
AGGREGATE OUTFILE = '!TEMP'
   /PRESORTED
   /BREAK = !BREAKVR
   /!CONCAT(!FUNC,'@') = !FUNC(!INVAR).

MATCH FILES FILE = *
   /TABLE = '!TEMP'
   /BY !BREAKVR.

!ENDDEFINE.

!TOTMAC BREAKVR=CLASS FUNC=MEAN INVAR=ABSENT FILE=SCHOOL.SAV.

COMPUTE DIFF = ABSENT-MEAN@.

LIST.

!TOTMAC BREAKVR=REGION FUNC=SUM INVAR=SALES FILE=SALES89.SAV.

COMPUTE PCT = SALES / SUM@.

LIST.
```

- In Figure D.8, syntax for declaring keyword arguments follows the name of the macro in DEFINE.
- !TOKENS(1) specifies that the value of an argument is a string following the name of the argument in the macro call. Thus the first macro call specifies CLASS as the value of BREAKVR, MEAN as the value of FUNC, and ABSENT as the value of INVAR.
- !CMDEND indicates that the value for FILE is the remaining text in the macro call (SCHOOL.SAV).
- TEMP is an optional argument that names an intermediate file to contain the summary statistics. Since TEMP is not assigned a value in the macro call, summary statistics are written to the default intermediate file *(TOTALS.SAV)*.
- In the body of the macro, GET FILE opens *SCHOOL.SAV*.
- SORT CASES sorts the file by *CLASS*.
- AGGREGATE computes the mean number of absences for each class. The name of the variable containing the means (*MEAN@*) is constructed using the !CONCAT function, which concatenates the value of FUNC and the @ symbol.
- MATCH FILES appends the means to student records.
- COMPUTE calculates the deviation from the classroom mean for each student (variable *DIFF*).
- LIST displays the deviation scores, as shown in Figure D.9. For example, John D., who was absent 12 times, had 6.75 more absences than the average student in classroom 102. Rich H., who was absent 4 times, had 1.25 fewer absences than the average student in classroom 102.
- The second macro call and remaining commands in Figure D.8 generate regional sales percentages for the 1989 sales data. As shown in Figure D.9, percentages are identical to those displayed in the bottom half of Figure D.7.

Figure D.9 Student absences and 1989 sales percentages

```
CLASS STUDENT     ABSENT      MEAN@      DIFF

 101  BARRY  G      3         3.50       -.50
 101  JENNI  W      1         3.50      -2.50
 101  ED     F      2         3.50      -1.50
 101  JOHN   O      8         3.50       4.50
 102  PAUL   Y      2         5.25      -3.25
 102  AMY    G      3         5.25      -2.25
 102  JOHN   D     12         5.25       6.75
 102  RICH   H      4         5.25      -1.25


YEAR  REGION       SALESPER   SALES      SUM@       PCT

1989  BATON ROUGE  GRAU        320       1459.00    .22
1989  BATON ROUGE  SMITH       800       1459.00    .55
1989  BATON ROUGE  RODRIGUEZ   339       1459.00    .23
1989  CHICAGO      JONES       300       1439.00    .21
1989  CHICAGO      STEEL       899       1439.00    .62
1989  CHICAGO      GREGORY     240       1439.00    .17
```

You can modify the macro call in Figure D.8 to specify a different data file, input variable, break variable, or summary statistic. To get a different summary statistic (such as standard deviation), change the value of FUNC (see the AGGREGATE command for more information on summary functions available in the AGGREGATE procedure).

Example 2: Testing Correlation Coefficients

While SPSS provides a large variety of statistical procedures, some specialized operations require the use of COMPUTE statements. For example, you may want to test a sample correlation coefficient against a population correlation coefficient. When the population coefficient is 0, you can use the CORRELATIONS procedure. When the population coefficient is nonzero, you can compute a Z statistic to test the hypothesis that the sample and population values are equal (Morrison, 1976). The formula for Z is

$$Z = \frac{0.5 ln\left[\frac{(1+r)}{(1-r)}\right] - 0.5 ln\left[\frac{(1+p_0)}{(1-p_0)}\right]}{1/(\sqrt{n-3})}$$

where r is the sample correlation coefficient, p_0 is the population coefficient, n is the size of the sample from which r is obtained, and ln signifies the natural logarithm function. Z has approximately the standard normal distribution.

Let's say you want to test an r of 0.66 obtained from a sample of 30 cases against a population coefficient of 0.85. Figure D.10 shows commands for displaying Z and its two-tailed probability.

Figure D.10 Commands for computing Z statistic

```
DATA LIST FREE / R N P.

BEGIN DATA
.66 30 .85
END DATA.

COMPUTE #ZR   = .5* (LN ((1 + R) / (1 - R))).
COMPUTE #ZP   = .5* (LN ((1 + P) / (1 - P))).

COMPUTE Z     = (#ZR-#ZP)/(1/(SQRT(N-3))).
COMPUTE PROB  = 2*(1-CDFNORM(ABS(Z))).

FORMAT   PROB (F8.3).
LIST.
```

- DATA LIST defines variables containing the sample correlation coefficient (R), sample size (N), and population correlation coefficient (P).

- BEGIN DATA and END DATA indicate that data are inline.
- COMPUTE statements calculate Z and its probability. Variables *#ZR* and *#ZP* are scratch variables used in the intermediate steps of the calculation.
- The LIST command output is shown in Figure D.11. Since the absolute value of Z is large and the probability is small, we reject the hypothesis that the sample was drawn from a population having a correlation coefficient of 0.85.

Figure D.11 Z statistic and its probability

```
    R        N         P       Z       PROB
   .66     30.00      .85    -2.41     .016
```

If you use the Z test frequently, you may want to construct a macro like that shown in Figure D.12. The !CORRTST macro computes Z and probability values for a sample correlation coefficient, sample size, and population coefficient specified as values of keyword arguments.

Figure D.12 !CORRTST macro

```
DEFINE !CORRTST ( R  =  !TOKENS(1)
                 /N  =  !TOKENS(1)
                 /P  =  !TOKENS(1)).

INPUT PROGRAM.
-    END CASE.
-    END FILE.
END INPUT PROGRAM.

COMPUTE #ZR  = .5* (LN ((1 + !R) / (1 - !R))).
COMPUTE #ZP  = .5* (LN ((1 + !P) / (1 - !P))).

COMPUTE Z    = (#ZR-#ZP) / (1/(SQRT(!N-3))).
COMPUTE PROB = 2*(1-CDFNORM(ABS(Z))).
FORMAT  PROB(F8.3).

TITLE SAMPLE R=!R, N=!N, POPULATION COEFFICIENT=!P.

LIST.

!ENDDEFINE.

!CORRTST R=.66 N=30 P=.85.
!CORRTST R=.50 N=50 P=.85.
```

- DEFINE names the macro as !CORRTST and declares arguments for the sample correlation coefficient (R), the sample size (N), and the population correlation coefficient (P).

- !TOKENS(1) specifies that the value of an argument is a string that follows the name of the argument in the macro call. Thus the first macro call specifies values of 0.66, 30, and 0.85 for R, N, and P.
- Commands between INPUT PROGRAM and END INPUT PROGRAM create a working data file with one case. COMPUTE statements calculate the Z statistic and its probability using the values of macro arguments R, N, and P. (INPUT PROGRAM commands would not be needed if COMPUTE statements operated on values in an existing file or inline data, rather than macro arguments.)
- A customized TITLE shows displays the values of macro arguments used in computing Z.
- The LIST command displays Z and its probability.
- The !CORRTST macro is called twice in Figure D.12. The first invocation tests an r of 0.66 from a sample of 30 cases against a population coefficient of 0.85 (this generates the same Z value and probability as in Figure D.11). The second macro call tests an r of 0.50 from a sample of 50 cases against the same population correlation coefficient. The output from these macro calls is shown in Figure D.12.

Figure D.13 Output from !CORRTST

```
SAMPLE R= .66 , N= 30 , POPULATION COEFFICIENT= .85

       Z        PROB
    -2.41       .016


SAMPLE R= .50 , N= 50 , POPULATION COEFFICIENT= .85

       Z        PROB
    -4.85       .000
```

Figure D.14 shows a modified !CORRTST macro that you can use to test a sample r against each coefficient in a *list* of population coefficients.

Figure D.14 !CORRTST macro with list-processing loop

```
DEFINE !CORRTST (R  = !TOKENS(1)
                 /N = !TOKENS(1)
                 /P = !CMDEND).
- INPUT PROGRAM.
-   END CASE.
-   END FILE.
- END INPUT PROGRAM.

!DO !I !IN (!P).
- COMPUTE #ZR = .5* (LN ((1 + !R) / (1 - !R))).
- COMPUTE #ZP = .5* (LN ((1 + !P) / (1 - !P))).

- COMPUTE Z    = (#ZR-#ZP)/(1/(SQRT(!N-3))).

- COMPUTE PROB=2*(1-CDFNORM(ABS(Z))).
- FORMAT  PROB(F8.3).
- TITLE SAMPLE R=!R, N=!N, POPULATION COEFFICIENT=!I.
- LIST.
!DOEND.

!ENDDEFINE.

!CORRTST R=.66 N=30 P=.20 .40 .60 .80 .85 .90.
```

- As in Figure D.12, DEFINE names the macro as !CORRTST and declares arguments for the sample correlation coefficient (R), the sample size (N), and the population correlation coefficient (P).
- !TOKENS(1) specifies that the value of an argument is a string that follows the name of the argument in the macro call. Thus, the macro call specifies the value of R as 0.66 and N as 0.30.
- !CMDEND indicates that the value for P is the remaining text in the macro call. Thus the value of P is a list containing the elements 0.20, 0.40, 0.60, 0.80, 0.85, and 0.90.
- Commands !DO !IN and !DOEND define a **list-processing loop**. Commands in the loop compute one Z statistic for each element in the list of population coefficients. For example, in the first iteration Z is computed using 0.20 as the population coefficient. In the second iteration 0.40 is used. The same sample size (30) and r value (0.66) are used for each Z statistic.
- The output from the macro call is shown in Figure D.15. One Z statistic is displayed for each population coefficient.

Figure D.15 Output from modified !CORRTST macro

```
SAMPLE R=  .66 , N= 30 , POPULATION COEFFICIENT= .20
          Z        PROB
       3.07        .002
SAMPLE R=  .66 , N= 30 , POPULATION COEFFICIENT= .40
          Z        PROB
       1.92        .055
SAMPLE R=  .66 , N= 30 , POPULATION COEFFICIENT= .60
          Z        PROB
        .52        .605
SAMPLE R=  .66 , N= 30 , POPULATION COEFFICIENT= .80
          Z        PROB
      -1.59        .112
SAMPLE R=  .66 , N= 30 , POPULATION COEFFICIENT= .85
          Z        PROB
      -2.41        .016
SAMPLE R=  .66 , N= 30 , POPULATION COEFFICIENT= .90
          Z        PROB
      -3.53        .000
```

Example 3: Generating Random Data

You can use SPSS command syntax to generate variables that have approximately a normal distribution. Commands for generating five standard normal variables (*X1* through *X5*) for 1000 cases are shown in Figure D.16. As shown in the DESCRIPTIVES output in Figure D.17, each variable has a mean of approximately 0 and a standard deviation of approximately 1.

Figure D.16 Data-generating commands

```
INPUT PROGRAM.
-    VECTOR X(5).
-       LOOP #I = 1 TO 1000.
-          LOOP #J = 1 TO 5.
-             COMPUTE X(#J) = NORMAL(1).
-          END LOOP.
-          END CASE.
-       END LOOP.
-       END FILE.
END INPUT PROGRAM.

DESCRIPTIVES VARIABLES X1 TO X5.
```

Figure D.17   Descriptive statistics for generated data

```
                                            Valid
Variable      Mean    Std Dev   Minimum   Maximum     N   Label

X1            -.01     1.02      -3.11      4.15    1000
X2             .08     1.03      -3.19      3.22    1000
X3             .02     1.00      -3.01      3.51    1000
X4             .03     1.00      -3.35      3.19    1000
X5            -.01      .96      -3.34      2.91    1000
```

The !DATAGEN macro in Figure D.18 issues the data-generating commands shown in Figure D.16.

Figure D.18   !DATAGEN macro

```
DEFINE !DATAGEN ().

INPUT PROGRAM.
-    VECTOR X(5).
-        LOOP #I = 1 TO 1000.
-            LOOP #J = 1 TO 5.
-                COMPUTE X(#J) = NORMAL(1).
-            END LOOP.
-            END CASE.
-        END LOOP.
-        END FILE.
END INPUT PROGRAM.

DESCRIPTIVES VARIABLES X1 TO X5.

!ENDDEFINE.

!DATAGEN.
```

In Figure D.18, data-generating commands are imbedded between macro definition commands. The macro produces the same data and descriptive statistics as shown in Figure D.17.

You can tailor the generation of normally distributed variables if you modify the !DATAGEN macro so it will accept keyword arguments, as in Figure D.19. The macro allows you to specify the number of variables and cases to be generated and the approximate standard deviation.

Figure D.19 !DATAGEN macro with keyword arguments

```
DEFINE !DATAGEN (   OBS   =!TOKENS(1)    !DEFAULT(1000)
                   /VARS  =!TOKENS(1)    !DEFAULT(5)
                   /SD    =!CMDEND       !DEFAULT(1)).
INPUT PROGRAM.
-   VECTOR X(!VARS).
-       LOOP #I = 1 TO !OBS.
-           LOOP #J = 1 TO !VARS.
-               COMPUTE X(#J) = NORMAL(!SD).
-           END LOOP.
-           END CASE.
-       END LOOP.
-       END FILE.
END INPUT PROGRAM.

!LET !LIST = !NULL.
!DO  !I    = 1 !TO !VARS.
-    !LET !LIST = !CONCAT(!LIST, ' ', X, !I).
!DOEND.

DESCRIPTIVES VARIABLES !LIST.

!ENDDEFINE.

!DATAGEN OBS=500 VARS=2 SD=1.
!DATAGEN.
```

- The DEFINE statement in Figure D.19 declares arguments that specify the number of cases (OBS), variables (VARS), and standard deviation (SD). By default, the macro creates 1000 cases with 5 variables that have a standard deviation of 1.
- Commands between INPUT PROGRAM and END INPUT PROGRAM generate the new data using values of the macro arguments.
- Commands !LET and !DO/!DOEND construct a variable list (!LIST) that is used in DESCRIPTIVES. The first !LET command initializes the list to a null (blank) string value. For each new variable, the index loop adds to the list a string of the form X1, X2, X3, and so forth. Thus, DESCRIPTIVES requests means and standard deviations for each new variable.
- The first macro call generates 500 cases with two standard normal variables. The second call requests the default number of variables, cases, and standard deviation. Descriptive statistics (not shown) are also computed for each variable.

As shown in Figure D.20, you can declare additional keyword arguments that allow you to specify the distribution (normal or uniform) of the generated data and a parameter value that is used as the standard deviation (for normally distributed data) or a range (for uniformly distributed data).

Figure D.20 !DATAGEN macro with additional keyword arguments

```
DEFINE !DATAGEN (OBS    =!TOKENS(1)    !DEFAULT(1000)
                /VARS   =!TOKENS(1)    !DEFAULT(5)
                /DIST   =!TOKENS(1)    !DEFAULT(NORMAL)
                /PARAM  =!TOKENS(1)    !DEFAULT(1)).
INPUT PROGRAM.
-     VECTOR X(!VARS).
-         LOOP #I = 1 TO !OBS.
-           LOOP #J = 1 TO !VARS.
-             COMPUTE X(#J) = !DIST(!PARAM).
-           END LOOP.
-           END CASE.
-         END LOOP.
-         END FILE.
END INPUT PROGRAM.

!LET !LIST = !NULL.
!DO !I = 1 !TO !VARS.
-    !LET !LIST = !CONCAT(!LIST, ' ', X, !I).
!DOEND.

DESCRIPTIVES VARIABLES !LIST.
!ENDDEFINE.

!DATAGEN OBS=500 VARS=2 DIST=UNIFORM PARAM=2.
```

- The **DEFINE** statement in Figure D.20 declares arguments **OBS**, **VARS**, **DIST**, and **PARAM**. As in Figure D.19, **OBS** and **VARS** represent the number of observations and cases to be generated. Arguments **DIST** and **PARAM** specify the shape and parameter of the distribution of generated data. By default, the macro generates 1000 observations with 5 standard normal variables.
- Statements between **INPUT PROGRAM** and **END INPUT PROGRAM** generate the new data using values of macro arguments.
- Remaining commands in the body of the macro obtain descriptive statistics for generated variables, as in Figure D.19.
- The macro call in Figure D.20 creates two approximately uniformly distributed variables with a range of 2. The output from the macro call is shown in Figure D.21.

Figure D.21 Descriptive statistics for uniform variables

Variable	Mean	Std Dev	Minimum	Maximum	Valid N	Label
X1	.99	.57	.00	2.00	500	
X2	1.00	.57	.00	2.00	500	

Topical Index

Add Cases procedure, 74–81
   case source variable, 79–80
   dictionary information, 76
   key variables, 78–79
   limitations, 76
   removing variables, 79
   renaming variables, 77–78
   selecting variables, 79
   unpaired variables, 76
   variables in the new file, 80–81
Add Variables procedure, 382–389
   case source variable, 388
   dictionary information, 383–384
   duplicate cases, 386
   excluded variables, 387–388
   file sort order, 384, 385
   key variables, 385–386
   keyed tables, 386
   limitations, 384
   renaming variables, 387
   variables in the new file, 389
aggregating data, 85–94
   aggregate functions, 90–92
   aggregate variables, 91–92
   break variables, 85, 88–89
   saving files, 88
   variable labels, 90
   variable names, 89–90
Akaike information criterion
   in Linear Regression procedure, 538
Ameniya's prediction criterion
   in Linear Regression procedure, 538
analysis of variance, 95–103, 461–470
   in Linear Regression procedure, 538
   in Means procedure, 418
   See also One-Way ANOVA procedure; Simple Factorial ANOVA procedure
ANOVA. See analysis of variance
area charts, 326
arithmetic functions, 46–47, 122–123
arithmetic operators, 45, 122

arrays. See vectors
ASCII text data files. See raw data files
assignment expression
   computing values, 119

backward elimination
   in Linear Regression procedure, 536
bar charts, 321–325
   in Frequencies procedure, 273–274, 275
   interval width, 273–274
   scale, 273–274
batch mode, 14–15
Binomial Test procedure, 444–445
   expected proportions, 445
   observed proportions, 444–445
Bivariate Correlation procedure, 127–132, 436–441
   case count, 438
   correlation coefficients, 127
   format, 130, 436, 439
   limitations, 128, 437
   matrix output, 130–132, 436, 440–441
   missing values, 130, 439
   random sampling, 436, 439
   rank-order coefficients, 436–441
   significance level, 438–439
   significance levels, 129, 436
   statistics, 129–130, 438–439
blank data fields
   treatment of, 633
blank lines
   displaying, 504–505
   See also printing cases
Blom's transformation, 512
BMDP files
   conversion to SPSS, 284–285
   format specification, 529
   numeric variables, 529
   reading, 283–288
   string variables, 529
boxplots

comparing factor levels, 225–226
comparing variables, 225–226
in Explore procedure, 229
outliers, 227
scale, 226

case identification variable, 525–526
case selection, 433–434
cases
　limiting, 433–434
　listing, 368–371
　sampling, 608–610
　selecting, 433–434, 625–629
　sorting, 648–649
　weighting, 685–687
character sets, 711–717
charts, 317–336
　area, 326
　bar, 321–325
　footnotes, 321
　functions, 318–319
　histograms, 333–334
　line, 326–329
　missing values, 336
　pie, 329–330
　resolution, 642
　scatterplots, 330–333
　subtitles, 321
　summary functions, 318–319
　templates, 334–336
　titles, 321
chi-square
　in Chi-Square Test procedure, 445–446
　in Crosstabs procedure, 141
Chi-Square Test procedure, 445–446
　expected proportions, 446
　observed proportions, 445–446
Cochran's Q
　in Tests for Several Related Samples procedure, 446–447
Cohen's kappa. See kappa
column percentages
　in Crosstabs procedure, 140
column-style format specifications, 160
command files, 21, 350–351
command order, 17–20, 703–710
command terminator

specifying, 640
commands, 11–20
　executing, 13–15
　that read data, 18–19
　that take effect immediately, 18–19
comments
　in commands, 116
complex raw data files, 520–528, 718–731
　case identification variable, 525–526
　defining, 202–203, 213–216, 216–217, 242–256, 520–528
　duplicate records, 527
　grouped, 247
　grouped files, 520
　missing records, 526–527
　mixed, 247
　mixed files, 520
　nested, 247
　nested files, 520
　repeating groups, 520
　skipping records, 524–525
　spreading values across cases, 527–528
　undefined records, 523–524
computing values, 45–58, 117–126
　arithmetic functions, 46–47, 122–123
　arithmetic operators, 45, 122
　assignment expression, 119
　conditional expressions, 196–198, 340–342
　converting numeric to string, 52
　converting strings to numeric, 52
　cross-case function, 56
　cross-case functions, 124
　date and time functions, 66–72, 125
　formats of new variables, 121–122
　functions, 117–119
　if case satisfies condition, 195–203, 340–345
　logical expressions, 52–56, 196–198, 340–342
　logical functions, 53–54, 124
　logical operators, 54–55, 195, 340
　loop structures, 372–381
　missing values, 121
　missing-value functions, 56–57, 123–124
　random-number functions, 47–48, 124–125
　relational operators, 54, 195, 340
　statistical functions, 47, 123
　string data, 120, 121–122
　string functions, 49–53, 126
　syntax rules, 120–121
　target variable, 119

condition index
  in Linear Regression procedure, 538
conditional transformations, 195–203, 340–345
  conditional expressions, 196–198, 340–342
  formats of new variables, 197, 342
  logical expressions, 196–198, 340–342
  logical operators, 195, 340
  missing values, 198, 342
  nested, 202
  relational operators, 195, 340
  string data, 196, 197, 341, 342
confidence intervals
  in Linear Regression procedure, 539, 541, 551
consecutive integers
  converting numeric data, 108–111
  converting string data, 108–111
contingency coefficient
  in Crosstabs procedure, 141
contour plots, 482
contrasts
  analysis of variance, 463–464
control variables
  in Crosstabs procedure, 139
converting data files. See data files
Cook's distance
  in Linear Regression procedure, 551
correlation, 127–132
  in Linear Regression procedure, 539, 544
  See also Bivariate Correlation procedure
counting occurrences, 133–134
  defining values, 133
  missing values, 134
counts
  in Report Summaries in Rows procedure, 592, 593
covariance
  in Linear Regression procedure, 538, 544
covariance ratio
  in Linear Regression procedure, 551
Cp. See Mallow's Cp
Cramér's V
  in Crosstabs procedure, 141
cross-case function, 56
cross-case functions, 124
cross-product deviation
  in Linear Regression procedure, 544
Crosstabs procedure, 135–145
  boxes around cells, 143
  column percentages, 140
  control variables, 139
  expected count, 141
  general mode, 139
  index of tables, 143
  integer mode, 140
  labels, 143
  layers, 139
  missing values, 142
  observed count, 140
  reproducing tables, 145
  residuals, 141
  row order, 143
  row percentages, 140
  statistics, 141–142
  suppressing tables, 143
  table format, 142–143
  total percentage, 141
  writing tables, 143–145
crosstabulation, 135–145
  in Means procedure, 416–417
  multiple response, 427–430
  writing to a file, 506–507
  See also Crosstabs procedure
custom currency formats
  creating, 637–638

d. See Somers' d
data
  inline, 112–113, 149, 150
  invalid, 633
data compression
  scratch files, 639
data files, 22–31
  aggregating, 85–94
  applying data dictionary, 104–107
  BMDP, 283–288, 529–530
  complex, 213–216, 242–256, 520–528, 718–731
  converting, 619–624
  dBASE, 311–312, 619–624
  default file extension, 639–640
  direct access, 360–365
  documents, 193–194, 209
  Excel, 310–311, 619–624
  file information, 190–192, 657
  grouped, 520
  INFORMIX, 289–292

INGRES, 289–292
keyed, 360–365, 487–490
labels, 241
Lotus 1-2-3, 310–311, 619–624
master files, 667–673
matrix, 26–31
merging, 74–81, 382–389
mixed, 520
Multiplan, 310–311
nested, 520
opening, 279–282
ORACLE, 289–292
OSIRIS, 293–298
raw, 22, 147–164
reading, 148, 279–316, 346–349, 360–365
repeating data groups, 520
SAS, 299–304
saving, 611–615, 696–701
SCSS, 305–308, 616–618
split-file processing, 650–652
spreadsheet, 310–311, 620–621
SPSS, 23, 25–26, 279
SPSS portable, 23, 234–239, 346
SPSS/PC+, 346
SQL, 289–292
subsets of cases, 257–258, 625–629
SYBASE, 289–292
SYLK, 310–311, 619–624
tab-delimited, 312, 621
transaction files, 667–673
updating, 667–673
working, 23–24
data formats. See data types; display formats; input formats; output formats
data records
  defining, 153–154, 520–528
data transformations, 45–58
  arithmetic functions, 46–47, 122–123
  arithmetic operators, 45, 122
  clearing, 115
  computing values, 117–126
  conditional, 195–203, 340–345
  conditional expressions, 196–198, 340–342
  consecutive integers, 108–111
  converting numeric to string, 52
  converting strings to numeric, 52, 108–111, 518–519
  counting occurrences, 133–134
  counting the same value across variables, 133
  cross-case function, 56

cross-case functions, 124
date and time functions, 66–72, 125
functions, 117–119
if case satisfies condition, 195–203, 340–345
logical expressions, 52–56, 196–198, 340–342
logical functions, 53–54, 124
logical operators, 54–55, 195, 340
loop structures, 372–381
missing-value functions, 56–57, 123–124
random-number functions, 47–48, 124–125
recoding values, 108–111, 514–519
relational operators, 54, 195, 340
repeating, 204–208
statistical functions, 47, 123
string functions, 49–53, 126
data types, 35–44, 147–148
  custom currency, 637–638
  date and time, 59–64
  numeric, 35–41
  string, 42–44
database files, 621
date and time functions, 125
dBASE files
  reading, 309–316
  saving, 622
decimal indicator
  specifying, 638
decimal places
  implied, 161–163
Define Multiple Response Sets procedure, 425–426
  categories, 425–426
  dichotomies, 425–426
  set labels, 425–426
  set names, 425–426
delimiters, 17
descriptive statistics, 183–189
  in Explore procedure, 230
  See also Descriptives procedure
Descriptives procedure, 183–189
  display order, 188–189
  format options, 186–187
  index of variables, 187
  limitations, 184
  missing values, 189
  output width, 186–187
  saving Z scores, 185–186
  statistics, 187–188
detrended normal plots

in Explore procedure, 229
dfBeta
   in Linear Regression procedure, 551
dfFit
   in Linear Regression procedure, 551
direct-access files
   reading, 360–365
display formats, 265–268, 501–503
documentation
   online, 352–355
documents
   dropping, 209
   for SPSS data files, 193–194
   retaining in aggregated files, 89
domain errors, 48
Durbin-Watson statistic
   in Linear Regression procedure, 553

eigenvalues
   in Linear Regression procedure, 538
end-of-file control
   in input programs, 154–156
erasing files, 222
error messages, 24
errors
   displaying, 634–635
   maximum number, 633–634
eta
   in Crosstabs procedure, 142
   in Means procedure, 418
exact-size sample, 608
examining data, 223–232
   See also Explore procedure
Excel files
   read range, 314–315
   read variable names, 314
   reading, 309–316
   saving, 622
expected count
   in Crosstabs procedure, 141
Explore procedure, 223–232
   factor variable, 225
   frequency tables, 227–228
   limitations, 224
   missing values, 231–232
   plots, 229–230

   scaling plots, 226
   statistics, 228, 230–231
exploring data, 223–232
   See also Explore procedure
extreme values
   in Explore procedure, 230

F ratio
   in Linear Regression procedure, 538, 539
   in Means procedure, 418
file handle, 240
file information
   SPSS data files, 657
   working data file, 190–192
file specifications, 240
file transformations, 667–673
   aggregating, 85–94
   applying data dictionary, 104–107
   merging files, 74–81, 382–389
   subsets of cases, 625–629
Fisher's exact test
   in Crosstabs procedure, 141
fixed format, 149, 149–150, 151–152, 157–158
forced entry
   in Linear Regression procedure, 536
forced removal
   in Linear Regression procedure, 537
formats
   of new variables, 121–122, 197, 342
   See also data types; display formats; input formats; output formats
FORTRAN-like format specifications, 160–161
forward selection
   in Linear Regression procedure, 536
fractional ranks, 510
freefield format, 149, 150, 151–152, 158–159
Frequencies procedure, 269–278
   charts, 273–275
   condensed format, 272
   display order, 272
   general mode, 270–271
   index of tables, 273
   integer mode, 270–271
   limitations, 271
   missing values, 278
   page format, 272

statistics, 277–278
suppressing tables, 273
value labels, 272
writing tables, 273
frequency tables, 270–273
format, 272–273
in Explore procedure, 227–228
increment, 227–228
starting value, 227–228
writing to a file, 506–507
Friedman test
in Tests for Several Related Samples procedure, 447
F-to-enter
in Linear Regression procedure, 540
F-to-remove
in Linear Regression procedure, 540
functions, 117–119
date and time, 66–72
examples, 122–126
missing values, 48, 52, 57–58
missing values in, 121
numeric, 46–49
string, 49–53

gamma
in Crosstabs procedure, 142
general mode
Crosstabs procedure, 139
Frequencies procedure, 270–271
Means procedure, 412, 413, 416
Goodman and Kruskal's gamma. See gamma
Goodman and Kruskal's lambda. See lambda
Goodman and Kruskal's tau
in Crosstabs procedure, 141
grouped files, 247, 520

H. See Kruskal-Wallis H
harmonic average
in analysis of variance, 466
help, 337–338
hierarchical files. See nested file
histograms, 333–334
in Explore procedure, 229
in Frequencies procedure, 274–275
in Linear Regression procedure, 552–553

interval width, 274
scale, 226, 274
with normal curve, 275

implied decimal format, 161–163
Independent-Samples T Test procedure, 663–666
dependent variables, 665
grouping variables, 665
limitations, 664
missing values, 666
variable labels, 666
independent-samples t test. See t test
indexing clause
in loop structures, 374–379
INFORMIX files
reading, 289–292
INGRES files
reading, 289–292
initialization
suppressing, 366–367
initializing variables, 459–460, 653–654
formats, 459, 460, 653–654
numeric variables, 459–460
scratch variables, 459
string variables, 653–654
inline data, 112–113, 149, 150
input formats, 34–44, 147–148, 159–164
binary, 38–41
column-style specifications, 160
date and time, 59–64
FORTRAN-like, 44
FORTRAN-like specifications, 160–161
hexadecimal, 38–41, 44
numeric, 35–41, 161–163
string, 42–44, 163–164
input programs, 356–359
end-case control, 212–219
end-of-file control, 154–156, 220–221
examples, 155–156, 203, 206, 213–219, 221, 358–359, 376–378, 379, 380–381, 460, 488–489, 682–683
input state, 357
integer mode
Crosstabs procedure, 140
Frequencies procedure, 270–271
Means procedure, 412, 413, 416
interaction effects

analysis of variance, 98
interactive mode, 13–14
invalid data
    treatment of, 633

journal file, 641
journal files, 21–22

kappa
    in Crosstabs procedure, 142
Kendall's tau-*b*
    in Bivariate Correlation procedure, 438
    in Crosstabs procedure, 141
Kendall's tau-*c*
    in Crosstabs procedure, 141
Kendall's *W*
    in Tests for Several Related Samples procedure, 450–451
key variables, 667–673
keyed data files, 487–490
    defining, 487–490
    file handle, 489
    file key, 487, 488–489, 489–490
keyed files
    reading, 360–365
keyed tables, 386
keywords, 16
    reserved, 32
Kolmogorov-Smirnov *Z*
    in One-Sample Kolmogorov-Smirnov Test procedure, 448–449
Kolmogorov-Smirnov *Z*
    in Two-Independent-Samples Tests procedure, 449
Kruskal-Wallis *H*
    in Tests for Several Independent Samples procedure, 449–450
kurtosis
    in Descriptives procedure, 188
    in Explore procedure, 230
    in Frequencies procedure, 277
    in Report Summaries in Rows procedure, 592

lambda
    in Crosstabs procedure, 141
Levene test
    in Explore procedure, 229
leverage values
    in Linear Regression procedure, 551
likelihood-ratio chi-square
    in Crosstabs procedure, 141
Lilliefors test
    in Explore procedure, 229
limitations. See individual procedures
line charts, 326–329
Linear Regression procedure, 531–548, 549–557
    case selection, 544–545
    constant term, 541–542
    dependent variables, 535
    format, 547–548
    histogram, 552–553
    matrix input, 545–547
    matrix output, 545–547
    missing values, 546–547
    model criteria, 539–541
    plots, 552–555
    residuals, 549–557
    saving new variables, 556
    statistics, 537–539, 543–544
    tolerance, 539, 540, 541
    variable selection methods, 536–537
    weights, 542–543
linearity test
    in Means procedure, 418
List Cases procedure, 368–371
listing cases, 368–371
listing files, 24–25
local documentation, 352, 354
logical expressions, 52–56, 196–198, 340–342
    in loop structures, 374
    missing values, 55–56
    selecting cases, 625
logical functions, 53–54, 124
logical operators, 54–55, 195, 340, 625
    missing values, 198, 342
    string data, 120
loop structures, 372–381
    increment value, 378–379
    indexing variable, 374–379
    initial value, 375
    logical expression, 374
    macro facility, 180–182
    terminal value, 375

looping structures
   terminating, 114
loops
   maximum number, 634
Lotus 1-2-3 files
   read range, 314–315
   read variable names, 314
   reading, 309–316
   saving, 622
lower case
   specifying, 636–637

macro facility, 165–182
   assigning defaults, 175–176
   conditional processing, 180
   display macro commands, 641–642
   examples, 732–746
   keyword arguments, 170–171
   loop structures, 180–182
   macro call, 167
   macro definition, 166–167
   macro expansion, 641–642
   positional arguments, 171–172
   SET command, 178–179
   string functions, 176–178
   tokens, 172–175
Mahalanobis distance
   in Linear Regression procedure, 551
Mallow's Cp
   in Linear Regression procedure, 538
Mann-Whitney U
   in Two-Independent-Samples Tests procedure, 451
Mantel-Haenszel chi-square
   in Crosstabs procedure, 141
master files, 667–673
matrices
   correlation, 127–132, 436–441, 471–478
   covariance, 129–130
   split-file processing, 651
matrix data files, 26–31
   converting correlation to covariance, 409–411
   converting covariance to correlation, 409–411
   raw, 390–408
   See also raw matrix data files
maximum
   in Descriptives procedure, 188
   in Explore procedure, 230

   in Frequencies procedure, 278
   in Report Summaries in Rows procedure, 592
MCA. See multiple classification analysis
McNemar's test
   in Two-Related Samples Tests procedure, 452
mean
   in Descriptives procedure, 188
   in Explore procedure, 230
   in Frequencies procedure, 277
   in Linear Regression procedure, 543
   in Means procedure, 417
   in Report Summaries in Rows procedure, 592
mean substitution
   in Linear Regression procedure, 547
Means procedure, 412–419
   crosstabulation, 416–417
   general vs. integer mode, 412, 413, 416
   labels, 418–419
   layers, 416
   missing values, 418
   statistics, 417–418
median
   in Explore procedure, 230
   in Frequencies procedure, 277
   in Report Summaries in Rows procedure, 592
median test
   in Tests for Several Independent Samples procedure, 452–453
merging data files
   files with different cases, 74–81
   files with different variables, 382–389
   raw data files, 77, 385
   See also Add Variables procedure
M-estimators
   in Explore procedure, 230–231
minimum
   in Descriptives procedure, 188
   in Explore procedure, 230
   in Frequencies procedure, 278
   in Report Summaries in Rows procedure, 592
missing values
   and aggregated data, 92–94
   and logical operators, 198, 342
   counting occurrences, 134
   defining, 420–422
   in charts, 336
   in functions, 48, 52, 57–58, 121
   in logical expressions, 55–56

Topical Index

in loop structures, 380
in Multiple Response Crosstabs procedure, 430–431
in Multiple Response Frequencies procedure, 430–431
system-missing, 420
user-missing, 420–422
See also individual procedures
missing-value functions, 56–57, 123–124
mixed files, 247, 520
mode
in Frequencies procedure, 277
in Report Summaries in Rows procedure, 593
Moses test
in Two-Independent-Samples Tests procedure, 453–454
Multiplan files
read range, 314–315
read variable names, 314
reading, 309–316
saving, 622
multiple classification analysis
analysis of variance, 103
multiple comparisons
analysis of variance, 464–466
multiple *R*
in Linear Regression procedure, 538
multiple regression, 531–548
See also Linear Regression procedure
multiple response analysis, 423–432
defining sets, 423–424
multiple category, 423–424
multiple dichotomy, 423–424
See also Define Multiple Response Sets procedure; Multiple Response Crosstabs procedure; Multiple Response Frequencies procedure
Multiple Response Crosstabs procedure, 427–430
cell percentages, 429–430
defining value ranges, 426–427
matching variables across response sets, 429
missing values, 430–431
percents based on cases, 430
percents based on responses, 430
value labels, 431
Multiple Response Frequencies procedure, 427
missing values, 430–431
table format, 431–432
value labels, 431

multipunch data, 240

nested conditions, 202
nested files, 247, 520
noninteger weights, 686
nonparametric tests, 18, 436–441, 442–458
normal probability plots
in Explore procedure, 229
in Linear Regression procedure, 553
normal scores, 510
notes, 24
numeric data
input formats, 147–148, 161–163
output formats, 265–268, 501–503, 693–695

observed count
in Crosstabs procedure, 140
in Linear Regression procedure, 544
One-Sample Kolmogorov-Smirnov Test procedure, 448–449
test distribution, 448
One-Way ANOVA procedure, 461–470
contrasts, 463–464
defining factor ranges, 462–463
display labels, 466
factor variables, 462–463
harmonic means, 466
limitations, 462
matrix input, 467–470
matrix output, 467–470
missing values, 467, 469
multiple comparisons, 464–466
polynomial contrasts, 463
statistics, 466–467
online documentation, 352–355
online help, 337–338
opening files
data files, 279–282
options, 630–643
displaying, 644–647
See also preferences
ORACLE files
reading, 289–292
OSIRIS files
conversion to SPSS, 294–295
reading, 293–298

outliers
   identifying, 227
   in Linear Regression procedure, 553, 554
output files
   borders for tables, 643
   chart characters, 642–643
   destination of, 634–635
   display command syntax, 634–635
   display output page titles, 637
   letter case, 636–637
   page size, 635–636
output formats, 34–44, 149, 501–503, 693–695
   binary, 38–41
   custom currency, 265, 501, 693
   date and time, 59–64
   displaying, 502, 694
   format specification, 501, 693
   hexadecimal, 38–41, 44
   numeric, 35–41
   print (display), 265–268
   string data, 42–44, 265
   types, 266–267
   write, 265–268, 693–695
overlay plots, 330, 332, 482

page ejection, 498–500
   missing values, 499
   variable list, 499
page size, 635–636
Paired-Samples T Test procedure, 663–666
   limitations, 664
   missing values, 666
   variable labels, 666
   variable list, 665–666
paired-samples *t* test. See *t* test
part correlation
   in Linear Regression procedure, 539
partial correlation, 471–478
   in Linear Regression procedure, 539
   See also Partial Correlations procedure
Partial Correlations procedure, 471–478
   control variables, 473
   format, 475
   limitations, 472
   matrix input, 476–478
   matrix output, 476–478
   missing values, 475, 477
   order values, 473
   significance levels, 474
   statistics, 474
Pearson chi-square
   in Crosstabs procedure, 141
Pearson correlation coefficient
   in Bivariate Correlation procedure, 127
   in Crosstabs procedure, 142
Pearson's *r*. See Pearson correlation coefficient
percentages
   in Crosstabs procedure, 140–141
   in Report Summaries in Rows procedure, 593
percentiles
   break points, 228
   estimating from grouped data, 275–276
   in Explore procedure, 228
   in Frequencies procedure, 276–277
   methods, 228
phi
   in Crosstabs procedure, 141
pie charts, 329–330
polynomial contrasts
   analysis of variance, 463
portable files
   saving, 234–239
post-hoc tests. See multiple comparisons
predicted values
   adjusted, 550
   standard errors, 551
   standardized, 551
   unstandardized, 550
preferences, 630–643
   blank data fields, 633
   borders for tables, 643
   charts, 642
   command terminator, 640
   custom currency formats, 637–638
   data compression, 639
   decimal indicator, 638
   default file extension, 639–640
   default variable format, 636
   display errors, 634–635
   display macro commands, 641–642
   display resource messages, 634–635
   display statistical results, 634–635
   display warnings, 634–635
   displaying, 644–647
   errors, 633–634
   graphics, 642, 642–643

invalid data, 633
journal file, 641
letter case, 636–637
macro expansion, 641–642
maximum loops, 634
output, 634–635, 637
output page size, 635–636
preserving, 491, 607
random number seed, 638–639
restoring, 491, 607
sort program, 639
thousands separator, 638
warnings, 633–634

print formats. See output formats

printing cases, 492–497, 504–505
column headings, 498–500
displaying blank lines, 504–505
formats, 492, 494, 690
missing values, 493
number of records, 496
output file, 492, 496–497, 504
page ejection, 498–500
strings, 492, 495
summary table, 492, 497

probability of F-to-enter
in Linear Regression procedure, 540

probability of F-to-remove
in Linear Regression procedure, 540

procedure output
output file, 506–507
writing to a file, 506–507

procedures
update documentation, 354

program states, 703–710

proportion estimates, 510

proportional sample, 608

Q. See Cochran's Q

R
in Means procedure, 418

r. See Pearson correlation coefficient

R^2
in Linear Regression procedure, 538

random number seed
specifying, 638–639

random sampling
in nonparametric tests, 458

random-number functions, 47–48, 124–125

range
in Descriptives procedure, 188
in Explore procedure, 230
in Frequencies procedure, 278

ranking data, 508–513
missing values, 513
proportion estimate, 512–513
ranking direction, 509
ranking methods, 510–511
saving variables, 511–512
subgroups, 509
summary tables, 513
tie handling, 512

raw data files, 22
blanks, 149–150
data types, 147–148
fixed format, 149, 149–150, 151–152, 157–158
freefield format, 149, 150, 151–152, 158–159
reading, 147–164
variable definition, 156–164, 520–528

raw matrix data files, 390–408
factors, 402–404, 406–407
format, 390–391, 393–401
N, 408
record types, 404–408
split files, 401–402
within-cells records, 404, 406–407

recoding values, 514–519
converting strings to numeric, 108–111, 518–519
limitations, 516
missing values, 515–516
numeric variables, 515–519
string variables, 516–519
target variable, 517–518

records
defining, 153–154, 520–528
duplicate, 527
missing, 526–527
skipping, 524–525
types, 520–528

regression coefficients
in Linear Regression procedure, 538

regression plots, 482–483

relational operators, 54, 195, 340, 625

relative risk ratio

in Crosstabs procedure, 142
repeating data, 560–573
  case identification, 572–573
  defining variables, 568
  input file, 568–569
  repeating groups, 520, 567–569
  starting column, 566–567
  summary table, 573
Report Summaries in Rows procedure, 574–600
  column contents, 584–585, 588
  column headings, 575, 585, 588–589
  column spacing, 576
  column width, 576, 576, 585–586, 589
  defining subgroups, 587–591
  footnotes, 598–599
  format, 580–582
  limitations, 579–580
  missing values, 576, 578, 600
  output file, 578, 582–584
  page layout, 582
  print formats, 596–598
  report types, 578
  string variables, 586–587
  summary statistics, 578, 591–598
  summary titles, 595–596
  titles, 598–599
  variable list, 584–586
reports, 574–600
  See also Report Summaries in Rows procedure
re-reading records, 601–606
  input file, 604–605
  starting column, 605–606
residuals
  deleted, 550
  in Crosstabs procedure, 141
  standardized, 551
  Studentized, 551
  Studentized deleted, 551
  unstandardized, 550
row percentages
  in Crosstabs procedure, 140
runs test
  in Runs Test procedure, 454–455
Runs Test procedure, 454–455
  cutting point, 455

sample
  exact-size, 608

proportional, 608
sampling cases, 608–610
  See also selecting cases
SAS files
  conversion to SPSS, 300–304
  reading, 299–304
Savage scores, 510
saving files
  aggregated data files, 88
  dBASE format, 619–624
  Excel format, 619–624
  Lotus 1-2-3, 619–624
  SCSS format, 616–618
  spreadsheet format, 619–624
  SYLK format, 619–624
  tab-delimited data files, 619–624
saving SPSS data files, 611–615, 696–701
  data compression, 615, 700–701
  dropping variables, 613–615, 698–699
  keeping variables, 613–615, 698–699
  limitations, 698
  renaming variables, 614–615, 699–700
  variable map, 700
  variable summary, 615
scatterplots, 330–333, 479–486
  contour plots, 482
  control variables, 481–482
  cutpoints, 483–484
  horizontal axis, 481, 485–486
  limitations, 480–481
  missing values, 486
  overlay plots, 482
  plot resolution, 479
  plot scaling, 485–486
  plot types, 480
  regression plots, 482–483
  symbols, 483–484
  titles, 486
  vertical axis, 481, 485–486
Schwarz Bayesian criterion
  in Linear Regression procedure, 538
scratch variables, 34
SCSS files
  conversion to SPSS, 305–306
  reading, 305–308
  saving data files as, 616–618
seed. See random number seed
selecting cases, 608–610

exact-size sample, 608
limitations, 609
proportional sample, 608
temporary sample, 608
semi-partial correlation. See part correlation
settings, 630–643
   displaying, 644–647
   See also preferences
Shapiro-Wilk's test
   in Explore procedure, 229
Shapiro-Wilk's test
   in Explore procedure, 229
sign test
   in Two-Related-Samples Tests procedure, 455–456
significance level
   in Linear Regression procedure, 544
Simple Factorial ANOVA procedure
   covariates, 98, 98
   defining factor ranges, 97–98
   display labels, 103
   factor variables, 97–98
   interaction effects, 98
   limitations, 96–97
   methods, 98–100
   missing values, 103
   multiple classification analysis, 103
   statistics, 100–103
   sums of squares, 98–100, 101
   treatment effects, 103
skewness
   in Descriptives procedure, 188
   in Explore procedure, 230
   in Frequencies procedure, 277
   in Report Summaries in Rows procedure, 592
Somers' d
   in Crosstabs procedure, 142
sorting cases, 648–649
   sort keys, 648
   sort order, 648
   specifying sort program, 639
Spearman correlation coefficient
   in Bivariate Correlation procedure, 436
   in Crosstabs procedure, 142
Spearman's rho
   in Bivariate Correlation procedure, 438
split-file processing, 650–652
   break variables, 650

matrices, 651
scratch variables, 650
system variables, 650
temporary, 658–659
spread-and-level plots
   in Explore procedure, 229
spreadsheet files
   read ranges, 314–315
   read variable names, 314
   reading, 309–316
   saving, 619–624
SPSS data files, 23, 25–26
   documents, 193–194, 209
   reading, 279–282
SPSS portable files, 23
   reading, 346–349
   saving, 234–239
SPSS/PC+ files
   reading, 346–349
SQL files
   reading, 289–292
standard deviation
   in Descriptives procedure, 188
   in Explore procedure, 230
   in Frequencies procedure, 277
   in Linear Regression procedure, 544
   in Means procedure, 417
   in Report Summaries in Rows procedure, 592
standard error
   in Explore procedure, 230
   in Linear Regression procedure, 538, 539
standard error of the mean
   in Descriptives procedure, 188
   in Frequencies procedure, 277
stand-in variable, 204–205
statistical functions, 47, 123
stem-and-leaf plots
   in Explore procedure, 229
   scale, 226
stepwise selection
   in Linear Regression procedure, 536
string data
   computing values, 120, 121–122, 125–126
   conditional transformations, 196, 197, 341, 342
   converting to numeric, 108–111
   in logical expressions, 120
   input formats, 147–148, 163–164

missing values, 420
output formats, 265, 501–502, 693–694
value labels, 83–84, 674
string functions, 126
macro facility, 176–178
strings
in command specifications, 16–17
subcommands, 16
subsets of cases
conditional expressions, 625–626
filter status, 257–258
filtering unselected cases, 257–258
if condition is satisfied, 625–629
selecting, 625–629
subtitles, 655–656
apostrophes in, 655
length, 655
quotation marks in, 655
suppressing, 655
with inline data, 655
sum
in Descriptives procedure, 188
in Frequencies procedure, 278
in Report Summaries in Rows procedure, 592
survival tables
writing to a file, 506–507
sweep matrix
in Linear Regression procedure, 538
SYBASE files
reading, 289–292
SYLK files
read range, 314–315
read variable names, 314
reading, 309–316
saving, 622
syntax charts, 11–12
syntax files. See command files
system-missing value, 420

t test
in Independent-Samples T Test procedure, 663
in Paired-Samples T Test procedure, 663
tab-delimited files
reading, 309–316
saving, 621, 622
table lookup files, 386

target variable
counting values, 133, 134
target variables
computing values, 119
formats, 121–122
tau. See Goodman and Kruskal's tau
tau-b. See Kendall's tau-b
tau-c. See Kendalls' tau-c
templates
in charts, 334–336
temporary transformations, 658–660
temporary variables, 658
Tests for Several Independent Samples procedure, 449–450, 452–453
grouping variables, 450, 453
Tests for Several Related Samples procedure, 446–447, 450–451
thousands separator
specifying, 638
titles, 661–662
apostrophes in, 661
displaying, 637
length, 661
quotation marks in, 661
with inline data, 661
See also subtitles, 661
tolerance
in Linear Regression procedure, 539, 540, 541
total percentage
in Crosstabs procedure, 141
transaction files, 667–673
transformations
temporary, 658–660
translating data files. See data files
transposing cases and variables, 261–264
treatment effects
analysis of variance, 103
trimmed mean
in Explore procedure, 230
Tukey's transformation, 512
Two-Independent-Samples Tests procedure, 449, 451, 453–454, 456
grouping variables, 449, 451, 454, 456
outlier trimming, 454
Two-Related-Samples Tests procedure, 452, 455–456, 457

Topical Index

U. See Mann-Whitney *U*
uncertainty coefficient
    in Crosstabs procedure, 141
update documentation, 352, 354
updating data files, 667–673
    dropping variables, 672
    flag variables, 672–673
    input files, 670
    keeping variables, 672
    key variables, 667–673
    limitations, 669
    master files, 667–673
    raw data files, 670
    renaming variables, 671–672
    transaction files, 667–673
    variable map, 673
upper case
    specifying, 636–637
user-missing values, 420–422

V. See Cramér's *V*
value labels, 82–84, 674–676
    adding, 674–676
    apostrophes in, 674
    concatenating strings, 674, 675
    length, 674
    revising, 82–84
    string data, 83–84, 674
Van der Waerden's transformation, 513
variable labels, 677–678
    apostrophes in, 677
    concatenating strings, 677, 678
variables, 32–34
    controlling default format, 636
    date and time, 64–66, 72–73
    defining, 156–164, 459–460, 520–528, 653–654
    naming rules, 32, 156–157
    scratch, 34
    system, 33
    temporary, 658
variance
    in Descriptives procedure, 188
    in Explore procedure, 230
    in Frequencies procedure, 277
    in Linear Regression procedure, 538, 544
    in Means procedure, 417

in Report Summaries in Rows procedure, 592
variance inflation factor
    in Linear Regression procedure, 538
vectors, 679–684
    index, 679, 683–684
    variable list, 679

W. See Kendall's *W*
Wald-Wolfowitz test
    in Two-Independent-Samples Tests procedure, 456
warnings, 24
    displaying, 634–635
    maximum number, 633–634
weighted least-squares
    in Linear Regression procedure, 542
weighting cases, 685–687
    missing values, 686
    noninteger weights, 686
    non-positive values, 686
    temporary weighting, 685
    weight variable, 685
Wilcoxon test
    in Two-Related-Samples Tests procedure, 457
working data files, 23–24
write formats, 693–695

Yates' correction for continuity
    in Crosstabs procedure, 141

Z scores
    in Descriptives procedure, 185–186
    saving as variables, 185–186

Syntax Index

A (format), 42–43
A (keyword)
   DESCRIPTIVES command, 189
   SORT CASES command, 648
ABS (function), 46
ADD (function)
   REPORT command, 594
ADD FILES (command), 74–81
   BY subcommand, 78–79
   DROP subcommand, 79
   FILE subcommand, 77
   FIRST subcommand, 80
   IN subcommand, 79–80
   KEEP subcommand, 79
   key variables, 78–79
   LAST subcommand, 80
   limitations, 76
   MAP subcommand, 80–81
   RENAME subcommand, 77–78
   with DATA LIST command, 77
   with SORT CASES command, 76–77, 649
   working data file, 77
ADD VALUE LABELS (command), 19, 82–84
   compared with VALUE LABELS command, 674
   limitations, 83
   string variables, 83–84
ADJPRED (keyword)
   REGRESSION command, 550
AEMPIRICAL (keyword)
   EXAMINE command, 228
AFREQ (keyword)
   FREQUENCIES command, 272
AFTER (keyword)
   ANOVA command, 98
AGGREGATE (command), 18, 85–94
   BREAK subcommand, 88–89
   DOCUMENT subcommand, 89
   functions, 90–92
   MISSING subcommand, 92–94
   OUTFILE subcommand, 88
   PRESORTED subcommand, 89
   variable definitions, 89–92
   with MATCH FILES command, 87–88
   with SORT CASES command, 649
   with SPLIT FILE command, 87, 650–651
AHEX (format), 44
ALIGN (keyword)
   REPORT command, 581
ALL (keyword)
   ANOVA command, 98, 102
   CORRELATIONS command, 130
   CROSSTABS command, 141, 142, 144
   DESCRIPTIVES command, 188
   EXAMINE command, 229, 230, 231
   FREQUENCIES command, 278
   INFO command, 354
   MEANS command, 417, 418
   MULT RESPONSE command, 430
   NPAR TESTS command, 444, 458
   ONEWAY command, 466–467
   PARTIAL CORR command, 474
   PLOT command, 481
   PRINT command, 493
   WRITE command, 689
ALPHA (subcommand)
   REFORMAT command, 529–530
ALPHANUMERIC (keyword)
   PLOT command, 483
ALSCAL (command), 18
   matrix output, 26
ANALYSIS (keyword)
   NPAR TESTS command, 458
   ONEWAY command, 467
   PARTIAL CORR command, 475
   T-TEST command, 666
AND (keyword)
   logical operator, 55
ANDREW (keyword)
   EXAMINE command, 231
ANOVA (command), 18, 95–103
   cell means, 102
   covariates, 102–103

Syntax Index

COVARIATES subcommand, 98
FORMAT subcommand, 103
interaction effects, 98
limitations, 96–97
MAXORDERS subcommand, 98
METHOD subcommand, 98–100
MISSING subcommand, 103
multiple classification analysis, 103
sums of squares, 98–100
VARIABLES subcommand, 97–98
with AUTORECODE command, 110
ANOVA (keyword)
   MEANS command, 418
   REGRESSION command, 538
ANY (function), 54
   missing values, 58
APPEND (subcommand)
   MCONVERT command, 411
APPLY DICTIONARY (command), 104–107
   formats, 106
   FROM subcommand, 107
   missing values, 105–106
   value labels, 105
   variable labels, 105
   weight, 106
AREA (keyword)
   GRAPH command, 326
ARSIN (function), 47, 49
ARTAN (function), 47
ASRESID (keyword)
   CROSSTABS command, 141
asterisk (filename)
   in ADD FILES command, 77
   in MATCH FILES command, 385
AUTOMATIC (keyword)
   REPORT command, 581
AUTORECODE (command), 18, 108–111
   compared to RECODE, 108
   compared to RECODE command, 514
   DESCENDING subcommand, 111
   INTO subcommand, 111
   missing values, 109
   PRINT subcommand, 111
   VARIABLES subcommand, 111
   with ANOVA command, 110
   with MANOVA command, 110–111
   with TABLES command, 109–110
AVALUE (keyword)
   CROSSTABS command, 143
   FREQUENCIES command, 272
AVERAGE (function)
   REPORT command, 594

BACKWARD (keyword)
   REGRESSION command, 536
BADCORR (keyword)
   PARTIAL CORR command, 474
   REGRESSION command, 544
BAR (subcommand)
   GRAPH command, 321–325
BARCHART (subcommand)
   FREQUENCIES command, 273–274
BASE (subcommand)
   MULT RESPONSE command, 430
BCOV (keyword)
   REGRESSION command, 538
BEGIN DATA (command), 18, 112–113
   in a prompted session, 113
   in interactive mode, 13
   with INCLUDE command, 113
   with SUBTITLE command, 655
   with TITLE command, 661
BINOMIAL (subcommand)
   NPAR TESTS command, 444–445
BIVARIATE (keyword)
   GRAPH command, 330
BLANK (keyword)
   REPORT command, 587
BLANKS (subcommand)
   SET command, 633
   SHOW command, 645
!BLANKS (function)
   DEFINE command, 178
BLKSIZE (subcommand)
   SHOW command, 645
BLOCK (subcommand)
   SET command, 642
   SHOW command, 645
BLOM (keyword)
   RANK command, 512
BOTH (keyword)
   NONPAR CORR command, 438
   SET command, 635
BOX (keyword)

CROSSTABS command, 143
BOX (subcommand)
  SET command, 643
  SHOW command, 645
BOXPLOT (keyword)
  EXAMINE command, 229
BREAK (command), 114
  with DO IF command, 114
  with LOOP command, 114
BREAK (subcommand)
  AGGREGATE command, 88–89
  REPORT command, 587–591
!BREAK (command)
  DEFINE command, 180–182
BREAKDOWN (command)
  see MEANS
BRKSPACE (keyword)
  REPORT command, 582
BTAU (keyword)
  CROSSTABS command, 141
BTUKEY (keyword)
  ONEWAY command, 465
BUFFNO (subcommand)
  SHOW command, 645
BY (keyword)
  ANOVA command, 97–98
  CROSSTABS command, 139–140
  EXAMINE command, 227
  LIST command, 371
  LOOP command, 378–379
  MEANS command, 416
  MULT RESPONSE command, 427–429
  NPAR TESTS command, 444
  PARTIAL CORR command, 472–473
  PLOT command, 481, 482
  RANK command, 509
  SORT CASES command, 648
  SPLIT FILE command, 650
  WEIGHT command, 685
BY (subcommand)
  ADD FILES command, 78–79
  MATCH FILES command, 385
  UPDATE command, 670–671
!BY (keyword)
  DEFINE command, 180–182

CASE (keyword)
  FILE TYPE command, 252–253
CASE (subcommand)
  FILE TYPE command, 249–251
  RECORD TYPE command, 525–526
  SET command, 636–637
  SHOW command, 645
$CASENUM (system variable)
  defined, 33
  in PRINT EJECT command, 500
  with SELECT IF command, 626
CASES (keyword)
  MULT RESPONSE command, 430
CASES (subcommand)
  LIST command, 370–371
CASEWISE (subcommand)
  REGRESSION command, 553–554
CC (keyword)
  CROSSTABS command, 141
CC (subcommand)
  SET command, 637–638
  SHOW command, 645
CDFNORM (function), 48
CELLS (keyword)
  CROSSTABS command, 144
CELLS (subcommand)
  CROSSTABS command, 140–141
  MATRIX DATA command, 404
  MEANS command, 417
  MULT RESPONSE command, 429–430
CENTER (keyword)
  REPORT command, 585, 589, 598–599
CFVAR (function), 47
  missing values, 57
CHA (keyword)
  REGRESSION command, 538
CHALIGN (keyword)
  REPORT command, 581
!CHAREND (keyword)
  DEFINE command, 172
CHDSPACE (keyword)
  REPORT command, 582
CHISQ (keyword)
  CROSSTABS command, 141
CHISQUARE (subcommand)

Syntax Index

NPAR TESTS command, 445–446
CI (keyword)
  REGRESSION command, 539
CIN (keyword)
  REGRESSION command, 541
CLEAR TRANSFORMATIONS (command), 115
CLUSTER (command), 18
  matrix output, 26
!CMDEND (keyword)
  DEFINE command, 172
CNLR (command), 18
COCHRAN (subcommand)
  NPAR TESTS command, 446–447
CODE (subcommand)
  GET BMDP command, 286
COEFF (keyword)
  REGRESSION command, 538
COLLECT (keyword)
  REGRESSION command, 535
COLLIN (keyword)
  REGRESSION command, 538
COLSPACE (keyword)
  REPORT command, 581
COLUMN (keyword)
  CROSSTABS command, 140
  MULT RESPONSE command, 429
COLUMN (subcommand)
  REREAD command, 605–606
COLUMNWISE (keyword)
  AGGREGATE command, 92, 93–94
COMM (keyword)
  EXPORT command, 237
  IMPORT command, 347
COMMA (format), 37–38
COMMA (keyword)
  SET command, 638
COMMENT (command), 116
COMPARE (subcommand)
  EXAMINE command, 225–226
COMPRESSED (subcommand)
  SAVE command, 615
  XSAVE command, 700–701
COMPRESSION (subcommand)
  SET command, 639
  SHOW command, 645

COMPUTE (command), 117–126
  functions, 117–119
  missing values, 121
  with DO IF command, 122
  with STRING command, 121–122, 126
CONCAT (function), 50
!CONCAT (function)
  DEFINE command, 177
CONDENSE (keyword)
  FREQUENCIES command, 272
  MULT RESPONSE command, 432
  RANK command, 512
CONDENSED (keyword)
  PARTIAL CORR command, 475
CONTENT (subcommand)
  GET BMDP command, 286
CONTENTS (subcommand)
  MATRIX DATA command, 404–408
CONTINUED (subcommand)
  REPEATING DATA command, 570–572
CONTOUR (keyword)
  PLOT command, 482
CONTRAST (subcommand)
  ONEWAY command, 464
CONVERT (keyword)
  RECODE command, 518–519
COOK (keyword)
  REGRESSION command, 551
CORR (keyword)
  CROSSTABS command, 142
  MATRIX DATA command, 404–405
  PARTIAL CORR command, 474
CORRELATION (keyword)
  REGRESSION command, 544
CORRELATIONS (command), 18, 127–132
  FORMAT subcommand, 130
  limitations, 128
  matrix output, 28, 130–132
  MATRIX subcommand, 130–132
  MISSING subcommand, 130
  PRINT subcommand, 129
  significance tests, 129
  STATISTICS subcommand, 129–130
  with REGRESSION command, 545
COS (function), 47
COUNT (command), 133–134
  missing values, 134

COUNT (function)
  GRAPH command, 318
COUNT (keyword)
  CROSSTABS command, 140
  MATRIX DATA command, 405
  MEANS command, 417
  MULT RESPONSE command, 429
COV (keyword)
  MATRIX DATA command, 405
  REGRESSION command, 544
COVARIATES (subcommand)
  ANOVA command, 98
COVRATIO (keyword)
  REGRESSION command, 551
CRITERIA (subcommand)
  REGRESSION command, 539–541
CROSSBREAK (subcommand)
  MEANS command, 416–417
CROSSTABS (command), 18, 135–145
  cell percentages, 140–141
  CELLS subcommand, 140–141
  expected count, 140–141
  FORMAT subcommand, 142–143
  general mode, 139
  integer mode, 140
  limitations, 137
  MISSING subcommand, 142
  residuals, 140–141
  STATISTICS subcommand, 141–142
  string data, 42
  TABLES subcommand, 139–140
  VARIABLES subcommand, 138
  with PROCEDURE OUTPUT, 143, 144–145
  with PROCEDURE OUTPUT (command), 506
  with WEIGHT, 145
  WRITE subcommand, 143–145
CTAU (keyword)
  CROSSTABS command, 141
CTIME.DAYS (function), 69
CTIME.HOURS (function), 69
CTIME.MINUTES (function), 69
CUFREQ (function)
  GRAPH command, 318
CUPCT (function)
  GRAPH command, 318
CUSUM (function)
  GRAPH command, 318

CUTPOINT (subcommand)
  PLOT command, 483–484

D (keyword)
  CROSSTABS command, 142
  DESCRIPTIVES command, 189
  SORT CASES command, 648
DATA (subcommand)
  GET OSIRIS command, 296
  GET SAS command, 300
  REPEATING DATA command, 568
DATA LIST (command), 23, 147–164
  column-style formats, 160
  END subcommand, 154–156
  FILE subcommand, 150–151
  FIXED keyword, 151–152
  fixed-format data, 149, 149–150, 151–152, 157–158
  FORTRAN-like formats, 160–161
  FREE keyword, 151–152
  freefield data, 149, 150, 151–152, 158–159
  inline data, 149, 150
  LIST keyword, 151–152
  NOTABLE subcommand, 152–153
  RECORDS subcommand, 153–154
  TABLE subcommand, 152–153
  variable definition, 156–164
  variable formats, 147–148, 159–164
  variable names, 156–157
  with ADD FILES command, 77
  with INPUT PROGRAM command, 154–156, 202–203
  with MATCH FILES command, 385
  with NUMERIC command, 460
  with POINT command, 488
  with RECORD TYPE command, 520–528
  with REPEATING DATA command, 560, 561–562, 563–565
  with REREAD command, 601–606
  with UPDATE command, 670
  with VECTOR command, 683–684
DATABASE (subcommand)
  GET CAPTURE command, 290
DATE (argument)
  REPORT command, 599
$DATE (system variable)
  defined, 33
DATE.DMY (function), 66

DATE.MDY (function), 67
DATE.MOYR (function), 67
DATE.QYR (function), 67
DATE.WKYR (function), 67
DATE.YRDAY (function), 67
DB2 (keyword)
    SAVE TRANSLATE command, 622
DB3 (keyword)
    SAVE TRANSLATE command, 622
DB4 (keyword)
    SAVE TRANSLATE command, 622
DECIMAL (subcommand)
    SET command, 638
DEFAULT (keyword)
    DESCRIPTIVES command, 188
    FREQUENCIES command, 278
    MEANS command, 417
    PLOT command, 482
!DEFAULT (keyword)
    DEFINE command, 175–176
DEFINE (command), 165–182
    !BREAK command, 180–182
    !BY keyword, 180–182
    !CHAREND keyword, 172
    !CMDEND keyword, 172
    !DEFAULT keyword, 175–176
    !DO command, 180–182
    !DOEND command, 180–182
    !ELSE keyword, 180
    !ENCLOSE keyword, 172
    !IF command, 180
    !IFEND command, 180
    !IN keyword, 181–182
    !LET command, 182
    limitations, 167
    macro arguments, 169–176
    !NOEXPAND keyword, 176
    !OFFEXPAND keyword, 176
    !ONEXPAND keyword, 176
    !POSITIONAL keyword, 169–172
    string functions, 176–178
    !THEN keyword, 180
    !TO keyword, 180–182
    tokens, 172–175
    !TOKENS keyword, 172
    with SET command, 178–179
DEPENDENT (keyword)
    MEANS command, 418
DEPENDENT (subcommand)
    REGRESSION command, 535
DESCENDING (subcommand)
    AUTORECODE command, 111
DESCRIPTIVES (command), 18, 183–189
    FORMAT subcommand, 186–187
    limitations, 184
    MISSING subcommand, 189
    SAVE subcommand, 185–186
    SORT subcommand, 188–189
    STATISTICS subcommand, 187–188
    VARIABLES subcommand, 185
    with SET WIDTH command, 186–187
    Z scores, 185–186
DESCRIPTIVES (keyword)
    CORRELATIONS command, 129
    EXAMINE command, 230
    NPAR TESTS command, 457
    ONEWAY command, 466
    PARTIAL CORR command, 474
DESCRIPTIVES (subcommand)
    REGRESSION command, 543–544
DFBETA (keyword)
    REGRESSION command, 551
DFE (keyword)
    MATRIX DATA command, 405
DFFIT (keyword)
    REGRESSION command, 551
DFREQ (keyword)
    FREQUENCIES command, 272
DIAGONAL (keyword)
    MATRIX DATA command, 400
DICTIONARY (keyword)
    DISPLAY command, 190
DICTIONARY (subcommand)
    GET OSIRIS command, 296
dictionary formats
    in Save As Data File procedure, 690
DIGITS (subcommand)
    EXPORT command, 239
DISCRIMINANT (command), 18
    matrix output, 27
    with MATRIX DATA command, 394
DISPLAY (command), 190–192
    VARIABLES subcommand, 191–192
    with PRINT FORMATS command, 502
    with WRITE FORMATS command, 694

DISPLAY DICTIONARY (command), 25
DIVIDE (function)
    REPORT command, 594
!DO (command)
    DEFINE command, 180–182
DO IF (command), 195–203
    logical expressions, 196–198
    missing values, 198
    nested, 202
    string data, 196, 197
    with ELSE command, 199–200
    with ELSE IF command, 200–202
    with INPUT PROGRAM command, 203
    with PRINT command, 495
    with PRINT EJECT command, 498–500
    with PRINT SPACE command, 504–505
    with SAMPLE command, 609–610
    with SELECT IF command, 629
DO REPEAT (command), 204–208
    PRINT subcommand, 207–208
    stand-in variable, 204–205
    with INPUT PROGRAM command, 206
    with LOOP command, 206
DO REPEAT command
    with XSAVE command, 697
DOCUMENT (command), 19, 193–194
DOCUMENT (subcommand)
    AGGREGATE command, 89
DOCUMENTS (keyword)
    DISPLAY command, 190
!DOEND (command)
    DEFINE command, 180–182
DOLLAR (format), 37–38
DOT (format), 37–38
DOT (keyword)
    SET command, 638
DOUBLE (keyword)
    FREQUENCIES command, 272
    MULT RESPONSE command, 431
DOWN (keyword)
    SORT CASES command, 648
DRESID (keyword)
    REGRESSION command, 550
DROP (subcommand)
    ADD FILES command, 79
    EXPORT command, 237–238
    GET BMDP command, 286–287
    GET command, 280–281
    GET OSIRIS command, 296–297
    GET TRANSLATE command, 315–316
    IMPORT command, 348
    MATCH FILES command, 387–388
    SAVE command, 613–614
    SAVE SCSS command, 617–618
    SAVE TRANSLATE command, 623
    UPDATE command, 672
    XSAVE command, 698–699
DROP DOCUMENTS (command), 19, 209
    with MATCH FILES command, 384
    with UPDATE command, 668
DUMMY (keyword)
    REPORT command, 584–585
DUNCAN (keyword)
    ONEWAY command, 465
DUPLICATE (subcommand)
    FILE TYPE command, 252–253
    RECORD TYPE command, 527
DURBIN (keyword)
    REGRESSION command, 553
DVALUE (keyword)
    CROSSTABS command, 143
    FREQUENCIES command, 272

E (format), 36–37
EDIT (command), 210–211
EFFECTS (keyword)
    ONEWAY command, 466
ELSE (command)
    see DO IF command
ELSE (keyword)
    RECODE command, 515
!ELSE (keyword)
    DEFINE command, 180
ELSE IF (command)
    see DO IF command
EMPIRICAL (keyword)
    EXAMINE command, 228
!ENCLOSE (keyword)
    DEFINE command, 172
END (keyword)
    REGRESSION command, 539
END (subcommand)
    DATA LIST command, 154–156

Syntax Index

END CASE (command), 212–219
   with LOOP command, 380–381
   with VECTOR command, 213–216, 218–219
END DATA (command), 13, 112–113
   in interactive mode, 14
END FILE (command), 220–221
   with END CASE command, 221
   with LOOP command, 380–381
END FILE TYPE (command)
   see FILE TYPE command
END IF (command)
   see DO IF command
END INPUT PROGRAM (command)
   see INPUT PROGRAM command
END LOOP (command), 372–381
   see also LOOP command
END REPEAT (command). See DO REPEAT command
ENDCMD (subcommand)
   SET command, 640
   SHOW command, 645
!ENDDEFINE (command), 165–182
   See also DEFINE command
ENTER (keyword)
   REGRESSION command, 536–537
EQ (keyword)
   relational operator, 54
ERASE (command), 222
ERRORS (keyword)
   INFO command, 354
ERRORS (subcommand)
   SET command, 634–635
   SHOW command, 645
ETA (keyword)
   CROSSTABS command, 142
!EVAL (function)
   DEFINE command, 178
EVERY (keyword)
   PLOT command, 484
EXAMINE (command), 18, 223–232
   COMPARE subcommand, 225–226
   FREQUENCIES subcommand, 227–228
   ID subcommand, 227
   limitations, 224
   MESTIMATORS subcommand, 230–231
   MISSING subcommand, 231–232
   NOTOTAL subcommand, 227
   PERCENTILES subcommand, 228
   PLOT subcommand, 229–230
   SCALE subcommand, 226
   STATISTICS subcommand, 230
   TOTAL subcommand, 227
   VARIABLES subcommand, 225
EXCLUDE (keyword)
   ANOVA command, 103
   CORRELATIONS command, 130
   EXAMINE command, 232
   GRAPH command, 336
   ONEWAY command, 467
   PARTIAL CORR command, 475
   RANK command, 513
EXECUTE (command), 18, 233
EXP (function), 47, 49
EXPECTED (keyword)
   CROSSTABS command, 141
EXPECTED (subcommand)
   NPAR TESTS command, 445–446
EXPERIMENTAL (keyword)
   ANOVA command, 98–99
EXPORT (command), 18, 23, 234–239
   compared to SAVE SCSS command, 616
   DIGITS subcommand, 239
   DROP subcommand, 237–238
   KEEP subcommand, 237–238
   MAP subcommand, 238–239
   OUTFILE subcommand, 237
   RENAME subcommand, 238
   TYPE subcommand, 237
EXTENSIONS (subcommand)
   SET command, 639–640
EXTREME (keyword)
   EXAMINE command, 230

F (format), 36–37
F (keyword)
   REGRESSION command, 539
FACILITIES (keyword)
   INFO command, 354
FACTOR (command)
   matrix output, 27, 28
FACTOR(command), 18
FACTORS (subcommand)
   MATRIX DATA command, 402–404

FGT (function)
    AGGREGATE command, 90
FIELDNAMES (subcommand)
    GET TRANSLATE command, 314
    SAVE TRANSLATE command, 623
FILE (keyword)
    SYSFILE INFO command, 657
FILE (subcommand)
    ADD FILES command, 77
    DATA LIST command, 150–151
    FILE TYPE command, 248
    GET BMDP command, 285
    GET command, 280
    GET TRANSLATE command, 313
    IMPORT command, 347
    INCLUDE command, 351
    KEYED DATA LIST command, 364
    MATCH FILES command, 384–385
    MATRIX DATA command, 399
    POINT command, 489
    REPEATING DATA command, 568–569
    REREAD command, 604–605
    UPDATE command, 670
FILE HANDLE (command), 240
    MODE subcommand, 240
    with POINT command, 489–490
FILE LABEL (command), 241
FILE TYPE (command), 242–256
    CASE subcommand, 249–251
    DUPLICATE subcommand, 252–253
    FILE subcommand, 248
    GROUPED keyword, 247
    MISSING subcommand, 253–255
    MIXED keyword, 247
    NESTED keyword, 247
    ORDERED subcommand, 255–256
    RECORD subcommand, 248–249
    subcommand summary, 247–248
    WILD subcommand, 251–252
    with RECORD TYPE command, 520–528
    with REPEATING DATA command, 560–561, 564
    with SAMPLE command, 609
FILTER (command), 257–258
FIN (function)
    AGGREGATE command, 90
FIN (keyword)
    REGRESSION command, 540

FINISH (command), 259–260
FIRST (function)
    AGGREGATE command, 91
FIRST (keyword)
    ANOVA command, 98
FIRST (subcommand)
    ADD FILES command, 80
    MATCH FILES command, 388–389
FITS (keyword)
    REGRESSION command, 556
FIXED (keyword)
    DATA LIST command, 151–152
FLIP (command), 18, 261–264
    NEWNAMES subcommand, 263–264
    VARIABLES subcommand, 262–263
FLT (function)
    AGGREGATE command, 90
FOOTNOTE (subcommand)
    GRAPH command, 321
    REPORT command, 598–599
FORMAT (subcommand)
    ANOVA command, 103
    CORRELATIONS command, 130
    CROSSTABS command, 142–143
    DESCRIPTIVES command, 186–187
    FREQUENCIES command, 272–273
    LIST command, 370
    MATRIX DATA command, 399–401
    MEANS command, 418–419
    MULT RESPONSE command, 431–432
    NONPAR CORR command, 439
    ONEWAY command, 466
    PARTIAL CORR command, 475
    PLOT command, 482–483
    REPORT command, 580–582
    SET command, 636
    SHOW command, 645
    T-TEST command, 666
FORMATS (command), 19, 265–268
    with REFORMAT command, 529
FORWARD (keyword)
    REGRESSION command, 536
FOUT (function)
    AGGREGATE command, 90–91
FOUT (keyword)
    REGRESSION command, 540
FRACTION (subcommand)

RANK command, 512–513
FREE (keyword)
    DATA LIST command, 151–152
    MATRIX DATA command, 399
FREQ (keyword)
    FREQUENCIES command, 274, 274
FREQUENCIES (command), 269–278
    BARCHART subcommand, 273–274
    FORMAT subcommand, 272–273
    general mode, 270–271
    GROUPED subcommand, 275–276
    HBAR subcommand, 275
    HISTOGRAM subcommand, 274–275
    integer mode, 270–271
    limitations, 271
    MISSING subcommand, 278
    NTILES subcommand, 277
    PERCENTILES subcommand, 276
    STATISTICS subcommand, 277–278
    VARIABLES subcommand, 272
    with PROCEDURE OUTPUT (command), 506
    with PROCEDURE OUTPUT command, 273
FREQUENCIES (subcommand)
    EXAMINE command, 227–228
    MULT RESPONSE command, 427
FREQUENCY (function)
    REPORT command, 593
FRIEDMAN (subcommand)
    NPAR TESTS command, 447
FROM (keyword)
    EXAMINE command, 227
    LIST command, 371
    SAMPLE command, 608
FROM (subcommand)
    APPLY DICTIONARY command, 107
FTSPACE (keyword)
    REPORT command, 582
FULL (keyword)
    MATRIX DATA command, 399

GAMMA (keyword)
    CROSSTABS command, 142
GE (keyword), 54
    relational operator, 54
GET (command), 23, 25, 279–282
    DROP subcommand, 280–281
    FILE subcommand, 280
    KEEP subcommand, 280–281
    MAP subcommand, 282
    RENAME subcommand, 281–282
GET BMDP (command), 23, 283–288
    BMDP to SPSS conversion, 284–285
    CODE subcommand, 286
    CONTENT subcommand, 286
    DROP subcommand, 286–287
    FILE subcommand, 285
    KEEP subcommand, 286–287
    LABEL subcommand, 286
    MAP subcommand, 288
    RENAME subcommand, 287
    SCAN subcommand, 285–286
GET CAPTURE (command), 289–292
    DATABASE subcommand, 290
    LOGIN subcommand, 290
    PASSWORD subcommand, 290
    SELECT subcommand, 290
    SERVER subcommand, 290
GET OSIRIS (command), 23, 293–298
    DATA subcommand, 296
    DICTIONARY subcommand, 296
    DROP subcommand, 296–297
    KEEP subcommand, 296–297
    limitations, 295–296
    MAP subcommand, 297–298
    OSIRIS to SPSS conversion, 294–295
    RENAME subcommand, 297
GET SAS (command), 23, 299–304
    DATA subcommand, 300
    SAS to SPSS conversion, 300–304
GET SCSS (command), 23, 305–308
    $ convention, 307–308
    MASTERFILE subcommand, 306
    SCSS to SPSS conversion, 305–306
    VARIABLES subcommand, 307–308
    WORKFILE subcommand, 306–307
GET TRANSLATE (command), 22, 309–316
    database files, 311–312
    DROP subcommand, 315–316
    FIELDNAMES subcommand, 314
    FILE subcommand, 313
    KEEP subcommand, 315–316
    limitations, 313
    MAP subcommand, 316
    RANGE subcommand, 314–315
    RENAME subcommand, 316
    spreadsheet files, 310–311

tab-delimited files, 312
TYPE subcommand, 313–314
GRAPH (command), 317–336
   BAR subcommand, 321–325
   count functions, 318
   FOOTNOTE subcommand, 321
   HISTOGRAM subcommand, 333–334
   LINE subcommand, 326–329
   MISSING subcommand, 336
   PIE subcommand, 329–330
   SCATTERPLOT subcommand, 330–333
   SUBTITLE subcommand, 321
   summary functions, 318–319
   TEMPLATE subcommand, 334–336
   TITLE subcommand, 321
GREAT (function)
   REPORT command, 594
GROUPED (keyword)
   FILE TYPE command, 247
   GRAPH command, 322
GROUPED (subcommand)
   FREQUENCIES command, 275–276
GROUPS (keyword)
   EXAMINE command, 225
GROUPS (subcommand)
   MULT RESPONSE command, 425–426
   T-TEST command, 665
GT (keyword)
   relational operator, 54

HAMPEL (keyword)
   EXAMINE command, 231
HARMONIC (subcommand)
   ONEWAY command, 466
HAVERAGE (keyword)
   EXAMINE command, 228
HBAR (subcommand)
   FREQUENCIES command, 275
!HEAD (function)
   DEFINE command, 178
HEADER (subcommand)
   SET command, 637
   SHOW command, 645
HELP (command), 337–338
HIERARCHICAL (keyword)
   ANOVA command, 98, 99–100

HIGH (keyword)
   RANK command, 512
HIGHEST (keyword)
   COUNT command, 133
   MISSING VALUES command, 422
   RECODE command, 515
HIGHRES (subcommand)
   SET command, 642
HISTOGRAM (keyword)
   EXAMINE command, 229
   REGRESSION command, 552–553
HISTOGRAM (subcommand)
   FREQUENCIES command, 274–275
   GRAPH command, 333–334
   SET command, 642–643
   SHOW command, 646
HISTORY (keyword)
   REGRESSION command, 539
HOMOGENEITY (keyword)
   ONEWAY command, 466
HORIZONTAL (subcommand)
   PLOT command, 485–486
HOST (command), 339
HSIZE (subcommand)
   PLOT command, 484–485
HUBER (keyword)
   EXAMINE command, 231

IB (format), 39
ICIN (keyword)
   REGRESSION command, 551
ID (keyword)
   REGRESSION command, 553
ID (subcommand)
   EXAMINE command, 227
   REPEATING DATA command, 572–573
IF (command), 340–345
   compared to RECODE command, 514
   logical expressions, 340–342
   missing values, 341, 342
   string data, 341, 342
   with LOOP command, 344
IF (keyword)
   LOOP command, 374
!IF (command)
   DEFINE command, 180

Syntax Index

!IFEND (command)
    DEFINE command, 180
IMPORT (command), 23, 346–349
    DROP subcommand, 348
    FILE subcommand, 347
    KEEP subcommand, 348
    MAP subcommand, 349
    RENAME subcommand, 348–349
    TYPE subcommand, 347
IN (keyword)
    ONEWAY command, 467–470, 546
    PARTIAL CORR command, 476
    REGRESSION command, 545–547
IN (subcommand)
    ADD FILES command, 79–80
    KEYED DATA LIST command, 365
    MATCH FILES command, 388
    UPDATE command, 672–673
!IN (keyword)
    DEFINE command, 181–182
INCLUDE (command), 350–351
    FILE subcommand, 351
INCLUDE (keyword)
    ANOVA command, 103
    CORRELATIONS command, 130
    CROSSTABS command, 142
    DESCRIPTIVES command, 189
    EXAMINE command, 232
    FREQUENCIES command, 278
    GRAPH command, 336
    MEANS command, 418
    MULT RESPONSE command, 431
    NONPAR CORR command, 439
    NPAR TESTS command, 458
    ONEWAY command, 467
    PARTIAL CORR command, 475
    PLOT command, 486
    RANK command, 513
    REGRESSION command, 547
    T-TEST command, 666
INCREMENT (keyword)
    FREQUENCIES command, 274
INDEX (function), 51
    missing values, 57
INDEX (keyword)
    CROSSTABS command, 143
    DESCRIPTIVES command, 187
    DISPLAY command, 190
    FREQUENCIES command, 273
!INDEX (function)
    DEFINE command, 177
INFO (command), 13, 352–355
    known errors, 354
    local documentation, 352, 354
    new releases, 354–355
    OUTFILE (subcommand), 355
    procedures, 354
    update documentation, 352, 354
INFORMIX (keyword)
    GET CAPTURE command, 289–292
INGRES (keyword)
    GET CAPTURE command, 289–292
INLINE (keyword)
    MATRIX DATA command, 399
INPUT PROGRAM (command), 356–359
    examples, 155–156, 203, 206, 213–219, 221
    with DATA LIST command, 202–203
    with END subcommand on DATA LIST, 154–156
    with NUMERIC command, 459
    with REPEATING DATA command, 560–561, 563–565
    with REREAD command, 601–606
    with SAMPLE command, 609
    with STRING command, 653
    with VECTOR command, 682–683
INTO (keyword)
    RANK command, 511–512
    RECODE command, 517–518
INTO (subcommand)
    AUTORECODE command, 111

$JDATE (system variable)
    defined, 33
JOURNAL (subcommand)
    SET command, 641
    SHOW command, 646

KAPPA (keyword)
    CROSSTABS command, 142
KEEP (subcommand)
    ADD FILES command, 79
    EXPORT command, 237–238
    GET BMDP command, 286–287
    GET command, 280–281

GET OSIRIS command, 296–297
GET TRANSLATE command, 315–316
IMPORT command, 348
MATCH FILES command, 387–388
SAVE command, 613–614
SAVE SCSS command, 617–618
SAVE TRANSLATE command, 623
UPDATE command, 672
XSAVE command, 698–699
KENDALL (keyword)
    NONPAR CORR command, 438
KENDALL (subcommand)
    NPAR TESTS command, 450–451
KEY (subcommand)
    KEYED DATA LIST command, 364–365
    POINT command, 489–490
KEYED DATA LIST (command), 360–365
    direct-access files, 360–361
    FILE subcommand, 364
    IN subcommand, 365
    KEY subcommand, 364–365
    keyed files, 360, 361
    NOTABLE subcommand, 365
    TABLE subcommand, 365
K-S (subcommand)
    NPAR TESTS command, 448–449
KURTOSIS (function)
    REPORT command, 592
KURTOSIS (keyword)
    DESCRIPTIVES command, 188, 189
    FREQUENCIES command, 277
K-W (subcommand)
    NPAR TESTS command, 449–450

LABEL (keyword)
    REPORT command, 584, 588
LABEL (subcommand)
    GET BMDP command, 286
LABELS (keyword)
    ANOVA command, 103
    CROSSTABS command, 143
    DESCRIPTIVES command, 187
    DISPLAY command, 190
    MEANS command, 418
    MULT RESPONSE command, 431
    ONEWAY command, 466
    T-TEST command, 666

LAG (function), 56
    missing values, 58
LAMBDA (keyword)
    CROSSTABS command, 141
LAST (function)
    AGGREGATE command, 91
LAST (subcommand)
    ADD FILES command, 80
    MATCH FILES command, 388–389
LE (keyword)
    relational operator, 54
LEAST (function)
    REPORT command, 594
LEAVE (command), 19, 366–367
    scratch variables, 34
LEFT (keyword)
    REPORT command, 585, 589, 598–599
LENGTH (function), 51
LENGTH (keyword)
    REPORT command, 581
LENGTH (subcommand)
    REPEATING DATA command, 569
    SET command, 635–636
    SHOW command, 646
$LENGTH (system variable)
    defined, 33
!LENGTH (function)
    DEFINE command, 177
!LET (command)
    DEFINE command, 182
LEVER (keyword)
    REGRESSION command, 551
LG10 (function), 47, 49
LIMIT (keyword)
    FREQUENCIES command, 273
limitations. See individual procedures
LINE (keyword)
    DESCRIPTIVES command, 187
    REGRESSION command, 539
LINE (subcommand)
    GRAPH command, 326–329
LINEARITY (keyword)
    MEANS command, 418
LIST (command), 368–371
    CASES subcommand, 370–371
    compared to PRINT command, 492

Syntax Index

FORMAT subcommand, 370
VARIABLES subcommand, 369–370
with SAMPLE command, 370
with SELECT IF command, 370
with SPLIT FILE command, 370
LIST (keyword)
DATA LIST command, 151–152
MATRIX DATA command, 399
REPORT command, 581, 600
LISTING (keyword)
SET command, 634
LISTWISE (keyword)
CORRELATIONS command, 130
DESCRIPTIVES command, 189
EXAMINE command, 231
GRAPH command, 336
NONPAR CORR command, 439
NPAR TESTS command, 458
ONEWAY command, 467
PARTIAL CORR command, 475
PLOT command, 486
REGRESSION command, 547
T-TEST command, 666
LN (function), 47, 49
LOCAL (keyword)
INFO command, 354
LOGIN (subcommand)
GET CAPTURE command, 290
LOOP (command), 372–381
examples, 213–219
increment value, 378–379
indexing clause, 374–379
initial value, 375
logical expressions, 374
missing values, 380
nested, 373, 376–377
terminal value, 375
with END CASE command, 380–381
with END FILE command, 380–381
with SET command, 634
with SET MXLOOPS command, 372, 373–374, 375
with VECTOR command, 679, 680–681
LOW (keyword)
RANK command, 512
LOWER (function), 50
LOWER (keyword)
MATRIX DATA command, 399

LOWEST (keyword)
COUNT command, 133
MISSING VALUES command, 422
RECODE command, 515
LPAD (function), 50
missing values, 57
LSD (keyword)
ONEWAY command, 465
LT (keyword)
relational operator, 54
LTRIM (function), 50
missing values, 57

MACROS (keyword)
DISPLAY command, 191
MAHAL (keyword)
REGRESSION command, 551
MANOVA (command), 18
matrix output, 27
with AUTORECODE command, 110–111
MANUAL (keyword)
REPORT command, 581
MAP (subcommand)
ADD FILES command, 80–81
EXPORT command, 238–239
GET BMDP command, 288
GET command, 282
GET OSIRIS command, 297–298
GET TRANSLATE command, 316
IMPORT command, 349
MATCH FILES command, 389
SAVE command, 615
SAVE TRANSLATE command, 624
UPDATE command, 673
XSAVE command, 700
MARGINS (keyword)
REPORT command, 581
MASTERFILE (subcommand)
GET SCSS command, 306
MAT (keyword)
MATRIX DATA command, 405
MATCH FILES (command), 382–389
BY subcommand, 385
DROP subcommand, 387–388
duplicate cases, 386
FILE subcommand, 384–385
FIRST subcommand, 388–389

IN subcommand, 388
KEEP subcommand, 387–388
LAST subcommand, 388–389
limitations, 384
MAP subcommand, 389
RENAME subcommand, 387
table lookup files, 386
TABLE subcommand, 386
with DATA LIST command, 385
with DROP DOCUMENTS command, 384
with SORT CASES command, 649
working data file, 385
MATRIX (command), 18
MATRIX (keyword)
   CORRELATIONS command, 130
   GRAPH command, 331
   NONPAR CORR command, 439
   PARTIAL CORR command, 475
MATRIX (subcommand)
   CORRELATIONS command, 130–132
   MCONVERT command, 410–411
   NONPAR CORR command, 440–441
   ONEWAY command, 467–470
   PARTIAL CORR command, 476–478
   REGRESSION command, 545–547
MATRIX DATA (command), 390–408
   CELLS subcommand, 404
   CONTENTS subcommand, 404–408
   data-entry format, 399
   entering data, 393–396
   FACTORS subcommand, 402–404
   field separators, 393
   FILE subcommand, 399
   FORMAT subcommand, 399–401
   matrix shape, 399–401
   N subcommand, 408
   ROWTYPE_ variable, 391–392, 397–399
   scientific notation, 393
   SPLIT subcommand, 401–402
   VARIABLES subcommand, 396–399
   VARNAME_ variable, 397
   with DISCRIMINANT command, 394
   with ONEWAY command, 396, 470
   with REGRESSION command, 395
MAX (function), 47, 51
   AGGREGATE command, 90
   missing values, 57
   REPORT command, 592
MAX (keyword)

DESCRIPTIVES command, 188, 189
   PLOT command, 485
MAXIMUM (function)
   GRAPH command, 318
MAXIMUM (keyword)
   FREQUENCIES command, 273, 274, 278
MAXORDERS (subcommand)
   ANOVA command, 98
MAXSTEPS (keyword)
   REGRESSION command, 541
MCA (keyword)
   ANOVA command, 102
MCIN (keyword)
   REGRESSION command, 551
MCNEMAR (subcommand)
   NPAR TESTS command, 452
MCONVERT (command), 18, 409–411
   APPEND subcommand, 411
   MATRIX subcommand, 410–411
   REPLACE subcommand, 411
MDGROUP (keyword)
   MULT RESPONSE command, 431
MEAN (function), 47
   AGGREGATE command, 90
   GRAPH command, 318
   missing values, 57
   REPORT command, 592
MEAN (keyword)
   ANOVA command, 102
   DESCRIPTIVES command, 188
   FREQUENCIES command, 277
   MATRIX DATA command, 405
   MEANS command, 417
   NPAR TESTS command, 455
   RANK command, 512
   REGRESSION command, 543
MEANS (command), 18, 412–419
   CELLS subcommand, 417
   CROSSBREAK subcommand, 416–417
   FORMAT subcommand, 418–419
   general vs. integer mode, 412, 413, 416
   limitations, 414
   MISSING subcommand, 418
   STATISTICS subcommand, 417–418
   TABLES subcommand, 416
   VARIABLES subcommand, 415–416
MEANSUBSTITUTION (keyword)

Syntax Index

REGRESSION command, 547
MEDIAN (function)
  GRAPH command, 319
  REPORT command, 592
MEDIAN (keyword)
  FREQUENCIES command, 277
  NPAR TESTS command, 455
MEDIAN (subcommand)
  NPAR TESTS command, 452–453
MESSAGES (subcommand)
  SET command, 634–635
  SHOW command, 646
MESTIMATORS (subcommand)
  EXAMINE command, 230–231
METHOD (subcommand)
  ANOVA command, 98–100
  REGRESSION command, 536–537
MEXPAND (subcommand)
  SET command, 178, 641–642
  SHOW command, 646
MIN (function), 47, 51
  AGGREGATE command, 90
  missing values, 57
  REPORT command, 592
MIN (keyword)
  DESCRIPTIVES command, 188, 189
  PLOT command, 485
MINIMUM (function)
  GRAPH command, 318
MINIMUM (keyword)
  FREQUENCIES command, 273, 274, 278
MISSING (function), 57
  missing values, 58
MISSING (keyword)
  COUNT command, 133, 134
  RECODE command, 515–516
  REPORT command, 582
MISSING (subcommand)
  AGGREGATE command, 92–94
  ANOVA command, 103
  CORRELATIONS command, 130
  CROSSTABS command, 142
  DESCRIPTIVES command, 189
  EXAMINE command, 231–232
  FILE TYPE command, 253–255
  FREQUENCIES command, 278
  GRAPH command, 336

MEANS command, 418
MULT RESPONSE command, 430–431
NONPAR CORR command, 439
NPAR TESTS command, 458
ONEWAY command, 467
PARTIAL CORR command, 475
PLOT command, 486
RANK command, 513
RECORD TYPE command, 526–527
REGRESSION command, 547
REPORT command, 600
T-TEST command, 666
MISSING VALUE (command)
  with RECODE command, 516
MISSING VALUES (command), 19, 420–422
  value range, 422
MITERATE (subcommand)
  SET command, 179, 642
  SHOW command, 646
MIXED (keyword)
  FILE TYPE command, 247
MNEST (subcommand)
  SET command, 178, 642
  SHOW command, 646
MOD (function), 46, 49
  missing values, 57
MODE (function)
  GRAPH command, 319
  REPORT command, 593
MODE (keyword)
  FREQUENCIES command, 277
  NPAR TESTS command, 455
MODE (subcommand)
  FILE HANDLE command, 240
MODLSD (keyword)
  ONEWAY command, 465
MOSES (subcommand)
  NPAR TESTS command, 453–454
MPRINT (subcommand)
  SET command, 178, 641–642
  SHOW command, 646
MRGROUP (keyword)
  MULT RESPONSE command, 431
MSE (keyword)
  MATRIX DATA command, 405
MULT RESPONSE (command), 423–432
  BASE subcommand, 430

CELLS subcommand, 429–430
FORMAT subcommand, 431–432
FREQUENCIES subcommand, 427
GROUPS subcommand, 425–426
limitations, 425
MISSING subcommand, 430–431
multiple-dichotomy groups, 423–424
multiple-response groups, 423–424
PAIRED keyword, 429
TABLES subcommand, 427–429
VARIABLES subcommand, 426–427
MULTIPLE (keyword)
GRAPH command, 326
MULTIPLE REPONSE (command), 18
MULTIPLY (function)
REPORT command, 594
MULTIPUNCH (keyword)
FILE HANDLE command, 240
M-W (subcommand)
NPAR TESTS command, 451
MXERRS (subcommand)
SET command, 633–634
SHOW command, 646
MXLOOPS (subcommand)
SET command, 634
SHOW command, 646
with LOOP command, 372, 373–374, 375
MXWARNS (subcommand)
SET command, 633–634
SHOW command, 646

N (format), 36–37
N (function)
AGGREGATE command, 91
GRAPH command, 318
N (keyword)
MATRIX DATA command, 405
REGRESSION command, 544
n (keyword)
ANOVA command, 98
N (subcommand)
MATRIX DATA command, 408
RANK command, 510
SHOW command, 646
N OF CASES (command), 19, 433–434
with SAMPLE command, 433, 609
with SELECT IF command, 433–434, 626

with TEMPORARY command, 433–434
N_MATRIX (keyword)
MATRIX DATA command, 405
N_SCALAR (keyword)
MATRIX DATA command, 405
N_VECTOR (keyword)
MATRIX DATA command, 405
NAME (keyword)
DESCRIPTIVES command, 189
REPORT command, 590
NAMES (keyword)
DISPLAY command, 190
MEANS command, 418
NE (keyword)
relational operator, 54
NESTED (keyword)
FILE TYPE command, 247
NEW FILE (command), 435
NEWNAMES (subcommand)
FLIP command, 263–264
NEWPAGE (keyword)
FREQUENCIES command, 272
NGT (function)
GRAPH command, 319
NIN (function)
GRAPH command, 319
NLR (command), 18
NLT (function)
GRAPH command, 319
NMISS (function), 57
AGGREGATE command, 91
missing values, 58
NO (keyword)
SET command, 632
NOBOX (keyword)
CROSSTABS command, 143
NOCATLABS (keyword)
MEANS command, 418
NODIAGONAL (keyword)
MATRIX DATA command, 400
!NOEXPAND (keyword)
DEFINE command, 176
NOINDEX (keyword)
CROSSTABS command, 143
DESCRIPTIVES command, 187
NOLABELS (keyword)

Syntax Index

ANOVA command, 103
CROSSTABS command, 143
DESCRIPTIVES command, 187
FREQUENCIES command, 272
MEANS command, 418
MULT RESPONSE command, 431
ONEWAY command, 466
T-TEST command, 666
NOLIST (keyword)
    REPORT command, 581
NONAME (keyword)
    REPORT command, 590
NONAMES (keyword)
    MEANS command, 419
NONE (keyword)
    ANOVA command, 98, 102
    CROSSTABS command, 141, 142, 143
    EXAMINE command, 228, 229, 230, 231
    FREQUENCIES command, 278
    MEANS command, 418
    ONEWAY command, 466
    PARTIAL CORR command, 474
    REPORT command, 600
    SET command, 635
NONORMAL (keyword)
    FREQUENCIES command, 275
NONPAR CORR (command), 18, 436–441
    format, 436
    FORMAT subcommand, 439
    limitations, 437
    matrix output, 27, 436
    MATRIX subcommand, 440–441
    MISSING subcommand, 439
    missing values, 441
    PRINT subcommand, 438–439
    random sampling, 436, 439
    SAMPLE subcommand, 439
    significance tests, 436, 438–439
    VARIABLES subcommand, 437–438
    with RECODE command, 440
    with WEIGHT command, 686
NOORIGIN (subcommand)
    REGRESSION command, 541–542
NOREPORT (keyword)
    EXAMINE command, 232
    GRAPH command, 336
NORMAL (function), 48, 49
NORMAL (keyword)
    FREQUENCIES command, 275
    NPAR TESTS command, 448
NORMAL (subcommand)
    RANK command, 510
NORMPROB (keyword)
    REGRESSION command, 553
NOSIG (keyword)
    CORRELATIONS command, 129
    NONPAR CORR command, 438
NOT (keyword), 54–55
    logical operator, 54
NOTABLE (keyword)
    FREQUENCIES command, 273
NOTABLE (subcommand)
    DATA LIST command, 152–153
    KEYED DATA LIST command, 365
    PRINT command, 497
    REPEATING DATA command, 573
    WRITE command, 692
NOTABLES (keyword)
    CROSSTABS command, 143
NOTOTAL (subcommand)
    EXAMINE command, 227
NOVALLABS (keyword)
    CROSSTABS command, 143
NOVALUES (keyword)
    MEANS command, 419
NOWARN (keyword)
    FILE TYPE command, 251–255
    RECORD TYPE command, 526–527
    SET command, 633
NPAR TESTS (command), 18, 442–458
    BINOMIAL subcommand, 444–445
    CHISQUARE subcommand, 445–446
    COCHRAN subcommand, 446–447
    EXPECTED subcommand, 445–446
    FRIEDMAN subcommand, 447
    independent-samples test, 442–443
    KENDALL subcommand, 450–451
    K-S subcommand, 448–449
    K-W subcommand, 449–450
    limitations, 444
    MCNEMAR subcommand, 452
    MEDIAN subcommand, 452–453
    MISSING subcommand, 458
    MOSES subcommand, 453–454
    M-W subcommand, 451
    one-sample test, 442–443

pairing variables, 452
random sampling, 458
related-samples test, 442–443
RUNS subcommand, 454–455
SAMPLE subcommand, 458
SIGN subcommand, 455–456
STATISTICS subcommand, 457–458
WILCOXON subcommand, 457
with WEIGHT command, 686
W-W subcommand, 456

NPPLOT (keyword)
EXAMINE command, 229

NTILES (subcommand)
FREQUENCIES command, 277

NTILES(k) (subcommand)
RANK command, 511

NU (function)
AGGREGATE command, 91

!NULL (function)
DEFINE command, 178

NULLINE (subcommand)
SET command, 640
SHOW command, 646

NUMBER (function), 52
missing values, 57

NUMBERED (keyword)
LIST command, 370

NUMERIC (command), 19, 459–460
formats, 459, 460
with DATA LIST command, 460
with INPUT PROGRAM command, 459, 460
with SET command, 459

NUMERIC (keyword)
PLOT command, 483

NUMERIC (subcommand)
REFORMAT command, 529–530

NUMISS (function)
AGGREGATE command, 91

NVALID (function), 57
missing values, 58

OCCURS (subcommand)
REPEATING DATA command, 567–568

OFF (keyword)
SPLIT FILE command, 650
WEIGHT command, 685

!OFFEXPAND (keyword)
DEFINE command, 176

OFFSET (keyword)
REPORT command, 586, 589

ONEPAGE (keyword)
FREQUENCIES command, 272
MULT RESPONSE command, 432

ONETAIL (keyword)
CORRELATIONS command, 129
NONPAR CORR command, 439
PARTIAL CORR command, 474

ONEWAY (command), 18, 461–470
analysis design, 463
CONTRAST subcommand, 464
FORMAT subcommand, 466
HARMONIC subcommand, 466
limitations, 462
matrix input, 467–470
matrix output, 27, 467–470
MATRIX subcommand, 467–470
MISSING subcommand, 467
POLYNOMIAL subcommand, 463
RANGES subcommand, 464–466
STATISTICS subcommand, 466–467
with MATRIX DATA command, 396, 470

!ONEXPAND (keyword)
DEFINE command, 176

OR (keyword)
logical operator, 55

ORACLE (keyword)
GET CAPTURE command, 289–292

ORDERED (subcommand)
FILE TYPE command, 255–256

ORIGIN (subcommand)
REGRESSION command, 541–542

OTHER (keyword)
RECORD TYPE command, 523–524

OUT (keyword)
CORRELATIONS command, 131
NONPAR CORR command, 440
ONEWAY command, 467–470
PARTIAL CORR command, 476
REGRESSION command, 545–547

OUTFILE (subcommand)
AGGREGATE command, 88
EXPORT command, 237
INFO command, 355
PRINT command, 496–497

PRINT SPACE command, 504
PROCEDURE OUTPUT command, 506–507
REPORT command, 582–584
SAVE command, 613
SAVE SCSS command, 617
SAVE TRANSLATE command, 622
WRITE command, 692
XSAVE command, 698
OUTLIERS (keyword)
  REGRESSION command, 553, 554
OUTS (keyword)
  REGRESSION command, 539
OVERLAY (keyword)
  GRAPH command, 330
  PLOT command, 482
OVERVIEW (keyword)
  INFO command, 354

P (format), 41
PAGE (argument)
  REPORT command, 599
PAGE (keyword)
  REPORT command, 581, 590
PAIR (keyword)
  PLOT command, 481–482
PAIRED (keyword)
  MULT RESPONSE command, 429
  NPAR TESTS command, 444, 452, 455–456, 457
  T-TEST command, 665
PAIRS (subcommand)
  T-TEST command, 665–666
PAIRWISE (keyword)
  CORRELATIONS command, 130
  EXAMINE command, 231
  NONPAR CORR command, 439
  REGRESSION command, 547
PARTIAL CORR (command), 18, 471–478
  control variables, 473
  correlation list, 473
  FORMAT subcommand, 475
  limitations, 472
  matrix input, 476–478
  matrix output, 27, 476–478
  MATRIX subcommand, 476–478
  MISSING subcommand, 475
  order values, 473
  SIGNIFICANCE subcommand, 474
  STATISTICS subcommand, 474
  VARIABLES subcommand, 473–474
PARTIALPLOT (subcommand)
  REGRESSION command, 555
PASSWORD (subcommand)
  GET CAPTURE command, 290
PCT (format), 37–38
PCT (function)
  GRAPH command, 318
  REPORT command, 594
PEARSON CORR (command)
  see CORRELATIONS
PERCENT (function)
  REPORT command, 593
PERCENT (keyword)
  FREQUENCIES command, 274, 274
PERCENT (subcommand)
  RANK command, 510
PERCENTILES (subcommand)
  EXAMINE command, 228
  FREQUENCIES command, 276
PGT (function)
  AGGREGATE command, 90
  GRAPH command, 319
  REPORT command, 593
PHI (keyword)
  CROSSTABS command, 141
PIB (format), 39
PIBHEX (format), 39–40
PIE (subcommand)
  GRAPH command, 329–330
PIN (function)
  AGGREGATE command, 90
  GRAPH command, 319
  REPORT command, 593
PIN (keyword)
  REGRESSION command, 540
PK (format), 41
PLAIN (keyword)
  REPORT command, 597
PLOT (command), 18, 479–486
  control variables, 481–482
  CUTPOINT subcommand, 483–484
  FORMAT subcommand, 482–483
  HORIZONTAL subcommand, 485–486
  HSIZE subcommand, 484–485

limitations, 480–481
MISSING subcommand, 486
missing values, 486
plot labeling, 485–486
plot resolution, 479
plot scaling, 485–486
PLOT subcommand, 480–482
plot types, 480, 482–483
SYMBOLS subcommand, 483–484
TITLE subcommand, 486
VERTICAL subcommand, 485–486
VSIZE subcommand, 484–485
with SET command, 479, 485
PLOT (keyword)
REGRESSION command, 554
PLOT (subcommand)
EXAMINE command, 229–230
PLOT command, 480–482
PLOTWISE (keyword)
EXAMINE command, 226
PLOT command, 486
PLT (function)
AGGREGATE command, 90
GRAPH command, 319
REPORT command, 593
POINT (command), 487–490
FILE subcommand, 489
KEY subcommand, 489–490
with DATA LIST command, 488
with FILE HANDLE command, 489–490
POISSON (keyword)
NPAR TESTS command, 448
POLYNOMIAL (subcommand)
ONEWAY command, 463
POOLED (keyword)
REGRESSION command, 553
!POSITIONAL (keyword)
DEFINE command, 169–172
POUT (function)
AGGREGATE command, 90
POUT (keyword)
REGRESSION command, 540
PRED (keyword)
REGRESSION command, 550
PRESERVE (command), 491
macro facility, 179
with RESTORE command, 607

with SET command, 631
PRESORTED (subcommand)
AGGREGATE command, 89
PREVIOUS (keyword)
REPORT command, 598
PRINT (command), 492–497
compared to LIST command, 492
compared to REPORT command, 492
formats, 492, 494
missing values, 493
NOTABLE subcommand, 497
OUTFILE subcommand, 496–497
RECORDS subcommand, 496
string data, 42
strings, 492, 495
TABLE subcommand, 497
variable list, 493–494
with DO IF command, 495
with PRINT EJECT command, 498–500
with SET command, 493
with SORT CASES command, 649
PRINT (subcommand)
AUTORECODE command, 111
CORRELATIONS command, 129
DO REPEAT command, 207–208
NONPAR CORR command, 438–439
RANK command, 513
PRINT EJECT (command), 498–500
$CASENUM system variable, 500
missing values, 499
with DO IF command, 498–500
with PRINT command, 498–500
with SET command, 499
PRINT FORMATS (command), 19, 501–503
format specification, 501
string variables, 501–502
with DISPLAY command, 502
with PRINT command, 494
with WRITE command, 690
PRINT SPACE (command), 504–505
number of lines, 504–505
OUTFILE subcommand, 504
with DO IF command, 504–505
PRINTBACK (subcommand)
SET command, 634–635
SHOW command, 646
PROBIT (command), 18
PROBIT (function), 48, 49

PROCEDURE OUTPUT (command), 506–507
OUTFILE subcommand, 506–507
with CROSSTABS, 143, 144–145
with CROSSTABS command, 506
with FREQUENCIES command, 273, 506
with SURVIVAL command, 507
PROCEDURES (keyword)
INFO command, 354
PROPORTION (subcommand)
RANK command, 510
PROX (keyword)
MATRIX DATA command, 405
PROXIMITIES (command), 18
matrix output, 27, 28
PTILE (function)
GRAPH command, 319

QUARTILES (keyword)
NPAR TESTS command, 458
QUICK CLUSTER (command), 18
!QUOTE (function)
DEFINE command, 178

R (keyword)
REGRESSION command, 538
RANGE (function), 53
missing values, 58
RANGE (keyword)
DESCRIPTIVES command, 188, 189
FREQUENCIES command, 278
RANGE (subcommand)
GET TRANSLATE command, 314–315
RANGES (subcommand)
ONEWAY command, 464–466
RANK (command), 18, 508–513
FRACTION subcommand, 512–513
handling of ties, 512
MISSING subcommand, 513
missing values, 513
N subcommand, 510
NORMAL subcommand, 510
NTILES(k) subcommand, 511
PERCENT subcommand, 510
PRINT subcommand, 513
PROPORTION subcommand, 510
rank functions, 510–512

RANK subcommand, 510
ranking order, 509–510
RFRACTION subcommand, 510
SAVAGE subcommand, 510
saving rank variables, 511–512
TIES subcommand, 512
VARIABLES subcommand, 509–510
RANK (subcommand)
RANK command, 510
RANKIT (keyword)
RANK command, 512
RB (format), 41
RBHEX (format), 41
RECODE (command), 514–519
compared to AUTORECODE, 108
compared to AUTORECODE command, 514
compared to IF command, 514
limitations, 516
missing values, 515
numeric variables, 515–519
string variables, 516–519
target variable, 517–518
with MISSING VALUE command, 516
with NONPAR CORR command, 440
RECORD (subcommand)
FILE TYPE command, 248–249
RECORD TYPE (command), 520–528
CASE subcommand, 525–526
DUPLICATE subcommand, 527
MISSING subcommand, 526–527
SKIP subcommand, 524–525
SPREAD subcommand, 527–528
with DATA LIST command, 520–528
with FILE TYPE command, 520–528
RECORDS (subcommand)
DATA LIST command, 153–154
PRINT command, 496
WRITE command, 691–692
REFERENCE (keyword)
PLOT command, 485
REFORMAT (command), 529–530
ALPHA subcommand, 529–530
missing values, 529
NUMERIC subcommand, 529–530
with FORMATS command, 529
REG (keyword)
ANOVA command, 102
REGRESSION (command), 18, 531–548, 549–557

case selection, 544–545
CASEWISE subcommand, 553–554
CRITERIA subcommand, 539–541
DEPENDENT subcommand, 535
dependent variable, 535
DESCRIPTIVES subcommand, 543–544
diagnostic measures, 532
diagnostic variables, 550–551
matrix data, 545–547
MATRIX subcommand, 545–547
METHOD subcommand, 536–537
MISSING subcommand, 547
missing values, 532, 546–547, 550
model criteria, 539–541
NOORIGIN subcommand, 541–542
ORIGIN subcommand, 541–542
output format, 532, 534, 538, 547–548
PARTIALPLOT subcommand, 555
REGWGT subcommand, 542–543
RESIDUALS subcommand, 552–553
SAVE subcommand, 556
saving new variables, 556
SCATTERPLOT subcommand, 554–555
SELECT subcommand, 544–545
STATISTICS subcommand, 537–539
variable selection, 536–537, 540–541
VARIABLES subcommand, 534–535
weighted models, 542–543
WIDTH subcommand, 547–548
with CORRELATIONS command, 545
with MATRIX DATA command, 395
with SAMPLE command, 545, 550
with SELECT IF command, 545, 550
with SET command, 552, 554–555
with TEMPORARY command, 545
REGRESSION (keyword)
PLOT command, 482–483
REGRESSION(command)
matrix output, 27
REGWGT (subcommand)
REGRESSION command, 542–543
RELIABILITY (command)
matrix output, 27
REMOVE (keyword)
REGRESSION command, 537
RENAME (command)
SAVE TRANSLATE command, 623–624
RENAME (subcommand)
ADD FILES command, 77–78

EXPORT command, 238
GET BMDP command, 287
GET command, 281–282
GET OSIRIS command, 297
GET TRANSLATE command, 316
IMPORT command, 348–349
MATCH FILES command, 387
SAVE command, 614–615
SAVE SCSS command, 618
UPDATE command, 671–672
XSAVE command, 699–700
RENAME VARIABLES (command), 558–559
REPEATING DATA (command), 560–573
CONTINUED subcommand, 570–572
DATA subcommand, 568
FILE subcommand, 568–569
ID subcommand, 572–573
LENGTH subcommand, 569
NOTABLE subcommand, 573
OCCURS subcommand, 567–568
STARTS subcommand, 566–567
with DATA LIST command, 560, 561–562, 563–565
with FILE TYPE command, 560–561, 564
with INPUT PROGRAM command, 560–561, 563–565
REPLACE (subcommand)
MCONVERT command, 411
REPORT (command), 574–600
BREAK subcommand, 587–591
column contents, 584–585, 588
column headings, 575, 585, 588–589
column spacing, 576
column width, 576, 576, 585–586, 589
compared to PRINT command, 492
defining subgroups, 587–591
footnotes, 598–599
FORMAT subcommand, 580–582
limitations, 579–580
MISSING subcommand, 600
missing values, 576, 578, 600
OUTFILE subcommand, 582–584
output file, 578, 582–584
page layout, 582
print formats, 596–598
report types, 578
STRING subcommand, 586–587
string variables, 586–587
summary statistics, 578, 591–598

Syntax Index

SUMMARY subcommand, 591–598
  summary titles, 595–596
  titles, 598–599
  VARIABLES subcommand, 584–586
  with SET command, 577
  with SORT CASES command, 649
REPORT (keyword)
  CROSSTABS command, 142
  EXAMINE command, 232
  GRAPH command, 336
REREAD (command), 601–606
  COLUMN subcommand, 605–606
  FILE subcommand, 604–605
  with DATA LIST command, 601–606
  with INPUT PROGRAM command, 601–606
RESID (keyword)
  CROSSTABS command, 141
  REGRESSION command, 550
RESIDUALS (subcommand)
  REGRESSION command, 552–553
RESPONSES (keyword)
  MULT RESPONSE command, 430
RESTORE (command), 491, 607
  macro facility, 179
  with PRESERVE command, 607
  with SET command, 607, 631
RESULTS (subcommand)
  SET command, 634–635
  SHOW command, 646
RFRACTION (subcommand)
  RANK command, 510
RIGHT (keyword)
  REPORT command, 585, 589, 598–599
RINDEX (function), 51
  missing values, 57
RISK (keyword)
  CROSSTABS command, 142
RND (function), 46
ROUND (keyword)
  EXAMINE command, 228
ROW (keyword)
  CROSSTABS command, 140
  MULT RESPONSE command, 429
ROWTYPE_ (variable)
  MATRIX DATA command, 391–392, 397–399
RPAD (function), 50
  missing values, 57

RTRIM (function), 50
  missing values, 57
RUNS (subcommand)
  NPAR TESTS command, 454–455

SAMPLE (command), 608–610
  limitations, 609
  with DO IF command, 609–610
  with FILE TYPE command, 609
  with INPUT PROGRAM command, 609
  with N OF CASES command, 433, 609
  with REGRESSION command, 545, 550
  with SELECT IF command, 608
  with SET command, 608
  with TEMPORARY command, 608
SAMPLE (subcommand)
  NONPAR CORR command, 439
  NPAR TESTS command, 458
SAVAGE (subcommand)
  RANK command, 510
SAVE (command), 23, 611–615
  compared to SAVE SCSS command, 616
  compared to XSAVE command, 611, 696
  COMPRESSED subcommand, 615
  DROP command, 613–614
  KEEP subcommand, 613–614
  MAP subcommand, 615
  OUTFILE subcommand, 613
  RENAME subcommand, 614–615
  UNCOMPRESSED subcommand, 615
  with TEMPORARY command, 660
SAVE (subcommand)
  DESCRIPTIVES command, 185–186
  REGRESSION command, 555–556
SAVE SCSS (command), 23, 616–618
  compared to EXPORT command, 616
  compared to SAVE command, 616
  compared to SAVE TRANSLATE command, 616
  compared to XSAVE command, 616
  DROP subcommand, 617–618
  KEEP subcommand, 617–618
  missing values, 617
  OUTFILE subcommand, 617
  RENAME subcommand, 618
  reserved keywords, 617
  string variables, 617
SAVE TRANSLATE (command), 23, 619–624
  compared to SAVE SCSS command, 616

DROP subcommand, 623
FIELDNAMES subcommand, 623
KEEP subcommand, 623
limitations, 622
MAP subcommand, 624
missing values, 620–621
OUTFILE subcommand, 622
RENAME subcommand, 623–624
TYPE subcommand, 622–623
SCALE (subcommand)
   EXAMINE command, 226
SCAN (subcommand)
   GET BMDP command, 285–286
SCATTERPLOT (subcommand)
   GRAPH command, 330–333
   REGRESSION command, 554–555
SCHEFFE (keyword)
   ONEWAY command, 465
SCOMPRESSION (subcommand)
   SHOW command, 646–647
SCRATCH (keyword)
   DISPLAY command, 191
SD (function), 47
   AGGREGATE command, 90
   missing values, 57
SD (keyword)
   MATRIX DATA command, 405
SDBETA (keyword)
   REGRESSION command, 551
SDFIT (keyword)
   REGRESSION command, 551
SDRESID (keyword)
   REGRESSION command, 551
SEED (subcommand)
   SET command, 638–639
   SHOW command, 647
SEKURT (keyword)
   FREQUENCIES command, 278
SELECT (subcommand)
   GET CAPTURE command, 290
   REGRESSION command, 544–545
SELECT IF (command), 625–629
   limitations, 627
   logical expressions, 625–626
   missing values, 626–627, 628
   with $CASENUM system variable, 626
   with DO IF command, 629
   with N OF CASES command, 433–434, 626
   with REGRESSION command, 545, 550
   with SAMPLE command, 608
   with TEMPORARY command, 625
SELECTION (keyword)
   REGRESSION command, 538
SEMEAN (keyword)
   DESCRIPTIVES command, 188
   FREQUENCIES command, 277
SEPARATE (keyword)
   REGRESSION command, 553
SEPRED (keyword)
   REGRESSION command, 551
SERIAL (keyword)
   CORRELATIONS command, 130
   DESCRIPTIVES command, 187
   NONPAR CORR command, 439
   PARTIAL CORR command, 475
SERVER (subcommand)
   GET CAPTURE command, 290
SES (keyword)
   REGRESSION command, 539
SESKEW (keyword)
   FREQUENCIES command, 277
SET (command), 630–643
   BLANKS subcommand, 633
   BLOCK subcommand, 642
   BOX subcommand, 643
   CASE subcommand, 636–637
   CC subcommand, 637–638
   COMPRESSION subcommand, 639
   DECIMAL subcommand, 638
   ENDCMD subcommand, 640
   ERRORS subcommand, 634–635
   EXTENSIONS subcommand, 639–640
   FORMAT subcommand, 636
   HEADER subcommand, 637
   HIGHRES subcommand, 642
   HISTOGRAM subcommand, 642–643
   JOURNAL subcommand, 641
   LENGTH subcommand, 635–636
   MESSAGES subcommand, 634–635
   MEXPAND subcommand, 641–642
   MITERATE subcommand, 642
   MNEST subcommand, 642
   MPRINT subcommand, 641–642
   MXERRS subcommand, 633–634
   MXLOOPS subcommand, 634

MXWARNS subcommand, 633–634
NULLINE subcommand, 640
PRINTBACK subcommand, 634–635
RESULTS subcommand, 634–635
SEED subcommand, 638–639
UNDEFINED subcommand, 633
WIDTH subcommand, 635–636
with LOOP command, 634
with NUMERIC command, 459
with PLOT command, 479, 485
with PRESERVE command, 491, 631
with PRINT command, 493
with PRINT EJECT command, 499
with REGRESSION command, 552, 554–555
with REPORT command, 577
with RESTORE command, 491, 607, 631
with SAMPLE command, 608
with SHOW command, 630
with SUBTITLE (command), 655
with TITLE command, 661
with T-TEST command, 664, 666
with WEIGHT command, 686
with WRITE command, 689
with WRITE FORMATS command, 695
XSORT subcommand, 639
SHOW (command), 644–647
   BLANKS subcommand, 645
   BLKSIZE subcommand, 645
   BLOCK subcommand, 645
   BOX subcommand, 645
   BUFFNO subcommand, 645
   CASE subcommand, 645
   CC subcommand, 645
   COMPRESSION subcommand, 645
   ENDCMD subcommand, 645
   ERRORS subcommand, 645
   FORMAT subcommand, 645
   HEADER subcommand, 645
   HISTOGRAM subcommand, 646
   JOURNAL subcommand, 646
   LENGTH subcommand, 646
   MESSAGES subcommand, 646
   MEXPAND subcommand, 646
   MITERATE subcommand, 646
   MNEST subcommand, 646
   MPRINT subcommand, 646
   MXERRS subcommand, 646
   MXLOOPS subcommand, 646
   MXWARNS subcommand, 646
   N subcommand, 646
   NULLINE subcommand, 646
   PRINTBACK subcommand, 646
   RESULTS subcommand, 646
   SCOMPRESSION subcommand, 646–647
   SEED subcommand, 647
   SYSMIS subcommand, 647
   UNDEFINED subcommand, 647
   $VARS subcommand, 647
   WEIGHT subcommand, 647
   WIDTH subcommand, 647
   with SET command, 630
   XSORT subcommand, 647
SIG (keyword)
   CORRELATIONS command, 129
   NONPAR CORR command, 438
   REGRESSION command, 544
SIGN (subcommand)
   NPAR TESTS command, 455–456
SIGNIFICANCE (subcommand)
   PARTIAL CORR command, 474
SIMPLE (keyword)
   GRAPH command, 321, 326
SIN (function), 47
SINCE (keyword)
   INFO command, 354–355
SINGLE (keyword)
   LIST command, 370
SIZE (keyword)
   REGRESSION command, 552, 555
SKEWNESS (function)
   REPORT command, 592
SKEWNESS (keyword)
   DESCRIPTIVES command, 188, 189
   FREQUENCIES command, 277
SKIP (keyword)
   REPORT command, 590, 598
SKIP (subcommand)
   RECORD TYPE command, 524–525
SLK (keyword)
   SAVE TRANSLATE command, 622
SNK (keyword)
   ONEWAY command, 465
SORT (subcommand)
   DESCRIPTIVES command, 188–189
SORT CASES (command), 648–649
   with ADD FILES command, 76–77, 649
   with AGGREGATE command, 649

with MATCH FILES command, 649
with PRINT command, 649
with REPORT command, 649
with SPLIT FILE command, 650–652
with UPDATE command, 649, 669–670
SORTED (keyword)
    DISPLAY command, 191
SPEARMAN (keyword)
    NONPAR CORR command, 438
SPLIT (subcommand)
    MATRIX DATA command, 401–402
SPLIT FILE (command), 19, 650–652
    limitations, 651
    with AGGREGATE command, 87, 650–651
    with SORT CASES command, 650–652
    with TEMPORARY command, 650–651, 659
SPREAD (subcommand)
    RECORD TYPE command, 527–528
SPREADLEVEL (keyword)
    EXAMINE command, 229
SQL (keyword)
    GET CAPTURE command, 289–292
SQRT (function), 47, 49
SRESID (keyword)
    CROSSTABS command, 141
    REGRESSION command, 551
STACKED (keyword)
    GRAPH command, 322
STANDARDIZE (keyword)
    PLOT command, 486
STARTS (subcommand)
    REPEATING DATA command, 566–567
STATISTICS (subcommand)
    CORRELATIONS command, 129–130
    CROSSTABS command, 141–142
    DESCRIPTIVES command, 187–188
    EXAMINE command, 230
    FREQUENCIES command, 277–278
    MEANS command, 417–418
    NPAR TESTS command, 457–458
    ONEWAY command, 466–467
    PARTIAL CORR command, 474
    REGRESSION command, 537–539
STDDEV (function)
    GRAPH command, 318
    REPORT command, 592
STDDEV (keyword)

DESCRIPTIVES command, 188
FREQUENCIES command, 277
MATRIX DATA command, 405
MEANS command, 417
REGRESSION command, 544
STEMLEAF (keyword)
    EXAMINE command, 229
STEPWISE (keyword)
    REGRESSION command, 536
STRING (command), 19, 653–654
    with INPUT PROGRAM command, 653
STRING (function), 52
    missing values, 57
STRING (subcommand)
    REPORT command, 586–587
SUBSTR (function), 50
    missing values, 57
!SUBSTRING (function)
    DEFINE command, 177
SUBTITLE (command), 655–656
    with BEGIN DATA command, 655
    with SET command, 655
    with TITLE command, 655–656, 661–662
SUBTITLE (subcommand)
    GRAPH command, 321
SUBTRACT (function)
    REPORT command, 594
SUM (function), 47
    AGGREGATE command, 90
    GRAPH command, 318
    missing values, 57
    REPORT command, 592
SUM (keyword)
    DESCRIPTIVES command, 188, 189
    FREQUENCIES command, 278
    MEANS command, 417
SUMMARY (subcommand)
    REPORT command, 591–598
SUMSPACE (keyword)
    REPORT command, 582
SURVIVAL (command)
    with PROCEDURE OUTPUT (command), 507
SYBASE (keyword)
    GET CAPTURE command, 289–292
SYMBOLS (subcommand)
    PLOT command, 483–484

Syntax Index

SYSFILE INFO (command), 657
SYSMIS (function), 57
   missing values, 58
SYSMIS (keyword)
   COUNT command, 133, 134
   RECODE command, 515
SYSMIS (subcommand)
   SHOW command, 647
$SYSMIS (system variable)
   defined, 33

TAB (keyword)
   SAVE TRANSLATE command, 622
TABLE (keyword)
   CROSSTABS command, 142
   MEANS command, 418, 419
   MULT RESPONSE command, 431, 432
TABLE (subcommand)
   DATA LIST command, 152–153
   KEYED DATA LIST command, 365
   MATCH FILES command, 386
   PRINT command, 497
   WRITE command, 692
TABLES (keyword)
   CROSSTABS command, 143
TABLES (subcommand)
   CROSSTABS command, 139–140
   MEANS command, 416
   MULT RESPONSE command, 427–429
!TAIL (function)
   DEFINE command, 178
TAPE (keyword)
   EXPORT command, 237
   IMPORT command, 347
TEMPLATE (subcommand)
   GRAPH command, 334–336
TEMPORARY (command), 658–660
   scratch variables, 34
   with N OF CASES command, 433–434
   with REGRESSION command, 545
   with SAMPLE command, 608
   with SAVE command, 660
   with SELECT IF command, 625
   with SPLIT FILE command, 650–651, 659
   with WEIGHT command, 685
   with XSAVE command, 660
TERMINAL (keyword)

SET command, 635
TEST (keyword)
   REGRESSION command, 537
!THEN (keyword)
   DEFINE command, 180
THRU (keyword)
   COUNT command, 133
   MISSING VALUES command, 422
   RECODE command, 515
TIES (subcommand)
   RANK command, 512
$TIME (system variable)
   defined, 33
TIME.DAYS (function), 68
TIME.HMS (function), 68
TITLE (command), 661–662
   with BEGIN DATA command, 661
   with SET command, 661
   with SUBTITLE command, 655–656, 661–662
TITLE (subcommand)
   GRAPH command, 321
   PLOT command, 486
   REPORT command, 598–599
TO (keyword)
   LIST command, 371
   REGRESSION command, 535, 536
   RENAME VARIABLES command, 558
   STRING command, 653
   variable list, 32–33
   VECTOR command, 679
!TO (keyword)
   DEFINE command, 180–182
!TOKENS (keyword)
   DEFINE command, 172
TOLERANCE (keyword)
   REGRESSION command, 539, 541
TOTAL (keyword)
   CROSSTABS command, 141
   MULT RESPONSE command, 430
   REPORT command, 590
TOTAL (subcommand)
   EXAMINE command, 227
TREE (keyword)
   MEANS command, 419
TRUNC (function), 46
TSPACE (keyword)

REPORT command, 582
T-TEST (command), 663–666
  FORMAT subcommand, 666
  GROUPS subcommand, 665
  independent samples, 664, 665
  limitations, 664
  MISSING subcommand, 666
  paired samples, 664, 665–666
  PAIRS subcommand, 665–666
  VARIABLES subcommand, 665
  with SET command, 664, 666
TUKEY (keyword)
  EXAMINE command, 231
  ONEWAY command, 465
  RANK command, 512
TWOTAIL (keyword)
  CORRELATIONS command, 129
  NONPAR CORR command, 439
  PARTIAL CORR command, 474
TYPE (subcommand)
  EXPORT command, 237
  GET TRANSLATE command, 313–314
  IMPORT command, 347
  SAVE TRANSLATE command, 622–623

UC (keyword)
  CROSSTABS command, 141
UNCOMPRESSED (subcommand)
  SAVE command, 615
  XSAVE command, 700–701
UNDEFINED (subcommand)
  SET command, 633
  SHOW command, 647
UNDERSCORE (keyword)
  REPORT command, 582, 589
UNIFORM (function), 47–48
UNIFORM (keyword)
  EXAMINE command, 226
  NPAR TESTS command, 448
  PLOT command, 485
UNIQUE (keyword)
  ANOVA command, 98–99
UNNUMBERED (keyword)
  LIST command, 370
!UNQUOTE (function)
  DEFINE command, 178
UP (keyword)

SORT CASES command, 648
UPCASE (function), 49–51
!UPCASE (function)
  DEFINE command, 178
UPDATE (command), 667–673
  BY subcommand, 670–671
  DROP subcommand, 672
  FILE subcommand, 670
  IN subcommand, 672–673
  KEEP subcommand, 672
  limitations, 669
  MAP subcommand, 673
  RENAME subcommand, 671–672
  with DATA LIST command, 670
  with DROP DOCUMENTS command, 668
  with SORT CASES command, 649, 669–670
UPLOW (keyword)
  SET command, 636
UPPER (keyword)
  MATRIX DATA command, 399
  SET command, 636

VALIDN (function)
  REPORT command, 592
VALUE (function), 56
  missing values, 58
VALUE (keyword)
  REPORT command, 584, 588
VALUE LABELS (command), 19, 674–676
  compared with ADD VALUE LABELS command, 674
VALUES (keyword)
  MEANS command, 419
VAR (keyword)
  REPORT command, 600
VARIABLE (keyword)
  DESCRIPTIVES command, 189
  GRAPH command, 336
VARIABLE LABELS (command), 19, 677–678
VARIABLES (keyword)
  DISPLAY command, 190
  EXAMINE command, 226
VARIABLES (subcommand)
  ANOVA command, 97–98
  AUTORECODE command, 111
  CROSSTABS command, 138

Syntax Index

DESCRIPTIVES command, 185
DISPLAY command, 191–192
EXAMINE command, 225
FLIP command, 262–263
FREQUENCIES command, 272
GET SCSS command, 307–308
LIST command, 369–370
MATRIX DATA command, 396–399
MEANS command, 415–416
MULT RESPONSE command, 426–427
NONPAR CORR command, 437–438
PARTIAL CORR command, 473–474
RANK command, 509–510
REGRESSION command, 534–535
REPORT command, 584–586
T-TEST command, 665
VARIANCE (function), 47
  GRAPH command, 319
  missing values, 57
  REPORT command, 592
VARIANCE (keyword)
  DESCRIPTIVES command, 188, 189
  FREQUENCIES command, 277
  MEANS command, 417
  REGRESSION command, 544
$VARS (subcommand)
  SHOW command, 647
VECTOR (command), 19, 679–684
  examples, 213–216, 218–219
  index, 679, 683–684
  short form, 681–683
  TO keyword, 679
  variable list, 679
  with DATA LIST command, 683–684
  with INPUT PROGRAM command, 682–683
  with LOOP command, 679, 680–681
VECTOR (keyword)
  DISPLAY command, 191
VERTICAL (subcommand)
  PLOT command, 485–486
VSIZE (subcommand)
  PLOT command, 484–485
VW (keyword)
  RANK command, 513

WARN (keyword)
  FILE TYPE command, 251–255
  RECORD TYPE command, 526–527

SET command, 633
WAVERAGE (keyword)
  EXAMINE command, 228
WEIGHT (command), 19, 685–687
  missing values, 686
  non-positive values, 686
  scratch variables, 34
  weight variable, 685
  with CROSSTABS, 145
  with NONPAR CORR, 686
  with NPAR TESTS, 686
  with SET command, 686
  with TEMPORARY command, 685
WEIGHT (subcommand)
  SHOW command, 647
WIDTH (subcommand)
  REGRESSION command, 547–548
  SET command, 635–636
  SHOW command, 647
$WIDTH (system variable)
  defined, 33
WILCOXON (subcommand)
  NPAR TESTS command, 457
WILD (subcommand)
  FILE TYPE command, 251–252
WITH (keyword)
  ANOVA command, 98
  CORRELATIONS command, 130–131
  NONPAR CORR command, 438–440
  NPAR TESTS command, 444, 452, 455–457
  PARTIAL CORR command, 473
  PLOT command, 481–482
  T-TEST command, 665
WK1 (keyword)
  SAVE TRANSLATE command, 622
WKS (keyword)
  SAVE TRANSLATE command, 622
WORKFILE (subcommand)
  GET SCSS command, 306–307
WR1 (keyword)
  SAVE TRANSLATE command, 622
WRAP (keyword)
  LIST command, 370
WRITE (command), 688–692
  formats, 690
  missing values, 689
  NOTABLE subcommand, 692

OUTFILE subcommand, 692
RECORDS subcommand, 691–692
strings, 691
TABLE subcommand, 692
variable list, 689–690
with SET command, 689
WRITE (keyword)
FREQUENCIES command, 273
WRITE (subcommand)
CROSSTABS command, 143–145
WRITE FORMATS (command), 19, 693–695
format specification, 693
string variables, 693–694
with DISPLAY command, 694
with SET command, 695
writing cases, 688–692
See also Save As Data File procedure
WRK (keyword)
SAVE TRANSLATE command, 622
W-W (subcommand)
NPAR TESTS command, 456

XDATE.DATE (function), 72
XDATE.HOUR (function), 70
XDATE.JDAY (function), 71
XDATE.MDAY (function), 70
XDATE.MINUTE (function), 71
XDATE.MONTH (function), 70
XDATE.QUARTER (function), 71
XDATE.SECOND (function), 71
XDATE.TDAY (function), 72
XDATE.TIME (function), 72
XDATE.WEEK (function), 71
XDATE.WKDAY (function), 71
XDATE.YEAR (function), 70
XLS (keyword)
SAVE TRANSLATE command, 622
XPROD (keyword)
CORRELATIONS command, 129
REGRESSION command, 544
XSAVE (command), 23, 696–701
compared to SAVE command, 611, 696
compared to SAVE SCSS command, 616
COMPRESSED subcommand, 700–701
DROP subcommand, 698–699

KEEP subcommand, 698–699
limitations, 698
MAP subcommand, 700
OUTFILE subcommand, 698
RENAME subcommand, 699–700
UNCOMPRESSED subcommand, 700–701
with DO REPEAT command, 697
with TEMPORARY command, 660
XSORT (subcommand)
SET command, 639
SHOW command, 647
XTX (keyword)
REGRESSION command, 538
XYZ (keyword)
GRAPH command, 331

YES (keyword)
SET command, 632
YRMODA (function), 69

Z (format), 40–41
ZPP (keyword)
REGRESSION command, 539
ZPRED (keyword)
REGRESSION command, 551
ZRESID (keyword)
REGRESSION command, 551